# THE CRIMINAL CROWD
## AND OTHER WRITINGS ON MASS SOCIETY

THE LORENZO DA PONTE ITALIAN LIBRARY

SCIPIO SIGHELE

# THE CRIMINAL CROWD AND OTHER WRITINGS ON MASS SOCIETY

Edited, with an Introduction and Notes, by Nicoletta Pireddu
Translated by Nicoletta Pireddu and Andrew Robbins
With a Foreword by Tom Huhn

UNIVERSITY OF TORONTO PRESS
Toronto Buffalo London

Toronto Buffalo London
utorontopress.com

ISBN 978-1-4875-0318-5

The Lorenzo Da Ponte Italian Library

---

**Library and Archives Canada Cataloguing in Publication**

Sighele, Scipio, 1868–1913, author
The criminal crowd and other writings on mass society/Scipio Sighele; edited, with an introduction and notes, by Nicoletta Pireddu and Andrew Robbins; with a foreword by Tom Huhn.

(The Lorenzo Da Ponte Italian library)
Translated from the Italian.
Includes bibliographical references and index.
ISBN 978-1-4875-0318-5 (cloth)

1. Crowds. 2. Social psychology. 3. Criminal psychology. 4. Crime. 5. Criminals. I. Pireddu, Nicoletta editor, translator II. Title. III. Series: Lorenzo Da Ponte Italian library

HV6084.S54 2018 364.3 C2018-900610-2

---

This volume is published under the aegis of Agincourt Press Ltd. and with the financial assistance of Cav. Vivian Cardia.

University of Toronto Press acknowledges the financial assistance to its publishing program of the Canada Council for the Arts and the Ontario Arts Council, an agency of the Government of Ontario.

Canada Council for the Arts Conseil des Arts du Canada

Funded by the Government of Canada Financé par le gouvernement du Canada

# Contents

# Acknowledgments

This volume about crowds would not have become reality without a little multitude of special people to whom I am deeply grateful for helping me spread the benefits of ... cultural *suggestion.*

First of all, Professors Luigi Ballerini and Massimo Ciavolella, the enlightened intellectual *meneurs,* who, with their compelling Lorenzo Da Ponte Italian Library series, have magnetized the interest of an international audience in a lineage of notable Italian writers worthy of being rediscovered, and have welcomed Scipio Sighele to the group. And, to be sure, Andrew Robbins, the other half of the *translating couple,* for having enthusiastically agreed to embark on this substantial project *à deux* at an incredibly busy stage of his academic career, and for having been a reliable and insightful interlocutor throughout this long process.

As Sighele already understood, groups can also work long distance, increasingly so. Multitudes are not only disruptive: they play a constructive role as producers of culture. From the West Coast, Heather Sottong contributed to my first English version of *La folla delinquente,* making it possible for me to resume this editorial project after unexpected setbacks. From Italy, Dr Caterina Tomasi at the Biblioteca della Fondazione Museo Storico del Trentino in Trento has been extraordinarily kind and helpful before, during, and after my consultation of the Scipio Sighele archive, and has provided precious unpublished documents including the photo of Sighele reproduced in this volume. From New York, Tom Huhn generously added his precious insights into the "otherness" emerging from Sighele's thought. From unknown locations, the two anonymous readers gave me much appreciated feedback. From Toronto, Richard Ratzlaff patiently awaited the final manuscript, offering encouragement and valuable advice throughout the publication process, and Mark Thompson enthusiastically supervised the final stage. With their insights and care for details, Anne Laughlin and Kate Baltais made the book production phase a rewarding experience.

Closer to my desk, the staff at Lauinger Library and Interlibrary Loan office at Georgetown University—in particular, Mr Jeffrey Popovich and Ms Elsbieta Stafford—have efficiently managed my incessant search for materials and my possible and impossible renewal requests. The Graduate School and the Faculty of Foreign Languages and Linguistics at Georgetown University supported various stages of this project with Summer Research Grants. My colleagues Louise Hipwell and Sylvie Durmelat helped me solve some linguistic conundrums in my tangle of English, French, and Italian. The proximity of Honoré Daumier's painting was a pleasant surprise, and the cooperation of the Phillips Collection for its reproduction on the cover of the book is much appreciated.

Last, but not least, my thanks to the crowd of students and friends with whom I could share my passion for that medley of extraordinary intuitions and bizarre inconsistencies that make up the fin de siècle, and that the writings of Scipio Sighele egregiously epitomize. It is not necessary to identify with an epoch or culture to learn from them and reappraise our own.

I wish to dedicate this volume to my own *coppia criminale*: Ester and Ilaria.

# Foreword

TOM HUHN

Grant that Scipio Sighele labours over many intriguing ideas concerning social relations. Still, we find in his writings collected here a particularly salutary feature, namely, a concept, now pervasive and popular—and thoroughly modern—which his thinking nonetheless strenuously navigates away from: the idea of the *other*. Sighele is not concerned with the blank slate of the other as a figure upon whom we project; he is instead interested in the nature and effects of our *proximity* to one another, especially the ways in which social relations have historically induced us to continue to expand towards and overlap with each another. Sighele's notion of the criminal crowd—an expansion of what he discovers in the criminal couple—gives voice to a deep modern ambivalence regarding the source and extent of our vulnerability towards one another. Sighele's insight and achievement, well formulated by Nicoletta Pireddu, is to have conceived the crowd as "a new criminogenic subject," and thereby to have uncovered a novel platform on which still further features of human sociability might become visible.

Sighele's sociological method takes as its unstated starting point the modern bureaucratic increase in control over the fate of individual lives, glimpsed first in the distinction between a "born" criminal and a person who becomes criminal only because of her susceptibility towards others. The deepest impress of this bureaucratic administration Sighele then finds between the living cells that we inhabit in our relations with one another. The criminal couple and the criminal crowd are expressions of the fact that the fate of the individual is now administratively joined with that of all other human beings. Our susceptibility towards others is of a piece with the complicity that entertains our stake in administrative order. Our relations with one another have taken on, mimetically, the contours of the administrative power over us. Now, it is not some other person, or even their behaviour that we have to fear, as it is rather our own susceptibility towards one another, enhanced by the administrative controls over us, that makes us truly vulnerable to whatever is "criminal" in society. Recall here the absolute unknowability of the bureaucracy in Kafka's *Castle*, and especially of how that unknowability mimetically permeates and infects all human relations. Under modern bureaucratic administration, our shared existence is presented less with the threat of some *direct* harm to any one of us and more, somehow, with the still greater threat of an *indirect* harm: that each of us might well lose hold of ourselves. The prospect of losing oneself is a threat more powerful than anything coming from some imagined other.

A fear of the loss of one's self first becomes prevalent in the eighteenth century. Enlightened thinkers such as David Hume and Adam Smith wrote of it as the result of a contagion—here following Thomas Hobbes's formulation of the body politic—that some foreign feeling or passion could be transfused uncontrollably from breast to breast. Such uncontrolled transfusions become possible only in a society large enough to have sufficient anonymity among its members. The logic of how such a contagion could happen seems to be as follows: our vulnerability to contagion from others cannot truly ignite when we know our neighbours since the boundaries that demarcate one person from another are visible in and by the recognizable face of the neighbour. Regardless the extent of the knowledge of, or familiarity we have with, our neighbour, anonymity is a term designating a certain insufficiency of what we know of others. And yet this insufficiency in turn inflames our sympathy, or at least our inclinations towards others. On the face of it anonymity would seem to be at odds with our natural inclinations towards sympathy and fellow feeling. But Sighele's formulation of the modern crowd instead implies that anonymity and sympathy fuel one another, that we become still more inclined towards fellow feeling the less we know of one another. Anonymity makes us more susceptible to the passions of others. Knowing someone presumably means some kind of knowledge of or at least familiarity with the person and their passions. The infamous anonymity of the crowd—and we might likewise say of modern society—withdraws all knowledge of persons; it thereby instead promotes our experience of others as primarily an emotional, passion-based exchange, or better: transfusion. The sympathy or fellow feeling crucial to Smith's and Hume's vision of what constituted the bonds in a society was premised upon just our inability to control our sympathetic inclinations towards others.

That the passions of others might somehow invade us (in Sighele this means one's susceptibility to becoming criminal) is possible only because of our natural predisposition towards sympathetic fellow feeling. And Smith's justly famous notion of the internal spectator is premised in turn upon a certain degree of anonymity between actor and audience, which, continued inwardly for each of us—via the "impartial" spectator—this anonymity between people implies a like anonymity within each person, hence a rather high degree of opacity towards oneself. Our natural sympathy towards one another, or what we might also call our susceptibility towards each other, is where the bonds that tie us to one another are first forged. And yet, the very means by which we come to bind ourselves to one another are turned against us by the modern administrative order of society. When a society achieves a sufficient degree of anonymity among its members, the sympathy that was deployed towards one another is supplanted instead by an administrative bureaucracy. The suggestion here is that there is a kind of equivalence, and even a complementarity, between the anonymity of modern society and the facelessness of modern administrative bureaucracies. That our neighbours are no longer recognizable to us—and this without any diminishment of our capacity for fellow feeling—makes it all the easier for us to have a kind of sympathy towards the administrative powers over us. The social inclinations that foster our being so readily administered are one and the same as our long-standing inclinations towards one another. This might well explain how it is that we became so adept at being administered; the means by which we forge connections with one another have been redeployed by and towards that which has power over us. Indeed, and bluntly, we might best describe our relation to modern bureaucratic administered society as an instance of the Stockholm syndrome.

According to Sighele, another prominent feature of the phenomenon of the crowd is that it includes what he describes as the simultaneity of experience. Two thoughts come immediately to mind, the first being that simultaneous experience is sometimes taken to be the signal achievement of modernity, as well as an explicit goal in a great many works of modernist art. One need only recall Stephen Kern's book, *The Culture of Space and Time, 1880–1918*, to find a rich source that surveys the many technological developments, such as the telegraph and telephone, etc., as well as the literary examples of Proust, Woolf, and Joyce, among others, that eclipsed the spatial and temporal constraints that kept one experience demarcated from another. In this light, the hallmark of the modern era is the technical and cultural erasure not only of the boundaries between experiences, but so, too, the boundaries between individuals. The second thought to arise in response to the crowd's simultaneity of experience is to acknowledge that Sighele intends something more cohesive and comprehensive with this phrase than merely the notion that individual experiences are somehow coordinated or synchronized in and by the crowd. The stronger version of this idea is to recognize that the novelty of the modern crowd carries with it the novelty of an experience—as well as a *simultaneity* of experience—not previously possible. The crowd makes possible a new form of unity of experience. And this particular unity leads us naturally to Freud, and especially to his notion of the oceanic as the fullest expression of the unity of experience. The crowd, in other words, beckons to us like the oceanic.

We might appreciate the most pointed formulation of this kinship in Elias Canetti's famous explanation, in his *Crowds and Power*, that the phenomenon of crowd occurs in just that moment when human beings crowded together overcome their inhibitions towards being touched and jostled by others and thereby achieve a kind of transcendent euphoria of crowd unity. For Freud the oceanic unity is always a return to an earlier stage of life, to an organic and even an inorganic state of existence. Freud writes of the oceanic as something we long for, a quest for the means by which we might lower the barriers between us in service of connecting or reconnecting with people as well as with things. The unity promised by the oceanic is a regression to an earlier state. But so, too, we might say that the crowd allows us to *progress* towards unity by means of our organic and inorganic memories of non-individuation. The crowd is then the prototypical modern phenomenon that exposes an enhanced, updated version of our primeval sociability. Thus, although the oceanic may well be a site of longed-for unification, the crowd is more like an administratively enforced one.

If the crowd comes about by means of the lowering of the barriers as well as the distinctions between and among us, then so, too, in the crowdedness of modern life does the individual transcend certain boundaries within herself. Thus, to whatever extent our responses to the world, its people, and things have become aesthetic, we might credit the lowering of the distinctions between our various faculties that have come into existence through evolutionary transformations. Our expansiveness becomes possible only with the lowering of the boundaries outside as well as within us. Although the crowd might sometimes appear as a kind of barbaric atavistic regression, Sighele reveals in us, in the end, an *ambivalence* about our very connectedness to other people, as well as an *ambivalence* towards the separateness or continuity within the individualized, segmented portions of each person's own psychology. Sighele's sociological focus then lights upon the crowd as a proto-aesthetic phenomenon insofar as the crowd partakes of the same dynamic of transcending separateness for the sake of a rejuvenated and rekindled unity. Further, Sighele's studies imply that our ambivalent relation to sociability extends to ambivalence towards the condition of being human. We might say that Sighele helps uncover in us an ambivalence regarding our own expansiveness. As our previously somewhat organic sense of community, or at least of clan and family, weakens, and the idea of the stranger and the unknown other achieve a greater proximity to each of us, it becomes possible to fear the prospect of becoming something else. Vulnerability towards the *other* is also vulnerability towards what each of us might yet become.

# Introduction: Alchemies of the Collective Soul: Scipio Sighele's Crimes and Punishments

NICOLETTA PIREDDU

When Mr Barnstaple, the protagonist of H.G. Wells's 1923 novel *Men Like God*, arrives in the parallel universe of Utopia, he finds himself in a "fortunate world" where "there is no Crowd" (*Men* 285). If for the stunned Earthling such felicitous discovery constitutes the most extraordinary feature of this civilization many thousand years ahead of his, it also triggers a comparison with his own society, which "alas still is, the world of the Crowd, the world of that detestable crawling mass of un-featured, infected human beings" (285). The contempt for these amorphous collectivities that in Utopia only survive through film and photographs preserved in history museums is summarized by Barnstaple's agitated explanation to Crystal, a young Utopian:

> You have never seen a Crowd, Crystal; and in all your happy life you never will. You have never seen a Crowd going to a football match or a race meeting or a bull-fight or a public execution or the like crowd joy; you have never watched a Crowd wedge and stick in a narrow place or hoot or howl in a crisis. You have never watched it stream sluggishly along the streets to gape at a King, or yell for a war, or yell quite equally for a peace. And you have never seen the Crowd, struck by some Panic breeze, change from Crowd proper to Mob and begin to smash and hunt. (285–86)

The mobs that Crystal sees only in the reproductions of thirty centuries before, "streaming over downs after a great race meeting" (286) or "rioting in some public square and being dispersed by the police"

(286) are, indeed, the protagonists of late nineteenth-century Western societies, where sociologists, psychologists, anthropologists, and philosophers begin to reinterpret the mass from a mere aggregation of singular individuals to an autonomous entity worthy of scientific inquiry. The scholars most commonly associated with the pioneering studies of crowds in that period are the French Gustave Le Bon (1841–1931) and Gabriel Tarde (1843–1904). It has been documented, for instance, that Le Bon's *Psychologie des foules* (1895) [*The Crowd: A Study of the Popular Mind* (1896)] played a crucial role in the development of Mussolini's political ideas, inspired Hitler's *Mein Kampf*, and was among Lenin's Parisian readings (Ginneken 185–86). Yet also representatives of democracy like Theodore Roosevelt avowed their admiration for the French social psychologist. No matter how faithful to the complexities of Le Bon's vision, supporters of totalitarian and representative regimes alike for several decades after the publication of *Psychologie des foules* have seen in Le Bon the pivotal contributor to the problem of the relationship between the internal discipline of the individual self and the external discipline that becomes necessary to cope with collective social manifestations under the assumption that self-organization of masses is unrealistic. Even now, the so-called age of crowds[1] still evokes primarily the late nineteenth-century French context, with the fearful popular uprising leading to the Paris Commune and the numerous disturbing images of masses in novels by Balzac, Sue, Maupassant, Zola, Huysmans, and Adam, among others.[2]

What is certainly less known by the international audience is that, four years before Le Bon's seminal text, Italian criminologist, sociologist, jurist, journalist, and literary critic Scipio Sighele (b. Brescia 1868, d. Florence 1913) had published *La folla delinquente: Saggio di psicologia collettiva* [*The Criminal Crowd: An Essay on Collective Psychology*, this volume], to be followed by numerous other explorations of the psychological mechanisms of collective behaviour and the power of social suggestion—among them *La coppia criminale* (1892) [*The Criminal Couple*, this volume], *La delinquenza settaria* (1897) [*Sectarian Criminality*, this volume], and *L'intelligenza*

1 Le Bon himself adopts this expression to connote the social situation of the European fin de siècle. For additional discussions of the age of crowds in a broader cultural and philosophical context, see Moscovici, *Age*; Schnapp and Tiews, eds., *Crowds*; Bodei, *Destini*.

2 Beyond France, Charles Dickens's 1841 historical novel *Barnaby Rudge* is also worth remembering for its gripping descriptions of the frightening mobs in the Protestant anti-Catholic Gordon Riots of 1780.

*della folla* (1903) [*The Intelligence of the Crowd*, this volume]. Born into a politically and socially active family originally from Nago, in the province of Trento, and supporting the Italianness of the region while it was still under the Austrian regime, Sighele grew up in various areas of Italy, owing to his father's frequent relocations as a magistrate. In 1890 Sighele gained a law degree in Rome, under the supervision of Enrico Ferri (1856–1929), a criminologist, politician, and writer who, like Guglielmo Ferrero (1871–1942) and Adolfo Zerboglio (1866–1952)—two other mentors of Sighele's—had studied with Cesare Lombroso (1835–1909), the renowned physician, anthropologist, and jurist considered to be the father of Italian criminology. Sighele taught at the Universities of Pisa and Rome and at the Istituto di Scienze Sociali in Florence, and he held courses in criminal sociology and collective psychology at the Institut des Hautes Études in Brussels.[3]

The title of Sighele's first and best known book, *La folla delinquente* (1891) [*The Criminal Crowd*, this volume], recalls, indeed, texts like *L'uomo delinquente* [*Criminal Man*] and *La donna delinquente: La prostituta e la donna normale* [*Criminal Woman, the Prostitute, and the Normal Woman*] in which Lombroso studied the category of deviance using a descriptive, clinical method. Yet, Sighele distances himself from the Lombrosian anthropometric approach, as well as from his master Enrico Ferri. Shaped by positivist thought, Lombroso interprets social anomalies almost exclusively in physiological and psychological terms, locating the signs of criminal behaviour in the subject's somatic features, and treating the propensity to criminality as a hereditary pathology. For his part, Ferri is more interested in the connection between socioeconomic influences and crime rates, and maintains that, rather than devising punitive methods for criminals, a culture of legality can be established through crime prevention. At the same time, Ferri remains loyal to Lombroso's biological positivism, according to which human behaviour is regulated by a deterministic sequence of causes and effects. Swerving from both his predecessors, Sighele rejects an anthropological interpretation of

3 Details about Sighele's international standing as a lecturer can be found in the archival material of the Fondo Sighele at the Biblioteca della Fondazione Museo Storico del Trentino, especially in the first album, "In memoria del mio Scipio," compiled by Sighele's devoted wife Antonietta Rosmini. Among Sighele's conferences, Rosmini lists ten in Brussels in 1899, one in 1900, eight in 1901, six in 1907, and she highlights his acclaimed talk at the Congress of Criminal Anthropology in Amsterdam on 4 September 1901.

crime and questions the abstract idea of an integral, rational subject. Sighele realizes that it is not enough to identify atavistic signs of deviance so as to distinguish between normal and anomalous subjects, insofar as individual behaviour can be temporarily altered. Therefore, he investigates the psychological foundations of individual and collective actions at the same time, focusing on the criminal attitudes developing from their interplay in particular social contexts. He conceptualizes an unpredictable multitude that magnifies the conflicting, destabilizing drives latent in the individual psyche, and that emerges as something qualitatively different from a mere sum of self-contained singularities while, at the same time, not coterminous with the idea of society. With Sighele, the crowd itself becomes a distinct and problematic subject, anonymous and chiefless, yet powerful enough to preserve social order or to generate social changes.

Not by chance the group begins to be studied as an agent of subversion worthy of a designated discipline—collective psychology—to which Sighele will devote his entire career. Sighele writes in a newly born Italy trying to negotiate between the patriotic dreams of the Risorgimento and the disappointing reality of the post-unification period. From the unification to the First World War, Italy attempts to achieve political and social stability through inclusive coalitions able to give voice to and at the same time contain very diverse forces, including the growing economic and social power of the middle class; a conservative, nostalgic, pro-Bourbon South; and a mounting popular unrest in response to increasing taxation, parliamentary corruption, financial scandals, and favouritism towards agricultural and industrial oligarchies to the detriment of farm and factory workers. Between 1893 and 1894, after an economic and agricultural depression, the upheaval of the Sicilian "Fasci"—leagues of peasants, miners, artisans, industrial workers, and intellectuals with a socialist, anarchist, and often millenarian orientation demanding social justice in reaction to low wages, exploitation by landowners, and protectionist tariffs—fostered the fast spread of riots in other agricultural and industrial areas of the Italian peninsula. Order was restored with the intervention of the Italian army that escalated to numerous summary executions and extensive arrests targeting association leaders, crowds of protesters, and alleged sympathizers. In May 1898 Milan was the theatre of the so-called Bava-Beccaris massacre, the suppression of massive riots protesting against the rise in food prices. Aggressive group reactions to appalling working conditions had already occurred in previous decades. Violent farmers' strikes in northern Lombardy in 1871 and 1877 were followed by more widespread and worrisome episodes in southern Lombardy and Veneto from 1884 to 1886, which showed the power of socialist and anarchic ideas, and culminated with trials in Venice (Virgilii 6). On 8 February 1889, a thousand unemployed workers in Rome committed acts of vandalism instigated by some leaders, although, as Sighele himself mentions in *The Criminal Crowd*, they ultimately regained reason and calm upon the intervention of an armed soldier. Things went differently in the French town of Décazeville, where, in 1886, a group of miners suddenly turned into fierce murderers owing to the "unknown and powerful influence of the crowd" (*Crowd* 54).

The increase in mass movements—demonstrations, strikes, riots, but also peaceful group manifestations like juries, committees, and theatre spectators—draws the attention of the scientific and juridical community towards collectivity as the social, political, and often subversive subject of modernity par excellence. This new entity demands a reconceptualization of criminalization and of responsibility, and the development of legal answers adequate to the passage from the individual to the group. In this context, between psychology and sociology, Sighele develops an interest in collective behaviour and crime resulting from associative forms of diverse extensions, yet always characterized by complicity as a distinguishing feature.

The scant attention to Sighele throughout the twentieth century and to date is the more surprising given the international visibility of this figure during his lifetime. This came not only as a result of Sighele's participation in international congresses and his recurring teaching appointments in collective psychology and criminal sociology at the Institut des Hautes Études at the University of Brussels, but also because of an intriguing international editorial controversy that the American magazine *Popular Science Monthly* summarized in the following terms: "Sighele made his name with an admirable book *The Criminal Crowd* which a French writer has thought fit to appropriate in outline and almost entirely in substance, obtaining for it the honor of translation into English, while the real author has been left out in the cold" (Zimmern, "Criminal Anthropology in Italy" 758). The author of this 1898 article, German-British writer and translator Helen Zimmern, is here referring to Sighele's diatribe against Gustave Le Bon himself—whose plagiarism from Sighele was publicly recognized, as we will see—in contrast to his more cordial relationship with equally renowned French sociologist Gabriel Tarde, who will at least acknowledge Sighele as a precursor. Zimmern's recognition of Sighele's ground-breaking ideas hits the mark, as the widespread echo of *The Criminal Crowd* was also promptly attested by many translations in French, Spanish, German, Russian, Polish, and Dutch; none, however, in the English-speaking world.[4]

The entry of Sighele's works into the anglophone world is hence highly overdue, together with a reappraisal of his writings able to foreground not only his contributions to the domain of sociology and criminology, but also his wider-ranging engagement with broad European intellectual debates on paramount issues that were becoming increasingly relevant to Italy in his time, such as the role of urbanization in the development of criminality, the problematic borders between individual and collective accountability in mass society, the legal and ideological constraints in the education and emancipation of women, the social and institutional challenges to the care and upbringing of children, and the responsibility of literary representation in the relationship between aesthetic standards and ethical norms.

There are also questionable aspects of Sighele's thought that make him a spokesperson of the ideologies of his time—for instance, as we will see, his contradictory approach to gender equality and his resistance to feminism, or his hostility to parliamentarism and his nationalistic overtones. Although far from negligible, once these controversial viewpoints are contextualized within a well-rounded portrait of the author, they can provide a more dynamic perspective on turn-of-the-century Italian and European culture as a transitional period facing the new simultaneously with fear and excitement. Through Sighele's eyes we catch a glimpse of the complexity of modernity, with which Italy was coming to terms as a recently unified nation.

## 1 The Italian "Man of the Crowd"

This old man [...] is the type and genius of deep crime. He refuses to be alone. *He is the man of the crowd.* [...] I shall learn no more of him, nor of his deeds.

—Edgar Allan Poe, "Man of the Crowd"

4 See Ginneken 83; McClelland 119. Contrary to Chiara Gallini's assertion (15), there are no English translations of *La folla delinquente.* Therefore, the reference to Sighele's English title *The Criminal Crowd* with the date 1894 in McPhail's *The Myth of the Madding Crowd* (2) is also incorrect.

According to Georg Lukács, the French Revolution rendered history for the first time "*a mass experience*, and moreover on a European scale" (*The Historical Novel*, 23; original emphasis). The multitude's storming of the Bastille comes to symbolize the power of an impulsive collectivity, frightening for its might as much as for its irrationality, but destined to become the protagonist of nineteenth-century European events because, as Lukács argues, the increasingly frequent mass upheavals are no longer perceived as "a 'natural occurrence'" (23). Rather, the mass acquires visibility, a consciousness of itself as a "historical character" (23). Indeed, when Sighele begins to write about the crowd, not only history but also literature, even in Italy, has already offered memorable demonstrations of the threatening and at times even bestial behaviour of the masses, from Alessandro Manzoni's *I promessi sposi* [*The Betrothed*] and *Storia della colonna infame* [*The Column of Infamy*], Iginio Ugo Tarchetti's *Una nobile follia* [*A Noble Folly*], and Edmondo De Amicis's *La vita militare* [*Military Life in Italy: Sketches*], to Gabriele D'Annunzio's *Novelle della Pescara* [*Tales of My Native Town*].

Yet, the crowd also captivated writers for whom the vast multitude of the populace embodied the revolutionary democratic impetus able to bring about social improvement. Karl Marx's utopian proletarian revenge represents the paramount example of a redemptive turning point able to overturn class relationships. Even before *The Capital* and the civil uprising of June 1848 that put Paris at the mercy of the mob, Jules Michelet (1798–1874) had expressed his messianic vision of the people—a poor, voiceless creature, laborious and despised but, in fact, grandiose and innumerable, ultimately coinciding with humankind itself—in lectures that preceded the more systematic argument of works like his 1847 *History of the French Revolution*. Likewise, Italian intellectual and political activist Giuseppe Mazzini (1805–1872), who posits a direct link between God and the people as the only synergy able to bring freedom to Italy, forcefully asserts that "nothing now succeeds if not supported by the masses" ("Europe" 455), since, just as "thought is the action of the individual" (456), action is "the thought of the people" (456).

Between the two extremes represented by the brute destructive force of the mob and its redemptive collective might, Sighele places his own vision of the crowd, blending liberal and undemocratic elements. On the one hand, he assumes human multitude's predisposition to commit evil and does not exonerate single individuals from the responsibility for their negative actions as members of a group. On the other hand, however, he admits that legal provisions have to take into account the extent of each participant's involvement, and the reasons for it. *The Criminal*

*Crowd: An Essay on Collective Psychology* remains Sighele's most iconic work, even if it may seem rather succinct and often impressionistic. Its first edition consists, to a large extent, of pronouncements by other European intellectuals with whom Sighele engages. Yet, his pioneering theorization of the crowd as a new criminogenic subject at the crossroads of psychology and sociology had great resonance. As he himself explains four years later in the preface to the second Italian edition (1895), science and tribunals had never before contemplated that the defendant could be a crowd, instead of a single person (*Folla* II ed., i). Sighele situates himself against the backdrop of previous theorizations of the social dimension, such as romantic readings of peoples as products of a collective soul often determined by race, or organicist interpretations of the social as the result of a progressive evolution from a simple biological entity to a complex, rational collectivity. For instance, Sighele refutes the correspondence between individual and social psychology through which Herbert Spencer (1820–1903) conceptualizes human aggregates as stable constructs made of homogeneous components. Sighele assumes that an aggregate of individuals is different from the sum of the single selves, and that not all collectivities are the same. In the case of "*heterogeneous* and *inorganic*" (*Crowd* 12) groups of people—Sighele's specific object of study—the laws of sociology are for him not applicable and need to be replaced by those of collective psychology, a term he borrows from Enrico Ferri's theory, and further explores.

Therefore, not all the elements in Sighele's argumentation are new,[5] yet he systematizes them within a new interpretive framework. *The Criminal Crowd* can be considered an incubator of ideas that Sighele further elaborates in subsequent works, and its relevance can be fully appreciated

5 Although Gallini maintains that it was Sighele who coined the expression *collective psychology* (17), as we can also infer from *The Criminal Crowd* (9), in a note following Sighele's correspondence with Tarde, Ferri explicitly acknowledges that he gave that name to the discipline in the second edition of his volume *Nuovi orizzonti* (1884) and that Sighele made it blossom ("Nota di Enrico Ferri," *Folla* II ed., 157). Sighele himself substantiates this fact in his response to Ferri, as he mentions his master's "felicitous distinction between *collective psychology* and *social psychology*, which was the spark of my book on the criminal crowd" ("Ancora sull'intelligenza e la moralità della folla," *Folla* II ed., 171). Sighele also explicitly maintains that, while he studied collective psychology, Ferri defined it. Along the same lines, *The Criminal Crowd*—and most of Sighele's subsequent works—are in dialogue with a surprising array of European sociologists, scientists, and humanists.

if it is read in connection with Sighele's overall thought.[6] Only a year after it first appeared, a French expanded version brings Sighele's discussion under the international spotlight. Sighele himself continues to present his investigations as work in progress—given that collective psychology is still "a science in its infancy" (*Folla*, II ed., i),[7] and crowd psychology "has just been born" (ii)—yet without overlooking their cogency and cumulative effect, as "logical applications of a single thought and of a doctrine resulting from extensive musings" (*Settaria* 10). For instance, by assuming that imitation is one of the strongest instincts in human nature, Sighele elaborates on the work of anthropologist and psychologist Giuseppe Sergi (1841–1936) on the reflexive receptivity of the psyche, and on suggestion as its acute phase,[8] highlighting the gradual shift from isolated instances to the collective, epidemic manifestations of the phenomenon. Likewise, building on the claims of alienists like Giuseppe Seppilli (1851–1939), Henry Maudsley (1835–1918), and Gerard Van Swieten (1700–1772) about the influence of an insane person upon his entourage, Sighele concludes that suggestion is a universal phenomenon that acts in the same way in states of insanity and in normal conditions, reaching its climax with crowd behaviour.[9] Since emotional intensity increases commensurate with the number of individuals experiencing it in a particular circumstance, suggestion promotes collective crime and combativeness because it instils in each member of the crowd the belief in one's own omnipotence and impunity. Sighele emphasizes that those feelings of self-aggrandizement are not the cause but, rather, the consequence of the emotional contagion that derives from one influential person's instigation, be it a cry, a word, or a bold action. He also adds, however, that a single prompt is not enough to influence a multitude's

---

6 Furthermore, as Sighele will explain in *La teoria positiva della complicità* [The Positive Theory of Complicity], *The Criminal Crowd* was conceived as the first volume of a collection to be titled *Le società criminali* [Criminal Societies], dealing with biological, sociological, and juridical aspects of collective crime, which would also include *The Criminal Couple* and *Sectarian Criminality*.

7 Hereafter, all parenthetical titles in Italian refer to quotations from sections of Sighele's books not included in our volume. English translations are my own.

8 For instance, Sergi, in his 1889 article "Psicosi epidemica" maintains that the suggestion observed in hypnosis is, in fact, a cardinal phenomenon of any individual's psychic life (154). It is so pervasive that Sergi even defines it as "un morbo epidemico di natura psicologica" [an epidemic disease of a psychological nature] (160).

9 It is precisely this all-encompassing power of suggestion as a practically universal, hence almost magical force that Georg Simmel, while upholding the centrality of crowd behaviour, will criticize in Sighele's argumentation, to the detriment of more solid explanations like interaction (see Borch 87).

behaviour, hence suggestion alone cannot account for the degrading collective manifestations. In the crowd "the microbe of evil can easily thrive and [...] the microbe of good almost always dies" (*Crowd* 32), because, Sighele concludes, "the good qualities of the individuals, rather than adding up, cancel one another out" (32).

Sighele explains this radical behavioural change through a parallel, which Sergi had already introduced, between suggestion and hypnosis, a captivating phenomenon for turn-of-the-century European scientists from Lombroso to Sigmund Freud (1856–1939), in the wake of the studies by French neurologist Jean-Martin Charcot (1825–1893).[10] *The Criminal Crowd* assumes that, just like human personality is not "entirely extinguished, but only diminished" (*Crowd* 69) under hypnotic suggestion, the impetus of the crowd favours crime even among individuals who are not born criminals, but simply weak. People are "easily or very easily prone to the suggestions of the external environment, according to the cases and degrees" (71). In *The Criminal Couple* he will reiterate this connection by treating cases of "suggestion in the state of wakefulness" (*Couple* 87) like those of "hypnotic suggestion" (87).

Together with the references to hypnosis, as well as to other scientific phenomena like contagion and microbial infections,[11] a recurring simile taken from chemistry (and already adopted by Ferri) highlights the difficulty of ascribing juridical responsibility to the individual members of an assembled group: "just as chemical reactions among various elements result in new and different substances, so, too, the psychological reactions among various feelings result in new and terrible emotions, unknown to the human soul until that moment" (*Crowd* 37). Sighele's essay *Contro il Parlamentarismo* [*Against Parliamentarism*] will foreground "the very complicated laws of chemistry" (*Sectarian* 198) that govern the human psyche even in political contexts, resulting in "always surprising, and often unexplainable, phenomena that are called combinations and fermentations" (*Sectarian* 198)—a claim that reappears almost verbatim

10 Freud had referred to hypnotic suggestion since his studies with Charcot at the Parisian Salpetrière Hospital in 1885–86 and started using hypnosis to treat nervous diseases in 1887.

11 Another scientific term that Sighele frequently adopts to describe mass behaviour or the effects of suggestion upon the individual is the verb "to polarize," which we have preserved in our translations, whenever we deemed appropriate, so as to highlight Sighele's multifaceted idea of a certain transmission and accumulation of energy (alternatively connoted in biochemical or electromagnetic terms) characterizing the collective experience.

in *Modern Eve* (this volume). Given Sighele's insistence on the unexplainable complexity of a group's conduct,—suggestion is an "arcane force" (*Couple* 79), as he claims in *The Criminal Couple*—, his "psychological chemistry" (*Sectarian* 205) is ultimately closer to alchemy, since, as we read also in *The Intelligence of the Crowd*, "although the phenomena of collective psychology resemble chemical phenomena a great deal, for their unexpected *precipitates* [...], what is possible in chemistry is impossible in collective psychology, namely, to know the required dose of the various substances in order to obtain the new substance" (*Intelligence* 254).

Significantly, although the starting point of Sighele's theory is the intrinsic difference between the behaviour of the crowd and that of the single subject, these ungraspable forces, in fact, undermine both the social order and the individual's coherence. In *The Criminal Couple* turmoil and fragmentation emerge as permanent factors in the single self. Even a love relationship reveals to us the illusion of spontaneous action. We believe we are autonomous, while "the suggestive charm has already started to act" (*Couple* 96). Debunking the absolutist aspirations of psychology, hence implicitly also the adequacy of positivist science to account for the complexity of reality, in *Sectarian Criminality* Sighele admits that all in our world is contradictory, because even a "brief pronoun" like "I" contains "an enormous mystery" (*Sectarian* 150)—it is a synthesis of our organism, but we ignore its "psychological formula [...] as invisible as air, as impalpable as fire, and nonetheless, as mighty and eternal as life" (150). In these lyrical phrases, which reveal more fascination than uneasiness for this feeling of self-dispossesion, we can see the prelude of the more thorough Freudian investigation that in less than a decade would disclose "the royal road to the unconscious" (*Interpretation* 608). Significantly, "incosciente" ["unconscious"] as both adjective and noun is already frequent in Sighele's works, although without overt psychoanalytical implications.

As we can see from his correspondence with Tarde and Ferri, included in the second edition of *The Criminal Crowd*,[12] Sighele's scholarship had by then an undeniable international relevance, which also entailed an international dispute with Gustave Le Bon. Unquestionably, by the

12 The second edition of *The Criminal Crowd* reproduces the entire text of the first version, with only minor changes and a slightly longer conclusion. Part II of the volume collects selected correspondence between Sighele, Ferri, and Tarde on the intelligence and morality of the crowd, the physiology of success, and contagion in popular riots, followed by the texts of several Italian court rulings on collective crimes.

time Le Bon publishes *Psychologie des foules*, other scholars—among them Taine, Fournial, and Tarde in France, and Sergi, Ferri, and Sighele himself in Italy—had already circulated their theories on group behaviour. Therefore, Le Bon's claim that his book was tracing a furrow "sur un terrain bien vierge encore" [on an almost still virgin soil] (*Psychologie* 10) sounded rather suspect, especially once Sighele's ideas became even more accessible through the very successful French translation of *The Criminal Crowd*. In his detailed account of this quite intricate affair, Jaap van Ginneken has convincingly documented, in chronological order, Sighele's interaction with Tarde on matters of crowd psychology and collective crime, the existence of French reviews of Sighele's *The Criminal Crowd* even before its French translation (followed by even greater visibility in French journals after his translated edition), and Tarde's appropriation of Sighele's research for his presentation at the Third International Congress of Criminal Anthropology in Brussels in 1892, which he frankly acknowledged (Ginneken 119–21). All this intriguing background makes Le Bon's obliviousness rather puzzling. As has been observed, although *Psychologie des foules* tackles the same subjects as Sighele's, Le Bon does not mention Sighele's treatment of the crowd's crimes, yet, in fact, he produces very similar argumentations, often corroborated by the same examples from previous scholars—the critic and historian Hippolyte Taine (1828–1893) among them (Ginneken 122; Palano 348). The resentment that Sighele expresses in his article "Una pirateria letteraria" [Literary piracy] is hence justifiable. Among the different forms of crime that he analyses, he cynically places intellectual theft substantiating it with the case of "Mister Gustave Le Bon [...] who [...] copied all or almost all that could be copied from an Italian book titled *The Criminal Crowd* ("Pirateria" 171) forgetting to cite the author's name. In *Sectarian Criminality*, Sighele resumes his polemical references to Le Bon's theft of intellectual property, sarcastically adding that, given that one appropriates what is considered accurate, Le Bon's plagiarism attests to the validity of his own observations on the psychopathology of the crowd.

In *Psychologie des foules*, however, Le Bon also takes a different direction, offering a new explanation for the behaviour of both occasional collective formations and entire peoples or races. Where Sighele focuses on the leader's influence upon the mass, Le Bon emphasizes two factors on which the psychological structure of a collectivity depends, namely, beliefs and opinions. While beliefs are deeply ingrained in a civilization and can only be modified with violent revolutions, opinions for Le Bon are fleeting standpoints that a crowd occasionally endorses (*Psychologie* 132, 179). Yet, since he foregrounds the mainly religious nature of the crowd's beliefs, Le Bon, like Sighele (and in contrast to Lombroso) assumes that any form of group behaviour derives from an irrational, emotional force. In any case, the tension between their respective standpoints seems to dissipate from the perspective of Sigmund Freud who, in *Group Psychology and the Analysis of the Ego* (1921), despite his extensive discussion of Le Bon's "deservedly famous work" (*Group* 11), adds that "none of that author's statements bring forward anything new" (32), and that, in particular, the idea of "the collective inhibition of intellectual functioning and the heightening of affectivity in groups, had been formulated shortly before by Sighele" (32). Yet, Freud is ultimately more focused on what both Sighele's and Le Bon's approaches share, namely, their attention to "groups of a short-lived character, which some passing interest has hastily agglomerated out of various sorts of individuals" (35). For his part, Freud upholds the continuity between individual and group, interpreting suggestion and emotional contagion as particular manifestations of a more elementary and universal force—the libido—transcending the specific kind of group.

*The Criminal Crowd* well shows the occasional nature of the group that Freud criticizes in Sighele and his contemporaries. Here the unpredictable outburst of mass brutality derives neither from a conscious intent to revolt nor from its leader's genetic predisposition to criminality. Rather, in Ferri's footsteps, Sighele explains mass behaviour as a transitory state that, because of external perturbations, alters the ordinary social equilibrium and the individual's psychic stability. Sighele, however, conceives the mind as a progressive superimposition of psychic layers, implying that any episode of collective emotional turmoil occurs because suggestion brings back to the surface the most ancestral elements inherent to the individual and the species as a whole: the crowd "descends with a dizzying speed down the rungs that lead it to the most cowardly brutality" (*Crowd* 49), hence suddenly exposing "the savage [...] from underneath the skin of civilized man" (39). This account of the evolution and relapses of civilization into savagery is one of the recurring themes in turn-of-the-century intellectual discourse, itself evolving from the depiction of atavism as an endemic, regressive force that threatens to disaggregrate civilization—as in Taine and Lombroso—, down to Nietzsche's evocation of ancient, noble roots as the model for future regeneration. For his part, Freud will reinterpret atavism not only as dormant relics of destructive primitive instincts brought to the surface by the individual's group experience, as in his *Group Psychology and the Analysis of the Ego*, but also as a productive anachronism that, by manifesting the disruptive relationship between the modern subject's traumatic past and its present mental and behavioural distress, fosters self-awareness (in the episode of the Wolf Man, for example). Arguably, Sighele partakes of both these perspectives, because, although he sketches a negative portrait of the crowd, he also maintains that the crowd promotes social change.

Sighele's interest in group behaviour soon transcends the mere dichotomy between individual and collectivity and begins to focus on specific social associations that become the object of *The Criminal Couple* and *Sectarian Criminality*. Elaborating on his previous observations about group suggestion as the extension of the *delirium à deux*, Sighele now justifies his focus on couples as the opposite extreme of the criminal crowd: "the crime by two and the crime by a thousand [...] close the chain of all the innumerable varieties and forms of criminal societies" (*Couple* 76). As the most elementary form of group association and supposedly the embryonic stage of all other more complex alliances, the couple allows Sighele to further explore the dynamics leading to the individual's influence on the mass, be it for legal, illegal, or criminal activities. While *The Criminal Crowd* discusses crowd behaviour as a temporary condition that may affect anyone, hence representing a mitigating factor in the individual's responsibility,[13] *The Criminal Couple* narrows its focus to unhealthy social environments where particular categories of subjects commit crimes as a couple. Resuming his earlier discussion of the power of suggestion, Sighele establishes a correspondence between physiological and pathological behaviour, maintaining that the captivating power that a notorious murderer exerts on a criminal is analogous to that of a charismatic artistic or scientific figure on a normal individual. Both respond to the need for an ideal, be it glorious or infamous, and made further attractive by the ascendancy that these models can have on those who are in direct contact with them.

Sighele's criminal couple functions according to a kind of Hegelian master-slave dialectics that highlights the asymmetry and simultaneously the interdependency between the two parties.[14] Just as the cohesion of two people in love derives, for Sighele, from a conscious or unconscious

13 An English summary of Sighele's support of penal leniency on unpremeditated mob criminals, penned by Robert Ferrari, appeared as "Sighele on Adulteration of the Positive Doctrines in Collective Crimes" in a 1912 issue of the *Journal of the American Institute of Criminal Law and Criminology*.

14 Significantly, Sighele himself alludes to the interdependence of master and slave in his analysis of Balzac's *Human Comedy* when he describes the criminal couple represented by Vautrin and Lucien de Rubempré (*In Art and in Science* 405).

negotiation between the superiority of one person and the submissiveness of the other, the wicked individual and his morally and intellectually weak counterpart are reciprocally enslaved. As it creates a spiritual and intellectual dependence between the two, this apparent imbalance enables "magnetic communications from soul to soul (*Couple* 93). The visceral syntony caused by unconscious reciprocal imitation can easily propel both constructive and destructive emotions, and lead to homicide and even suicide, which, according to Sighele, are often committed by the weaker individual under the influence of the more compelling partner. Although Sighele considers insanity to be the cause of social alienation par excellence, he maintains that even the insane couple is held together by this intimate social bond between what he presents as the *succubus*—the person who instigates—and the *incubus*—the individual subjugated to the partner's influence.[15] Upon these premises Sighele substantiates "the universality of the *form à deux* of suggestion" (89) and shows the path that transforms mere diversity of personality into criminal suggestion, according to a tug of war between corrupting and being corrupted that does not diminish either partner's moral and legal responsibility. If "[u]nity is strength in good as well as in evil" (143), a crime committed by a couple is more serious and deserves harsher punishment.

Assuming the lack of intrinsic difference between the born and the occasional criminal—in contrast to Lombroso—, Sighele illustrates a series of cases in which suggestion influences a couple's crime, blurring the emotions and the degree of accountability of the two individuals, and maintaining that the subject is neither completely manoeuvred by forces beyond its control nor totally autonomous in its decisions. From the murderous lovers to the infanticidal couple, he thus throws light upon social, legal, and moral challenges in Italy and Europe overall at that time, for instance, the increase in abortion cases in urban environments and the need to address male complicity and liability. At the same time, however, Sighele falls back to the positivist Lombrosian rigidities as soon as he

15 Sighele already introduces the terms *succubus* and *incubus* in a note to *The Criminal Crowd* (26n58) where he connects the effects of suggestion in normal and insane states, as well as in suicide and crime, also explicitly associating the condition of the *succubus* to that of a slave. Significantly, in the 5th edition of his *L'uomo delinquente* (1897), Lombroso quotes extensively from Sighele in his discussion of the criminal couple as an instance of occasional crime committed by "criminaloids," that is, individuals predisposed to crime but carried away by circumstances—in this case by reciprocal suggestion.

confronts the anomalies and excesses of what he defines as degenerate couples, a veritable "other" reality with respect to social norms. From prostitutes and their pimps to same-sex partnerships, Sighele highlights what for him are dangerous psychological perversions through which allegedly unhealthy social components threaten healthy and righteous individuals.

The wider group associations mentioned at the opening of *The Criminal Couple* become the object of investigation in *Sectarian Criminality*, which Sighele conceives as the *trait d'union* between his study of the crowd and that of society at large. Referring—this time in peaceful terms—to Le Bon's latest studies on crowd psychology, together with contributions by the only two other scholars whom Sighele recognizes in the field, namely, Henry Fournial (1866–1932) and Gabriel Tarde, Sighele here reinterprets the dynamics of collective criminality beyond the simple re-emergence of violence as a temporary halt of, or deviation from, human evolution. Sighele now distinguishes between the atavistic brutality of lower social layers and the perverse deviance of more elevated classes, claiming that the former constitutes one particular stage of the evolutionary process—"the crisis of a young organism that is growing and progressing" (*Settaria* 24), hence is the intimation of renewal, the dawn of a new social era—, while the latter is a pathological manifestation confirming that the current social system has reached its terminal phase, "the index of a sunset, [...] a sign of the degeneration of an already old organism" (24). As it manifests the energy and boldness with which lower classes can prevail upon a superior but exhausted social layer, the crowd's psychological dynamics substantiates the widespread anxiety that perturbs the turn of the century, "that obscure complex of causes that the French define as *fin de siècle*, Nordau end of race" (20) and Sighele "less poetically, but more realistically—*end of the bourgeois regime*" (20, original emphasis). This observation about the fragility of the apparently monolithic, rational, self-controlled bourgeois subject, the protagonist par excellence of the European late nineteenth century, is particularly insightful in connection with the social dynamics of post-unification Italy, where the Italian subject, and the bourgeoisie in particular, were in their nascent state. As Susan Stewart-Steinberg observes, the national subject that emerges from the project of making Italians is "an ego of anxiety" (*Pinocchio Effect* 4) living in a post-liberal environment. Where exactly does Sighele situate himself in this vision of a conflictual European society allegedly on the verge of implosion? What future does he delineate for the Italian mass society approaching the new century?

With an interesting conflation of space and time, Sighele assumes that every society reproduces synchronically its own diachronic evolution.

Hence the alleged savage tribes that constitute for him the primitive ancestors of advanced civilizations reappear as the lowest classes within modern societies. Anything but neutral despite his declared objectivity, this social layout conveys Sighele's own judgment and fears as he attempts to shake the middle and cultivated class from its indifference to the looming social threat. Inspired by the Goncourt brothers' depiction of workers' crowds as the barbarians of modern society, Sighele here underscores, but does not endorse the renewing effects of their disruptive potential. Rather, through the study of collective psychology, Sighele pursues at once a criminological and a social objective, namely, to understand the illness of civilization and to find remedies. Yet, the predominant feeling that emerges from his argumentation is a sense of belatedness and of an impending defeat at the hands of "the future wreckers of our civilization, or—at least—its future masters" (*Settaria* 45). If the power of masses constitutes the only invincible and increasingly respected force that holds the destiny of the world in its "unconscious hands" (43), the only resource left to withstand such an ungovernable entity is to use knowledge as a protection against the danger of being too much governed by it.

With his intellectual work, Sighele therefore now strives to fill the many persisting gaps between crowd psychology and sociology, examining other forms of group psychology that are for him necessary to understand such an apparently dangerous social movement that, however, also constitutes an inevitable step in social evolution. For instance, he presents the modern state as the ultimate and most perfect human aggregate that developed out of the primitive and savage crowd, transforming the latter's transitory and unconscious scope into a stable organization of individuals. In overtly Darwinian tones after his influential reading of *On the Origin of Species*, Sighele explains the evolution of other intermediate associations—sects, castes, and classes—which he defines as homogeneous and permanent in opposition to the heterogeneous and occasional social formations examined in *The Criminal Crowd*. The sect is crucial for Sighele, as it represents the "*nucleus* and the *yeast* of every crowd" (*Sectarian* 151), "the chronic form of the crowd" (*Settaria* 55), just as, conversely, the crowd can be seen as "the acute form of the sect" (55). When individuals of different social extraction or education share a common ideal generated by religious, scientific, or political faith, they acquire remarkable compactness and power. No matter whether it is composed of criminals, martyrs, or instigators, the sect—Sighele argues—always represents the first phase of the development of an idea, which requires a unique rule and scope in order to consolidate itself.

Because of its total devotion to an ideal, the sect's actions are never impulsive. Even when it resorts to violence, it does not commit unnecessary atrocities, unlike the crowd. At the same time, with respect to castes and classes, the sect is "always *innovative*" (*Sectarian* 173) because, thanks to the psychological strength and unity of its members, it nourishes a spirit of revolt that, aiming at social dissolution, promotes renewal. The sect is hence the negative soul of any revolution, necessary as much as its crimes, despite its "inferior and retrograde tactic" (170), and Sighele prides himself on being the first to demonstrate the utility of political crime for human progress.

Yet, Sighele's apparent endorsement of social unrest as a factor of innovation coexists with a deep uneasiness at the individual's increasing lack of autonomy. The potential mobility between different kinds of human association confirms with a vengeance what Sighele presents as the crisis of the subject, overthrown by multiple forms of collectivism. Elaborating on his recurring thoughts about the constraints of the self, Sighele here effectively maintains that the "poor human brain" (*Sectarian* 149), deprived of free will, is no longer "an absolute king" (149), but, rather, "a constitutional king" (149), with only a semblance of freedom and, in fact, subject to a plurality of external factors, fermenting in his brain and awakening simultaneously. Significantly, even the sect leader, who apparently exerts his authority on the group's thoughts, is, in fact, subordinated to the influence of the idea itself. The "*meneur* [...] is, above all, a *mené*" (159). Possessed by fixed ideas, he no longer belongs to himself—an effective image of self-alienation with which Sighele synthesizes the subject's lack of control over the influence of the multitude—what Remo Bodei connotes as the colonization of consciousness (*Destini* 12).

Furthermore, just as collective psychologies change according to the particular social aggregate, morality differs not only among individuals of various epochs and social environments, but even within a single subject in relation to its roles and conditions. In particular, building on his conviction that collectivity is always morally worse than a single agent, Sighele elaborates on the difference between the malleability of public moralities (deliberately in the plural) and the greater rigidity of individual morality. Sectarian morality foregrounds the centrality of cultural and conceptual borders in determining moral resolutions, as the sect highlights the dualism between internal and external relationships, and consequently, the relativity and arbitrariness of moral codes. Hence patriotism, which Sighele considers no less sectarian than a religion, shows how easy it is for the cult of love inside the homeland borders to turn into a religion of hate against what lies beyond them.[16] Likewise, the equally sectarian political morality arbitrarily justifies governmental corruption, a particularly hot topic in Sighele, which, as we will see, nourishes his hostility towards parliaments.[17]

In *Sectarian Criminality* Sighele reiterates the inevitable discrepancy between public and private morality, and presents history as an incessant struggle between inferior classes, which fight with barbarous means to promote change from below, and superior ones, which, with more civilized strategies, set obstacles from above to slow down progress. Nevertheless, in *The Intelligence of the Crowd* Sighele transcends the destructive action of belligerent crowds, maintaining that, as a legacy of the nineteenth century, the "multiform and complex" (*Intelligenza* 17) collective soul already holds the destiny of society in hand, and its power now manifests itself even in peaceful circumstances—as meetings, elections, and public opinion. He hence aims to devise ways to render this despotism "more conscious and worthy" (16), by elevating it morally and intellectually.

Sighele contextualizes his discussion of the collective social dimension within the Italian unification process, offering a critical view of that redemptive notion of "the people" that propelled the Risorgimento. A comparison with other modern European nations shows for him that the proverbial creativity and resilience of the Italian individual has failed to translate into a prosperous common homeland. This Italian psychological paradox, according to which better elementary components generate a much worse product, derives, in his view, from the endemic fragmentation of the peninsula. While France, Germany, or England fostered

16 These statements provide a more nuanced image of Sighele than that of a fanatic nationalist.

17 See section 4 below for a discussion of Sighele's *Against Parliamentarism*. In *Sectarian Criminality*, Sighele mentions the scandal of the Panama Canal to demonstrate how honest people can give in to political vice and crime losing any restraint when they participate as a collectivity. The main reason why the affair was denounced, in his view, is that the dealings were not successful, while the politicians involved in the analogous case of the Suez Canal were acquitted. Sighele decries the same imbalance between private and public morality in Italian politics. For instance, he was deeply struck by the political-financial scandal of the Banca Romana that impaired Italy's stability. The bank had loaned large sums to property developers but was left with huge liabilities when the real estate bubble collapsed in 1887. Fearing that publicity might undermine public confidence, Prime Minister Crispi tried to keep the information secret but the scandal broke out in parliament in 1892.

cohesion of individual energies towards a great collective soul able to inscribe the national character into each single component, Italy has remained a cluster of independent planetary systems, in which regional bonds prevail and every individual bears above all "the stigma of his province" (*Intelligenza* 20). Yet, the real problem, for Sighele, lies in Italy's disavowal of its own anthropological and psychological variety, and in the false patriotic rhetoric that has ensued. Unmasking the alleged lies on which Italy has been feeding since 1870, Sighele maintains that his country cannot achieve authentic unity through a uniform educational, political, and legal system. The prejudice of this unnatural and impossible evenness can only create "a single Italian type that does not and cannot exist" (22), while, in fact, an administrative federalist system would for him facilitate the development of different kinds of Italian subjects able to shape Italy as a flexible organism harmoniously combining their various energies.

Convinced that the real strength of his country lies outside the atrophying effect of national institutions, Sighele urges a more practical and modern mass education rather than bookishness, so as to foster the birth of "a free and unconstrained people" (*Intelligenza* 29) endowed with a veritable collective consciousness. Sighele here seems to retrieve but also revise Mazzini's claims on the end of the epoch of the individual, replaced by the modern "mondo *sociale*" [*social* world] (Mazzini, "Pensieri" 98; original emphasis). While Mazzini's insistence on the need to educate the people starts from the belief in the latter's edifying potential, Sighele's multitude is never intrinsically good and reliable. Even when Sighele gives credit to collective works, he does not question that, generally, "the crowd is morally worse than the individual" (*Intelligence* 226), although he admits that sometimes the former surpasses the latter and displays the highest human qualities. We see this duplicity—the obscure, "mysterious divinity of the collective soul" (*Intelligenza* 33)—in Sighele's treatment of the relationship between art and the crowd and in the role of public opinion.

Sighele reconsiders even the apparent incompatibility between art and the crowd, from a standpoint that recalls Oscar Wilde's maxim, "Art should never try to be popular. The public should try to make itself artistic" (Wilde 248). Discussing the strife between individualism and socialism, which for him is one of the many tensions that nourish "the great doubt" (*Intelligence* 223) into which the new century is born, Sighele challenges the contrast between the haughtiness of the artist and the faithfulness of his crowd of followers, highlighting the "unconscious work" (223) of collective production. Despite the frequent Nietzschean overtones in his overall oeuvre,[18] here Sighele goes as far as to attack the "supermen" (233) who despise the multitude as a jumble of brutes unworthy of the gift of a work of art. Rather, the genius reveals truths that, in fact, are asleep in everybody's consciousness and that the collective soul has only partially sketched or glimpsed but will ultimately embrace with time, as any idea has to struggle against adversity before imposing itself and gaining collective approval. Having bridged the gap between crowds and society, as much as between the individual and the collective mind, Sighele transcends the stigma of the multitude univocally as an agent of crime and, rather, validates its positive, constructive role as a contributor to civilization and as a producer of culture, in competition with single great figures for the advancement of progress (McClelland 172).

By redeeming the intellectual function of collectivity, Sighele now paves the ground for his discussion of public opinion, focusing once again on the ambivalence of the multitude as a whimsical supporter of error much more frequently than of truth. Sighele's investigation of the notion of "public" as a synonym of either crowd or people according to the context owes to the categories that, more than a decade earlier, Gabriel Tarde had discussed in articles he would later collect in *L'opinion et la foule* (1901). For Tarde, after the psychology of the crowd it was time to study the psychology of the public, to be interpreted not so much as any static assembly like the audience at a theatre performance (for him still an instance of crowd), but rather as an endlessly growing collectivity composed of physically separated individuals brought together by a mental cohesion.[19] Endorsing Tarde's main standpoints and terms on communication and social influence, Sighele invokes the positive method to separate the vague and protean nature of the public from other collective entities, like the crowd or the people in general. The crowd requires physical contact, but the public—a more advanced form of association

18 In addition to several references to Nietzsche in his books, Sighele authored the essay "Nietzsche e le teorie biologiche moderne," which appeared in his posthumous collection *Letteratura e sociologia*. There, he maintains the Lamarkian and Darwinian foundation of the German philosopher's thought, explaining the theory of the superman as "a logical consequence of evolutionary transformism" (34).

19 "The public […] is a dispersed crowd, in which the influence of minds on one another has become a remote action, at increasing distance. Ultimately, Opinion—which results from all those remote or direct actions—is for crowds and publics what thought is, somehow, for the body" (Tarde 7, my translation). "We have made the psychology of crowds; now we have to work at the psychology of the public, […], as a purely spiritual collectivity, a dissemination of physically separated individuals, whose cohesion is entirely mental" (8–9, my translation).

from the evolutionary point of view—is comprised of people who share an idea or common feeling, thanks to an “invisible, mental cohesion” (*Intelligence* 240). With an argument that anticipates Benedict Anderson’s observations (*Imagined Community*, 39–46) on the role of print culture for the construction of the nation as an imagined community, Sighele connotes reading as an “invisible, intellectual thread” (*Intelligence* 242) binding individuals unknown to and distant from one another—a much more effective and up-to-date representation of universal suffrage than parliament, Sighele provocatively adds. Unlike the crowd, the public does not necessarily react in unison, even though, Sighele admits, new means of communication like the railroad, telegraph, and telephone are beginning to transport thought more efficiently, providing the public with the unity of time that it lacked.

Yet, the press and other media also allow the *meneur*’s voice to spread more extensively, hence multiplying the forms of suggestion. Significantly, as Sighele draws attention to the complex social structure of his time, he pinpoints interesting situations that transcend the standard *succubus-incubus* polarization. Do newspapers and journalists shape the public or vice versa? Sighele concludes that no single individual, however great, can influence the collectivity. The two parties develop out of a particular social and cultural conjuncture. In so doing, Sighele questions the clear-cut, qualitative difference between the discerning abilities of cultivated and uncultivated publics. As shown by the Dreyfus affair in France and by the Italian reactions to Prime Minister Antonio di Rudinì’s colonial policy after the Adwa debacle of 1896, the majority, no matter how educated, may be wrong, and public opinion can impose itself even without consensus. Therefore, even the apparent distinction that progress has enabled between a barbaric, atavistic crowd and a civilized, modern public can vanish. Just as the most brutal mob can perpetrate murder, the public can inflict insults and commit defamation, which Sighele considers a moral murder. Sighele thus concludes that, in order to understand the formation of public opinion, it is imperative to combine the psycho-physiology of the public with that of the crowd that he delineated in earlier works.

Distinguishing his perspective from both Le Bon’s monolithic categorization of the age of the crowd and Tarde’s equally static age of the public, Sighele defies univocal standpoints by defining his time both the age of the publics and the age of the crowds. Civilization may as well have transformed the crowd into the public, but the public reverts to its atavistic crowd stage when it can no longer contain itself, just as civilized individuals at times may regress to barbarism. It is precisely to the public that Sighele turns at the outset of the new century, after abandoning his criminological interest in the crowd to embrace an intense journalistic activity through which he popularizes the most crucial sociological and psychological issues that were animating contemporary Italian intellectual debates—in particular, the status of women, the impact of feminism on gender relationships, the bleak conditions of children, and the challenges of early childhood education.

## 2 Eve's Unconscious Power: Woman's World between "Folla" and "Follia"

> [...] This Hydra with one thousand heads, of sublime altruism at times, quite often of frightening ferocity, and always little responsible for her actions.
>
> —*Letteratura tragica*, 191

If the behaviour of the multitude, albeit inferior to the individual's, can as easily attain high ideals as it can degrade to savagery, for Sighele, this is because of its contradictory and extreme psychology. For its inability to keep emotions and reactions under control, the crowd is ... a woman, because, precisely like a woman, it is "capable only of excesses" (*Intelligence* 226), as prone to abnegation as to ferocity, but almost never mediocre and measured in her feelings. Whether Sighele refers to collective resurgences of mankind's buried past or to an overt present, where even the more civilized public opinion has an "undefinable" and "elusive" (234) character, he not only posits a binarism between Western civilization and its external cultural alterity—the savage, tribal, primitive world—but also reinforces this hierarchical comparison, so widespread in fin de siècle discourse, with a gendered simile. The crowd and woman as interchangeable entities embody modernity's internal "other," whom Sighele connotes as endowed with a tremendous unconscious power that they cannot manage by themselves, and that is hence tragically dangerous to social equilibrium.

Whenever woman does not comply with the two roles endorsed by a patriarchal society, namely, the subservient wife and the fertile mother, she becomes the embodiment of the wild, insane unruliness that qualifies the crowd's "negative, destructive action" (*Settaria* 44). She is thus degraded to her biological function of "femmina" (*Intelligenza* 14). Likewise, "the crowd is never a spouse or a mother; it is only a female" (*Settaria* 43). No matter how terrible and immense, neither crowd nor female, can produce on its own, hence they both require to be controlled by knowledge.

Just as through the study of mass psychology Sighele strives to develop a defence against the future masters and destroyers of modern civilization, the exploration of the female subject reveals his anxiety vis-à-vis this disquieting new social agent and his attempt to prevent practices that overstep the codified expectations of a male-dominated society. The female lack of moderation already appears in *The Criminal Crowd*, where Sighele mentions women who purportedly surpass their male counterparts in audacity and cruelty during the French Revolution. Curiously, even the political assembly of the Italian parliament is for him "psychologically a female and often a hysterical one" (*Sectarian* 211)—a derogatory connotation that recurs in subsequent works specifically devoted to woman's condition, such as *La donna nova* (1898) [*The New Woman*, this volume] and *Eva moderna* (1910) [*Modern Eve*, this volume].

Sighele lives in the most eventful decades for the emergence of the woman question. Although support of women's emancipation develops more slowly in post-unification Italy than in other European countries, in 1868 Gualberta Alaide Beccari (1842–1906), a social reformer and spokesperson for women's rights, had launched the journal *La donna*, which for decades promoted progressive ideas also abroad through translations of its articles in one of the first British feminist journals, *The Englishwoman's Review*. Among the contributors to *La donna* was activist Anna Maria Mozzoni (1837–1920), the founder in 1881 of the League for the Promotion of the Interests of Women [Lega promotrice degli interessi femminili], and a strong advocate of a reform of the laws regulating prostitution, to whom Sighele often refers in his writings. Other associations were soon created in favour of women's civic and political rights, such as the Association for Women [Associazione per la Donna] (Rome, 1897)—soon to become the National Association for Women [Associazione Nazionale per la Donna]—, the National Female Union [Unione femminile nazionale] (Milan, 1899), and the National Council of Italian Women [Consiglio Nazionale Donne Italiane] (1903). Cultural and social initiatives, however, in favour of female advancement clashed with male intellectuals' widespread resistance to innovation, in the name of the stereotypical image of the submissive, romantic, maternal, family-oriented woman. Giuseppe Sergi's 1898 article "Il movimento femminista" effectively synthesizes this struggle. Precisely in compliance with nature's norms and normality, he strenuously defends woman's "supreme ministry" (5) as "mother and lady of the house" (5) and condemns the feminist agitators as dangerous rebels against human nature, who are marked even physically by alleged anomalies that render them incompatible with their mission. The outset of the new century does not entail a radical change of mentality, if we think of Filippo Tommaso Marinetti (1876–1944) and his declared contempt for women and hostility to feminism since the 1909 Founding Manifesto of Futurism (*Futurism* 51), or even Luigi Pirandello (1867–1936) and his critique of women's emancipation in "Feminismo" (*Saggi* 1068–72). Precisely like the two male protagonists in Pirandello's essayistic novella, Sighele expresses the masculine fear of female independence with often contradictory statements.

Sighele's writings contribute to the intellectual debate on women and feminism by blending ideological clichés like the feminization of violent collective behaviour with the analysis of woman as a new social subject worthy of enfranchisement. Sighele's endorsement of woman's need to overcome the status of savage instinctuality typical of the crowd attests not only to the sociologist's progressive views, but also to his desire to tame the fair sex, putting it in the service of social stability. Therefore, he often sanctions the less threatening female aspirations while he opposes the more problematic and transgressive ones. The feminine world becomes the receptacle of the main stereotypes and ambivalences in Sighele's thought. Yet, from Sighele's diverse reactions across time, we can also measure the impact of the social, cultural, and political questions of which woman becomes a protagonist between the two centuries.

In *The New Woman*, where, with his customary approach, Sighele draws individual and collective psychological features from pathological manifestations, the female mindset reflects a "*psychology of extremes*" (*New Woman* 266) that renders woman either "awful or excellent" (266), "more cynical, more cruel, more brutal, and more depraved than man" (266) and simultaneously able to surpass men in virtue and moral greatness. The cause lies, not surprisingly for an avowed positivist, in her environment. Does this evaluation aim to challenge or to consolidate woman's current status? Sighele maintains that the morally and intellectually narrow space where woman can act—the family—only allows her to concentrate her affectivity on her next of kin, instead of stimulating her brain with broader issues and theoretical discussions. Even woman's greater capacity to withstand pain derives, in Sighele's view, from her lower sensitivity than man's, ultimately confirming the scientific verdict that "woman is of lesser *anthropological* value than man" (272, original emphasis).[20]

Therefore, Sighele's argumentation at this stage of his career is anything but a denunciation of female alleged inferiority. By granting more

20 Not accidentally, these are truisms endorsed by numerous nineteenth-century intellectuals, from Schopenhauer to Nordau and Weininger, to whom Sighele refers rather frequently in his writings.

freedom and opportunities, female emancipation for Sighele would erase all gender differences apart from the physiological one, which would not suffice to preserve male attraction to the other sex. Sighele patronizingly co-opts even factual observations like woman's lack of autonomy in order to legitimize man's authority. For instance, man's institutionalization of marriage, despite its often inflexible laws, is for Sighele a great advantage for woman, since it protects her from the danger of free love and of loneliness and misery in old age. Furthermore, physiology accounts not only for the codified contrast between female and male behaviour, but also for allegedly more worrisome female anomalies—veritable "*perversions*" (*Donna nova* 81; original emphasis) such as the gender-neutral spinster ["zitella"] (46) or the immoral "half virgins" (48).

To be sure, such aberrations can suffice to dismiss Sighele's position altogether as reactionary and biased, but they also show the difficulty of adjusting to the remarkable changes that were undermining deeply ingrained Italian customs and expectations, partially a result of the influence of more socially advanced Western nations. In the mutable contemporary woman, it is impossible to recognize the woman of yesterday—Sighele asserts with considerable uneasiness. Through his ideological refractions we can glimpse not only the crucial issues with which Italian society was already grappling, but also the developments looming on the horizon. As in the case of the power of crowds, Sighele reluctantly acknowledges the centrality of the so-called woman question in the intellectual discourse of his time and above all woman's expanding social conquests, although he defers them to an undefined future or to foreign cultural spaces, especially England or France.[21]

With the same ambivalence, his 1910 volume *Eva moderna* [*Modern Eve,* this volume] expands on a discussion that Sighele initiated in an eponymous chapter of *The New Woman,* contributing to the widespread

---

21 In the last chapter of *La donna nova,* after acknowledging more progressive foreign manifestations of female freedom such as French and German associations for the defence of women's rights or New Zealand women's brilliant performance in public administration, Sighele lingers on two milestones in the lives of American women, namely, the right to vote in presidential elections and the practice of divorce. Wavering between recognition of feminism as a worthy cause and condemnation of it as a pathological deviation that is even gaining ground in stern England (198), Sighele reduces the new woman's subversive impact by defending the solidity of marriage in Italy and by strategically projecting the need for reforms to a vaguely near future able to accommodate the claims of women.

turn-of-the-century co-optation of the archetypical figure of Eve as the model of modern femininity that synthesizes the major ideological tensions on the woman question.[22] Censoring feminists' obsession with the sexual problem, which has allegedly degraded "woman" to "female," Sighele extols woman's nobler desire for freedom predicated on the conquest of the rights of the soul in addition to those of the body, but he confines woman's demand for love to her institutionalized domestic roles of spouse and mother, assuming her indifference to multiple lovers.

Much of Sighele's patriarchal argumentation about women is founded upon the triad of imposed social functions—mother, virgin, prostitute—that contemporary French feminist critic Luce Irigaray challenges precisely because it reinforces an androcentric economic network of gender relationships that commodifies women: the mother represents use value, the virgin exchange value, and the prostitute both of them ("Women" 186–87). Sighele attempts to lay bare this biased system of values, yet predictably, he does not go so far as to subtract woman from the mercantile logic of patriarchy. He presents virgins and prostitutes as excessive, but interdependent contributors to a system of sexual production, whereby, while the former category of workers is on strike, the latter has to work twice as much. Attention to the female status on the market of values emerges, for instance, in his critique of Alexandre Dumas's three female categories of vestal, matron, and courtesan (*Eve* 299), where he presents virginity as a negligible good that becomes valuable only when it begins to circulate through marriage. Sighele, indeed, seems to foreshadow Irigaray's polemical argument when he denounces that men enjoy "this *value* that marriage has circulated" (37, original

22 From an equally contradictory standpoint, the internationally known physiologist and anthropologist Paolo Mantegazza had also extensively discussed the biological and social role of the "daughters of Eve" in works like *Fisiologia dell'amore* [*The Physiology of Love*] (1873) and *Fisiologia della donna* [The Physiology of Woman] (1893). He glorified the feminine unconditional disposition to give love, which renders women superior to men in the emotional domain, and simultaneously considered women inferior creatures because of their sensitivity, seen as an impediment to their intellectual development. Likewise, Mantegazza denounced social and educational inequalities between the two sexes, yet he opposed all those opportunities that, by promoting women's emancipation, risked compromising the female figure as "the true and great priestess of love" (*Physiology of Love* 226). See N. Pireddu, "Paolo Mantegazza: A Scientist and His Ecstasies," 23–29. Sighele explicitly refers to Mantegazza in *The New Woman* (274).

emphasis), while, in fact, maidens, too, should have the right to free love before, and even instead of, tying the knot. Yet, Sighele implicitly legitimizes the status quo as he ultimately admits the family and society's resistance to such a hypothesis, and thus opts for the lesser evil, namely, the chance to dissolve marriage through divorce rather than the prospect of woman's total freedom through the abolition of the marriage contract altogether.[23] Not surprisingly, this argument, which Sighele was also repeatedly upholding in public lectures, had already stirred polemical reactions among Italian feminists, as shown by philosopher and jurist Teresa Labriola (1874–1941), who in her 1907 piece in *Rivista di Roma* writes, "Scipio Sighele concluded with an invocation to the eternal flame—love—, which must spring from the female soul. But please tell me, readers, is it possible to limit woman's psychic life [...] to love alone?" ("Cronaca" 49, my translation).

Sighele's reticent openness to the customs of the modern Eve also characterizes his approach to the question of adultery. It is for him a blatant example of gender inequality at the time, insofar as it was accepted for men but condemned for women. On the basis of his positivist observation of facts against idealism, Sighele supports adultery as a right for both sexes, yet once again, with many caveats. The occasion for his pronouncement is, significantly, a survey on married women's happiness launched by Danish journalist Rosalia Jacobsen as a follow-up to her controversial article in *Vita femminile italiana* in defence of Italian writer Sibilla Aleramo's novel *A Woman.*[24] Sighele praises the moral battle of Aleramo's female protagonist in favour of personal freedom beyond marriage constraints at the cost of losing custody of her son, yet he does not endorse the implications of Aleramo's message for society at large. *A*

23 It should, however, also be recognized that in *Eva moderna*, as he attempts to embrace a more progressive stance on the feminist cause, Sighele finds it unconceivable that women who are increasingly taking on paid jobs outside their homes still need to remain under the economic tutelage of their husbands (142, 144), and that, ironically, no safeguarding legal measure in favour of women is contemplated whenever they are victims of male material or sexual exploitation.

24 Jacobsen's article in support of Aleramo, published in the July–Aug. 1907 issue of *Vita femminile italiana*, denounced women's discrimination in marriage and met the hostility of the journal's director, who warned readers not to identify with the novel's protagonist. Jacobsen then conducted a survey on married women's happiness titled "Inchiesta sulla donna e il problema dell'amore: Lettera aperta alla Direttrice della *Vita femminile italiana* Signora Sofia Bisi Albini," the results of which appeared in *Pagine Libere: Rivista quindicinale di politica, di scienza ed arte* on 1 November 1908.

*Woman* may as well be one of the best novels penned by an Italian female author, but it narrates an exception that should not legitimize the many cases of female rebellion dictated by vice and immorality. Sighele does not consider adultery a crime, yet he deplores the lies at its foundation and prefers, instead, the sincerity of free love. Ironically, however, he seems to reinstate the male's exclusive property right over the female commodity, as he ultimately laments the loss of voluptuousness once all constraints and mystery dissolve in a relationship.

Although Sighele never fully overcomes his prejudices about gender differences, he sounds increasingly sympathetic to juridical problems affecting women in a rapidly evolving post-unification Italy. His public interventions on the legal unfairness that has relegated women to a condition of inferiority, like the slaves of antiquity or black people in America (*Eva moderna* 129), gained Sighele the reputation of a progressive thinker, as shown, for instance, by the echo of his 1906 conference at the Società di educazione della donna ("Cronaca" 63).[25] Now Sighele foregrounds the tragic consequences of the imbalance between male and female juridical responsibility. When women cannot find the strength to rebuild their lives marked by the stigma of male deceit, they react with violent, even homicidal, instincts against their partners or their illegitimate children, the innocent but blatant evidence of their shame.

These alarming social ills prompt Sighele to advocate for voting and legal rights for women, which at the time were entering a heated international debate. While New Zealand was the first country to recognize unlimited female suffrage in 1893, followed by Finland in 1906, Italy would have to wait until the advent of the Republic in 1946, but ferments in favour of female suffrage were already widespread at the beginning of the twentieth century. For instance, in 1907 the trade unionist and social activist Adelaide Coari proposes a "Programma minimo femminista" [Minimial Feminist Program] requesting women's right to vote in local elections, which in the 1920s Benito Mussolini ended up granting temporarily until a reform reassigned that right to the government.[26] As for political voting, the patriot and journalist Salvatore Morelli (1824–1880)

25 Teresa Labriola herself, commenting on Sighele's lecture on feminism in front of Queen Margherita, found his sincere defence of women's rights all the more surprising, given his anti-feminist past ("Cronaca" 49).

26 See Annamaria Isastia, "La battaglia per il voto nell'Italia liberale," 31–51.

had already proposed a bill in favour of equal juridical rights between men and women back in 1867.[27] For his part, Sighele underscores serious inconsistencies in the Italian legal system. Although both sexes came of age at twenty-one, de facto it was as though women were recognized to be mentally inferior, given their inadequacy to exercise voting rights, while paradoxically a man of the lowest intelligence had no impediment. Beyond the juridical steps necessary to reach the milestone of universal suffrage, however, the major obstacle that Sighele highlights is women's own indifference to the problem, the result, above all, of the illiteracy of more than half the Italian female population. Sighele may have not yet digested the prospect of college-educated women he had earlier dismantled in *La donna nova*, but he is now at least ready to put aside his perplexities about schooling opportunities for women.

Indeed, Sighele denounces Italy's shameful backwardness with respect to other European nations, where the duration of mandatory education was at least twice as long.[28] As he blames the absolutely inadequate three years' elementary schooling introduced at the time of Italy's unification, Sighele demythifies the Risorgimento nation-building enterprise. The greatness of the motherland—he polemically asserts—does not derive from patriotic military heroism but rather from a strong culture, which in his view is not even adequately served by the 1904 extension of mandatory education until age twelve.[29] The need to change the Italian mentality about schooling also implies integration of women as agents and beneficiaries of education. Since this has to happen outside the family, Sighele supports co-educational classes as a more accurate reflection of actual social dynamics: This authentic and fuller life experience enabled by better culture and consequently by enhanced working opportunities is precisely what can help women gain more independence and

27 See http://www.salvatoremorelli.org/parlamentoitaliano.html (last accessed 22 Jan. 2017). Although unsuccessful on that occasion, Morelli continued to introduce legislation in favour of women's rights.

28 For instance, with the 1880 Elementary Education Act, England required mandatory school attendance from 5 to 10 years of age. In France, the "loi Ferry" of 28 March 1882 mandated primary education for both sexes from age 6 to 13.

29 Amid intense discussions about the status of Italian schools, it was the "legge Orlando," from the name of Italian jurist and politician Vittorio Emanuele Orlando, at the time minister of education, that in 1904 extended mandatory education to the age of 12. This law also guaranteed equal salary compensation to teachers across class levels, school location, and gender.

respect, beyond their confinement to the domestic sphere and their simple sexual function.

Yet, Sighele's apparently progressive argumentation also reveals the enduring legacy of the *mater salvifica* ideology that had informed the rhetoric of national identity during the Risorgimento, ascribing to women a moral and political mission through their roles as mothers and educators (Romani 394). Sighele, indeed, hopes that, just as the heroes and martyrs who fought for a united Italy were animated by a patriotic faith "that their mothers' lips had instilled in them" (*Eva moderna* 123), the new generation, too, will rely on the maternal figure's guidance to promote harmony. These observations seem to resurrect, almost verbatim, Giuseppe Mazzini's idealization of woman as a source of moral and intellectual inspiration at once for the family and for the homeland. For instance, in *The Duties of Man* Mazzini extolled the mother as the initiator of the future precisely for her pivotal educational responsibilities towards her child as a budding virtuous citizen.[30] This idea was further elaborated by female pedagogues in the nineteenth century like Giuliana Molino Colombini, Erminia Fua Fusinato, or Caterina Franceschi Ferrucci, who championed the education of women not only for the sake of their independence, but also for their central role in the renewal of their nation. Neither aim, however, was supposed to compromise woman's main mission as angel of the hearth, in charge of the happiness of her family's male components thanks to her moral qualities. Although Sighele agrees that the starting point of feminism is emotional and mental equality between men and women, in fact, he explicitly preserves a hierarchical difference between the two sexes. He intends to rescue the woman from rigid patriarchal impositions, but he cannot accept her brutal competition with man. Woman's aspiration to dignity and freedom of choice in relationships should leave unscathed "all her female attractiveness" (*Eva moderna* 155), and, like his predecessors, Sighele ascribes to society the "duty to shape the girl as a future spouse and mother" (181).

Precisely with an eye to the family, Sighele delves into another challenge inherited by the new century, namely, the social problems of childhood in Italy. The abandonment of infants, child abuse in the family, and juvenile delinquency are sensitive topics that he had already tackled

30 "From the Mother's kiss, Man learns the lesson of hope and faith in life; and hope and faith create that yearning after progress, and that power to achieve it step by step, that future, in short, whose living symbol is the infant, our link with the generations to come" (*Duties* 97). The mother is "for each of us the Initiatrix of the Future" (97).

in his 1899 volume *Mentre il secolo muore* [As the Century Dies] and that will continue to engage him, as also shown in *La crisi dell'infanzia e la delinquenza dei minorenni* [The Crisis of Childhood and the Delinquency of Minors] (1911). For its magnitude, the question of abandoned infants was paramount throughout the Italian peninsula. Its main causes were not only the poverty of the biological parents or prostitution, but also the strict moral codes that would condemn procreation outside of marriage and label as dishonourable a woman's decision to raise her illegitimate child, independently of her social class. Furthermore, even when foundlings were adopted, especially by peasant families, the main underlying motif was often far from humanitarian: they were considered a good investment as future workers in agriculture. Those who remained in orphanages avoided exploitation but had to live in appalling sanitary conditions, correlated to high mortality rates (Gorni and Pellegrini 5–8). Very attentive to these ordeals and to solutions implemented by other nations, Sighele repeatedly advocates for an increase in public assistance to pregnant women—following similar measures in Paris—to help them keep and raise their children. In *Eva moderna*, Sighele denounces the negative effect of modernity—urbanization and industrialization, in particular—upon parent-child relationships, urging a re-examination of criteria for bringing up children in bourgeois and working-class families, broken apart by both male and female employment outside the home.

Sighele believes that it is necessary to transcend the opposition between two stereotypical extremes in the care of children, namely, the idealization of children's innocence and perfection and the demonization of children's selfishness and unruliness. Reiterating that nothing is absolute in psychology, and that "the human organism is a complicated, delicate, mysterious machine" (*Modern Eve* 326), Sighele opposes the projection of logical reasons on the inconsistencies of child behaviour and recommends, instead, to address the causes of those contradictions. Admittedly, his own inquiry into the child's mind still adopts the most pervasive analogy in post-Darwinian social sciences, namely—in line with the atavism he supports in his theorization of the crowd—, that between the psychology of the child and that of the primitive, impulsive savage, a surpassed stage in the mature individual's development yet retrievable at least as a trace precisely through the study of infantile behaviour.[31] Nevertheless, beyond the undeniable limits of these

31 Sighele had already expressed this idea in "I bambini selvaggi," in *Mentre il secolo muore* 180–81.

unproblematic assumptions, Sighele also makes intriguing observations about children's spontaneous creativity that are in syntony with the ideas of pioneering European child psychologists. For instance, Sighele decriminalizes children's lies, explaining them as the construction of an illusory reality through autosuggestion. His referents in his exploration of the infantile creative mind are English associationist psychologist James Sully (1842–1923), author of works like *Studies of Childhood* (1895) and *Children's Ways* (1897); Swedish feminist and suffragist Ellen Key (1849–1925), supporter of a child-centred approach to upbringing and education; and French psychologist Théodule-Armand Ribot (1839–1916) who, in his ground-breaking *Essai sur l'imagination créative* (1900), which appeared in English translation in 1906 as *Essay on the Creative Imagination*, explained creativity as being the result of three psychological factors: the individual's emotions, intellect, and unconsciousness. Furthermore, Sighele even seems to intuit the premises of what Freud would introduce as primary narcissism when he associates childhood and imagination with the "age of the dream" (*Eva Moderna* 265), but he also highlights the child's cruel selfishness and the often boundless projection of the child's personality over its object of desire.

Overall, Sighele calls for a more empathetic relationship with children, based on love and identification with their imaginary world, in contrast with the accelerated maturation imposed by the abstract rules and the dehumanizing rhythms of contemporary civilization. He thus contributes to an intense ongoing debate that, since the Italian unification, had foregrounded the importance of education, physical health, and hygiene for an adequate psychological and moral development of youth. This holistic project of "making Italians" by shaping the new generation involved building values with the aid of the following: literature, well exemplified by novels like Carlo Collodi's *Le avventure di Pinocchio* [*The Adventures of Pinocchio*], Edmondo De Amicis's *Cuore* [Heart], and Paolo Mantegazza's *Testa* [Head]; proper care of the body, through a variety of approaches to physical exercise, by Emilio Baumann, Angelo Mosso, Ferdinando Abbondati, and Alberto Gamba;[32] and proper care of the mind through education, as with the ground-breaking educational methods and logistical arrangements (the "Case dei bambini") pioneered

32 An interesting English synthesis of an 1893 report by the Italian Commission on Physical Education, edited by A.F. Chamberlain, appeared that same year in the *Journal of Genetic Psychology*.

33 For a discussion of these issues in post-Risorgimento Italian society, see Stewart-Steinberg, *The Pinocchio Effect*.

by Maria Montessori (1870–1952).[33] For his part, Sighele makes families (especially mothers) aware of the physiological causes behind their children's indiscipline before reacting with excessive severity or indulgence. From foreign cultures, especially the Anglo-Saxon, Italian society for Sighele could learn how to promote children's free expression rather than imposing uniform roles and predetermined notions. The major problem that Sighele identifies in Italian education is the strength of traditions and prejudices, which makes it difficult to apply new theories. Although his views may not sound particularly progressive to us today—and in some cases quite reactionary, as we have seen—, they were, in fact, much more advanced than the pedagogical projects circulating in the positivist circle from which he had emerged. An eloquent example is Costantino Melzi's *Antropologia pedagogica* (1899), which applied Sergi's anthropometric method to measure students' intellectual, moral, and physical growth using technical instruments.

Nevertheless, although Sighele transcends rigid, dogmatic positivism in the sociological and psychological domains, he remains faithful to its methodology in a particular area of inquiry, namely, literary criticism. Starting from the premise that "the artist can and must be an object of scientific analysis" (*Tragic Literature* 332), Sighele examines the works of leading European writers through the lens of his theories of collective behaviour, focusing on characters and situations that substantiate criminal anthropology and, in particular, his interpretation of associative crime.

## 3 The Crowd in the Literature Laboratory

Art and science are two grandiose rivers, which, despite having different courses, come from an identical source and flow towards a single—invisible and perhaps unattainable—estuary.

—*Tragic Literature* 333

The urgent social questions that Sighele tackles in his writings involve not only the real world, but also the literary domain. With an approach already adopted by the criminological school of Lombroso, and by positivist psychiatry in general,[34] many of Sighele's critical works, now mostly

34 See, e.g., Lombroso, "Il delinquente e il pazzo nel dramma e nel romanzo," and Enrico Ferri, *I delinquenti nell'arte.*

neglected, offer insightful sociological analyses of European masterpieces that reveal his gifts as a perceptive literary and cultural critic with an international vision. In works like *Letteratura tragica* (1906) [*Tragic Literature*, this volume], *Nell'arte e nella scienza* (1911) [*In Art and in Science*, this volume], and the posthumous *Letteratura e sociologia* [Literature and Sociology] (1914), the central questions of Sighele's scientific investigations, namely, the crowd, criminality, and the condition of women, reappear as literary *topoi* crafted by nineteenth-century European authors, as there is no "better document of truth than an artist's intuitions, which anticipate the theories in which we believe" (*Nell'arte* vii). Convinced that "the external environment influences our moral and intellectual sphere, just as it does with our body" (*Sociologia* 11), Sighele defends the "right to analyse works of art sociologically" (*Letteratura tragica* 7) because art for him has a social function.

Sighele synthesizes the main premises of what is still recognized as sociological criticism, which aims at understanding literature by placing it in a wider social context and by analysing the literary strategies adopted to depict social constructs. To be sure, if for Sighele art is "an iridescent reflection of life" (*Letteratura tragica* 148), he remains the child of his time for his often narrow treatment of the literary work as a natural phenomenon worthy of scientific attention, and as a confirmation of predetermined scientific hypotheses. At times, however, Sighele problematizes the relationship between aesthetics and science or the underlying social forces, and even seems to deploy the distinction that, already with Friedrich Engels (1820–1895), transcended the static Marxian dichotomy between economic structure and aesthetic superstructure. Just as for Engels ("Against" 39) art not only reflects but also influences real life and the course of its historical struggles, Sighele's argumentations often underscore the active role that literature and culture can play to modify the social context.[35]

On the one hand, in *Letteratura tragica* Sighele defines the literature of his time as "a clinic" (150) because of its almost exclusive focus on mephitic emotional contexts and degrading urban environments in which

35 We notice this two-directional dynamics at work also in Sighele's discussion of public opinion, where journalists and their audience are described as influencing each other: "every public produces journalists who have its instincts, its tendencies, its talents, and its flaws, [...] but once the public has, so to speak, given birth to its journalist, he, like the son towards his parents, will start to influence the public, to guide and modify its opinions" (*Intelligence* 253).

individuals are victims rather than protagonists. On the other hand, he also dissociates himself from what he portrays as notorious enemies of art like Max Nordau (1849–1923) or Cesare Lombroso. He intends to show that aesthetic activity can be analysed according to scientific parameters without affecting its beauty, even when, as in the case of modern literature, its objects of study are the abnormal and degenerate aspects of life, the "ugly, morbid, or evil" (*Tragic Literature* 333) instances of reality rather than the idealized realm of the good and the beautiful. Given his interests in the anthropological, psychological, and contextual causes of deviant human behaviour, Sighele's main field of investigation is therefore what, since the theories of Émile Zola (1840–1902), has come to be known as the experimental novel, engaged in a dialectical relationship with science, aiming at an objective reproduction of the real according to the laws of nature, and morally committed to act on social phenomena. Sighele endorses what for him are socialist and naturalist writers, as well as their forerunners, who compassionately expose moral illnesses not to punish vice, but rather to heal society. Among these brave allies of science, for him equipped with powerful intuitions and a documented knowledge of psychopathology, we hence find Émile Zola, Eugène Sue, Honoré de Balzac, and also the writer whom Sighele considers *the* Italian genius, namely, Gabriele D'Annunzio.

The portrait that Sighele provides of this kaleidoscopic figure, who ferries Italian literature from naturalism to symbolism and aestheticism and, ultimately, to modernism, may sound particularly intriguing to readers of our time, generally much more attuned to the Dannunzian apostle of beauty, the exceptional individual divorced from social problems and collective manifestations. For Sighele, life in D'Annunzio consists of a duel between the individual and his two fatal enemies—woman and the crowd—which propel progress and bring together aesthetic, anthropological, and political concerns. In the second edition of *L'intelligenza della folla* (1911), Sighele is captivated by D'Annunzio's ability to grasp the tumultuous emotional contradictions of the individual confronted with the multitude as much as with woman.[36] Both trigger male desire to possess and conquer. Sighele highlights the centrality of collective psychology in D'Annunzio's works, from the superhuman contempt for

36 Arguably Sighele shares with D'Annunzio the "inconfessato amore e [...] desiderio inconscio" (*Intelligenza* 57) [unavowed love and [...] unconscious desire] that even the most self-centred of authors is said to conceal behind his alleged hatred for the multitude and for woman alike.

the revolting mob in *Le vergini delle rocce* [*The Virgins of the Rocks*] (1895) and *La Nave* [The Ship] (1908)—the symbol of an overwhelming democracy—to the fecund communion between the artist and an inspiring multitude that reinvigorates individual creativity thanks to its mysterious choral force.[37] Already in *Tragic Literature*, indeed, D'Annunzio's works are said to blend realistic types with characters and situations deriving from an "unlikely and unnatural" (336) imagination. Although Sighele does not appreciate the more symbolistic developments of D'Annunzio's writings, he endorses these marked contrasts as evidence of the aesthetic novelty of his time, namely, the ability of art and even its authority to engage in a dialogue with science.

Thus, besides representing the scientifically perfect "moral neurasthenic" (*Tragic Literature* 337), D'Annunzio's eponymous protagonist of *Giovanni Episcopo* also engages in a conflictual relationship with his rival Giulio Wanzer that epitomizes the dynamics of Sighele's degenerate couple. The *succubus* ends up savagely revolting against the suggestion of the *incubus*, ultimately killing him. For their part, the remorseless premeditation and the egoism that lead Tullio Hermil to infanticide in *L'innocente* [*The Intruder*] pertain to the typology of the born criminal, refined rather than brutal, but genetically devoid of moral sense and able to conceal his perversity under his elegance and ingenuity. With no less psychiatric accuracy despite its implausibility, the oneiric tragic poem *Sogno di un mattino di primavera* [*Dream of a Spring Morning*] (1914), a one-act play, for Sighele convincingly documents Isabella's downfall from extreme happiness to the paralysis of intellectual faculties at the sight of her lover's murder, and the lucidity with which she relives the most heart-rending moments—an almost photographic "artistic resurrection" (*Tragic Literature* 342) of events that occur in mental asylums.

Once D'Annunzio ceases to be faithful to real phenomena validated by experimental observation, his characterization for Sighele succumbs to exaggeration, beyond positive truth. Yet, Sighele does not give up categorizing Dannunzian characters according to anthropological parameters. Giorgio Aurispa, in D'Annunzio's *Trionfo della morte* [*The Triumph of Death*] (1894), can thus represent the abortive madness of the "superior degenerate" (*Tragic Literature* 343) who self-inflicts psychological

37 To D'Annunzio's *La Nave*, Sighele also devotes a chapter in *Nell'arte e nella scienza* [*In Art and in Science*], where he praises the author's ability to draw "all the turmoil of collective life with the precision of a physiologist who plots on paper, in the oscillating lines of a diagram, the emotions of the human heart" (*Nell'arte* 178).

torture through an unforgiving self-analysis, while on the entirety of *The Virgins of the Rocks*—for Sighele the most incomprehensible and emptiest of D'Annunzio's novels—there looms the nightmare of a collective hereditary insanity that overturns the author's intent to highlight the vitality of an aristocratic race.[38] Predictably, therefore, Sighele cannot a fortiori come to terms with the "abnormal idea" (*Tragic Literature* 345) of Nietzschean superhumanism. He censures it as an acritically imported foreign theory that, in properly Sighelian terms, exerts its power of suggestion upon D'Annunzio and, as an alleged illness affecting his characters, ends up infecting him as well from the psychological, aesthetic, and moral point of view.

Without overcoming his taxonomic bias, at the apex of D'Annunzio's art Sighele finds exceptional individuals or pathological moods, rather than physiological and psychological normality. While he disapproves of D'Annunzio's aesthetic turn, Sighele underscores the precision with which the author reconstructs and analyses environment, objects, behaviours, and moral parameters by dissecting scenes, dialogues, and impulses even in his least verisimilar works like *Francesca da Rimini* or *La Figlia di Iorio* [*The Daughter of Jorio*] (1904). Likewise, in *La fiaccola sotto il moggio* [The Torch under the Bushel] (1905)—for Sighele the least convincing because of its technical and at times melodramatic excesses—Sighele lingers on strong passions like hate or jealousy, and crimes like uxoricide, examining characters as defendants in a trial. Sighele thus proves more engaged and open-minded than a more recent sociological critic like Georg Lukács, who condemns modernist literature in bulk precisely for the "abstract particularity" ("The Ideology of Modernism" 1230) of its eccentric, singular protagonists—alienated personalities whose psychopathology distorts rather than portrays the typicality of realism, with its dialectical unity of character and environment. Sighele maintains that at the outset of the century "we are all more or less deranged or neurotic" (*Letteratura tragica* 149), hence implying that what Lukács would later decry as "the disintegration of personality" ("Ideology" 1229) and the subjective world-view it entails are the rule instead of exceptions.

Undeniably, however, Sighele's sympathies go to depictions of humble and even morbid characters that still place social and moral conditions at the centre of representation as forms of what Lukács endorses as

38 Sighele adopts a similar approach in his chapter "I tipi femminili nell'opera di Gabriele D'Annunzio" (*Nell'arte* 105–62) on D'Annunzio's female characters, which are made to comply, even more rigidly than their male counterparts, with behavioural and moral typologies.

"concrete criticism" ("Ideology" 1224) rather than "rejection of reality" (1224). For diametrically opposite reasons to his evaluation of D'Annunzio, it is in Eugène Sue (1804–1857) that Sighele locates a precursor of the positivist approach. Although he finds the French novelist quite insignificant from the point of view of form, Sighele foregrounds the scientific value of his ideas which, as exemplified by his masterpiece *The Mysteries of Paris*, foreshadow pivotal issues in criminal anthropology—the analogy between the barbarian "other" and the criminals of his time, the arrested development that confines the criminal to a state of savage brutality, and the connection between physiognomy and temperament in the typologies of degeneracy that Sue sketches "with Lombrosian precision" (*Letteratura tragica* 100). Sue's novels, therefore, are for Sighele a "copious reserve of documents" (115) that, inspired by real life, study phenomena like prostitution, sexual crimes, violent murders, and civil injustices with an approach that foreruns modern sociology. Furthermore, Sighele praises the brilliant intuitions with which Sue transcends rigid categories (like that of the born criminal) and, rather, underscores the complexity of moral attitudes, hence also the contradictions of criminal psychology. The examples of suggestion he draws from Sue help Sighele validate the main point of his theory, namely, the treatment of collective psychology as the psychology of the unexpected that suddenly modifies the individual's moral choices for good or bad. Sighele endorses, for instance, Sue's hostility to penitentiaries as dangerous spaces of suggestion, and his promotion of alternative social establishments, like provident institutions and agricultural colonies to aid the poor or rehabilitate former convicts. The displacement of Sue's character Chourineur from the deleterious Parisian environment to an African farm, represents for Sighele a successful redirection of violent instincts towards socially useful activities, showing Sue's enduring involvement in the prevention of evil and the promotion of the common good through an art of hope rather than of fear.

In this way, Sighele distances himself from mere literary depictions, dissections, and diagnoses, which for him typify a superficial naturalism and, rather, urges the novel to move from social pathology to therapy. French literature offers Sighele other exemplary models of criminal and spoiled settings drawn from the world of true suffering by authors committed to the social function of literature. Émile Zola's works lucidly present the indissoluble link between heredity and environment without drifting into psychological absolutism or falling back into simplistic atavism. Zola's representation of the "fearsome unknown of the collective soul" (*Letteratura tragica* 158) so crucial to Sighele does not produce "infinite copies of a single type" (156), but, rather, connotes each character and action taken individually, like multiple rays emanating from the iridescent prism of life. Zola's detailed analysis of the remorse that stops the homicidal instinct in *Jacques Lantier* or the crime of the mob of miners degraded by work and inflamed by the redemptive communist promises even beyond their *meneurs'* intentions in *Germinal* demonstrate for Sighele that Zola's art can divulge scientific truth not only by highlighting its two conquests—namely, the discovery of the anthropological type of the criminal and the creation of collective psychology—but also by humanely judging the obscure depths of the multitude's soul and the material causes that awaken it, calling for remedies.

On these principles, in *In Art and in Science* Sighele intends to revive the work of Honoré de Balzac (1799–1850), surprisingly overlooked by both Lombroso and Ferri in their anthropological and psychological studies of literary texts. Sighele himself admits having neglected, until then, the colossal *Human Comedy,* which he defines as the most extensive and complete representation of life produced by a writer who "*carried an entire society in his brain*" (*Art* 377). Balzac's genius—Sighele insightfully claims—lies in its ability to condense at once the spirit and morals of his time and the psychological truths of ours, expressing both of them through his characters' actions and personalities instead of preaching in the first person. It is hard to believe that certain statements "with a flavour of liberalism and socialism" (*Art* 403) in the *Human Comedy* do not come from an extreme left-wing deputy but, rather, from "a conservative and reactionary author who did not hide his sympathy for the Bourbons" (*Art* 403). In these poignant observations we hear echoes of Engels's praise of Balzac as a great master of realism for his depiction of emerging popular masses "against his own class sympathies and political prejudices" ("Realism" 40) in favour of a nobility doomed to extinction.

Among the numerous issues that Balzac tackles in his novels, Sighele predictably lingers on those that are in syntony with his field of investigation—at times magnifying his own idiosyncracies. Thus, in the claims of the Count of La Palferine on women and love, for instance, Sighele finds truths that substantiate his own theory of female psychology revolving around the excesses, volubility, and attachments of the female heart. Likewise, Sighele praises the acumen with which Balzac grasps the peculiar behaviour of criminals, who are always ready to declare their innocence. Sighele, for his part, confirms this regularity by foregrounding the exception represented by the "aristocracy of crime," that is, the tendency of the most fearsome and perfidious criminals to boast of their offences. For his ability to differentiate the psychology of great criminals from that of common delinquents Balzac therefore deserves a place in a genealogy of jurists, physicians, and anthropologists—from Prosper Despine (1812–1892) and Gabriel Tarde to Cesare Lombroso and Enrico Ferri—who have substantiated his hypothesis. Furthermore, Sighele finds in Balzac a poignant precursor of his own inquiries into the deleterious effects of detention upon the convict's psyche. In open polemics with the legislators of his time, Sighele, indeed, reiterates his denunciation of the economic and social inefficiency of the prison system, further elaborating on his claims on Eugène Sue.

The climax in Balzac's characterization of the prison environment is, predictably, Vautrin, for Sighele a masterpiece not only of psychological accuracy, but also of aesthetic creation. Much more effectively than through physiognomy, Balzac provides the moral portrait of a "poet of evil" (*Art* 399) who, thanks to remarkable intuition and absolute unscrupulousness, can manipulate people to his advantage. Vautrin's undeniable attractiveness even leads Sighele to endorse a notion that he had earlier deplored in his analysis of D'Annunzio, namely, that of the "superman against the crowd" (400), which here connotes an exceptional "truthful soul" (401) able to abstract from the particular to the universal. Vautrin is an "unconscious ironist" (402) who can denounce with philosophical cynicism the selfishness and wickedness that are ingrained within the majority, yet hypocritically silenced. Vautrin is equally pivotal to substantiate the typical dynamics of Sighele's criminal couple, since, as Vautrin himself declares, he needs an accomplice, a creature he can model at his own will. His future succubus is Lucien de Rubempré, caught in the magnetic bond of the suggestion *à deux* that for Sighele synthesizes more extended human associations, and ultimately driven to suicide. Even the fact that Vautrin escapes incrimination despite his ruthlessness belongs for Sighele to the logic of verisimilitude rather than of implausibility, since real life presents no less unbelievable legal cases, like that of the criminal and criminalist Eugène François Vidocq (1775–1857). With his strength and charisma, Vautrin clearly validates the law of inequality that Balzac masterfully captures through the inverse relationship between genius and morality. Hence, Vautrin ultimately takes revenge against a cowardly and impotent society that has failed to punish him.

These provocative statements on the inefficiency of laws and magistrates transcend the literary realm. In this interpretation of Balzac's message we can also hear Sighele's polemical stance towards legal and political measures in the society of his time. Like Sighele, indeed, Balzac the great expert of collective psychology fully perceives the gap between individual and political morality, and expresses reservations about the role of parliament, given the unpredictability of the crowd and the risks entailed by its own sovereignty. The author of the *Human Comedy* becomes Sighele's soulmate, as Sighele himself had earlier attacked the parliamentary system, stirring strong reactions in the political and social sphere.

## 4 Collective Bodies, Collective Souls: Sighele, Politics, and Their Aftermath

We need to campaign here, among the populace [...] if we really want to save the Italianness of the country, and, with it, its ideal.

—Sighele's unpublished letter to Giovanni Pedrotti, 30 Aug. 1908

For Sighele 1895 is quite an upsetting year. It shadows his international scientific recognition with the publication of Le Bon's book, and also provides ample evidence of Italy's political dysfunctionality. The transfer of power from the king to the government, which, for decades already, had given more autonomy to the parliament, had led to continued violations of the basic rules of the system. In particular, the closing of parliament had become a dangerous habit that prevented confrontations between the government and its opposition, often entailing the dissolution of the two chambers. All pending bills would decay and the government could no longer perform its functions. Prime Minister Crispi frequently exploited this strategy between January 1894 and June 1895, but he was certainly not the only one.[39] These parliamentary abuses prompt Sighele to publish the pamphlet *Against Parliamentarism: An Essay on Collective Psychology*,[40] where he denounces not only the flaws of the current Italian political system but, more generally, the inefficiency of the parliamentary form itself.

Sighele is certainly not alone in condemning the government, hence dealing yet another blow to the ideal of a respected unified Italy. Many other intellectuals and writers criticized Italian politics in the same

39 See Merlini, "Il governo costituzionale," 19–20.

40 Later republished in *Sectarian Criminality*.

period, from Matilde Serao (1856–1927) with her depiction of the inefficiency and hypocrisy of the government in *Il ventre di Napoli* [The Belly of Naples] (1884) and of Italian politicians' careerism in her parliamentary novel *La conquista di Roma* [The Conquest of Rome] (1885), to Paolo Mantegazza (1831–1910) with his ironic recollections of his experience as a senator in *Ricordi politici di un fantaccino del parlamento italiano* [*Political Memoirs of a Foot-soldier in the Italian Parliament*] (1896), and V.G. Sanfelice's critique of the deputies' ignorance in *La coltura degli uomini politici* [The Culture of Politicians] (1897). Sighele, however, does not only intend to denounce the selfishness and immorality of individual politicians or political parties. He is more in line with the "Italian School of Elitists," including political scientists Gaetano Mosca (1858–1941) and Vilfredo Pareto (1848–1923), who challenged the parliament as an intrinsically flawed institution, doomed to further degeneration along with the extension of suffrage and the consolidation of mass political parties. In his 1883 *Sulla teorica dei governi e sul governo parlamentare* [On the Theory of Governments and on Parliamentary Government], Mosca denounces the group interests behind the parliamentary systems and upholds greater power to the king and to an educated, independent political minority. Similarly, Pareto associates the failure of the parliamentary system with the lack of actual differentiation among Italian political parties and of private initiative, highlighting, instead, widespread connivance for specific personal interests. His critique contains the premises of his subsequent vision of history as an alternation of aristocracies opposed to masses in *The Rise and Fall of the Elites* (1901).

For his part, with even stronger undemocratic implications, Sighele highlights the inadequacy of the parliament as a collective organism, doubting that many people can decide better than one. The psychic elements of individuals gathered in an assembly generate for him "an unknown quid" (*Sectarian* 198) that annuls single intelligences and the intellectual value of the decision at stake, hence determining an inevitable mediocrity. Although he does not avow a preference for the authoritarianism of the single individual, Sighele sees parliament as the locus of a potential tyranny of the many, of numbers, of the mass. In line with his psychological theory on collective behaviour, the majority's right in politics seems to Sighele not only illogical, but also dangerous because the volatile emotions and opinions of the assembly members may erratically overturn decisions at any time, with uncontrollable consequences. The sudden randomness in the functioning of parliament does not only pertain to the deputies' deliberations, according to Sighele, but also to their election. For him, to vote is not a free action but, rather, the result of a hypnotic force that, through speeches and newspapers, influences and manipulates the audience (*Settaria* 254). Electoral behaviour hence exemplifies the functioning of public opinion that he describes in *The Intelligence of the Crowd*, even if he considers the judgment of a scattered audience more reliable, because impressions and reactions are more intense when they are in unison. The power of suggestion affects with equal strength parliament's morality, which for Sighele is tainted by social corruption, voting frauds, and hypocritical libelling and praises.

Sighele is so carried away by this alleged example of sectarian criminality that he indulges in quite daring similes aimed at reinforcing the connotation of parliament as an unmanageable, degenerate collectivity. The Chamber of Deputies is not only psychologically female and hysterical—as we have seen—but also like a group of children whose propensity to evil increases when they form a group. Both images support Sighele's deterministic conviction that no remedy exists to the ills of that intrinsically flawed political institution, yet he indicates ways to limit its damage to the nation: either to reduce the number of parliamentarians or to promote regional autonomy so as to let the corrupted fixers stew in their own juice in Rome—, an intriguing idea for our own times, considering the current debates about the so-called devolution in Italian politics and the separatist regionalism of the Northern League, but certainly contrary to the unifying impulse that had recently made Italian nationhood a reality.

Not surprisingly, *Against Parliamentarism* raised a remarkable controversy that also tarnished Sighele's scientific reliability. Italian socialist politician Leonida Bissolati (1857–1920) attacked Sighele's premises and the almost non-existent scientific seriousness of his applications ("Pseudopositivismo" 88), maintaining that parliament was not born in reaction to hereditary and individual tyrannies but, rather, as a result of human spontaneous gregariousness, and by the action of the bourgeoisie. For his part, Italian deputy Francesco Ambrosoli (1854–1908) responds with *Salviamo il Parlamento!* [Let's Save the Parliament!], where he criticizes Sighele's unilateral view and his simplistic explanation of the parliament's procedures: Sighele should have at least limited his condemnation to Latin regions instead of generalizing to include even the prototypical, fully functioning English model (*Salviamo* 6–7). Furthermore, Sighele equates the parliament to the Chamber of Deputies without mentioning the Senate. Overall, Ambrosoli urges Sighele to look beyond the problems of the specific Italian government that probably triggered his attack, and to consider edifying examples of great deliberations offered by political institutions at large across time.[41] Ettore Lombardo Pellegrino (1866–1952), too, deplores Sighele's axiomatic approach to deputies' irrational behaviour which for him is, in fact, neither extendable to parliament in general nor, a fortiori, tantamount to human nature, but, rather, only an altered and modifiable state (*Parlamentarismo* 64). Even the more sympathetic Pietro Chimienti (1864–1938), who defended Sighele's intelligent and original application of collective psychology to criminal crowds, is puzzled by Sighele's pessimistic drift and by the death sentence he inflicts to parliamentary institutions. He objects to Sighele that collective psychology cannot be reduced to crowd behaviour. While the crowd acts upon few and simple emotional elements, a complex political assembly has intellectual, critical, and moral faculties. Life cannot be understood from such a narrow perspective (*Vita politica* 319).

Antiparliamentarism is not the only controversial aspect of Sighele's intellectual trajectory. The other burning issue is his notoriety as a nationalist, mainly deriving from his irredentism and at times approached unilaterally by critics without enough contextual evidence. Sighele's attachment to his unredeemed Trentino region, which had been under the Austrian regime since the Third War of Independence (1866) despite its Italian indigenous population, prompts him not only to adhere to local Italian cultural institutions like the Società Dante Alighieri, but also to contribute to the creation of an Italian university in Innsbruck in 1903 and to envisage a similar initiative in Trieste. Both projects aborted, because of the strong opposition by local Austrian authorities and students, as Sighele recollects in his *Pagine nazionaliste* [Nationalistic Pages] (1910). Sighele regularly hosted sympathizers of the irredentist cause in his villa at Nago, on the coast of Lake Garda in the province of Trento. After several trials for his subversive activity, in the summer of 1913 an order from the Austrian commissioner gave Sighele eight days to leave

41 The magnitude of the echo created by Sighele's pamphlet is such that Ambrosoli's intervention stirs, in its turn, the reaction of Filippo Turati who, while not strenuously defending Sighele, attacks Ambrosoli's bourgeois ideology. See Turati, "Micrologia politica," *Critica Sociale* (16 March and 1 April 1895). Other critics of Sighele's antiparliamentarism include E. Pinchia, *La bancarotta del Parlamento?* (Roux, 1895); Leonida Bissolati, "Pseudopositivismo," in *Critica Sociale* (1 May 1895); and V. Miceli, "Come salvare il Parlamento," in *Riforma Sociale* (10 Sept. 1895).

the region.[42] This was the final blow to his already precarious health. Scipio Sighele died in Florence a few months later, on 21 October 1913.

To resurrect the hopes of his unredeemed land is, not accidentally, the main impulse animating *Pagine nazionaliste*, Sighele combined Risorgimento patriotism with a liberal form of irredentism that grew particularly fervent after Austria's annexation of Bosnia Herzegovina in 1908. In order to gain Italy's consensus and support for the cause of Trento and Trieste, Sighele joined the Associazione Nazionalista Italiana, led by the reactionary writer and politician Enrico Corradini (1865–1931), and participated in its 1910 congress in Florence despite his dissent with Corradini himself. On that occasion, Sighele expressed the main theoretical ideas that would then converge in his volume, namely, his hostility to impulsive imperialism and the pivotal role of culture and institutions in the defence of Italian nationality in the unredeemed areas of the country. The growth, however, of antidemocratic right-wing tendencies in the association induced Sighele to abandon it,[43] and to keep alive his political commitment through writing. In *Pagine nazionaliste*, addressing new generations in particular, Sighele aspires to promote consciousness of and pride in the nation. Writing from Nago, he foregrounds his condition

42 The echo of Sighele's expulsion was remarkable, as demonstrated by the numerous Italian newspaper articles on the episode, as well as telegrams and letters of support sent to Sighele and collected by his wife, currently archived at the Fondo Sighele. Some of those texts emphasize that, since Sighele is a naturalized Italian citizen, by expelling such a high-profile and much respected intellectual, Austria deliberately attacked the Italian people as a whole, demonstrating all its hatred against them.

43 Both Palano and Bosc attempt to draw a more articulated profile of Sighele, beyond unilateral examinations of his political ideals as consistently anti-democratic, nationalist, and imperialist. Palano explains Sighele's alleged antiparliamentarism not as an authoritarian stance but, rather, as an application of his own theories on political crime to a critique of Italian politicians' parasitism, in the attempt to reduce, at least, the number of parliamentarians (*Potere* 340–41). Bosc provides details about Sighele's relationship with Corradini, and his ultimate separation from the Association once its reactionary orientation condemned the three values that Sighele wanted to preserve, namely, democracy, socialism, and internationalism (Bosc *Foule* 347–48). Already Cipriano Giachetti, commemorating Sighele in *La Nuova Antologia* a few months after his death, had underlined how his nationalism was "a theoretical and practical sublimation of his Italianness" ("Sighele" 99) but did not coincide with a political party, hence his worries about the anti-proletarian tendencies of the Italian right. Likewise, in his biographical introduction to Sighele's posthumous collection *Letteratura e sociologia*, Gualtiero Castellini, Sighele's nephew, highlights the continuity in Sighele's concerns with his small and great homeland (respectively, Trentino and Italy), in the framework of a nationalism with a philosophical foundation outside political parties (*Letteratura* xiii).

as a border intellectual, showing the complexity of Italy well beyond the abstract simplification of its unification, in contrast to the prevailing ignorance of politicians and citizens about geopolitical boundaries and the ordeal of territories still unfairly subject to Austria. Sighele describes the Trentino region as the slave of Tyrol, given the inadequate number of deputies to represent it, the scarcity of its economic resources, and the availability of exclusively German newspapers to its Italian population. Yet, he explains that, unlike the irredentism of the Risorgimento period, the struggle he defends and foresees for the Trentino region is not a military but a legal one, in defence of economic and administrative rights, as well as of nationality.

Sighele connects Italy's indifference towards the Trentino's struggle for liberation from Austria to a wider discussion of the political and cultural importance of internationalism. In his view, Italy neither feels nor understands foreign policy, because its citizens travel very seldom, read very little, and do not invest enough in culture, while other nations enjoy higher profiles thanks to well-respected cultural institutions. A narrow psychology keeps Italy hostage to a parochial pride in visceral petty ideals that translates into political myopia and lack of authentic patriotism. Sighele interprets nationalism in much broader terms than either mere anti-Austrian sentiment or French reactionary legitimism. Nationalism to Sighele amounts to the creation of "a collective national soul" (*Pagine* 235). Significantly, on the one hand, in line with the premises of his collective psychology, Sighele implies that local individualities (citizens or regions) are better than their national whole. On the other hand, however, here he re-evaluates the positive potential of collectivity as he envisages an Italian soul able to overcome the mediocrity of the present by rising above regional vanities. Between echoes of the unfulfilled Risorgimento dream and intimations of the patriotic mirage that would soon degenerate into the nightmare of Fascist dictatorship and of its colonial enterprise, a nationalist for Sighele is "a man who feels proud of his own race and Latin civilization, and wants to defend them against foreigners, who attempt to denaturalize them" (222). Sighele

---

For his part, in *Il nazionalismo e i partiti politici*, Sighele will go as far as to justify imperialism as self-defence (80–81), and war as a necessary consequence, a matter of survival for Italy. The occupation of Tripolitania appears to him almost like a moral obligation after Italy's sacrifices for the Triple Alliance (87). Yet, in her detailed reconstruction of Sighele's political thought, Maria Garbari substantiates Giachetti's and Castellini's views, interpreting Sighele's controversial stance on both nationalism and imperialism in a Risorgimental perspective ("Pensiero" 545).

thus provocatively avows no fear of being accused of imperialism, if this term describes Italy's attempt to lead its politics beyond the humiliating stereotype of a "little boat trailing behind the grand Austro-Hungarian ship" (182) or of a powerless garden of Europe, and gain its own dignity. Halfway between cowardly resignation and defiant provocation, Sighele claims the right to one's own defence without being a medieval warmonger or silently accepting injustice.

Critics maintain that Sighele allegedly resisted the appeal of extreme right-wing politics and defended the kind of moderate, liberal, international thought that Fascism would later attack as an example of positivist democracy (Bosc, "Foule" 45). It cannot be neglected, however, that the theoretician of crowd psychology ultimately falls into the trap of collective suggestion when, less than a year after these pronouncements, Prime Minister Giolitti rekindles Italy's expansionist ambitions obtaining vast support thanks to a huge lobbying operation by the Italian press, able to turn public opinion into mass opinion, in proper Sighelian terms. The invasion of Libya inflames Sighele to such an extent that, despite his poor health, he travels to Tripoli to see the battle with his own eyes. A probable surrogate target for his unredeemed region, the prospect of an Italian Tripoli confirmed to him that his nation could successfully employ equal energy for other victorious enterprises closer to home and to his heart.[44]

Scipio Sighele died as a forty-five-year-old exile, six years before history began to realize his irredentist dream, but inevitably with the use of military force and at a very high price. The Trentino region was annexed to the Kingdom of Italy in 1919, at the end of the First World War, with deep social lacerations within the region, torn between Trentino soldiers fighting in the Austrian army and irredentists on the Italian side, and ultimately penalized by heavy repressions on both fronts, internment, and the massive exodus of Trentino refugees. As for Trieste, its ordeal will not end with the 1920 ratification of its liberation. More foreign occupations will follow after the Second World War. More criminal crowds, manipulated by extremist political ideas, will exert their

44 See his argument about irredentism and the war in Libya in "La nouvelle psychologie irrédentiste depuis l'expédition tripolitaine" (145). Significantly, a note of Sighele's wife on the archived copy at the Fondo Sighele specifies that a lecture he had earlier prepared to deliver in Milan on the same topic was prohibited. He hence published it abroad in article form, yet it enraged Austria nonetheless, and was probably the decisive factor that determined Sighele's expulsion from Trentino.

violence before this last portion of Italy could move to the coveted side of that disputed border.

Crowd psychology did not have a considerable following in Italy after Sighele's death. His notable disciple, who died prematurely in 1905, is Pasquale Rossi (b.1867), who further developed Sighele's ideas on collective psychology in works like *Psicologia collettiva* [Collective Psychology] (1898), *Psicologia collettiva morbosa* [Morbid Collective Psychology] (1901), and the posthumous *Sociologia e psicologia collettiva* [Sociology and Collective Psychology] (1909). Rossi differentiates between sociology as the study of collective bodies and collective psychology as the study of collective souls. He modifies Sighele's theory by assuming that the crowd has a soul and rational faculties, hence it can be educated and is not necessarily prone to crime. With this twist he erases Sighele's distinction between homogeneous and heterogeneous subjects.

Sighele was mentioned quite regularly by the foreign press in his lifetime. Whereas in France his intense correspondence with Gustave Le Bon and Gabriel Tarde and the numerous translations of his works reinforced his scientific profile as a criminologist and sociologist, his reception in the anglophone world, where none of his volumes were translated, sketches a more superficial yet multifaceted portrait. In the American journal *Popular Science Monthly*, Helen Zimmern places turn-of-the-century Italy at the forefront of criminal anthropology and of other branches of social sciences to which Sighele contributes, in her view, as a highly cultivated and fine observer. Nonetheless, he often "jumps to conclusions too rapidly" ("Criminal Anthropology in Italy" 758), especially on "matters English and American of which he has but the most superficial and second-hand knowledge" (758). In a previous article for *Blackwood's Edinburgh Magazine*, Zimmern had devoted an extensive discussion to the "truly remarkable" ("An Indictment of Parliaments" 227) work of *Signor* Scipio Sighele on collective psychology, applied in particular to the institution of parliament. In much more favourable tones than her Italian contemporaries, Zimmern qualifies Sighele's argument as theoretical rather than militant, and adopts it to undermine England's overconfidence in its own representative government, given the intrinsic weakness of the parliamentary institution in general as an unpredictable "assemblage of many persons" (228). In August 1896, *Reynold's Newspaper* announces the English publication of Sighele's article "Individual Morality and Political Morality—A Sociological Problem" in the journal *To-morrow*, offering a synopsis of its major theoretical points. Likewise, on 10 September 1901 the *London Daily News*, reporting on the papers presented at the Fifth International Congress of Criminal Anthropology in Amsterdam, summarizes Sighele's theory of collective crimes, highlighting the relationship between *succubus* and *incubus*, the role of suggestion, and the reduction of individual responsibility in a crowd.

Yet, it is once again for political reasons that Sighele's thought stands out, often co-opted with rather tendentious aims. In a survey of international opinions on Great Britain on the occasion of the Anglo-Boer War, the *Morning Post* (30 Oct. 1899) praises "the eminent Professor of Sociology and Anthropology" (3) Scipio Sighele for his endorsement of Britain's attack on the assumption that "the more civilised nations have the right to absorb the less civilized" (3). Over two decades later, Micklem and Morgan's volume *Christ and Caesar*, which supports the idea of an intimate relationship between the individual and mankind through the mediation of the nation, assimilates Sighele's nationalism to an extreme form of "Jingoism and imperialism" (137), inspired "by a desire for power much after the manner of Nietzsche" (137). Sighele, they conclude, "is as indignant with pacific and humanitarian sentiment in the political realm as is Sorel or Lenin with any show of mildness in the industrial sphere" (137).

However, the aggressive affirmation of national sovereignty that here seems to taint the Italian intellectual's reputation appeared under a quite different light in the commemorations of his death. On 13 November 1913, the American weekly periodical the *Nation* remembers "one of the most distinguished Italian sociologists, [...] banished by the Austrian government for asserting his ideals of political liberty" (457). Besides sympathy for Sighele's political vicissitudes, the author of the obituary, Harvard University scholar Rudolph Altrocchi (1882–1953), extols his high patriotic ideals, including his glorious manifestation of nationalism in the Tripoli campaign. Altrocchi provides a flattering portrayal of Sighele as "both scientist and artist" (457), not only "a pioneer" (457) in collective psychology, but also a deep connoisseur of literature and a psychological critic who skilfully analysed "social evils and the character of crowds" (457) in real life as well as in fiction. Altrocchi's edifying obituary equally upholds the political repercussions of Sighele's sociological vision, rectifying that the psychological inferiority of the group with respect to the individual does not lead in Sighele to a pessimistic philosophy of government. Rather, it is propelled by a proactive "ideal philanthropy" (458) that moves from the improvement of the individual to that of social and political collectivity.

In the United States, Scipio Sighele's works initially became known mostly through their French translations, as we can see from a review article by American scholar Albert Schinz (1870–1943) in an 1897–98 issue of the *American Journal of Psychology*. Schinz introduces *Psychologie des sectes*, the French translation of Sighele's *La delinquenza settaria*, in the framework of the current reinterpretation of individual and collective crime. Schinz acknowledges Sighele's ground-breaking contribution in Italy and his claim to priority over Le Bon in the study of crowd psychology; nevertheless, he ranks Le Bon's truly scientific approach higher than Sighele's voluble and repetitive argumentation (597). Curiously, however, an anonymous piece in an earlier issue praises Sighele's "interesting and comprehensive review of collective psychology, past and future" (416), penned by a "more critical and detailed" (416) author than Le Bon. In 1901 the periodical the *Humanitarian* publishes an article in English by Sighele, "The Moral Problem of Collective Psychology," followed a year later, by a political piece in the *International Monthly* on "Latin Europe and American Imperialism." Here Sighele extends to international policy the psychological dynamics of the crowd that in *Sectarian Criminality* explain the relationship between lower and higher social strata: "the humbler among the nations may supersede the greater, corrupted and weakened by excess of power and by their overweening pride" (670). Sighele maintains that "[e]very nation that flourishes inevitably becomes imperialist, just as every man who succeeds in life absorbs and centralizes subordinate elements" (662), hence, from a philosophical point of view, imperialism should not be condemned a priori, but rather examined lucidly.

Between acclaim and controversies, Sighele can be said to gain canonical status in the United States in the 1920s, after a section from his *Psychologie des sectes*, translated into English and titled "Types of Social Groups," appears in *Introduction to the Science of Sociology*, edited by Robert Park and Ernest Burgess and published in 1921. Inclusion in this volume, which was conceived as "a systematic treatise" (v) rather than "a mere collection of materials" (v), consecrates Sighele as an internationally renowned scholar, and the only Italian one, among eminent figures like Émile Durkheim, John Dewey, Alfred Binet, William James, Ferdinand Tönnies, and Théodule-Armand Ribot. Indeed, as the editors write, "Tarde and Le Bon in France, Sighele in Italy, and [Edward Alsworth] Ross in the United States were the pioneers in the description and interpretation of the behavior of mobs and crowds" (213), a topic in which the editors acknowledge "an increasing interest" (213).

Yet, to be sure, the past tense "were" also underlines that, by then, those innovative theories of collective psychology had become history. As Ernesto Laclau claims, an "ideological anti-popular bias" (*Populist* 10) shaped those argumentations upon the rigid dichotomy of the rational, normal individual and the irrational, pathological crowd. More flexibility was necessary in order to render the study of mass phenomena "a catalogue not of social aberrations but of processes which, in different degrees, structure *any* kind of socio-political life" (40, original emphasis). This turn will come with Freudian psychopathology as an interpretive key for human behaviour in general. Sighele is not Freud, but he addresses the need for a nuanced approach to forms of human aggregation, and provides numerous poignant examples that break down the dualism between social homogeneity and social differentiation.[45]

While theories of crowd behaviour evolved considerably since *The Criminal Crowd*, masses have continued to captivate, alarm, or repel twentieth-century's intellectuals, from Émile Durkheim's collective effervescence and Ortega y Gasset's revolt of the masses, down to Elias Canetti's analysis of crowd dynamics in relation to the power of rulers, Hannah Arendt's treatment of masses as the quintessential totalitarian phenomena, and Michel Maffesoli's studies of the irrational, tribal behaviour of contemporary Western collectivities, among many others.

Significantly, both the crowd's unpremeditated boundless destructiveness and more sophisticated and intentional forms of collective behaviour investigated by Sighele continue to intrigue contemporary historians and sociologists, who, however, problematize abstract univocal definitions. Neither a savage rabble nor a fully purposeful collectivity emerges, for instance, from the historian George Rudé's 1956 analysis of the Gordon Riots, the most devastating outburst of urban violence in British history, against the repeal of the 1778 Papists Act aiming to reduce anti-Catholic discrimination. Determined to offer a portrait of pre-industrial rioters, identifying their patterns and motives rather than treating them in bulk as mob (Rudé "Gordon" 94), Rudé seems to substantiate Sighele's views when he dismisses the hypothesis of premeditation and rather supports the idea of an impulsive multitude managed by local leaders "by temporary circumstance" (103). But, ultimately, he explains the crowd's drive "to destructive violence" (106) as the conscious expression of a desire for social justice propelled by a variety of political and economic, rather than merely religious, grievances. Rejecting the interpretation of a "fickle, irrational, violent" (*Crowd* 252) mob, Rudé tempers the generalizations of late nineteenth-century collective psychology by highlighting

45 It is surprising, therefore, that Laclau himself mentions Sighele only once, and extremely superficially, in his discussion of the Lombrosian school, while he pays attention to nuances in Tarde's treatment of public opinions that in his view anticipate Freud's theories.

the different social and historical contexts and the multiple coexisting motivations behind public disorders.

Along similar lines, although E.P. Thompson acknowledges the role of particular individuals acting as initiators of sudden upheaval, like Sighele's suggestionizers,[46] his concept of "the moral economy" (*Customs* 185) of the eighteenth-century English crowd in his seminal 1971 study refutes the "spasmodic view of popular history" (185) by invalidating the reductive image of riots prior to the French Revolution as "compulsive, rather than self-conscious or self-activating" (185) interventions, and by ascribing, instead, a "complex, culturally mediated function" (187) to mass insurrections. Well beyond elementary, instinctive, violent reactions to the basic stimulus of hunger and distress, for instance, Thompson offers an interpretation of eighteenth-century English food riots as sophisticated patterns of collective behaviour propelled by "custom, culture, and reason" (187), expressing grievances against the breakdown of shared "social norms" (188) and "moral imperatives" (269) that regulated and negotiated economic roles among the different parties within the community.

Nonetheless, the empirical and theoretical implications of Scipio Sighele's analysis of mass society and the power of crowds as both agents of destruction and promoters of change have not lost their relevance, if we consider, for instance, the dynamics and effects of the soccer fan riots that periodically erupt in Europe, the violent popular uprisings that overthrew Romanian dictator Ceausescu in 1989, the "people power" movements that toppled Philippine presidents Marcos in 1986 and Estrada in 2001,[47] or the more recent massive demonstrations that

46 For the coinage of this term as the English rendition of Sighele's "suggestionatore," see "A Note on the Texts and Their Translations" in this volume.

47 Both the crowd's influence upon political events and its manipulation (what in Sighele would be suggestion) for specific agendas emerge from a recent study of the "People Power II" movement, focusing on the attempt by the middle class to co-opt the masses to support their demands to the state by using communication technologies. See Vincent Rafael, "The Cell Phone and the Crowd" (2003). I am grateful to the anonymous reader who directed me to this article.

Likewise, contemporary news shows us that Sighele's attention to the dynamics of crimes *à deux* is more than ever timely. One emblematic Italian "criminal couple" that corroborates Sighele's *succubus-incubus* relationship can be found in the 2001"Novi Ligure murder," in which 16-year-old Erika De Nardo slaughtered her mother and brother with the complicity of her suggestionable 17-year-old boyfriend Omar Favaro, whom she had brainwashed. Similarly, in the January 2017 double murder at Pontelangorino, husband Salvatore Vincelli and wife Nunzia Di Gianni were killed by their 16-year-old son and his allegedly weaker-minded 17-year-old friend.

contributed to the downfall of Egyptian President Mubarak in 2011. Recent scholarship in the humanities and social sciences confirms the relevance of Sighele's contribution beyond a mere historical interest for its own sake. In his book *The Crowd and the Mob,* an examination of the idea of the crowd in history from Plato to Canetti, J.S. McClelland foregrounds the pivotal role that Sighele played in the shift from a mere criminological approach to crowds to a more general sociological theory treating collectivities as permanent and modern, rather than occasional, social factors (162–65). Even more radically, Christian Borch in *The Politics of Crowds* inserts Sighele in a trajectory of scholars who demonstrate that crowds are not just exceptional phenomena, In fact, crowds have been and continue to be central to the understanding of society.

Scipio Sighele did not just write for his own time. He can and should still be read—with his insights, inconsistencies, and even inadmissible claims—as a reference figure in the Italian and European history of an idea that has not ceased to speak to us. The radical oppositional power of sectarian violence, the effects of suggestion exerted by group ideologies upon easily influenced minds, the power of collectivities as agents of innovation, and the danger of mass fanaticism undermining individual freedom and democratic ideals are issues more relevant than ever in our globalized but deeply fragmentary present.

## Bibliography

Altrocchi, Rudolph. "An Eminent Sociologist." *The Nation.* 97, 2524 (13 Nov. 1913): 457–58.

Ambrosoli, Francesco. *Salviamo il Parlamento! In risposta all'opuscolo di S. Sighele Contro il Parlamentarismo.* Milan: Treves, 1895.

Anderson, Benedict. *Imagined Communities.* London: Verso, 1991 [1983].

Bissolati, Leonida. "Pseudopositivismo." *Critica sociale* (1 May 1895).

Bodei, Remo. *Destini personali.* Milan: Feltrinelli, 2002.

Borch, Christian. *The Politics of Crowds: An Alternative History of Sociology.* Cambridge: Cambridge University Press, 2012.

Bosc, Olivier. *La foule criminelle: Politique et criminalité dans l'Europe du tournant du XIXe siècle.* Paris: Fayard, 2007.

– "De la foule criminelle à la foule nationaliste: Scipio Sighele, théoricien de l'irrédentisme." *Matériaux pour l'histoire de notre temps* 43 (1996): 44–45.

Castellini, Gualtiero. "Introduzione biografica." In Scipio Sighele, *Letteratura e sociologia.* Milan: Treves, 1914, i–xxi.

Chamberlain, A.F. "Report by the Italian Commission on Physical Education." *Journal of Genetic Psychology* 3 (1893): 164.

Chimienti, Pietro. *La vita politica e la pratica del regime parlamentare.* Turin: Roux Frassati e Co. Editori, 1897.

Engels, Friedrich. "Against Vulgar Marxism." In *Marxist Literary Theory.* Edited by Terry Eagleton and Drew Milne. Oxford: Blackwell, 1996, 39.

– "On Realism." In *Marxist Literary Theory.* Edited by Terry Eagleton and Drew Milne. Oxford: Blackwell, 1996, 40–41.

Ferrari, Robert. "Sighele on Adulteration of the Positive Doctrines in Collective Crimes." *Journal of the American Institute of Criminal Law and Criminology* 3, 4 (Nov. 1912): 616–17.

Ferri, Enrico. *I delinquenti nell'arte.* Genoa: Libreria Editrice Ligure, 1896.

– "Nota di Enrico Ferri." In Scipio Sighele, *La folla delinquente* II ed. Turin: Bocca, 1895, 157–66.

Freud, Sigmund. *Group Psychology and the Analysis of the Ego. The Standard Edition of the Complete Psychological Works of Sigmund Freud,* vol. XVIII (1920–22). Translated by James Strachey. London: Hogarth Press, 1949.

– *Interpretation of Dreams* (1900). *The Standard Edition of the Complete Psychological Works of Sigmund Freud.* Translated by James Strachey. London: Hogarth Press, 1955.

Gallini, Chiara. "Introduzione." In Scipio Sighele, *La folla delinquente.* Edited by Chiara Gallini. Milan: Marsilio, 1985, 7–42.

Garbari, Maria. "Il pensiero politico di Scipio Sighele." *Rassegna storica del Risorgimento* LXI (1974): 391–426, 523–61.

Giachetti, Cipriano. "Scipio Sighele." *La Nuova Antologia* 49, 1009 (1 Jan. 1914): 94–102.

Ginneken, Jaap van. *Crowds, Psychology, and Politics, 1871–1899.* Cambridge: Cambridge University Press, 1992.

Gorni, Mariagrazia, and Laura Pellegrini. *Un problema di storia sociale: L'infanzia abbandonata in Italia nel secolo XIX.* Florence: La Nuova Italia, 1974.

Irigaray, Luce. "Women on the Market." In *This Sex Which Is Not One.* Translated by Catherine Porter. Ithaca: Cornell University Press, 1985.

Isastia, Annamaria. "La battaglia per il voto nell'Italia liberale." In *Dal diritto di voto alla cittadinanza piena.* Edited by Marisa Ferrari Occhionero. Rome: Università la Sapienza, 2008, 31–51.

Jacobsen, Rosalia. "Inchiesta sulla donna e il problema dell'amore, " *Pagine libere. Rivista quindicinale di politica, scienza e arte,* 21 (1 Nov. 1908): 1–12.

Labriola, Teresa. "Cronaca del femminismo." *Rivista di Roma* 11 (Jan. 1907): 48–51.

Laclau, Ernesto. *On Populist Reason*. London:, Verso, 2005.
Le Bon, Gustave. *Psychologie des foules*. Paris: Alcan, 1895.
Lombroso, Cesare. “Il delinquente e il pazzo nel dramma e nel romanzo.” *Nuova antologia* XXXIV (1889): 665–81.
Lukács, Georg. *The Historical Novel*. Translated by Hannah and Stanley Mitchell. Lincoln: University of Nebraska Press, 1983.
– “The Ideology of Modernism.” In *The Critical Tradition: Classic Texts and Contemporary Trends*, David H. Richter, ed. 3rd ed. Boston: Bedford/ St Martin’s Press, 1218–32.
Mantegazza, Paolo. *The Physiology of Love*. In *The Physiology of Love and Other Writings*. Edited and introduced by Nicoletta Pireddu. Translated by David Jacobson. Toronto: University of Toronto Press, 2007.
Marinetti, Filippo Tommaso. “The Founding and Manifesto of Futurism.” In *Futurism: An Anthology*, Lawrence Rainey, Christine Poggi, and Laura Wittman, eds. New Haven: Yale University Press, 2009, 49–53.
Mazzini, Giuseppe. *The Duties of Man*. London: Chapman and Hall, 1862.
–.“Europe: Its Conditions and Its Prospects.” In *Five Views on European Peace*, Sandi E. Cooper, ed. New York: Garland, 1972.
– “Pensieri: Ai poeti del XIX secolo.” In *D’una letteratura europea e altri saggi*, Paolo Maria Sipala, ed. Fasano: Schena, 1991, 93–118.
McClelland, J.S. *The Crowd and the Mob*. London: Unwin Hyman, 1989.
McPhail, Clark. *The Myth of the Madding Crowd*. New York: DeGruyter, 1991.
Melzi, Costantino. *Antropologia pedagogica*. Arona: Tipografia Economica, 1899.
Merlini, Stefano. “Il governo costituzionale.” In *Storia dello Stato italiano dall’unità a oggi*, Raffaele Romanelli, ed. Rome: Donzelli, 1995, 1–72.
Miceli, V. “Come salvare il Parlamento.” *Riforma Sociale* (10 Sept. 1895).
Micklem, Nathaniel, and Herbert Morgan. *Christ and Caesar*. New York: Macmillan; London: Swarthmore Press, 1921.
Moscovici, Serge. *The Age of the Crowd*. Cambridge: Cambridge University Press, 1985.
Palano, Damiano. *Il potere della moltitudine*. Milan: Vita e Pensiero, 2002.
Park, Robert E., and Ernest W. Burgess, eds. *Introduction to the Science of Sociology*. Chicago: University of Chicago Press, 1921.
Pellegrino, Ettore Lombardo. *La questione del Parlamentarismo*. Florence: Casa Editrice Libraria “Fratelli Cammelli,” 1896.
Pirandello, Luigi. “Feminismo.” In *Saggi, poesie, scritti varii*. Edited by Manlio LoVecchio Musti. Milan: Mondadori, 1977, 1068–72.
Pireddu, Nicoletta. “Paolo Mantegazza: A Scientist and His Ecstasies.” In Paolo Mantegazza, *The Physiology of Love and Other Writings*. Edited and introduced by Nicoletta Pireddu. Translated by David Jacobson. Toronto: University of Toronto Press, 2007, 3–53.

Poe, Edgar Allan. "The Man of the Crowd." In *Selected Tales.* Oxford: Oxford University Press, 1980, 97–104.

Rafael, Vincent. "The Cell Phone and the Crowd: Messianic Politics in the Contemporary Philippines." *Public Culture* 15, 3 (2003): 399–425.

Romani, Gabriella. "Interpreting the Risorgimento: Blasetti's *1860* and the Legacy of Motherly Love." *Italica* 79, 3 (2002): 391–404.

Rudé, George. *The Crowd in History: A Study of Popular Disturbances in France and England.* New York: Wiley, 1964.

– "The Gordon Riots: A Study of the Rioters and Their Victims: The Alexander Prize Essay." *Transactions of the Royal Historical Society* 6 (1956): 93–114.

Schinz, Albert. "Psychological Literature." *American Journal of Psychology* IX (1897–8): 416.

Schnapp, Jeffrey, and Matthew Tiews, eds. *Crowds.* Stanford: Stanford University Press, 2006.

Sergi, Giuseppe. "Il movimento femminista." *Rivista politica e letteraria* (April 1898): 3–12.

– "Psicosi epidemica." *Rivista speciale di opere di filosofia scientifica* 8 (1889): 151–72.

Sighele, Scipio. *Eva moderna.* Milan: Treves, 1910.

– *Il nazionalismo e i partiti politici.* Milan: Treves, 1911.

– "Individual Morality and Political Morality – A Sociological Problem." *To-morrow: A Monthly Review* (Aug. 1896; Oct. 1896): 218–25.

– *La coppia criminale: Saggio di psicologia morbosa.* Turin: Bocca, 1892.

– *La delinquenza settaria.* Milan: Treves, 1897.

– *La donna nova.* Rome: Enrico Voghera Editore, 1898.

– *La folla delinquente: Saggio di psicologia collettiva.* Turin: Bocca, 1891; II ed. Turin: Bocca, 1895.

– "La nouvelle psychologie irrédentiste depuis l'expédition tripolitaine." *La Revue* 6 (15 March 1912): 145–56.

– "Latin Europe and American Imperialism." *The International Monthly: A Magazine of Contemporary Thought* (Jan. 1902): 655–70.

– *Letteratura e sociologia.* Milan: Treves, 1914.

– *Letteratura tragica.* Milan: Treves, 1906.

– *L'intelligenza della folla.* II ed. Turin: Bocca, 1911.

– *Nell'arte e nella scienza.* Milan: Treves, 1911.

– *Pagine nazionaliste.* Milan: Treves, 1910.

– *Mentre il secolo muore.* Milan-Palermo: Remo Sandron Editore, 1899.

– "The Moral Problem of Collective Psychology." *The Humanitarian* (April 1901): 242–52.

– "Una pirateria letteraria: Le Bon, *La Psychologie des foules.*" *La scuola positiva* V, 3 (1895): 171–73.

– Unpublished letter to Giovanni Pedrotti, 30 Aug. 1908. Fondo Sighele, Biblioteca della Fondazione Museo Storico del Trentino, Trento, Italy.

Stewart-Steinberg, Susan. *The Pinocchio Effect.* Chicago: University of Chicago Press, 2007.

Tarde, Gabriel. *L'opinion et la foule.* Paris: PUF, 1989 [1901].

Thompson, Edward Palmer. *Customs in Common.* New York: New Press, 1991.

Virgilii, Filippo. "Lo sciopero nella vita moderna." *Studi senesi* 14 (1897): 4–40.

Wells, H.G. *Men Like Gods.* New York: Macmillan, 1923.

Wilde, Oscar. "The Soul of Man under Socialism." In *The Complete Works of Oscar Wilde*, vol. 4. Edited by Josephine M. Guy. Oxford: Oxford University Press, 2007.

Zimmern, Helen. "An Indictment of Parliaments." *Blackwood's Edinburgh Magazine* 58 (Aug. 1895): 227–33.

– "Criminal Anthropology in Italy." *Popular Science Monthly* 52 (April 1898): 743–60.

# A Note on the Texts and Their Translations

NICOLETTA PIREDDU

As this is the first and long overdue English edition of Scipio Sighele's writings, the texts included in our volume aim to offer an overview of the author's contributions to topics that have consistently engaged him in his career as a public intellectual, namely, the crowd, the woman question, sociological literary criticism, and politics.

With the exception of *La folla delinquente: Saggio di psicologia collettiva*, which we have translated in its entirety because of its seminal role in Sighele's overall investigation,[1] the excerpts here collected are chapters from works that highlight Sighele's major theoretical breakthroughs at pivotal moments in his epistemic journey. They aim to show the continuity but also intriguing turning points in his thought, and at the same time the breadth and interconnectedness of the original topics he explores. Within each area of Sighele's investigation, texts are arranged in chronological order and trace the emergence of the author's conceptualization of the crowd as a criminogenic subject and of the laws able to explain

1 In order to give readers an idea of how Sighele's pioneering ideas on the crowd were first circulated in book form, we have chosen to translate the first edition of *La folla criminale*, where all the main points of Sighele's overall argumentation are already clearly expounded. As mentioned in the introduction to this volume, apart from minor changes and a slightly longer conclusion, the second edition reproduces the first and adds selected correspondence between Sighele, Ferri, and Tarde on the intelligence and morality of the crowd, the physiology of success, and contagion in popular riots, followed by the texts of several Italian court rulings on collective crimes.

collective behaviour from couples to masses, as well as other crucial highlights such as analogies between the crowd and the public; the application of collective psychology to the study of female behaviour amid the ideological tensions in the turn-of-the-century woman question; the power of crowds as both agents of destruction and promoters of change in the social, political, and literary domains; and, hence, ultimately, an understanding of crowds not only as occasional regressive aggregations, but also as forward-looking models of mass society that epitomize modernity.

Our interventions as translators have involved the following three main areas, of which we provide here some representative examples.

## 1 Word Choice

Sighele draws terminology from many disciplines such as science, sociology, criminology, law, and philosophy. Finding English equivalencies often required much debate and no less creativity.

As Sighele follows in the steps of Italian positivist criminology, he alternates two kinds of terms in his discussion of individual and collective deviant behaviour, namely, "delinquente" and "delinquenza," on the one hand, and "criminale" and "criminalità," on the other. Since his word choice does not seem to lay out a systematic difference between the two notions in his argumentation, we have decided to privilege "criminal" and "criminality" throughout his texts. In so doing, we think we are aligned with the most recent English translations of Cesare Lombroso's own pioneering works, which inaugurated the Italian school of criminal anthropology. Lombroso's *L'uomo delinquente* has been mostly rendered in English as *Criminal Man*, especially in most recent decades, down to its 2006 English translation by Mary Gibson and Nicole Hahn Rafter, who throughout their book also adopt "criminal" to qualify all the categories of anomalous behaviour for which Lombroso had originally used the term "delinquente."

In his shift from individual to collective deviance, Sighele maintains an evident connection with the tenets of Lombroso's investigations, starting from the titles of his own books. We thus felt it crucial to reflect such connection by translating *La folla delinquente* as *The Criminal Crowd*, and proceeding accordingly for his other works, so as to foreground also the continuity of his thought. Moreover, even when anglophone critics refer to his works in Sighele's time and later, they translate "delinquente" and "delinquenza" in his titles as "criminal" and "criminality." One example among many can be found in *Literary Digest*, vol. 16 (2 April 1898), 401.

For their part, the English "delinquent" and "delinquency" mainly evoke, respectively, a minor crime, and the tendency to commit it, typically by a young individual, while Sighele adopts those terms for *any* kind of offender and *any* degree of wrongdoing. Therefore, we have designated with "delinquent" and "delinquency" only those social phenomena that Sighele explicitly associates with youth, whenever they clearly appear as not attributable to atavistic deviance à la Lombroso, but, rather, as misdemeanours caused by the environment—initially not serious, but potentially degenerating into criminality.

For the Italian expression "a due," with which Sighele defines any criminal action performed by two people—be they perverse, insane, immoral, or simply weak—under their reciprocal influence, we have adopted the French "*à deux*" because this is the locution that widely circulated in that period and that is still being used in current psychiatric scholarship. Sighele's own *La coppia criminale* [*The Criminal Couple*] was translated into French as *Le crime à deux*.

Other crucial and frequent terms in Sighele's thought are the verb "suggestionare," the noun "suggestionatore," and the adjective "suggestionabile." Given their pivotal role, it was necessary for our English equivalents to be as faithful as possible to the originals. Starting from the English verb "to suggestionize," we have hence coined "suggestionizer" and "suggestionable."

Whenever Sighele refers to the charismatic, spontaneous leader of a crowd, he adopts the French term *meneur*. Since he borrows it from Gabriel Tarde, we have kept it.

As for the term "follia," although more politically correct terms could be chosen for mental illness in our time, we have usually translated it as "madness," as it is contextually more relevant to the nineteenth-century lexicon and culture. Likewise, whenever Sighele refers to a subject in its singularity (either "uomo" or "individuo"), we have not eliminated the evident masculine bias in our translation. Apart from those occasions where Sighele explicitly designates an all-inclusive collectivity or mankind as a whole, we felt it would be ahistorical to opt for gender-neutral alternatives, a fortiori because Sighele devotes separate discussions to the female subject.

## 2 Style

Sighele's expository style is quite verbose and at times redundant. His tone is often oratorical and sententious, particularly in the texts that were originally conceived as public lectures, but also, more generally, whenever he engages with his sources, trying to persuade his audience of his own standpoint.

In our translations, we have preserved Sighele's rhetoric, yet we have simplified his longest and most convoluted claims, which often make it difficult even for an Italian native speaker to identify the main idea. For instance, in the case of very long sentences with numerous incidental and subordinate clauses nested into one another, we have decided to break them into multiple statements, and to reconnect their respective ideas more clearly. Likewise, we have rephrased frequent negative rhetorical questions.

Another area that required considerable intervention was Sighele's quite idiosyncratic use of punctuation. In all his works, we frequently found multiple sentences connected through colons, each of them comprising, in their turn, several subordinate clauses connected by dashes or semicolons. In order to render the main subject, verb, and object more evident, we have restructured those long paragraphs, separating sentences by full stops, and, whenever necessary, by adding some transitional expressions that serve to clarify the relationships between the different ideas.

## 3 Citations

Sighele's argumentation results from an intense dialogue with a surprising array of European scientists, sociologists, and humanists. His writings are a collage of often very extended citations that are an integral part of his reasoning. *The Criminal Crowd* is paradigmatic in this respect, but we see this tendency throughout his oeuvre. As most scholars of his time, Sighele is well versed in French language and culture but does not seem to know English. Whenever foreign works (especially English and German) are not available in Italian, he reads and quotes them in French. This additional linguistic filter is often a hindrance in the translation process. Indeed, Sighele is frequently not faithful in his transcriptions. At times he quotes from the same work in French and at other times in Italian without distinguishing his own translations from the official ones, and he does not quote passages in their original sequence. Furthermore, he does not always signal ellipses, he alters some terms, and at times he does not provide page numbers or specify his textual source altogether—as happens systematically in his essay on Honoré de Balzac, for instance.

We have traced back the original texts of the scientific, sociological, and philosophical works to which Sighele refers most frequently and extensively in his writings—such as those by Hyppolite Taine, Herbert Spencer, Arthur Schopenhauer, and John Stuart Mill—and have provided the English translations already available. We have proceeded likewise for the quotations by literary writers—such as Gabriele D'Annunzio and Honoré de Balzac, among several others. We have given our own English translations of Italian and French citations from other foreign scholars' works that, besides being less known and more difficult to find, did not present particular lexical sophistication or ambiguity. For the sake of documentation, however, we have kept all of Sighele's footnotes with the bibliographical references of the editions from which he is quoting.

We hope that our juggling between domestication and foreignization will pleasantly carry readers across two quite different languages and cultures without carrying them away too much from either one.

As Sighele already includes peritextual material, Nicoletta Pireddu's notes (as new, self-standing additions to Sighele's own or as supplemental comments in brackets within Sighele's original notes) aim to add information without excessively overburdening the primary works. In most cases, their main function is to identify individuals, places, and contexts with which the general public today might not be familiar and for which Sighele provides no details. Additional editing was necessary to highlight and rectify several incorrect references, terms, and titles, and to standardize the spelling of some foreign names.

Biographical and historical information derive from *Enciclopedia Treccani*, *Encyclopedia Britannica*, *Biographie universelle ancienne et moderne*, and various editions of Albert Bataille's *Causes criminelles et mondaines*.

With the exception of *L'intelligenza della folla*, of which we used the second edition amended and expanded by Sighele in 1911,[2] our translations are drawn from the following first editions of Sighele's works (the numbers in square brackets below indicate where translations from each work can be found in this volume):

2 In the preface to the second edition of *L'intelligenza della folla*, which Sighele defines as more complete and organic than the previous one (*Intelligenza* 9), he rearranges chapters and adds a new one on "La folla and Gabriele D'Annunzio" [The Crowd and Gabriele D'Annunzio], as well as his essay *Contro il Parlamentarismo* [*Against Parliamentarism*], which had already appeared in *La delinquenza settaria*.

*La folla delinquente.* Turin: Bocca, 1891. [3–75]

*La coppia criminale.* Turin: Bocca, 1892:

"Prefazione": vii–viii. [76–77]

"Introduzione. La suggestione nel delitto": 1–14. [77–78]

Capitolo I "La coppia sana, la coppia suicida e la coppia pazza": 15–30. [88–100]

Capitolo II "La coppia criminale": 31–52. [100–17]

Capitolo III: 53–78. [117–37]

Capitolo IV "La coppia criminale (continuazione e fine)": 79–92. [137–47]

*La delinquenza settaria.* Milan: Treves, 1897:

Capitolo II "Psicologia della setta": 69–121. [148–73]

Capitolo IV "Il delitto settario": 181–227. [173–95]

Appendice *Contro il Parlamentarismo*.: 231–74. [195–220]

*L'intelligenza della folla.* Turin: Bocca, 1911:

Capitolo II "L'arte e la folla": 35–56. [221–33]

Capitolo IV "L'opinione pubblica": 65–119. [233–64]

*La donna nova.* Rome: Enrico Voghera Editore, 1898:

"Ottime o pessime?": 13–42. [265–71]

"La questione femminile: 75–95 [271–75]

*Eva moderna.* Milan: Treves, 1910:

"La donna e le ingiustizie della legislazione": 129–57. [276–89]

"L'istruzione della donna": 161–91. [290–303]

"Per i nostri figli": 227–56. [304–17]

"L'anima del fanciullo": 259–87. [317–30]

*Letteratura tragica.* Milan: Treves, 1906:

Capitolo I "L'opera di Gabriele D'Annunzio davanti alla psichiatria": 3–94. [331–76]

*Nell'arte e nella scienza.* Milan: Treves, 1911:

Capitolo II "Leggendo Balzac": 37–102. [379–411]

## Bibliography of Sighele's Major Single-Authored Books and Their Translations

*Un paese di delinquenti nati: Con quattro figure nel testo.* Turin: Bocca, 1890.

In French: *Un pays de criminels-nés.* Lyon: A. Storck, 1896.

*Note critiche di diritto penale.* Civitavecchia: Strambi, 1891.

*La folla delinquente.* Turin: Bocca, 1891. [2nd enlarged ed., 1895.]

In French: *La foule criminelle: Essai de psychologie collective.* Translated by Paul Vigny. Paris: Alcan: 1892. [2nd ed., 1901.]

In Spanish: *La muchedumbre delincuente: Ensayo de psicología colectiva.* Translated by Pedro Dorado Montero. Madrid: La España Moderna, 1892.

In Russian: *Prestupnaâ tolpa: Opyt kollektivnoĭ psikhologīi.* Translated by Aleksandr Petrovič Afanas'ev. St Peterburg: Izd. F. Pavlenkova, 1893. [2nd ed. 1896.]

In Polish: *Tłum zbrodniczy: Szkic psychologii zbiorowej.* Translated by Antoniny Morżkowskiej. Warsaw: G. Centnerszwer, 1895.

In German: *Psychologie des Auflaufs und der Massenverbrechen.* Translated by Hans Kurella. Dresden: Reissner, 1897.

In Dutch: *De menigte als misdadigster: Een studie over collectieve psychologie.* Translated by Anna Sophie Polak. Amsterdam: Mij. voor Goede en Goodkoope Lectuur, 1906.

*La coppia criminale: Saggio di psicologia morbosa.* Turin: Bocca, 1892. [2nd ed., 1897; 3rd ed., 1909.]

In French: *Le crime à deux: Essai de psychologie morbide.* Translated by Vincent Palmet. Lyon: A. Storck; Paris: G. Masson, 1893. [2nd. ed., *Le crime à deux: Essai de psycho-pathologie sociale.* Paris: V. Giard et E. Brière, 1910.]

In Spanish: *El delito de dos: Ensayo de psicología morbosa.* Translated by Pedro Dorado Montero. Madrid: La España Moderna, 1895.

*La teoria positiva della complicità.* Turin: Bocca, 1894. [2nd expanded book-length edition of Sighele's thesis "La complicità," published in *Archivio di psichiatria, scienze penali ed antropologia criminale* IX (1890).]

In Spanish: *La teoría positiva de la complicidad.* Translated by Pedro Dorado Montero. Madrid: La España Moderna, 1894.

*Contro il Parliamentarismo: Saggio di psicologia collettiva.* Milan: Treves, 1895.

*La morale individuale e la morale politica: Saggio di sociologia.* Rome: Casa editrice italiana, 1896.

*La delinquenza settaria.* Milan: Treves, 1897.

In French: *Psychologie des sectes.* Translated by Louis Brandin. Paris: V. Giard et E. Brière, 1898.

*La donna nova.* Rome: Enrico Voghera Editore, 1898.

*Mentre il secolo muore.* Milan-Palermo: Sandron, 1899. [2nd revised ed., *Idee e problemi di un positivista.* Milan: Sandron, 1907.]

*I delitti della folla. studiati secondo la psicologia: Il diritto e la giurisprudenza, e coll'aggiunta di tutte le sentenze pronunciate dai tribunali e dalle Corti d'appello in tema di delitto collettivo.* Turin: Bocca, 1902.

*L'intelligenza della folla.* Turin: Bocca, 1903. [2nd revised and enlarged ed., 1911.]

*Letteratura tragica.* Milan: Treves, 1906.

In French: *Littérature et criminalité.* Translated by Erick Adler. Preface by Jules Claretie. Paris: V. Giard et E. Brière, 1908.

In Spanish: *Literatura trágica.* Madrid: Enrique Teodoro y Alonso, 1910.

*Eva moderna.* Milan: Treves, 1910.
In Spanish: *Eva moderna.* Translated by Cristóbal de Castro. Madrid: Calpe, 1921.
*Il nazionalismo e i partiti politici.* Milan: Treves, 1911.
*La crisi dell'infanzia e la delinquenza dei minorenni.* Florence: La rinascita del libro, 1911.
*Nell'arte e nella scienza.* Milan: Treves, 1911.
*La donna e l'amore.* Milan: Treves, 1913.
In Spanish: *La mujer y el amor.* Translated by Pedro Pedraza y Paez. Madrid: Imp. La Morena y Manzanares, 1921. [2nd ed., 1931.]

Information was taken from WorldCat, Index Translationum, and the catalogues of the national libraries of France, Great Britain, Germany, Spain, and the Netherlands.

WorldCat and the catalogue of the Biblioteca Nacional de España also list a Spanish volume by Sighele with the title *Las Ciencias sociales y sus aplicaciones*, translation and appendix by Alberto Lasplaces (Montevideo: Claudio García, 1917). No information is given about the original work in Italian.

In the last decade, new editions and translations of Sighele's works have appeared in Europe, including: a Spanish translation of *Eva moderna*, published in Madrid in 2005 by Editorial Espasa Calpe; a reprint of the German 1897 edition of *The Criminal Crowd—Psychologie des Auflaufs und der Massenverbrechen*, translated by Hans Kurella—published in 2007 and in 2015 by VDM Verlag Dr Müller in Saarbrücken.

Through a partnership between Hachette Livre and Bibliothèque nationale de France the first French translations of several of Sighele's works have been reprinted, including:

*Littérature et criminalité* (2010, 2016)
*La foule criminelle* (2013)
*Le crime à deux* (2013)
*Psychologie des sectes* (2013)

A French edition of *Sectarian Criminality*, as *Psychologie des foules*, appeared in 2015 by Éditions Dupleix.

Many of Sighele's works have been recently reprinted or re-edited in Italian, including the following titles:

*L'intelligenza della folla* (Genoa: Name, 1999; Reink Books, 2017)
*Il nazionalismo e i partiti politici* (Nabu Press, 2010)

*La complicità* (Nabu Press, 2010; Reink Books, 2017)
*Pagine nazionaliste* (Nabu Press, 2010)
*Contro il Parlamentarismo: Saggio di psicologia collettiva* (Kessinger Publishing, 2010; Nabu Press, 2012)
*I delitti della folla* (Nabu Press, 2012)
*Un paese di delinquenti nati: Con quattro figure nel testo* (Nabu Press, 2012)
*La folla delinquente* (La Vita Felice, 2015)
*La coppia criminale* (Musso, 2008; Yume, 2016)

# THE CRIMINAL CROWD
## AND OTHER WRITINGS ON
# MASS SOCIETY

Scipio Sighele. Undated photograph (c. between 1905 and 1913). Fondazione Museo Storico del Trentino, Trento.

# 1 *The Criminal Crowd: An Essay on Collective Psychology*

## Introduction: "Sociology and Collective Psychology"

In psychological events, the result of a gathering of individuals can never be equal to the sum of each of them.

—Enrico Ferri

*I*

Out of bricks, well burnt, hard, and sharp-angled, lying in heaps by his side, the bricklayer builds, even without mortar, a wall of some height that has considerable stability. With bricks made of bad materials, irregularly burnt, warped, cracked, and many of them broken, he cannot build a dry wall of the same height and stability. The dockyard-labourer, piling cannon-shot, is totally unable to make these spherical masses stand at all as the bricks stand. There are, indeed, certain definite shapes into which they may be piled—that of a tetrahedron, or that of a pyramid having a square base, or that of an elongated wedge allied to the pyramid. In any of these forms they may be put together symmetrically and stably; but not in forms with vertical sides or highly-inclined sides. Once more, if, instead of equal spherical shot, the masses to be piled are boulders, partially but irregularly rounded, and of various sizes, no definite stable form is possible. A loose heap, indefinite in its surface and angles, is all the labourer can make of them. Putting which several facts together, and asking what is the most general truth they imply, we see it to be this—that the character of the aggregate is determined by the characters of the units.

> (...)
> This truth is again exemplified by aggregates of living matter. In the substance of each species of plant or animal, there is a proclivity towards the structure which that plant or animal presents (...). The perpetually-cited case of the polype, each part of which, when it is cut into several, presently puts on the polype-shape, and gains structures and powers like those of the original whole, illustrates this truth among animals. Among plants it is well exemplified by the Begonias. Here a complete plant grows from a fragment of a leaf stuck in the ground (...).
> Among such social aggregates as inferior creatures fall into, more or less definitely, the same truth holds. (...) Given the structures and consequent instincts of the individuals as we find them, and the community they form will inevitably present certain traits; and no community having such traits can be formed out of individuals having other structures and instincts.[1]

Now, those who have thrown off the yoke of theological and metaphysical prejudice, and who know that there does not exist one law for the universe and another for humanity, or even those who have only a basic familiarity with the theory of evolution, will be neither surprised nor repulsed by the idea of also including human aggregates in Spencer's model.

To say that the properties of the single parts determine the properties of the whole is, indeed, to state a truth that can be applied to human society, as well as to everything else. Spencer based his conception of sociology precisely on this truth, by positing as a scientific axiom that the principal characteristics of societies correspond to the principal characteristics of man.[2] Thus, he confirmed the idea of Auguste Comte, who in different words but summarizing the same thought, has said, "human society must be considered a *single man*[3] who has always existed throughout the centuries."[4]

Nor, if we leave aside for the moment the question of whether the analogy between man and society goes so far as to allow us to speak of a

1 [Herbert Spencer, *The Study of Sociology* (London: Henry S. King, 1873), chapter III, 48–50. Sighele does not seem to read English. All the English works to which he refers in his writings appear mostly in French translation and occasionally in Italian. In this case, Sighele quotes from H. Spencer, *Introduction à la science sociale*, VII ed. (Paris: F. Alcan, 1885), chapter III.]

2 Spencer, op. cit., 55.

3 [All emphases are Sighele's, or as originally found in Sighele's work, unless otherwise specified.]

4 A. Comte, *Système de politique positive* (Paris, 1851), 129 and ff.

veritable organism,[5] is it possible to challenge the idea that in every society there is a group of phenomena that is the natural result of phenomena exhibited by the members of the society in question. In other words, the aggregate has a series of properties that are determined by the series of properties of its parts. We only need ask ourselves what would happen if man had had a preference for those who do him harm, in order to understand that social relations would be completely different (if at all possible) from today's social relations, which are established by the inherent tendency of every man to prefer those who bring him the most pleasure. We only need ask ourselves what would happen if, instead of seeking the easiest means to reach an end, men sought the most difficult means, to guess that such a society (supposing that a society could actually exist under such circumstances) would not resemble at all the societies we know.[6]

This analogy of structure, and therefore of functions, which seems evident and undeniable between man and society, repeats itself not only with regards to general characteristics, but also to some particular characteristics, between the individuals belonging to a given class and this same class considered as a collective entity.

We know that society is not a homogeneous whole of equal parts, but rather "a sedimentary rock formed slowly by debris deposited by an indefinite series of beings,"[7] an organism that, like the animal body, has tissues of different structures and of varied sensitivity. Now, these tissues, either layers or social groups—which have been forming little by little over the course of time by means of that continual and progressive shift

5 Gabba, *Intorno ad alcuni più generali problemi della scienza sociale* (Florence, 1881); Gumplowicz, *Grundiss der Sociologie* (Vienna, 1885); De Greef, *Introduction à la sociologie* (Paris, 1886); and Letourneau, *L'évolution du mariage et de la famille* (Paris, 1888),—to cite only the major writers—all dismissed the resemblance between the animal organism and social organism as *pure metaphor*. Ferri in *Nuovi orizzonti* (2nd ed., 115n) and Sergi in the article *La sociologia e l'organismo della società umana*, inserted in the volume *Antropologia e scienze antropologiche* (Messina, 1889), responded to them rather well.—That society is a veritable organism, has been magnificently demonstrated not only by Comte and Spencer, but also by Schäeffle in his masterpiece *Bau und Leben des socialer Körpers* (Tubingen, 1875), and by Espinas in the historical introduction to his volume *Des Sociétés animales* (Paris, 1878).

6 See Spencer, op. cit., chapter III.

7 G. Sergi, *Antropologia e scienze antropologiche* (Messina, 1889), 128. [Giuseppe Sergi (1841–1936) was a renowned Italian anthropologist, famous for his physiological theory of emotional and psychic phenomena, as well as for his elaboration of a Mediterranean racial identity. See the introduction to this volume.]

from the simple to the complex, from the homogeneous to the heterogeneous, in accordance with the law of evolution,[8] like the tissues of plants and animals—possess organic and psychic characteristics of their own that reproduce the specific characteristics of the individuals that make up these groups.

The most trivial observation demonstrates this fully. Who does not know that the aristocracies (of intellect, money, or birth), the magistracy, the clergy, the military, in short, all social classes—which represent today in an elective and spontaneous manner the ancient casts determined solely by hereditary relationships—reflect in their spirit and in their collective manifestations not only the general characteristics of man, but also the peculiarities of the aristocrat, the magistrate, the priest, and the soldier? Who does not know that the habits, the ideas, the sentiments, the tendencies, in a word, the functions proper to each of these classes differ from those of all the others?[9]

Therefore, the axiom that the characteristics of the aggregate are determined by the characteristics of the units that comprise it is applicable not only to the collective social organism, but also to its partial sub-components.

And it cannot be otherwise, because if all the natural laws that apply to the organic world are necessarily valid for human society (which is merely a fragment of the universe, or in other words, an episode of universal evolution), then the general laws must hold true in the partial organisms of human society, just as—according to a felicitous expression by Enrico Ferri—in the fragments of a crystal the mineralogical characteristics of the entire crystal must inevitably be reproduced.

---

8 See in this regard: Spencer, *Les premiers principes,* chapter XIV, and Ardigò, *Opere filosofiche,* vol. II, *La formazione naturale nel fatto del sistema solare.*

9 This truth—in itself evident, as I said—is confirmed by all sociologists indistinctly. See M.A. Vaccaro, *Genesi e funzione delle leggi penali* (Rome: Fratelli Bocca, 1889), chapter I—Tocqueville says: "classes in a society always form like many distinct nations" (*La démocratie en Amérique,* vol. I, chapter VI).—See also Bagehot, *Lois scientifiques du développement des nations,* 5th ed. (Paris: F. Alcan, 1885) [originally published in English in 1872 as *Physics and Politics*], and Spencer, *Introduction à la science sociale,* chapter XI, *Les préjugés de classe.* [Walter Bagehot (1826–1877) was a British journalist, essayist, and businessman, who also became editor-in-chief of *The Economist.* He was one of the first to study the relationship between the natural and the social sciences from a sociological perspective and also devised a distinct theory of central banking. In his 1872 volume *Physics and Politics,* Bagehot applied the principles of evolution to human societies. Sighele frequently refers to Bagehot's ideas in other works, among them *The Criminal Couple* and *Sectarian Criminality.*]

From this point of view and according to these principles, sociology seems to be a reproduction—mostly faithful at a general level, but immensely more complex and vast—of psychology. Psychology is the study of man and sociology is the study of the social body; but we know that the characteristics of the former must necessarily be determined by those of the latter. The structure and the functions of the social organism are, therefore, analogous to those of the human organism. Social individuality, Espinas would say, is parallel to human individuality; thus sociology is nothing more than psychology on a larger scale, in which the principal laws of the individual psyche are amplified and complicated. As Tarde so wonderfully has phrased it, sociology is "the solar microscope of psychology."[10]

## *II*

But just how far can this analogy between the qualities of the aggregate and those of its individual units be stretched? Is the relationship between the psychological laws that govern an individual and those that govern a group of individuals always constant? Is it always true that a group of men possesses specific characteristics that result from the characteristics of the group members taken individually? In short, are there ever any exceptions to the aforementioned principle?

Before responding to these questions, I would like to discuss several fairly common psychological phenomena that will help us find the answer, or better still, will themselves be the answer.

Everyone is aware of the absurdities frequently committed by juries. Often their errors derive from individual incompetence or from the intrinsic difficulty of the questions posed to them. But other times, intelligent people issue an absurd and erroneous verdict on questions that require no more than a bit of common sense to be resolved.

I, for example, happened to witness the acquittal of three youngsters, who were *convicted* and who *confessed* to having inflicted the utmost offences upon an unfortunate girl, and, after this, to having tortured her in the vilest of ways, burning her with quicklime in extremely delicate areas. Do you believe that, if confronted individually, the jurors would have acquitted these criminals? I am doubtful.

10 G. Tarde, *La philosophie pénale*, 1st ed. (Paris-Lyon: Storck-Masson, 1890), 118. [English translation by Rapelje Howell, *Penal Philosophy* (London: William Heinemann, 1912), 118.] The solar microscope is the magic lantern, which, illuminated by the sun's rays, magnifies images of very small objects.

Garofalo reports an experiment performed on a board of distinguished doctors, among whom were several illustrious professors who were invited to give a verdict regarding a case of theft, and acquitted him, despite the evident proof that the accused was guilty, but later admitted they had made a mistake.[11]

What do these and many other similar episodes, which could be cited and observed by any of us,[12] prove? Simply this: that twelve intelligent men of common sense can issue a stupid and absurd verdict. An assembly of individuals can, therefore, produce a result opposite to that which each of them would have given alone.

The same phenomenon occurs within the many committees (artistic, scientific, or industrial), which are one of the most grievous social evils of our administrative system. It frequently happens that the strangeness of their decisions surprises and dumbfounds the public. Why—one asks—can men, like those who are part of a committee, reach a similar conclusion? Why do ten or twenty artists, ten or twenty scientists, altogether reach a verdict that conforms neither to the principles of art, nor to those of science?

These questions, as of yet, have not been answered by anyone, but the facts have been observed and remarked by all.[13]

Not only juries and committees, but also political assemblies are at times guilty of acts that are in open and absolute contrast to the individual opinions and tendencies of the majority of their members. An ancient maxim says: *Senatores boni viri, senatus autem mala bestia,*[14] and today people repeat and confirm this observation when, with regard to certain

---

11 R. Garofalo, *Un giurì di persone colte*, in *Archivio di psichiatria, scienze penali ed antropologia criminale* II, 3: 374. [Italian criminologist and jurist Raffaele Garofalo (1851–1934) was a follower of Cesare Lombroso.]

12 The absurd verdicts of the jurors are in the thousands. See some referred to by Lombroso, *Sull'incremento del delitto in Italia* (Turin: Bocca, 1879), 49 and ff.; in L. Carelli, *Verdetti di giurati*, in *Archivio di psichiatria, scienze penali ed antropologia criminale* VIII, 6; in V. Olivieri, *Un verdetto negativo in tema di furto qualificato,* in the same *Archivio* IX, 1.

13 Among others, by A. Gabelli, *La libertà in Italia,* in *Nuova Antologia* (1 Nov. 1889), and by Turiello, *Governo e governati in Italia,* vol. 1, 2nd ed. (Bologna, 1889).

14 ["Senators are good men, the senate, on the other hand, is an evil beast." This assertion (of uncertain origin yet sometimes attributed to Cicero) recurs in Sighele's writings, as it clearly summarizes his overall standpoint regarding collective behaviour. See, e.g., *Against Parliamentarism* (201, this volume) and *In Art and in Science* (386, this volume).]

social groups, they affirm that, while independently individuals are honest men, collectively they are scoundrels.[15]

If, furthermore, we move from such meetings, which at least follow certain criteria for the selection of individuals, to other gatherings that are determined only by chance, such as, for example, the audience of a meeting, spectators in a theatre, and the crowds in unplanned assemblies in piazzas and public streets, we shall see that the phenomenon in question offers new and more glaring confirmations. These agglomerations of people certainly do not reproduce (since everyone knows this, it is useless to demonstrate it) the psychology of their single members.

Thus, there is no doubt that often enough the overall result of a gathering of men can be quite different from that which, strictly speaking in terms of abstract logic, should result from the simple sum of individuals; namely, there is no doubt that oftentimes the Spencerian principle "that the character of the aggregate is determined by the characters of the units"[16] is largely contradicted.

Enrico Ferri has this truth in mind when he writes: "a gathering of generally capable men is not always a solid guarantee of the overall and definitive capacity of the group; an aggregate of individuals of common sense can result in an assembly that is anything but reasonable, just as in chemistry the union of two gases can result in a liquid."[17] And for this reason he notes that between psychology, which studies individuals, and sociology, which studies a whole society, there exists another branch of science that could be called *collective psychology. Collective psychology* should deal precisely with groups of individuals, such as juries, assemblies, meetings, and theatre audiences, which in their manifestations deviate from the laws of individual psychology, as much as from the laws of sociology.[18]

But what is the reason why these groups of individuals give results that contradict Spencer's axiom?

The reasons are many, as there are always many causes behind every phenomenon; but in our case, they can be substantially reduced to two: the gatherings in question are *heterogeneous* and *inorganic.*

It is evident and not even necessary to point out that the analogy between the characteristics of the aggregate and those of its individual

15 E. Ferri, *Nuovi orizzonti,* 2nd ed., 484.

16 [H. Spencer, *The Study of Sociology,* 48.]

17 Ferri, op. cit., 483.

18 See Ferri, ibid., 351n1.

units is only possible when these units are the same, or, more exactly, when they are very similar to each other. Dissimilar units joined together not only could not yield an aggregate that reproduces the various characteristics of these units, but could not even result in an aggregate of any kind. A man, a horse, a fish, and an insect cannot form an aggregate. This is the equivalent of what occurs in arithmetic, where in order to have a sum, it is necessary for each addend to be of the same type. Books cannot be added to chairs, nor coins to animals: the sum, even if done physically, would be a number devoid of any meaning.

Now, if the analogy between the characteristics of the units and those of the aggregate is possible only when these units possess at least a certain degree of similarity (if they were, for example, all men), then it is easy enough to infer as a logical consequence that the analogy would increase or decrease in accordance with an increase or decrease in the similarity, the *homogeneity*, between the single units that compose the aggregate.

A cosmopolitan gathering cannot obviously reflect as a whole the various characteristics of the individuals that comprise it with the same proportional accuracy with which a group comprised only of Italians or only of Germans reflects, as a whole, the specific characteristics of those Italians or those Germans. The same can be said of a jury in which blind chance placed a grocer next to a scientist, in front of a board of experts; the same can be said of a theatre audience that comprises individuals of every condition and culture; the same can be said for all multiform gatherings of men, compared with those composed of members of the same class of people. The heterogeneity of the psychological elements (ideas, interests, tastes, habits), in one case, renders impossible the correspondence between the characteristics of the aggregate and those of the units, while the homogeneity of the same psychological elements makes this correspondence possible in the other case.

In order to establish an analogy between the characteristics of the aggregate and those of the units it is not enough, either, for the units to be very similar to one another; they must also be linked by a permanent and organic connection.

Spencer, in the example mentioned at the beginning of this study, notes—as proof that the qualities of the whole are determined by the qualities of the parts which compose it—that with hard, well-baked, rectangular bricks, one could construct, even without mortar, a wall of a fair height, which would be impossible to do with irregular stones. But it is self-evident that the possibility of constructing a wall in the first case does not depend on the fact that equal bricks are used in the place of shapeless stones; rather, it depends, above all, on the fact that these bricks are placed one right next to the other and one on top of the other, according to a given norm, namely, that the bricks be *firmly united.* Indeed, it goes without saying that if the same bricks were piled up haphazardly, the resulting aggregate would differ very little or not at all from what could be obtained by piling up the stones of various forms and sizes.

Applying this observation to the field of sociology leads us to the conclusion that random and inorganic groups of individuals, such as those of a jury, theatre [audience], or crowd, in their manifestations cannot reproduce the characteristics of the units that constitute the group, just as the confused and disordered agglomerate of several bricks cannot reproduce the rectangular shape of the brick. Just as, in the case of the bricks, a *stable union* and *regular placement* are necessary in order to build a wall, so in the former case, in order for the aggregate to take on the qualities of the individuals, it is necessary that these individuals be linked by *permanent* and *organic* relationships, such as those that exist, for example, among the members of a family or of a particular social class.[19]

Therefore, in order for the aggregate to reproduce the characteristics of its units, it is necessary to have both *homogeneity* and an *organic union* among the units.

## *III*

The simple and logical conclusion deriving from these observations can be briefly summarized as follows: Spencer's principle—that the characteristics of the aggregate are determined by the characteristics of the units which compose it—is quite correct and can be applied to its full extent when dealing with aggregates composed of *homogeneous* and *organically* linked units; however, it loses its accuracy and only has limited application whenever aggregates are *hardly homogeneous* and *hardly organic*; finally, it becomes absolutely false and inapplicable when the aggregates are completely *heterogeneous* and *inorganic.*

This evolution in the applicability of the Spencerian principle to human aggregates clearly indicates that the laws of sociology—which we defined

19 Bentham, speaking of the political assemblies and English juries, hinted at the big difference between the manifestations of political bodies that have a *permanent* existence, and those that have an *occasional* and *ephemeral* existence. He stated that the former—more easily than the latter—give results that correspond to the true interests and the true tendencies of their members.—See *Tactique des Assemblées politiques délibérantes,* excerpts of manuscripts by J. Bentham, by Et. Dumont (Brussels, 1840), chapter II.

as parallel to, although more complex than, those of individual psychology—are valid when these aggregates are homogeneous and organic. Yet, as the aggregates become less and less homogeneous and less and less organic, it is no longer possible to apply the laws of sociology, hence, in such cases, they are replaced by the laws of *collective psychology*, which we established to be completely different from the laws of individual psychology.

Collective psychology, therefore, pertains to a different field and, in its development, follows a trajectory diametrically opposed to that of sociology: it expands where the other retreats, and the maximum domain of its laws coincides with the minimal domain of the laws of sociology. The more temporary, accidental, and inorganic a gathering of individuals is, the more it will divert from Spencer's axiom and enter, instead, the area of investigation of collective psychology.

Therefore, if we are not mistaken, among the more or less heterogeneous and inorganic aggregates of individuals that we mentioned—namely, juries, committees, theatre spectators, but also occasional and transitory meetings of any kind—the one that, more than any other, escapes the laws of sociology and must be subject to the laws of collective psychology is, without a doubt, the crowd.

The crowd, indeed, is an aggregate of men that is *heterogeneous par excellence*, as it is composed of individuals of every age, sex, class, social condition, morality, and culture; and it is *inorganic par excellence*, as it is formed suddenly, instantaneously, and with no prior arrangement.

To study the psychology of the crowd, therefore, means to study the *collective psychology* of the phenomenon that, better than any other, can reveal its laws and shed light on their mode of functioning.

And this is what we modestly propose to do in this study, with the aim of accurately explaining the nature and social danger of the crimes that a crowd can commit.

## Chapter 1: "The Psycho-Physiology of the Crowd"

The problem of criminal liability is relatively simple when the author of the crime is a single individual; it becomes more complicated when multiple individuals are involved, as it must examine, in this case, the complicity of each person in the criminal action. It becomes an infinitely more difficult problem to solve when the authors of a crime are no longer a few, nor many, but a massive, indefinite number of individuals that escapes every precise assessment; in other words, when the crime is the work of a crowd.

Judicial repression, easy in the first scenario and slightly more difficult in the second, assumes in the third scenario the semblances of an almost absolute impossibility, because one cannot find and punish the true culprits.

According to what criteria, then, should one proceed?

One option is to adopt the stupidly soldierlike method of decimation, striking only those few whom the agents of the public force can manage to arrest, not always justly, in moments of confusion or fear; another method, which is more logical, though not totally exact, is that of Tarquinius, who believes in winning over his enemies by striking off *the tallest poppies*,[20] that is to say, the instigators who are always present in a crowd.

Faced with these two solutions, which are either illogical or insufficient, the popular judges frequently acquit the accused, thereby confirming Tacitus's saying that "where many sin, nobody is punished." And, Pellegrino Rossi[21] would say, this is one of the cases in which one arrives at impunity by way of absurdity.

But is impunity just? If it is, for what reason? If it is not, what then is the proper way to react to the crimes committed by a crowd?

The purpose of this study is to answer these questions.

## *I*

The classical school of criminality never posed the question of whether the crime of a crowd should be punished in a different way from the crime of an individual who acts alone. It was natural. The study of crime as a judicial entity was enough; the criminal was secondary, an unknown variable whom no one wanted or knew how to decipher. It did not matter if the criminal was the son of epileptics or alcoholics or healthy parents, if he was born of one race or another, in a torrid or cold climate, if he had, from then on, a deplorable or commendable conduct. Therefore,

20 [Lucius Tarquinius Superbus, seventh king of Rome, was walking in his garden when a messenger sent by his son Sextus inquired how to deliver the city of Gabii in his hands. Instead of replying, Tarquinius kept striking off the heads of the tallest poppies with his stick. Sextus understood he meant eliminating the chief men of Gabii, and successfully subdued the city.]

21 [Pellegrino Rossi (1787–1848) was an Italian economist, jurist, and politician, and a naturalized French citizen. After becoming chair in political economy at the Collège de France and professor of constitutional law at the Sorbonne, in 1843 he was appointed dean of the faculty. In 1845 he served as ambassador of France for the Papal States and, finally, as minister of justice under Pope Pius IX.]

for the classical school the conditions under which the criminal committed his crime must also have been of little importance. Whether he acted alone or in the midst of a mob that instigated and intoxicated him with their screams, it was always and solely his own free will that determined his criminal actions. Hence in both cases the cause is identical, and the punishment as well.

Given the principle, this line of reasoning could not be more logical; but, once the principle failed, so, necessarily would the reasoning, too. And this is what happened. After demonstrating that free will is an illusion of consciousness, and unveiling the world of the physical, anthropological, and social factors of crime, unknown until then, the positive school elevated to a judicial principle the idea that was previously and unconsciously felt by all, but could not find a place in the jurists' rigid formulas: that is, the idea that the crime committed by a crowd should be judged differently from that committed by a single individual, because the anthropological and social factors of the former case differed from those of the latter.

It is Giuseppe A. Pugliese who, in a brief pamphlet,[22] first developed the doctrine of criminal liability in collective crimes. He concluded his fine work by supporting the semi-responsibility of all those who commit a crime under the impetus of a crowd. "When it is a crowd, a population, that rebels"—he wrote— "the individual does not act as such, but rather as a drop of water in the great flood, and the arm with which he strikes is an unconscious instrument."[23]

Completing, perhaps, the thoughts of Pugliese and attempting, in any event, to provide with a simile the anthropological reasons behind his theory, I later compared the crimes committed under the impetus of a crowd with those committed out of passion by an individual.[24]

Pugliese adopted the term *collective crime* to describe the strange and complex phenomenon of a crowd that, dragged by the bewitching words of a demagogue or exasperated by a fact that is (or seems to be) an injustice or an insult, commits a crime. I preferred to call it simply the *crime of the crowd* insofar as, in my opinion, there are two forms of *collective crimes*, and need to be kept separate: there is the *crime by congenital tendency of*

---

22 *Del delitto collettivo* (Trani, 1887). [Giuseppe Alberto Pugliese (1845–1931) was an Italian lawyer and member of parliament for six legislatures.]

23 Ibid.

24 See my "La complicità," in *Archivio di psichiatria, scienze penali ed antropologia criminale* XI, 3–4.

*the collectivity*, which include banditry, the Camorra, and the mafia, and there is the *crime of the passion-driven collectivity*, which is precisely a crime committed by a crowd. The former is analogous to the crime of a born criminal, the latter to the crime of an occasional criminal.[25] The former is always premeditated, the latter never is. In the first case, the anthropological factor is predominant, while in the second case the social factor is. The first reveals a constant and severe dangerousness[26] in its perpetrators, the other a momentary dangerousness, which is occasional and not severe.

The semi-responsibility Pugliese invoked for the crimes committed by a crowd is, therefore, right, if not in itself, at least certainly as a means to the proposed end.

Given our penal code and given a special circumstance (such was the reason that prompted Pugliese to conceive his theory), one could not achieve the goal of punishing the crimes of a multitude with different and milder criteria than those adopted to punish the crimes of single individuals, other than by invoking semi-responsibility.

Yet, scientifically, semi-responsibility is an absurdity, above all, for us positivists who maintain that every man is wholly responsible for his actions.[27]

The positivist theory must be based on other principles.

We must not ask ourselves if the perpetrators of a crime committed under the impetus of a crowd are responsible or semi-responsible (old formulas for wrong concepts); we must only ask ourselves what specific and best-suited form of reaction they deserve.

These are the terms of the problems we will attempt to solve.

---

25 [Here Sighele is explaining crowd behaviour in the framework of Cesare Lombroso's and Enrico Ferri's categories of criminals—in particular the difference between born criminals and occasional ones. As Lombroso writes in *Criminal Man*, "[T]he occasional criminal is a weak version of the born criminal" insofar as, according to Ferri as well, he does not resist "'external incentives to commit crime, while the latter is driven by an internal compulsion to find a crime and commit it.'" Cesare Lombroso, *Criminal Man*, translated by Mary Gibson and Nicole Hahn Rafter (Durham: Duke University Press, 2006): 294.]

26 [Sighele is here adopting a leading concept in positivist criminology, namely, the notion of *temibilità*, that is, the degree of dangerousness upon which, as we can see in Lombroso, a typology of criminals is constructed.]

27 On this point see Ferri, *Nuovi orizzonti*, 2nd ed., 128 and ff. The French positivists (especially Tarde) do not admit that "man is *always* responsible for every anti judicial action he commits," and they maintain that there are cases of *irresponsibility*. We will see in chapter III what value such a theory has.

## *II*

Before defining a disease and proposing cures, it is necessary to make a diagnosis; before discussing what the crime of a crowd is and before mentioning the methods for repressing such a crime, it is necessary to study it in its manifestations.

We will hence examine, first and foremost, the sentiments under the influence of which a crowd acts, and, if possible, we will explain its strange psychology. "A crowd"—writes an acute philosopher—

> is a phenomenon which is difficult to comprehend. It is an aggregation of heterogeneous elements, unknown to one another and, nonetheless, as soon as a spark of passion bursts forth from one of these elements, and electrifies the entire mass of individuals, by spontaneous generation, a sort of organization is immediately produced.
>
> Incoherence becomes cohesion, a confused noise becomes a distinct voice and, all of a sudden, the thousands of people previously divided by sentiment and idea come to form a single and unique person, a nameless and monstrous beast that runs towards its aim with an irresistible finality.[28]
>
> The majority of these men had assembled out of pure curiosity, but the fever of some of them soon reached the minds of all, and in all of them there arose a delirium. The very man who had come running to oppose the murder of an innocent person is one of the first to be seized with the homicidal contagion, and moreover, it does not occur to him to be astonished at this.[29]

The incomprehensibility of the crowd lies precisely in its unpremeditated organization. In the crowd there is no orderly and pre-existent common goal, thus, as an anonymous author observes in the journal *The Lancet*, the crowd cannot truly possess a collective will determined by the highest elementary faculties of all the brains that are a part of it. And yet, we see a unity of action and scope in the middle of the infinite variety of its movements, and we hear a single note—if I may say so—among

28 Flaubert, the scientist-novelist, wrote about the crowd in analogous terms: "This gathering of heterogeneous, human particles finds itself so well cemented by its own acts, that it forms a coherent mass: a crowd that first was only curious, is dragged behind an orator whose words it does not understand, and participates in the acts of whoever surrounds it without knowing why."

29 G. Tarde, *La philosophie pénale* (Paris-Lyon, 1890), 320. [*Penal Philosophy*, 323.]

its discordant thousands of voices.[30] The same collective name of *crowd* indicates that the single personalities of the individuals who take part in it are concentrated in and identified by a single personality. Therefore, we must inevitably recognize in crowds the action of *some thing* that acts temporarily as a common thought, although it cannot be explained. "This *some thing* is not the intervention of the lowest mental energies, and could not aspire to the dignity of a true intellectual faculty. It is not possible to define it other than by the name: *soul of the crowd*."[31]

But what produces this soul of the crowd? Does it arise miraculously, and is it a phenomenon whose causes cannot be discovered, or does it originate in some primordial faculty of man? How does one explain that a sign, a voice, a cry—emitted by one person—can almost unconsciously carry away an entire population and often lead it to the most horrible excesses?" It is the faculty of imitation"—replies Bordier—

> which, just as diffusion in a gaseous environment equalizes the tension of the gases, tends to equalize the social environment in all of its parts, to destroy originality, to level out the characteristics of an epoch, of a nation, of a city, of a small circle of friends. Every man is individually inclined to imitation, but this faculty reaches its *maximum* among gathered men. Proof of this can be found in theatres and public meetings, where a single applause or whistle is enough to stir up the participants and sway them in one direction or another.[32]

It is an unquestionable and undisputed truth that the tendency of man to imitate is one of the strongest tendencies of his nature.[33] It suffices to

30 "Une foule a la puissance simple et profonde d'un large unisson" [a crowd has the simple and profound power of a wide unison]. G. Tarde, ibid., 321.

31 From a published study from *The Lancet*, a journal of medicine. See: *Contribuzione alla dottrina della responsabilità penale nel delitto collettivo*, by the lawyer Pugliese, in *Rivista di giurisprudenza* (Trani, 1889).

32 A. Bordier, *La vie des sociétés* (Paris, 1888), 76.

33 "And one sign of it"—Bagehot observes shrewdly—"is the great pain that we feel when our imitation has been unsuccessful. A cynical doctrine maintains that most men would rather be accused of wickedness than of *gaucherie*. And this is but another way of saying that the bad copying of predominant manners is felt to be more of a disgrace than common consideration would account for its being, since *gaucherie* in all but extravagant cases is not an offence against religion or morals, but is simply bad imitation." W. Bagehot, *Physics and Politics; or, Thoughts on the application of the principles of "natural selection" and "inheritance" to political society* (New York: Appleton, 1873), 92. [In French in Sighele's text. See *Lois scientifiques du développement des nations*, 5th ed. (Paris: Alcan, 1885), 101–102.]

observe our surroundings to realize that the social world is nothing but a fabric of *similarities*—similarities that are produced by imitation in all of its forms: custom-imitation or fashion-imitation, sympathy-imitation or obedience-imitation, precept-imitation or education-imitation, spontaneous-imitation or conditioned-imitation.[34]

Serious people and frivolous people, the old and the young, the cultivated and the ignorant, everyone ultimately—although to different degrees—succumbs to the instinct to imitate what they see, what they feel, and what they know. The so-called *currents of public opinion*, both in politics and in business, are determined by this instinct. Today you find enthusiastic politicians or stockbrokers, full of ardour for an idea or speculation; later you see them disappointed, tired, disheartened. If you search for the reasons behind their ardour and their depression, you can distinguish them only with great difficulty, and if you do, these reasons have, indeed, little value. In reality, it is not reason or logic that has produced this change, but it is the instinct of imitation. Something occurred, at first, that seemed a good omen: in this case the optimists, those who always dare and hope, took to crying loudly, and the public followed in the same tone. Then, when they began to tire of seeing everything in a rosy glow, something occurred that seemed a bad omen; and at that time the pessimists, those who always fear and are always prudent, began to chatter, and everyone repeated what they said.[35]

This is what occurs in politics and business, and in all things as well. From the style of a dress to a form of government, from honest actions to crimes, from suicide to insanity, all manifestations of life—the least and the most important, the painful and the happy—are a product of imitation.[36]

---

34 See G. Tarde, *Les lois de l'imitation* (Paris: Alcan, 1890). [English translation by Elsie Clews Parson, *The Laws of Imitation* (New York: Henry Holt, 1903), 14.]

35 See Bagehot, *Physics and Politics*, 95 and ff.

36 Affirming the universality of the instinct of imitation, it seems to me that one upholds, implicitly, the existence of *misoneism* in human nature. Tarde, however, who so commendably explained the laws of imitation, maintains that these laws contradict *misoneism*, given that, he says, if one imitates all and always, one imitates not only that which is old, but also that which is new. Now I do not deny that a part of our acts of imitation are determined by the *love of the new*, but I do deny that the existence of this *philoneism* excludes the existence of *misoneism*. The majority is *misoneistic* for an important innovation, and *philoneistic* for an innovation of little or no importance. The two phenomena proceed in a distinct and parallel manner; it is not possible, therefore, to confound them. And it would not be necessary to say more if I did not feel the need to refute an observation—seemingly very acute—that Tarde made regarding Lombroso ("*Le délit politique*," in *Revue scientifique*, Oct. 1890). "As an example of national neophobia"

It is, therefore, natural that this faculty—which is innate in man—not only explains its efficacy, but also copies and multiplies it in the middle of a multitude, where every fantasy is stimulated and where the unity of time and place immensely accelerates and renders the exchange of impressions and feelings almost instantaneous.

Nevertheless, to say that man *imitates* is, in our case, an insufficient explanation. It is important to know *why* man imitates; we need an explanation that does not stop at the superficial causes but finds the initial cause of the phenomenon.

In observing how imitation sometimes takes on acute forms, both in its intensity and in the extent to which it spreads, and noticing, moreover, that this imitation, rather than being voluntary, is in a few instances unconscious, many writers have attempted to explain it by resorting to the hypothesis of moral contagion. "There is, in the phenomenon of imitation," —says Doctor Ebrard—

> something mysterious, a sort of attraction that can only be compared to that blind and powerful instinct that compels us, almost unbeknownst to us, to repeat the acts we witnessed and that deeply impressed our senses and fantasy. We all endure, to a greater or lesser degree, the yoke of this fascination, against which weak characters cannot and do not know how to defend themselves.[37]

And more explicitly Joly writes: "Imitation is a true contagion that finds its means of transmission in the example, as smallpox is spread by a virus. And just as diseases exist in our organism that need only a small cause to start developing, so do passions exist inside of us, which remain dormant while reason indisputably reigns, but can wake up and explode simply on account of imitation."[38]

---

national neophobia"—writes Tarde—"Lombroso cites the French population, which, since Strabo's times, has remained in the same, vain, bellicose, and *in love with novelty*. Here the contradiction is so strong that one must attribute it to a *lapsus calami*" [in French in Sighele's text]. Indeed, there is no contradiction if one reflects on the distinction made above. A nation can be *misoneistic* and a *lover of novelty* at the same time, just like a lady who loves changing her *toilette* according to the fashion, who remains incredulous in the face of the discoveries of science, and who is offended if one tells her that religion is nothing but a heap of prejudices and falsities.

37 N. Ebrard, *Le suicide considéré aux points de vue médical, philosophique, religieux et social*, chapter VII.

38 Joly, "De l'imitation," in *Union médicale* VIII (1869), 369. [Henri Joly (1899–1925) was a French sociologist and philosopher known for his studies in criminology.]

In addition to Ebrard and Joly, there follow Despine, Moreau de Tours, and many others,[39] who unanimously agree that moral contagion is as certain as in any physical disease. "Just as"—writes Despine—

> the resonance of a musical note makes that same note vibrate in all the soundboards that, being susceptible to it, are under the influence of the sound, the manifestation of a feeling or a passion excites the same instinctive element, puts it into action, makes it vibrate—so to speak—in any individual who, because of his moral constitution, is likely to experience more or less intensely the same instinctive element.[40]

With this fitting if not profound metaphor that better clarifies the hypothesis of moral contagion, many believed to have explained not only the common, natural, and constant cases of imitation, but also and, above all, the rarest and oddest cases, those veritable *epidemics* that develop every now and then in connection with a specific phenomenon.

In this way, the epidemics of suicides, which followed the suicide of someone famous who deeply fascinated and moved public opinion,[41] were said to be attributable to moral contagion; the many crimes that followed an atrocious crime reported by all newspapers[42] were said to

---

39 Doctor Prosper Despine in his two works *De la contagion morale* (1870) and *De l'imitation considerée au point de vue des différents príncipes qui la déterminent* (1871); Moreau de Tours, in his volume: *De la contagion du suicide à propos de l'épidémie actuelle,* Thèse de Paris (1875), and in his short paper "Un mot sur la contagion du crime et sa prophilaxie," in *Union médicale* XXII, no. 88.—Before these authors, the phenomenon of contagion in suicide was alluded to by Brierre de Boismont, *Du Suicide et de la folie suicide,* 2nd ed. (Paris, 1865), 258 and ff.,—and the contagion of madness by Calmeil in the volume—even today marvelous in its freshness—*De la folie considérée sous le point de vue pathologique, philosophique,* etc. (Paris, 1845). Among recent works, Aubry's *La contagion du meurtre* (Paris: Alcan 1888), deserves attention.

40 P. Despine, *De la contagion morale,* 13 [in French in Sighele's text].

41 The efficacy of moral contagion is perhaps more evident in suicide than in any other phenomenon. The case is well known of those 15 invalids who in 1772 hanged themselves in succession and in a short time span from a beam in a ward of the hospice where they lived. Likewise, it is known that after a lord, tired of life, committed suicide by jumping into a crater of the Vesuvius, many British followed suit. Examples could be multiplied. In addition to the already cited works by Ebrard and Brierre de Boismont, see Morselli, *Il suicidio* (Milan: Dumolard, 1879).

42 As for crime epidemics, I do not think it is necessary to prove it with examples. We all may have observed it ourselves on numerous occasions. It suffices to hint at the two analogous epidemics of homicides and injuries committed with handguns or with vitriol by women on their lovers. These epidemics occurred in France especially

be caused by moral contagion; the political and religious epidemics that suddenly stirred up a mob behind the heated words of some enthusiast or behind the bad faith of some instigator were said to be the result of moral contagion.

Therefore, we also can—and even more so—attribute the unexpected and apparently incomprehensible manifestations of the crowd to moral contagion.

But can we be satisfied with this explanation? Is, perhaps, *moral contagion* different from *imitation* beyond its verbal expression?

It is self-evident that, in order for this explanation to satisfy us, it is necessary to understand the manner and means by which this moral contagion is spread. Otherwise, we would be back to where we started.

Giuseppe Sergi felt this necessity and, as a true positivist psychologist, he understood that in order to speak scientifically of *moral contagion*, the physical foundation of this contagion had to be established.

This is what Sergi has attempted to do, and we believe that he succeeded in his endeavour. "The psyche"—writes Sergi—

> is a general mode of activity identical to any other organic activity, without a single exception. Whosoever is knowledgeable about this mode of activity knows that every organic tissue is activated by means of stimuli; when it receives a stimulus from an outside agent, its reaction corresponds to the nature and energy of the stimulus. An obvious example is muscular tissue, which contracts in particular muscles only when an exterior stimulation awakens its inherent ability. This is how the psyche functions as well, considered in connection with its organs. Nothing is spontaneous, nothing is autonomous; it is activated by received stimuli and manifests itself exteriorly according to the nature of these stimuli.
>
> We call *receptivity* the ability to receive impressions that come from outside; we call *reflection* the ability to manifest a stimulated activity according to the impressions received. Both of these states can be included in a fundamental law, the *reflexive receptivity* of the psyche.

---

after Marie Brière in 1880 killed with three gunshots her seducer who abandoned her, and after Clotilde Andral, in the same year, disfigured her lover with vitriol. See Bataille's collection of *Causes criminelles et mondaines*. I recall in this regard that according to Professor Brouardel the starting point of the series of *vitriol* attacks is, allegedly, a novel by Karr that narrates the story of a betrayed husband who takes revenge disfiguring his wife with vitriol.

> Alienists for some time now have been dealing with the phenomenon of hypnotic suggestion, and they have generally maintained that it occurs only when their subjects are hypnotized. They have not realized that what they call *suggestion* is a more acute phenomenon than the fundamental state of the psyche, *receptivity*, analogously to what tends to occur in all morbid states, in which phenomena take on an exaggerated form and become more evident than in a normal state. Hypnotic suggestion only shows the disposition of the psyche, its fundamental conditions, through which it operates and moves. Suggestion is relative to the receptivity here described, and complies with the general law of every organism, which does not act spontaneously but, rather, by received stimuli.[43]

Now, according to Sergi, every idea and emotion of the individual is but a *reflection* of an external impulse he has received. Nobody moves, functions, thinks, if not because of a *suggestion* that can be produced by seeing an object, hearing a word or a sound, by any occurrence whatsoever outside of our organism. And this suggestion can influence a single individual, many, or a multitude, and it can spread far among people like a true epidemic, leaving a few entirely immune, others mildly affected, and others violently overcome. The phenomena produced in the last case, however strange and terrible they may be, are only the highest degree, the most acute expression of the simple and unobserved phenomenon of suggestion that is the primary cause of every manifestation of our psyche. While the intensity varies, the nature of the phenomenon is always the same.

All forms and kinds of human activity confirm Sergi's fitting intuition that renders the imitation of the many a phenomenon equal to, although more acute than, the imitation of one individual, and thereby connects epidemic imitation to sporadic imitation, explaining both in terms of suggestion, of which Sergi reveals the reasons and the conditions.

Who will deny that the relationship between teacher and pupil and the latter's imitation of the former—an imitation of fondness and of unconscious and instinctive admiration—has the characteristics of true suggestion? And who will deny that this relationship, which is initially established between two people only, is the primitive and embryonic form, if I may say so, of the suggestion that is later established between one and many, between the head of a scientific, political or religious school

43 G. Sergi, *Psicosi epidemica* (Milan: Dumolard, 1889), 4.

and his disciples, his adepts, his co-religionists? Who cannot see that this epidemic suggestion is the last step of that first isolated suggestion?

Who does not feel and does not know that this epidemic suggestion can grow in extension and intensity, wherever favourable environmental circumstances or particular characteristics of the person or persons keep it alive?

Political and religious sects have sometimes gone as far as to turn into veritable madness epidemics. From Arab and Indian holy men to medieval demonomaniacs, whose last descendants could be found until not too long ago in Italy,[44] from Barkers, to Perfectionists, to the Shakers of North America,[45] to the Stundists, Cholaputs, and Skoptsy of Russia,[46] from the crowds led by Judas the Gaulanite and by Theudas, which foreshadowed the revolution of Christ, to those who, guided by a strange and morbid fetishism for Klopstock,[47] announced the German Renaissance,[48] we have an infinite variety of moral epidemics, of *epidemic psychoses*, that surprise us first of all for the atrocities and infamies they commit, but that, when examined in depth, prove to be nothing more than pathological exaggerations of the phenomenon of suggestion, the most universal law of the social world.

And just as in the sphere of normal life it is possible to rise from the suggestion of a single person upon another, of a teacher upon a pupil, of a strong man upon a weak man, to the suggestion of a single individual upon a multitude, of a genius of thought and sentiment upon all his contemporaries, of a sectarian leader upon his members, so in the sphere of pathology it is possible to shift from the power of suggestion

44 I am alluding to the convulsive epidemic of 1878 when the women of the small town of Verzenis in Friuli [Verzegnis, a municipality in the province of Udine] were roused by the sermons of a madman and by certain religious practices. See Franzolini, "La epidemia di demonopatia in Verzenis," in *Rivista sperimentale di freniatria e di medicina legale* (Reggio, 1878). Other similar epidemics could be cited, like that of Lazzaretti.

45 See C. Lombroso and R. Laschi, *Il delitto politico* (Turin: Bocca, 1890), 130.

46 They are sects of individuals more or less exalted and sick, who accompany the nihilist movement in Russia. The *Stundists* want everything in common; the *Cholaputs* are ecstatic worshipers of the spiritual saints; the *Skoptsy* emasculate themselves. See Tsakni, *La Russie sectaire.*

47 [Friedrich Gottlieb Klopstock (1724–1803) was a German poet best known for his epic work *Der Messias.*]

48 See Lombroso and Laschi, ibid.—It is worth noting that this mad uprising that foreshadowed the German Renaissance takes its name from *Stürmisch,* or *period of the storm.* This is further confirmation of the German language's reputation as a philosophical language.

of a single madman over another madman to that of a madman upon all those around him.

This is proof not only of the fact that pathology follows the same laws as physiology, but also of the universality of the phenomenon of suggestion.

Legrand du Saulle so wonderfully describes the *delirium à deux*,[49] this strange form of madness, produced by the influence that a man has on an individual—naturally already inclined to the contagion—who little by little loses reason and takes on the identical form of madness as his suggestionizer.[50] A bond of dependence is established between these two unfortunate men; one dominates the other, who is nothing more than an echo of the first, and carries out what the first carries out. The power of imitation is sometimes so strong that it transfers the same hallucinations from one to the other.[51]

From this *madness à deux* (which corresponds in the field of pathology to the power of suggestion one has over another—the master upon the disciple, a lover upon his lover—in the normal sphere) we rise to madness of three, of four, of five,[52] which occurs by the same process as the

49 Legrand du Saulle, *Le délire des persécutions*. [Legrand du Saulle (1830–1886) was a French psychiatrist famous for his studies of phobias and other personality disorders. He also contributed to the advancement of forensic psychiatry.]

50 [For an explanation about the choice of this term in the English translation of Sighele's works, see "A Note on the Texts and Their Translations," lxxv in this volume]

51 Euphrasie Mercier, an insane assassin, had this power over her friend Elodie Ménétret, who was destined to remain her victim. See the trial against her in Bataille's *Causes criminelles* (1866), 54. Tebaldi provides a typical example of *delirium à deux*. "Here is a *form à deux*," he writes, "where imitation"—we would say suggestion—"was the treacherous weaver: in a small village in the Veneto region, there was the case of a pair born under the same unlucky star, a pair who shared in the same misery, who struggled against the same straitened circumstances; husband and wife were seized by pellagra, and the worry of their misfortunes led them to ascribe their causes to the injustices of the Municipality, to a false distribution of aid to the poor. Each under the influence of the other, got carried away, and they concocted a plan to go into the piazza, make a scandal, imprecating and threatening authorities in the name of coarse but articulated communist principles. That same plan led them to the hospital; they said their goodbyes with the enthusiasm of someone who would meet again in Eldorado, and in the same delirious manner, they entered into their respective rooms." See [A. Tebaldi,] *Ragione e pazzia* (Milan, 1884), 143. [Augusto Tebaldi (1833–1895) was an Italian professor of psychiatry at the University of Padua who studied mental illness through physiognomy and expression.]

52 Roscioli refers to a case of madness involving four people (in *Manicomio* no.1, 1888). The married couple N., honest and hard-working farmers, had three daughters. One day, the 18-year-old second-born, while in church, was suddenly struck by a strong maniacal exaltation and was taken back home. At the sight of such a sad spectacle,

*madness à deux*. It is always a madman who influences his relatives, those who usually live with him, and his example enables those morbid ideas to arise in these individuals along with sensory disorders. Little by little their consciousness is blocked out, leaving free rein to the sphere of insanity, which is either the exact reproduction of the instigator's madness or a pale and colourless reproduction thereof.[53]

And apart from these true cases of multiple, simultaneous madness, produced by suggestion, all of the alienists concur that the madman has a power of suggestion—less intense but more general—over all those around him. Usually living with people who think wrongly, reason badly, and act accordingly— writes Rambosson—, our brain, which constantly receives the blowbacks of theirs, tends to yield to the same movement that, through its influence on our intellectual faculties, leads us to act like them.[54] "The sight of the sick person,"—writes Seppilli—"the ideas that he manifests provoke in the brains of those around him the same psychic, sensory, and motor images that, depending on their intensity and duration, can more or less transform the individuals."[55] And, before them, Maudsley wrote on the subject of living with the insane: "No one can acquire the habit of being inconsequent in his thoughts, feelings, or

---

her father remained so shaken that after eight days he fell prey to a state of anxiety with panophobia. It wasn't long before the mother succumbed to the same malady, and finally, after fifteen days, the eldest daughter was also struck by the same maniacal agitation. Many other similar cases that I have not consulted can be found in the works of Jörger, Tuque, Martinenq, and Verner, quoted by Seppilli ("La pazzia indotta," in *Rivista sperimentale di freniatria* (1890), nos. 1, 2), which I was unable to consult.

53 Regarding these forms of insanity—especially the *madness à deux*—after Lasègue and Falret's communication on this subject at the Academy of Medicine ("De la folie à deux," in *Ann. med. psych.*, 1877), there has been no shortage of either works or discussions on what clinical name to give it. Some wanted to call it "communicated madness," others "imposed madness," others "simultaneous madness," see Regis, *La folie à deux ou folie simultanée* (Paris: Baillière, 1880), and they assigned it different causes and reasons. Venturi was the first to raise the hypothesis of suggestion (adopted later by Sergi) in his work "L'allucinazione a due e la pazzia a due," in *Manicomio* (1886), no. 1. See also the previously cited work by Seppilli. [Sighele's attention to Silvio Venturi's studies of suggestion is quite pertinent. The Italian alienist made an enduring contribution to the field. See, e.g., the references to his work in Sante de Sanctis's "La psichiatria contemporanea," in *Rivista d'Italia* V, vol. II (1902): 907.]

54 J. Rambosson, *Phénomènes nerveux, intellectuels et moraux, leur transmissions par contagion* (Paris: Firmin-Didot, 1883), 230 [in French in Sighele's text].

55 Op. cit.

actions without affecting the sincerity and integrity of one's nature, or diminishing the strength and lucidity of one's intelligence."[56]

Finally, in addition to general contagion, which is slow, unperceived, and not very intense, we have immediate, instantaneous contagion among the insane, particularly among epileptics. It is a phenomenon different from those discussed so far, but the origin and cause are always the same: suggestion.

Van Swieten reports the observation of convulsive movements in several children, which were repeated by all those who were unfortunately present.[57] And no one ignores the often-mentioned case of the girl in a Harlem hospital who, during an an epileptic seizure, instantaneously *suggestionized* the other patients, who showed symptoms of the same condition.

Without citing other examples, I believe I may conclude that our description of the suggestive forms in *insanity* corresponds exactly to that of the suggestive forms in a normal state.[58] In insanity, as in a normal

---

56 H. Maudsley, *Le crime et la folie,* 214.—The following authors made identical observations regarding madness: Leuret, *Du traitement de la folie*; Flourens, *Psychologie comparée*; Vigna, *Il contagio della pazzia* (Venice, 1881).

57 See G. van Swieten, *Dictionnaire des sciences médicales,* cited by Rambosson, op. cit.

58 The development and parallel spreading of the phenomenon of suggestion—from one to another, from one to several, to many, or to a multitude,—which we have described in the *normal state* and in the *insane state* also occurs in *suicides* and *crimes.* Regarding suicide—there is the *suicidal couple*—two lovers, one of whom persuades the other to die with him;—which today has become extremely frequent (V. Chpolianski, *Des analogies entre la folie à deux,* Paris, 1885); there is the *suicide by three, four, and five,* entire normal families who, because of the state of destitution they find themselves in, resolve to die: it is the father, generally, who first has the idea of suicide and who communicates it to his wife and children and convinces them to accept it. Two typical examples of this multiple suicidal suggestion are the cases of the Hayem family (father, mother, and four children) who committed suicide with coal during the winter of 1890 in Paris, and of the Paul family (father, mother, and three children) who committed suicide in 1885 in Brittany by throwing themselves into the sea. Finally, there is the *epidemic suicide,* which occurred in more than a few cases, according to Ebrard, in Lyon, where women disgusted with life threw themselves into the Rhône, two or three at a time, and in Marseille, where young girls committed suicide together in the name of love. As for crime, all I have said about suicide also applies. There is the *criminal couple* (Corre): the born criminal who influences and corrupts the occasional criminal, making him a slave (*incubus* and *succubus*); there is the *criminal association,* in which the leader drags young occasional criminals into a crime by his sheer willpower and by the moral dominion he has over them: this is the case of Lacenaire with Avril and the others of his band; there is, ultimately, the *criminal epidemic,* which develops, above all, in gangs with a large number of criminals

state, suggestion begins with a simple event that one could call, generally speaking, an instance of imitation. Little by little, as this imitation develops and spreads, it arrives at collective and epidemic forms, at forms of true delirium, in which actions are involuntary and, I dare say, performed by an irresistible force.

Therefore, is it not evident that this suggestion—which we wanted to describe, perhaps too extensively, in order to demonstrate its universality—must also be the cause of the manifestations of the crowd? Is it not evident that also in the midst of a multitude, the cry of one individual, the word of one speaker, the act of some bold man, could *suggestionize* all those who witness that cry, that speech, or that act, and could lead them—like an unconscious herd—to perform wicked actions? And is it not, indeed, evident that in the crowd suggestion will attain its maximum effect and instantly go from the *form à deux* to the *epidemic form*, because—as we said—the unity of time and place and the immediacy of contact between individuals lead the velocity of emotional contagion to its limit?

I hope nobody will want to respond negatively to this question. However, to further explain how suggestion functions in a crowd—namely, the way in which any emotion manifested by a single individual, whether fear or anger, can spread throughout a multitude—I wish to reproduce several splendid pages by Alfred Espinas.

In these pages we will find the clear and precise physiological explanation of the psychology of the crowd.

The renowned French naturalist Espinas, when describing societies of wasps (which he categorized as a maternal domestic society), notes that among these animals the division of work reaches a high degree of perfection, given that there are individuals whose sole occupation is to ensure the security of the community. The nest, as a matter of fact, is guarded by sentinels that enter the nest to warn the other wasps in case

---

and in libidinous crimes. When an unfortunate girl falls victim to some criminals, they are not satisfied with violating her: it is enough that one of them has the idea for some horrible abuse, for all of his companions to imitate him, I would almost say in a fit of true delirium. This is the case of the woman who was kidnapped and violated by a gang of fifteen criminals and who was subjected to the most obscene jokes. Lit matches were inserted into her genitals and pins stuck all over her body. Only one of the men gave the example: the others, competing, followed, singing and dancing around the body of the unfortunate girl. See Henry Fouquier, *Les moeurs brutales* in *Le Figaro* (4 July 1886). Elsewhere, we will deal extensively with the various forms of *criminal association* attributable to suggestion.

of danger. Once alerted, the other wasps exit the nest, all irritated, and sting their aggressors.

Espinas then asks:

> How can the sentinels alert their companions about the enemy's presence? Do they perhaps have a language so precise that they are able to communicate warnings? Wasps cannot use their antennae to convey their impressions with the subtlety with which ants do; in the case of wasps, a precise language is useless. And here is why. To explain the phenomenon, we need only understand how an emotion such as alarm or anger is communicated from one individual to another. Every individual, immediately affected by this rapid impression, will rush out and follow the general impulse. He will throw himself at the first person he encounters, preferably at a fleeing individual. All animals are carried away by movement. Hence the only thing left to explain is: how are emotions communicated to a multitude? *By the mere spectacle of an irritated individual*—we answer. *It is a universal law in all kingdoms of intelligent life that the representation of an emotional state provokes an identical state in the witness.* In realms inferior to those where intelligence begins, in order to have a conformity of impressions, external circumstances must act separately on each and every individual simultaneously. But when representation is possible, it is enough for a single one to be upset by external circumstances in order for the same reaction to be immediately generated in all. Indeed, "the alarmed individual externally manifests his state of consciousness in an energetic manner. The buzzing of the wasp, for example, signifies a state of anger or agitation: the other wasps hear it and produce the same buzz; but they cannot represent this buzz unless their nerve fibres which produce this sound are stimulated to a greater or lesser degree." A physiological phenomenon easy to observe in superior animals is that the performance of any act involves a cause of execution of this act: a goat offered a piece of sugar and a dog offered a piece of meat, lick their lips and salivate as if they were actually eating. A child and a savage accompany with mimicry the story they tell. Chevreul[59] demonstrated that

59 [Michel-Eugène Chevreul (1786–1889) was a French chemist best known for his research on animal fats and for his scientific explanations of involuntary muscular reactions that the spiritualism of his time wrongly interpreted as magical movements. He also studied the laws of colour contrasts.]

> an adult in a state of perfect rest need only think of the possible movement of his arm to make this movement to begin to happen. "We do not think only with our brain, but with our entire nervous system. As the image, by means of the perceiving sense, suddenly invades the organs that ordinarily correspond to the perception, it inevitably provokes in them the proper movements, which only an energetic counter-command can suspend." The weaker the concentration of the thought, the more the movements born in this way impetuously follow their course. Our wasps, seeing one of their own enter the nest and then exit in rapid flight, will thus be dragged outside, and the buzzing produced by the first wasp will result in all of them buzzing in unison. From this, a general effervescence of all the members of the society ensues.[60]

This excellent description by Alfred Espinas sufficiently explains, I believe, the psychology of the crowd.

Just as among wasps or a flock of birds caught by an invincible panic at the smallest wing flap, so does an emotion spread *suggestively* among a crowd of humans by means of sight and sound, even before the motives for this emotion are known; and the impulse ensues from the sole representation of the imitated action, in the same way that we cannot look out over the edge of a cliff without experiencing the vertigo that attracts us to it.[61]

---

60 A. Espinas, *Des Sociétés animales*, 2nd ed. (Paris: Germer-Baillière, 1878), 358 and ff. [Sighele's emphasis.] [Significantly, the term "effervescence," which Sighele here connects to mass psychology through Espinas's example of animal collective behaviour, will become the foundational concept in Émile Durkheim's theory of religion as a social phenomenon and of the sacred as the organizing principle that excites and unifies the community. See Durkheim, *The Elementary Forms of Religious Life* (1912).]

61 Rambosson, in his work *Phénomènes nerveux, intellectuels et moraux: Leur transmission par contagion*, has applied the law of transmission and of transformation of expressive movement to the nervous and mental phenomena that spread like contagion. He maintains (I am summarizing his theory) that each psychic state corresponds to a cerebral movement that manifests itself externally with changes in the physiognomy, behaviour, gestures, all coordinated in a special way. This movement does not stop, but, rather, propagates in space and is transmitted, without modifications, to another brain, causing the same phenomenon. Laughter, yawn, pain spread according to this law. The remote propagation of cerebral movement is the cause of the diffusion of all phenomena, from the simplest to the most complex, of all spheres of nervous activity. As we can see, this theory, after all, corresponds to that of Espinas, who has explained it in a few pages more clearly than Rambosson in an entire volume.

## *III*

But, one might say, what you have been discussing so far is enough to explain certain movements, certain acts of the crowd, though not all of them. It sufficiently explains why, if one applauds, everyone applauds, why, if one flees, everyone flees, why the anger of one shows instantly on the faces of many. But it does not explain why this anger drives people to actions, to violence, to homicide; it does not sufficiently explain why a crowd arrives at such extremes as murder and massacre, at those unthinkable atrocities of which perhaps the most terrible example is the French Revolution. Your theory regarding these cases, that an emotion is communicated suggestively by one individual to a multitude by a single display of this emotion and that the impulse results from the mere performance of the imitated act, is insufficient. You cannot claim that one kills only because one sees someone else kill or attempt to kill; it takes more to turn a man into a murderer.

This objection (which has a kernel of truth, as we shall see) spontaneously presented itself to those authors who attempted to analyse the motives behind the crimes committed by a crowd. They dimly sensed that a savage and cruel act cannot be produced solely by exterior circumstances, but it must have other causes rooted in the particular constitution of the organism that commits such an act. "What happens in the hearts of men"—Barbaste asks himself—

> when they are collectively driven to homicide, to the spilling of blood? Where is this power of imitation born, this power that subjugates them and leads them to destroy one another? *The culminating point of the research stops at a primordial, homicidal inclination, a sort of instinctive fury, a fatal characteristic of humanity that finds a powerful aid in imitative tendency.* External circumstances of every sort, acting on these virtual faculties, cause them to break out in the world. At times it is the mere sight of blood that gives birth to the desire to shed it; yet in other cases it is proselytism, the party spirit that stirs up evil passions of every type and incites man to take up arms; elsewhere, it is an imagination continually instigated by an irritable temperament, which is

62 Barbaste, *De l'homicide et de l'anthropophagie* (Paris, 1856), 97. [Mathieu Barbaste (1814–1889) was a French physician, member of the Medical Faculty of Montpellier, and famous for his research on anthropology.]

upset by the narrative of some sinister event or gets fired up by publicity, able to transform in an instant the most timid man into a ferocious beast.[62]

Even before Barbaste, Lauvergne applies the idea of man's primordial, homicidal inclination to explain the crimes of the crowd.

> The organs of cruelty and combativeness present themselves at the forefront along with that of imitation. In times of anarchy and revolution, all of the crimes committed are the work of these three mental faculties that govern reason and intelligence. Such being the case, man *who is born cruel … rolls up his sleeves and becomes a provider for the guillotine.* His imitators will be the crowd of those who want a model or an impetus to commit that which they felt able to carry out but which they did not dare perform alone or before anybody else. His victims will be the weak men, the sheep men, the men whose wisdom and reason have made them human and whose organs of cruelty and combativeness, if they ever had them, had to yield to the arduous work of intelligence and feeling.[63]

To be sure, what Barbaste and Lauvergne say is true, profoundly true. As distant precursors of the new science of criminal anthropology, they do nothing but attribute a portion of the causes of human phenomena to the physiological and psychological constitution of the individual, rather than leaving all of them indistinctly to the social environment, as some would still want.

But before turning to the anthropological factor for explanations, I believe we must take some other considerations into account—which explain, if not by themselves at least mainly, how a crowd can be driven to acts of savagery and cruelty.

First of all, it is necessary to underline that every crowd is generally more disposed to evil than to good. Heroism, virtue, and kindness can be the qualities of individuals; they are never, or almost never, the qualities of a throng of individuals. Ordinary observation attests to this: you are

63 Lauvergne, *Les forçats, considérés sous le rapport physiologique, moral et intellectuel* (Paris: Baillière, 1841), 206.—See also Attomir, *Theorie der Verbrechen auf Grundsätze der Phrenologie basiert* (Leipzig, 1842). Like Barbaste and Lauvergne, Lombroso writes, "The primitive yeasts of theft, homicide, lust, that are harboured as an embryo in each individual until he lives isolated, especially if tempered by education, magnify all of a sudden in contact with others; they become virulent in excited crowds" See *Il delitto politico*, 140.

always afraid of a multitude, and you rarely trust it. Everyone has heard and knows—unfortunately from experience—, that the example set by a wicked man or a madman can drive a crowd to crime; very few believe, and it rarely occurs, that the voice of a peacemaker or some courageous soul can persuade the crowd to calm down.

Collective psychology, as we demonstrated in the introduction, is full of surprises; a hundred, a thousand assembled men can commit acts that none of the hundred or thousand individuals would have committed alone. But usually these surprises are painful. From a gathering of good men, you will almost never see a good result; you will often see a mediocre result and at times an awful one.

The crowd is a ground where the microbe of evil can easily thrive and where the microbe of good almost always dies, unable to find the right living conditions.

Why?

Without getting into a discussion on the various elements that constitute a crowd, in which next to the compassionate are the indifferent and the cruel, and next to the honest, fairly often, are the vagabonds and the criminals, and limiting ourselves for now to a general observation, we can respond to the question posed to us by saying that in a multitude the good qualities of the individuals, rather than adding up, cancel one another out.

First, they cancel out on account of a natural, and I would say, arithmetic necessity. Just as the average of many numbers cannot obviously be equal to the highest of these numbers, so, too, an aggregate of men cannot reflect, in its manifestations, the highest qualities that only some of these men possess; what will be reflected are the average qualities that reside in all or at least the majority of the individuals. The ultimate and best strata of one's character, Sergi would say, those that civilization and education manage to form in some privileged individuals, remain overshadowed by the intermediate strata that are common patrimony of all; in the sum of individuals, the latter prevail while the former disappear.

The good qualities of the individuals are also suppressed for a second reason. Whoever is good, gentle, or compassionate in a crowd does not dare to show himself as such, because *he is afraid of being called a coward.* How many, during a demonstration in a public square amid utter turmoil, shout "*life*" or "*death*" because they fear that, if they did not shout, then those around them would accuse them of being cowards or spies! And how many, for the same reason, go from cries to action! Extraordinary strength of character is necessary in order to resist the excesses of the crowd, and few are strong enough. Most of them *sense* that they are doing wrong, but they do it anyway because the mob compels them to do it. They know that if they do not follow the current, not only will they be called cowards, but they will also become victims of the others' anger. The material fear of being beaten up and wounded combines with the moral fear of being branded as cowards.[64]

---

64 The moral and physical impossibility that prevents the good members of a crowd from reacting against the majority that is madly drawn to criminal actions is masterfully described in the following page of Manzoni's *The Betrothed*, which is worthwhile reproducing in its entirety:

> There was a general retreat and detention, asking and answering of questions, a kind of stagnation, sighs of irresolution, then a general murmur of consultation. At this moment an ill-omened voice was heard in the midst of the crowd: "The house of the superintendent of provisions is close by; let us go and get justice, and lay siege to it." It seemed rather the common recollection of an agreement already concluded, than the acceptance of a proposal. "To the superintendent's! To the superintendent's!" was the only cry that could be heard. The crowd moved forward with unanimous fury towards the street where the house, named at such an ill-fated moment, was situated. (...) "The superintendent! The tyrant! The fellow who would starve us! We'll have him, dead or alive!" (...) Renzo found himself this time in the thickest of the confusion (...). At the first proposal of blood- shedding, he felt his own curdle within him; as to the plundering, he had not exactly determined whether, in this instance, it were right or wrong; but the idea of murder aroused in him immediate and unfeigned horror. And although, by that fatal submission of excited minds to the excited affirmations of the many, he felt as fully persuaded that the superintendent was an oppressive villain, as if he had known, with certainty and minuteness, all that the unhappy man had done, omitted, and thought; yet he had advanced among the foremost, with a determined intention of doing his best to save him. (...) Among these appeared one, who was himself a spectacle, an old and half-starved man, who, rolling about two sunken and fiery eyes, composing his wrinkled face to a smile of diabolical complacency, and with his hands raised above his infamous, hoary head, was brandishing in the air a hammer, a rope, and four large nails, with which he said he meant to nail the vicar to the posts of his own door, alive as he was. "Fie upon you! Shame!" burst forth from Renzo, horrified at such words, and at the sight of so many faces betokening approbation of them; at the same time encouraged by seeing others, who, although silent, betrayed in their countenances the same horror that be felt. "For shame! Would you take the executioner's business out of his band? Murder a Christian! How can you expect that God will give us food, if we do such wicked things? He will send us thunderbolts instead of bread!" "Ah, dog! traitor to his country!" cried one of those who could bear, in the uproar, these sacred words, turning to Renzo, with a diabolical countenance, "Wait, wait! He is a servant of the superintendent's, dressed like a peasant; he is a spy; give it him! give it him!" A hundred voices echoed the cry. "What is it? where is be? who is he?—A servant of the superintendent!—A spy!—The superintendent disguised as a peasant, and making his escape!"—"Where is he? where is he ? give it him! give it him!" Renzo became dumb, shrank into a

We can all see how easily, in this condition, the wicked passions prevail in the crowd, how they crush and suffocate some individuals' good intentions.

But there is another consideration that better explains the victory of brutal instincts.

We have demonstrated, at least I hope I did, in which ways any given emotion felt and manifested by an individual is immediately propagated to a multitude. No matter whether this emotion is fury or anger, in an instant the face and attitude of every individual will manifest an expression of anger with tense and tragic nuances.

One must not assume that this expression is not authentic: the real state of emotions always follows the acts that express it, even when the origins of these acts are proven fictitious. We can simulate, through willpower, an emotion that we do not feel, but we cannot remain indifferent to an emotion that we exteriorly simulate. Just as the representation of any emotional state stimulates the nervous fibres that normally produce this state, so these nervous fibres, once stimulated, cause the individual to actually *feel* the emotion that their physiognomy outwardly expresses.

Maudsley explains this well when he claims, "The special muscular action is not only representative of passion, but also an essential part of it. Let physiognomy assume a particular emotional expression—that of anger, amazement, annoyance—and the emotion thus imitated will not fail to come upon you; and as long as your features are fixed in this expression, every attempt to call to mind another emotion will be in vain."[65]

Analogously, Espinas writes:

> In the same way that a man who draws a sword in a fencing match becomes animated and experiences something quite close to his feelings in a real duel—in the same way that a hypnotized man moves through all the states corresponding to the positions commanded of him, becoming proud when he is made to stand up straight, humiliating himself when he is made to kneel—so do animals quickly experience all of the emotions they portray in exterior signs. The monkey, the dog, the cat, simulating battles in their games, quickly arrive at a real state of anger, given the close connection between a state of

---

mere nothing, and endeavoured to make his escape; some of his neighbours helped him to conceal himself, and, by louder and different cries, attempted to drown these adverse and homicidal shouts. But what was of more use to him than anything else, was a cry of "Make way, make way!" which was heard close at hand (...). [Alessandro Manzoni, *The Betrothed*, edited by Charles W. Eliot (New York: P.F. Collier & Son, 1909), 215–22.]

65 H. Maudsley, *Corpo e mente*, lectures translated by Dr Collina (Orvieto, 1872), see Lecture 1, 33.

> consciousness and the actions and attitudes that express it; these two halves of a single, identical phenomenon, easily generate one another.[66]

Espinas is clear—a crowd that experiences an emotion such as rage or anger will be, after an instant, not only *exteriorly* agitated and moved, but *truly* irritated.[67] And it is easy to understand, even before turning to the anthropological factors, how this can lead to crime.

---

66 A. Espinas, op. cit., 360. In this respect, Spencer writes:

> The effect must be that if, in connection with a group of impressions and the nascent motor changes resulting from it, there is habitually experienced some other impression or motor change; this will, in process of time, become so coherent to the group, that it too will become nascent where the group becomes nascent, or will render the group nascent if it is itself induced. If, along with the running down and laying hold of certain prey, there has always been experienced a certain scent; then, the presentation of that scent will render nascent the motor changes and impressions that accompany the running down and laying hold of the prey. If the motor changes and impressions that accompany the catching of prey, have been habitually followed by those bitings, and strugglings, and growlings, accompanying the destruction of prey; then, when they are rendered nascent, they will in their turn render nascent the psychical states implied in bitings, strugglings, and growlings. And if these have similarly been followed by those involved in eating; then those involved in eating will also be made nascent. Thus, the simple olfactory sensation will make nascent those numerous and varied states of consciousness that accompany the running down, catching, killing, and eating of prey: the sensations, visual, aural, tactual, olfactory, gustatory, muscular, constantly accompanying the successive phases of these actions, will be all partially aroused at the same time—will be present to consciousness as what we call ideas—will, in their aggregate, constitute the desires to catch, kill, and devour —and will, in conjunction with that olfactory sensation which aroused them all, form the motor impulse which sets going the limbs in pursuit ... See *Principes de psychologie*, vol, 1, part 4, chapter VIII, section 214. [In French in Sighele's text. English translation in Herbert Spencer, *The Principles of Psychology* (London: Longman, Brown, Green, and Longmans, 1855), 598.]

This fragment by Spencer contains the law of psycho-physiology, which Charcot summarized in this way: "Every external movement communicated to our muscles, every nervous force developing in the organism by an excitation extraneous to our spontaneity, determines a series of cerebral states and mental modifications that are susceptible to translation into attitudes and expressive movements that usually accompany this movement." See G. Campili, *Il grande ipnotismo* (Turin: Fratelli Bocca, 1886), 43. Janet poses the same law as the basis of the suggestive theory. See Paul Janet, in *Revue politique et littéraire*, nos. 4–7 (1884).

67 Joly, intuiting the physiological phenomenon that we have just described, makes the following statement about the individual as member of the crowd and carried away by it: "in his case it is no longer the will that provokes the act; it is the act that triggers the imaginative part, and perhaps even more to the physical component of the will." See *La France criminelle* (Paris: L. Cerf, 1899), chapter XV, 406 [in French in Sighele's text].

The psychological condition of all the individuals in a crowd is analogous to that of anyone who was individually provoked or offended. For this reason, the crime that they commit is not an incomprehensible act of barbarism, but rather a reaction (just or unjust, but in any case natural and human) against the cause or the alleged cause of the provocation that, on account of fatal contagion, they have suffered.

The anthropological factor will certainly play a part in this crime, but the principal motive behind it will always be the *real* state of anger and irritation in which the multitude finds itself; a state of anger renders the crimes of the crowd in all respects similar to those of occasional criminals, who—as we all know—do not commit crimes unless induced by exterior circumstances or provocation.

Thus a first veil is lifted from the mystery of the unexpected crimes of a crowd: now we begin to see why these crimes are committed. One last consideration will help us explain this phenomenon even better.

It is a psychological law of indisputable truth that the intensity of an emotion increases in direct proportion to the number of persons who feel this emotion in the same place at the same time.

This is the reason behind the extremely high degree of frenzy that enthusiasm or disapproval sometimes reach in a theatre or at an assembly.

As an example and proof of what we affirm, let us look at what happens in a hall where an orator is speaking.

> Let us assume that the emotion felt by the speaker when he is in front of the public can be represented by the number 10, and that with his first words, his first flashes of eloquence, he communicated half of his emotion to his listeners, who will be, let us suppose, 300. Each will react by applauding or by doubling his attention, and this will produce what the reports of the event call a movement (*sensation*). But this movement will be felt by everyone at the same time, given that the listeners are just as concerned about the rest of the audience as they are about the speaker, and their imaginations will be immediately struck by the spectacle of these 300 people, all prey to one emotion. This spectacle can only produce a real emotion within each one, thanks to the stated law. Supposing that each listener only feels half of this emotion, the shock he receives will be represented no longer by 5, but by half of five multiplied by 300, that is, 750. And if we were to apply the same law to the man standing and speaking in the middle of this silent assembly, it would no longer be the figure 750 that expresses his internal agitation, but 300 x 750/2, since he is the fire where all the impressions, felt by 300 listeners, converge.[68]

68 See Espinas, op. cit., 361.

Certainly, in a crowd, the communication of emotions does not occur in this manner from everyone to only one person, and, therefore, this character of organic concentration is not present.

An aggregate is turbulent, and the majority of emotions—it must be acknowledged—cannot be felt by everyone, hence remain without echo. Therefore, the intensity of the emotion no longer offers the identical relationship with the number of the individuals, and the acceleration of passionate movements is much less rapid. But this does invalidate the general law. It becomes more indeterminate, more confused, more uncertain, but this very uncertainty and this very confusion will have their own effects. Every cry, every noise, every act, precisely because it is not understood or not interpreted correctly, will produce an effect that is perhaps more severe than it really should be. Every individual will feel his imagination get excited, it will be easily influenced by suggestion, and pass from idea to action with a terrifying swiftness. We will then be witnesses to what Enrico Ferri has called *psychological fermentation*: the leaven of all the passions will rise from the depths of the psyche; and just as chemical reactions among various elements result in new and different substances, so, too, the psychological reactions among various feelings result in new and terrible emotions, unknown to the human soul until that moment.[69]

It is in these cases that—since it becomes impossible not only to reason but also to correctly see and hear—even the smallest occurrence takes on enormous proportions, and every little provocation leads to crime. It is in these cases that the innocent man is put to death by a crowd without being heard because—as Maxime Du Camp has said—"any suspicion is sufficient, any protest is futile, conviction is profound."[70]

It is, therefore, obvious to conclude that the irritation and the anger of a crowd—which we have demonstrated to be not only apparent but *actually felt*—will escalate in no time at all to a true fury, by the sole influence

69 Schützenberger, in his work on fermentations writes: "The simpler the organization is, the fewer orders of special cell it contains, the simpler, easier to disentangle and to isolate by experience chemical reactions are. By contrast, the more varied and diverse the histological constitution is, the more distinct compounds we see, as products of multiple chemical phenomena which occur in the various tissues" ("Les fermentations," *Bibl. scient. intern.*, 2nd ed., 2) [in French in Sighele's text]. From this one can easily deduce that in the human organism – which is among all organisms that which has the most complex and heterogeneous constitution – psychological reactions, too, will reach the apex of complexity and heterogeneity.

70 M. Du Camp, *Les convulsions de Paris*, vol. IV, 5th ed. (Paris: Hachette, 1881), 155.

of numbers. And it will no longer be surprising to see a crowd go so far as to commit the most horrible of crimes.

This terrible influence of numbers, which is—I believe—intuitive for everyone and which we have attempted to explain, is confirmed by the observations of all naturalists. It is well known that the courage of every animal increases in direct proportion to the quantity of companions the animal knows to have nearby, and it decreases in direct proportion to the degree of isolation in which the animal finds himself.[71]

And the most brilliant evidence of this law according to which the animosity of soldiers is proportional to their number is provided to us by Forel in an experiment he conducted and discussed in his wonderful work on ants. He took seven ants from two armies of *formica pratensis,* which were engaged in a fierce battle, four of them from one army and three from the other. Placed in a jar, the seven ants, initially bellicose and irritated, treated one another in friendly terms.

What better proof could we have that it is the number that causes the instincts of cruelty and combativeness to explode in a crowd?

## Chapter 2: "The Criminal Crowds"

### *I*

The general observations made thus far were necessary for a good comprehension of that strange and terrible inner force that is inherent in crowds.

Now it is necessary to examine, in light of the facts, not only how this inner force manifests itself, but also which other factors, if any, contribute to the production of a multitude's crimes, because only after such an inquiry will it be possible to answer the question we asked at the beginning of this study, that is, to determine the most appropriate form of social reaction to such crimes.

And, before anything else, we must take into account that the number of individuals not only has the *arithmetic* effect that we described, namely, to increase hundredfold the intensity of an emotion, but also that the number itself can generate new emotions. The number provides

71 "The same ant that will let itself be killed ten times when it is surrounded by its companions, will be extremely timid and will avoid the minimum danger, when it is only twenty meters from its nest." See Forel, *Les fourmis,* 249.

all the members of a crowd with the awareness of their sudden and extraordinary omnipotence; and this omnipotence—which they can impose without control, as they know it has to remain unquestioned and hence unpunished— leads them to commit even those actions that in the depths of their souls they feel to be unjust.

Every dictatorship must necessarily abuse its power and commit injustice, because it is a psychological law that whoever can do everything, will dare to do everything.

"To be able to do evil is a great invitation to do evil," writes Alfieri, and it is natural that a hundred, a thousand, ten thousand individuals gathered together by chance, know their own strength. Finding themselves all of a sudden masters of a situation, they believe to have even the right to be judges and at times executioners. "Sudden omnipotence and the liberty to kill"—writes Taine—"are a wine too strong for human nature; giddiness is the result; men *see red*, and their frenzy ends in ferocity."[72]

It is in these moments, when the most brutal and savage passions germinate, that all of a sudden we see the savage resurface from underneath the skin of civilized man. In order to explain this phenomenon, we are almost obliged to apply the hypothesis—already put forth by Barbaste and Lauvergne—of a sudden atavistic resurrection of the primordial, homicidal instinct that was latent like a fire smouldering beneath the ashes, ready to explode at the slightest spark.[73]

Crimes committed by a crowd are certainly attributable to this, as well as to the aforementioned *external* causes, because if the stratification of character, which Sergi describes,[74] is a positive fact and not merely a beautiful simile, then it is logical and natural to assume that the lowest strata of character rise suddenly to the surface when a psychological storm turns our entire organism upside down.[75]

---

72 H. Taine, *Les origines de la France contemporaine*, vol. I, 2nd ed. (Paris: Hachette, 1878), 58. [English translation by John Durand in Hyppolite Taine, *The Origins of Contemporary France*, vol. 1, *The French Revolution* (Indianapolis: Liberty Fund, 2002), 51.]

73 Carlyle says, I cannot remember where, that man's civilization is "only a wrappage, through which the savage nature of him can still burst, infernal as ever." [See T. Carlyle, *The French Revolution: A History in Three Volumes*, vol. III (Boston: Dana Estes, [ca.] 1895), 247.]

74 See G. Sergi, "La stratificazione del carattere e la delinquenza," in the volume *Antropologia e scienze antropologiche* (Messina, 1889).

75 Here I am only hinting at the hypothesis of character stratification, as I will discuss it in the next chapter.

> No man, and especially a man of the people, rendered pacific by an old civilization, can, with impunity, become at one stroke both sovereign and executioner. In vain does he work himself up against the condemned and heap insult on them to augment his fury; he is dimly conscious of committing a great crime, and his soul, like that of Macbeth, "is full of scorpions."[76]
>
> Through a terrible self-shrinking, he hardens himself against the inborn, hereditary impulses of humanity; these resist while he becomes exasperated, and, to stifle them, there is no other way but to "sup on horrors," by adding murder to murder. For murder, especially as he practises it, that is to say, with a naked sword on defenceless people, introduces into his animal and moral machine two extraordinary and disproportionate emotions which unsettle it, on the one hand, a sensation of omnipotence exercised uncontrolled, unimpeded, without danger, on human life, on throbbing flesh, and, on the other hand, an interest in bloody and diversified death, accompanied with an ever new series of contortions and exclamations.[77]

So writes Hippolyte Taine—but it is not always true that man wants to or, more importantly, *can* rebel against the internal voice that advises him to be humane and compassionate; it is not always true that man yields to the atavistic, homicidal instinct.

If sometimes the multitude commits unforeseen atrocities never before foreseen or dreamed up by even the most cruelly fervid imagination, at other times it refrains from such monstrous crimes even though nothing restrains it.

Similar to the blind, brutal, and uncontrollable crowd that has lost a sense of justice and has attained a crazy fury, there is the crowd that does not trespass a certain limit, that mends its ways after having committed the first offence, and that lets itself be dominated by whomever invites it to return to calm.

The history of all insurrections and riots—small or large, whether with political, religious, or economic goals—proves this. And such diversity of manifestations demonstrates to us implicitly and clearly that the crimes of a crowd are not caused solely by suggestion, the influence of number,

---

76 [See Act 3, scene ii in Shakespeare's *Macbeth.*]

77 H. Taine, op. cit., vol. II, 301, 302. [English translation *The Origins of Contemporary France*, cit., II, *The French Revolution*, 678–79.]

and the moral intoxication (which Taine so masterfully describes) that derives from the instantaneous victory of atavism over the slow work of centuries of education.

There are other causes—and these depend on the particular makeup of each crowd and on the different characters of its individual components, sometimes firmly honest and compassionate, sometimes predisposed to crime by their own nature.

We will now concern ourselves with these causes, with their importance and their efficacy, examining the different criminal manifestations of the multitude in different cases.

## *II*

As I wish to discuss, first and foremost, the crowd that, with a dreadful velocity, commits the most horrible acts of barbarism and cruelty, no example could better serve this purpose than that of certain events of the French Revolution.

At that time the population was a wild beast, insatiable in its thirst for plunder and blood. Nothing and no one could stop it. After satisfying its bloodthirsty and ferocious instinct, it would lash out more terribly than before.

But was it merely the sheer number of persons and the reawakening of homicidal instincts that drove the crowd to such extremes, to such excesses? Was it really a population of honest workers that became, all of a sudden, a monster of perversity? Or was it, rather, that these upstanding individuals were corrupted by the lowest members of society, *le troisième dessous*, as Victor Hugo would say,[78] who were mixed in among them, and who (whenever there is turmoil or an uprising) emerge from the taverns and the brothels where they are wont to spend their time, just as the mud at the bottom of a pond rises to the surface when the water is stirred up?

"In peaceful times," writes Carlier,

78 [In "Patron Minette," Book Seven of Victor Hugo's *Les Misérables*, the "troisième dessous" (166) connotes the lowest depths (at once physical and metaphorical) of the city of Paris, "the great cavern of evil" (167) where the worst criminal groups dwell, distinct from the diffuse criminality emerging from the masses at large. Victor Hugo, *The Works of Victor Hugo*, vol. II, *Les Misérables* (New York: The Kelmscott Society, 1887).]

> when pacified political passions do not offend the authorities on a daily basis, the police exert a moral influence on the vagabonds, the *souteneurs*, on all the ignoble and strange rabble that surrounds the great masses of criminals, which somewhat restrains them. As they live only in hiding, the arrival of an officer makes them flee. But as soon as public opinion reawakens, as soon as the press gets aggressive towards the authorities and undertakes a campaign against the police, then they immediately become arrogant and raise their heads. They will resist the officers and fight against them: they will take part in every uprising, and if they are by chance convicted, they will play the victim. If a revolution breaks out, they, along with their lovers whom they drag along, will become the most cruel and fearsome agents.[79]

Each of us can know how true all this is, from our own personal experience. When a cloud emerges on the political horizon foreboding a coming storm, and an unusual bustle and scuffle permeates the streets full of gatherings and brawls, one suddenly notices some sinister figures never seen before. Everyone asks themselves: where on earth did these individuals come from? And, as the only response, everyone thinks instinctively about those filthy animals that emerge from their lairs, drawn out by the odour of a rotting carcass.

In Paris, during the terrible days of 1793, these individuals were the life and soul of all the atrocities that were committed.

"A great number of vagabonds, foreign to the city of Paris, who settled there after the first signs of the revolution"—narrates an eyewitness—"roamed the various quarters and grew in number when they joined with the workers leaving the factories. They obtained all kinds of weapon and bellowed out cries of revolt. The residents fled as they approached, all doors were closed, and wherever these frenzied hordes were not seen, the streets seemed deserted and uninhabited. When I arrived home, in the neighbourhood of Saint-Denis, one of the most densely populated of Paris, many of these scoundrels were firing gunshots into the air to frighten the population."[80]

---

79 Carlier, *Les deux prostitutions*, 229. On this topic, see also Macé's book *Le service de la société* (Paris, 1885), chapter XII, and that of Cère, *Les populations dangéreuses et les misères sociales* (Paris, 1872), chapters IX and XVIII.

80 Mathieu-Dumas, *Souvenirs*, vol. I, 431.

These loathsome people were not limited to such little deeds. Droz[81] numbers them at 40,000 individuals, and Bailly[82] and many others after him believed they had been recruited without knowing by whom. They broke into houses and public offices, stealing everything they managed to carry away with them: the rest they destroyed, often setting fire to the ransacked properties. The authorities attempted to give work to twenty thousand of these individuals on the hills of Montmartre, but a great number of them joined forces with smugglers and raided the city.

"They enter the convent of Saint Lazare"—writes Taine—"and they plunder it. They force their way into the furniture storage and devastate it. We see people get out in rags, some covered with ancient armours, others wearing weapons precious for their value or as historical mementos: one of them had the sword of Henry IV in his hands."[83]

"And these habitual criminals"—Joly rightly states—"are the authors of massacres. They are the ones who surround the guillotines and compete for the honour of shootings."[84] And their women do not hesitate to intervene, because those who, under one name or another, make a living from prostitution, have at their disposal masses of individuals ready to add theft and murder to debauchery.

Not only do the women accompany the men in these instances, but they also push and encourage them to commit evil acts, and often surpass them in audacity and cruelty. "In more than one case," writes Maxime du Camp, "the victim could have been saved if the woman had not

---

81 Droz, *Histoire du règne de Louis XVI*, vol. II, 230.

82 Bailly, *Memoires*, vol. I, passim. [See *Intelligence of the Crowd*, 245 and 245n25.]

83 Taine, *La Révolution*, vol. I, 18 [in French in Sighele's text. Our translation].

84 H. Joly, *La France criminelle* (Paris, 1889), 408. M. Du Camp, exaggerating this true concept by Joly, wrote on the topic of the atrocities committed by the Communards in 1870:

> They were evildoers who invoked pretexts because they could not provide a good reason: the murderers said that they struck the enemies of the people, and they killed the most honest people of the country; the thieves said that they recovered the good of the nation, and they plundered public treasuries, emptied private buildings, and robbed the municipal coffers; the arsonists said that they raised obstacles against the monarchical army, and they set fire all over; only the drunks were in good faith: they said that they were thirsty, and they emptied the barrels. All of these obeyed the impulses of their perversion: but the political matter was the last thing on their minds." See *Les convulsions de Paris*, vol. 1, xii [in French in Sighele's text].

intervened, saying to the hesitating men: 'You are cowards!' and if she had not often struck the first blow."[85]

And, among the degenerates, not only the criminals but also the insane took part in the revolution. Having escaped from the madhouses because the revolutionary mob had opened the doors, they had free rein to vent their raving madness in the squares and streets, rather than in the solitude of their cells. Many of these wretches ran through Paris bringing confusion and terror with them wherever they went.

"The son of a madwoman," writes Tebaldi,[86] "who used to divide his time between the asylum and the prison, was one of the most ruthless participants in the ransacking, in the massacres, in the fires." And the most notorious of all was Lambertine Théroigne, a heroine of blood, who led the mob in the assault on the gate of the Invalids and in the storming of the Bastille, and who ended up at La Salpêtrière, dragging herself along naked on her hands and knees, and rummaging about in the rubbish.[87]

---

85 See *Les convulsions de Paris*, vol. IV, 152. The same author recounts this episode from the Commune:

> the Sentinels caught sight of a man who was walking apace: "Ho there!" They interrogated him, they examined him. He had a mustache, thus he was a guard. The crowd screamed: "shoot him! He's a guard! He must be put down!" In that group a woman distinguished herself by her rantings; she had a rifle in hand and an ammunition belt around her waist; she was called Marceline Epilly. It is superfluous to say that the man was condemned to death unanimously. He was led to the rue de la Vacquerie and put against a wall. He was energetic, he threw himself on his executioners and overturned several of them hitting them with his head. They tripped him and shot him. Bleeding and with a shattered left arm, he got back up. Marceline cried: "let me do it! let me do it!" She put the rifle on the poor man's chest and fired. He fell, and since he was still moving, she gave him the final blow (88) [in French in Sighele's text].

The observation that woman, when she is perverse, is more perverse than man, was already made (by Lombroso among others) regarding individual crime. One can repeat this for collective crime. If blood enraptures her, woman becomes a hyena, and she knows neither limits nor restraints.

86 Tebaldi, *Ragione e pazzia* (Milan: Hoepli, 1887), 87.

87 See Esquirol, *Des maladies mentales* (Paris, 1838). In table IV of the *Album*, one can find the portrait of Théroigne. For major particulars on the influence of the madmen in revolutions and on the part that they take in them, see the work of Jules Clerc: *Les hommes de la Commune, biographie complète de tous ses membres* (Paris, 1871); by J.V. Laborde, *Les hommes de la Commune ou l'insurrection de Paris devant la psychologie morbide* (Paris, 1872); and by M. Du Camp, "La Commune à l'Hôtel de Ville," in *Revue des Deux Mondes* (1879). [La Salpêtrière was originally a gunpowder factory, which was converted into a hospital by Louis XIV. At the time of the Revolution, it was the world's largest hospital, hosting not only patients but also convicts, prostitutes, and mentally ill people.]

Thus, criminals, madmen, children of madmen, victims of alcoholism,[88] the dregs of society, devoid of moral direction, used to every crime, constituted a great part of the rebels and revolutionaries.

Now, mix these individuals to the crowd, which is heedless and by its nature easily subject to every stimulus, and they will transmit to it their ferocity and madness. Hence, why should we be surprised that the actions of the crowd are cruel?

Wherever, in the confusion of people and voices, no one commands and no one obeys, the savage passions run free like noble passions, and, unfortunately, the heroes—who are not lacking—find themselves unable to restrain the murderers. While the latter act, the majority watches, unable to rebel, like automata that let themselves be dragged along.

To augment the ferocity of the true criminals and the irritation of everyone, besides the moral intoxication resulting from the number of people, we can add physical intoxication, wine drunk in overabundance, orgies over corpses, and all of a sudden "we see rising out of this unnatural creature the demon of Dante, at once brutal and refined, not merely a destroyer, but, again, an executioner, instigator, and calculator of suffering, and radiant and joyous over the evil it accomplishes."[89]

"During the long hours of firing,"—Taine writes

> the murderous instinct has become aroused, and the wish to kill, changed into a fixed idea, spreads afar among the crowd that has hitherto remained inactive. It is convinced by its own clamour; a hue and cry is all that it now needs; the moment one strikes, all want to strike. "Those who had no arms,"

88 It should be observed that the number of crazy people is always large in revolutions and revolts, not only because those who take part in them—when they can—are *already crazy*, but also because the great public commotions, either political or religious, drive crazy many of those who were *only predisposed*, even remotely, to insanity. This was statistically proven by many authors. Belhomme in his work *Influences des commotions politiques* (Paris, 1872) reveals the great upsurge in madmen awoken by the revolution of 1831, 1832, and 1848. Bergeret notes the same phenomenon, in "La politique et la folie," in the *Gazette des hôpitaux* (March and April, 1886) for the same revolution of 1848. Lunier, in the volume, *Influences des événements et des commotions politiques sur le développement de la folie* (Paris, 1879) says that the sad events of 1870–1871 provoked the explosion of 1,700 to 1,800 cases of insanity from 1 July 1870 to 31 Dec. 1871. Ramos-Meyia, in *Las neurosis de los hombres celebres en la historia Argentina* (Buenos Aires, 1878) raised a similar opinion regarding the effects of the revolutions that happened in Buenos Aires after 1816.

89 H. Taine, *Les origines de la France contemporaine*, vol. II, 302. [English translation by John Durand in Hippolyte Taine, *The French Revolution* , vol. 2 (Indianapolis: Liberty Fund, 2002), 679.

> says an officer, "threw stones at me; the women ground their teeth and shook their fists at me. Two of my men had already been assassinated behind me. I finally got to within some hundreds of paces of the Hôtel-de-Ville, amid a general cry that I should be hung, when a head, stuck on a pike, was presented to me to look at, while at the same moment I was told that it was that of M. de Launay," the governor. The latter, on going out, had received the cut of a sword on his right shoulder; on reaching the rue Saint-Antoine "everybody pulled his hair out and struck him." Under the arcade of Saint-Jean he was already "severely wounded." Around him, some said, "his head ought to be struck off"; others, "let him be hung"; and others, "he ought to be tied to a horse's tail." Then, in despair, and wishing to put an end to his torments, he cried out, "Kill me," and, in struggling, kicked one of the men who held him in the lower abdomen. On the instant he is pierced with bayonets, dragged in the gutter, and, striking his corpse, they exclaim, "He's a scurvy wretch (*galeux*) and a monster who has betrayed us; *the nation* demands his head to exhibit to the public," and the man who was kicked is asked to cut it off. This man, a cook out of place, a simpleton who "went to the Bastille to see what was going on," thinks that as it is the general opinion, the act is *patriotic,* and even believes that he "deserves a medal for destroying a monster." Taking a sabre that is lent to him, he strikes the bare neck, but the dull sabre not doing its work, he takes a small black-handled knife from his pocket, and, "as in his capacity of cook he knows how to cut meat," he finishes the operation successfully. Then, placing the head on the end of a three-pronged pitchfork, and accompanied by over two hundred armed men, "not counting the populace," he marches along, and, in the rue Saint-Honoré, he has two inscriptions attached to the head, to indicate without mistake whose head it is. They grow merry over it: after filing alongside of the Palais-Royal, the procession arrives at the Pont-Neuf, where, before the statue of Henry IV, they bow the head three times, saying, "Salute thy master!"—This ends the mockery: some of it is found in every triumph, and beneath the butcher the buffoon becomes apparent.[90]

When the crowd is reduced to this state and it is no longer content to kill, but wants to accompany death with the most atrocious forms of torture and horrible derision—when the thirst for blood reaches such frenzy—

90 H. Taine, op. cit., vol. I, 58–60 [in French in Sighele's text]. [English translation by John Durand in Hippolyte Taine, *The French Revolution,* vol. 1 (Indianapolis: Liberty Fund, 2002), 51–53.]

libidinal instincts are quick to follow. Cruelty and lasciviousness arise, and the one augments the vigour of the other. Just as a degenerate devastates the intimate poetry of love with torments and blood,[91] the crowd augments the baseness of the murder with indecent behaviour. This obscene madness, lecherous and bloody, finds at times its most extreme state of degradation in cannibalism.

> All the monstrous instincts that grovel chained up in the dregs of the human heart, not only cruelty with its bared fangs, but also the slimier desires, unite in fury against women whose noble or infamous repute makes them conspicuous; against Madame de Lamballe, the Queen's friend; against Madame Desrues, widow of the famous poisoner; against the flower-girl of the Palais-Royal, who, two years before, had mutilated her lover, a French guardsman, in a fit of jealousy. Ferocity here is associated with lewdness to add debasement to torture, while life is violated through outrages on modesty. In Madame de Lamballe, killed too quickly, the libidinous butchers could outrage only a corpse, but for the widow, and especially the flower-girl, they revive, like so many Neros, the fire circle of the Iroquois.—From the Iroquois to the cannibal, the gulf is small, and some of them jump across it. At the Abbaye, an old soldier named Damiens, buries his sabre in the side of the adjutant-general la Leu, thrusts his hand into the opening, tears out the heart "and puts it to his mouth as if to eat it"; "the blood," says an eyewitness, "trickled from his mouth and formed a sort of mustache for him." At La Force, Madame de Lamballe is carved up. What Charlot, the

91 Lombroso, in "Delitti di libidine e di amore," in *Arch. di psich.* IV, and then more fully in *L'uomo delinquente*, vol. I, studied the union of libido with the homicidal instinct, showing how sometimes homicide accompanies rape, and other times it substitutes it, provoking the same gratifications in the perpetrator. "Some man, whom prostitutes call the executioner, would precede every encounter with the martyrdom or the killing of hens, pigeons, or geese; another one, over the course of a few months, seriously wounded fifteen girls with a knife in the vulva, because it satisfied, as he confessed, his sexual instincts." This venereal pleasure of bleeding, wounding, and biting before coitus is—according to Lombroso—purely atavistic, from the times in which love would come from fighting and blood. Therefore, as in some libidinal born criminals, it resurfaces in the crowd, hence showing another analogy between individual criminal psychology and collective criminal psychology.

Parini—who sang the following lines about the Roman matrons, intoxicated with the blood of the circus: "So, after dissolving all decency from the souls / Cruelty gathered vigor from libido,"—described with a poet's intuition that union of ferocity with lasciviousness, which today the scientists explain as a morbid deformation of sentiment. See Tebaldi, op. cit., 71.

wig maker who carried her head, did to it should not be described. I merely state that another wretch, in the rue Saint-Antoine, bore off her heart and "ate it."[92]

In that regard, one can repeat what Maxime du Camp has said about an analogous episode: "that they were insane, and that they had an assigned place at Charenton in the ward for the seriously disturbed."[93]

Indeed, this is no longer the moral madness of the born criminal, which leaves the intellectual faculties intact; rather, it is a true delirium that alienates from their companions those who commit these nefarious actions. That the crowd is in a state of true madness is proven not only by the enormity of its crimes, but also by the unconscious manner in which they are committed. The crowd prefers to kill its friends (or at least those believed to be friends) along with its enemies, rather than waiting to make a distinction. "During the shootings of the hostages, a rebel, having thrown his rifle to the ground, seized each one of the priests' bodies with his hands and, applauded by the crowd, lifted them up, and shoved them over the wall where they were sent to their death. The last priest put up a struggle and fell, dragging the insurgent down with him; the murderers were impatient, they fired ... killing their companion as well."[94]

This is precisely the mad crime, without reason and without purpose: it is the frenzy and unconscious impulse that arises as the almost-natural consequence of the intoxication that is produced by the blood and the shooting, by the cries and the wine; it is the *madness of dust*—as the Arabs would say—that develops after a battle; it is madness, as we say, that takes man back to his atavistic instincts, because it manifests itself after the fight with the same characteristics as in the basest animals. "It is often at the end of combat," writes Forel, "that Amazonian ants (*Rufi-barbe*) are overcome by a true fury that pushes them to blindly bite everything around them: larvae, their fellows, even their slaves that try to calm them

92 H. Taine, *Les origines de la France contemporaine*, vol. II, 303–304. [English translation by John Durand in Hippolyte Taine, *The French Revolution*, vol. II, 680–81.]

93 M. Du Camp, *Les convulsions de Paris*, vol. IV, 151. [Charenton was an insane asylum in the French province of Val-de-Marne, founded in 1645. Under the direction of the Abbé de Coulmier, in the 1800s, it had a good reputation for treating patients humanely. The Marquis de Sade spent the last decade of his life there.]

94 M. Du Camp, op. cit.

attempt to seize them by the legs and hold them still until their anger has subsided."[95]

A crowd also reaches such a state, and it is the ultimate phase of its intellectual and moral perversion.

## *III*

In the face of this multitude that knows no limit and that descends with a dizzying speed down the rungs that lead it to the most cowardly brutality, let us now recall other crowds that managed to resist the strange and powerful influences that drove them to criminality.

This comparison will not prove futile.

"In May of 1750," writes Lacretelle in his *Histoire du dix-huitième siècle,*[96]

> the Paris police reacted with excessive violence to one of their periodic mass arrests of mendicants. With no apparent reason for such barbarism, children were ripped from their mothers' arms: they filled the streets and squares with their cries of desperation. The people had united and the mobs grew bigger; the men were extremely irritated, and among them one could see the desolate mothers everywhere. Some told of how the police officers demanded money for the return of their kidnapped children; others lost themselves in imagining their fate. An odious rumour spread through the crowd: Louis XIV was depicted as a new Herod who would repeat the massacre of the innocents. People said that his doctors prescribed him baths in human blood to regain his health, which he had lost to excesses of libertinism and vice. The population was furious with the police; many guards were mistreated; the home of M. Berrier (prefect of police) was besieged; he escaped by fleeing through the garden. But the anger of the assailants went to extremes: there was talk of scaling the walls, so an officer, braver than his boss, saw to it that all of the gates were thrown open. Upon seeing this, the people calmed down, almost as if under a spell, and they respected the boundaries of the open house; slowly they dispersed, wandering far away in the direction of Place Vendôme.

95 Forel, *Les fourmis,* cited by Ferri—"Evoluzione nell'omicidio," in *Archivio di psich* III, 292.

96 Charles Lacretelle, *Histoire du dix-huitième siècle.*—See *Mémoires tirés des Archives de la Police de Paris,* by F. Pleuchet, vol. II, 129.

"This conduct," adds Lacretelle, "is quite understandable if one considers that, just as wolves are scared off with flintlocks, emotions that have cruelty or folly as a cause and end cease at the first manifestation of tranquility and energy."

And certainly this behaviour is easily explainable, but not in the way Lacretelle explains it. If only cruel emotions always gave way to a manifestation of tranquility and energy! Unfortunately, as we have seen in the preceding pages, this happens very rarely, and when it does, the cause is not an external influence that suddenly wins over and dominates the crowd, but it lies in the innermost faculties of the crowd itself.

During the great revolution of 1793 and the small revolt of 1750, the reason why the multitude became agitated, although different, can be considered psychologically equivalent. Indeed, I believe that the thought of one's children being abducted and forced to serve the cannibalistic whim of the king has more power to incite a people to revolt than the abstract thought of a political reform, no matter how keenly it is desired. Thus, equal in both cases is the external coefficient that drove the two crowds to crime, but the event was not the same. Why? Because these two crowds were *anthropologically* different. This is the only explanation that can be logically given.

The throngs that flooded the streets of Paris in 1793 were made up, in a large part, of criminals, ready to vent their evil instincts in any way. There were also a great number of madmen and degenerates of every type, easily excitable, and, on account of their psychic weakness, easily driven to excesses. The crowd that descended into the streets in 1750, on the other hand, was composed only of common people, of workers, of fathers and mothers who feared for the lives of their children ...

This multitude, which a saintly reason made rebellious and which, if further provoked, might have arrived at criminal acts by the inevitable influence of number,[97] found itself disarmed of its anger in the face of

97 Manzoni, in the following page from *The Betrothed* (chapter XIII), admirably describes the composition of the crowd, and he shows what are, in the majority of cases, the reasons why the multitude sometimes ends up committing crimes, and other times it calms down and disperses:

> In popular tumults there is always a certain number of men, who, either from overheated passions, or from fanatical persuasion, or from wicked designs, or from an execrable love of destruction, do all they can to push matters to the worst; they propose or second the most inhuman advice, and fan the flame whenever it seems to be sinking: nothing is ever too much for them, and they wish for nothing so much as that the tumult should have neither limits nor end.

the official's act of courageous confidence and was horrified at the enormity of the crime it had been about to commit.

Such behaviour, on a collective level, reflects that which sometimes happens individually to a criminal by passion. His anger immediately subsides and he drops the weapon he is holding if you turn up defenceless in front of him, or if in any other way you manage to soothe his irritation and lead him back to his normal state, because the crime that he was on the brink of committing was the consequence of a momentary madness, and, once this has passed, he no longer has the courage to commit it, *he cannot* commit it.

---

But, by way of counterpoise, there is always a certain number of very different men, who, perhaps, with equal ardour and equal perseverance, are aiming at a contrary effect: some influenced by friendship or partiality for the threatened objects; others, without further impulse than that of a pious and spontaneous horror of bloodshed and atrocious deeds.

Heaven blesses such. In each of these two opposite parties, even without antecedent concert, conformity of inclination creates an instantaneous agreement in operation. Those who make up the mass, and almost the materials of the tumult besides, are a mixed body of men, who, more or less, by infinite gradations, hold to one or the other extreme: partly incensed, partly knavish, a little inclined to a sort of justice, according to their idea of the word, a little desirous of witnessing some grand act of villainy; prone to ferocity or compassion, to adoration or execration, according as opportunities present themselves of indulging to the full one or other of these sentiments; craving every moment to know, to believe, some gross absurdity or improbability, and longing to shout, applaud, or revile in somebody's train. "Long live," and "Down with," are the words most readily uttered; and he who has succeeded in persuading them that such a one does not deserve to be quartered, has need of very few words to convince them that he deserves to be carried in triumph: actors, spectators, instruments, obstacles, whichever way the wind blows; ready even to be silent, when there is no longer anyone to give them the word; to desist, when instigators fall; to disperse, when many concordant and uncontradicted voices have pronounced, "Let us go"; and to return to their own homes, demanding of each other—"What has happened?" Since, however, this body has, hence, the greatest power, nay, is, indeed, the power itself; so, each of the two active parties uses every endeavour to bring it to its own side, to engross its services: they are, as it were, two adverse spirits, struggling which shall get possession of, and animate, this huge body. It depends upon which side can diffuse a cry the most apt to excite the passions, and direct their motions in favour of its own schemes; can most seasonably find information which will arouse or allay their indignation, and excite either their terror or their hopes; and can give the word, which, repeated more and more vehemently, will at once express, attest, and create the vote of the majority in favour of one or the other party. [Alessandro Manzoni, *The Betrothed*, edited by Charles W. Eliot (New York: F. Collier & Son, 1909), 224–25.]

Now, this voluntary renunciation to a criminal act, just as it is not possible for someone who is a born criminal, is not possible for a crowd made up of true criminals and that has already reached a high degree of paroxysm. To think that one can subdue the crowd with tranquility and energy is like thinking one can, by the same means, subdue a murderer who assaults you in the street at night, or a raging madman that threatens you. The throat slitters of September 1793 in Paris "could not stop themselves," says a historian, and the heroically serene conduct of the victims did nothing to appease their thirst for blood. It was without a doubt the inebriation of those horrible moments that reduced them to such a state, but it was also their physiological and psychological organization that permitted them, even drove them, to act as executioners.

I would like to mention two recent trials that may serve as irrefutable evidence of what I have been explaining: two trials with similar causes and different outcomes: that of the strikes of Décazeville in 1886 and that of the *events of 8th February* in Rome in 1889.[98]

On 26th January 1886, the miners of Décazeville decided to stop work. Led by Bedel, a miner who had been laid off, the miners sought out the engineer Watrin, who was the head manager of the mines. They forced him to leave his office and dragged him screaming to the town hall. There the workers formulated their complaints. Their first demand was that Watrin resign immediately. Their request was not granted, as it was his duty to remain. When he exited the town hall, 1,800 strikers greeted him with cries of death. Watrin fled to a nearby house and climbed up to the second floor. The furious crowd below threw stones against the house; they shattered the window panes and placed a ladder against the wall so that some of the strikers could climb up. Others broke down the door like a rushing river bursts its banks. They were led by a miner armed with a club. Watrin heard the crowd coming up the stairs and courageously, with that admirable cold blood that would never abandon him on his last day, opened the door of the room and faced his assailants.

This act of tranquility and energy should have caused the crowd to withdraw, according to Lacretelle. Yet, unfortunately in this case, it was not the sort of crowd that repents and retreats.

Bedel struck Watrin with a piece of wood, exposing his frontal bone. The engineer Chabaud attempted to aid Watrin, but in vain. Another worker, Bassinet, hurled the room door at him. The mayor of Décazeville

98 [For additional comments on these and other instances of sudden collective riots, see the introduction to this volume, xix.]

begs Watrin to back down and give his resignation. Watrin, nearly unconscious and blinded by blood, let himself be dragged to a table and prepared himself to write. The mayor ran to the window and, hoping to calm the crowd, announced that Watrin was resigning.

The response was a furious clamour: "It's not his resignation we want, it's his hide!"[99]

Watrin was seized by three wretches who dragged him to the window and threw him into the street head first. He smashed his cranium on the pavement and lay there motionless and wheezing. The infamous crowd surrounded him, trampling him, ripping his clothes, tearing out his hair … finally someone was able to rescue the dying man from the beasts and take him to the hospital.[100] At midnight he was dead.

---

99 [In French in Sighele's text.]

100 In a wonderful framework of *Germinal*, Émile Zola describes this pathological perversion of the crowd that, not content with having killed he whom they hated, perpetrated the most obscene cruelties to the body:

> His brain had spurted out. He was dead. (...)They were stupefied at first. (...) And the cries ceased, and silence spread over the growing darkness. All at once the hooting began again. It was the women, who rushed forward overcome by the drunkenness of blood. (...) They surrounded the still warm body. They insulted it with laughter, abusing his shattered head, the dirty-chops, vociferating in the face of death the long-stored rancour of their starved lives. "I owed you sixty francs, now you're paid, thief!" said Maheude, enraged like the others. "You won't refuse me credit any more. Wait! wait! I must fatten you once more!"
>
> With her fingers she scratched up some earth, took two handfuls and stuffed it violently into his mouth. "There! eat that! There! eat! eat! you used to eat us!" The abuse increased (...).
>
> But the women had another revenge to wreak on him. They moved round, smelling him like she-wolves. They were all seeking for some outrage, some savagery that would relieve them.
>
> Mother Brulé's shrill voice was heard: "Cut him like a tomcat!" "Yes, yes, after the cat! after the cat! He's done too much, the dirty beast!" Mouquette was already unfastening and drawing off the trousers, while the Levaque woman raised the legs. And Mother Brulé with her dry old hands separated the naked thighs and seized this dead virility. She took hold of everything, tearing with an effort which bent her lean spine and made her long arms crack. The soft skin resisted; she had to try again, and at last carried away the fragment, a lump of hairy and bleeding flesh, which she brandished with a laugh of triumph. "I've got it! I've got it!" Shrill voices saluted with curses the abominable trophy. (...) They showed each other the bleeding fragment as an evil beast from which each of them had suffered, and which they had at last crushed, and saw before them there, inert, in their power. They spat on it, they thrust out their jaws, saying over and over again, with furious bursts of contempt: "He can do no

So who were his assassins? Perhaps honest workers who until that time had led an exemplary life and who were suddenly transformed into ferocious criminals by the unknown and powerful influence of the crowd?

Here are the murderers: *Granier*, a worker with a terrible reputation: "an owl's head, a bad man who beat his wife"; *Chapsal*, previously sentenced three times for wounding others and for theft; *Blanc*, known as *Bassinet*, already sentenced for wounding someone: "a flattened head, and a wild beastlike jaw"; and *Louis Bedel*, sentenced once for theft and twice for wounding someone, who offered "to kill, no matter whom, for 50 francs," who wanted to form a gang "to steal in the countryside," and who, immediately after committing a crime, went to a café to play cards.[101]

All the individuals, thus, had reasons for the excesses committed within themselves, and the crowd's excitation did nothing but offer the occasion to reveal their nature.

Very different from the behaviour of the strikers of Décazeville was that of the unemployed workers in Rome in 1889.

These men, exasperated by a long-lasting economic crisis that showed no signs of subsiding, were exalted and suggestionized by the speeches given by their leaders at Prati di Castello, speeches that incited them to demand by force all they had not succeeded in obtaining by peacefully expressing their desires and needs. On the afternoon of 9th February 1889, armed with sticks, tools, and stones, they marched across Rome, from the Ripetta Bridge to Piazza di Spagna, easily overcoming the weak resistance of a few law enforcement officers who had in vain attempted to prevent them from crossing the bridge. The workers were not many, but because they proceeded without encountering obstacles, they aroused a great deal of fear.

---

more! he can do no more!—It's no longer a man that they'll put away in the earth. Go and rot then, good-for-nothing!" Mother Brulé then planted the whole lump on the end of her stick, and holding it in the air, bore it about like a banner, rushing along the road, followed, helter-skelter, by the yelling troop of women. Drops of blood rained down, and that pitiful flesh hung like a waste piece of meat on a butcher's stall. [In French in Sighele's text. See Émile Zola, *Germinal*, part 5, chapter 6, http://www.ibiblio.org/eldritch/ez/g56.html.]

101 For all the details of this trial, see A. Bataille, *Causes criminelles et mondaines de 1886: La Grève de Décazeville*, 136. Very similar episodes can be found in the anarchists' actions in Lyon in 1883 (see Bataille *Causes criminelles et mondaines de 1883: Les procès anarchists*) and in the strikes of Monteceau-les-Mines (Bataille, 1882). From the latter, Zola must have certainly drawn not only the idea for his *Germinal*, but also the scenes that he depicts in some chapters.

All doors and windows were shut; whoever found themselves in the street fled to their homes, giving the workers free rein to commit any excess. The panic of the citizens naturally increased the boldness of the strikers who threw stones at the lamps and broke all the store windows.

From Piazza di Spagna, they climbed up to Via delle Quattro Fontane and proceeded towards Piazza Vittorio Emanuele with all the deafening noise of a mob waiting for the right moment to vent a load of resentment that had been latent for some time. Once they reached the Galleria Regina Margherita, they turned threateningly towards the entrance of the Grande Orfeo Café in order to raid it. A soldier, who by chance found himself at the door, unsheathed his sword and ordered the crowd to retreat. There were a thousand workers and they were armed; but not one stone was thrown, and not one act of rebellion was attempted; they all withdrew and continued on their way, and not much later they dispersed.

Even in this case, just as in the one described by Lacretelle, the calm and courageous act of one individual was enough to calm them down, because that rabble of people felt the enormity of what they were about to commit. And just as when water is thrown into a drunkard's face, they regained their normal—I would even say individual—senses.

Now, thirty-two of these workers were tried for devastation and ransacking, violations that they were indeed guilty of; but the records of all thirty-two men were clean. And this, I believe, is one of the reasons why they could, in the heat of the moment, break a few lamps and store windows, but yet could not be driven to homicide like the workers of Décazeville.

It seems evident, therefore, that the *anthropological* composition of the crowd influences the actions that it commits: a multitude of good men can become corrupt, but it will never reach the degree of perversity of a multitude consisting mostly of criminals.[102]

102 As for the *anthropological* composition of the crowd, it must be noted that its consequences can be menacing not only because of the presence—in a multitude—of true criminals, but, moreover, because of the presence of those who, although honest, do not have, by organic constitution, a repugnance to blood and are not shocked to see it flow. Many of them, in a pacific and honest environment, give legitimate outlet to their tendency, doing those trades or professions that a very sensible and excessively pitiful individual would find cruel: the butcher, the soldier, the surgeon. If they find themselves in a crowd, it is evident that transcending to crime will be less difficult for them than for others. See on this topic Andral, *Pathologie interne*, vol. III, 59, and Corre, *Les Criminels* (Paris, 1889), 179.

It is, however, always true that the very soul of the crowd causes the good to be worse and the potentially wicked to become such.

In other words, the judicial problem still remains unresolved: what is the responsibility for the crimes committed under the impetus of a crowd?

We will attempt to answer this question in the following chapter.

## Chapter 3: "Juridical Conclusions"

### *I*

Napoleon, in a famous phrase dictated by his studies on the Convention said: "Collective crimes engage no one."

It was the observation of a fact; it was not and could not have been a scientific doctrine.

Science feels that the irresponsibility for the crimes committed by a crowd cannot be proclaimed because science knows that the social organism—just like any other organism—always reacts, in this case just as in any other, against anyone who threatens its conditions of life. To be the object of this reaction means to be responsible: if the reaction is, therefore, fatal and necessary, so, too, is the responsibility.

But who is responsible?

With one of those summary judgments that, if oftentimes erroneous, are just as often correct because they reflect what was first determined by intuition and will later be proven by a positive examination of facts, common sense responds: the entire crowd must be responsible. And science, after attempting to unravel the mysterious complexity of causes that determine the crimes committed by a crowd, and after seeing how these causes are so interrelated and blended that their individual value cannot be determined, is also forced (if it is to remain accurate and sincere) to give the same response as common sense: the entire crowd must be responsible.

The response cannot go beyond this collective name for the crowd, this vague and undetermined entity, given that only the crowd contains *all* of the anthropological and social factors that participate in the production of crimes committed by its members. It seems that to attribute the responsibility to a more determined and precise entity—the individual—would be an error, because *all* the elements of these crimes do not exist in the individual: the individual would only be one of the causes rather than the whole set of causes.

But is it possible for the crowd to be responsible? Is this collective responsibility a possibility in today's world?

In the past, collective responsibility was the only form of responsibility. Even when it was known that a certain crime was committed by a single individual, it was not only this individual who had to answer to the crime, but his entire family, his *clan*, his tribe. Ancient legislations extend the same torture or punishment that the condemned man received to the wife, the children, the siblings, and sometimes even the relatives of a criminal.[103]

In those primitive epochs, every naturally formed group, such as the tribe and the family, constituted an indivisible and indissoluble entity. The individual was a part rather than a whole; one did not conceive of the individual as an organism, but as an organ. To accuse the individual alone, then, would have seemed absurd, just as today it would seem absurd to single out only one limb of the man.

Subsequently, however, with the advancement of civilization, responsibility became more and more individualized. Some traces of the ancient doctrine survived up until the last century, especially regarding certain political and religious crimes,[104] but today this has completely disappeared.[105] Nowadays the families of the condemned are no longer

103 The semi-civil states of the Ancient Orient inflicted the same punishment on the wife and children of the condemned as he had to endure. Also in Egypt the conspirator's whole family was condemned to death.—On the topic, see Thonissen, *Droit criminel des anciens peuples de l'Orient*, vol. I, passim, and Letourneau, *Évolution de la morale* (Paris, 1887).

104 It is known that up until the last century, in almost all the European countries, families of condemned politicians were exiled from the state.

105 Tarde believes one can currently find a residue of the collective responsibility of the ancients, in parliamentary immunity, in virtue of which a deputy or senator cannot be processed without the authorization of the assembly of which he is a part, as if it would consider him liable together with it.—See *La philosophie pénale*, 137 [*Penal Philosophy*, 139.] Beyond this, there are—I believe—currently many other residues of the old theory of collective responsibility, above all, in prejudices. It is notable that, in antiquity, each member of a tribe believed that his actions or someone else's, when they were taken to bring either fortune or disgrace, would have their favourable or baleful efficacy not only on their perpetrator, but on the entire tribe. Therefore, even today, one believes from the people—and unfortunately, even from the educated classes—that certain actions, held as a good or bad omen, bring fortune or misfortune not only to whomever commits them, but to all those present: for example, pouring wine or salt on the table. "There are people to this day"—Bagehot writes on this issue—"who would not permit in their house people to sit down thirteen to dinner. They do not expect any evil to themselves particularly for permitting it or sharing in it, but they cannot get out of their heads the idea that some one or

banished; the law does not stigmatize the children of a criminal: only custom still preserves a hostile prejudice against those who are born into a family of criminals. Is it, perhaps, an unconscious internal voice that senses the power of the law of heredity? We do not know. Certainly, this bias is not merely an unjust social prejudice.

The law, nowadays, has individualized responsibility:[106] one cannot say any longer that a certain family is responsible for a crime and, thus, all should be punished. Instead, we must say: that individual is responsible, so let us punish him alone.

If, however, today the ancient and absurd concept of collective responsibility has disappeared, it has been superseded by another concept, in some respects analogous to the first and certainly much more scientific. I am referring to the concept of the responsibility of the environment.

We know that every crime, just like every human action, is the result of two forces: the individual character and the social environment. We attribute the responsibility of every crime—although in different proportions in each case—to this *character* and this *environment*; therefore, even today, it is a matter of collective responsibility. At the outset of criminal law, one would have said: the individual who committed the crime and all of his family or all of his tribe are guilty. Now that criminal law has reached its highest phase of development, we say: the individual who committed the crime is guilty along with the environment that made it possible for him to commit it.

---

more of the number will come to harm if the thing is done. This is what Mr Tylor calls survival in culture. The faint belief in the corporate liability of these thirteen is the feeble relic and last dying representative of that great principle of corporate liability to good and ill fortune which has filled such an immense place in the world." See Bagehot, *Physics and Politics*, 139.

106 Tarde adds, "it will always go in the direction of greater individualization, leaning on criminal anthropology, which will permit us to distinguish the individual in this association, the diverse elements, if not separable, of which it is composed, to take them apart and apply to the special treatment of each person the appropriate remedy" (op. cit., 147). Of course, I also believe that the science of the future will localize the causes of human actions better than today: but I do not believe for this that the liability can be transferred from the individual to his brain or to a given convolution of his brain. The *pathological responsibility*, if I can say so, can be reduced to this or that part of the man, but the *social responsibility* will always remain with the whole individual, given that *the individual*—according to Schäeffle's fine expression—is the *atom* of the social organism, and just as in chemistry it is not possible to divide the atom, so in sociology it is not possible to divide man.

The terms have changed, although less drastically than it would seem. Above all, what has changed are the grounds for the two conclusions, but both point to the same identical thing: a collective responsibility.

There is, however, a great practical difference in the consequences of these two conclusions.

In ancient times, the individual and his family were considered responsible, and the reaction fell equally on the two;[107] today, we consider the individual and his environment responsible, but the reaction, the *punishment*, to use this old word, falls solely on the individual. In ancient times, the responsibility of the individual and the family was *joint* and *actual* (in the sense that the individual and the family were subjected to the same punishment). Today, the responsibility of the environment is *illusory* (in the sense that the environment is never subjected to retribution; it can never be punished), and, rather than being joint, the individual and the environment have an inverse relationship, since the more the environment is responsible, the less the individual is, and vice versa. That is, the more the environment is to blame for a given crime, the less severe is the social reaction against the individual.

In the case of a murder committed for profit, all or almost all of the causes lie in the individual who committed this crime, and none or very few causes can be attributed to the environment; thus, in this case, the social reaction against the criminal is very strong. In the case of a homicide committed in the heat of passion, however, most causes lie with the environment and only few with the individual. Therefore, in this case the social reaction against the criminal would be minimal. If it can be proven that the motives for a certain crime reside entirely in the environment, that the environment is *entirely* responsible, then no social reaction can occur against the individual. In other words, the individual would not be criminally responsible. Such is the case with legitimate self-defence. If a robber assaults me in the middle of the night in the street, and in repelling his attack I kill him, I am not responsible (in other words, I cannot be subjected to social reaction for this homicide), given that the causes, that is, the responsibility of murder, all lie in the environment, in the robber's unjust aggression.

107 "At the beginning"—Tarde writes—"collective responsibility has always been understood in the sense that *all* relatives were to be punished at the same time. Later on, when customs became milder, it was interpreted more humanely, in the sense that *any* member of the family had to be punished" (op. cit., 137) [in French in Sighele's text].

Departing from these general considerations and returning to our specific case, we can, in summary, draw the following conclusion: when we stated that the *entire* crowd must be held accountable for the crimes committed by its members, we did nothing other than apply the modern theory of collective responsibility to a particular and more evident case. This theory sees and recognizes that the causes for every crime are to be found not only in the individual but also in the environment; but just as the environment, as a general rule, cannot, on account of the modern individualization of responsibility, be subjected to any reaction, so, too, in this particular case there can be no reaction against the crowd. Thus, the individual will be the only one held *effectively* responsible; but since his responsibility is inversely proportional to that of the crowd (the environment), we must examine whether the responsibility of a crime lies *entirely* with the crowd, because in such a case the individual could not be held accountable; or, rather, we must determine *which part* of the responsibility lies with the crowd, in order to gauge the social reaction against the individual.

In short, it is the criminal's degree of dangerousness that we must determine, in this case just as in every other—a dangerousness that, according to the positivist school,[108] increases or decreases in inverse relation to any increase or decrease in the number and intensity of external circumstances in the etiology of a crime.

108 It is useful to note that, while it was the positivist school that openly introduced the criterion of the criminal's dangerousness as the basis for juridical repression, this criterion also existed, although veiled by more or less abstruse formulas, in the doctrines of the classic criminologists. (See Carrara, *Programma*, spec. part, paragraph 2085, 2111, 2115; Pessina, *Elementi di diritto penale*, book II; Rossi, *Trattato di diritto penale*, vol. II, chapter IV). And if I am not wrong, this criterion is also hidden in the theories of those positivists, I will say *dissidents*, who wanted to base responsibility upon different principles from those adopted by the Italian positivist school. I am referring to the criterion of *identity* put forward by Tarde. *Personal identity*, indeed, which Tarde requires for an individual to be responsible, is a condition that can be right only when we mean that if an individual carrying out the crime has become totally different from himself, that is, going from *dangerous* to *no longer dangerous*, one must declare him not responsible. Tarde maintains, for example, that sentences should be short for crimes committed by prepubescents, and he supports this opinion by saying that, when an individual becomes an adult, he is no longer the same as when he was a child. If you punish, he writes, a 20-year-old man for a crime he committed when he was 10, you punish a person who is not the perpetrator of that crime, since the 10-year-old child no longer exists, either physically or morally, in the 20-year-old man. *Personal identity* is lacking in such a case. Now, it seems to me that, rather than legitimating this regulation with the principle of *non-personal identity*,

## *II*

The problem then can be stated in the following way: is the individual who committed a crime under the impetus of a crowd to be feared, and if so, to what degree is he to be feared? In other words, once this man is removed from the wild and inflamed environment in which he found himself, once he is freed from the power of suggestion that drove him to crime, once he has returned to his normal state, does he still present a threat to society? Is it possible that even an honest individual can be swayed by the crowd to commit some evil, almost as if in a fit of momentary madness, which, once ended, leaves no trace and thus cannot be grounds for penal action?[109]

To respond adequately, we must know, not only in theory but in every single case, what is the suggestive force of the crowd and its power to pervert the individual; we must know if, under its terrible and strange spell, a steadfastly compassionate man can be converted into a murderer.

Can the crowd perform this miracle?

We said in the first chapter that the influence exerted by the crowd over the individuals of which it is composed corresponds to the phenomenon of suggestion. We can, therefore, respond to our question by examining the effect of suggestion on an individual and how far it reaches. It is not

---

one might legitimate it with the *non-dangerousness* of an adult who has grown up normal and honest, but who had committed a crime as a child (when everyone was a bit delinquent). The same applies to the hypothesis, unfortunately rare, of a madman who, after having committed a crime in delirium, recovers sanity. Once cured, namely, once he is no longer dangerous, society does not have the right to punish him. As one can see, Tarde's *personal identity* understood within these limits is nothing but a different name given to the criterion of *dangerousness*. Understood, instead, in the broader sense that Tarde ascribes to it, namely, in the sense that the madman must *always* be considered not responsible, even if his madness persists after the crime, only because madness creates in him an *abnormal I* that is different from the *normal I* that existed before, the theory of *personal identity* seems to me an error and an absurdity in its consequences: an absurdity from the deterministic point of view, since determinism does not admit that there are, for any reason, irresponsible individuals; and an error from the social point of view, since society always reacts against whatever offence made to its existence, be it from a criminal or a madman.

109 I say *penal action* (*reazione penale*) only, because *punishment* (*pena*), no longer has its reason for being when the danger revealed by the crime has disappeared, but the *compensation for civil damages* (*risarcimento civile*), instead, always has its reason for being, even when the author of the crime is no longer dangerous. The punishment is inflicted uniquely *ne peccetur* [so that no offence will be committed], the compensation is inflicted *ne peccetur* and, above all, *quia peccatum* [because an offence has been committed].

possible to conduct this inquiry for individuals in a state of wakefulness, as few studies exist in this regard. Instead, we shall investigate hypnotic suggestion, which offers us a vast field of experiments and observations.

This will not alter in any way the efficacy of our examination. No one ignores that the suggestion that takes place in a crowd happens in a state of wakefulness, and, indeed, we did mention this, that such suggestion is of the very same nature as hypnotic suggestion. It is, indeed, the first degree of it. The reasoning that works for one hence also holds true for the other. The only difference is that suggestion in the state of magnetic sleep is more powerful than in the normal state. "Hypnotic suggestion," writes Ladame, "acts in the same way on diseased and fatigued brains as ordinary suggestion, the one everybody knows and practices whenever they hope to convince others by telling them certain things. Hypnotic suggestion is of the same nature as persuasion in the state of wakefulness, except that it greatly enhances our power of persuasion over others by removing the resistances that exist in the state of wakefulness."[110]

Now, can we make a man under hypnotic suggestion do whatever we wish? Can we entirely suppress his personality and lead him to commit acts that he would never have committed in a wakeful and conscious state?

If we endorse the opinion of the Nancy school, then we must respond affirmatively.

Liébeault writes, "The hypnotist can develop anything in the minds of sleepwalkers and put it into effect not only in their state of sleep, but after they got out of it."[111] According to Liébeault, the man under hypnosis blindly obeys suggestion: "He performs his task with the inevitability of a falling stone."[112]

Richet[113] and Liégeois[114] refer to examples that prove how, thanks to the power of suggestion, an individual's active principles can be forced: he can be induced to forget the feelings he holds most sacred and to abdicate his most basic precepts of morality. A docile and virtuous daughter,

---

110 Cited by Laurent, "Les suggestions criminelles," in *Archives de l'anthrop. crim. et des sciences pén.* (15 Nov. 1890) [in French in Sighele's text]. [Paul-Louis Ladame (1842–1919) was a Swiss neurologist who studied the medical applications of hypnosis and of electricity.]

111 Liébeault, *Du sommeil et des états analogues*, 519 [in French in Sighele's text].

112 Ibidem.

113 Richet, *L'homme et l'intelligence* (Paris, 1884). [Charles Richet (1850–1935) was a French physiologist, renowned for his contributions to immunology and winner of the Nobel Prize in Physiology or Medicine in 1913.]

114 Liégeois, *De la suggestion hypnotique dans ses rapports avec le droit civil et le droit criminel* (Paris, 1884).

at the command of the hypnotist, shot a handgun at her own mother; an honest youth attempted to poison his aunt for whom he felt the most profound affection; a woman killed a doctor because he failed to cure her; another poisoned a stranger.[115]

But were these results easily obtained, without any difficulty, as soon as the hypnotist gave the command? Oh no, certainly not! He had to struggle at length against the will of the hypnotized, which still fought against him. Campili writes,

> It is only through a repeated and gradual suggestive process that the subject may be pushed down the road of these dangerous and risky suggestions. Every time that he puts forth some objection or refuses to follow a command without reserve, the suggestion is repeated with relevant details that render it more qualified and acceptable. In other words, the content of the suggestion of a given act is supplemented by a logical series of retroactive suggestions, positive or negative. To the first words of the hypnotist, the somnambulist sometimes reacts with an outright refusal; but when the statement is repeated with stern insistence, his mind and expression become troubled. He grows pensive and seems to recall a memory that has slipped his mind. In the end, bewildered by the incessant and bothersome suggestions of the hypnotist, he gives in automatically.[116]

He gives in automatically—and we add—but not without repulsion, and not without suffering a hysteria attack afterwards. This attack proves just how much effort it cost him to obey the command he was given, and this is the *belated refusal*, if I may say, of an organism that has involuntarily committed an act against which he rebels, the very thought of which horrifies him.[117]

Therefore, if it is true at times that even when the subject resists, one can, by insisting and stressing the suggestion, make him execute an order, it is false, as Beaunis says, that "the automatism is absolute, that the subject only preserves the degree of spontaneity or will that the hypnotizer chooses to leave him, and that he realizes, in the strict sense of

---

115 These last two cases were brought up by Gilles de la Tourette in his work *L'hypnotisme et les états analogues* (Paris, 1887), 139, 133.

116 G. Campili, *Il grande ipnotismo e la suggestione ipnotica nei rapporti col diritto penale e civile* (Turin: Bocca, 1886), 18–19.

117 See the cases of these attacks of hysteria that follow the implementation of a repugnant suggestion in the work cited by Gilles de la Tourette, chapter IV.

the word, the famous ideal: to be like a walking stick in the hands of a traveller."[118]

The hypnotized *always remains someone*,[119] given that he manifests his will in his effort to resist the suggestions, and, if he sometimes gives in, this proves only his individual weakness, but it does not testify to the omnipotence of the suggestion, because, in fact, he commits the imaginary crimes with repugnance and afterwards will never again relapse into such behaviour.[120]

Moreover, the cases in which the subject gives in to a suggestion that conflicts with his moral sense are extremely rare compared with the instances in which he has the strength to resist. These cases, observed in particular by the followers of the Salpêtrière school, demonstrate that the opinions of the Nancy school are wrong. Against the affirmations of Liébeault, Liégeois, and Beaunis, are those of Charcot, Gilles de la Tourette, Brouardel, Féré, Pitres, Laurent, and Delboeuf. "The somnambulist," writes Gilles de la Tourette, "is not a simple machine that one can turn in all directions: he possesses a personality, reduced, it is true, to its basic constituents, but in certain cases it remains intact."[121] "The somnambulist," writes Féré, "can resist a certain suggestion that contradicts a profound sentiment";[122] "and"—adds Brouardel—"he only yields to the suggestions he finds pleasant or to which he is indifferent."[123] Finally, Pitres affirms that "the irresponsibility of hypnotized subjects is never absolute."[124]

In summary, the *normal I* always outlives the *abnormal I* created by the hypnotist. If you attempt to make this *abnormal I* commit an action to which the *normal I* is profoundly and organically opposed, you will not succeed in your endeavour. A great number of examples can prove this. Let us select a few.

---

118 Beaunis, *Du sonnambulisme provoqué: Études physiologiques et psychologiques*, 181. [Henri-Étienne Beaunis (1830–1921) was a French physiologist and psychologist, member of the École hypnologique de Nancy.]

119 Gilles de le Tourette, op. cit., 137.

120 On this topic, see Lombroso, *Studi sull'ipnotismo*, 3rd ed. (1887), and Lombroso and Ottolenghi, *Nuovi studi sull'ipnotismo e la credulità* (Turin, 1889).

121 Op. cit. 136.

122 Ch. Féré, *Les hypnotiques hystériques considérés comme sujets d'expériences en médecine mentale.* Note communiquée à la Société médico-psychologique, 28 May 1883.

123 Brouardel, *Gazette des hôpitaux* (8 Nov. 1887), 1125.

124 Pitres, *Les suggestions hypnothiques* (Bordeaux, 1884), 61. Also see identical conclusions in: Bianchi, "La responsabilità nell'isterismo," in *Riv. sperim. di fren. e di med. leg.* vol. XVI, fasc. III; Laurent, "Les suggestions criminelles," in *Arch. de l'anthrop. crim. et des sciences pén.* (15 Nov. 1890); Delboeuf, *L'hypnotisme et la liberté des représentations publiques*; and Richer, *Études cliniques sur la grande hystérie ou épilepsie* (Paris, 1885). [Paul Richer (1849–1933) was a French physiologist and anatomical artist who studied hysteria and epilepsy with Charcot.]

"We had in our care," writes Pitres, "a young woman who was very easily hypnotized and with whom we could, without any difficulty, achieve movements of imitation, illusions, and hallucinations. But it was impossible to get her to hit someone. If we commanded it energetically, she would raise her arm which then would fall immediately into a state of lethargy."[125]

The episode related by Féré is analogous: "One of our patients," he writes, "was consumed by a great affection for a young man: she had suffered greatly, but her passion did not die. If the presence of this man was evoked, she gave signs of great affliction: she wanted to flee, but it was impossible to make her commit any act whatsoever that may have been harmful to the man who made her suffer; but, apart from that, she obeyed all other orders automatically."[126]

In these two cases, it is the feeling of compassion that prevents suggestion from being effective.

The identical phenomenon occurs when the suggested idea conflicts with any other sentiment whatsoever, provided that this sentiment is profound and alive within the hypnotized individual.

To demonstrate this resistance against suggested actions, Pitres relates the following experiment:

> I sent my subject (a girl) to sleep, and, after having placed a silver coin on the table, I said to her: "when you awake, you will go to the table to take the coin that someone has forgotten; no one will see you; you will place the coin in your pocket: it will be a small theft with no painful consequences."—Then I woke up the subject.
>
> She headed towards the table, searched for the coin and placed it in her pocket with hesitation. But immediately she pulled it back out and gave it to me, saying that the money was not hers and that we must find the person who left it on the table.—"I don't want to keep this money," she said: "it would be stealing and I am no thief."[127]

Gilles de la Tourette reports a case similar in every way to this one. "One day," he writes,

> we told W. under hypnosis that it was very hot. Indeed, she wiped her face as if she were sweating and declared that it was unbearably hot.
>
> —Let's go for a swim.

125 Pitres, op. cit., 55.
126 Féré, ibid.
127 Pitres, op. cit., 54.

—What, together with you?

—And why not? You know well that men and women can swim together without any scruples.

She did not seem convinced.

—Come on! Get undressed.

She hesitated. Then she undid her hair and took off her socks; but then she stopped.

—Come on! I command you to take off all your clothes.

She blushed and seemed to confer with great difficulty; finally, confused, she took off her dress.

—Keep going, keep going!

At this brutal order, she became troubled and seemed to suffer bitterly; she was about to obey, but her will reacted. Her modesty was stronger than the suggestion: her body stiffened, and I did not have the time to intervene in order to prevent an attack of hysteria.[128]

Gilles de la Tourette adds: "W. is fairly modest. Obviously that is why she has had an almost unconscious rebellion, leading to the result that we know; because in similar circumstances, Sarah R. does not hesitate to leave her clothes and take an imaginary bath."[129]

In our case, then, it was W.'s strong sense of modesty that prevented her from carrying out the suggestion. Sarah R., on the other hand, in whom this sentiment was weaker, was able to perform the suggested order. The same can be said of the other cases: the sentiments of pity or probity, in accordance with their relative weakness or strength, rebel against the suggestions or permit that these suggestions take place following more or less numerous attempts. In other words, in the last analysis, there is an *organic predisposition*, however latent, weak, or indistinct it may be, that allows or does not allow the realization of the suggestion. When an individual is absolutely unresponsive to an idea, it is thoroughly impossible for this idea, even if suggested under the hypnotized state, to

128 Gilles de la Tourette, op. cit., 140. Pitres brings up an experiment that is almost identical to the cited case. "One day," he writes, "I ordered one of our sick hypnotized patients to kiss one of our assistants after she woke up. Once woken up, she got close to the designated assistant, took his hand, then hesitated, she looked around, she seemed bothered by the attention with which she was being observed. She remained for a while in that position, with an anxious air, prey to intense distress. Pressed with questions, she ended by confessing, blushing, that she had wanted to kiss the assistant, but that she would never commit such an inconvenience."

129 [In French in Sighele's text.]

be transformed into action. This is the conclusion that almost all of today's most illustrious supporters of hypnotism concur upon, and which Janet summed up in his famous phrase: "An unknown idea will not suggest anything."[130] "Suggestions," writes Campili, "must harmonize with the inner world of the subject: not all of them, therefore, achieve the effect proposed by the hypnotist, but only those that the individual, given certain conditions, would have carried out some time in his life."[131]

To alter the personality, to diminish human will to the point of being almost unable to say whether or not it exists, this is what suggestion can do. But this personality and this will shall always show they are not totally dead, either by tenaciously resisting certain suggestions that the subject finds repulsive or—if the subject yields to them—by reacting through subsequent phenomena that represent the *repentance of the organism* for having committed acts in contrast with his normal nature.

Just as today we can no longer say that contagion is "an act by which a given disease is communicated from one individual affected by it to another individual *who is healthy*," but we must, instead, define it as "an act by which a disease is communicated from one individual affected by it to another individual *who is more or less predisposed to it*,"[132] it is not true that suggestion can make an individual perform *any action*. Suggestion can only cause an individual to commit an action to which he is *more or less predisposed*. Of course, predisposition in this case need not be as marked as it was in the first case; it is enough for it to exist even in minimal proportion, but it is, nonetheless, necessary.

What occurs in the hypnotic state, on account of the hypnotist's dominance over the subject's will, also occurs in the states of dreaming, somnambulism, and intoxication, although for different reasons. In these states a man carries out actions that he would not have committed in his normal state, but nevertheless his *I* always survives, however pathologically perverted his state may be. His *I* is altered, but not suppressed.[133]

---

130 Paul Janet, in *Revue politique et littéraire*, nos. 4 and 7 (1884).

131 Campili, op. cit, 48.

132 See the old definition of *contagion*, given by Gallard in *Dictionnaire de médecine et de chirurgie pratiques*, and Aubry's critique of it in the volume *La contagion du meurtre* (Paris: Alcan, 1888), 9–10.

133 The comparison I make between the hypnotic state and the states of the dream, of somnambulism, and of intoxication might seem inexact. One could, indeed, observe that the actions completed in the hypnotic state are performed because of the interposition of the will of a third person, who undoubtedly alters, with his intervention, the relations that make action depend on the moral characteristics of the individual

Colaianni puts it very well in speaking of alcohol, "that it removes or diminishes, according to the intensity and duration of its action, *the inhibiting moral force*, acquired hereditarily or developed through education, which restrains us from indulging in those tendencies that may lead to criminal acts or simply to acts of impropriety."[134]

One can say the same of suggestion, adding to it what Ribot notes, "that in the hypnotic state, the passage from one idea to the other is all the more swift, as there is nothing to obstruct it, no force to hold it in check, because the suggested idea alone reigns supreme in the consciousness of the sleeping subject."[135]

It is, therefore, easier under suggestion, than in any other pathological state, to make the individual perform acts that he deems repulsive; but this individual, as in sleep, somnambulism, and intoxication, will always reveal his own self, albeit more feebly.

---

(Campili), while in the states of dreams, somnambulism, and intoxication, this intervention of the will of an external person is missing, and the physical man—although pathologically altered—is always in full and direct correlation with the moral man. However, if all this constitutes an essential difference between the *causes* that produce those diverse states, it does not at all invalidate *the analogy* that exists between the *consequences* of those states. And the analogy (as I said quickly in the text) consists in this: that in suggestion, as in the dream, somnambulism, and intoxication, the normal conditions of the organism do not manage to abolish the personality completely. They only diminish it, and they certainly do so much more in suggestion than in the other pathological states. Rather, in these, more than diminishing it, one could say that they alter it by *accentuating it.* Indeed, in the dream, for example, the most pronounced characteristics of the individual are reflected, and habit, taken as the unique standard of psychic activity, ensures that the moral personality of the dreamer is entirely reproduced in a faithful depiction, although shadowed and confused in the middle of the most complicated changes of scenery. And, therefore, Bouillier (in *Revue philosophique,* 1883, no. 2) admitted that there exists a special form of responsibility for crimes committed in the dream. The same thing can be said for somnambulism and, more extensively, for intoxication. No one ignores the old and very valid proverb *in vino veritas,* and the entire positivist school (see Ferri *Nuovi Orizzonti,* 2nd ed., chapter III; Lombroso, *Uomo delinquente,* vol. II (1889); Garofalo, *Criminologia,* 2nd ed.; Marro, *I caratteri dei delinquenti,* and *Riv. delle. Discipl. carcer.* (1885), nos. 10 and 11); and Albano, *Ubbriachezza e responsabilità nel progetto di Codice penale Zanardelli* (Turin, 1888) agrees with Colaianni in maintaining that "spirituous beverages render the sentiments of man more energetic and lively, and they only diminish the calculating reflex that ordinarily makes us abstain from committing an action for various motives." *L'Alcoolismo* (Catania: Tropea, 1887), 125.

134 Op. cit., 127.

135 Ribot, *Les maladies de la volonté,* 6th ed. (Paris: Alcan), 137. [See *In Art and in Science,* 406 and 407n37.]

If we cannot say for suggestion what we can say for spontaneous somnambulism, for sleep, and for intoxication, namely, that man restores the image of his own individuality as in a mirror, we could at least say that the man demonstrates to which actions his character is naturally and organically opposed.

## *III*

The conclusion of what we have stated thus far is, I believe, evident and spontaneous. If under hypnotic suggestion—which is the strongest and most powerful form of suggestion—the human personality cannot be entirely extinguished but only diminished, a fortiori this personality will survive under the power of suggestion in a state of wakefulness, even if this suggestion reaches, as happens in a crowd, its highest intensity.

A part of the causes, however small, of the crime committed by an individual under the impetus of a crowd will, therefore, always be attributable to the physiological and psychological constitution of its perpetrator. Therefore, he will always be legitimately responsible.

A truly honest man, just as he does not yield to the orders of the hypnotist, will not bend even when confronting that whirlwind of emotions he experiences in the midst of a multitude. "When nature has well and tenaciously shaped this organism of the spirit"—says Tommasi—"any event may shake us, but we will remain on our feet."[136]

Should we, therefore, conclude that all those who, indistinctly, commit crimes driven by the crowd are true criminals?

This would be a serious mistake. Often in crowds there are born criminals, but we cannot say that whoever in the crowd commits an offence is a criminal.[137] We can only say that they are weak.

136 Cited by Virgilio, *Sulla natura morbosa del delitto*, 9.

137 Benedikt, at the 1st Congress of Criminal Anthropology (see *Actes du Congrès*, 140, 141), maintained that all criminals are *born criminals*; and he was right in this sense: that in every crime the anthropological factor always matters. But the habit is by now invalid to designate with the name *born-criminal* only that criminal in whose crime the anthropological factor represents *the most important and largest part* of the causes. The other criminals are defined as: habitual, occasional, or passionate; and with that one does not intend to exclude in them the anthropological, individual factor, but only to indicate that it is secondary in the etiology of the crime. Such is the sense that Enrico Ferri gave to his classification of criminals, and, if I am permitted to say so, all those who criticized it—before Benedikt—demonstrated their misunderstanding of its meaning and scope.

Every individual draws from nature a certain character that gives intonation and physiognomy to his behaviour, and that is its innermost stimulus—I daresay—according to which man acts and operates in life. The stronger a man's innermost stimulus, that is, the more steadfast and well-rounded his character is, the more the individual behaves in conformity with it without succumbing to external influences, in the same way that a projectile with a higher initial velocity is not so easily deviated by any obstacles it may encounter along its trajectory.[138]

Unfortunately, persons of robust temper, who win over every temptation and who know how to avoid all derailments, are quite rare. If there exist, as Balzac has said, men who are oaks and others who are shrubs,[139] the majority certainly falls into the latter category. For most individuals, life is nothing more than a fabric of compromises, insofar as, since they do not have the power to force the environment to adapt to them, they must necessarily adapt to the environment in their turn.

In this vast class of weak people—from those whom Benedikt calls *moral neurasthenics*, whose resistance to exterior impulses is naught, to those whom Sergi[140] brands with the name of *serviles*, who cowardly submit to the will of others and always opportunistically turn where the favourable wind blows; from good but timid and cruel beings who accept every idea

---

[Moritz Benedikt (1835–1920) was a professor of neurology at the University of Vienna, who also practised as a physician with the Austrian army during the Italian Second War of Independence. Like Lombroso, he contributed to criminal anthropology with controversial studies that posited differences between normal and criminal brains. He was one of the first physicians to use hypnosis since the 1860s to explore the past of mentally disturbed patients, even though he later discarded it as an unreliable method.]

138 And that is true, not only for the honest man in the most absolute sense of the word, but also for the criminal with a congenital tendency. Indeed, in this regard, one can establish an identity between the true gentleman and the born criminal, because both are equal before the modifying influences of the external world, as—I believe—there are only very rare circumstances, not to say none at all, which could force the one or the other to deviate from his path.

139 [Cf. Balzac, "Il y a des hommes-chênes, je ne suis peut-être qu'un arbuste élégant," in *Les Illusions perdues* in *Oeuvres Complètes de Honoré de Balzac*, vol. VII (Paris: Calmann-Lévy, 1879), 693. "Some are men like oaks, I am a delicate shrub it may be," Honoré de Balzac, *Lost Illusions*, in *Honoré de Balzac in Twenty-Five Volumes*, vol. 10 (New York: Peter Fenelon Collier & Son, 1900), 370. Sighele also refers to this comparison in his chapter on Balzac in *In Art and in Science* (394, this volume) and in *Against Parliamentarism* (215, this volume).]

140 G. Sergi, *Le degenerazioni umane* (Milan: Dumolard, 1889).

imposed upon them, to the individuals who change because of their inconstant and irritable temperament—, the gradations are infinite.[141]

But—be it more or less despicable, or more or less profound—the weakness of character has for all these individuals the same infallible result: to render them easily or very easily vulnerable to the suggestions of the external environment, according to the cases and degrees.

As Ribot remarks[142] about the weakening of the will, for every act committed by someone with incipient abulia, the role of the individual character is *minimal*, while the role of the external circumstances is *maximum*. Likewise, we can affirm by analogy that in the actions committed by all these weak individuals who lack a congenital and strong tendency towards a certain kind of life, the part played by the individual character is *minimal*, and, by contrast, the *maximum* part is the one left to external circumstances and suggestions.

Put these individuals in a favourable ambience, under the influence of good suggestions, and they will remain honest, at least before the Code of Law.[143] Put them in an unfavourable ambiance, under the influence of unhealthy suggestions, and they will become occasional criminals or criminals by passion.

Because of the weakness of their character, which makes them prone to absorb all that surrounds them, good as well as evil, their adoption of one lifestyle as opposed to another is left to the mercy of external circumstances.[144]

---

141 Will, like intelligence, Ribot says, has its idiots and its geniuses with all the possible shades from one extreme to another.—See *Les maladies de la volonté*, 6th ed. (Paris, 1889), 86.

142 Ribot, op. cit., 36.

143 The opposite of occasional criminals, "[l]atent criminals are those offenders who do not reveal their criminalistic tendencies, either because they lack an opportunity or because wealth or power gives them the means to satisfy their depraved instincts without breaking the law. I know three men with all the physical and psychological anomalies of the born criminal but whose high social position protects them from imprisonment. One confessed that 'if I had not been rich, I would have been a thief.'" Lombroso, *L'uomo delinquente* (ed. 1889), vol. II, 432 [*Criminal Man*, English translation by Mary Gibson and Nicole Hahn Rafter (Durham: Duke University Press, 2006), 295.]

144 This easy adaptation to the environment—no matter whether good or bad—manifests itself to a truly exceptional degree in hysterical women. It is worthwhile bringing up the following page by Laurent:

> Put a hysteric in a convent, this hysteric, even if she were depraved with loose morals, as soon as she breathes the odour of incense, will undergo a complete change; in a few days she will abandon her old habits with surprising facility, and take up the

Now, if this is what happens during a calm, regular, and normal life, what will happen in a crowd that, in a single moment, concentrates a power of suggestion not found in any other instance? Is it not evident that all of these individuals will yield to suggestion, and that crime will be committed even by those who are good but weak—those very individuals who tomorrow may have a magnificent altruistic impulse for the same reason that today they are carried away by a current of hatred?[145] "I remember seeing in 1870"—narrates Joly—"a crowd pursue the carriage of a general from whom they wanted to extract a political promise at any cost. In the crowd, there was a young man I knew well, an enthusiastic but gentle boy, tidy, industrious, and good, perfectly honest. Suddenly he began to ask for a revolver to shoot the recalcitrant

---

habits and tastes of the house; she will love mass and the church as she once loved ballet and theatre; she will love prayer as she once loved vice; in short, according to a Doctor of the Church, she will liberate herself from the former woman. And she will not be a common devotee; she will not be pious without ostentation; she will pray with clamour as she once sinned with scandal; her religion will be a mysticism full of exaltation. So were Mary Magdalene, Mary of Egypt, and many others whose legends have not survived. Take the same woman and put her in a brothel among bad women and prostitutes. A new metamorphosis. In less than a week she will have placed a new mask on her face. So sudden and complete is her transformation, one could say that the brothel walls have infected her. In a few days will she have acquired the language, the tastes, and habits of the house. In Troyes, some years ago, I met a type of hysteric who was the model of the entire religious community. One lovely day, forced by a sister, she migrated from the convent to the city brothel. As in the convent she had been a model of devotion and virtue, so in the brothel she was a pearl, the most dissolute, and, as a consequence, the most sought-after and coddled. See *Les suggestions criminelles*, op. cit. [in French in Sighele's text].

145 Although very rare and exceptional, it should not be forgotten that there is also the case of an individual whom the crowd's impetus draws to good rather than to evil. In a political revolution, for instance, in the most supreme and acute moments of patriotic sentiment, as a consequence of the enthusiasm and excitement that the multitude stirs in him, a man may raise to the level of a hero or martyr, while in normal times he would simply be a good citizen, or even a bad one if he had lived in an unhealthy and corrupted environment. In this respect, Moreau wrote about the classical type of the Parisian *gamin*, who "in time of peace, at sixteen becomes a pimp, a thief, an assassin, and from the age of eighteen, enters the Grande Roquette where he takes a ticket for New Caledonia; in times of barricades, this kid dies as a hero." (See *Le Monde des prisons* by the Abbé G. Moreau, Paris, 1887, 81). This proves once again (as I demonstrated in chapter 1) that it is the influence of number that increases courage and awakens in man the instinct of combativeness; and, according to different circumstances and people, courage and instinct can be put in the service of an abject or sublime objective. [For Abbé Moreau see also 81n14, this volume.]

general. If he had had the weapon in his hands, I do not know what would have happened."[146]

Many individuals find themselves in the situation of this young man, and many, unfortunately, use the weapon they have in their hands! Are they evil for this?

No; I reiterate: they are simply weak in character. The sentiments of compassion and integrity exist in them, but only superficially.

The new layers of character, which constitute the physical foundation of these sentiments, have not had the possibility to organize themselves and completely cover the old layers, which represent the debris of the most distant generations. And an external incident, any occasion whatsoever that deeply disturbs the psyche of individuals, is enough to disrupt their character and reshuffle its layers, and the lowest ones, suddenly rising to the surface, give way to savage and cruel manifestations.[147]

What happens in a crowd *via revolution* happens in ordinary life *via evolution*. The disorganization of character at first begins slowly, because of the influence of bad examples or the solicitations of an already perverted companion. After corrupting the individual on one occasion and opening up the path of no return, it expands even further to the point of radically changing the individual, annihilating his very character. In a crowd, all this happens in a matter of instants.

Rather than the slow and gradual disintegration that turns an honest man first into an occasional criminal, and then into a habitual one, we have in the crowd an instantaneous disintegration that turns a still honest man into a criminal by passion.

Such is, in my opinion, the process by which most individuals in the crowd come to commit crimes.

And if this is true, what social reaction do they deserve?

The positivist school, I believe, cannot respond with a firm answer. They maintain, generally speaking, that the crimes committed under the impetus of the crowd must be considered crimes committed out of passion,[148]

146 H. Joly, *La France criminelle* (Paris: L. Cerf., 1889), 406n1 [in French in Sighele's text].

147 See in this regard, G. Sergi, *La stratificazione del carattere e la delinquenza* (Milan, 1883). The new strata of the character would have been easily overcome by the ancients, also because all that in the organism is of a more recent formation disappears and dissolves before what is of more ancient formation. "The functions born last," Ribot said (op. cit., 61), "are the first to degenerate."

148 Hence the repressive means to be mainly applied against those crimes are the ones that have been proposed for criminals under the impetus of passions.

but they also maintain that, according to this criterion, to dictate a single formula applicable to all cases is a mistake.

In a crowd there can be—and we have seen this—born criminals and occasional criminals. It is of little importance that they committed the same crime: the punishment, in our opinion, should be established by judging not so much the objective severity of the crime committed, but rather, the criminal's dangerousness, which can only be evaluated case by case.

Let us add that, in the collective crime, it is not even possible to take as guides those few general norms, which, in the case of individual crimes, we can sometimes deduce from the manner in which the crime was carried out.

For example, the isolated criminal who kills a few people without an apparent motive—*out of brutal wickedness*, as the classic phrase goes—should *always* receive the maximum punishment, because it can be affirmed a priori that he, with his crime, proved to be a born criminal or a mad criminal.

For collective crimes, on the other hand, to apply the same principle would be inexact in some cases.

In a crowd, a man can commit many murders and not be a born criminal. The moral intoxication of which he is a victim can drive him to such excesses, and only after having committed them does he comprehend—as if he woke up from a dream—the enormity of his crime. He then experiences sincere repentance and remorse, unknown to a congenital criminal.

Taine tells of an extremely honest man who, during the revolution of 1793, killed five priests in one day and then died of remorse and shame.[149]

Just as the nervous fit—which the suggestionized subject suffers after having committed an imaginary crime under the action of hypnosis—demonstrates his organic repulsion for his action, so this remorse and repentance after a real crime prove that the man was not entirely evil. Life imprisonment would have been an unjust punishment for him.[150]

---

149 "... a local commissioner, a very honest man, but was carried away, then got drunk and panicked, kills five priests, and dies of it one month later, unable to sleep, with foam in his mouth, and trembling all over." Taine, *Les origines de la France contemporaine*, vol. II, 2nd ed. (Hachette, 1878), 295.

150 In the crimes of the crowd we should always remember Holtzendorff's words: "We cannot ever say, from the moral point of view, that in whatever circumstance a certain crime is worse than another." See *L'assassinio e la pena di morte*, translated by R. Garofalo (Naples, 1877), 173. [For Holtzendorff see also 298n28, this volume.]

We cannot, therefore, dictate any absolute norm in the abstract. It is necessary—here more than elsewhere—to comply with the supreme principle of our school, namely, to indicate the form and measure of retaliation according to the nature of each individual criminal.[151]

In conclusion, the positivist school examines, acknowledges, and patiently considers the infinite causes of the crimes in a crowd; all of this is necessary to pass a more competent judgment. But positivism does not have the arrogance to attempt to draw an exact conclusion that is applicable to each and every case from the study of these causes.

As for the current state of affairs—still dominated by the classical school—it is necessary to provide a general criterion, and this criterion must be the one proposed by Pugliese, that is, to rule that the crimes of a crowd are always committed by individuals who are semi-responsible.

The excuse of mental illness will reflect less poorly than any other, at least in its consequences, the sound judgment and intention of the positivist school.

Surely, as we have said, this excuse is a scientific absurdity, not only because of the imperfection of the adopted formula,[152] but, above all, because this formula will be used for occasional criminals (in which case its penal consequences will be just), but also for born criminals (in which case its use would be an injustice and one of the many felicitous outcomes of legal dispositions).

But to this we must resign ourselves, until the day when, with the triumph of the positivist school, our ideas are no longer only partially accepted and through means which, adapted to institutions of a different nature, hence partially illogical, reveal the deplorable yet necessary scientific opportunism that encourages the application of one's own theories to the extent that the empire of commonly accepted ideas permits.

---

151 We must also take into account the sex and age, since it is known that women and children are more prone to suggestion than adult men. "Childhood," Rambosson writes (op. cit., 247), "is the molten metal that we pour into the mould and that takes on all forms … All the temperaments that resemble those of the child, such as the woman's and the young man's, are the most susceptible to external influences and to all outbreaks." [in French in Sighele's text]. Lauvergne (*Les forçats* etc., 216) defined children as *educable sponges*; a very appropriate phrase that could also be applied, in part, to women.

152 By now everyone knows that modern psychiatry has demonstrated the opinion of ancient psychiatry to be erroneous, which maintained that a man could be more or less insane, or insane and mentally sane at the same time: insane, namely, regarding certain sentiments or certain ideas, and sane regarding other sentiments and other ideas. These days everyone recognizes with Maudsley that *when one is insane, he is insane up to the tips of his fingers*. See *Corpi e mente*, Lecture II, 45.

# 2 From *The Criminal Couple: A Study in Morbid Psychology*

To my master Enrico Ferri, trusting that my veneration as a disciple and my affection as a friend will suffice to forgive my pride in dedicating such a negligible work to such a great name.

## "Preface"

The present study is only one chapter in a volume on the *associated criminal*,[1] which I had hoped to publish this year.

Reasons that are useless to provide here forced me to delay said publication, hence in the meantime I am presenting this small portion of my work to the public, since I think it can stand alone, as an essay on the psychology of criminal association.

Last year, in a modest book of mine,[2] I attempted the analysis of the most complex form of this association; now I will attempt the analysis of its simplest form. The *criminal couple* and the *criminal crowd*—the crime by two and the crime by a thousand—are, indeed, the extreme links that close the chain of all the innumerable varieties and forms of criminal societies.

1 [All emphases are Sighele's, or as originally found in Sighele's work, unless otherwise specified.]

2 *La folla delinquente* (Turin: Bocca, 1891) [*The Criminal Crowd*]. I take the liberty to announce that this book is about to be published by Alcan in Paris, in a French revised edition of the Italian original.

If I have worked—before others—on these two themes, it is because no one so far has believed it necessary to tackle this subject, hence I felt I perhaps had something—I do not know whether good or right, but at least new—to say about it.

Rome, July 1892—Scipio Sighele

## "Introduction"

### *"Suggestion in Crime"*

### *I*

"Universal history," Carlyle writes, "the history of what man has accomplished in this world, is at bottom the History of the Great Men who have worked there. They were the leaders of men, these great ones; the modellers, patterns, and in a wide sense creators, of whatsoever the general mass of men contrived to do or to attain."[3]

Without completely endorsing Carlyle's overly unilateral idea, it is certain that Spencer exaggerated when he ridiculed this theory of *the great man,* reducing the influence of genius on the evolution of society to a negligible factor.[4]

If geniuses are undeniably a necessary product of the environment in which they arose, and sons of their time, so to speak, one cannot deny that they are, moreover, fathers of what follows them, that is, men who are not only representative, as Emerson called them, but also active; not only actors, but also authors of the drama of history.[5]

"There is an odd idea"—Bagehot says rather well, clearly alluding to Spencer's opinion—"that those who take what is called a 'scientific view' of history need rate lightly the influence of individual character. It would be as reasonable to say that those who take a scientific view of nature need think little of the influence of the sun."[6]

---

3 Thomas Carlyle, *On Heroes, Hero-Worship, and the Heroic in History* (London: Chapman and Hall, 1893), Lecture 1, 1.

4 Spencer, *Introduction à la science sociale,* 7th ed. (Paris: Alcan, 1885), 31 and ff.

5 See the study by A. Chiappelli: "Gesù Cristo e i suoi recenti biografi," in *Nuova antologia* (1 April 1891).

6 Bagehot, *Physics and Politics,* 96. See my article "Il delitto politico," in *Archivio giuridico* XLVI (1891).

Indeed, we see in all eras and within all populations that every phase of progress is personified in the name of some hero who triggered it. In the epochs of war, it is a famous captain; in the artistic epochs, a painter or a poet; in the great revolutions of thought, it is a scientist who leads his contemporaries and forces them to follow.

"How many great men," Tarde writes, "from Ramses to Alexander, from Alexander to Muhammad, from Muhammad to Napoleon, have polarized in their own way the soul of their people! And how many times an entire population has fallen into catalepsis after staring for a long time at that luminous point that is the glory or genius of one man!"[7]

One can fight the irrational fetishism with which we sometimes admire the great figures of history; one can disapprove of the methods with which history has thus far been written, attributing the causes of every occurrence solely to one or a few men; but one cannot disavow the immense efficacy exerted by those great men on the era from which they arose. One cannot deny that they represent, as [John] Stuart Mill says, "the salt of the earth; without them human life would become a stagnant pool."[8]

This influence of the individual on the masses, which reaches a high level when the individual is a genius and the mass surrounding him is prepared to follow him, can be found partially and in minor proportions also in normal, modest, everyday life, outside of the great historical events.

If we look at human society from an intellectual and moral point of view, we see that it can be subdivided into many fractions, each of which is composed of one or more commanding leaders and of many gregarious followers who blindly obey.

The medieval regime—when whoever had the strongest arm and the boldest heart constructed his hawk's nest[9] at the top of the mountain, while the humble built their huts all around him and looked up at him in awe—is alive and true even today, although customs have changed. Even today, he who is more ingenious or brave or cunning, and inspires more confidence, places himself at the top and drags the crowd behind him.[10]

---

7 G. Tarde, "Qu'est-ce qu'une société?" in *Revue philosophique* (Nov. 1884).

8 [John] Stuart Mill, *La libertà* (Turin, 1865), chapter II, 95. [English original, *On Liberty* (Boston: Ticknor and Fields, 1863), 124.]

9 [The original Italian term here is "falco," hawk, even though the image that Sighele evokes seems closer to an eagle's nest.]

10 This simile was suggested to me by an analogous line of thought from an article by E. Scarfoglio. The idea contained in this simile could make one suppose that we believe that in human society the Darwinian law of the struggle for existence acts as in the animal and vegetable world, leading to survival of the fittest, and therefore that those

In religion and science, in politics and business, in any manifestation of the human spirit, you will see the many group around a few or just one, in the formation of a church or a school, a class or a party; and they fight, like soldiers in battle, under the orders of a captain who represents and is able to lead an interest, a feeling, or an idea to victory.

Given this spontaneous organization of society, one could almost say that our tiny earth wants to imitate the grand harmony of the universe, to be like a gathering of planetary systems where an infinite number of minor stars revolve around suns.

Now, what can be the reason why, no matter what place or moment of social life we examine, we catch sight of this fatal disposition of many individuals who act and think under the direction of only one?

It is certainly not through terror or deception that a select few have morally and intellectually ruled, and still do, over the masses, since in such cases the masses' complete dedication is spontaneous and excludes every suspicion of despotism.

The real reason lies, I believe, in the charm that certain men exude. Whether lasting or ephemeral, we almost never know how to express or explain this charm, but we experience it in the semi-obscurity of emotion and foreboding. They are men who have in their mind the power that certain natural spectacles or certain masterpieces of art exert over the eyes, making us ecstatic in mute contemplation. They are men who reflect and summarize, so to speak, that heap of vague and indistinct aspirations, which lie latent in the sparse energies of single individuals,[11] and towards whom we feel irresistibly attracted, as nature towards the sun from which it knows it receives its life and warmth.

In short, it is the arcane force of suggestion, possessed by some, that, like a magnet, attracts and withholds around them those who approach

---

who *arrive*—to use an expressive word—and place themselves high, are the best. Instead, in our opinion (and the reality unfortunately demonstrates it amply), in the struggle for existence, if the best sometimes win, the worse often lose. Of course, he who wins in the social battle is a strong person (and in this sense the application of Darwinian theory is true), but his strength can consist as much in a great ingenuity and in a great morality, as in a great slyness and in a knowing and masqueraded perversity. And, disgracefully, this second hypothesis is not less frequent than the first.—On this topic see G. Cimbali, *Il diritto del più forte* (Roux, 1891), and the controversy between the author of this book, A. Zerboglio and Filippo Turati, in *Critica Sociale* (1891).

11 It was brilliantly said that "a genius is an unconscious foreshortening of humanity," meaning, in other words, that in him all tendencies (artistic, political, or religious) of a given epoch are personified.

them. And the number of followers is either greater or smaller depending on the intensity of this force of suggestion, which could be defined as the true measure of individual value. From Christ, who disseminates his doctrine to a huge part of the world and to future centuries, to any one of the current leaders of a political party or a scientific school, who, in comparison, exert a small and transient influence, everything in the world, art, thought, and action circles around a few people who give the signal and the direction of the movement, and none of us can deny looking at a man as to our own beacon when we want to follow his ideas and imitate him.

## *II*

If this is what happens in the world of honest people, why does it not happen, as well, in the world of criminals?

Criminal psychology has by now shown how, even in the social world, the following principle remains effective: pathology follows the identical laws of physiology. Criminal activity is predicated upon phenomena analogous to those that make honest activity grow and develop.[12] Therefore, although the criminal differs from other people in psychological and physiological constitution, he cannot escape the laws that govern the actions of all individuals, from a general point of view. And for the same reason why a normal man feels full of admiration for the noble figure of an artist or a scientist, the criminal will be subjected to the charm of a famous bandit or murderer, and will attempt to imitate them. Every profession has its ideal: the soldier dreams to be a colonel, the merchant hopes to become as rich as the millionaire who lives next door, the scholar aspires to have the fame of his mentor. Even crime is, unfortunately, a profession for many of those who commit it; crime must, therefore, have its ideal, but, instead of a glorious ideal, it has an infamous one.

Just as the neophyte in a church or school would like to attain the perfection of the superior man whose doctrines inspire him, the new recruits in the army of criminality aspire to imitate and surpass in atrocity the great evildoers whose name they know and repeat with a sense of terror and admiration.[13]

---

12 On this topic see Lombroso, *L'uomo delinquente* [*Criminal Man*], vol. I, and Ferri, *Nuovi orizzonti.*

13 It must be noted that, if it is true that the great majority of mediocre criminals admire and desire to imitate the celebrated criminals, all the celebrated criminals are not always admired and imitated indistinctly by all the mediocre criminals. Thieves, for

The Abbé Moreau, in his precious book about the prisons of Paris, talks extensively about the pernicious influence that great criminals have over the other convicts. In the page I reproduce here, he sculpts it masterfully:

> When at the *Grande-Roquette*[14] the news spread that Blind, the celebrated murderer, had arrived, there was a great turmoil among all the prisoners. They knew about Blind's past, his audacity, his fortune to have never been caught until then; in that atmosphere he appeared as a hero (...). The door to the big room opened, around ten convicts entered—"Which one is Blind?" everyone was asking—"I am Blind, who wants me?" responds one of average height with two lively eyes fixed deeply in his superciliary arches. He advanced boldly and sat down in an empty chair. Glances of envy were cast on the privileged ones who managed to sit near him. The conversation was about to start. All ears were taut. Blind asked some news about the *modus vivendi* at the *Grande-Roquette*. The ice was broken, but he had not yet spoken of his conviction or of his successful homicide attempt. Finally he yielded to the requests and began to narrate his crime ... A long silence ensued after the narration. No one dared to inquire as to the particulars. Little by little each of the criminals rose and went to recount the crime to others. His place was soon occupied. The audience was thus completely renewed. New questions: new story. The conversation livened up; the details were exposed. Blind felt like the king of that crowd; he dominated them, he charmed them, they were at his feet.[15]

---

example, have sometimes, not admiration, but repugnance for murderers; and vice versa the criminals against people despise criminals against property. A murderer to whom was asked if he had stolen, responds disdainfully: "Steal? But I am an honest man!" And the celebrity thief Corbière refused to evade prison because it was necessary to kill the guards: "Violence," he said, "is not my system" (V. Despine, *Psychologie naturelle*, vol. III, 191). In general then, one must think that among criminals there are two categories, thieves and murderers, each of which has its unique ideal. Unfortunately, however, there exist the more dangerous types who indifferently combine robbery with homicide, and for whom the best type to imitate is the robber, *l'escarpe*, who robs and kills.

14 [A prison in the 11th arrondissement in Paris, which was opened in 1830 and closed in 1974. The Abbé Georges Moreau was the chaplain of the Grande Roquette. In his 1887 book *Le Monde des prisons*, he denounced the hardships and abuses of criminal life in the prison, and created a scandal. Also Havelock Ellis quotes from that book in his *The Criminal*.]

15 Abbé Moreau, *Le monde des prisons* (Paris, 1887), 29.

Outside of prison, conditions may be different, but the *suggestion* exerted by great evildoers on petty criminals has identical effects.[16] Even crime has an aristocracy, behind which one places the envious multitude of the mediocre. The deeds of a Lacenaire or an Abadie[17] are recalled in the criminal world analogously to those works of illustrious men that honest people recall. And the murderers and thieves who acquired sad notoriety feel compelled to be examples and instructors for their companions. They are, I daresay, conscious of their influence and keep exerting it even in supreme moments with daring audacity.

Who ignores how beneficial it is to the infamous notoriety of a criminal to know how to die courageously on the scaffold? The public that attends capital punishments exposes itself not only to the deleterious consequences that come from the spectacle of a horrible, bloody tragedy, which revives all the cruel feelings in the human soul, but also to the danger of admiring like a martyr the murderer who does not lose his serenity even when standing before the executioner. A criminal who approaches his extreme torture without trembling is certain to leave a lasting memory behind him among his companions, and his name will be remembered as that of a courageous person who must be loved and imitated.[18]

---

16 See a trove of examples in Vidocq, *Les moyens de diminuer les crimes*; Gisquet, *Mémoires*; Claude, *Mémoires*; Andrieux, *Souvenirs d'un préfet de police*; Yves Guyot, *La police*; Macé, *Un joli monde, Mon musée criminel, Le service de la sûreté, Mes lundis en prisons*; Moreau Christophe, *Le monde des coquins*; M. du Camp, *Paris, ses organes, ses fonctions et sa vie* (Paris), vol. III; P. Cère, *Les populations dangereuses*; Laurent, *Les habitués des prisons de Paris* and *L'année criminelle*; Joly, *Le crime, La France criminelle*, and *Le combat contre le crime*; O.Z., *Les bas-fonds de Berlin*; J.D. Lewis, *Les causes célèbres de l'Angleterre*; the collection of *Causes criminelles et mondaines* by Bataille; Émile Gauthier, *Le monde des prisons*; Th. Dostoevsky, *La maison des morts*; D'Haussonville, *L'enfance à Paris*; Guy Tomel and H. Rollet, *Les enfants en prison*; A. Guillot, *Les prisons de Paris et les prisonniers*; Raux, *Nos jeunes detenus*; Ch. Desmaze, *Les criminels et leurs grâces*; J. Peuchet, *Mémoires tirés des Archives de la police de Paris*.

17 [Pierre François Lacenaire (1803–1836) was a French murderer with a poetical vein, whose rebellious personality and deeds inspired Balzac, Hugo, Dostoevsky, Gautier, Stendhal, Corbière, and Prévert, among others. Émile Abadie was one of three working-class men on trial for the gang murder of a grocer's boy and a newspaper vendor. Detained at La Roquette, he was also portrayed by Edgar Degas for his studies of degenerate and criminal physiognomy. See, e.g., Degas's painting *Head of a Criminal: Émile Abadie*.]

18 On the effects of capital punishment in public, see Du Camp and Moreau, op. cit.; Garofalo, *Contro la corrente!* (Napoli, 1888); Aubry, *La contagion du meurtre* (Paris: Alcan, 1888); and Ferri, "La ghigliottina a Parigi," in *Intermezzo* (Alessandria, March 1890).

Not infrequently, the degenerated popular imagination is not content with transmitting oral narratives about its admiration for great evildoers; rather, it writes poems for them, narrating their lives.[19] Such was the case of Cartouche,[20] who came to be celebrated in a poetic work of twelve cantos, the last of which describes him among the torments of torture, and ends with these lines:

Of the horror of such a deed he becomes the winner,
We cannot but admire his great courage.[21]

A born criminal is thus described as a hero! And it is easy to imagine the effect of similar apologies.

But it is in the associations of evildoers where the charm exerted by some criminals over the mass of the others shows itself most clearly.

In these associations, the leader, recognized as such by the unanimous suffrage of his companions, is blindly obeyed, like a general by his army or the master by his disciples, and he is obeyed not only out of fear or for the sake of discipline, but also by true force of suggestion, because he possesses the faculties that increase his subordinates' esteem.[22] Is there, perhaps, a

---

Avril, when he knew about his sentence for death, sent a message to Lacenaire in prison: "My dear Lacenaire, you who have the spirit, write me a song that I can sing when I go to the scaffold." Lacenaire wrote back: "Dear Avril, I do not want to write you a song: one sings when one is afraid, and I hope that neither of us will sing."—In these words we see that the will to die is strong, that it is a big part of the suggestion exerted by the great criminals. [Pierre Victor Avril was a henchman who met Lacenaire in prison and later became his accomplice.]

19 Lombroso, in chapter XII, part III of vol. I of *L'uomo delinquente* (4th ed.), hinted to this literature that forms around the great criminals, and that is, if I can say so, an outburst of the latent, criminal tendencies of the population; and he cited many poems, songs, and ballads that illustrate the most celebrated evildoers.

20 [Louis Dominique Garthausen, a.k.a. Cartouche (1693–1721) was a legendary highwayman who, under different pseudonyms, stole from the rich and gave to the poor during the French Regency period of Philippe d'Orléans, and became a popular subject in literature and the visual arts.]

21 See *Répertoire général des causes célèbres anciennes et modernes* (Paris, 1834), vol. II, biography of Cartouche.

22 Fouquier (in *Causes célèbres*) says that ferocity and experience in crime are the conditions that enable a criminal to impose himself on another. I add that the moral and, above all, the physical insensibility of born criminals are gifts that in themselves confer a halo of superiority. When we see pain being heroically endured, a sentiment of admiration is born in us, given that we believe that everyone suffers as we suffer. It is thanks to this fortunate insensibility that many illustrious captains owe much of their ascendancy to their soldiers.

need to commemorate the times of brigandage to prove how there truly exist individuals who are destined to crime by nature, who have the horrible privilege of knowing how to dominate a bunch of perverts or weaklings, lead them from crime to crime, gain respect, and be venerated by them?[23] Or is it, perhaps, that they are quite different from legendary chieftains, those who direct the mafia or the Camorra with remarkable organization, and know how to have their orders punctually executed, surrounded by mysterious formalities that thus increase their prestige?[24] Or, perhaps, do not the last and most civil manifestations of criminal associations, such as the international gangs of a Gasco or a Catusse,[25] also prove that in the criminal industry, as in every other form of human effort, there are a few who rule the many thanks to the influence they have over them?

## *III*

Nevertheless, the analogy between the suggestion that takes place among honest people and in the criminal world does not stop here.

---

23 On this see Marc Monnier, *Histoire du brigandage dans l'Italie méridionale* (Paris, 1862); Locatelli, *Il brigantaggio e la maffia* [*sic*] (1875); Saint-Jorioz, *Il brigantaggio nelle provincie meridionali* (1864); Lestingi, "L'associazione della Fratellanza di Girgenti" (*Arch. di psich.*, vol. V, 1884); the *Chronique des Tribunaux* (Brussels, 1830), for crimes committed by the *Chouans*, and the article "Le brigandage en Turquie," by E. Dutemple (in the *Supplément* of *Le Figaro*, 15 Aug. 1891), where he speaks of the fascination of two current Turkish gang leaders, Kattiegani and Psitchi-Osman, and their followers.

24 See the two works by Alongi on the *Camorra* and the *Maffia* [*sic*]. [Sighele is here referring to Giuseppe Alongi's *La Maffia nei suoi fattori e nelle sue manifestazioni* (Turin: Bocca, 1887) and *La Camorra: Studio di sociologia criminale* (Turin: Bocca, 1890). The circulation of books on such topics confirms widespread awareness and overt recognition, already in Sighele's time, of those two social problems plaguing southern Italy. For Camorra, see also 88; *Criminal Crowd*, 15; *Sectarian Criminality*, 196, this volume.]

25 The gang of thieves headed by Catusse was discovered in Paris by Goron [Marie-François Goron, officer of the French National Police] in 1888; it had ramifications in London, Calais, Spa, and Brussels. The Gasco gang, also of thieves, and about which Joly speaks (*Le crime* 160), represents the ultimate form that an international criminal organization can take on. It has its headquarters in London and sends its affiliates all over Europe. In Italy, fortunately, we have not yet arrived at these extreme manifestations of international organization. However, last year in Bari we had the trial of the *Mala vita*, and now in Rome a trial is being prepared against 150 members of an association of thieves, which proves that crime is assuming frightening forms even among us.

Among honest people, aside from the general and indirect influence coming from the sole prestige that the names of certain men exude, we find the limited and direct influence that they exert on those who approach them, inciting them with words and examples to put them on their path.

This also occurs in the criminal environment.

Many individuals endowed with poor intelligence and weak moral sensibility, if they have the misfortune of running into an ingenious criminal, who possesses what Despine calls *active perversity*, will soon become totally deprived of morality. They do not always have the spontaneous desire to imitate he who has become their master. Rather, at first, they sometimes feel an instinctive repulsion towards him. But they are subjugated little by little by promises of gain or fear of punishment; they are brutally ridiculed for their scruples; they feel their already poor moral sense slowly decline; hence they become what he wants them to become.

Among the convicts at Mazas,[26] Aubry recounts, one finds an 18-year-old belonging to a noble family who showed signs of sincere repentance. This miserable boy tells M. Goron that, after letting himself be dragged into his first theft, he had been forced into further thievery, threatened by one of the main dealers if he tried to return to an honest life. And then, "you know," he added as a final argument, "our association's code is clear: desertion is death."[27]

The Lemaire Gang, whose boss was Villert, organized and carried out plots and forced others to crime—Joly writes. Lemaire himself lacked initiative and courage and thus allowed Villert to drag him along, instigating him, putting his self-respect to severe test and giving him wine. "He made me drink," Lemaire said to the audience, "and if I hesitated he laughed at me."[28]

A 20-year-old peasant, Gibrat, who was convicted of robbery, complicity in a homicide, and attempted homicide, crimes that he always committed in the company of evildoers, was interrogated by Lauvergne about those crimes. He responded alluding to his accomplices: "He was stronger than me; I followed him like a dog."[29]

---

26 [A Paris prison designed by Émile Gilbert. Inaugurated in 1841, Mazas was located close to the Gare de Lyon and destroyed in 1900.]

27 Aubry, *La contagion du meurtre*, 44.

28 Joly, *Le crime*, 137. Also Lemaire's aunt encouraged her nephew, telling him: "*Marche Henry, marche toujours!*" [*March Henry, always march!*].

29 Cited by Ferri, *L'omicidio*, part I: *L'omicidio come fatto naturale.*

And Avril, for the same reason, became the companion and loyal executor of Lacenaire's feats: "'I will be the head, you the arm,' he told him in the prison of Poissy, coercing him to combine their interests."[30]

What more? In the Campi trial, Arnaud, a spy placed in prison in an attempt to discover his secret, testified that Campi had excited the prisoners so much that one of them, fresh out of prison, decided to kill his wife—against whom he had suppressed an ancient bitterness.[31]

This revelation proves once again, if there was even the need to do so, how true that criminal's thought on prison is (no. 357 of the Tables of *L'omicidio* by Ferri): "Here the most educated teach to the most ignorant the best way to commit further crimes; they do nothing else."

Victor Hugo wrote that a great criminal in prison is like a painter in his studio: *he is always dreaming of a new masterpiece.* And it is true: "The well-executed crimes, the famous thief Maillot confessed, are thought out and planned in prison."[32] But Victor Hugo had to add that the artist is never alone in the design of a new masterpiece, because he associates himself with all of the convicts. Prison is a wonderful breeding ground for crimes, where one cannot enter without perverting oneself and where one does not leave without eventually coming back.[33]

Occasional criminals are at first surprised and appalled by speeches they hear around them, but then,

> they receive advice, encouragements from their new companions, they familiarize themselves with them, they narrate some details of their sentencing, proclaiming their innocence (since, out of modesty, they want to call themselves innocent) until it becomes a lie against them, a reason for scorn and contempt on the part of the older criminals who despise the company of honest people. Then, encouraged by experience, confused for not having measured up to the sentiments of their friends, they essentially strip themselves of their remaining morality; they open their hearts and ears to

---

30 De-Pine, *Psychologie naturelle,* vol. II, 433.

31 Aubry, op. cit., 42.

32 Moreau, op. cit., 16.

33 Setti rightly compares prison to the jackal, the filthy animal that would immediately eat vomited food.—See "La condanna condizionale," in *Rivista di discipline carcerarie.*—Criminals know that they can perfect their craft in prison: See *Mémoires de M. Gisquet, écrits par lui-même* (Brussels), vol. VI, 220.—On the deleterious influence of prison, consult Laurent, *De l'action suggestive des milieux pénitentiaires* (communication made to the international conference on hypnotism held in Paris, 1889) and the exhaustive book by Lombroso, *Palimsesti del carcere.*

the lectures of the wise and the advice of superiors, and in little time they are able to profess, in their turn, the same maxims of conduct and put them into practice.[34]

If the simile did not seem far-fetched,[35] I would say that occasional criminals, those who fell into crime for the first time more out of weakness than of perversity, whenever they have the misfortune of being in those environments—like a prison or criminals' gathering places, where the most ferocious and cunning among them rule and command the others—must model themselves upon the habits, tastes, and feelings of their already perverted companions, by a fatal law of *psychic mimicry*. Just as some animals acquire the colour of the surrounding environment to avoid attracting the looks of their potential enemies, and better defend themselves,[36] so men of weak character and underdeveloped moral sense slowly take on the moral tint of their companions, to avoid embarrassment in front of those who are more wicked.

It is the old fable of the rotten and healthy pears, that is, the already over exploited theory of the environment's influence, though under a less vulgar aspect.

We do not think it is necessary, for the moment, to go deeper into this argument, or to bring up other examples of suggestion in crime, as no phenomenon was more widely studied than this one in the few years after the scientific world admitted that, beyond hypnotic suggestion, there was also suggestion in the state of wakefulness.[37] To linger on such an argument would, therefore, mean to repeat things that have already been said, and, in any case, the few novelties we have to add will be developed in a later section of this work.

The preceding pages were written because it seemed useful to us to present the phenomenon of suggestion in the world of honest people as well

34 Appert, *Bagnes, prisons et criminels*, vol. III, 12.

35 [The simile to which Sighele is referring is the one that he explicitly describes at the end of this long and complex sentence, that is, the parallel between occasional criminals and animals that camouflage.]

36 On mimicry, consult: Weismann, *Studien zur Descendenz Theorie* (Leipzig, 1876), 10 and ff.; Girard, *La nature* (1878), 109; Darwin, *On the Origin of Species*, [Italian translation] (Turin, 1875), 467; Canestrini, *La teoria di Darwin*, 2nd ed. (Milan: Dumolard, 1887), 263.

37 To cite all the works that deal with suggestion in crime would be long and useless; some were mentioned earlier, and the most important ones will be cited over the course of this work. We will say only that all French works on criminal sociology indistinctly deal with the phenomenon of suggestion, after the example given by Tarde in 1884.

as in the world of criminals in a logical and orderly fashion, starting from its more general and widespread form and descending to the more direct and limited one. And, above all, it was necessary to talk about this phenomenon before individually studying the diverse forms of criminal association, of which suggestion is one of the principal factors, if not the only one.

## Chapter 1: "The Healthy Couple, the Suicidal Couple and the Insane Couple"[38]

### *I*

What occurs in sociological phenomena occurs in all other phenomena, that is, they are perceived only, or especially, when their manifestations reach an acute level. It is the highest note that strikes our timpani; it is the brilliant light that strikes our eyes. Average sounds and colours do not make an impression on us; they go unnoticed.

The phenomenon of the association between criminals attracted the attention of scholars only in its most severe forms: when the associations are many; when the association has extended its network to multiple places; when the crimes committed are atrocious. They spoke rarely and briefly about smaller associations between a few individuals, committing only one or a few crimes.

I do not deny that it is natural and logical to preoccupy ourselves with the most dangerous and rarest of criminal associations before all the others. I only affirm that we must not neglect the latter. The doctor who studies the worst diseases with great care is, nonetheless, not ashamed to examine the least dangerous.

Furthermore, it is an undisputed rule that in order to have a complete and exact idea about any event, it is necessary to go back to its origins, to its initial forms. Going gradually from the simple to the complex is not only the law that presides in the development of all organisms, but it is, moreover, the law that regulates any acquisition of precise knowledge.

Therefore, I believe that dealing only with mafia, Camorra, banditry is not enough to intimately understand that complex phenomenon represented by the association between criminals. If one really wants to

38 This chapter includes some ideas that I had already hinted at in other works. I hope readers will forgive these repetitions, which are necessary to the understanding of our topic, and which I have attempted to keep to a minimum.

understand its innermost reasons and to know all its secrets, it is necessary to go as deep as the embryonic forms from which the criminal bond arises, still weak and indistinct, and then accompany it in all its subsequent transformations as it strengthens and becomes clearer. Only in this way are we able to judge it, having formed not an incomplete idea—as when we consider an organism in its last stage of development—but a clear and complete picture that takes shape when we observe the organism from its birth and follow through all the phases of its life.

By studying the association among criminals with these criteria, it is obvious that the first form we must examine is the association between two single individuals. There is no simpler phenomenon than this association, and it is from this association that all the others necessarily and inevitably originate.

How and why does an alliance form between two criminals? What are the psychological characteristics of what I call *the criminal couple*?

The object of our work lies in these questions. I anticipate here a response that should logically come in the end, but the ideas I exposed in my introduction already allow me to formulate it. I maintain that the alliance between two criminals is caused by the phenomenon of suggestion.

A wicked person who corrupts a weak person, an evil genius who instigates someone with mediocre intelligence and an inadequate moral sense to commit a crime, a born criminal who makes a slave and an instrument out of an occasional criminal—these instances define the criminal couple.

Apart from that, this *form à deux* of suggestion is not limited to the criminal world: it also occurs—though in different ways and with different effects, but for the same reason—in the honest world and in noncriminal forms of degeneration like suicide and mental illness.

Now, since our method is to study concurrently all the phenomena caused by suggestion, no matter whether they pertain to the physiology or the pathology of the social organism, we will analyse the *form à deux* of suggestion in each of the areas in which it manifests, confident that this examination will then help us better understand and explain the *form à deux* of suggestion in the criminal world.

## *II*

Let us begin in the normal field.

Do we not see many times, in daily life and in the honest world, a bond develops between two individuals because of the charm or domination that one exerts over the other?

Where do amorous love and its pale and chaste reflection that is the love between a brother and sister derive if not from an unconscious suggestion that one of the lovers or siblings exerts over the other, with the effect of bringing two people's hearts together in a strange unity of thoughts and feelings?

What is friendship, what is a disciple's devotion to his master, if not the result of this unknown force that we feel without explanation and that pulls us without giving us the chance to rebel?

We say that in love there is always one who loves and one who is loved. This phrase is psychologically truer than it appears. It is not to say that between lovers there is always an altruist who gives everything and an egoist who accepts without reciprocating—this would be an erroneous interpretation because it is too absolute. But it means that in all the great and true affections that tie two people together, there is always one who unconsciously maintains a sense of superiority over the other, and the other unconsciously recognizes it. The will of one is more often accomplished over that of the other, not so much because the first imposes it, but because the second anticipates it. The tendencies and habits of the two gradually become the same, not because one came before the other, but because the tendencies and habits of the one sweetly triumphed over those of the other.

Sometimes these two psychological currents, which are more or less alive and profound in every passion, reach such a high degree of intensity that they represent two absolutely different forms of love. Therefore, we see that, while the one enjoys sacrificing all of his being for the loved person, enveloping the latter with an affection made of humility and tenderness, the other, instead, accepts this complete dedication and reciprocates it with an affection in which there is no humility and tenderness, but protection and support.

This is the case with almost all the loves of famous men. As fame magnifies their effective moral and intellectual superiority, it makes them appear to the fervid and often hysteric female fantasy as idols worthy to be more than loved, that is, adored. And, indeed, their lovers show endless veneration and devotion for them, happy to be repaid with just a word or a smile. "God knows it!"—wrote Héloïse in one of her letters to Abelard in which she transfused all of her soul—

> in you I search for nothing but you, nothing of you but yourself, such was the object. I did not want an advantage, not even the knot of matrimony; I did not think, you know, to satisfy my will nor my desires, but only yours. If the name "spouse" is holier, I found that your "lover" is sweeter, that—do

> not be offended—of your mistress, or your whore. The more I humiliated myself for you, the more I hoped to win your heart. Yes: when the world's ruler, when the very emperor wanted to bestow on me the honour of being your spouse, I would have preferred to be called your lover, rather than your spouse and empress ...[39]

Furthermore, without focusing on the exceptional cases—which are nothing else but sick exaggerations of a universal event—, we can convince ourselves, only by an examination of the most frequent and common cases, that in the amorous couple there is always one who psychologically depends on the other.

It is a trivial observation that two people take a liking to one another when, although having fundamental aspects of a similar character, they have, however, different qualities and defects. Two temperaments of identical character could not join together—they would break each other. In order for two gears to turn together regularly, one needs to have the tooth where the other has the hollow: "For such a truly passionate inclination to arise"—Schopenhauer says—"something is required which can only be expressed by a chemical metaphor: two persons must neutralize each other, like acid and alkali, to a neutral salt."[40]

Common sense intuited this truth, creating the proverb "opposites attract.".

Opposites attract—I believe—because, in the end, love is *the desire to complete oneself* physiologically and psychologically,[41] and two individuals complete each other precisely when the one has what the other is missing.

39 *Heloissae*, Epistle 1 [in Italian in Sighele's text].—From G. Ferrero, "La crudeltà e la pietà nella femmina e nella donna," in *Archivio di psichiatria*, vol. XII, sections V–VI.—Regarding love for geniuses, see also Silvio Venturi, *Le degenerazioni psico-sessuali* (Bocca, 1892), 304.

40 Schopenhauer, *Il mondo come volontà e come rappresentazione* (Milan: Dumolard, 1888), book III, 298. [English translation by R.B. Haldane and J. Kemp, in Arthur Schopenhauer, *The World as Will and Idea*, vol. 3 (London: Kegan Paul, Trench, Hübner, 1906), 356. [See also *Sectarian Criminality* 163.]

41 And this instinctive desire was placed in man by that same fatality that wanted every living species to propagate itself.—"Instinct," writes Schopenhauer—"(...) is to be regarded as the sense of the species, which presents what is of benefit to *it* to the will." And elsewhere, referring in particular to love, he said: "The delusive ecstasy which seizes a man at the sight of a woman whose beauty is suited to him, and pictures to him a union with her as the highest good, is just the *sense of the species*, which, recognizing the distinctly expressed stamp of the same, desires to perpetuate it with this

Now, granted that opposites love each other, the result clearly is that one has to maintain a certain moral dominance over the other. If, indeed, some elements of their respective temperaments, minds, and hearts are different, then the intellectual and psychological functions that the two lovers will perform while aiming at the same goal will also be necessarily different: one will have the will, the other the fulfilment; one will be the head, the other the arm.

This diversity of functions that we find in the *healthy couple* is the first embryonic form of that division-of-labour phenomenon that attains even further specialization as it ascends to larger associations.

Every alliance has its reason for being: in utility or agreement; and agreement—as in Espinas's[42] profound observations—is, ultimately, nothing but the presentiment of future utility, which, I daresay, is almost divined in the obscurity of the unconscious, by those beings who feel very attracted to one another.[43] Even the smallest of communities—like the one composed of only two people and also created by sympathy, which we are discussing here—is uniquely motivated by interest or utility, although it could seem rather strange to many people. And because this utility is reduced to a division of labour (and to the perfecting process it entails), it is natural that, even in the amorous couple, one member exerts some different specific functions that are *therefore* superior, in a sense, to the functions of the other.

I said *therefore* because diversity implies the concept of superiority. Organization, according to a positivist philosopher, is a synonym for subordination: the two terms are equivalent.[44] If more organs compete to form an organism, although all are necessary, it is certain that each will have, physiologically, a greater or lesser importance than that of the others. If more individuals compete to form a community, although all are necessary, it is certain that their single social value will be different, namely, greater or lesser than that of all the others.

---

individual." See Schopenhauer, op. cit., 290. [English translation by Haldane and Kemp, 346, 347.] Therefore, the sense of the species pushes the individual, who alone is sterile, to complete himself with another individual, because in completing himself he perpetuates himself.

42 A. Espinas, *Des Sociétés animales*, 2nd. ed. (Paris: Germer Baillière, 1878), 173.

43 According to the acute and brilliant Schopenhauerian hypothesis just now mentioned, also in this case it would be *the sense of the species* that, under sympathetic forms, presents to the individual a phenomenon that is useful to him.

44 V. Espinas, op. cit., 176.—It is furthermore an intuitive truth that no society can exist if there is not a direction on one part and a subordination on the other.

The same must also happen, by logical necessity, in the simplest of human societies, the one that brings together two individuals.

But, let us leave aside these strictly scientific considerations, through which we only wanted to offer a cursory overview of the origins of the psychology of the association, and return to the phenomenon of suggestion. I believe it is not possible to deny that we owe to suggestion that relationship of spiritual and intellectual dependency that is sometimes established between two individuals, and that is more or less strong depending on whether it derives from simple affinity or from irresistible charm.

Attempting to prove it would be useless because this seems to me to be a truth that one feels and does not show.

Suggestion can be so strong in some cases that it harmonizes not only tastes and habits, but also expression, poise, voice, and even thoughts. "Daily relations," writes Roger, "the continual frictions of existence, establish an involuntary assimilation of nature between two people through a long series of imitative exchanges, and this is reflected in the organization and in the very sound of the voice."[45] And who among us, while speaking with the person to whom we are tied by affinity, has not exclaimed, all of a sudden, "I was thinking about this thing," and to be interrupted by the other person with those words: "Strange, I had precisely the same idea![46]

These magnetic communications from soul to soul, the coincidence of tastes and habits, the aligning of equal, external expressions of emotion, like voice and physiognomy—from what can they all derive if not from suggestion? Is it not evident that one will have unconsciously imitated the other?

## *III*

I do not know if I managed to express my thought with sufficient clarity: I certainly believe that everybody has had the chance to verify, in their turn, the phenomenon I have observed.

When no extraordinary event perturbs the uniformity of normal life, it is perhaps difficult to linger on the single cases of suggestion from

45 Roger, *Traité des effets de la musique sur le corps humain*, 265.

46 See on this topic Brierre de Boismont, *Du suicide*, etc., 2nd ed., 25 and ff.; and Rambosson, *Phénomènes nerveux, intellectuels et moraux, leur trasmission par contagion* (Paris, 1883).

individual to individual, because the form of such a phenomenon is weak and indistinct. When, instead of flowing calmly and serenely, love has the strange and impetuous force of a raging torrent, suggestion manifests itself with greater acuity, and everyone recognizes its paramount role.

And yet, the phenomenon is identical in both cases: the difference lies in its degree of intensity.

If we think about those not very rare dramas in which a woman drags a man along, rendering him a slave, making him forget his marital or filial duties, making him neglect his dignity as a man and as a citizen, obliging him to commit all of her insanities, we do not hesitate to affirm for one minute that in this case we are facing a cold and astute person who ties a weakling or an enthusiast to her wagon, supplying herself with all the weapons that nature or art can offer. We do not hesitate to affirm that this man succumbed to suggestion. He does not lack ingenuity and honesty, and he, nevertheless, slowly penetrates into a net that always grows tighter and from which he can no longer escape. Although he sometimes has a fit of rebellion, he is, nonetheless, subdued like a beast domesticated by his female tamer's gaze, and forgets everything and everyone, having polarized his mind according to the desires and whims of another person, like the hypnotized succumbing to the will of the hypnotist.

Now, if suggestion, by unanimous consensus, has this power, will it be strange and unlikely to affirm that it can also guide a lover to suicide if the other so desires?[47]

Why then should *the suicidal couple*, this *form à deux* of degeneracy that today has, unfortunately, become too frequent, not depend on the same phenomenon on which the healthy couple depends?

I believe that this analogy should not be surprising in any way.

Given two people who understand and love one another, the great law that regulates relationships between them cannot be ignored only because these people, instead of having obtained a normal constitution by nature and a happy life from events, were, unfortunately, born with abnormal tendencies and lived in an atmosphere of disillusionment and pain that made them, or at least one of them, desire death.

47 Obviously, in order to be persuaded to commit suicide, a person must be more or less predisposed to it. I neglect to speak of the anthropological factor (here, as in the rest of this work), above all, because, for us positivists, the existence of this factor is implied, and admitted a priori indistinctly in all human actions; second, because this study intends to focus on the efficacy of the social factor, that is, of suggestion.

Indeed, a psychological analysis of the motives that led the two lovers to suicide shows us that suggestion exerts its power also in these cases, and that in this emotional drama, where apparently each lover has to play the same role, one's conduct is, instead, always different from the other's. Furthermore, here we have the more intelligent individual who exerts his influence over the other—a well-determined will that subdues a weaker one, a hand that performs while the thought commands.[48]

The idea of suicide never arises simultaneously in the minds of both; it springs up first in the mind of one and, from this, it is then transmitted to the other who, through slow and continuous suggestion, accepts it. To one the sacrifice of life is repugnant, either because of religious prejudices or of love of family, or of a strong survival instinct. To the other, death seems the only way to salvation, and such a thought overpowers and chases away any opposite idea. The latter (and it is often the woman, rarely the man) dominates the former, who follows her and is sometimes a blind instrument. Indeed, one of the strangest particulars about these cases of double suicides consists in the fact that he who decides to commit suicide and persuades the other is almost never the material author of one's own or of the other's killing. The person who deals the blow to the lover and then to himself is always the weaker one, the one who does not want to die and who allowed himself to be driven to the extreme act by the other's pressure.[49] This phenomenon is new proof of the division of functions we already discussed, which we will see at work in the criminal couple, as well. There, as in the suicidal couple, one member has the idea, the other performs the action. The executor of the crime, as in suicide, is almost always he who at first rebelled against the idea of the crime itself. The instigator limits himself to planting in the soul of the other a germ that gradually grows and eventually seizes him, and when the former sees that his work of suggestion is complete and only needs

48 See on this topic: Chpolianksi, *Des analogies entre la folie à deux et le suicide à deux*, thèse de Paris (1885); Garnier, "Le suicide à deux," in *Annales d'hygiène publique* (March 1891);—and my study: *L'evoluzione dal suicidio all'omicidio nei drammi d'amore* (Turin: Bocca, 1891), reprinted with additions in the appendix of the 3rd ed. of *Omicidio-Suicidio*, by Ferri.

49 In my study cited before, I collected four cases of the *double suicide* carried out materially by the one who, between two lovers, obeyed to the suggestion of the other, namely, the double suicide of Doctor Bancal and Zélie Trousset, of Cesira M. and Pierre S., of Marguerite Vagnair and Tony Auray, and of E. Kleist and Mme Vogel.—Bierre de Boismont (*Du suicide*, etc., 130) also records a fact similar to the previous ones.

to be turned into reality, he withdraws and lets the other act. By then, his part is finished.

If the proportions of this study allowed it, we could cite many events in support of what we have just affirmed! How many human documents could attest to the truth of our observations![50] But we want to arrive soon at the real topic of our work and, moreover, we have already discussed this rather interesting argument elsewhere, and, perhaps, one day we will resume it with greater vigour.

At this point it is enough to observe how the double suicide of lovers is the last degree, the extreme manifestation that can reach that *form à deux* of suggestion in which all the intimate and often unknown psychology of love is enclosed.

This suggestion is at first born weak and latent so that it still gives us the illusion of acting spontaneously. When, indeed, we strive to pre-empt the desires of our loved one, we believe we are autonomous. We do not think that the suggestive charm has already started to act precisely because it has already instilled that invincible desire in us. As a result, influence becomes stronger and increases even simply out of habit, and then we feel the sweet domination that manipulates our thoughts and feelings, and their physical expressions as well. In the end, when love degenerates, for whatever cause, into morbid passion, then even the force of suggestion takes on an exaggerated and pathological form, hence it becomes powerful to the point of causing the downfall of one of the two lovers, or their double suicide.

Such is the trajectory that the suggestion of love will, or can, follow.

---

50 As for suggestion in suicide, facts can be found, in addition to the already cited study by Bierre de Boismont—a veritable mine of information—, in Ebrard, *Le suicide considéré au point de vue médical, philosophique,* etc., especially chapter VII; in Primerose, *Maladies des femmes;* in Spon, *Histoire des antiquités de la ville de Lyon,* and in the *Gazette de santé.*

For the general phenomenon of suggestion, and especially the phenomenon of suggestion of one over the other, see–together with the recent works by Tarde (*Les lois de l'imitation,* Alcan, 1890), Sergi (*Psicosi epidemica*),and Rambosson (op. cit.)—, Roger (op. cit.); Bouchut (*De la contagion nerveuse et de l'imitation dans leurs rapports avec les maladies nerveuses,* 1862); the article on "Imitation" in *Dictionnaire des sciences médicales;* Lucas (*De l'imitation contagieuse, ou de la propagation sympathique des névroses et des monomanies,* Paris, 1833); Calmeil (*De la folie considérée sous le point de vue pathologique, philosophique,* etc., Paris, 1845); Despine (*De la contagion morale,* 1870, and other works by him); Joly ("De l'imitation," in *Union médicale,* 1869), and Moreau de Tours (also in *Union médicale,* vol. XXII).

## *IV*

If it is quite natural that the suicidal couple has similar psychological characteristics to those of the healthy couple, both being but extreme links of the same chain, it is, instead, rather strange to find a third couple, the *insane couple*, next to the other two aforementioned couples.

The madman has the unique characteristic of never associating with anyone. He lives by himself, lost in his sad dream, and if the surrounding environment has the power to produce sensations in him, they never allow him to establish any stable relationship with other people. The very term *alienated* reveals it to us; he is alien to what others say or do; he has separated and removed himself from the world.

Paying a visit to an insane asylum is enough to convince ourselves of the truth in this observation. Those poor recluses rarely speak to each other, and if they do speak to one another, it is about indifferent things, not to exchange about an idea to be carried out together, nor is it to plan a conspiracy. Joining with others in order to attain an objective more easily is an unknown action for them.

This distinctive characteristic of madness, which Tarde very aptly defines as "an isolator of the soul,"[51] is so constant and absolute that it apparently has no exceptions. It represents one of the most reliable norms to distinguish the madman (in the narrow sense of he who is stricken by mental insanity) from the born criminal or the moral madman, who, on the contrary, easily associate with companions.

There seems to be, however, an exception regarding epileptic madmen. They are not always isolated, but, instead, they try to form relationships among themselves, and they sometimes speculate together about breaking out of the asylum.[52] Nevertheless, this fact, which seems

51 G. Tarde, *La philosophie pénale*, 1st ed., 239. [English translation by Rapelje Howell, *Penal Philosophy* (Boston: Little, Brown, 1912), 242.]

52 "Epileptics are the only inmates in insane asylums"—writes Lombroso—"who seek each other out and associate, as do criminals in prisons. They conspire not only with other epileptics but also with the morally insane." See *L'uomo delinquente*, vol. II, 27. [*Criminal Man*, English translation by Mary Gibson and Nicole Hahn Rafter (Durham: Duke University Press, 2006), 256.]—In the health spa of Schönberg, four madmen conspired to escape and they set fire to the house that was hosting them: of these, three were morally insane, one was epileptic. (See *Allgem Zeit. fur Psych.*, 1884). —In *Archivio di psichiatria*, vol. VIII, 1, one reads the history of an epileptic who conspired with two other epileptics and one morally insane person from his room at Mombello, to provoke a true uprising that needed to be suppressed with force.

to contradict an unsaid principle in schizophrenic science, was interpreted by Cesare Lombroso with one of his not so rare and felicitous intuitions. His new theory that places epilepsy at the base of criminality, and renders criminality as nothing else but a form of epilepsy, explains why, among madmen, the epileptics always assemble. Indeed, the kind of degeneration that afflicts them is precisely the first cause of all criminal forms, and it is, therefore, natural that they also have the innate tendencies of criminals.[53]

Therefore, it is not really an exception to the rule that madmen do not associate with one another; the exception—if we do want to call it that—exists, but it is much different.

It is comprised in that phenomenon of the *delirium à deux*, which Legrand du Saulle I believe described for the first time.[54] It is a very strange form of madness, which corresponds, both in its cause and manifestation, to the healthy couple and the suicidal couple. It deals with two individuals, one of whom is already insane, and the other who is naturally predisposed to insanity. The first usually has a certain ingenuity, the second is lacking in intelligence; the second, simply as a result of his contact with the first and of the incessant blow of his dissolute and confusing ideas, is led to act like his companion, and slowly assumes an identical form of madness. A dependent bond is formed between these

---

53 See Lombroso's diagram illustrating increasing degrees of epilepsy from Criminal by Passion and Criminaloid to Born Criminal, Morally Insane Criminal, and Epileptic Criminal. In this design, however, the distinction between the *born criminal* and the *morally insane criminal* surprises me, as they always coincided in Lombroso's view.

As for the *nature of criminality* and the many, too many explanations that one wants to give them, I declare (now that the occasion presents itself) to accept in full the explanation of Enrico Ferri, who interprets criminality as "a truly specific form of biological anomaly distinct from every other form of anomaly or pathology or degeneration, and that determines precisely the concrete crime, when it finds itself in the specific physical and social environment that provides the individual disposition with the circumstances and means to turn into action. Therefore, not to give an explanation on the essence or nature of criminality, but uniquely because it is necessary to give a name to one's own thought, I believe that the most precise and positive concept, on the biological side, is still that of a 'criminal neurosis,' distinct from any other pathological, atavistic, degenerative or other form." (See *Nuovi orizzonti*, 3rd ed., chapter "Il tipo criminale e la natura della delinquenza.")

54 Legrand du Saulle, *Le délire des persécutions* (Paris: Délahaye, 1873), chapter VI, 217 and ff.

two poor wretches: one dominates the other, who becomes nothing else but the echo of the first and does what the first does.[55]

We are actually, even here, in the presence of an *incubus* and a *succubus*, of an individual who influences another individual, precisely as in the case of the amorous couple.

One could truly argue that in the insane couple the bond between the *incubus* and the *succubus* is, above all formal, since it does not create an actual alliance, but only a simple relation of resemblance. Of the two madmen, one could say, one is the mirror and the other is the reflection, but nothing more: between the two there is no intimate agreement or intent from which the association originates.

But is this argument correct? Legrand du Saulle[56] and Dagron refer to a case in which the *madness à deux* does not solely represent a parallel coexistence of two similar delusions, but it establishes a real alliance that has a clear and determined scope.

> A girl, taken by delusions of persecution, accuses her father of having put her to sleep and of introducing a man (the sub-prefect of the city) into her room so that he could violate her. After some time, her sister convinced herself that she had endured the same fate: she also accused the father in the same terms. The two girls wanted to avenge themselves and they planned to lure the sub-prefect into a house and kill him. One of them wrote to him on behalf of the other; they armed themselves with handguns and prepared to go through with it. Fortunately, the designated victim thwarted the danger.[58]

> A woman was convinced that everyone was spying on her every time she left her house; she could not encounter anyone without regarding them as an enemy. Some months later, her daughter, who always accompanied her and at first attempted to dissuade her from this imaginary danger, was caught by the same delusion of persecution, which augmented to such a point that

55 On the *madness à deux*, see an article by Doctor Ball (in *Encéphale*, 1886); Lasègue and Falret ("De la folie à deux," in *Annales méd. psich.*, 1877); Régis (*La folie à deux ou folie simultanée*, Paris, 1880); Venturi ("L'allucinazione a due e la pazzia a due," in *Manicomio*, 1886, no. 1); Seppilli ("La pazzia indotta," in *Rivista speriment. di freniatria*, 1890, vols. I–II); Tebaldi (*Ragione e pazzia*, Milan, 1884); and Manaceine (*Le surmenage mental dans la civilisation moderne*, Paris, 1890, translated from Russian by E. Joubert).

56 Op. cit.

57 Dagron, *Archives cliniques des maladiès mentales et nerveuses* (1861). [Jules Dagron (1814–1884) was a French psychiatrist, the first director of the Prémontré asylum. For him mental alienation had moral causes, which the physician had to identify and control through a personalized relationship with the patient.]

58 Legrand du Saulle, op. cit., 243.

> it drove both to suicide. Together they prepared all that was necessary for the gruesome plan: the mother ordered her daughter to go and buy coal; they locked themselves in a room and plugged the cracks in the door and windows; they lay down together on the bed and waited for death.[59]

These two cases—and many others that are noteworthy—are, I hope, enough to convince us that in the insane couple, as in the healthy couple and the suicidal couple, the relationship between the two individuals is not one of purely exterior resemblance, but consists of an intimate and real associative bond.

The phenomenon of one's suggestion over the other always manifests identical characteristics—although with different degrees of intensity—in all three of the forms we have studied. In the healthy couple, the suicidal couple, and the insane couple, we have always found, clearly distinguished, the two types of *incubus* and *succubus*, and the same psychological relationships persist between the two.

To demonstrate the universality of the *form à deux* of suggestion, now we must examine whether it occurs among criminals as well.

This is what we will do in the following chapters.

## Chapter 2: "The Criminal Couple"

Up until now we have attempted a psychological analysis of the *form à deux* of suggestion without first discussing the events, or discussing very few, that intend to prove these ideas. We did this for two rather simple reasons: first, because the events that would have confirmed our observations have already been observed and reported by others before us and thus must already be known; second, because our objective, as we have already said, is not to study the healthy couple, the suicidal couple, or the insane couple. These were discussed briefly so as to provide an analogy to what will be the principal, or better, the only objective of our work: the criminal couple.

Now that we are discussing the criminal couple, our methodology will be first to highlight the facts and events, thereby leaving observations and reflections until the end.

59 Ibid., 251.

Many authors have already spoken in passing, incidentally, about the demoralizing influence that a criminal can have over another; no one thought to make it the objective of a specific study.[60] The subject is thus new and unexplored, which renders it an interesting topic of research. It is all the more interesting insofar as research in criminal psychology has not progressed as much as we would have hoped in recent years. Not much else has been done after Enrico Ferri's masterful classification of criminals.[61] The five categories that he proposes represent the fundamental divisions that can be traced in the criminal world, but much diversity exists among the same criminals in each of these categories! "I try to place our convicts in different categories;"—writes Dostoevsky—"is this possible? The reality is so infinitely varied that it escapes the most ingenious deductions of abstract thinking: it cannot be subjected to clear and precise classifications."[62]

Now, it is precisely a patient, minute, and exact study of this *infinitely diverse* reality that has to be undertaken, not so much to draw clear and precise classifications, which would be wrong like all absolute affirmations, but only to appreciate the criminal's strange psychology in a way

60 Only Aubry, in his already cited work *La contagion du meurtre* (135), hinted to a form of *crime à deux*: abortion actually, committed by the pregnant woman and by a midwife or doctor, maintaining that in this case the woman is almost always under the suggestion of her accomplice. In no other author have I found a word that refers to the existence of the criminal couple.

61 I speak especially for Italy, and naturally I would not express this disheartening opinion if Enrico Ferri had published at least the first volume of his *L'omicidio*, which is a complete, exhaustive, psychological study of criminal homicide. [Ferri had begun this monumental work—which he considered the first study of a specific kind of murder with the methods of criminal anthropology—back in 1882 but, after numerous interruptions, he managed to publish it only in 1895.] In France criminal psychology can rely on many precious volumes; and it is a curious phenomenon that there the *criminal man* is studied above all by someone who is foreign to penal sciences, and by the adversaries of the positivist school, by those indeed who, believing in free will, should not believe at the same time in the existence of the anthropological criminal type. Furthermore, since it is in the character of the French to be analytical, and in the character of Italians to be concise, it is not surprising to find thinkers among us who, like Lombroso, continually launch new ideas with the prodigality of great gentlemen, without evaluating them first through a minute examination of facts, while in France, instead, there are writers who collect these ideas in order to support or combat them with a series of experimental observations.

62 T. Dostoevsky, *Souvenirs de la maisons des morts*, 4th ed. (Paris), 303 [in French in Sighele's text].

that is less vague than the definition of a criminal as insane, instinctive, habitual, occasional, or passionate.[63]

I hope this work will serve such a scope, at least in a small way.

The facts that we have collected to prove the existence of the criminal couple are many and are diverse among themselves in many respects: for the quality of the crimes, the people who commit them, their motives, and the means of execution.

It is, therefore, necessary to divide couples into various groups and to study each of them individually. Afterwards we can perhaps bring them together in a unique synthesis.

The first group we intend to analyse is the one formed by a woman and her lover planning to kill a husband or a rival.

In these homicides, the suggestion of love plays a big role; and it is from these types of murders that I have decided to begin, precisely because it offers an easy and evident transition from the study of the healthy couple and the suicidal couple to that of the criminal couple.

In the previous chapter we saw how a lover can drive the other to suicide; here we will see how a lover is able to push the other to crime.

## *I The Murderous Lovers*

1—Mrs Aveline, 35 years old, wife to a much older man, fell in love with Garnier, a handsome 24-year-old soldier. Not satisfied with adultery, which her unaware husband did not even suspect, she was jealous of her young lover whom she wanted to have all to herself forever. Her dream was to marry him when she became a widow. A widow! This idea, as soon as it materialized, never left her head. She at first spoke shyly to her lover, without daring to completely clarify her plan; then, gradually, her audacity increased and her determination took shape. One day the great word was uttered: Mr Aveline was an obstacle, Mr Aveline had to disappear.

Garnier, dominated by this ardent, seductive, and voluptuous woman, was timid and afraid at the thought of the crime; he meekly took part in the sinister plan. Although promising to help her, he tried to delay. When she said to him: "Kill him, then, kill him immediately!" he responded:

63 [Here Sighele clearly lists Lombroso's categories while attempting to transcend them.]

"Why? I am still in the army until next winter; let's wait … I couldn't marry you now anyway."[64] And he asserted that the poor Mr Aveline would not be killed until January 1885.

But the woman was in a hurry. "I will not have the courage, she writes, to wait until next year. I need you all to myself. Let's move faster, I beg you!"

Garnier resisted, however.[65] So she decided to try the crime alone. Her husband often hunted. She thought of putting dynamite in the cartridges of his rifle, so that at the first shot he would explode. If this attempt did not work, she would poison him; if she did not manage to poison him, Garnier would kill him.

During July and August, Mrs Aveline asked Garnier for dynamite, but he always responded that he could not obtain it; perhaps he did not want to. "Tuesday is the anniversary of the first month of our love, I am sending you a flower as a souvenir, I will try everything I can to be all yours. Oh! How much I'd like to be free! Is it so difficult to have *the thing*?"

*The thing* was the dynamite. But, tired of constant refusals, Mrs Aveline, instead, tried poison. The same night when she had put a small dose of poison in her husband's soup, she wrote to Garnier: "I am about to attack the enemy, but I don't know whether I'll be victorious. If I succeed, I will send a letter to tell you. If I fail, you know *what it means*."[66]

Mrs Aveline did not succeed, as she had feared, and Garnier understood *what that meant*. It was on him to try now.

Armed with a rifle, he was led by his lover to a path where her husband would pass when returning from the hunt. There he waited; as soon as he saw the husband coming, recognizing that it was, indeed, Mr Aveline, he pointed the rifle but then suddenly he lacked courage, dropped it, and fled.[67]

His lover found him some days later, and she incited him once again to commit the crime; he finally agreed, after she intoxicated him with a night of love.

One night, at the Avelines' home, a loud detonation was heard. The steward ran outside and, a few steps away, found Aveline's body in a pool of blood.

64 Note Garnier's passive but continuous resistance to the suggestions of his lover.

65 See the previous note.

66 [All exchanges between Garnier and Aveline are in French in Sighele's text.]

67 This is precisely an example of the physical repugnance that an organism experiences when committing a crime.

> Garnier spontaneously confessed everything, exhibiting sincere regret. In prison he attempted suicide;[68] he opened his veins with scissors; the rhythmic din of his blood dripping drop by drop onto the pavement woke up an inmate. He was cured and healed.

Physically "he had the appearance of a young bull, from the enormous neck to the stupid eye." Morally he was weak: "his lover, an energetic and resolute woman who responded to the audience with cold imperturbable blood, did to him what she had wanted."[69]

2—In the following event—more terrible than the previous—it was not the woman, but the man who instigated the lover to kill the rival. Love mixed with infamous motives and the means to implement the crime are strangely ferocious.

---

68 Suicide, in this case, is a new sign of sincere regret: it is almost the penalty that the culprit feels the need to inflict on himself.

69 The reader will have noted that Aveline and Garnier perfectly correspond to the two types of *incubus* and *succubus:* she, a born criminal, he, prone to suggestion. The crime, wanted by the woman, is materially carried out by Garnier, which confirms the observation made above, regarding the double suicide, on the division of functions in the suicidal and the criminal couple.

I said that Aveline was a born criminal. She wrote erotic letters to Garnier, lavishing the most obscene expressions, entering into cynical details that demonstrate the insatiable needs of her temperament. Her correspondence with her lover illuminates many sides of criminal psychology. One day she wrote to Garnier: "He [her husband] was sick yesterday; I thought God was beginning his work." Another day: "This week I went to Nôtre-Dame-des-Victoires, and I lit a candle for the realization of our projects." Obscenity united with religious sentiment: God invoked as an accomplice to a misdeed. Even Pompilia Zambeccari "had vowed to bring a chalice of gold to Our Lady of Loreto if she succeeded in poisoning her husband." (See Toselli, *Racconti estratti dall'Archivio bolognese,* Bologna, 1868, vol. II, 181, cited by Ferri, *Il sentimento religioso negli omicidi.*) And in the pamphlet *Un paese di criminali-nati,* I cited the analogous case of a woman who had made a vow to carry out a homicide.—Aveline, together with religiosity, had poetic and sentimental ideas, which would appear only in noble, exquisite souls: "I am jealous of the nature that seems to enrage us with its beauty. Don't you think, my dear, that this beautiful weather is made for lovers and talks about love?" And elsewhere: "How much I would like to be at the end of the *business* (the murder of her husband!) that will make us free and happy! I need to get there, heaven is at the end. Down the road there are roses ..." (V.A. Bataille, *Causes criminelles et mondaines de 1884,* 314 and ff.).

Sougaret—a murderer from the small village of Ascain (in the low Pyrenees)—revealed one day to his lover Marie Noblia how he had killed his mortal enemy, Jolimon. The authorities thought it had been a suicide and Sougaret was never suspected. After some time, Sougaret got tired of Marie and threw her out of the house, substituting her with one of her relatives, Françoise Elissalde. Marie was quite distressed and offended; she threatened to reveal the former lover's fatal secret if he did not abandon Françoise and take her back.

Sougaret was so weak that he confessed his crime to the second concubine;[70] he feared that if he threw Françoise out, then she would reveal his secret. So he conceived a monstrous plan to keep one of the two women, while stopping the other from ever talking, that is, by killing her.

He sacrificed Françoise. But in order to secure Marie's silence, he wanted her to take part in the crime. Over the course of a week, he stirred the jealousy of this energetic and impassioned Basque girl, and instigated her to take revenge on the one who took her place. After making all of her resentments, jealousies, and hate resonate in her soul, he bought her a rope, taught her how to tie a noose, and said to her: "We will see if you have the heart! You can strangle Françoise tomorrow ... come to my house and I'll open the door for you." For a month Marie resisted the suggestion, but Sougaret was constantly tormenting her, telling her that she did not have any courage, and that she did not love him anymore because she did not want to do what was necessary for them to return to their old life.

Finally, Marie surrendered and went to Sougaret's house. Françoise was standing with her back turned; Marie threw herself on her rival, and, before she could move, Marie put the noose around Françoise's neck and pulled the rope hard ...

After the crime, Sougaret said, referring to the victim's corpse: "Let's go and bury it tonight, for now let's hide it here somewhere. Let's go! Get her feet!" Marie wanted to obey, but she could not. A nervous tremor seized her; some sort of anxiety choked her throat. Seeing the inert body made the horror of her crime appear all at once and, as if an invincible force

70 This improvidence is common in homicides, and it constitutes rather one of their characteristics (see Ferri, *L'omicidio*, part I).—Gamahut, who escaped from Paris after the crime, said to a labourer whom he met: "In Paris they searched for the murderer of Madame Ballerich: and so, you have him before you."—Prado, the night that he killed Marie Agaëtan [Aguétant], re-entered the house of his lover Eugénie Forestier, and, when she noticed a scratch on his hand, he replied: "It's nothing, I just butchered a woman." [See also *The New Woman*, 270 and 270n8, this volume.]

had pushed her, she fell to her knees onto the body.[71] When she got up she was like a madwoman; she fled through the streets of the village shouting savagely and, upon her arrest, she confessed to the horrible crime.[72]

3—The Fenayrou trial—celebrated in the criminal annals of contemporary France—offers us a third example of murder committed by a man and a woman, one of whom was influenced by the other.

Actually, here the victim is not the husband, as in the Aveline trial, nor is it the case of two lovers who kill a rival, as in the Sougaret trial; rather it is a husband who forces his wife to help him kill her lover.

With Garnier and Marie Noblia we saw two types of individuals who, lacking a strong moral sense, after a more or less long time surrendered to the pressure of whoever had instilled in them the mirage of a calm and happy life, or had arisen in them the demon of jealousy.

With Gabrielle Fenayrou we will find a nature equally lacking—even totally devoid of—moral sense, who surrendered to her husband for an obscure complex of emotions: a bit of terror, a bit of remorse, a bit of mysticism, and above all a hatred for the lover who had abandoned her, a hatred that is nothing else but a transformation of ancient love.

"... She had that vague sentimentalism of characters without energy, who would like to open up but do not dare, who would like to say no, and who find no other strength than that of tears."[73] "A witness, who"

71 This reaction after the crime is something more than simple remorse, because it is not only moral, but physical: she represents, if I can say so, the *posthumous regret* of the organism, and demonstrates that the crime intimately disgusted he who committed it because of suggestion. Even in hypnotic suggestion, the hypnotized, after having committed an imaginary crime, presents the identical phenomenon. See Gilles de la Tourette, *L'hypnotisme et les états analogues* (Paris, 1887); Pitres, *Les suggestions hypnotiques* (Bordeaux, 1884).

72 See, for all the details, Bataille, op. cit. (1881), 312 and ff.

73 [In French in Sighele's text.]

74 Bernheim, *De la suggestion et de ses applications à la thérapeutique* (Paris: Doin, 1886), 191. [Quotations are in French in Sighele's text.]

75 [In French in Sighele's text.]

—writes Bernheim[74]—“was derided at the hearing because he was not understood, said of her: ‘*She was soft dough, leaning towards vice as much as towards virtue.*’”[75] Translated into psychological language—Bernheim adds—this means: she was prone to suggestion, all the more so insofar as the moral sense did not counterbalance this excessive tendency to suggestion.

Forcibly married to Marin Fenayrou, a pharmacist she did not love, Gabrielle proved to be an obedient and docile wife during the first years of marriage, although she was rather cold. She dreamed of a more elevated position, of a man less uncouth and vulgar than her own husband. He, easily distracted away from home, was a heavy gambler and drinker, and began to neglect her after some time.

He had hired a youth named Aubert to help manage his store. Gabrielle was always in the store with him while her husband was off enjoying himself. The ground was favourable for the lovers’ triumph. The fall became fatal during one of those days that culminated with a *tête-à-tête* between the two youths. And Gabrielle fell.

(…) The years went by; Aubert got tired of his friend; he left the Fenayrou pharmacy and opened his own, which prospered while Fenayrou’s was slowly falling apart because of his neglect.

One day he found out that Aubert had taken a wife and, at the same time, came to discover that Aubert had also been Gabrielle’s lover. Perhaps he also knew his misfortune before—or at least suspected it—; but now that Aubert was competing with the Fenayrou pharmacy, he began to harbour a desire for revenge. Thus, in order to satisfy it, he tried to ingratiate himself to Gabrielle. He persuaded her that Aubert was the cause of their misfortune, that it was necessary to kill him, and the crime would be the price of her rehabilitation as an adulterous woman. If she did not consent to sacrifice Aubert, Fenayrou would kill her and the children.

Marin Fenayrou was a brutal and authoritative man who seriously commanded fear. Gabrielle felt like a slave in his hands: “She was”—a witness said—“her husband’s *object.*” And, for some strange psychological perversion to which her mysticism contributed a great deal, she was able to find her adultery more unforgivable than the crime for which she was to be the instrument. Rather, the latter would be the just punishment for the former.

Under Fenayrou’s dictation, she wrote a love letter to Aubert in which she reproached him for his coldness and invited him for a tryst at an isolated villa not far from Paris.

Aubert refused.

So Fenayrou forced Gabrielle to write a second letter to her lover, even more tender than the first.

Another refusal.

By the third letter Aubert finally accepted.[76]

Gabrielle, on the given evening, departed with Aubert for Chatou. Fenayrou had arrived with his brother Lucien not long before the two lovers.[77]

Once at Chatou, Gabrielle made Aubert enter the house her husband had rented. Upon reaching the vestibule where Fenayrou was hiding, he hurled himself at Aubert and killed him with a hammer. They stripped the body, brought him to the Seine River and threw him in. Then the accomplices returned to Paris.

After the crime Gabrielle felt no remorse, no regret; she was cold and cynically serene. She is thus—one will say—a born criminal, and there was no need for her husband's suggestion to coerce her into committing the murder. Certainly, she was a born criminal, because she had had from birth—as Brouardel would say—a *moral blindness*, but, I believe, whoever maintains that in another environment, among other people, and with other ideas, she would have in any case committed a crime, would be wrong. Hers is a passive, latent perversity, which can remain such for an entire lifetime, if the conditions are favourable; but it can reveal itself if the occasion allows. "The man without moral sense," writes Despine—"and whose perversity is not active, may never commit criminal acts if his perversity is not awakened by any exciting cause of some

76 One could say that the first chapter of Zola's *La Bête humaine* is taken from the Fenayrou trial. It also deals with a husband who forces his wife to write to her former lover in order to kill him at a rendezvous.

77 This Lucien Fenayrou did not participate in the material execution of the crime: he helped only to transport the body of Aubert and to throw it in the river. He is a secondary and insignificant figure that the brother brought along in case of need. On this issue, I note a particular that reveals the congenital perversity and moral insensibility of Marin Fenayrou. The day of the crime, he went to the station of Saint-Lazare with his wife and brother. Gabrielle was supposed to wait for Aubert and to depart with him for Chatou with the 8:30 train. Marin and Lucien departed an hour earlier, on the 7:25 train. Marin, however, wanted to buy the tickets for everyone: he purchased three round-trip tickets (for himself, his wife and his brother), giving one to Gabrielle, together with a simple *one-way* ticket for the unfortunate Aubert, who did not have to return.

importance, and this undoubtedly happens to a certain number of people devoid of this superior feeling."[78]

Gabrielle Fenayrou was among these people; she did not possess an organic repulsion for crime, but she did not have the need until it nudged her. She resembled those hysterical women who, when placed in a convent, become fervently religious, and, when put in a brothel, become the most obscene of prostitutes,[79]–like reeds that bend to the side where the wind pushes them; blank slates—so to speak—on which the environment writes what it wants. Indeed, these traits are particularly dangerous and easy prey for the first villain who wants to utilize them. Gabrielle surrendered to Aubert and became his lover not out of passion, but out of innate weakness; she surrendered to her husband for the same reason.[80]

She truly represents, in the tragedy of Chatou, the hand that performs while the thought commands.[81]

4—The couple of Josephine P. and her steward Guillet—who both murdered Josephine's husband—is in many ways psychologically similar to the Fenayrou case.

Despine describes the origin and cause of the crime in this way: "Josephine P., 17 years old, fatherless, was seduced by an older man, whom she then married. But the life that followed the marriage was unhappy; the husband was always living the good life while the wife stayed at home alone. This young woman, deceived by her illusions, without guidance or support, gave in to the pernicious influence of boredom, to the stimuli of a romantic imagination and a fantasizing temperament. A daughter was born; the husband refused to acknowledge his paternity.

78 Despine, *Psychologie naturelle* (Paris: F. Savy, 1868), vol. II, 259 [in French in Sighele's text].

79 Laurent, "Les suggestions criminelles," in *Archives* of Lyon (15 Nov. 1890).

80 And she conceded then to Macé, head of public security, confessing the crime in detail to him, while heading to Chatou from Paris on the train. Gabrielle Fenayrou greatly resembles Gabrielle Bompard, another *moral blind* who "does good or bad depending on who leads her." Also, Bompard conceded before Eyraud, murdering Gouffé together with him; she conceded then to her new lover Garanger, confessing her crime in part to him; she conceded in the end to the judge, completely telling him how the crime was carried out.—See, on the topic of the Gouffé trial, the psychiatric appraisal of Bompard by Brouardel, Motet, and Ballet (in *Archives* of Lyon, 1891). The illustrious professors, together with Charcot, deny that Bompard could be susceptible to Eyraud's suggestion: but they speak of hypnotic suggestion, and we speak of suggestion in the waking state, and of the weakest form of this suggestion.

81 For the particulars of this trial, other than Bernheim already cited, see Macé, *Mon Musée criminel* (Paris: Charpentier, 1890); Bérard des Glajeux, *Souvenirs d'un Président d'Assises* (Paris: Plon, 1892), chapter V; and Bataille, op. cit., 1882.

Tired of, and disgusted by each other, the spouses separated. The wife lived alone and gradually began to indulge in a licentious lifestyle without moral restraint, but her husband forced her to live on a monthly pension of 30 francs. She had been rich and renowned for her luxury and elegance. Misery and hunger ensued. These extremely poor living conditions explained in part the disordered lifestyle that Josephine led from then on.

> The steward Guillet was her lover; he was an avid peasant with ferocious instincts. Dominated by this man, in her will she left him a sum of 50,000 francs. Guillet wanted to enjoy this money as soon as possible, and he hoped to marry Josephine as soon as she was widowed. The idea to murder her husband had germinated and settled in his soul; there was nothing left to do but make her accept. Because of his power over her, his perfidious and repeated insistences, and to her dereliction, he succeeded in convincing her. Together they plotted to lure the husband to them and then kill him.[82]

During the trial, Josephine confessed, regretting her involvement: "God will forgive me"—she said—"because I was too unhappy! I had no resources, I was alone and without bread. Whenever I asked my relatives for help, they wouldn't give me anything. This is how this man (hinting at Guillet) made me lose myself. The origin of all my misdeeds, the cause of the crime, is him—you are the guilty one, the monster of crime!"

Despine noted that Josephine was sincere when she uttered those words. She belonged in the group of those with a weak moral sense; the environment in which they live moulds them. Guillet, instead, is the true example of a born criminal.[83]

5—I said that the Josephine P. and Guillet couple resembled the Fenayrou couple, and that—as one will come to understand—the individual characteristics of the protagonists are analogous (although Mrs Fenayrou was much more perverse than Josephine P.), though not for the murder they committed, as it was done to the husband rather than the lover, which actually reflects Mrs Aveline and Garnier's crime.

Now we will see in the Quérangal trial an almost identical reproduction of the Aveline trial in terms of its execution, the type of victim, and the psychological implications.

82 Despine, *Psychologie naturelle*, vol. II, 220.
83 Despine, op. and loc. cit.

In the tiny village of Saint-Hervé lived the Simon couple. The wife, 35 years old, was a Messalina: her lovers were uncountable. The husband was a suffering, weak being; she hated him and hurried his death not only with desire, but also by encouraging with all possible means the vice he had, namely, drinking. She would force him, morning and night, to drink a sort of drug she prepared, which was composed of eau de vie, juniper, and some other unknown, strong, unhealthy liquors.

Of all the lovers that Mrs Simon had had, there was not one she had not asked for help to get rid of her husband. A witness recalled how she had promised him—for the crime—five francs! And marriage right after. It seems that this second promise did not matter as much as the first, because the witness responded: "I do not want reheated soup!"

Aimée Quérangal—the last of her lovers—received, like all of his predecessors, Simon's proposal; but unfortunately, rather than refusing her, he accepted. He was hereditarily predisposed to crime. His father had had the wife of the executioner of Saint-Brieux as his lover; his mother, a dissolute woman, had been condemned for public outrage and various thefts committed with her daughter. Another sister of Aimée Quérangal's had been accused of killing her husband. A family of criminals—as you see—or, better, of lunatics, as some details of the trial justify the latter assumption more than the former. Aimée Quérangal himself had always appeared honest, but he was weak and unbalanced. Given those precedents and accounting for the fact that he was twenty years old and idolized a woman of thirty-five, who was his first love, it is easy to understand how Mrs Simon managed to persuade the young man to be the instigator of her crime, and it is thus useless to dwell any further on it.

We will only say that Quérangal did not succeed the first time he tried to kill Mr Simon; it was the second time that, having perhaps become more skillful and courageous, he was able to strangle him.[84]

6—To complete this review of cases in which a lover becomes the instrument in the execution of a crime for the other, we believe it is also necessary to mention the trial of the widow Gras.

The widow Gras, whose nom de guerre was the Baroness Eugénie de Breville de Lacour [Delacour], was a gallant woman by then in elderly decline[85] who wanted to marry her last *beloved lover*, a poor worker named

84 See Bataille, op. cit., 1882.

85 Like Aveline, she also combined religious sentiment with *débauche*, which, in any case, is typical of many prostitutes. "The faldstool of the widow Fras"—Joly recounts,—"contained rosaries and hymnals, mixed with salacious books and a stock of cantharis." See *Le crime*, 271. [The widow Gras's full name is Eugénie Amenalde Brécourt, veuve Gras dite Delacour.]

Gaudry. However because of her financial situation she could not afford this luxury. What did she do then? She convinced a young, rich boy of ailing health, de la Roche, to marry her; then, by means of a contract, she planned to gain control of his fortune and once they were married, it would be all too easy to make her husband's health decline. But to convince this rich, young man to marry her, despite the difference in age and position, Gras deemed it necessary to render him ugly enough so that he would think no other woman would want to marry him. Vitriol was the weapon in this attempt, and the accomplice would be the worker she wanted to marry … "My little man," Gras said one day to Gaudry, "I have to make a large fortune for us to get married. Here's how: I know a twenty-four-year-old fool who is called Viscount René de la Roche. We will disfigure him. When he is so ugly that no woman will want him, I'll marry him. He is fragile and will die quickly. Then …"[86] Gaudry, was flattered by the love of this beautiful woman, and, attracted by the idea of marriage, he agreed.

One night the Viscount de la Roche stopped at Gras's home to take her to a ball. Eugénie de Lacour made him wait in the living room while she went to get dressed in her bedroom. Gaudry was hiding in an adjacent closet and she gave him a bottle of sulphuric acid.

While she was getting dressed, Gras was going back and forth between the two men, lavishing words of love to the one and giving words of encouragement to the other.

At midnight, smiling, wearing a pink cape, with flowers in her hair, Eugénie raised the cover that was concealing the closet where Gaudry was hiding and threw an imperious look at him, full of promises. Then she walked into the living room and took de la Roche's arm.

… At 3 in the morning, when they returned from the ball, while de la Roche, after letting Gras in first, was about to enter the house, he suddenly felt a skin-burning liquid thrown onto his face …[87]

***

So far we wanted to describe couples of murderous lovers rather minutely, because it seemed necessary for us to bring to light the psychology of these crimes as much as possible, to underline the diversity of character of the two associated individuals, and to follow the more or less slow path of criminal suggestion.

86 [In French in Sighele's text.]
87 Aubry, op. cit., 115.

Now that we have offered at least some elements that can help readers draw conclusions by themselves, we will limit ourselves to succinct summaries of the other collected episodes.

7—In Belgium, a woman wanted her lover to murder her husband. When it was time to act, the lover hesitated in front of the victim. She yelled: "Such an opportunity, and not be able grab it, what nonsense!" And she took him to dinner, she got him drunk and coerced him, under the influence of alcohol, into committing the crime. In front of her husband's bed, she held a lantern in one hand and a hammer in the other, which she gave to the murderer. Having accomplished the misdeed, she dragged her lover to her bed.[88]

8—At Groslay near Montmorency, a woman, a certain X …, had adulterous relationships with B. Her husband scolded her, which aroused in her desire to kill him. While she was lying next to her husband, B. hid in an adjacent room. At midnight he went into the bedroom of his lover. B. placed a rope around the husband's neck and the woman cried: "Come on, pull, you made it!"[89]

9—Mrs Ballanger, a woman of very liberal morals, made Mauclair, the one man who courted her without success, understand that her husband must be killed and that she would give herself to him, *when he had done his job.*[90]

10—Anne Beausoleil, two months after her marriage, made a young boy kill her husband, and promised herself to him as soon as the crime was committed. The husband, very sick with consumption, had bequeathed all of his fortune to her.[91]

11—In February 1889, Chevalier and his lover Martine appeared before the Criminal Court at Caen because he had coerced her into killing her husband. Martine had been for a long time separated from her husband, who did not even live in the same town any longer, hence she had to describe him to her lover, who did not know what he looked like. Chevalier departed, found the man, and asked him if he really was Martine's husband. Upon his affirmative response he shot him with a handgun.

88 Darras, *Causes célèbres de la Belgique*, 216.
89 Aubry, "De l'homicide commis par la femme," in *Archives* of Lyon (1891), no. 34.
90 Criminal Court of Tours, March 1888 (see Aubry, op. cit.).
91 Criminal Court of Dordogne, Oct. 1888 (see Aubry, op. cit.).

12—In May of 1890, the Criminal Court at Le Puy condemned Cédot and Mrs Queyran—the former for having killed the husband of the latter, and the latter for having instigated the murder.

13—In April of 1888, the Criminal Court at Caen condemned a Mr Corbet, who was coerced by his lover Sorel into murdering her own husband.[92]

14—Françoise Rodet was romantically involved with a Mr Froment, a violent and brutal man who forced her to get rid of her husband. One day, after making Mr Rodet morally and tangibly suffer every sort of humiliation, she killed him because of Froment's insistent pressure.[93]

15—Jeanne Dubernet flattered her lover so much that he, who was barely 20 years old, unable to resist his married lover, was coerced into killing her husband.[94]

16—A certain L., whose lover wanted to force her to kill her husband, accepted a bottle of sulphuric acid from him, promising she would make her husband drink it. After having poured it into a glass of wine, her courage failed her, and let the glass drop, subsequently confessing everything.[95]

In this last case, criminal suggestion was able to pervert an honest soul to the point that she attempted a crime, but did not manage to make her commit it. The woman's innate moral sense won at the decisive moment, and she rebelled.

What difference between this wife and Gabrielle Fenayrou, who succumbed easily and who afterwards had no remorse! What difference also between this wife and the others who were swayed by suggestion, and, after a more or less long resistance, yielded to the will of their suggestionizers![96]

---

92 For the last three paragraphs, see Aubry, op. cit.

93 Despine, *Psych. natur.*, vol. II, 350.

94 *Repertorio di cause celebri*, vol. IV, 281.

95 Ferri, *L'omicidio*, part I.

96 A magnificent example of murderous lovers (which has come to our knowledge too late in all its minute particulars to be able to be inserted with the others in the text) is offered to us by the trial of the poisoner of Aïn-Fezza, Madame Weiss (Jeanne Daniloff), who under the suggestion of her lover, the engineer Roques, tried to poison her husband. Tarde spoke about this famous trial months ago (see "Les affaires Weiss et Achet," in *Archives* of Lyon), but he did not focus on the respective parts taken in the crime by the two culprits. The most recent publication of some epistolary exchanges between Jeanne Daniloff and Roques, and, above all, some autobiographical pages written in prison by Weiss, show us who was the true character of this crime. Jeanne Daniloff, according to Doctor Lacronique's evaluation, "*is deranged: her nervous system is very impressionable and excitable; she can easily be put in a hypnotic trance, but her*

And yet, except for the degree of intensity, how identical the phenomenon of suggestion is in all the observed cases! In these murderous, amorous couples, the protagonists always resemble, respectively, the two types of the *incubus* and *succubus*, which we found in the healthy couple, the suicidal couple, and the insane couple. One plays the Mephistophelian role of the provocateur, who educates to evil, and drives to crime. The other is gradually won over by evil genius. Almost like a thread binding these two existences and enslaving one to the other, it is a sentiment of love, never pure, almost always guilty, and often monstrous or shameful.

---

*mental state is intact; she acts with full knowledge*" [in French in Sighele's text, original emphasis].—We do not have data on engineer Roques's personality because he killed himself the day of his arrest; however, the fact that he was the instigator of the crime emerges from Weiss's writings, which cannot but be sincere, since this woman never attempted to apologize and committed suicide the very day of her condemnation, unable to survive her remorse and sorrow.— "I obeyed"—she wrote—"the orders of the man I loved; those imperative orders are still reiterated in the letters that have arrived since my arrest. For an entire year I have fought against the force that controlled me. Did I not have at hand that terrible cyanide? And who can know how many times, after swearing this would be the end, I put down the bottle I had grabbed with a hand determined to obey? No matter how much I fought, I did not belong to myself anymore. Mr Roques had generated in me a woman I ignored, a violently passionate woman, passively subdued; he had shaken not only my existence, but also my entire intimate being. And it is indeed his harmful influence that has shattered my life, taking me away from all whom I loved ... Sometimes Roques wanted to act alone! But if I had no fear for myself, I feared for him. I did not want him to expose himself, and I preferred one thousand times to brave the dangers of action and the consequences of crime by myself. And because *I had to*, because one last time my master gave me an ultimate deadline, at the end of October I abruptly made up my mind, I closed my mind and heart, I plugged my eyes and ears, and I obeyed. But what an awakening! Oh! If I have tried to kill myself, it is not to elude public vengeance, but rather to end this life that now offers itself to my eyes. Alas! Death has not come; but for weeks I have endured sufferings of unimaginable intensity ...." [in French in Sighele's text, original emphasis].—Roques's last letter to Weiss said: "Will this letter be the last I will write you in Algeria? I hope so with all my heart. *It will always bring you the same order*" [in French in Sighele's text, original emphasis]. And Weiss answered: "Oh! Félix, love me, because the atrocity of my deed is becoming apparent to me; I want to shut my heart, my mind, my eyes, I want to erase the memory of what it has done for me, because I adore you! I feel such a flow of absolute intimacy between you and me that words seem useless between us; the thoughts of one will be read by the other as in an open book; to stop this flow would be like stopping my life, and even without this moral need for you, my body cannot live without your body. *I may have horror of myself later, but it is impossible for me to desist.* Console me, support me, let me overcome the inevitable crisis of discouragement, embrace me with your yoke. Inebriate me with your caresses. That is your only strength ...." [in French in Sighele's text, original emphasis].

One could perhaps summarize the psychological characteristics of the previous examples and draw consequences. But we must examine other cases of criminal couples, and only after this examination can we come to a conclusion.[97]

## "Addendum to Chapter 2"

It is evident—and it would be almost futile to observe—that criminal suggestion from one lover to another happens not only in the murders of husbands or rivals, but also in the crimes that have their principal cause in jealousy, revenge, or any other feeling that derives from passionate love.

Two lovers very often are brought together for more foul and antisocial motives (e.g., greed). We did not speak about these other crimes because they do not matter directly to our objective. We want, however, to touch briefly on them in this addendum, citing three examples that appear similar to the psychological characteristics of the criminal couple.

I—A certain Lavoitte advised Albert, her lover, to kill an old woman, her neighbour, so she could rob her. Albert refused at first to commit the crime. "One kills in war," she exclaimed, "and it is not a sin! God will forgive; he knows that we are poor!" Albert was still hesitant. So she made him drink eau de vie, and she made him change clothes and disguise

97 While I am revising the proofs, I learn from the *Archivio di psichiatria* (vol. XII, V–VI) that Mr Raymond de Rykère has published a monograph entitled *La criminalité féminine* (in the *Belgique judiciaire*), in which he studies, among others, some cases of homicides committed by two lovers on the husband or rival. It is impossible for me to consult de Rykère's work. Therefore, I limit myself to reporting from the review that the *Archivio* made of a case that seems it could fall among those I've already collected: "Louise Fraikin, a woman of liberal habits, got married to an old man who wanted to forget the past, and she soon returned to the arms of promiscuity. She became the lover of one of her husband's employees, a certain Wehent, to whom she offered herself. Although the husband was not too much of an inconvenience, Fraikin wanted to get rid of him, and she gave the task of carrying out the crime to a certain Béniers, who was afraid, however, at the moment of action and refused to do it. Fraikin said to him: "And why will you not do it? You will have 1,500 francs immediately after." She looked for somebody else, but also this one did not have the courage; so the woman taunted him by asking: "To have such a perfect opportunity and to let it get away is beastly!" (Note the strangeness of the phrase, which is identical to one uttered by that Belgian woman whom I cited in the text, n7). "Finally, she found an accomplice and the murder was carried out."

his face to make sure that he would not be recognized and discovered. Indeed, the police did not manage to find the perpetrators of the murder; it was Albert who later confessed his crime.[98]

II—The prostitute Ribos and her lover Maffei planned to murder and rob the cashier of a bank. At first, the woman, who was to carry out the crime, hesitated and threw away the weapon. Maffei encouraged her; he gave her a razor and she sliced the victim's throat. Maffei finished off the moribund cashier with a revolver.[99]

III—Louise Feucher, at the whim of her cousin and lover Bénoît, helped to murder her aunt; she died soon after, torn by remorse and prey to a most profound melancholy.[100]

## Chapter 3: "The Criminal Couple" (Continuation)

### *II The Infanticidal Couple*

The murder of a husband or rival is, if I may say so, the specific crime of the amorous couple. The husband and the rival are intruders, and it is natural (from the criminals' point of view) that they want to make them disappear.

But there is another crime that is a spontaneous, if not necessary consequence, of illicit love. I am speaking about infanticide and abortion.[101]

Very often it is the proof of guilt that must disappear. The baby, coming into life, accuses the mother, so it must be killed.

What can one do then?

In the countryside, where morality is stricter than anywhere else, pregnant girls generally hide their pregnancy for the entire nine long months, and only when they give birth, only when they see in front of them the

98 Note the spontaneous confession, which demonstrates a certain regret.—See Abbé Crozes, *Souvenirs de la petite et de la grande Roquette*, vol. II, 306.

99 Court of Trieste, 1888.—Cited by Aubry, *De l'homicide commis par la femme* (Lyon: Storek, 1891).

100 *Repertorio di cause celebri*, vol. VI, 950.—Cited by Ferri, *L'omicidio*, part I.—Another similar case is cited by Lacassagne, "Du dépéçage criminel," in *Archives de l'anthr. crim.* (1888): 239).

101 I unite these two crimes because, similar from the juridical point of view, they are almost identical from the social point of view: they constitute a killing that takes a different name according to the victim's age. Abortion is, indeed, but a premature infanticide.

witness of their mistake, alive and screaming, in an impulse of legitimate defence[102] that muffles nature's voice, do they sometimes have the sad courage to kill the newborn.

In cities, where immorality is most diffuse and civil egoism has enjoyed the aid of a thousand sources of welfare and prevention, one does not wait until childbirth to get rid of the child. It is obviously more convenient, easier, and less dangerous to extinguish the hope of life at its roots, rather than waiting for life to form before suffocating it.[103] Infanticide, a crime that reveals crude and simple customs, is substituted with abortion, a crime that the legal codes deem milder than infanticide, but that is morally more deplorable, because under the varnish of lesser cruelty it can hide, as often happens, a more refined perversity.

I understand and excuse the mother who, after having suffered all the moral and physical anguishes of a guilty pregnancy, kills the baby when it is finally born, sacrificing it for her own honour. But I do not understand, nor do I excuse a mother who, as soon as she feels the fruit of her love move inside of her, decides to get rid of it. She has not yet suffered at all, or very little. She can hope for a stillborn, but immediately, coldly, thoughtfully, she condemns it to death. The law can say that she did not kill a human being, but rather a fetus, and in this biological diversity finds a reason for a milder punishment. Sentiment, I believe, does not make these subtle distinctions, or, better, it makes them but for the opposite reason.[104]

---

102 Obviously, I am alluding to the legitimate defence of honour. Society demands of the young mother, with a brutal dilemma, either her dishonour or the sacrifice of the child's life. If she kills, it is then, indeed, to save her honour.—See my study on "Infanticidio," in *Archivio giuridico* XLII (Bologna, 1889): 177–209.

103 That infanticide is more frequent in the countryside than in the city was demonstrated by Lambert, Guerry, and others. See Carrara, *Programma*, P.S., par. 1213n. Recently, Socquet conducted a statistical study on French criminality for the years 1851–55 and 1875–80, and found an average of 30 per million inhabitants who committed infanticide in the countryside, and an average of 20 in the city. For Italian statistics, see Balestrini, *Aborto, infanticidio ed esposizione d'infante* (Turin: Bocca, 1888). The Italian statistics for the last four years (1885–88) gives identical results. [We have summarized and interpreted the data from two tables that Sighele transcribed from Socquet and Balestrini.]

104 All this has to be interpreted from a moral point of view. Juridically we believe that abortion must not be punished for the reasons adopted by Balestrini in his already cited work and that here it is useless to reproduce.—We observe on this issue that, as infanticide is substituted in the cities by abortion (a less serious crime than the first,

Nevertheless, while infanticide is in most cases the exclusive work of the mother, and one can only accuse her, abortion is, instead, a crime that is often committed by the mother and other people.

Rarely does a woman want and know how to carry out an abortion without help from accomplices. She perhaps has an idea, a confused idea, which seems like the only way to salvation but which she shuns at first, because she feels and knows it is criminal. As time passes, however, the idea returns with the insistence of an autosuggestion. Then, in the pregnant woman's soul, one of these phenomena occurs, one could call it a compromise with conscience. She decides to go to a midwife or to a doctor only to consult them about her pregnancy, but with the secret desire to have them help her get rid of her unborn child. She does not confess this second objective openly to herself, as it is still indistinct in her mind; if someone were to accuse her, she would indignantly and sincerely reject the accusation.

Sometimes the idea of a crime crosses, like a sinister lamp, even the clear sky of an honest conscience;[105] it vanishes immediately if no personal interest retains it; it can linger there, if the interest exists and if someone knows how to make it germinate.

The midwife or the doctor, with whom the woman consults, senses the psychological condition of this misfortunate woman, but the word "abortion" is not uttered. Sometimes, they pretend to doubt the pregnancy and advise the patient to take a medication, alleging that it will only help the woman resume menstruating ... The next month the internal

---

and one that reveals major foresight), so abortion is being substituted now by the Malthusian system in all its various forms, which for some is certainly not a crime, and represents—if I can say so—the peak of foresight. To kill the newborn baby—to kill it before it is born—to impede its birth—these are the phases of evolution that followed and will follow, I believe, always more frequently, the crime of infanticide.

105 "To every man, although pure and honest," writes Ferri in *Nuovi orizzonti*, "in certain enticing occasions, the fleeting thought of a dishonest or dangerous action presents itself."—And Lombroso recalls, to give an example, the case of the alienated Morel who, as he himself narrates, passing one day by a bridge in Paris and having seen a labourer who was leaning on the railing, felt his brain traversed by the flash of a homicidal idea, and ran away so as not to succumb to the temptation to throw him into the river. And an equally known case is that of Humboldt's wet nurse who, upon seeing and touching the newborn's rosy flesh, was taken by the temptation to kill it, and rushed to leave it to someone else's care, in order to avoid a tragedy.—See "I Criminaloidi," in *Arch. di psich.* X, 121.—However, it is good to add with Ferri that if this deleterious idea attacks the psychic constitution of an individual, it means that this individual is not solidly honest, given what Victor Hugo says: "Before duty, to doubt is to be defeated."

cure has not succeeded; the woman looks for an excuse, thinking that it is the midwife's or the doctor's responsibility. The first visit makes the second easier, and, having already taken, consciously and unconsciously, an abortive substance, she removes the final hindrance to using a more direct and secure method.

"Do we not see"—Aubry says rather well—"a hesitant woman, still retaining some honest feelings, who was persuaded and ruled by a matron, an expert in the art of abortions, who knows, with a skilful and very feminine policy, how to dispel the last scruples of her client and turn her into a criminal?"[106]

Here we have the first type of the infanticidal couple:[107] the pregnant woman and the less scrupulous doctor, or one of those matrons who made a lucrative profession out of their shameful job.[108]

If abortion, together with adultery, were not a crime that remains almost always unpunished and is almost never revealed to judicial authorities, I believe one could prove that in many cases they are committed in the way that I have previously described.[109]

Sometimes, instead of the doctor or midwife, or in addition to them, it is the lover who advises and instigates the woman to have an abortion. Robert Gentien attempted to force Marie Bière to eliminate the fruit of their love. Fouroux, the mayor of Toulon, whose trial last year in France provoked a very serious scandal,[110] instigated and forced his

106 Aubry, *La contagion du meurtre*, 136 [in French in Sighele's text]. This form of the criminal couple—as I have said—is the only one that has been mentioned by writers so far. This is why I am talking about it only briefly.

107 It would be more exact to say *fetus-cide* rather than infanticide. However, we have already explained the reason for combining the two.

108 It is remarkable that the fact of the abortion committed on a woman by a midwife has recently become (Jan. 1892) the object of a comedy staged at the Realist Theatre in Paris, called *L'Avortement*. This comedy, reproducing with too much cruelty the particulars of the crime, generated a trial. The author Chirac was condemned to 15 months of prison, and the two actresses who represented the parts of the *midwife* and the *sufferer* were condemned to one month's and two months' prison. I said this fact is notable because it proves indirectly the frequency and notoriety of this form of *crime à deux*.

109 Years ago, in Milan, an aristocratic lady and a famous physician were tried for procured abortion. The circumstances of the fact reflected precisely my hypothesis. The case was stopped at the investigative phase. Bataille, in his collection, reports two trials on abortion charges occurring in France in 1881, each against a physician and the woman, as accomplice. One ended in acquittal; the other, that of Dr Chopart and Anne Chaumont, with the condemnation of both defendants.

lover Madame Jonquières to go to a midwife and made her perform an abortion.

Who could say how many lovers have done, and still do the same?

We can only hint at this idea, because we lack—it is not our fault—the examples with which to prove it.[111]

There are, however, other more serious and ignoble cases of abortion or infanticide than those we have already talked about, and which fortunately do not always remain unknown. Also, in these cases, the guilty parties are two, and the woman is dragged to crime by her accomplice.

I allude to those obscene dramas that begin with incest and finish with abortion or infanticide. It is the father or the mother's lover who has an obscene fancy for the daughter. A man addicted to all vices, he wants to experience the acute and refined pleasure, typical of senile degeneration, to lay with a child. The promiscuity of life in common offers him the occasion to release his libidinal urges, sometimes in the brutal form of rape, often employing a thousand arts and pitfalls, and managing to corrupt the unconscious ingenuousness of a girl who yields to him without knowing that it is bad. After committing the crime and possessing the daughter, the relapses happen naturally, spontaneously. The girl sees her seducer as a master who wants to subject her to his desires; she knows that if she does not satisfy them, then abuses and beatings await her; she endures the male with the primitive docility of the female, and she bends as a slave before her master, an instrument of his will. It is a slow degeneracy that develops in her and prepares her to be an accomplice to other crimes later in life. If she gets pregnant, it will be he, once again, who will convince her and force her to kill the baby; and she will always surrender out of fear and because of suggestion.

Laurent[112] recalls a story about a girl, Georgette Boges, accused of infanticide, whose accomplices were her mother and her mother's lover, a worker named Plot. The lovers lived together and Georgette with them: "Plot was seduced by the juvenile graces of the barely nubile child.[113] Ardour grew in his horny male brain, and one day he possessed her, almost under her mother's eyes ... The little girl had probably seen him

110 See Bataille, *Causes crim. et mondaines de 1891.*

111 We will speak elsewhere and diffusely about the associations that form in large cities and that have the scope of procuring abortion.—See "Die Verbrecherwelt von Berlin," in *Zeitschrift* of Liszt IV (1888).

112 *L'année criminelle* (1889–1890), 235.

113 Georgette was 12 years old.

several times with his mother doing the act he proposed; she might have noticed that she enjoyed it. Why would she not do like her mother? And she submitted docilely and obediently, suffering the caresses of the man without disgust and without pleasure ... From this moment Georgette was entirely his. He could do what he wanted with her. He could lead her to crime and he did so."[114]

Indeed, Georgette got pregnant and gave birth surreptitiously, and, forced by her lover, helped him kill the baby. Plot had, therefore, rendered the girl blindly obedient to his orders. It managed to terrorize her in such a way that, in front of the judge, she declared to be the only guilty one, denying any complicity by Plot and the mother. It was during the trial that their involvement came to light.

It is a strange phenomenon, and at first incomprehensible, to see the victim pardon the man who made her suffer, to defend the one who is the cause of her pain. There is something Christianly sublime in this supine resignation, in this complete absence of every legitimate feeling of revenge or hate.

And yet, the phenomenon is not rare. It also happened during the trial of Désirée Ferlin, analogous to that of Georgette Boges.

Ferlin, a man lost in vices, a criminal who abused his wife and lovers,[115] lured his daughter to bed one day, suffocating her screams by putting his hand over her mouth, paralyzing her with threats and then raping her.

Désirée, an 18-year-old girl, blonde, puny, pale, and tired-looking, and of very mild character, had to share her father's caresses with his other lover. Disgusted by this wretched life, she tried to run away from home, but her father brought her back. She got pregnant and, tired of futile resistances, consented to let her father perform an abortion. Ferlin burned the fetus.

One would think that during the trial the daughter would accuse her father and throw all of the responsibility for her conduct onto this foul man. On the contrary, Désirée at first refused to speak of him; forced to confess the truth, she tried to excuse him: "As for me"—she said to the jury—"if you believe me guilty, take me, but I beg you, have mercy on the white hair of my father who was carried away by his unfortunate passion!"

114 [In French in Sighele's text.]

115 Ferlin was the terror, not only of his parents, but of the entire town. He had served in the gangs of the province and bragged, as a title of glory, of being "one of the first to kill the inhabitants of Versailles and one of the last to abandon a burning Paris."

And the first time she had to confront Ferlin, instead of reproaching him, she said, "I have prayed for thee!"[116]

Superficial observers might say that it is a magnificent generosity of forgiveness; it is, in my opinion, nothing but an effect—of course, the most difficult and rare—of suggestive force.

The most terrible prerogative of these imperious and evil characters—who know how to impose themselves on weaklings and lead them to do what they want—does not lie in their ability to make their *succubus* consent to their vagaries. Rather, it lies in the mysterious charm against which the affected person—even from afar, even when there is nothing to fear anymore—lacks the courage to rebel. And one's fear becomes respect, one's hate transmutes into love.

Just as the dog licks the hand of the one who beat it, the victim sometimes venerates the executioner. They seem psychological aberrations, but in fact are fatal consequences of an encounter between two opposite characters.

We hinted, in chapter 1, at the relationships that generally develop between geniuses and their lovers; the disdain or neglect that geniuses have for their lovers increases the latter's devotion. And it is a bizarre rule of love that the more one is neglected, the more one loves. Even in mystical love and in religious faith, the more torment one believes that divinity inflicts, the more this divinity is adored. It is the pleasure of martyrdom that increases the reverence for those who make one suffer.

Thus, in the pathological and criminal world, the more a wretch endures the physical and moral tortures of an evildoer, the more he loses

116 [In French in Sighele's text.] On this trial, see Bataille, op. cit., 1880, 231.—Here is the touching letter that Désirée, from prison, wrote to her father, also in prison: "Poor father, the sorrow you have caused me has not extinguished pity in my heart. I have done all I could to save you: talking to justice, I have not had the thought of taking revenge against you. Vengeance belongs to God only; I have asked him the grace to have mercy on you. I dare hope he has listened to my prayer! O my father! confide to him all your sorrow; he, alone, will lighten your burden. Believe me, if God punishes you in life, it is to spare you a dreadful eternity, it is to bring your poor lost soul back to him. He could have allowed you to continue your sad life, and hit you with death at the least predictable moment, without a single instant for you to repent! Be hence contrite. Repent. There is no sin that God does not forgive. And you, forgive, as I forgive my mother, who, out of weakness, did not dare stop you on the fatal slope! May she turn my brothers into honest people, and give them good examples, so that they will not fall into the evil where you have fallen!" [In French in Sighele's text.]

self-awareness and the consciousness of his rights, he annihilates himself before his master, and lives only in him and for him.[117]

Suggestion arrives at this degree of degradation and, if the comparison does not seem paradoxical, I would like to say that in these *degenerate couples*, the identical phenomenon that happens in collective form between the despot and the population here happens in individual form. The long habit of bondage muffles every ambition of revolt; the yoke has for too long prevented the muscles of the neck from straightening out. Where a tyrant rules, rebellions are fewer; the majority of the population is organically and hereditarily a servant. Not only do they obey their master, but they exalt and adore him. We see it in Russia: the subjects fear the Czar as the representative of God on Earth. All the tyrannies, all the infamies they must endure do not diminish, but increase their docile and religious respect. They say: "We must live like this because he wants so; we cannot do anything but obey and love him."[118] It is the Catholic

117 Among the many additional examples that could be cited to prove what we affirm, the most celebrated, tragic episode is that of Mademoiselle Doudet. She was a governess, at the service of Doctor Marsden, a very rich Englishman. Doctor Marsden had five children, and—as a widower—not being able to take care of their education, he entrusted them to Doudet, a young girl whose references were optimal, and who had been at the court of the Queen of England for several years. The children adored their governess and sang her highest praises to their father. After some time, Doctor Marsden started receiving anonymous letters, accusing Doudet of mistreating the children entrusted to her: they said that she tied their hands and feet and kept them for entire hours in a dark room, that she beat them and starved them. Doctor Marsden did not believe it, the accusations seemed even absurd and unlikely. The children, however, were pale and scrawny. Mademoiselle Doudet attributed this fact to disgusting habits for which she had repeatedly reproached them, in the father's presence. Doctor Marsden asked his children whether they had anything to complain about: they all responded no, repeating their declarations of affection and gratitude for Doudet. It seemed beyond doubt that the anonymous letters were slander. It was necessary for one of the children to die before suspicions were reawakened. Doctor Marsden took the children away from their instructor and left them in the care of relatives. In the new house, the children, on principle, continued to say a world of good about Doudet, and they wrote her letters full of affection: only after some months, back in health and encouraged by the healthy environment and outside of any danger, did they decide to reveal, with crushing depositions, how they had been victims of Doudet's vileness. This woman's singular power of suggestion was finally overcome.—See the very interesting trial (from 1855) in the *Revue des grands procès contemporains* (1886), by Lèbre, vol. IV.

118 See on this issue the magnificent book *Siberia* by George Kennan (Lapi, Città di Castello, 1891); and, on the suggestion of the despot, see also Bagehot, *Physics and Politics*.

morality in its meanest and most inept manifestation; it is the debasement of man to the level of the brute and the automaton.

To be sure, only the weakest characters stoop to this point, and fortunately suggestion does not have the same effects on everyone. If it is rare to have the energy needed to rebel, it is less rare that citizens curse tyranny, at least in their hearts, despite not having the courage to say it out loud.

For the same reason, if there are victims like Georgette Boges or Désirée Ferlin who love their fathers in spite of all and defend them,[119] there are also, and more frequently, miserable girls who are raped and forced by their fathers to commit infanticide. Although unable to escape from the tyranny of their evil genius, they dare at least to accuse him once free, and they actually do so with real satisfaction.

In the *Chronique des Tribunaux* of 1835, the trial against Jean Baptiste and Victorine Lemaire is described in great detail: the former was accused of having raped his daughter when she was 13 years old and of having lived with her for 14 years; they were both accused of having committed an abortion and infanticide.

It is futile to extensively talk about the facts, as they resemble those of the Boges and Ferlin affairs.

Lemaire's cruelty was unimaginable.[120] He forced his daughter into absolute isolation. Only one time did she dare leave the house and go to the main village square and on returning home she found her father furious. This monster made her kneel on the sharp edge of a sickle and ask forgiveness for her disobedience. Victorine tried to escape from him in vain. One day she wanted to exclaim: "Oh how I would love it if you were shot by a rifle! I would then be free!"

She was a slave but she hated her master!

During the trial she confessed to having had an abortion and to having killed her second child upon her father's recommendation, but the excruciating story that revealed Lemaire's brutalities granted her acquittal.[121]

---

119 It is necessary to note that Ferlin was a true hysteric, which explains, in large part, why her father managed to attain such a grand power of suggestion over her. Placed in a convent, already depraved, she became fervently devoted, and got intoxicated, so to speak, by mysticism.—"The monastery"—Bourget brilliantly says—"is the alcohol of hysteric women."—She sent her father a small medallion of the Virgin Mary, and wrote to him letters in which the religious sentiment manifests in pathological and exaggerated forms.—See above on this topic.

120 He let his wife die of a broken heart: one day he struck her on the head with a sword.—"The expression on his face is hideous" the reporter said—"on seeing him, one experiences involuntary horror" [in French in Sighele's text].

121 See *Chronique des Trib.*, already cited, vol. I, 392.

And I confess that I do not blame the jury. Of course, this—like the other aforementioned situations—is a case in which one could almost say that the responsibility for the crime falls entirely on only one of the two individuals who comprise the criminal couple, as the other individual only supplies—by force—his unconscious and mechanical assistance.[122]

## *III The Family Couple*

Less tragic and less pitiful, but still owing to suggestion, are the examples of the criminal couples that we will now examine.

The bond which unites the *incubus* to the *succubus* in the couples described so far was amorous love in its guilty or pathological forms, and the committed crime always had its origin, or at least one of its causes, in this love, whether it was mutual and paid or born of one lover and imposed on the other.

Another bond that fosters, so to speak, the formation of a criminal couple is that of the family.

If it is quite common that out of two lovers—one of whom is perverse and the other weak—one becomes the instrument of the other, it is also quite common that, in a family where an individual of scarce moral sense is next to an evildoer, the latter manages to corrupt the former and sometimes makes him an accomplice to a crime. Passion in one case, familiarity and common lifestyle in the other, are truly favourable conditions to the arousal and development of criminal suggestion.

Much has been said about the influence that the example and the education of the family can have on the predisposition to crime, even if initially very low, and facts have been collected to prove this assertion,

---

122 However, we will see further ahead how the truly honest individual does not even succumb under moral and physical pressures, even stronger than those adopted by Plot, Ferlin, and Lemaire, against their daughters. That—and I note it incidentally—confirms the thesis (already formulated elsewhere) that no form of suggestion manages to entirely suppress the personality, the *normal I* of the individual, and thus to render it irresponsible.

Whoever would want to see other examples of infanticidal couples, which I have described, should consult the collections of trials I have already cited. I will recall here only three other cases: that of Doctor Vigouroux and his niece—and lover—Philomène (see Bataille, *Les faiseurs d'anges de Langognes*, 1885, 183); Bastide and Adolphine V. (see Laurent, *L'année criminelle*, 259); and the famous *Affaire Castellan* (see *Revue des grands procès*, already cited) which, however, deals with true hypnotic suggestion rather than suggestion in the waking state.

already intuitive by itself. The contagion of evil, which is already so strong in the vast and diverse environment of society, can better and sooner propagate in the restricted and uniform family environment.

Now, of this contagion, which until now has been discussed in very general and vague terms, we will provide the simplest cases, where contagion occurs between only two individuals, as they reflect the form of criminal association we are studying.

Victor Meille and his mother appeared before the Criminal Court in the Var Department in August 1876, both being accused of patricide and the mother of being the instigator of the crime.

Since he left his family home, said Meille, he had always lived under his nightmarish mother, who had never ceased to turn him against his father, repeating that he would disinherit him and his sister. "He must be killed"—she told him—"so that he does not make arrangements against you." And because the son refused to follow that advice, she continued even more animatedly: "Come on! How can you be so ingenuous? Is it possible to look at what is happening with such indifference? Do you not understand that your father will give everything he has to your aunt? You and your sister could have something, but if *you let him act*, you will get nothing!" Then she added, "Oh! If only I weren't afraid to mess up, I would have killed him already!"

Meille added detailed instructions to her previous advice: "Your father has two heifers that lead him at night to the pasture; get your cousin's rifle and take advantage of this moment to wait for your father and kill him."

But Victor Meille resisted.[123]

Finally, one day when he had gone to visit his mother, she reiterated her advice and instructions more insistently, and, to give a decisive influence to her words, she went to look for the rifle in her son-in-law's room and delivered it to her son. This time he succumbed, committing the crime according to his mother's suggestion.[124]

An identical reproduction of the Meille patricide is offered to us by the Enjalbert trial.

123 During the trial, it emerged that Meille, who had planned the plot to kill her husband for a long time, thought of recruiting someone else for her plan rather than her son, when he seemed unwilling to be her accomplice.

124 From Aubry, *La contagion du meurtre*, 23.

Enjalbert was a 45-year-old man, but sickly and unable to work. His wife, a woman of awful morals, wanted to get rid of him as she thought he was a useless weight, and to live more comfortably with her lovers. The last of these lovers, although he agreed to give her money, refused to give enough to support Enjalbert as well. She then attempted to poison her husband; but, after failing, she devised to kill him with the aid of her son François.

François was a 17-year-old youth, not very developed and weak-minded; his mother promised him a happy life and no obligation to work if he consented to help her in the murder of Enjalbert. A month later, he no longer resisted the idea, and the crime was decided.

One night, father, mother, and son departed from Gabian to go to Mézières. The mother had hidden a revolver under some clothes; the son brought only a stick. At a certain point, the mother begged her husband to tie her shoe; while he was bent over, she shot him on the nape three times. The son struck him on the head with the stick.

After the crime François spontaneously confessed everything.[125]

In addition to the wives who lead their sons to crime, there are also the wives who push their husbands.

Rose Plancher, wife of Jean Faure, hated her brother-in-law Claude. He was rich and highly respected in the village for his honesty. Jean, instead, was poor and had a bad reputation. Against the will of his brother, he married Plancher, whose family was known for some sinister legend,[126] and he became a slave to this woman.

---

125 From Laurent, *L'année criminelle*, 247. Despine (*Psych. nat.*, vol. II, 299), recalls a similar event: the killing of L. Nazet by his wife and son, the latter under the suggestion of the former;—Aubry in his recent work, *De l'homicide commis par la femme*, recalls also the murder committed by Leger and her son, the former instigating the latter.

126 It is important to refer to this legend because, if it is true, it constitutes an eloquent proof in favour of atavism in crime. At the beginning of the century, in Peyrebelle, a village in the mountains of the Ardèche region, there existed a hotel that was later called *the hotel of murderers*. Travellers who slept there for the night never woke up. The hotel manager with his wife would strangle them in their sleep, burn their bodies in the oven, and throw their bones off the cliff. In 1833, after 25 years of murders, the hotel owner, his wife, and accomplices were arrested and died on the scaffold on October 2nd.—Now, the legend says that Rose Plancher is a descendant of these hotel murderers. The strange thing is that she is also said to have thrown her cousin's bones off the cliff, after having boiled his corpse. There would thus be an atavism also in the execution methods of the crime. What is certain is that a great-uncle of Plancher was condemned to life in prison for having burned a woman.

Rose Faure thought of having her husband kill her brother-in-law so as to seize his wealth and to discharge the profound aversion she had towards him.

Every night for months she told Jean to terminate his brother. She often reproached him because he had not killed him at night when they were returning home along dangerous mountain paths. One day she threatened to poison him if he did not agree to kill her brother-in-law.

Jean Faure did not resist his wife's insistent pleads and threats for very long. His brother's wealth was tempting him and, after all, having already demonstrated that he was not the best of gentlemen, it was natural that sooner or later he would give in.

On the night of the crime, however, he felt he lacked the strength and courage to commit fratricide, thus Rose made him drink. Excited by the wine, he struck and killed his brother.[127]

What is monstrous in this trial is Rose's demeanour after the crime: "a woman with the cowardice and ferocity of a hyena." She boiled her brother-in-law's body and gave it to the pigs to eat; she brought the bones to an almost inaccessible mountain peak, where she disposed of them in the crevasses and fissures.[128]

Another typical example of *the criminal couple* is represented by the Schneiders, *the murderers of the maidservants,* condemned to death in January of 1892 by the Criminal Court in Vienna. Here is how an intelligent Italian journalist who attended the trial describes these two criminals:

> Franz Schneider came from the lowest people, with no education. He cannot read or write. He has no ideas of his own. He does not act unless upon suggestion. He is cynical, brutal, crude, and strong. He has an ox's neck and a powerful hand. His lower jaw is very prominent. His hair is thick and red. He started stealing from a young age. From stealing he went on to burglary.
>
> It was in this period—as soon as he left prison, after eight months' detention—that he met Rosalie Schneider. She was a waitress, six years his senior. She liked the younger, robust butcher. She imposed her discrete education and vivacious intelligence on him, who was half stupid. After all, they had understood each other. Their marriage was nothing but a criminal alliance.

127 Other than Faure, Rose's brother also participated in the crime, who committed suicide as soon as he was arrested. He was a relatively honest young man (suicide is, in all probability, proof of this), who was led astray by his sister to take part in the crime. It seems, however, that he did not even place a hand on the victim. His figure resembles that of Lucien Fenayrou (see chapter 2), an accomplice under the suggestion of an evildoer, who has with this a rather pronounced analogy.

128 From Bataille, op. cit. (1886), 384.

Rosalie was the first to conjure up murderous ideas. She proposed that her husband should lure into the woods of Neulengbach the girls who came to the capital from provinces in search of a maidservant's position, and to rob them. Rosalie would tell a victim that she had a perfect family in mind who could employ her; she would lead the victim into a tavern, make her drink and eat, and then the two would take a walk in the woods with her husband. And at that point the poor girl would be strangled by the two human monsters. Three were the girls killed in such a way.

At the hearing, Franz Schneider appeared as a thoughtless brute whose wife made him do what she wanted. Devoid of any moral sense, even incapable of comprehending the horrible severity of his misdeeds, he strangled because Rosalie told him to *strangle,* and she was giving the example.

We could refer to many other instances of women who dragged their husbands to crime,[129] or of men who persuaded their wives, or of brothers who pushed their brothers.[130] But, apart from the individual details, the fact always remains the same from a psychological point of view.

---

129 See in the *Chronique des Tribunaux,* vol. I, 293 and 380, the two trials of the spouses Henry and Soulet, murderers. It is the wife, in both cases, who instigates the husband to crime.—Corre (*Les criminels,* 183) also cites a crime committed by a husband and wife, and since the case is odd and interesting for criminal psychology, I reproduce it verbatim: "Pious people can reconcile crime with religion, and this does not erase ferocious instincts; rather, it exalts them, as it doubles with a sort of fanaticism the feeling of resentful vengeance. In the affair of the *Crucified of Hengoat* (Saint-Brieuc, 1883), a young woman, who had been a novice, induces her husband, who had considered becoming a member of the Institute of Christian doctrine, to strangle her brother, whom they had accused of perjury regarding a score settling. The corpse was then tied, arms outstretched, to the shafts of a cart. The couple had already attempted to obtain from Saint-Yves the punishment of the guilty relative, but, since the saint had refused to intervene, they decided to resort to murder. Two days later, the woman was going to Communion. The jury acquitted the accused." [In French in Sighele's text.]

130 Despine (op. cit., vol. II, 301) narrates the following event: "Two brothers Jacques and Simon Bonnefoy are irritated with their mother because she wants to marry for a third time, and they foresee the unfavourable economic consequences of such a marriage. Jacques is the more ferocious: he threatens and beats his mother, and forces Simon and their sister to abandon the paternal house. The mother, now free, gets married. Jacques's anger increases: he says to his sister that their mother's money will not be taken by the new husband, because he will kill her. He activates Simon's hate and forces him, who is shier, to go to their mother's house and throw out the husband. After a violent scene, Simon says to Jacques that he doesn't want to be involved. But the brother reignites the hate in him, he persuades Simon that he must kill their mother and one day drags him with him to the crime."

In these family crimes—in which the scope is almost always profit, in which there is almost never a spark of a less foul passion that could offer the culprits even a feeble excuse—, more than the encounter of a perverse person and a weak one and the slow corruption of the latter by the former, there occurs the encounter of two perverse people who do not need much time to understand and associate with each another. A feeling of dependency certainly exists between them as well, and one acts on the impulse of the other, but the individual roles are not so different or distinct as in the other cases.

"When two individuals devoid of moral sense and animated by perverse feelings meet,"—Despine says—"they soon agree to plan the crime. The one whose perversity is more active is the leader, and the other, whose active principles are similar to those of his companion, promptly adopts the latter's thoughts without repulsion."[131]

In these words, the physiognomy of the crimes of Meille, Enjalbert, Faure, and Prager, is carved.

We are not lacking examples, however, in which the suggestive influence of one over the other is—also in the family couple—much more intense, and in which we really find the two types of the *incubus* and *succubus* with their most pronounced characters.

In this respect, I shall only refer to one event that will offer us an occasion for hopefully not useless considerations.

Pierre Gironde appeared before the Criminal Court in Limoges on serious charges of parricide. Evidence was scarce and a condemnation seemed dubious. But a dramatic scene happened at the hearing. Martin Gironde, brother of the accused, was cited as a witness. "It is definitely Pierre," he said, "who killed our father. I witnessed the crime; I participated; my brother forced me to kill my father with an ax."

"Why did you not speak up before?" the president asked.

"I was afraid of my brother," he responded. "He would have killed me if I had accused him. Today I am choking with remorse, and, come what may, it's necessary for me to tell the truth."

---

In Berlin, in January 1892, the famous trial took place against Mrs Prager—a gallant and very well-known woman—and her brother, accused of having tried to kill his brother-in-law, and the other of having instigated him to this crime. Prager, astute and intelligent, persuaded her brother, a semi-idiot, to hide himself in her husband's bedroom and to stab him with a knife while he was asleep. Her brother was hesitant; she encouraged him, and manoeuvred by her, he hit him.

131 Op. cit., vol. II, 250 [in French in Sighele's text].

Martin Gironde explained that his father had gone down to the cellar when Pierre, who had followed him, threw himself on him and killed him with an axe. Attracted by the screams of father and son, Martin realized what had happened. When Pierre saw him, he gave Martin the axe, telling him: "Because you know everything, you also need to strike him. I want your silence. Kill him or I'll kill you." Martin, terrified, struck.

The truth of the narrative was confirmed. Furthermore, it spoke in favour of Martin and of his sincere remorse and behaviour after the crime; he sat at his father's side all night, crying like a child. A witness testified that Martin, weak and inoffensive, was truly subdued by Pierre, whom he was following like a lamb.[132]

Someone reading this fact will probably be surprised to see that I cited this among the other phenomena attributable, at least in part, to suggestion. It is physical violence, one will say, not moral violence that Pierre Gironde exerted over his brother; suggestion, therefore, has nothing to do with it.

Had it been a kind of physical violence to which it was impossible to resist, I could accept this criticism. It is understandable that man is impotent before a superior force, which frees him of any responsibility. But Martin Gironde could have rebelled against his brother, and he would have done so if he had been a person who knew no weaknesses or hesitations.

Without a doubt, suggestion in this case, instead of manifesting itself in a slow and continuous way, was instantaneous, and can ultimately be assimilated to "terror," but can the different degree of intensity or the different duration of a phenomenon change its inner nature?

To succumb to the will of another person, after this person employed the weapon of persuasion for some time, or to immediately obey a will expressed imperiously and reinforced by threats: are these two actions perhaps not uniquely caused by the weak individual's proclivity to succumb to suggestion?

In the first case, a truly honest person would not yield to corruption, and, in the second case, the honest person would be able to resist without hesitating not even for an instant.

Despine recalls an event that most eloquently proves my assertion.

Two barbershop boys one day killed a certain Donney while they were trimming his beard, and they threatened with death one of their companions, who was also at the shop, if he did not help them tie up and hide the victim. This companion, horrified at such ferocity, resolutely refused to become an accomplice to their misdeed, despite his legitimate fear.

132 From Bataille, op. cit. (1882), 237.

Hence the murderers tied him up as well and locked him up along with Donney's body. Fortunately, the owner discovered the crime and the poor young man was saved, but he went mad.[133]

This is the conduct of an honest man in the most absolute sense of the word. This is how an adamant character behaves in face of a seemingly irresistible suggestion.[134]

## *IV The Friend Couple*

To complete our overview of criminal couples—which we wanted to distinguish according to the emotional bonds that unite the *succubus* and the *incubus*—we only need to discuss the criminal couple formed by two friends,[135] which most frequently develops in the prison environment or in those taverns where criminals gather with vagabonds, misfits, and sloths, in other words, all candidates who are waiting to join the army of crime.

For friendship we can repeat, although to a different degree, what we said about amorous love or familial kinship: it is, too, a condition that can foster criminal suggestion whenever one of the friends is wicked and the other is psychologically weak.

Already in the introduction to our work, we hinted at the perverting influence that a corrupt individual can have over his companion, and we referred to some representative examples.

Here we will only add a few instances, as we deem it useless to dwell on this type of suggestion *à deux*, because it is the most common and observed of all.

Ferri, in his *L'omicidio*,[136] cites two cases: that of Andony, a young man endowed with Herculean strength but with a very docile character, who

---

133 Despine, op. cit., vol. II, 261. Despine took the event from a newspaper from Illinois in 1858.

134 Regarding the major or minor power of suggestion, both hypnotic and wakeful, see my work *La foule criminelle* (Paris: Alcan, 1892), chapter III. Here I reconfirm, with the incontrovertible argument of an event, the thesis that I developed at length in that volume.

135 As the reader will see, we have dedicated a special study, in the *Appendix* to this volume [but not included herein], to the criminal couple formed by parents who mistreat their children. The importance, not only psychological but also social, that these crimes currently have, advised us to treat them separately, although the logical order of the work would have required to include such a study into the previous section, among the cases of family couples.

136 Part I.

led an honest life until he reached a mature age when, subdued by the murderer Latour, he became an accomplice to a murder; and that of Rousselet, who killed his mother after succumbing to Édouard Donon's insistences and confessed at the trial: "I cannot tell how many ways he employed to make me do it."

The *Chronique des Tribunaux*,[137] when speaking about the Lacenaire gang, recalled how the gang corrupted François, a weak but not entirely perverse individual. One time, Lacenaire wanted François to help him kill someone. François finally gave up after many refusals, although he would not directly take part in the crime, but, rather, only guard the door. Lacenaire, after slitting the victim's throat, said with great disdain to his companion: "*Coward that you are; you will never do anything to mount the scaffold!*"[138]

Laurent[139] tells a story about a hysterical man who was forced into crime by a girl with whom he had lived a long time.

Despine[140] talks about the peasant Girbas who killed his boss after Collas coerced him.

But the most typical case is that of Porcher and Hardouin, and it is worthwhile referring to it at length.

Porcher, 20 years old, was arrested for theft and in prison got to know Hardouin, who asked Porcher to kill his in-laws, and promised a compensation of 1,500 francs. Porcher hesitated to accept. To combat his reticence, Hardouin told him stories of the many unpunished crimes committed by men *who were not afraid as he was*. Porcher did not respond. One day Hardouin said to him: "It is absolutely necessary for you to kill them for me; they keep disrespecting me; they made my wife go mad."—"These words scared me"—Porcher said later—"I reflected, *but I couldn't kill people I didn't know and without a personal motive.*"[141] Another time Hardouin said to Porcher: "You must decide; if you don't kill my in-laws as soon as you leave prison, I will kill you." Porcher was convinced that Hardouin's threat was serious; as soon as he was freed (because he had served his time), he went to his house, got a rifle, and headed to

137 Vol. II, 222.

138 [In French in Sighele's text.]

139 Laurent, "Les suggestions criminelles," in *Archives de l'anthrop. crim. et des sciences pen.* (15 Nov. 1890): 625.

140 Op. cit., vol. II, 288.

141 Note how the reasons why Porcher *could not decide to kill* the Chaumiers are determined by simple considerations regarding the quality of the people, rather than by an intimate repulsion for homicide.

the Chaumier residence, Hardouin's in-laws. But then he stopped and reflected, acknowledging how he was about to commit a serious crime, and turned back.

"The day after"—he recalled—"at four in the morning, I got up to do what I hadn't had the courage to do the day before. I walked by the village church. The sight of this church, where I had my first communion, inspired remorse in me.[142] I knelt down praying to God to send me good inspiration. *But I don't know what pushed me to the crime.* I set off again. I proceeded without fear of making mistakes, since Hardouin had described the place to me. *I retraced my steps ten times, but the more I hesitated, the more I felt the desire to continue.* I arrived. I saw the servant exiting the house: I took her for Hardouin's mother-in-law, so I fired and killed her."[143]

The homicide by Porcher undoubtedly had Hardouin's prodding as its primary cause, but then one could almost say that it was owed to an idea rooted in Porcher's soul. External suggestion slowly transformed into autosuggestion. The words reveal it: "*But I don't know what pushed me to the crime ... the more I hesitated, the more I felt the desire to continue.*"

This phenomenon of transformation from one suggestion to another is rare, but not isolated. Another example, even more obvious, can be seen in the trial of the *acid throwers* Marie Moyen and Julie Bila.

Marie Moyen was a girl abandoned by her lover Lecrique, who thought it was better to take a wife. The pain of abandonment, or perhaps the delusional hopes of marriage, spurred on the vendetta. She had a friend: Julie Bila. She was a young girl of little intelligence but of impassioned character, who greatly loved Moyen, her companion since childhood. Marie shared her unhappy love affair with her; she depicted Lecrique as completely hateful, crying for the child to whom she allegedly had given birth, and whose father had disowned it. Julie Bila got excited about this store. She had only hate for her friend's lover, she empathized with the situation as if it were her own, and when, after a few days, Moyen asked Julie to help with her vendetta, she agreed. And it was she, under the influence of Marie, who killed the poor Lecrique with vitriol. As soon

142 This phenomenon is contrary to what usually happens to born murderers, who use religion to reinforce their deleterious criminal proposals and pray to God to help them in their misdeeds. It could thus be proof that in Porcher's soul every light of honesty was extinguished.

143 Despine, *Psych. natur.* II, 355.

as she committed the crime, she made an ample confession and tried to pass it off as if she were the only guilty one.[144]

Apart from the motive, the psychological similarity with Porcher's crime is evident.

With both Julie Bila and Porcher, the companion's suggestion is just the incentive, the spark that ignites a criminal idea in their heads, which then develops on its own and becomes—I daresay—autonomous. It is an obsession they are prey to, an obsession that naturally vanishes as soon as the crime is done, leaving in its place a satisfying feeling comparable to lifting a great weight off of one's chest. "The dormant faculties, fascinated by a fixed idea, wake up; and the perpetrator of the crime considers his work as if coming from a disgrace that is *within him*, but that is not him, and he does not even know it."[145]

Indeed, after the homicide, Porcher felt liberated from the inner voice that never granted him peace and that insistently pushed him to crime. And Julie Bila, with her immediate and spontaneous confession, and with her desire to be the only punishable offender, showed regret for her actions, having been driven, more than by will, by an inner impulse she could not explain. Neither Porcher nor Julie Bila speak of, or even hint at the origin of their suggestion. As the principal, if not unique, cause of their offence, they accuse another *I* that lies within them and forces them to crime.

These cases of suggestion in the waking state are very close to those of hypnotic suggestion. A proposal made by Hardouin and repeated several times,—a request made with some insistence by Moyen—is enough to force Porcher and Julie to murder, just as the hypnotist's orders are enough to make the hypnotic commit an imaginary crime to which he is predisposed. As he carries out the crime, this hypnotic subject does not know that another imposed it on him; he only feels invincibly pushed to commit it. Porcher and Bila almost no longer remember who put the homicidal idea into their heads; they only have an acute and irresistible desire to kill. After the crime, the hypnotic has a reaction that

---

144 From Bataille, op. cit. (1880), 194.—The Moyen-Bila pair is one of the very rare *criminal couples* formed by two women: Corre cites another (*Archives* of Lyon, 1890, 133) formed by two girls who killed a man, who was the lover of both.

145 See Laurent, in the work just cited, 634. There Laurent, speaking about autosuggestions, situates anger and vendetta among these, when they burst some time after the provocation from which they were born. Accepting such an opinion (and it seems possible to me), the premeditation would not be in some cases but an autosuggestion.—See, in this respect, Alimena, *La premeditazione in rapporto alla psicologia, al diritto e alla legislazione comparata* (Turin: Bocca, 1887).

demonstrates the effort made by his *normal I* in succumbing to suggestion; Porcher and Bila repent and sincerely accuse only themselves for the crime.

In such cases, suggestion has the effect of splitting the personality of the succubus. This is the extreme phenomenon that suggestion in the waking state can produce, which makes it overlap with hypnotic suggestion. Thus, it demonstrates that, ultimately, suggestion in the waking state is nothing but a weakened form of hypnotic suggestion.

## Chapter 4: "The Criminal Couple" (Continuation and End)

### *I*

Our objective in collecting the long series of facts we have talked about thus far was to bring a modest contribution to criminal psychology. Persuaded, as we are, that one must study criminals so as to effectively judge crimes and the various legal entities they can represent, we thought it would be useful to highlight the psychological genesis of some crimes that have their own physiognomy, and that, unfortunately, are not very rare.

It is clear, however, that simple enumeration is not enough and that, after our analysis, a synthesis is required to summarize, coordinate, and interpret the single observations. This work is all the more necessary because, as we were proceeding in our study, we were increasingly digressing from—apparently almost forgetting—the fundamental idea from which we had started, to express the considerations suggested each time by the special cases.

In the first chapter, we analysed the healthy couple, the suicidal couple, and the insane couple, affirming that we would find analogous characteristics of the *form à deux* of suggestion in the criminal world as well.

Was our affirmation incorrect?

We do not believe so.

For us it is an axiom that the association between two individuals—in whatever domain it occurs—is attributable to the phenomenon of suggestion.[146] It is certain, however, that this association can be formed either by absolute predominance of the one and thus the absolute awe of the other, or by an agreement between the two that almost equalizes

146 And—that is—not only the association between two individuals, but all the forms of associations. See on this: Tarde, "Qu'est qu'une société?" in *Revue philosophique* (Nov. 1884).

their importance, even though their functions are different. Namely, suggestion can be explained either as totally and always by one over the other, or as mutual influence between the two.[147]

Already in the brief pages devoted to the amorous suggestion, we noted that the spiritual union in which two lovers fatally converge—becoming, according to the overused yet true phrase, "two bodies in one soul"—can derive from the exclusive dominance that one exerts over the other, as much as from their mutual fascination. In the first case, we have an *absorption* of the weaker individual into the more energetic one; in the second case, a *fusion* of the two individuals. The conclusion in both cases is always the same, since, for both *absorption* and *fusion*, the two individuals form an organic whole, and their alliance produces a single psychological figure. By contrast, the means, or, better, the elements that constitute this organic whole and this figure are, in either case, different. They derive almost exclusively from only one of the lovers in the case of *absorption*, and from both in the case of *fusion*.

Therefore, criminal couples always give a unique result, and they are, indeed, formed to perform a unique action—the crime—, but this result, this action, may depend mostly on one of the criminals, or almost to the same extent on both.

We have seen some examples of couples of murderous lovers—and even more of couples of infanticidal lovers—where it was clear that the crime always had to be entirely attributed to only one of the criminals, given that every will, every emotion of the other had been *absorbed* into the will and emotions of the first. We have also seen examples of criminal couples where, if the idea had originated from the person who also directed the execution of the crime, the other did not have to exert much effort or to suppress his *I* in order to adhere, but his tendencies had gradually and spontaneously *fused* with those of his partner.[148]

147 With all the possible gradations from one extreme to the other.

148 In the comparison between the healthy couple and the criminal couple, we chose, as an example of the first, the couple of two lovers, although—as we briefly said above (chapter 1)—there are couples of siblings, master and disciple, friends, that also reflect the phenomenon of suggestion *à deux*. The reason for this choice lies in the fact that the couple of two lovers presents those characteristics in a more pronounced and acute way, which are common also in the more attenuated forms of couples. Also among criminal couples, the psychological tie that unites two lovers is always stronger than between two relatives or friends. And the reader will have noted that—exceptions apart—in the couples of murderous or infanticidal lovers, the influence of the energetic character (*incubus*) over the weak character (*succubus*) is always stronger than in other couples, not because the succubus is more prone to suggestion and

The gang leader Villert forced Lemaire to murder and only needed to deride Lemaire's character when he hesitated. Gabrielle Fenayrou succumbed almost immediately to her husband and sacrificed her lover, later showing neither remorse nor repentance. Jean Faure was led by his wife to commit fratricide and a glass of wine gave him enough courage to commit the crime. In addition to all of these and other similarly vulgar criminals, we get to Garnier, who resisted Aveline's pressure for months and, after committing the crime, regretted it and asked for forgiveness; to Louise Feucher, who died after committing the crime because her entire organism was too repulsed by it; and finally, to that woman who, after succumbing to her lover's will and promising to kill her husband for him, did not have the moral and physical force to make him drink the poison, and collapsed confessing everything. We have examined a fair quantity of *criminal couples* which, if they all attained their objective and had their raison d'être in the phenomenon of suggestion, they nonetheless reached this goal in different ways and presented this phenomenon in always different degrees of intensity.

While for some of them the influence exerted by the words and incitements of another represented only the guide and direction necessary to evoke the already pre-existing and very strong disposition for crime, for others this same influence perverted their honesty—weak honesty, certainly, but which otherwise would have remained such, instead of going so far as criminal activity all by itself.

Our work should at least demonstrate that clear differences do not exist in nature between the born criminal, the occasional criminal, and the passionate criminal, but that all of these categories are conjoined through a gradual evolution of types, because the individual who represents and personifies a particular sentiment and character possesses every nuance of them and expresses them in all their diversity.

"It is the same thing with regard to delinquency"—Tarde says quite well[149]—"as it is with regard to predisposition and neurosis,—those pathological turncoats, whose transformations are infinite"[150]

---

the *incubus* is more imperious (these are circumstances that vary case by case), but solely because the sexual love that ties the two together is the strongest weapon of persuasion and suggestion.

149 Tarde, *Philosophie pénale,* 1st ed., 223. [*Penal Philosophy* 225.]

150 [In French in Sighele's text.]

## *II*

While accounting for single individual differences, there are, however, some psychological characteristics common to all criminals who represent the succubus in the criminal couple, whom I would define as *criminaloids,* according to Cesare Lombroso's felicitous neologism, which is the best term to describe them.

We will now briefly discuss these special characteristics, considering the behaviour of these criminaloids before and after the crime.

Enrico Ferri in *L'omicidio* remarks how in normal individuals "all the repulsive force of the homicide resides, on the one hand, in the intimate aversion of our moral conscience and of physical sensibility itself, and, on the other hand, in the forecast and fear of consequences that would ensue for us, both for the remorse of having massacred a man and for the sanctions represented in religious beliefs and applied by the law and public opinion. Therefore," he logically concludes, "the psychic state, in which the perpetration of a crime is possible, consists in *the lack of that moral aversion or of this fear for future consequences.*"[151]

Now, such a categorical and absolute affirmation, which reflects exactly the psychic state of a born murderer, is not viable in the cases we have examined. Of the two conditions deemed necessary for murder—lacking moral aversion to commit it and lacking fear for its potential consequences—, the former is not found in those who kill under the pressure and influence of another.[152]

Rather, they possess, certainly not so tenaciously as honest people but at least to some degree, this moral aversion or repugnance to crime, which is revealed in two symptoms that are its clearest expression.

The first symptom is *the time that is needed for them to choose to actualize a criminal idea.* If one truly lacked moral aversion to homicide, then, once proposed, it would be undoubtedly accepted, as actually happens with all born criminals who do not show any repugnance for a similar action. Rather, committing it is, for them, what the completion of the simplest and most natural act is to us: "I kill a man like drinking a glass of wine,"

151 Enrico Ferri, *L'omicidio,* vol. I.

152 We do not find the second either, in many cases.—The fear of consequences for the crime is very frequent in the *succubi,* and we saw some examples (see 116, the case of Lavoitte and her lover Albert). Here we limit ourselves to highlighting the existence of the moral aversion to crime, because is it the most important psychological characteristic.

Lacenaire said. "To cut off a man's head, what is it?"—Prévost the murderer said—"It's chocolate, it's velvet!"[153]

Instead, when an action recommended to us contradicts the average of our sentiments, we immediately push it back disdainfully—and this is the case of the honest man—or we require a long period of time to get used to it and to be able to accept it. And so we saw, among others, Porcher and Meille resist for a long time, one against his friend, the other against his mother, before committing homicide and patricide. Likewise, Marie Noblia and Garnier slowly succumbed to their lovers' charms before agreeing to their evil designs.

The second symptom, which proves the non-absolute lack of aversion to crime, is *the uncertainty in the execution* as soon as the decision is made. This is the case of Porcher who, while at the crime scene (when he had already succumbed to Hardouin's insistences), was assailed by remorse and turned back, and for a day he did not dare attempt murder. Likewise, Jeanne Daniloff grabs the cyanide vial several times to poison her husband, and then puts it down, horrified at the simple thought of what she was about to do. And Garnier, after aiming the rifle at his victim, drops it and runs far away.

This latter symptom differs from the former. The latter is, I would say, the belated physiological refusal with which the organism obstructs he who believes he can accomplish an evil action and thought about it and wanted it. The former symptom, instead, is the repugnance that the honest man feels from the beginning, and that the weakest individuals feel less intensely, when simply thinking about the crime. A criminal idea—we have already said—can come in a flash even in the mind of an honest man, and can even settle in the mind of an occasional criminal. At the moment of execution, however, the one (always) and the other (often) will feel an invincible repulsion, because it is one thing to think about doing something, and quite another to actually do it. This proves—and I claim it incidentally—that in every man there is an absolute impossibility to perform certain actions; in other words, free will does not exist.

After the crime (during which we see no trace of the cynical verbal expressions and the abuses that characterize, by contrast, the true born criminal or the morally insane), those who acted under someone else's impulse understand all the horror of their misdeed, rather than remaining indifferent and impassive. It looks as though they are awakening from a dream and only then are they able to realize what they have done. A sort of reaction is triggered, which grows in strength in proportion to

153 [In French in Sighele's text.] See *In Art and in Science*, 400 and 400n36, in this volume.

the intensity of the external influence that led them to crime. We have the example of Marie Noblia, who, upon seeing the body of her victim, was stricken with a nervous tremor and ran screaming madly through the village; and the example of Martin Gironde, who spent an entire night crying and kneeling next to his father whom he had killed. In the cases in which the psychological reaction does not reach this degree, we, nonetheless, always find that the conduct after the crime radically differs from that of the born criminal, as it shows true remorse—showing all the characteristics that distinguish it from simple sorrow and from pseudo-remorse—, or at least a spontaneous and immediate confession without attempting to mitigate their complicity in the crime (Meille, Albert, Enjalbert, Gaudry, etc.).

## *III*

It is evident that these considerations, which roughly summarize the psychological aspects of the form of association that we have studied, do not provide us with sufficient elements to deduce the exact and precise judicial norms, but they will only serve as criteria for the modality and measure of repression in cases that are analogous to those examined here.

Above and before the behaviour of a criminal in committing a crime, we first need to take into account the motive for the criminal's action. And one understands that there is a big difference between whoever kills out of greed—like Faure, Meille, etc.—, whoever kills, like Garnier, because of an unavoidable passion that weighs on all his senses like a nightmare, and whoever kills because of a dominating terror, like Boges, Ferlin, Lemaire, and Gironde.

Yet, even if we need to reserve an examination of the criminal motives of a couple to each individual case and an examination of each guilty party's involvement in the crime together with it, we believe one can a priori express a general norm of repression that is indistinctly valid for all of these crimes.

The sole fact that a crime is committed by two people rather than one must, in our opinion, *always* constitute an aggravating circumstance.

It is an intuitive observation—and it would seem almost useless to illustrate it if it had not been so neglected thus far by criminologists[154]—

154 No one (and I affirm it categorically anticipating here the results of a study on the classic theories of complicity that I will develop in the juridical part of *Il delinquente associato* [The Associated Criminal—which Sighele ultimately never completed ]),

to say that the crime involving two or more people presents greater dangers than the crime that is designed and carried out by only one person. Unity is strength in good as well as in evil; a stronger reaction is needed to logically counteract a criminal force.

Classical jurists dealing with the question of complicity believed that it was enough to weigh each criminal's involvement in the crime on the goldsmith's scale, and to punish them adequately *solely* based on their involvement. In this way, the legal Code became—according to the witty phrase by the lawyer Porto[155]—a ledger where, for each of the individuals who contributed to the making of a drape, the metres of tailored fabric were recorded under *credit*, and the years of imprisonment in relation to the length under *debit*.

Now, we believe that this method is too mechanical and mercantile when considering the phenomenon of complicity.

Two individuals that get together to perpetrate a crime do not give a result that is either psychologically or socially equal to the *simple sum* of each of them.

In psychology and sociology there are no simple *mixtures*, that is, inorganic *convergences* of two or more bodies. There are only *combinations*.

---

no one among the writers on penal law has ever come close to hinting at the idea that complicity—when it does not attain the acute and extreme forms of associations of evildoers—must constitute an aggravated circumstance and thus entail a harsher punishment as a consequence.

Pessina, actually (*Elementi di diritto penale*, vol. II, 247), with a strange ingenuity, warns that "if a crime was committed by more people, the penalty is *not divided among them*," and Impallomeni (*Il Cod. pen. illustrato*, vol. I, 209), repeats that "*the penalty does not get divided among those involved*," almost as though one could even think that if a homicide—let's say punished with 15 years—is committed by three individuals, each would get five years!

The only declaration that all criminologists feel the need to make regarding more individuals involved in a crime is this: "each one is only responsible for one's own deed." But they do not realize that the first and most important deed of each participant is ... the association! Only Niccolini (*Questioni di diritto*, Livorno, 1853) hints at a practice of our theory, where he claims that a murder, when it is committed by more people, must be given the maximum penalty.

On the positive theory of complicity—at which here I hint very quickly—see Ferri, *Sociologia criminale* (Turin: 1892), 577, and my two articles: "La complicità" (*Arch. di. psich.*, 1890, XI, 262) and "La complicità nei reati colposi" (*Scuola positiva*, 1892, II, no. XII), in which I started to develop the idea expressed first by my mentor.

155 Vito Porto, "Note di cronaca," in *Appunti al nuovo Codice penale*, 2nd ed. (Turin: Bocca, 1889).

The action that results from the collusion of two people is, thus, never *an addition*, but it is always *a product.*

Just as the joint force of two horses—and I ask forgiveness for this trivial comparison, which, however, serves to express my thought rather clearly—is always greater than the simple sum of the forces of the one and of the other, and as the economic value of a pair of horses is always greater than the sum of the prices that each would have separately, thus the danger and the social importance of a criminal couple is always greater than the sum of the single criminal's individual energy.

An alliance of two people[156] possesses elements that do not exist in either of the individuals who compose the pair, and that, rather, are born and emitted—almost as psychological sparks—only at the moment when the two individuals, together, give life to the alliance.

Now, supposing that this alliance has a criminal objective, is it not logical that the legal Code should consider, above all, these new elements intrinsically present in the alliance, thus rendering the complicity of more people an aggravating circumstance?

I believe that one cannot but respond affirmatively to this question, because nobody fails to see the greater gravity of the crime committed by two people in comparison to a crime by only one.

There is more objective gravity, since the victim's self-defence is greatly impaired when confronted with two people, and the execution of a crime is, therefore, easier. There is subjective gravity, since, as a general thesis, the associated criminals are more perverse and dangerous than the isolated criminals.

"If there are solitary criminals"—says Joly—"it is, above all, among the accidental criminals that we encounter them. The idea of accident excludes the idea of premeditation and, therefore, the idea of mutual agreement"[157]

The born criminal and the habitual criminal associate with one another because those who live in an unhealthy environment find easy and spontaneous accomplices for any crime among their companions. The occasional criminal or the passionate criminal, instead, is not yet familiar with the criminal world, and, although committing a crime, feels the damage and shame, and rarely finds, and above all rarely looks for accomplices.

If there are associated, occasional criminals—like all of the *succubi* in the criminal couples—they do not truly represent the extreme type of

156 And, of course, a fortiori an association of many people.
157 Joly, *Le crime*, chapter V, 129 [in French in Sighele's text].

fortuitous criminal on which the environment almost *imposes* the crime, but, rather the type of weakling to whom the occasion—this touchstone of moral resistance[158]—only offers a way to reveal their nature.

The same can be said about crimes of passion committed by two people, of which we offered examples in the couples of murderous lovers. In these cases, if we observe well, it is almost never a noble passion that guides the murderous hand. Rather, it is a passion that only serves to give a scent of sentimentality to the egoism of the guilty parties, or the semblance of an excuse to the temperaments of two degenerates.

If I steal truly out of need or if I kill truly out of passion, I do not have the time, the means, or the desire to associate another person with my crime. To give an accomplice to Othello or to Jean Valjean—the classic types of sympathetic, fortuitous criminals—would be a psychological absurdity.

Therefore, we unwaveringly uphold the principle that the sole fact of committing a crime *with a partner* must always constitute an aggravating circumstance independently of whatever other reason.[159]

This is the unique judicial consequence that we feel we can deduce from the study of the criminal couple. "The law would be tyrannical or incomplete if it came down to detail," says Pellegrino Rossi.[160] And a fortiori it would be illogical and unjust if whoever writes on the basis of not just one fact but on a complexity of facts wanted to go into many details. To generalize is a necessity of science, but it is a necessity that inevitably contains errors, above all for a positivist, who knows that, as in nature two identical tree leaves do not exist, two actions that are psychologically equal cannot exist.

Before closing this summary, however, we want to make a modest observation about the *succubus*, which is the most interesting aspect of the criminal couple.

Without any doubt, this individual, who forcibly carries out the crime because of a more or less strong suggestion, is much less perverse than

158 Féré, *Dégénérescence et criminalité* (Paris: Alcan, 1888).

159 It would be absurd if we, who abhor every absolutism, were to maintain that there should not be or could never be exceptions to this principle. Earlier in chapter 3 (125–26), regarding the case of an *infanticidal couple*, we were saying that the *succubus* (Victorine Lemaire) deserved acquittal. Hence, we see that for the *succubus* the sole fact of being with another one, if it can be a reason for justification, can sometimes count even more as an excuse.—The principle we stated in the text thus applies to the majority of cases, and we believe to have supported it with good arguments.

160 P. Rossi, *Traité de droit pénal: Oeuvres complètes*, 3rd ed., vol. II, 216 [in French in Sighele's text].

the companion who slowly corrupted him. But is that individual any less dangerous?

If I am not mistaken, the concept of *dangerousness*—very justly regarded by the positive school as the first and foremost way to measure the reaction that society must inflict on a guilty person—has been, until now, almost identified with the concept of *perversity*.[161]

The more perverse a man is, the more dangerous he is. This is the affirmation that derives from the theories of Raffaele Garofalo.[162] We do not want to—or believe one could—contradict an affirmation with such clear evidence but it needs to be completed with this: the weaker a man is, the more dangerous he is.

Indeed, one can be dangerous in two ways, or, better, for two reasons, one of which is positive, the other negative—because we are by nature predisposed to *spontaneously* do evil, and because we are by nature predisposed to do evil *by suggestion*.

Thus far, we have brought to light the dangerousness of the active and energetic criminal without thinking much of the weak criminal prone to suggestion.

Now, even if we omit to note that active and energetic criminals are rather rare, while, instead, the bulk of the army of criminality is composed of weaklings, one cannot deny that in our social environment the

161 I believe that having identified the concept of *dangerousness* with that of *perversity* depends on a residue of the old ideas that have unconsciously survived also in positivist theory. The classics and metaphysicians punished man as he is and wants to be *an evildoer*. Although they deny free will and place at the foundation of an individual's punishability the *danger* that he represents, the positivists have not completely managed to shake off this idea of *wickedness*, which alone, even for them, often determines the measure of their reaction, above and beyond every consideration of dangerousness. Indeed, for the insane criminal (and I speak not of the morally insane, but of he who is struck by intellectual madness), no positivist had the courage to propose the death penalty that they propose for born criminals. Why? Evidently because if in the madman one recognizes a *dangerousness* often equal to or even greater than that of the born criminal, one does not equally recognize an intentional *perversity*. Hence, even the positivists—despite having substituted the word *defence* for the word *penalty*—cannot get rid of the sentiment that wants to reserve the greatest punishment to the *morally despicable* man, rather than to the *dangerous* man. Now—let's be clear—I confess I am the first to be guilty of this contradiction, given that one would need to be truly mad to maintain that madmen are to be given the most extreme penalty—but I recognize this contradiction, and I maintain that in some cases one can and must overcome it, defending oneself energetically even from the *dangerous* individual who is not very *perverse*.

162 [See *The Criminal Crowd*, 8n10.]

occasions for and suggestions to crime are many and so strong that the probability that a weakling will succumb becomes almost a certainty. Therefore, in many cases and from the point of view of danger, the weak and suggestible person is equal to a spontaneously perverse individual.[163]

Without a doubt, these weaklings, these moral neurasthenics, as Benedikt would call them, are less insensitive than the true born criminals, who are deprived of every sense of compassion and probity. They can always say: "I committed the crime because others forced me to do so."

But if this is an excuse that might matter a great deal for whoever wants to punish the *subjective guilt*, I believe it will sound almost irrelevant to the positivist, to anyone who—abandoning every idea of fault or merit—punishes, that is, defends himself from danger, and knows that a suggestible person tomorrow will find—as he found today—the occasion or person that will make him once again commit a crime.

Unfortunately, the world can truly be defined in just two words, as theologians do: *corrupt* and *be corrupted.* And whoever is easily corruptible cannot, from the utilitarian point of view, be treated very differently from he who corrupts.

163 Let's add that—if we abandon the criminal world and consider society as a whole from a wider point of view—we cannot disavow that the energetic character, despite its many flaws, can be more useful (and for me always more agreeable) than the weak character, even with many qualities. On this topic, [John] Stuart Mill has a very beautiful page: "It is not because men's desires are strong that they act ill; it is because their consciences are weak. There is no natural connection between strong impulses and a weak conscience. The natural connection is the other way. To say that one person's desires and feelings are stronger and more various than those of another, is merely to say that he has more of the raw material of human nature, and is therefore capable, perhaps of more evil, but certainly of more good. Strong impulses are but another name for energy. Energy may be turned to bad uses; but more good may always be made of an energetic nature, than of an indolent and impassive one. Those who have most natural feeling, are always those whose cultivated feelings may be made the strongest. The same strong susceptibilities that make the personal impulses vivid and powerful, are also the source from whence are generated the most passionate love of virtue, and the sternest self-control." [*On Liberty* 115–16.]

# 3 From *Sectarian Criminality*

## Chapter 2: "The Psychology of the Sect"

*I*

Epictetus said that what upsets men are not things, but the ideas that they derive from things.

*Things* do indeed—to use the Greek philosopher's words—always remain the same: it is *ideas* that change. And they change so much that not even a man, whose life is so short, is allowed to die with the ideas into which he was born and by which he lived. Everything changes and with immense velocity. In politics and science, what was considered an axiom yesterday is an error today, and human thought in its vertiginous race can very well resemble fashion, the fickle goddess who makes each new day bring new laws.

You speak about medicine? What brought death fifty or twenty years ago now brings life, and vice versa.

You speak about art? What was beautiful at the beginning or middle of our century today has become vulgar and commonplace.

You speak about the science of nature, from astronomy to biology? Discoveries induce more discoveries, and the old scientific belief is forced to transform itself and even makes religious belief vacillate, which, until a short time ago, was considered to be unwavering.

Criminology, too, had to follow the destiny of all ideas or, better yet, of all the systems of ideas created by human fantasy.

Until now, crime has been considered a strictly individual action—perhaps the most individual of all actions—and, among criminologists, the notion of the unshared crime was lost, just as the notion of collective sin among theologians was lost. When the attacks of conspirators or the misdeeds of a gang of robbers forced us to recognize the existence of collectively committed crimes, jurists rushed to break up this criminal *nebula* into nothing more than a sum of individual crimes.

Today the terms of the problem have changed; today the difficulty does not consist in finding collective crimes, but rather in discovering crimes that are not collective, that do not actually involve the complicity of the environment.[1]

What happened?

Something very simple, but with effects that brought about a revolution.

The belief in free will was destroyed, and that poor human brain that considered itself an absolute king, whose decrees were spontaneous and intangible, had to descend to the rank of a constitutional king, whose decrees were nothing but the necessary reflection of a multitude of physical, moral, and intellectual factors that leave him only with a semblance of liberty.

Today one could ask whether there are individual crimes, just as one asks whether works of genius that are not collective can exist.[2]

Without a doubt, any human action has an evident, definite, and precise cause: *a person.* But because this person has materially acted, can we, perhaps, say that all the infinite causes and conditions that produce the action can only be retraced to that person?

Is the individual—even when he operates alone, perhaps unbeknown to him or us—not motivated by an invisible and innumerable crowd, that of his ancestors compatriots, or educators, whose influences combine and accumulate in his brain, and suddenly arise altogether at particular moments, a true internal multitude that swarms and ferments in a cranium?[3]

Remove from a criminal all that belongs to external influences (education, instruction, activism, etc.) at the time of his crime, or from an inventor at the moment of his discovery, and what remains? A negligible

1 See G. Tarde, "Foules et sectes au point de vue criminel," in *Revue des Deux Mondes* (15 Nov. 1893).

2 On *intellectual collaboration,* see chapter I of my volume *La coppia criminale,* 2nd ed. (Turin: Bocca, 1897) [*The Criminal Couple,* chapter 1, this volume].

3 See the review to the 1st edition of my *Criminal Crowd* in *Revue philosophique* of 1891, by G. Tarde, and reprinted in the volume *Études pénales et sociales.*

thing, yet a thing that need not isolate itself in order to individualize itself: the *I*, this brief pronoun that, nonetheless, encapsulates an enormous mystery, this synthesis of our organism of which we ignore how it forms although we know its components, this psychological formula that no one until now could solve, that is as invisible as air, as impalpable as fire, and nonetheless as mighty and eternal as life.

Dozens, hundreds of people must have seen an apple fall from a tree under which they sat, or observed the isochronous oscillations of a lamp in a church; but only the genius, the *I* of Newton or Galileo could find in those common occurrences the revelation of a great physical law.

To thousands, to hundreds of thousands of people the current conditions of social life suggest and offer the pretext of a crime, but only the criminal tendency, the *I* of a Ravachol, of a Henry, or of a Palla[4] would be pushed to throw bombs or fire a handgun because of those conditions.

All actions, therefore, are collective in a sense and individual in another sense. They are the effect that comes from the impact of two forces—the individual and the environment—just as every disease is the consequence of a microbe's encounter with the terrain in which it was able to evolve.

Between the environment and the individual there exists a relationship that I would call of osmosis and endosmosis; sometimes it is the first that influences the second, at other times the second that influences the first. Of course, the individual, the *I*, needs to blend with the environment so as to acquire self-consciousness and the ability to fortify itself. Like every animal organism, *the individual feeds on that which alters him.*[5]

4 [Anarchist political criminals frequently mentioned by the major criminologists of Sighele's time include the following: The French anarchist François Claudius Koenigstein, known as Ravachol (1859–1892), who fought for the improvement of working conditions and was publicly guillotined, becoming an inspiration for many popular songs; Émile Henry (1872–1894), famous for several violent attacks, such as the detonation of a bomb at the Café Terminus in Paris's Gare Saint-Lazare and at the French Chamber of Deputies; Galileo Palla (1865–1944), who was considered one of the most dangerous Italian anarchists and participated in the 1894 Lunigiana uprising.]

5 This phrase by Tarde, which seems to me a good definition of animal life, suggests an analogy with intellectual life. Rousseau says, wrongly, that man must be used to a regime of solitude since his childhood. Like the brain, which must suggestionize itself with readings so that then, *by itself*, it can fix what it learned, in other words, change food into nourishment, so man must live in the world, *to nourish himself with what changes him*, except then to isolate himself in order to meditate on what he saw and felt. *Solitude is fertile only when it alternates with an intense life of relations, of which it is meditation.*

This alteration of the *I* occurs, in quotidian and peaceful forms of social life, by a slow process of widespread infiltration. I would say that the environment modifies the individual with that same law of gradual, unperceived, and imperceptible mutation with which nature makes him grow and evolve.

Looking at a child every day, do you realize how much he has grown since the day before. Studying a man every day, you cannot specify which new lines of development the environment is forming in his spirit.

But allow time to pass, and, after months or years, it will be easier to say how much that child and man have changed physically, mentally, and intellectually.

If, rather than in peaceful everyday life, you compare the man within a more limited and intense collectivity than society in its general meaning—if, that is, you consider him as a member of a nation, class, caste, sect, party, assembly, or crowd—you can see that the alteration of his *I*, by means of the environment that so closely surrounds him, no longer occurs by a slow process of widespread infiltration, but rather by a process that gradually increases in intensity of time and modality, to the point of resembling—in the extreme case of the crowd—a true, torrential flood that not only alters the *I*, but also suppresses or totally changes it.

So, to study this man, the notions of individual psychology and sociology are no longer enough, because a part of his actions are determined by the influence of collective psychology—whether this collectivity is a nation, class, caste, sect, or mob. Therefore, to understand his *I*, to retrace his part of responsibility, one must study the *alterations* within him that are produced by the specific environment in which he lived. Thus, if you are confronted with a *sectarian criminal*, you cannot be content with studying only his person in order to judge his crime, but you must consider his *sect*, which is the terrain where he grew up, *le bouillon* (as the French would say) where the microbe of his crime evolved, in other words, the totality of the most immediate factors that have *altered* his *I* and that have reduced it to his present state.

## *II*

We undertake the study of the psychology of the *sect* with greater pleasure, as it is the necessary complement to the study of the psychology of the crowd.

The crowd cannot be understood without the *sect*. One could say that a *sect* is the *nucleus* and the *yeast* of every crowd.

It is rare, very rare indeed, that actions, whether very good or bad, performed by a crowd were not motivated and initially caused by (a cause sometimes very distant and thus difficult to retrace) the idea of a sect. And if it is true that a crowd often put in motion by a group of fanatics surpasses them, absorbs them, and becomes headless, no longer appearing to have a guide, then it is also true, as Tarde elegantly says, "that it no longer has a guide, just as risen dough has no more yeast …"[6]

In the great historical crowds, as in the small crowds that form every day, you can find, when searching for it, the work of sects, which is sometimes evident and sometimes occult—or if not of sects, of certain corporations.

The crusades were attributable to monastic orders, the September Massacres to the Jacobins, the Expedition of the Thousand to a very few who firmly conceived and wanted it.[7]

"A great number of popular movements"—writes Proal[8]—"that seemed spontaneous, in fact, are nothing but assembled movements, instigated, prepared, or at least exploited by political parties. Riots rarely are sudden explosions of popular anger; they are often imposed by ambitious leaders. The 20th of June was prepared by Girondists, who wanted to impose themselves to the king as ministers. The 31st of May and the 2nd of June were conceived by Robespierre and by Danton …[9]

When you see a crowd attempt to extinguish a fire, the intelligent activity that it reveals is ascribed to the fire brigade, which by example—this mighty, silent suggestion—teaches and directs.

When workers on strike transcend absurd violence and go so far as to destroy things because, from their point of view, this is right—for

6 In this vein, Tarde himself wrote in his already cited article, "So to the chiefs of a gang or riot, we can always ask about the cunning and the ability it has shown in the execution of its massacres, plunderings, fires, but not always about the violence and the extent of harm caused by criminal contagions. One must honour only the general for its campaign plans, but not the bravery of its soldiers."

7 [The September Massacres were dramatic killings that occurred in Paris and other French cities in 1792 during the French Revolution. The Expedition of the Thousand refers to the volunteers led by Giuseppe Garibaldi who during the Italian Risorgimento landed in Sicily to overthrow the Bourbons.]

8 L. Proal, *Le crime politique* (Paris: Alcan, 1895), 104. [The correct title is *La Criminalité politique*. See 189n79.]

9 [On 20 June 1792 the French populace invaded the King's palace at the Tuileries and the halls of the Assembly. Between 31 May and 2 June 1793, one of the most important insurrections of the French Revolution took place, which decreed the fall of the Girondin party.]

example, the tools of those who did not want to participate in the strike—it means there is a labour union behind them, a workers' association.

When there is a demonstration in the streets, you can surmise that that those screams and threats result from the influence of a political circle or of a sect.

Examples could be endlessly multiplied.[10]

The danger (and in certain cases even the fortune) of sects consists precisely in their potential for expansion. They could do but little harm if they were reduced to their own forces; yet, a light yeast of perversity is enough to raise an enormous dough of destructive and absurd anger.

And it is in this sense, and for this reason, that the psychology of the sect completes the psychology of the crowd.

Studying the crowd is like judging a drama from what one sees on stage; studying the sect is like judging a drama from what happens backstage.

## *III*

Luigi Settembrini, in the first volume of his *Ricordanze*, writes these words:

> In free nations there are parts that are public and employ means that, if not always honest, have at least a legal semblance. In subjugated countries there are secret sects that, out of anger or corruption, do not care much about the quality of means. Sects are a necessity of servitude, and cease when the idea that formed them is no longer secret or exclusive to a few but, rather, public and general; it must spread and fly everywhere. If you want a butterfly you must first have the maggot ...[11]

In a narrow sense, Settembrini's affirmation could not be considered absolutely true.

Even in free nations there are sects: the anarchist sect is proof, which exists today in the free nations of France and Italy.

But in a broader sense, that affirmation is completely right because sects (which distinguish themselves from the parties almost solely because

10 See G. Tarde, art. cit.

11 Luigi Settembrini, *Ricordanze della mia vita*, 5th ed. (Naples, 1881), vol. I, 85–86. [Settembrini (1813–1877) was an Italian politician and literary scholar, imprisoned for conspiring against the Bourbon government. After the unification of Italy, he was appointed professor of Italian literature at the University of Naples, and he became a senator in 1875.]

they are secret) rise, indeed, where there is no freedom for the idea or for the ideas they support. And today, even in free nations, there is no freedom for the anarchist sect.

Rather, not only the anarchists, but also the socialists are, with respect to the current government, in the same sociological relationship in which the Italian patriots were half a century ago with respect to the foreign governments of Italy.

Their party can, thus, be better defined as a sect, precisely because in many cases it must act in secret, and because it is subject to the persecutions and repressions that are not inflicted on the so-called constitutional political parties.

Furthermore, from a psychological point of view, from which we intend to study sects, it is not important, nor would it be possible, to clearly distinguish them from parties.

We already hinted at it,[12] and we wish to reiterate that in psychology, above all in collective psychology, there are no clear-cut lines of separation, and it would be dangerous to give any definitions, which—apart from geometrical ones—are always inexact.[13]

*The sect and the party are but subsequent phases of an idea or a sentiment that arises.*

This is the unique difference that we believe we are able to ascertain.

The sectarian phase subsists until that idea or sentiment has not had the baptism of legitimacy; and often that phase is not surpassed and the idea or sentiment is extinguished with it, as when the idea was foolish, the sentiment was antisocial, or the time was not yet mature enough.

The phase of the party takes over when, the idea being right or the sentiment good, either one can win the misoneism of the majority and obtain—so to speak—the right to citizenship in the moral and intellectual world.

With time, this party—after having been recognized as legitimate—becomes the majority. And at this point, which marks the *zenith* of its trajectory, the party begins, little by little, inadvertently, to back down as

12 See above in chapter 1, and my polemic "Sull'intelligenza e moralità della folla," with Enrico Ferri, Gabriele Tarde, Silvio Venturi, and Pio Viazzi, in *Critica Sociale* (Nov. 1894).

13 The quote is by C. Lombroso, in response to my critiques of his and R. Laschi's volume called *Il delitto politico e le rivoluzioni.* (See my pamphlet *Il delitto politico*, Bologna, Fava and Garagnani, 1889, extract from *Archivio giuridico.*)

other sects arise all around that will become parties and, in their turn, will follow the same process to the detriment of their predecessor.

It is inevitable that everything that is born will die, that is, everything undergoes this transformation of death, which seems to mark an end. Social organisms are subject to it, as much as physical organisms. And for them old age is—as for individuals—a return to infancy.

The party that, after attaining omnipotence, sees its decline approaching, becomes a sect once again, just as at the time when it took its first steps. It will not be as violent and audacious as before, because it is no longer youthful, but it will substitute these gifts with the astuteness, cleverness, and force that come from holding power in hand, and it will defend the conquered terrain with that energy with which, in the past, it attempted to seize someone else's terrain.

This trajectory that parties follow also pertains to all men and all ideas. Even in science, when a theory or school is well established, it looks on the newly arisen theories and schools with diffidence or scorn, and attempts to fight them in every way. "Anyone," writes Enrico Ferri, "who dedicated their lives to obtaining a reform or any kind of progress, naturally succumbs to; only a few privileged minds can resist the illusion that their achievement is the ultimate goal of human improvement, and, believing they have attained the non plus ultra, a revolutionary of yesterday becomes a conservative today."[14] Everyone, even geniuses, having thus arrived at the end of their lives, defend the ideas for which they fought with an aversion to novelty, and do not admit that they can be modified as they had previously modified ancient ideas in their turn. Precisely in this sense Spencer said that every accomplished progress is an obstacle to future progress; and it is curious that Bagehot made the same observation in almost identical terms: "by the time a man of science attains eminence on any subject,"—he writes—"he becomes a hindrance upon it, because he is sure to retain errors which were in vogue when he was young, but which the new race has refuted."[15]

Taine says that "a revolution is nothing but the rising of a grand sentiment."[16]

The same definition could be attributed to sects, which are the soul of every revolution.

14 *Nuovi orizzonti*, 2nd ed., 7.

15 Bagehot, *Physics and Politics*, 60.

16 H. Taine, *L'idéalisme anglais*, 152.

They are, so to speak, its negative soul because they generally only have destruction in mind, following the biological truth that "destruction is fundamental for construction ..."[17]

But this negative work is also necessary in the beginning.

Negative work is pure madness, according to most. But in every revolution both insane and wise people are necessary, just as boldness and wisdom are necessary in all great things; "at the outset, however, only the insane are always needed."[18]

They will be called criminals or martyrs, apostles or instigators, according to the times and cases—just as those who have arrived at the top, who do not intend to surrender to the new sect that is moving forward to destroy their own, will be called defenders of order or exploiters of the people. But to the scholar's impartial eye, they will both look like different representatives of two moments—the first and the last—of every sect and every party. In other words, they will seem the atavistic residues of whoever fights with violence in order to conquer, or the civil and mature representatives of whoever fights with astuteness in order to preserve. And if politics must divide them in its judgment, science will reunite them and treat their differences as a mere question of form.

Sometimes—but it is a rare case—even when the sect has become a party and a majority, it keeps the systems of action with which it was born and developed. This happens in periods of brief and intense revolutions when power is gained by storm in a brief moment, and the sect that yesterday still had to defend itself from the contrary opinion of the majority, today finds itself sovereign and dominating. Therefore, there is no time—and no experience, either, which is the daughter of time—to change methods, and one remains in the government with the ideas and systems that they had in the scant ranks of the opposition.

Look at the Jacobins. They did not change their nature in order to change their status and political impact; violence was their line of conduct always and everywhere. They did not have time to grow old, either as men or as a party, hence they always remained young, they were always *psychologically* a sect, even when they synthesized and spoke for all of France.

Later we will study the evolution of the sectarian spirit from *violent* to *fraudulent*; for now we will limit ourselves to tracing what I believe are the general and fundamental lines of the psychology of every sect.

---

17 J. Moleschott, *La circolazione della vita*, 49.
18 L. Settembrini, op. cit., vol. I, 89.

## *IV*

It is a law of nature that, when a group of men are joined together, they will instinctually submit to the authority of one of them.

More than a law of nature, I would say that this is an animal law. As we ascend the zoological ladder, the organs of a social body, just as those of an individual body, differentiate themselves,[19] and *organization* takes shape, which includes the meaning of *subordination*, and is actually a synonym for it.[20]

A relatively advanced social group needs a leader, just as a relatively advanced animal body needs a brain.[21] "The existence of humanity "—writes Nordau—"is a combat which it cannot carry out without captains. As long as the combat is of men against men, the herd requires a herdsman of strong muscles and ready blow. In a more perfect state, in which all humanity fights collectively against Nature only, it chooses as its chief the man of richest brain, most disciplined will, and concentrated attention."[22]

The existence of this leader (which the French call *meneur*)[23] in every human group does not need to be demonstrated; it is a spontaneous consequence of the phenomenon of association.

---

19 The criterion of the vital perfection generally accepted by English philosophers is the level to which the division of labour and the specialization of functions are pushed in every individual. See H. Spencer, *Les premiers principes*, translated by Cazelles, 359.

20 See Espinas, *Des Sociétés animales*, 2nd ed. (Paris: Germer Bailiève, 1878), 174, 185, and 227. On page 185 of the same volume we read: "A society cannot but organize itself thanks to a direction, on the one hand, and a subordination, on the other." And on page 227: "Individuality is the dominant character in the last ranks of the animal kingdom—somewhat absolute individuality. Beings of different species and in prodigious numbers live in waters, on the ground, and on other animals in a state of complete isolation. A great number of foraminifera, whose carapaces have formed continents, are physiologically isolated. Such beings are weak because they are alone. However, since the first steps of the ladder of life, association appears. It manifests itself, alike, in the first phases of individual growth of all superior animals ..."

21 "The more imperfect the creature," says Goethe, "the more the parts are equal or similar and the more they hold together. The more perfect is the creature, the more dissimilar its parts become. The more the parts resemble each other, the less they are reciprocally subordinate. Subordination of the parts means a more perfect creature." —Maudsley, *Corpo e mente*, translated by A. Collina (1872), 202.

22 Max Nordau, *Degenerazione*, vol. I (Milan, 1894)I, 427. [English translation *Degeneration* (New York: Appleton, 1895), 472.]

23 The word is Tarde's, who is believed to have something new, affirming that in every crowd there is, clear or hidden, an instigator, a *meneur*. In fact, however, the discovery (moreover very easy) was made by others.—See on this *La folla delinquente* [*The Criminal Crowd*], 2nd ed. (Turin: Bocca, 1895), 133n2.

And, like all that originates from the inner nature of things, it occurs at first in an unconscious way, by everyone's tacit consensus, and then it becomes a conscious and deliberate fact.

I will explain. Primitive men—like animals—did not elect their leader and they did not ascribe functions, duties, and special rights to him. They were simply *subject*, by force of suggestion, to the prestige of the best among them,[24] and his authority arose from the instinctive subjection of the others. Then, gradually, this unconsciously endured authority became consciously desired, and developed into the form of elections and plebiscites, which—if sincere—are nothing but the conscious manifestation of the general will.

Even today, in human aggregates, if we have to recognize that there is always a leader, we must, moreover, recognize that this leader is sometimes nominated by the free and conscious will of whomever has that right, and sometimes he imposes himself thanks to his suggestive charm.

In general, *stable* and *legitimate* social groups, those that Tarde would call *corporations*, have their leader consciously nominated or wisely accepted. Every warehouse has its director, every convent has its superior, every regiment its colonel, every assembly its president, every court its king.

Social groups, instead, whether *unstable* or *illegitimate*, have a leader who arises, I would say, almost by spontaneous generation and to whom the members of the group unconsciously bow. Every salon has its conversational coryphaeus, every political party has its *leader*, every scientific or artistic school has its scientist or artist who is considered the master, every sect its man from whom sectarians await the Word as the disciples awaited it from Jesus.

If it were possible, in a few words, to define the difference between the leaders of individual social groups, I would say that in *legitimate* and *stable* groups the leader is always *consciously desired* and *visible*. In *illegitimate* and *unstable* groups, the leader is *visible* but founds his authority on the *unconscious subjection* of the many. Finally, in *crowds* (which are the most transitory and ephemeral of groups), not only is the authority of the leader based on *unconscious subjection*, but the *meneur* is often hidden, *invisible*.

And—a phenomenon that at first will seem strange—the prestige of this leader is generally inversely proportional to the legitimacy and consciousness with which he was elected. An office manager or president of

---

24 *Best* must be taken not in an absolute sense and in relation to abstract morality, but in a relative sense, and in connection with current and real situations.—See on this Vaccaro, *Genesi e funzioni delle leggi penali*, and Cimbali, *Il diritto del più forte*.

an assembly has less authority over the workers or members he presides over, compared with what a sect leader has over his affiliates or a *political party leader* over his fellow members; and these *leaders* have, in their turn, much less power than the obscure, unknown individual has over a multitude—the obscure and unknown individual who, on certain occasions, with a phrase or gesture, suddenly becomes the random and instantaneous despot of an entire crowd.

The reasons explaining this phenomenon are of two types: *personal* and *collective.* Namely, they belong to the intrinsic faculties of the head, of the *meneur,* or to those of the human group on which this head acts.

Clearly, the authority and prestige of a person over the individuals around him will be directly proportional to the enthusiasm and active faith that this person puts in the service of the ideas he wanted to divulge, or the goals he wanted to attain.

Now, do you believe that, in general, this enthusiasm and active faith are most present in the leader of a stable and legitimate social group, or rather in the *meneur* of an unstable and illegitimate group? Do you believe that the president of an assembly or of whatever other legitimate association has more power to attract the masses than a sect leader?

The response cannot be doubtful.

The *meneur* of a crowd or sect is, above all, a *mené.* He was, at one time, hypnotized by the idea under which he subsequently has become the apostle. And this idea has invaded him to such a point that everything beyond it vanishes or is obscured, and any contrary opinion seems an error or superstition. Such it was, for example, with Robespierre, who was hypnotized by Rousseau's philosophical ideas and employed the methods of the Inquisition to propagate them.[25]

The *meneurs,* furthermore, are usually not thinkers, but men of action. Their mind is neither vast nor limpid. Whoever is broad-minded and intellectually sharp is generally prone to tolerance, doubt, and inaction. Instead, the *meneurs* are intolerant, decisive, and active. And when a thought, goal, or theory enters into their heads, one can be certain that it will dominate them. It will not, indeed, encounter any obstacle because their brain is almost empty, and it will occupy them entirely because their brain is restricted. So, the *meneurs* "no longer belong to themselves but are mastered by it; it works in them and through them, the man, in the true sense of the word, being possessed. Something which is not himself, a monstrous parasite, a foreign and disproportionate conception, lives

25 See G. Le Bon, [*Psychologie des foules,*] op. cit., 106.

within him, developing and giving birth to the evil purposes with which it is pregnant. He did not foresee that he would have them."[26]

Suggestion, to which the *meneur* is victim, thus becomes from now on an *active force*, it becomes his passion, his vocation.

"What is a vocation"—Ribot wonders—"if not an attention that finds its path and orients itself for its entire life?"[27]

This attention to the *meneur* reaches its highest level, its extreme stage, in *the fixed idea.*[28]

Contempt and persecution do not affect him; rather, they do nothing but excite him. Personal interest, family, everything is sacrificed; even the preservation instinct is nullified in him, because the only compensation he often asks for is to become a martyr.

"The possessor of an obsession"—Nordau writes—

> is an incomparable apostle. There is no rational conviction arrived at by sound labour of intellect, which so completely takes possession of the mind, subjugates so tyrannically its entire activity, and so irresistibly impels it to words and deeds, as delirium. Every proof of the senselessness of his ideas rebounds from the deliriously insane or half-crazy person. No contradiction, no ridicule, no contempt affects him; obstacles do not discourage him, because even his instinct of self-preservation is unable to cope with the power of his delirium, and for the same reason he is often enough ready, without further ado, to suffer martyrdom.[29]

To create faith—be it religious, political, or social faith, faith in a work, an idea, or a man—is the main role played by the great agitators, who are always abnormal if not insane. And this is why their influence is always immense. Of all the strengths mankind possesses, faith has always been the

---

26 H. Taine, *Les origines de la France contemporaine: La Révolution*, vol. III, *Le gouvernement révolutionnaire*, 13th ed. [Sighele, in error, has 14th ed. here] (Paris, 1892 [1883]), 70. [English translation by John Durand in Hyppolite Taine, *The Revolution*, vol. 3 (London: Sampson Low, Marston, Searle and Rivington, 1885), 53.]

27 Ribot, *Psychologie de l'attention* (Paris: Alcan, 1889), 15.—Similarly, at another point Ribot writes, "The great attentions are always caused and supported by great passions."

28 See Buccola, *La legge del tempo nei fenomeni del pensiero.*—Ribot says that "the fixed idea is the chronic form of the hypertrophy of attention and ecstasy is the acute form" (op. cit., 138).—Esquirol says that "the fixed idea is the catalyst of intelligence."

29 Max Nordau, *Degenerazione*, vol. I, 61. [Nordau *Degeneration*, 31.]

biggest, and, rightly so, the Gospel attributes to it the power to transport mountains. Giving faith to a man increases his strength a hundred times.[30]

But, to instil faith, one must have it. The apostles who raised the soul of the crowds—Peter the Hermit, Luther, Savonarola, the men of the French Revolution, Garibaldi, Mazzini—did not exert their charm without having first been fascinated by an idea. Only then were they able to create faith, this formidable power that renders man a slave of his dream.

Now, this deeply felt faith, which spreads by suggestion, is the exclusive patrimony of the *meneurs*, namely, the leaders who arise by *spontaneous generation* as a result of their prestige, which is a gift of nature.

Legitimate leaders of stable social groups generally do not have it. They direct and command because they were nominated or elected to that position, but they are not animated or *possessed* by an intimate drive that can be the reason for their authority and the secret of their strength. They are followed and obeyed out of habit, fear, duty, or persuasion. In other words, leaders have around them a multitude of people who reflect and consciously adapt to their will, rather than a suggestionized population, which blindly throws itself headlong wherever the *meneur* wants to throw them.[31]

And this does not happen only for their intrinsic *personal* reason, but also for a *collective* reason.

The environment on which the *meneur* acts is very different from that on which the leader of a legitimate association usually acts.

The members of this association are often *dispersed*, while the members of a sect or crowd are almost always *gathered*, and it is useless to reiterate the evidence I presented elsewhere to demonstrate that suggestion is faster and more intense on individuals united by an immediate contact than on dispersed or distant individuals.[32]

---

30 See G. Le Bon, op. cit., 107.

31 To prove this assertion, which seems to me evident in itself, it is enough that in history the great people able to suggest, those who drag the crowds behind them, were in a large part *non-legitimate* leaders, meaning people who did not have the power by heredity or by legal nomination, but who conquered them with their own personal energy. The exceptions to this rule—which undeniably exist—do nothing but confirm it. To make an example close to home, Victor Emmanuel, legitimate king, exerted a charm on the multitude, and one could psychologically define him as a *meneur*; but his prestige derived from a faith, an enthusiasm, an ideal extraneous to his quality as a king, and which, indeed for this, made the population love him like a father, like a hero. His popularity, in other words, and his glory depended on the fact that he was something more and better than what kings ordinarily were.

32 See *La folla delinquente*, 2nd ed., 176 and ff.

Second, members of a stable and legitimate association are more cultivated and, above all, calmer, more sensible, and more reflective than the members of a crowd or sect. Personal charm, therefore, has a minor power over them; the inhibition centres are more active in them. Reason guides and restrains emotions, hence immediate and complete endorsement of a man, enthusiasm for a phrase, or fanaticism for an idea are difficult and rare.

Third, the leader of an association or a corporation acts solely on those who belong to those groups, and he knows more or less who they are. The sect leader or the *meneur* of a crowd acts, instead, on a much vaster and more undetermined public. He attracts potential disciples scattered everywhere. In a word, he gathers and creates his population, and he creates it by attracting all the weak, coercible individuals, all those—and there are many—who wander on the earth like moths in search of a light to fly around, until sometimes ... they burn themselves.

Therefore, the reason why a *meneur* has more influence than a legitimate leader of an association or corporation on those surrounding him resides in two orders of factors: the energetic and active faith that he possesses—(and Mazzini says that "true energy is like magnetism on the multitudes"[33])—and the weakness of will of those who compose the environment on which he acts.

After all, these are—energy on one side, weakness on the other—the factors of all associations, and the more they are exaggerated and, so to speak, intensified, the firmer, more uniform, and mightier is the human nucleus they form.

The ideal of every association is unison, meaning the formation of only one body and only one soul—to use the classic phrase—from two or more bodies and two or more souls.

Now, the unison does not form without domination, on the one hand, and subjugation, on the other.

Look at all the forms of association—from that *à deux* to that of 100 or 1,000, from the normal to the pathological ones—in love, suicide, madness, criminality: the phenomenon is identical.

In the amorous couple there is always one who *depends* psychologically on the other. It is a trivial observation that two people are drawn to each other when, although sharing some fundamental character traits, they have different qualities and defects. Two temperaments of

33 Writings by G. Mazzini, *Lettera di un italiano a Carlo Alberto di Savoja*, vol. I, 62.

identical character could not unite—they would break apart. In order for two gears to turn together regularly, one needs to have the tooth where the other has the hollow. "For such a truly passionate inclination to arise"—Schopenhauer says—"something is required which can only be expressed by a chemical metaphor: two persons must neutralize each other, like acid and alkali, to a neutral salt."[34] And common sense grasped this truth, creating the proverb: opposites attract. Opposites attract because—I believe—love is essentially nothing but the *desire to complete each other* physiologically and psychologically, and two individuals complete each other precisely when one has what the other lacks. Now, supposing that opposites attract, it is evident that one must maintain a certain moral dominance over the other. Indeed, if some elements of temperament, of intelligence, and of the heart differ, the psychic and intellectual functions the two will perform will necessarily also be different, although aiming for an identical end. The one will have the will, the other the execution; the one will be the head, the other the arm.[35]

In the *double suicide*, we attest to the same fact: the more intelligent individual exerts his influence over the other to push him to die; a very determined will subdues a weaker one; a hand executes while the thought commands.[36]

In the *madness à deux*, the phenomenon does not change. Legrain writes, "The explanation for the cases of *madness à deux* must be sought in the pre-existing inclination to delirium, on one the hand, and in the weakness of spirit that accompanies it, on the other."[37]

Likewise, in the *criminal couple* it is the born criminal who asserts himself and subjects the criminaloid to suggestion.[38]

---

34 Schopenhauer, *Il mondo come volontà e come rappresentazione* (Dumolard, 1888), Book III, 298, Italian ed. [English translation by R.B. Haldane and J. Kemp, in Arthur Schopenhauer, *The World as Will and Idea* (London: Kegan Paul, Trench, Hübner, 1906), vol. 3, 356. This quotation and the entire section already appeared in *The Criminal Couple* 91.]

35 See on this issue J. Rambosson, *Phénomènes nerveux, intellectuels et moraux, leur transmission par contagion* (Paris: Firmin-Didot, 1883).

36 See my study *L'evoluzione dal suicidio all'omicidio nei drammi d'amore* (Turin: Bocca, 1891).

37 Legrain, *Du délire chez les degénerés* (Paris, 1896), 173.

38 I will not bring proofs to support these ideas because they have already been affirmed in my volume *Le crime à deux*, and yet again in the 2nd Italian edition of *La coppia criminale* [*The Criminal Couple*] (Turin: Bocca, 1897), to which I refer the reader.

Now, move up from these simple cases to the more complex; shift from the *suicide à deux*, the *madness à deux*, and the criminal couple to suicides, epidemic madness, and associations of evildoers. Go from the suggestion of teacher upon his disciple to that of a sect leader upon his affiliates, and you will always find the identical law—although magnified. In every association you will find two forces, one active and one passive.[39]

And here I take the liberty to integrally transcribe a page by Gabriel Tarde that, while it illustrates my concept, also authoritatively endorses it:

> An idea always makes its men, like a fertilized egg makes its body. It sinks and gradually extends its roots in the soil that has been prepared for it. From the first one who conceived it, the idea passes, by imitative impressionability, to one catechumen first, then to two, three, ten, a hundred, a thousand.
>
> The first phase of this embryogeny is the association of two: this is the basic fact that one should study well because all subsequent phases are only its repetition. M. Sighele has devoted a volume[40] to demonstrating that in every association *à deux*—marital, loving, friendly, criminal—there is always a partner who suggestionizes the other and shapes him in his image. And it is good that this demonstration was made, no matter how superficial. This is unquestionably certain: beware of the household where there is neither *meneur* nor *méné*; divorce is not far away. In all couples, of whatever kind, there is a more or less apparent or erased distinction between suggestionizer and suggestionized. But as the association grows by the addition of further neophytes, this distinction is still verifiable. This plurality, ultimately, is but a great duality and, no matter how numerous a corporation or a crowd may be, it is also a sort of couple, where at times any member is suggestionized by the totality of all the others—a collective suggestionizer including the dominant leader—, and at other times the entire group is suggestionized by him.[41]

39 Nordau writes (op. cit. vol. I, 60): "The common, organic bases of these different forms of one and the same phenomenon—of the *folie à deux*, the association of neuropaths, the founding of aesthetic schools, the banding of criminals—is, with the active part, viz., those who lead and inspire, the predominance of obsessions: with the associates, the disciples, the submissive part, weakness of will and morbid susceptibility to suggestion." [*Degeneration*, 30.]

40 *Le crime à deux* (Lyon: Storek, 1893).

41 G. Tarde, *Essais et mélanges sociologiques* (Lyon: Storek, 1895), 46.

## *V*

Let's recapitulate.

We said that in every association there must be, and there is, one who commands and one who obeys. We added that any association is all the stronger the more forceful its leadership is, and the blinder its obedience. We showed that, for personal and collective reasons, in unstable and illegitimate groups, like a crowd or a sect, that leadership is forceful and that obedience is blind more than in any other stable and legitimate group.

We can, therefore, affirm that the crowd and the sect are among the strongest human associations, in the sense that uniformity and unison are the rule for them, and that *debate*—this quality of independent spirits—as well as *rebellion*—the consequence that the restless draw—are unknown to them.

Not too many words are needed to demonstrate the truth of what we have claimed. "A crowd or sect"—Tarde says—"has no other idea than what is suggested to them."[42]

The crowd, indeed, is easy prey for whoever manages to become its master. Let's cry *life or death*; let's go and kill Tom, enemy of the people; or, let's go and save Dick, friend of the poor; be it a crime or an act of heroism, the crowd will commit one or perform the other, according to the moment and its predisposition, but it will act *all together* with one of these passionate surges that assimilate its psychology to the explosion of a line of gunpowder whose fuse had, been lit. There is no contradiction, there is no possible discord, and, if there is, it is annihilated. The thousand voices have but one soul: the mysterious soul of the crowd. This *psychological unison* constitutes the invincible force of the crowd, and confers to its acts the tragic awfulness of irreparability.

In the sect, the identical phenomenon occurs, but with this single difference: that the actions are performed with more consciousness.

Indeed, in the sect, too, the words *debate* and *rebellion* are unknown. Its affiliates act on a simple sign of their leader, just as the individual in a multitude acts according to the cry of whoever suggestionized him. And, whether few or many, close or far, sectarians have one soul: the soul of the sect.

---

42 Art. cit.

In the crowd by unconscious suggestion, in the sect by conscious suggestion, we see that the inflexible principle that informed ancient societies resurges, or better, persists.

The sect wants docile and obedient men like the soldiers of an army or the monks of a convent. It wants *equal unities* directed by a sole commander, not *independent organisms* that can move by themselves. It realizes *dynamically*, in time, the uniformity that the crowd obtains *statically* for a single and brief instant. All sectarians serve their ideal with the precision and simultaneity of human machines, just as all the members of a crowd scream and act like automatons set in motion by a cry or sudden act of one of them.

"(...) [I]n the old Greek or Latin cities"—Taine writes—

> (...) human society was shaped after the pattern of an army or convent. In a convent as in an army, one idea, absorbing and unique, predominates: the aim of the monk is to please God at any sacrifice; the soldier makes every sacrifice to obtain a victory. Accordingly, each renounces every other desire and entirely abandons himself, the monk to his rules and the soldier to his drill. In like manner, in the antique world, two preoccupations were of supreme importance. In the first place, the city had its gods who were both its founders and protectors: it was therefore obliged to worship these in the most reverent and particular manner; otherwise, they abandoned it. The neglect of any insignificant rite might offend them and ruin it. In the second place, there was incessant warfare, and the spoils of war were atrocious; on a city being taken every citizen might expect to be killed or maimed, or sold at auction (...). Liberty, under such conditions, is out of the question: public convictions are too imperious; public danger is too great. With this pressure upon him, and thus hampered, the individual gives himself up to the community, which takes full possession of him, because, to maintain its own existence, it needs the whole man. Henceforth, no one may develop apart and for himself; no one may act or think except within fixed lines. The type of Man is distinctly and clearly marked out, if not logically at least traditionally; each life, as well as each portion of each life must conform to this type (...). In reality, not only in Greece and in Rome, but in Egypt, in China, in India, in Persia, in Judea, in Mexico, in Peru, during the first stages of civilization, the principle of human communities is still that of gregarious animals: the individual belongs to his community the same as the bee to its hive and the ant to its ant-hill; he is simply an organ within an organism. (...)

"Just the opposite in modern society";—Taine adds—"what was once the rule has now become the exception (...). Gradually, the individual has liberated himself (...); the antique system survives only in temporary associations, like that of an army, or in special associations, as in a convent,"[43] and—I add—in some temporary and spontaneous associations, like a sect. The sect, too, wants *the entire man* and wants him to obey the unique and supreme scope for which the sect was born; it wants him to be a blind and faithful instrument, and it wants him in its hands *perinde ac cadaver*, according to the famous phrase of the mightiest and longest of sects, the Jesuits.[44]

What did the Jacobins—this other mighty sect, albeit brief—do if not revive the authoritative system of the ancient Greek and Latin cities? What was their social conception if not the logical construction of a unique and identical type of man, who must sacrifice all of himself to the community or to the state?

There is certainly no more retrograde social construction, but also there is certainly no stronger social construction, either.

What one loses in elasticity and independence one gains in cohesion and compactness. Battles—not those of long-term progress, but those of immediate utility—are more easily won when we are all in accordance with whatever goal, rather than when we leave to individual initiative the choice and pursuit of higher goals and nobler ideals.

To the people of our times, who have progressively evolved, the fact that in the first stages of humanity, as in animal aggregates, the association between organisms manifests itself as complete dedication of the single parts to the whole they form seems crude and absurd, but back then it was a fatal necessity.

"How to get the obedience of men is the hard problem,"—Bagehot writes[45]—"what you do with that obedience is less critical."

A rigid, precise, and concise law is the first need of mankind: it is what is necessary, above all, to form a core of habits, customs, and ideas. All actions of life must submit to a single rule, in view of a single goal. If this regime bans freedom of thought, it is not an evil thing or, rather, although it is evil, it is the indispensable basis for a greater good. It forms

43 Taine, *Les origines de la France contemporaine: La Révolution*, vol. III, *Le gouvernement révolutionnaire*, 13th ed. (Paris: Hachette, 1892), 121–22. [English translation by John Durand in Hippolyte Taine, *The Revolution*, vol. 3 (London: Sampson Low, Marston, Searle and Rivington, 1885), 91–92.]

44 [In the manner of a corpse. The locution comes from the *Constitution of the Society of Jesus*, where Saint Ignatius of Loyola emphasizes abnegation and obedience to religious superiors and to the Pope as if one were a lifeless body.]

45 Bagehot, *Physics and Politics*, 26.

the substratum of civilization and hardens the still soft fibre of man from earlier times.

The centuries of monotony, equality, and slavery have had their utility because they have shaped man for the centuries in which he had to be free, independent, and original.

This historical necessity, which unfolded over time and which Bagehot has sculpted so well,[46] is also in action today.

Even now in war—which, despite its transformations, is still the most grandiose and genuine atavistic residue of the primitive epoch—we preserve the ancient tactic, namely, the blind obedience of everyone to only one individual in order to obtain a unique and supreme objective: victory. We feel and know that if discipline were not strict, and if command were not absolute like obedience, that objective would fail.

In this order of ideas it is remarkable that everyone by now recognizes how, in order to have a successful outcome in a war, there has to be a *single leader*. The plurality of deliberating minds can only produce damage, precisely because it removes unison, that is, the necessary uniformity of an aggregate of individuals who must be unanimous like a single man in their attempt to attain a given objective. Macaulay rightly said that often an army was fortunate under an incapable captain, but never has an army gained victory under the guidance of a deliberating assembly: this monster of a thousand heads always produces disastrous results.

The ancient tactic survives not only in war—which is a barbaric form of fighting—but also in its most civilized equivalents, namely, intellectual fights.

Even today, indeed, the retrograde organization of primitive men is necessary for the triumph of ideas that take their first step into the world: it is necessary that men blindly obey, that they are slaves to the objective they want to reach.

Whatever new direction arises—be it artistic, scientific, religious, or political—, it needs, above all, followers who *serve* and do not *discuss*

46 Ibid., Book I, passim.—I summarized with some phrases Bagehot's ideas on the argument I am discussing, and I wish to underline that this volume by Bagehot is truly a mine, from which many illustrious authors have drawn. Taine was certainly inspired by it in writing some chapters on the psychology of the Jacobins (see vol. III, of his *Révolution*), and Tarde owes the core of his sociological theory of imitation to it. Yet—strangely—Bagehot is rarely cited. A synthetic and suggestive writer, he can be considered one of the promoters of modern sociology, just as Despine—also not often cited—can be considered one of the promoters of the school of criminal anthropology.

the banner under which they enlisted; it needs absolute dependence and uniformity. On this sole condition can it hope to have an impact and succeed.

Such a phenomenon is too evident even for the most myopic observer to require further explanation. Taking only one example in our field—or, rather, in my personal field—I know that a youth, who is attracted by a new scientific trend, from the beginning welcomes, supports, and defends *indistinctly all* the ideas of whoever may have suggestionized him: like a true disciple, he swears *in verba magistri.*[47]

This is the psychology of the neophyte, and it could not be different, since it is this same exaggeration and absolutism that reveal his conviction and passion, and that give him the energy to work, to produce, in a word, to make his own way and to inspire disciples in his turn. Gradually—when the new theory gains ground and when the neophyte, from being a simple follower, ascends to a more elevated level—he feels he can afford the luxury to partially detach himself from the ideas of the master or masters and to support some on his own.

The period of scientific independence follows that of supine obedience, but the former cannot do without or skip the latter, just as in nature the fruit cannot exist without the flower.

Just as Bagehot said that the centuries of monotony, equality, and slavery produced those of originality, inequality, and liberty, so we can say that the phase of every doctrine in which its followers support identical ideas with equal enthusiasm produces the phase—more glorious but not more useful—in which single individuals elevate themselves and acquire their own personality.

It is the eternal law of progress according to which the homogeneous becomes heterogeneous—from a uniform mass of organic material, the different, specific organs gradually sprout.

What happens in science also happens in politics and art.

In art the phenomenon presents itself with more intensity and major expansion. Hence it should be underlined.

There was an epoch in which Italian painters took pride in *doing nothing else* but imitating their masters.

The fifteenth-century schools of painting present a character of such uniformity that they represent the most typical example of suggestion and obedience, or, better, of artistic *copy*. And it is, perhaps, this humbly but tenaciously desired uniformity that constitutes the secret of the

47 [By the words of the master; to accept opinion on authority.]

charm exerted by those schools. Paul Bourget, in his *Sensations d'Italie,* has a splendid page about it, which I reproduce in its entirety because the reader can see a reflection of that *sectarian psychology in art,* which I can here only briefly mention:

> The union of the ideal and the conventional was as dear to the artists of that time as originality, at any cost, is to us. They were content with transmitting, they desired nothing more than to transmit a tradition, to be each a branch of the same great tree—not even a branch, a flower among many other flowers, one minute of a great day, one stage in a great doctrine. Therefore it is that a large collection of their works produces so strong an impression, and that so great a power still resides in each separate work. Something semipersonal allows the last effort to be divined through the fragment we see, which alone could have rendered this fragment possible. Sometimes, even, as in the present instance, the fragment is so delightful that for a moment it seems to mark the highest point reached by art, and for this moment all the glory of all the schools centres on the name of the poor and modest worker who, by force of unpretending merit, has produced a work of genius, like the greatest of the great.[48]

These words, with few variants, could be applied to all the obscure but enthusiastic disciples of an idea. They, too,—like fifteenth-century painters—put their pride into serving humbly and devotedly their objective, that is, to be the branch of a great tree, the minute of a great day, or the stage of a great doctrine. And they act in this manner because an instinct warns them that only this complete dedication of themselves to their ideal will allow it to triumph. Later, when the ideal will have conquered the majority, they will afford the luxury of being *personal,* of abandoning the imitation of their masters, of showing, in other words, that, while unanimous on the main ideas, they are not so on the secondary ones.

Now, the sect—which always reflects the first phase of every idea that arises and blossoms—cannot have and does not have but one of these tactics, the first one.

It is an inferior and retrograde tactic—we repeat—but necessary and successful, because even in intellectual battles it is important to run to the assault of the enemy position, all in accordance with and trusting the command of one's own general (apart from later dissenting on the way the conquered land should be governed), and for this initial objective

48 [In French in Sighele's text. English translation: *Impressions of Italy.* Translated by Mary J. Serrano (New York: Cassell Publishing, 1892), 18.]

there is nothing more strategically useful than the organization of the sect, this uniform and compact human group that enters like a wedge into the social organism and that, like the Macedonian phalanx, breaks through it and, in destroying it, renews it.

## *VI*

Napoleon said that there is only one form of truly effective reasoning: repetition.

My readers will pardon me if I have employed this tactic too often in the attempt to be clear and persuasive. I believed that I had to insist on the fundamental character of the sect, namely, the psychological uniformity of its members, because this character constitutes all of its strength, it is the reason for its mode of being, and—by connecting the psychology of the sect to that of the crowd—renders it possible to explain the one by means of the other.

In the first chapter,[49] I wrote that the sect is *a crowd in the dynamic state.* After what I said in the previous paragraph, this definition should seem exact, and it will seem so even more if we illustrate it with examples. The crowd—when it unites not just for the sake of curiosity or entertainment, but to demand something or to protest against someone—is nothing but a *statically violent* form of collective struggle.

Do you recall the very serious riots that broke out in Sicily in the winter of 1893–94?[50] The multitude descended into the streets and squares, devastated, inflamed, wounded, and killed. Did it do good? Or bad? It is not important to answer here. Of course, that attempted revolt, although it was a crime, or, better, a heap of crimes, had the undeniable advantage of awakening from mental torpor all those who for thirty-three years should have thought about the appalling conditions of the island.[51] Without that semblance of civil war, we would still be going ahead for many years dragging the imperious necessities of Sicily.

Now, while the crowd performs this role as alarm to the ears of solemn governments with instantaneous acts, the sect performs it slowly over time. It is, therefore, a *dynamically violent* form of collective struggle.

49 [Not included in this volume.]

50 [The "Fasci siciliani" riots. See the introduction to this volume, xviii, and *Intelligence of the Crowd,* 247 and 247n28.]

51 [Sighele here is polemically alluding to the neglect that affected southern Italy since the nation was unified in 1861.]

From the primitive Christian sects to the recent ones of the Carbonari,[52] or the current anarchists, we see a continuous and obscure activity that manifests itself from time to time with political crimes, and that tends—as the crowd does in a more brutal and unexpected way—to win, with violence, the predominance of the majority in order to inaugurate the ideal and future reality of a minority.

And, precisely because the sect is a not momentary but a continual form of struggle, its effects go quite more deeply and far beyond those of the crowd.

The crowd acts on nothing but impulse, thus without common sense;[53] the sect always acts thoughtfully and often with premeditation. The sect has a factor to its advantage that the crowd does not have: time—a very important factor because generally it does not respect what is done in its absence. And the work that the sect carries out—not only because it is slower, but also because it is more conscious—has more certain and longer consequences than those of the work accomplished by the crowd.

Furthermore, the crowd only employs violence as a means of struggle; it ignores shrewdness. By contrast, the sect is always astute, but—whenever necessary—it can also be violent; it normally acts with the brain and, when it employs the arm, the brain guides it.

Finally, if it is true that the sect follows its *meneur* as the crowd does—that is, trusting in him and determined to obey him with heroic blindness—, it is also true that a sect's *meneur* has a clear and precise objective ahead of him, which the obscure and unknown *meneur* of a crowd almost always lacks. Therefore, while the crowd—following the cry or gesture of its sudden despot—can commit useless atrocities or harm to itself, the sect, instead, always being led by a man who is aware of what he does, with an objective that shines bright ahead of him, is rarely wrong in its tactics.

All of these considerations[54] show us, after the analogies, the differences that distinguish the sect from the crowd; they hence bring us back

---

52 [Carbonari (charcoal burners) were early nineteenth-century secret revolutionary groups in favour of Italian independence.]

53 Sometimes even the crowd can commit preordained or premeditated acts.—The example is offered to us by the lynching that often one decides to commit beforehand. See on this issue my *La folla delinquente*, 2nd ed., 138, and my *Teoria positiva della complicità*, 2nd ed., 125 and ff.—The pamphlet *La Ley de Lynch en los Estados Unidos* (Havana, 1892), by Dr Josè Gonzales y Lanuza, and the articles on the same argument published by R. Garofalo and P. Dorado in *Scuola positiva* (15 Aug. and 15–30 Sept. 1893).

54 One could discuss others, for example: *the physical factor* (climate, seasons, etc.) has more importance in determining the acts of the crowds than it does for sects—the opposite in the case of the *anthropological factor*. This difference can be explained

to the conclusions expressed at the end of the previous chapter,[55] where we said that the sect is the *trait d'union* between the most inorganic of human aggregates, which is a crowd, and the most organic aggregates, which are associations, castes, and classes.

If, however, the sect is close to these human aggregates for some aspects of its psychology, it differs from them basically for this reason: that it is always *innovative*, while castes, classes, and, in general, legitimate associations are always *conservative*.

The sect is the environment where that spirit of revolt—which the victories of civilization abandon as a necessary consequence—takes shelter, feeds itself, and develops.

For each step of that infinite ladder known as progress, behind those who ascend, there are those who fall and who—being trodden on—help others to rise. These unhappy people—if they manage to stand up again—united by the desire for revenge and the envy of those who contemplate them from above, form sects,[56] these associations of losers and dissatisfied individuals who, to the victorious and happy ones, appear, by egotistical illusion, to be the germs of their social dissolution, while, in fact, they are nothing but the germs of a fatal transformation and renewal. [...]

## Chapter 4: "The Sectarian Crime"

### *I*

In the previous chapter[57] we analysed private and sectarian morality, and we aimed to explain the possible coexistence of both in one individual.

Now it is time for us to attempt to draw a conclusion from the difference between the two.

---

recalling how the actions of the crowd are more passionate (and thus more susceptible to exterior influences) than the sect.—We do not insist on this fact because we do not want to go beyond our theme too much, which is strictly psychological, and because on this topic Lombroso and Laschi already made interesting observations in their *Delitto politico*, and also Tarde in his *Études pénales et sociales*, many times cited.

55 [Not included in this volume.]

56 Understand that we allude here more specifically to the political sects, which we almost always referred to in this chapter. But in any case, the observations made matter—with few variants—for all sects, whose content is always—as we have said—a minority's attempt to revolt against the majority. For religious (and insane) sects in Russia, see the articles by Jean Finot in *La Revue des revues* (1896).

57 [Chapter 3 is not included in this volume.]

The first law that the previous observations authorize us to make is this: "sectarian morality and, in general, political morality are always less developed than private morality."

Indeed, we saw that certain actions, which the consciousness of a population gradually rejects, *first* disappear from individual habits, and *later* from social and political habits, and actually they often survive in political life. For example, such is still the case of lies, just as, in the past centuries, was the use of poison. And the same can be said, in part and in some areas like the Romagna region, about homicide, which completely dishonours a man if it is committed for private and personal objectives, but does not dishonour him at all if it is committed for political objectives.[58]

In a word, man, as *a private individual*, is much more moral than as *political individual*. The wider the sphere of his action, the more indulgent his morality becomes.

This observation supports the theory that I have elsewhere stated and defended "that collectivity is always morally worse than the individual."[59]

I applied this theory to *crowds*, to *parliaments*, to *juries*, to *commissions*, to transitory and, so to speak, short-lived gatherings of individuals. Now, by a simple logical deduction of what I have been saying, I can also apply it to other social groups, not transitory but permanent. The members of a party, sect, or nation are—as such—much less moral than *private individuals*.[60]

A misanthrope would exploit this truth to hate men and the world even more. He would elaborate on one of the articles of Adrien Sixte's philosophical code by saying that "social ties are to be reduced to a minimum

---

58 See the article cited by Ferrero.

59 And also intellectually. See my volume *La folla delinquente*, 2nd ed. (Turin: Bocca, 1895), and my pamphlet *Contro il parlamentarismo* (Milan: Treves, 1895). [Later published in *La delinquenza settaria* [*Sectarian Criminality*] and included as an appendix here as *Against Parliamentarism*.]

60 I must note that in my studies on collective psychology, I have until now observed that the *overall product* of a given human group was worse than what logically should have given the simple sum of the moral and intellectual faculties of the individuals who comprise it, but on the other hand, I had recognized that the individual *considered singularly* remained, to use a phrase by Tarde, "identical to himself," meaning he did not alter his faculties. Now, instead, it is demonstrated that the individual—for the sole fact of his cohabitation in a given human group and beyond the perturbing phenomenon of collective psychology—alters his personal qualities, and naturally, for the worse. The two observations complete each other and have—as it is easy to see—very important consequences.

not only for those who want to know and tell the truth,"[61] but also for whoever wants to remain honest.

We, who are not misanthropes, remark, without fear, the fact that "the more social cohabitation and association extend among individuals, the less rigid morality becomes," and knowing that this painful phenomenon is compensated by other very useful ones, we exploit it only to judge with major serenity and impartiality those dishonest actions that are not accomplished out of a selfish, individual motive.

Writing for the first time, quite a while ago,[62] the phrase "the more social cohabitation and association among individuals extend, the less rigid morality becomes," I foresaw that it would attract harsh criticism.

Indeed, criticism fell on me as thick as a hailstorm, both from those pious souls who are afraid of every idea that assumes the form of a paradox, and from the socialist sociologists who in my affirmation wrongly saw a disavowal of the advantages of social cohabitation, hence they rose up against a theory that wrongly seemed to them the apotheosis of a foolish individualism.

At that time I did not respond to the attacks because I wanted to do so in this book, wherein the controversy will be useful to shed better light on my idea, and where the reader—knowing my entire argument—can be a competent and impartial judge.

My opponents—be they kind like my mentor and friend Enrico Ferri,[63] or violently unkind like a collaborator of *Critica Sociale*[64]—directed this counter-argument at me: "The affirmation that the more social cohabitation and association extends among individuals the less rigid morality becomes clashes against the universal fact that morality is, instead, the specific product of social cohabitation, and it progresses along with social cohabitation, because the isolated individual is neither moral nor immoral."[65]

61 P. Bourget, *Le disciple*. [In Bourget's novel, the materialist and positivist philosopher Adrien Sixte exerts a terrible influence over Robert Geslon, a mentally weak student who ends up playing a role in the death of a young woman.]

62 In the already cited pamphlet, *La morale individuale e la morale politica*.

63 See *Scuola positiva* VI, 6 (June 1896): 326 and ff.

64 See *Critica Sociale* (1 and 15 June 1896), and the polemic that followed, not so much on merit, more so on the form of its criticisms. [*Critica Sociale* is a left-wing Italian political journal founded by Filippo Turati in 1891 and still active today. In Sighele's years it collected articles by the most prominent Italian and foreign socialist intellectuals and covered the main political and social problems affecting Italy. See also the introduction to this volume, lixn41.]

65 E. Ferri, "Delinquenti ed onesti," in *Scuola positiva*, already cited.

With these words, my friend Ferri wanted to teach me something that he certainly knew I already know, and, furthermore, he wanted to misinterpret my thoughts—, which, frankly, I did not expect from him.

It is ingenuous to try to teach that "*morality is the specific product of social cohabitation*" not only to me, although I want to place myself among the most undeserving writers, but also to the most ignorant of students. This is so axiomatic that the attempt to teach it as a new finding to whomever is not illiterate resembles the celebrated effort of bringing vases to Samos and owls to Athens.[66]

But what has this axiom to do with my affirmation?

Did I perhaps deny that morality is "the specific product of social cohabitation"? You may rummage through my writings to check whether there is a similar scientific blasphemy, and, if it is found, I surrender. In my writings, I thought I could omit that premise, which is by now a banal truth, because—whenever possible—I do not repeat commonplaces.

Therefore, taking into account this well-known truth that now I want to reveal, I limited myself to collecting the facts and drawing a conclusion from them.

The facts proclaimed that an individual, as a private man, is more moral than when he acts as a member of a province, class, party, or nation. And I, therefore, concluded that private morality is superior to all other moralities, whether sectarian, regional, or patriotic; and that, consequently, *the larger the sphere in which an individual must think and act, the looser his moral consciousness becomes.*

I specifically concluded with the following words, words that stirred up a hornet's nest and are also synonyms for what I have just written: "the more social cohabitation and association among individuals are extended, the less rigid morality becomes."

My opponents, not being able to negate the facts,[67] clung (and I want to believe that some did so in good faith) to the conclusion, and, isolating

66 [The expression *Portar, come si dice, a Samo vasi, nottule a Atene, e crocodili a Egitto* [Bringing vases to Samos, owls to Athens, and crocodiles to Egypt], from Ludovico Ariosto's *Orlando Furioso,* means doing useless, redundant things, similar to "carrying coals to Newcastle."]

67 Ferri actually (loc. cit.) explicitly admitted: "It is very true"—he writes—"that political morality is always in a level of development inferior to that of individual morality." A writer from *Critica Sociale* makes an identical observation.—I feel the need to warn that Colaianni, although being a socialist, does not succumb to the misinterpretations of his coreligionists, and he does not attribute blunders to me that I did not commit: I thank him for that. See his article about my pamphlet in *Secolo* (17 May 1896).

it from the rest of my words, gave it an interpretation that, to whomever read attentively and honestly, was totally unthinkable.

The anecdote of Talleyrand, who says, "Show me two lines of a man's writing and I will have him condemned," may be old, but its applications are always timely.

There are, in the literary world no less than in diplomacy, clever people who, from many pages of a writer, extract two lines and, not taking into account what was written before or after that excerpt, present only those lines to the public, and they easily build an indictment on them, no matter how unfair the methods of the debate.

The clever ones rendered this service to me. From my pages they removed the well-known phrase that I will not repeat here for the one-hundredth time, and they said that with this phrase, "I proved I was a metaphysical sociologist—rather, an ugly species of theologian who conceives the individual as a perfect type coming out of the Creator's hands, and on whom human society can exert only a perverting influence."[68]

And all this happened because these clever people misinterpreted me and made me say something that I never even dreamed of thinking.[69]

Indeed—and this is what my opponents did not understand or at least pretended not to understand—it is one thing to admit that morality, like all the rest that is beautiful and useful in the world, is a product of social cohabitation (I bet! not only could an isolated man do nothing good, but ... it is inconceivable that he exists!),—and another thing is to say that the private man's morality is more rigid than that of the sectarian, the citizen, or the politician, and thus that the more the association between individuals extends—*in this sense*—, the more indulgent morality becomes.

The two affirmations are not at all contradictory. Rather, they mutually illuminate and reciprocally reflect the two points of view from which every social phenomenon must be considered.

From the *dynamic* point of view—meaning its evolution over time—it is axiomatically evident that "the more an association between individuals develops, the more morality progresses." From the *static* point of

68 See *Critica Sociale* already cited (1 June 1896).

69 There were also some impartial critics who recognized that some other critics had lent me ideas that I did not have. So, an anonymous person in *Coltura* (May 1896) wrote regarding my already cited pamphlet: "Critics have perhaps exaggerated a little too much in drawing consequences from this new theory and have made Sighele say more than he wanted." I thank the anonymous writer for having understood my thought better than others.

view—meaning a given historical moment—it is undeniable that "the more cohabitation extends, the less rigid morality becomes." Indeed, in the restricted family circle, that is, as a private individual, man is more moral than when he is considered in vaster environments, that is, as a member of an association, party, sect, or nation.

I hope that—after this—my opponents' misunderstanding[70] will be eliminated, because it seems to me to have been clear and, if I do not delude myself, also persuasive.

I now recapitulate.

Morality has increasingly developed as the association between individuals extended and perfected itself. And, to convince ourselves of this axiomatic truth, it would be enough to glance at the abyss that separates our morality from that of the first savage tribes. On its way towards perfection, however, which is perhaps a utopian notion, morality has not proceeded as a unique and indivisible organism, but rather as a body composed of many relatively independent parts. And, if all these parts have perfected themselves, each one has done so to a different degree, depending on the different social environments to which it was applied. This is why we see that private morality is more advanced than sectarian, patriotic, and political morality, and we can, therefore, affirm that *statically* "the more the social group extends where man thinks and acts, the less rigid his morality becomes."

This is my limpid and precise thought, and I challenge men of good faith to battle it.

---

70 A similar misinterpretation happened about another one of my publications, and it is useful to recount the story here because one will see how there is the tendency in some critics to interpret in an exaggerated way an author's thought for the sake of fighting him. In October of 1894, I was writing an open letter in *Critica Sociale* to Gabriele Tarde, entitled "Intelligenza e moralità della folla." In this letter, speaking about the crowd and generally about *static* unions of individuals (juries, commissions, parliaments, etc.), I wrote, "The union of men worsens each morally." It was nothing but the repetition of the principle in the introduction of my volume *La folla delinquente*, a principle that had obtained the unanimous approval of the scientific world. Ferri interpreted this phrase literally, he gave it a universal significance and—naturally—he combatted it without difficulty. I responded that he had misunderstood, and indeed, it was not even presumable that a man who was not crazy could say in an absolute way that "the union of men worsens." Why not, then, negate all of civilization! I meant to say that, when men are united *statically* (crowds, juries, etc.) their intellectual and moral level, instead of rising, decreases. More on this polemic, in the 2nd ed. of *La folla delinquente* (Turin: Bocca, 1895).—Well, this misinterpretation was useless; rather, it was followed by another one …

## *II*

Now that we have cleared the ground of these cumbersome critiques, we can continue our reasoning.

We have shown the inferiority of political morality to private morality. This is no novelty, however; many people had highlighted it more or less clearly.

Plato, who was persuaded that virtue is lost in contact with politics, recommended to the wise to distance themselves from public affairs. Saint-Just, the pupil of Robespierre—a fierce, cold calculator and a pure moralist in words—, gives the same advice: "Are the lessons imparted by history, the examples afforded by all great men, lost to the universe? These all counsel us to lead obscure lives; the lowly cots and virtue form the grandeurs of this world. Let us seek our habitations on the banks of streams, [and] rock the cradles of our children."[71]

La Bruyère writes with subtle irony: "I only consider superior to a great politician him who does not consider becoming one, and who is more and more persuaded that the world does not deserve that we care about it."[72]—Littré says with exaggeration, "Everything progresses except politics,"[73] and an old ambassador gives to Maxime du Camp this definition of art to which he had consecrated his life: "An affair of blackmail, bargaining, and often of robbery."[74]

This definition at first may seem too severe, but it is not. Indeed, politics in its origins, in its essence, and in its consequences—whether it descends from above or rises from below, whether it is sectarian or patriotic—has always been and still is immoral.

Examine its period of incubation, elections.

Montesquieu, with the ingenuity of the genius, writes that "the people is admirable for choosing its representatives."[75] Poor people! If only it were granted the freedom to truly choose its representatives, perhaps Montesquieu would be right. But since this liberty does not exist, and it is a vain noun without a subject, dust thrown into the eyes of the public,

71 See Buchez and Roux, vol. XXXII, 314, cited by Taine, *La Révolution*, vol. III, 247. [English translation by John Durand in Hyppolite Taine, *The Revolution*, vol. 3 (London: Sampson Low, Marston, Searle, and Rivington, 1885), 189n4.]

72 La Bruyère, *Des Jugements*.

73 Littré, *De l'établissement de la troisième république*, 363.

74 Maxime du Camp, *Le Crépuscule*, 250.

75 Montesquieu, *L'Esprit des lois*, vol. II, chapter II.

the French philosopher, unfortunately, is wrong. "The period of elections"—Ferrero correctly says,

> constitutes for all the candidates and their advocates a true phase of moral brutalization. Both,—even those whose conscience is more difficult—descend without repugnance to the most indecorous baseness, to lies, trickery, deception, knowingly failed promises, mental restrictions, falsifications, and fraud. I saw, for example, a Jewish candidate brought to a countryside borough where his race and religion would have done him damage, declare himself Catholic and go to mass on Sunday in the main centre of the borough during the entire election time. Let's not speak, then, of the falsifications of court transcripts, of the dead who vote, of the poorly read ballots, of the calculations made according to the party's arithmetic, and of many other frauds committed behind the approval of people who, elsewhere, would react with the more sincere conscience of having been wrongly insulted, if they had been called liars and swindlers.[76]

All of this—and much more could be said[77]—as far as the origin of political life is concerned.

Let us now examine the functions of politics.

Robert Walpole used to buy parliamentary consciences and boasted about knowing all the tariffs. Nonetheless, Macaulay judges his conduct with incredible indulgence: "Walpole governed by corruption,"—he writes— "because, in his time, it was impossible to govern otherwise. (...) His crime was merely this, that he employed his money more dexterously, and got more support in return for it, than any of those who preceded or followed him (...) [T]he House of Commons was in that situation in which assemblies must be managed by corruption, or cannot be managed at all. (...) [T]o blame those ministers who managed the Legislature in the only way in which it could be managed is gross injustice. They submitted to extortion because they could not help themselves."[78]

Modern corrupted and corrupters can console themselves; they have great lawyers. It is, moreover, the destiny of the great criminals!

---

76 Ferrero, loc. cit.

77 See my pamphlet *Against Parliamentarism.*

78 Macaulay, *Essais sur l'histoire d'Angleterre*, 459 and ff. [English original in Thomas Babington, *Lord Macaulay, Critical and Historical Essays* [1832] (London: Longman, Brown, Green, and Longmans, 1848), vol. 2, 121–24.]

Nowadays, people like Walpole do not exist, but there is, however, someone who resembles him. The Chambers of modern people will perhaps not be so venal as the House of Commons was then, but if their members cannot be bought with money, they can be with favours. In the meantime, for sure, money can buy journalists. It is true that we do not have illustrious historians like Macaulay who can justify these venalities, but servility and the public's tacit acquiescence allow them.

How do parliaments vote, given this venom of corruption and other ones that can contaminate it?

The most unjust laws—Proal writes[79]—were voted on by political assemblies with the greatest docility. All the despots, Roman emperors, Henry VIII of England, Robespierre, the Directory, Napoleon I, each found unconditional support in political bodies for the laws they wanted to propose. "When Henry VIII wanted to rid himself of his wives, the Parliament provided support; when he wanted to kill his ministers, the Parliament condemned them without trial; when finally he had the idea to promulgate laws at his will, the Parliament authorized him to do so."[80]

These sad words could be repeated even today, despite the difference that exists between those times and now. Even recently, we saw a parliament do everything its Henry VIII wanted, who was not a king but a minister.

A French writer, when speaking about corruption of laws through political means, says:

> The objective of the law should be the protection of the liberty and property of all citizens. By contrast, politics has always enacted laws in the interests of whoever had power, and filled the legislation with absurdity and hypocritical cruelty. Legal persecution is more hateful than brutal violence because it adds hypocrisy to iniquity. The legislators who give legal character to the persecution are more perverse than the executioners. What can be more monstrous than, for example, English laws that wish to suppress Catholicism in Ireland? Burke said about them that "they represented the ablest and mightiest instrument of oppression that has ever been invented by man's perverse genius to ruin, discourage and deprave a nation, and to corrupt in it the purest and most unalterable sources of human nature."[81]

79 L. Proal, *La Criminalité politique* (Paris: Alcan, 1895), 244.

80 John Russell, *Essai sur l'histoire du gouvernement et de la constitution britannique*, 23.

81 See Proal, op. cit., 239–40.

Do you not think that—still taking into account the different times—certain contemporary laws of the Russian Empire or the conduct of the Turkish government deserve Burke's blistering words? And do you not think that even in other nations—more civil than the bear of the north and Turkey—an analogous system was applied with diverse forms? Were the laws voted on by Bismarck against the socialists—which had, by fatal force, the opposite effect than what was hoped for—not also an iniquity?[82]

Let us now examine politics in its consequences.

Politics corrupts not only the judges—who, despite the rhetoric that wants them to be unsuspected and above suspicion like Caesar's wife, are employees suffering from the influence coming from above—but also the jurists, who are free individuals and should be independent.

No unjust law exists that was not commented on with the approval of jurists. They generally did not dare to formulate the slightest criticism. Grotius admitted slavery; Blackstone justified the assimilation of papism to a crime of high treason. Merlin—according to Albert Sorel—"lent his great knowledge and wonderful legislative abilities to the making of that masterpiece of insidious tyranny: the law of suspicions."[83] Chancellor Pasquier said about him: "I have never known a man with a lesser sentiment of right and wrong than he. Everything seemed well done and commendable to him as long as it was the consequence of a *text*."[84]

Thus—a worthy *pendant* in this welter of immorality to political advantage—just as parliamentary corruption found its praiseful historian, the most unjust laws found their approving jurist.

And how about judges?

Regarding the English tribunal before the 1688 revolution, Macaulay writes that "it was an unclean public shambles, to which each party in its turn dragged its opponents, and where each found the same venal and ferocious butchers waiting for its custom."[85]

---

82 According to Thomas More, all laws are iniquitous. [See, e.g., "Here now would I see, if any man dare be so bold as to compare with this equity, the justice of other nations; among whom, I forsake God, if I can find any sign or token of equity and justice. For what justice is this [...]?" Thomas More, *Utopia*, chapter II. The Harvard Classics, 1901–14, http://www.bartleby.com/36/3/10.html.]

83 Albert Sorel, *L'Europe et la Révolution française*, 3rd part, vol. II, chapter IV. [Philippe-Antoine Count Merlin (1754–1838) was a prominent jurist of the French Revolution and the Napoleonic period.]

84 *Mémoires du chancelier Pasquier*, vol. I, 268.

85 Op. cit., 306. [English original in Babington, *Lord Macaulay*, vol. II, 271. See also Proal, op. cit.]

I know that these phrases would be an anachronism and blasphemy if they were applied to the judiciary today. Nevertheless, wanting to limit our observations to Italy, I recall that our magistrature was defined as a *question mark* by a truly and organically honest minister. I recall an indictment by a general attorney in which someone said that the magistrates had made a delegation of power and *conscience*; I recall a judgment by the Court of Cassation in which they defined the socialists as *evildoers*; I recall the interrupted investigations of important trials—and it appears to me that all of this—if it does not justify insult—authorizes us at least to be sceptical about the independence of the magistrature, and makes us think about the words of Camille Desmoulins: "The least clever despots are the ones who use bayonets; the art of tyranny is to do the same with judges."

These are examples and teachings we can draw from the politics that could be called governmental, that is, the astute and civil politics of those who managed to grab power.

What will be of that politics that is called sectarian, and is performed by men who are not masters but oppressors, and who do not have power but desire it?

"Can you"—Bissolati asks[86]—"say that the group hostile to the bourgeoisie behaves like its opponent is in political life? Can you say that the proletarian party makes use of the same weapons that the bourgeoisie parties use? You could not say it without a ridiculous lie."[87]

The triumphant tone of this question is all wasted. I have, too often, maintained that dominating classes have a collective criminality different from that of dominated classes, hence I cannot be ascribed, not even hypothetically, the opinion that the former fight with the same weapons as the latter.

To different organisms, different functions—this is not a new physiological truth, which is also applicable and applied to sociology, and I have used many pages to bring it further to light.

86 See the already cited article in *Critica Sociale* (15 June 1896). [Leonida Bissolati (1857–1920) was a leading member of the socialist movement in turn-of-the-century Italy.]

87 And Bissolati added: "This therefore demonstrates that one thing is the politics of the conservative groups and another that of the progressive groups."—Amazing news, that Bissolati flaunts as if it were his brilliant discovery, and that he wants to teach me, even though I had already announced it in the *Archivio di psichiatria* of 1895 and in *Mondo Criminale italiano*, II series, also in 1895!

The oppressed will not employ astuteness, cleverness, and audacity like the oppressors, but rather violence. They will not steal money from banks, but they will descend into the square to attempt a revolt; they will not buy consciences, but they will throw bombs.[88]

It is another genus of fight—less unpleasant, I am the first to admit it—but the species will always be identical: immorality and crime.

"It must be confessed," Taine writes, "that Jacobinism, as they have practised it, was the religion of robbery and murder."[89]

This extreme judgment is even false if it refers to the intentions and finalities of Jacobinism, but it is partly true if it refers to the means employed by the Jacobins.

All sects, upon birth, employ more or less—by necessity—the Jacobins' means; indeed, all sects must act with violence, immorality, and crime. For minorities, legality is too long a path, when it is not a path that leads away from, rather than towards, the objective.

It is useless to insist upon this affirmation because our history and the history of the world provide the evidence.

## *III*

From the law that "sectarian morality and political morality are always less developed than private morality," it seems to me that one could deduce, as a logical and spontaneous corollary, this other principle, that "the sectarian and the politician cannot truly be moral men."

This principle will appear to many people, to everyone perhaps, as an outrageous paradox, but one that I express and maintain with full conviction and serenity.

I recall a declaration years ago by our prime minister: "*we may be incapable but we are honest,*" a phrase that made many smile, but that—like all naive statements—reflected a truth that many felt, although it was in nobody's interest to proclaim it. To be honest in politics—that is, to be frank and loyal as in private life—means, unfortunately, to be incapable.

*Ergo* whoever is honest is not able, meaning unable to be a true politician.

---

88 See the *Introduction.*

89 H. Taine, *Les origines de la France contemporaine: La Révolution,* vol. III, 13th ed. (Paris, 1892), 553. [English translation by John Durand in Hippolyte Taine, *The Revolution,* vol. 3 (London: Sampson Low, Marston, Searle and Rivington, 1885), 422.]

Yes, if it is true that geniuses and, in general, men of intelligence are rarely men of incorruptible honesty,[90] a fortiori it must be true that geniuses and political geniuses are rarely of adamantine character. Without arriving at Buckle's exaggeration, according to whom it is unlikely that a true politician is not also a criminal,[91] I believe that it would not be possible to find in history the name of a great statesman who always acted with the most scrupulous loyalty and with the calmest and most severe justice.

Let's be clear: I do not maintain that all politicians are scoundrels and that one could say of all of them exactly what Chateaubriand said about Talleyrand and Fouché when he saw them one day enter the quarters of Louis XVIII, arm in arm: "Here is vice leaning on crime."

I only affirm that politicians cannot adapt their conduct to the rigid and absolute rules of private morality, for the simple reason that one cannot govern a population with the same morality with which one governs a man.

If it is very unlikely for an able politician to be also honest, it is almost impossible for a sectarian to be honest. The former must, perforce, violate the sentiment of probity, because he must lie, buy the media or parliamentary conscience, while the latter must perforce violate the sentiment of pity, because without violence no sect will impose itself.[92]

The honest man type—according to private morality—is given by he who does not want to shed blood, who does not want violence or immoral acts committed in any way. Could this man be a sectarian? Evidently not.

I already said that sectarians adore courage, and this adoration is one of the causes that drag them to crime. Now, to be courageous, to despise one's own life and make an attempt on another's—in war where homicide is legitimate, in riots, revolutions, or attacks—one must be devoid

90 See Maudsley, *Le Crîme et la folie*, and the *Introduction*. Ferri, in his recent volume *I Delinquenti nell'arte*, which I am seeing now while I am proofreading this book, writes: "Just as to people with a very developed sentiment of altruism often corresponds a limited intelligence, so to whoever lacks moral sentiment, nature often provides a very acute and lucid intelligence, if not profound and balanced" (20).

91 [Henry Thomas Buckle (1821–1862) was a major positivist English historian who applied natural science methods to the study of historical processes. He is remembered for his unfinished *History of Civilization in England*.]

92 It is noted that Garofalo, in the analysis of instincts that constitute the moral sense, placed among the most important ones those of *pity* and *probity*, the partial or total absence of which gives place, respectively, to the criminal against people and the criminal against properties. We refer here to his theory of *natural crime* (see *Criminologia*, chapter I) because it seems that it can adapt itself to the two forms of political criminality, the violent and the fraudulent. In sectarian criminals, the sentiment of pity is, indeed, lacking or very weak; in political criminals of the elevated classes, instead, the sentiment of probity is lacking.

to the highest degree of that sentiment of pity, which is a slow conquest of civility, and which, while it improves the average of human morality, hinders or at least diminishes, the rising of heroic men. A truly and profoundly merciful sectarian would find himself in the condition of a truly and profoundly principled politician. The latter would not feel the need to strain his principles of probity, not even for an imperious need to govern—the former would not feel the need to strain his principles of pity, not even to achieve an ideal.

The sectarian—if diplomatic—would never lie and would let the interests of his homeland go downhill; he would be honest, but incapable. The politician would not dare conspire or act as a conspirator, and he would serve his sect rather poorly; he would then be like a sectarian, honest but incapable. And history would not have a Garibaldi at Aspromonte, nor an Antonio Carra, who suppressed the hated Duke Charles III,[93] nor a Cavour, who pretended to impede the hero of Caprera while secretly helping him.

One can recite this forever, but the truth is—both from the luminous post of ministers or rulers of nations, and from that darkness of conspirators or sectarians—one cannot think or act with the entire and rigidly moral conscience of the private man. "Everything in this world"—Settembrini writes—"takes a bit of deception, and this is like salt, which gives flavour in small amounts and makes things bitter if it is too much." Deception and immorality are necessary in political affairs—and only the Jesuits or the naive deny this.

## *IV*

Nevertheless, those who ably justify this deception and immorality are not lacking.

Mirabeau has said that *la petite morale tue la grande*, and he said it well, because small morality, meaning private, kills great morality, meaning political, in the sense that it gives us either honest but incapable ministers, or honest but fearful sectarians.

Great morality—which renders crime legitimate when it is committed for altruistic goals—is, in the eyes of true sectarians and politicians,

93 [Charles III, very unpopular Duke of Parma and Piacenza (1823–1854), reigned with the support of the Austrian regime and was assassinated by Antonio Carra and Ireneo Bochi, who both escaped prosecution because of unreliable witnesses.]

actually nobler than small morality, which would not permit it to be accomplished.

And one cannot deny that sectarians and politicians are right in certain cases.

If there is a field in which the maxim "*the end justifies the means*" must be applied, this field is politics. Ultimate protection of the homeland, for example, can justify any crime. But a restriction should be made to that maxim, which smells a bit too much like Jesuitism and Machiavellianism. It should say: the end justifies the means *necessary* for the objective. Necessity, in these cases, would limit abuses and safeguard morality. If a statesman or sectarian commits a crime in order to reach a goal that he could have equally reached in another way, that man would really, and also politically, be a criminal.

But one does not always decide based on these criteria.

What is important—above all in politics—is to succeed. Success absolves any crime, even useless ones; and, vice versa, failure puts the guilty on the dock.

The opening of the Suez Canal was a gigantic fraud, done with the same criminal arts as Panama; but it was exalted by general approval because it succeeded, while Panama sank into a scandalous trial because it was a fiasco.

In private life as well as in politics, it is necessary to be a great and ingenious evildoer if one wants crime to result not in jail, but in power and honour. Pickpockets appear in court; thieves of millions travel in carriages calling their thefts *speculations*.

Ingenious sectarians rise to omnipotence through one or multiple crimes, while mediocre sectarians are punished, or are ridiculed and alienated. Typical examples of these two cases are Napoleon and Boulanger.[94]

Thus, ministers or members of parliament who committed some indelicacy or crime but, since they are intellectually mediocre, did not

94 [George Ernest Jean-Marie Boulanger (1837–1891) was a French general and politician. After a military career, he became minister of war in 1886. The popularity he gained for his reforms turned him into the figure that could avenge the French defeat in the recent Franco-German war and overthrow the Third Republic. By the late 1880s, he was enjoying widespread right-wing support, and, when he became deputy in 1889, he was urged to take power. Even though he declined and preferred to spend the night with his mistress—a big disappointment for his followers—he had become, by then, a threat to the parliamentary government, and was denounced for conspiracy and treason. He fled abroad and committed suicide in Brussels.]

know how to exploit those immoralities in order to achieve political success, lose power and the public's consideration, while the ministers or members of parliament who committed more severe and numerous crimes but, being intellectually stronger, knew how to exploit them to their full advantage, remain powerful, flattered, and envied.

Despite our civilization, we are still at the moral stage of those savage tribes who highly praise and reward large-scale theft, and they despise and punish it if it is limited to stealing insignificant things.[95]

Even Lombroso maintains that the morality or immorality of certain political acts comes from their success or failure.

Speaking about revolts and revolutions, he said[96] that the former are distinguished from the latter specifically by outcome. Indeed, when an insurrectional movement breaks out in a political, religious, or economic arena, one cannot always know if it will be a revolution or a revolt. One will be able to predict it, not ascertain it. It is the outcome that will attribute the legal or illegal status to the movement. Victory gives an insurrection the label of revolution; defeat, the label of revolt.

Now, victory implies the adhesion of many; defeat necessarily implies the opposite; and since the main condition for an act to be antisocial, that is, a crime, is that it be the work of a minority, it follows that, if the majority approves it, it becomes a normal and legal action, and the revolution is seen as a normal act.

This rigorously logical reasoning can be accepted from an historical point of view for collective political motives, which are, indeed, revolts and revolutions. In these cases, the majority, that is, the number, is always the supreme, perhaps the only judge.

But what would it be if—in addition to the collective motions—we also wanted to apply this reasoning to people?

Can we affirm that—the French Revolution not being a crime, but considered a collective phenomenon—some of the authors of some of the bloodiest episodes were not criminals? Can we affirm that Napoleon I was a moral man only because France wanted him as consul and emperor?

---

95 "It is curious that the Teke people, who consider murder and pillaging means of existence, despise theft if it is reduced to stealing something from someone or removing an object from a bazaar." O'Donovan, *The Merw Oasis*, vol. II, 408, cited by Spencer, *La morale des différents peuples*, 79.

96 Lombroso and Laschi, *Il delitto politico* (Turin: Bocca), 189.

Here—everyone feels it—the criteria for success are no longer enough to legitimize and absolve a person. One can repeat for the judgment of history what an Italian minister used to say about the judgment of parliaments: moral debates cannot be solved with the support of the majority.

Thus, in vain, one attempts with a more or less acute and specious argument to bestow the laurel of morality on politics and its fortunate actors.

However, even if many admit that politics and politicians do not often adopt honest means, people maintain—I do not know with how much sincerity, and, I believe, with one of those kinds of hypocrisy that are a platonic homage to virtue—that politics must be and can be rigidly moral, and only when it is so can it generate goodness.

A philosopher paraphrased Rabelais's claim that science without conscience is the ruin of the soul, by writing that politics without morality is the ruin of society.

This is a dangerous axiom because, by accepting it, one must admit that the society from which it arose did not do anything else but bring it to ruin, there being always politics without morality.

And equally rhetorical, if not equally dangerous, is the phrase by Jules Simon that if political virtues do not have origins and are not confirmed in private virtues, then they are nothing but theatrical virtues.

I would have liked Jules Simon to demonstrate that most great politicians who were useful to their country were privately virtuous men: only then would he be right, but the evidence would be difficult to get.

Of course—for whom would it not be agreeable?—the ideal would be to have an honest politics: but could it be, at the same time, a politics of genius and, therefore, useful and fruitful? Can you imagine a great diplomacy without lies, a strong government without abuses, and a fortunate sect without violence?

In the past and present of course not; I fear for the future.

## V

Let us conclude.

I have demonstrated that political morality is inevitably far inferior to individual morality; I say and repeat that, in general, organically and truly honest men who give themselves to politics manage to do mediocre things, while politicians of genius are all—more or less—immoral.

Now, Buckle has shown that it is more dangerous for a population to have foolish and ignorant rulers than criminal rulers, given that the foolish ruler grants freedom of action to hundreds of scoundrels, while the rascal robs and commits the crime alone. Hence the latter rather than the former should be wished for a nation, leaving naive and sentimental people to support the contrary.[97]

Analogously, Renan said: "an immoral population is worthier than a fanatic population, because the fanatic multitudes befuddle the world, and a world condemned to stupidity no longer interests me: I prefer to see it dead."[98]

This is painful but inevitable, and perhaps less painful than it at first appears.

In nature there is a strange and mysterious law of compensation where good is sometimes born from evil, so much so that evil is often necessary to produce good.

According to Darwinian theory, nothing survives except the institutions and organs that have some utility, because—if they do not have it—natural selection atrophies and extinguishes them.

Since crime is continually increasing in extension, if not in intensity, and finds new forms as civilization progresses, it must be recognized that even crime must produce some useful effect.

This utility of crime, which is not easily noticeable in common crime,[99] can be easily discovered in political crime, which, be it sectarian or patriotic, has always been a mighty lever of human progress.

War is an entire cluster of crimes on a vast scale, and if it damages the already lush civilizations, it must be recognized that it pushes the semi-barbaric populations to extraordinary developments.

One could say the same thing about slavery: an atrocious crime today, a very useful necessity in the first stages of humanity, because it allowed a class of men—who did not work—to think. "The refinement of customs is not possible but with leisure, and slavery renders leisure possible for the first time. It creates a class of people who work so that others can think."[100]

---

97 The critic of *Critica Sociale* was shocked by this opinion. Since, however, it is Buckle who expressed it and it was accepted by Lombroso, I prefer their company to his.

98 E. Renan, *L'avenir de la science*, Préface, x.

99 And one cannot glimpse it because it is so rare. See, however, some examples of the utility of common crime in the article by C. Lombroso: "La funzione sociale del delitto," in the *Rivista di sociologia* (Nov. 1895), reproduced in the end of volume 3 of *L'uomo delinquente*.

Prostitution, an institution that, if one cannot call it criminal, is certainly depraved, manages a true prophylaxis, preventing a quantity of sexual crimes. Likewise, usury was the origin of the first great accumulations of capital from which the largest, human businesses derived.

100 *Lois scientifiques du dévéloppement des nations*, 79.

One could say the same thing about sectarian crime, which, if it diminishes public safety in the environment that produced it, it undeniably forces the rich and ruling classes to think about many political or social problems that otherwise would remain neglected or forgotten for a long time.

This happened a few years ago in Sicily, where revolt, homicide, fire, and plundering were necessary so that Italy could begin to think about the unfortunate island.

This happened politically in all of Italy, in the first half of this century; the crimes at that time against government oppressors awoke the population's spirit of independence and prompted help from the house of Savoy.

Finally, one can say the same thing about the genius statesman who, even though criminal or immoral, compensates his crimes or immoralities with the immense advantages he brings to the population, defeating enemies on the battlefield or on the more difficult ground of diplomacy, giving a new impulse to industries, arts, and commercial endeavours.

And it is, indeed, his immoralities that—making him despise and skip all moral obstacles that would stop a timid, honest soul—permit his genius to work and be fruitful for good.

There is thus a *social function of crime* that not only explains to us why crime subsists and increases with the progress of civilization, but—proving to us that, in part, it is useful—also renders less sad the certainty that it has a necessary supremacy in politics.

Cesare Lombroso, speaking for the first time about this social function of crime,[101] was afraid of being interpreted in the opposite sense. It would not have been a new thing for him! "Who knows"—he writes—"if my words, instead of being taken as an expression of protest against the muddy current that rises to our throat and defames us all, are not interpreted as a bizarre apology for evil, and an agglomerate of paradoxes attracting the careless attention of the many!"

Lombroso was not misunderstood this time, but it happened to me, who had resumed his idea and given it an application and a wider extension.

Our country is, sadly, so rhetorical that it revolts against whoever has the sincerity and courage to contest evil, rather than against those who have the perversity to commit it. Nobody dares say to political villains that they are villains. Rather, one tolerates and praises them, but

101 Article cited.

if someone affirms that their immorality is painfully necessary and adds that, in many ways, it is rich in good, then the simple Catos of the print will come out and proclaim that this is a dishonest theory, and, like unctuous seminarists, cry out anathema.

I will not defend myself against the accusation of having made the apology of political criminality.

If—observing the facts and not allowing myself to be seduced by false idealism—I contested (not for the first or only time) that the politician's inevitable immorality is often rather useful—it seems to me I did not speak in the criminal's defence, but only emphasized how good can sometimes come from evil.

Who today would dream to assert that Lombroso apologized for the madmen only because he showed that insanity is the inseparable companion to genius?

Just as it is not true that only health and normality are useful to the world, since the great, afflicted, and abnormal ones have always been the most effective engines of human progress, so it is not true that only honesty is the origin of everything that is beautiful and good among us. Even crime—sometimes—can do good.

Psychiatrists, for whom genius and, to a lesser degree, ingenuity are nothing but hereditary consequences and transformations of illnesses, do not only see the evil in that ballast of degenerates that civilization drags in its vertiginous course towards progress. They know that splendid manifestations of genius—like flowers from mud—will later be born from those degenerates.

Sociologists do not only see the immediate danger of crimes committed by a politician, they know that a more civil and elevated social rapport will arise from those crimes.

And it seems comforting and poetic to me to think that—like the pearl, which is an illness for the oyster—as genius is nothing but the transformation of the pains and misadventures that nature prepares with unknown and wise incubation, human progress is often the fruit of atrocious crimes.

But there is another accusation to which I am eager to respond.

We currently consider—some of my opponents say—that political morality is inferior to private morality, but we deny that this inferiority is eternal; rather, we affirm that the complete unification of these two moralities is attainable and will be attained.

Those who speak in such a way are the socialists, namely, the people who—entrenched behind a still-debated idea—for the unconscious necessity to fight, exaggerate its value and efficacy, and believe its realization has the power to change the face of the world. They believe indeed that, with the advent of socialism, together with other infamies of bourgeois society even its Machiavellian politics will disappear.

They reiterate—without noticing and by the inevitable law of nature—the illusion that has lulled all the apostles of any revolution.

Did the sincere apostles of the French Revolution not believe that the reign of liberty, equality, and fraternity would come?

And are the socialists not the first to recognize today that this liberty is very little, that this equality is a lie, and that this fraternity is Jesuitism?

Let's be clear.

One would have to be an idiot to deny the progress brought forth by the French Revolution, as by all revolutions, which are nothing other than the necessary crises of populations to rise one level up on the path of civilization, just as the crisis of puberty is necessary for a boy to become an adult.

But one should be very short-sighted to assert that the French Revolution—like every revolution—realized *all* the hopes of its precursors.

In collective life—as in private life—it is necessary to remember that if it is logical to ask *a great deal* to obtain *something*—then it is impossible to obtain all we ask.

Every revolution forgot that the social factor can do a great deal, but it cannot completely destroy the anthropological factor in a short time.

Man will remain such as the past centuries have gradually shaped him. To attempt to reduce him to an algebraic quantity, making him move according to the theorems of socialist theory, is to dream about an unrealizable future or a future so distant that it is useless for us to study it.

Therefore, I say to the socialists: your doctrine's foundation is true, you will have a revolution tomorrow—whether bloody or peaceful, it is in the hands of fate—which will be the best and most sacred after that of Christ; but if the world guided by your ideas becomes *better*, it will not become *perfect*.

One of you years ago wrote an ingenious book claiming that crime will disappear with socialism.[102]

Nowadays, another one of you wrote two very mediocre articles asserting that private morality and political morality will be the only morality in a socialist world.[103]

102 F. Turati, *Il delitto e la questione sociale*.

103 L. Bissolati, in *Critica Sociale*, loc. cit.

The error of the first writer was refuted by one of your current coreligionists,[104] and, in any case, it is blatant, because it amounts to saying that there will no longer be diseases with the development of medicine and surgery. It is not possible to picture an environment without crime, as it is not possible to imagine a physical climate without disease.

The error of the second writer is refuted by this positivist truth: "one cannot ever govern a great collectivity of men with the same laws with which one governs one man." In other words, political morality will always be different from private morality—and, therefore, inferior.

I am the first one to admit—and I have also demonstrated—that both of these moralities will rise, but they can never be united. They are two parallel lines following the law of evolution; they advance together, but will never touch.

The mathematical hypothesis that parallel lines meet at infinity is not applicable in sociology, and, even if it were, it would be a completely useless metaphysical satisfaction.

The Michelangelesque mind of Herbert Spencer may like to imagine a society in which morality is perfect—as a believer may like to fathom an *afterlife* in which the unknowable can be explained.

Personally, I do not imagine the realization of any of these hypotheses, and even if I did believe them, the realization would be too far off to render it a game of thought rather than practical utility.

Hence optimists may like to foresee an epoch with one unique morality, in which the whole world will be ruled by a unique code, and the millions of men who populate it will live in honest and fraternal friendship. But, leaving aside my personal scepticism, which would be worthless, to this too charming philosophy I oppose a fact that matters a great deal: the fact that many centuries will pass before this dream comes true, and that we must preoccupy ourselves with the immediate and foreseeable future, not of that far off and oneiric future. The great problem of our time—Renan says—is not God or nature, but humanity. And I permit myself to add: humanity as it is now and which will logically remain so for a long time.

This humanity does not—unfortunately—seem to follow the noble but metaphysical ideals of certain socialists, and on the other hand, even if it were better than what it is, I would not believe in the achievement of these ideals.

104 E. Ferri, *Socialismo e criminalità* (Turin: Bocca, 1883).

Melchior de Vogüé[105] says that war will be inevitable as long as there are a woman and a piece of bread between two men. We can say, with less absolutism and more truth, that competition and struggle among men will be inevitable as long as the intellectual, moral, or material superiority of some will excite the envy of others.

Now, since moral and intellectual equality is impossible, and material equality, even though possible, is very far off, history will continue to be for a long time—in attenuated but substantially equal forms—a struggle between the superior and inferior classes of society. We will always necessarily have a morality of class or politics that will be different and, therefore, less elevated than private morality.

The superior classes will fight with even more civil means, and the inferior classes with their barbaric weapons; the former will be able to call their true sectarian crimes legitimate actions, the latter will have the posthumous glory to have their crimes renamed as acts of heroism. And both will be necessary—the violent actions of those below, in order to promote progress, as much as the arrogance of those above, to halt progress, which would otherwise accelerate. But those worthiest of indulgence will always be the sectarian criminals at the bottom, because they bring with them a desire for the better and the grand altruism of sacrifice for posterity, which are the only things that distinguish man from the brute.

## Appendix – *Against Parliamentarism*

I do not know whether, as many hope and some believe, the hour is near when the parliamentary system must transform itself or die. Of course, I know that politicians and thinkers throw many accusations at this system, and that the grand majority of the public does not spare the system their bitter criticism or scornful contempt. It seems to me, however, that in this severe indictment the most serious charge has been forgotten.

Until now, parliamentarism has been attacked, above all, by fighting its people: the members of parliament—it has been said—are not, except with rare exceptions, the best of the nation; rather, they are often mediocre people. Once they win their seats, they pursue their own inter-

105 [Marie-Eugène-Melchior, Vicomte de Vogüé (1848–1910) was a French diplomat who served as attaché to the French legations in Egypt and in the Ottoman Empire. A travel writer, especially on Orientalist topics on which he wrote numerous books, he was a frequent contributor to *Revue des deux Mondes*.]

ests and not those of the voters, or they serve the latter's interests only when they can draw personal advantages. The discipline of the party is lacking or weak where it would be necessary, and one finds it instead in the shady form of the Camorra or in the ridiculous stubbornness of debates where great political ideas do not matter and where the extreme sectors of the Chamber of Deputies could agree without offending the logic and integrity of their character. Regionalism and parochialism, these two manifestations of wretched, myopic, collective egoism, dominate and command together with individual egoism, bringing immorality inside and outside parliament, and making its member, who should be a legislator conscious of his very high office, a man who does many favours, hopeful that they will be repaid by one: re-election. And all that without hinting at the ugliest and, unfortunately perhaps, no less widespread among the worms that gnaw away at the parliamentary system: vote buying in elections.

As far as I know, no one has thought to fight parliament in its essence as a collective organism, rather than in the people who constitute it. In other words, no one has raised this issue: supposing, as an unlikely hypothesis, that all the single members who comprise it were morally and intellectually the nation's *best*, could parliament give *excellent* results? In other words: is the reason for almost all its flaws not to be found in the very fact that the parliament is an assembly of many?

We will try to respond to this question.

## *I*

The belief that *more people* know how to decide better than *only one person* about any debate—which an optimist could attribute to human modesty and a pessimist to the desire not to take responsibility—is a trivial idea.

Four eyes see more than two—says a proverb, which is undoubtedly true in many cases but also false in many others, as happens in general with all proverbs, born of experience drawn from *some* facts, hence not applicable to *all*. And enlarging the embedded principle of this proverb, which seemed to be of axiomatic evidence, in every branch of civil life the rule has gradually developed that important decisions must be made by a college of individuals rather than only one. The judiciary branch, popular or stipendiary, was collegial; the problems that dealt with arguments about art, science, industry, or administration were submitted to the judgment of councils or committees; and even the laws, which are the most serious problems of populations, had to be submitted to the parliament, that is, to the vote of many people.

In so doing, the moral and intellectual dangers posited by a single-arbiter system were allegedly avoided. Adding up more intelligences—it has been said—will produce a better result than what would come from an individual mind, and, by uniting more people, they will control one another, thereby avoiding injustices, which would otherwise be rather frequent.

The reasoning—it is necessary to confess—was simple and apparently of irreproachable logic. But was it true in practice? I do not think so.

First of all, there are reasons that I will call extrinsic and that Aristide Gabelli[106] egregiously hinted at: "One says"—he writes—

> that the Councils and Committees, in one word, those who exert power together, are a guarantee against abuses. It may be true. But first we must see whether they are useful. The purpose for which powers are bestowed is, indeed, this: so that they can be used. When guarantees against abuses are such that they impede their use, it becomes futile to give them. Now, many powers are, indeed, a guarantee of this type, against the partisanships and discords ensuing from interests, opinions, and contrary moods. In their absence, one shows up, one does not, one is sick, another is travelling, and, frequently, debates and resolutions must be rescheduled, with an inestimable loss of time and often of opportunities and efficacy; because, if it is difficult to find intellect among all of them, it is even more difficult to find a resolution and firmness; because, not being personally responsible, whoever is able does search to protect oneself; because, whoever has the power and does not exert it, becomes nothing but an impediment to whoever must exert it; because, ultimately, without repeating reasons that everyone knows by now, *the forces of united men cancel each other out and do not add up*. This is so true that very frequently a mediocre result comes out of an assembly of that kind, so much so that each individual member would have done better alone. Men, Galileo said, are not like horses attached to a cart they all pull; rather, they are like loose, racing horses, one of which wins the *palio*.[107]

106 [Aristide Gabelli (1830–1891) was an Italian pedagogue who applied the principles of positivism to scholastic organization. He was elected member of parliament of the Kingdom of Italy in 1886 and 1890. Prime Minister Francesco Crispi appointed him to develop the curricula for the newly instituted mandatory primary education system.]

107 A. Gabelli, *L'istruzione in Italia* (Bologna: Zanichelli, 1891), part I, 257–58.

This last idea that Gabelli exposes only fleetingly is, in my opinion, the most profound and important. It is fine to say: when more minds are added up, they will give a better result than only one mind, but in sociology can we apply these purely and exclusively mathematical criteria? I do not believe so. "How many times"—the unhappy Guy de Maupassant writes—

> have I seen how intelligence expands and rises in the one who lives alone, while it decreases and falls as soon as we mingle again with other people! Personal contacts, everything we say, everything that we are forced to listen, to hear and respond, act on thought. A flux and reflux of ideas goes from head to head, and a level is established, an average intelligence for any large agglomeration of individuals. The qualities of intellectual initiative, of wise reflection, and even penetration of every isolated man, disappear once this man is mixed with a great number of other men.[108]

Maupassant only paraphrases two lines by Lamartine:

> One must separate from the crowd in order to think
> And mix in to act.[109]

The human psyche, indeed, is not a figure that can be subjected to the simple and elementary laws of the science of numbers. Rather it is a strange entity that governs itself by the very complicated laws of chemistry, and, by associating with other similar entities, it gives a place to those always surprising and often unexplainable phenomena that are called combinations and fermentations. Therefore, the result achieved by an assembly of men is never the sum, but is always a product, it is an unknown quid that emanates—almost as a sudden psychological spark—from the diverse individual psychic elements that meet and collide.

To whomever wants to know the reason for this phenomenon—certainly observed by everyone—, to whomever wants to know why, as Gabelli synthetically says, the forces of united men cancel each other out and do not add up, we could not respond in a better way than by citing a page by Max Nordau, the strong and acute scientist who makes the mistake of attempting to become, every now and then, a mediocre novelist. "Collect

---

108 Guy de Maupassant, *Sur l'eau,* 149 [in French in Sighele's text].

109 [Alphonse de Lamartine, *Recueillements poétiques,* "Utopie:" "Il faut se séparer, pour penser, de la foule / Et s'y confondre pour agir."]

four hundred Goethes, Kants, Helmholtzes, Shakespeares, Newtons, etc.,"—he writes—

> together, and have them discuss and decide upon concrete matters—their speeches will be perhaps—and even this is not certain—superior to those of any ordinary convention, but not so their decisions. Why? Because each one of them, besides his personal originality—which renders him the distinguished individuality that he is—has the inherited attributes of the race, which he shares not only with his neighbours in the assembly, but with all the nameless pedestrians on the street. We can express this mathematically by saying that all normal human beings possess a certain something of equal value in common, which we will call a, and the prominent characters a certain special something besides, different in each individual, that we will have to designate in each respectively, as b, c, d, etc. Suppose then, four hundred men assembled together, even if every single one be a genius, they could only be designated as 400 a's, with one b, one c, one d, etc. Then no other result would be possible but that the 400 a's should score a brilliant triumph over the one b, c, d, etc.—that is, that what is common to them as humanity, would put what is individual to flight, that the cotton night-cap would knock off the professional silk hat.[110]

For whomever doubts their exactness, these words, which seem axiomatic to me rather than a demonstration, are confirmed by a long series of facts. What are the very frequent, absurd verdicts of jurors the result of, if not the phenomenon so acutely explained by Nordau? I saw three young men be acquitted who had themselves confessed their guilt for inflicting the utmost violence upon a poor girl, and subsequently martyrizing her in an obscene way. Do you think that each juror, taken individually, would have acquitted these three miserable people? I allow myself to doubt it. Raffaele Garofalo[111] recalls his own experiment performed before a college of six distinct doctors who, being asked to evaluate a man accused of theft, declared him innocent despite the evident proof of guilt, and they later recognized their misjudgment.

In these cases—and in the endless other cases that I could cite—it is, indeed, the simple fact of being *some* rather than *alone* that causes these exaggerated verdicts. The union of many minds diminishes, rather than

110 Max Nordau, *Paradossi*, chapter II. [English translation in Max Nordau, *Paradoxes* (Chicago: L. Schick, 1886), 55–56.]

111 See *The Criminal Crowd* 8, this volume.

increases, the intellectual value of the decision to be made. And, just as in the assembly of geniuses dreamed up by Nordau, the result is probably what a mediocre man's brain would give, so in these juries of sensible men it is easy to obtain a verdict that descends not only below reasonableness, but also below common sense.

The identical phenomenon occurs—of course, because of identical causes—within the too many artistic, scientific, and industrial committees that are one of the most painful plagues of our administrative system. It often happens that their decisions surprise the public because of their strangeness. How is it possible—one asks—that men like those who take part in a committee were able to reach such an illogical and false judgment? How is it possible that ten or twenty artists, or ten or twenty scientists, can reach a verdict that is not compliant with the principles of art, nor with those of science?

The author of *The Conventional Lies of Our Civilization*[112] would respond that even here ... the worker's beret covers the professional silk hat.

Melchior de Vogüé, with his habitual acuteness, one day said, when speaking about one of the most recent French ministers: "These ministers, whose individual value I earlier liked to acknowledge, those men who, for the most part, show eminent administrative qualities in their respective departments, seem to have been struck by fulminant paralysis when they are gathered around the Council table or at the foot of the podium, to make a collective resolution."

Now, why should the same not happen in parliaments? Nordau's reasoning works even if we replace the number 20 with 100 or 500. Rather, the increase in number only exaggerates and renders the phenomenon more acute.

Lord Chesterfield,[113] in a letter to his son, noted this fatal elimination of the best intellectual qualities in any vast human assembly. "After me"—he writes—"Lord Macclefield took the floor. He had a large part in the preparation of the Bill and is one of the greatest mathematicians and astronomers in England. He spoke with great clarity and profound knowledge about the question. But, despite that, the preference was given to

112 [That is, Nordau, who in 1883 wrote *Die conventionellen Lügen der Kulturmenschheit* [*The Conventional Lies of Our Civilization*], a merciless attack on nineteenth-century institutions (in particular, organized religion), which he considered inadequate to meet human needs.]

113 [Philip Stanhope, 4th Earl of Chesterfield (1694–1773) was a celebrated British diplomat and man of letters, author of *Letters to His Son on the Art of Becoming a Man of the World and a Gentleman.*]

me, very unjustly I confess." Then he adds: "It will always be like this. Every assembly is a crowd; whatever personalities comprise it, one should never expect the language of reason from them; a collection of individuals does not possess the faculty to understand ..."

Indeed, popular experience has already intuited what the German philosopher has recently demonstrated and what Lord Chesterfield had observed since 1751. An old proverb says: *Senatores boni viri, senatus autem mala bestia.*[114] And today the public confirms this claim when speaking about certain social groups; it affirms that their individual members taken separately are gentlemen, while taken together they are rogues. Enrico Ferri was, therefore, correct to write that "the assembly of capable people is not a reliable promise of its overall and definitive capacity: from the union of sensible people, one can obtain an assembly that nonetheless lacks common sense, just as in chemistry when two gases unite one can obtain a liquid body."[115]

It is painful, but true; contrary to the laws of mathematical logic, a concentration of many people, albeit very intelligent, can only lead to an intellectually mediocre result.

## *II*

But then—the reader, being a political animal according to Aristotle, will immediately see the very severe political consequences that can derive from our observations—but then, if you condemn a priori the decisions made by more people, do you want to return to despotic, personal tyranny without any union or guarantee?

Do you want to appropriate Casti's quote: better between the claws of a lion than between the nails of a hundred mice?

I would not assert this because the conclusion would be exaggerated and too absolute; I just criticize what I believe to be the flaws of the current system.

This system was indeed born, on the one hand, for the aforementioned reason that one sees better with many eyes than with just one, and, on the

114 [See *The Criminal Crowd* 8n14, this volume.]
115 Enrico Ferri, *Sociologia criminale*, 3rd ed. (Turin: Bocca, 1892), 483.

other hand, to react to the dangerous, old tyrannical system where there was only one supreme judge.

Ancient tyrannies had two flaws: the fact of being hereditary and individual. The former was without a doubt more serious than the latter—and the better but almost impossible way of correcting it would have been to make Carlyle's dream come true by turning geniuses into despots, rather than the sons of the previous despot. Instead, society wanted to correct both vices—the second above all—thus power was given to the people. The tyranny of one was substituted with the tyranny of many; the prejudice of the king's divine right—Spencer would say—was substituted by the prejudice of the parliaments' divine right. At one time, one would be sovereign by birth, today by number. Arithmetic has dethroned heritage.

Indeed, there are still some solitary aristocratic spirits who cannot see the reason for throwing this sceptre, perhaps imprudently, to the masses. Why should the vote of 100 shoemakers be as valuable as that of 100 cultivated men? "I prefer to court Mr Guizot than my porter"—Beyle says, thus summarizing with his fiery irony the apparent paradox that, placing the origin of power at the bottom, seems to enslave intelligence to number. We know the proud *boutade* of that orator who, upon hearing the crowd's applause, interrupted himself to exclaim: "They applaud me? Have I thus said nonsense?" There are many minds that, disdaining public opinion like him, appropriate the superb lines of the poet:

I do not like anything but that which can displease
The judgment of the rude populace.[116]

But were these disdainful souls really right and, therefore, truly sincere? Is the despised *philistine* not perhaps the fertile field on which they work, the necessary condition of their own existence, because they owe him the palm of triumph and the consecration of glory?

If I am not wrong, at the roots of this theory, as of any other one that supports the majority's absolute right, there lies a misunderstanding. Both aristocrats and democrats (we call them such for the sake of

116 [In French in Sighele's text. See Joaquim du Bellay: "Rien ne me plaît, hors ce qui peut déplaire / Au jugement du rude populaire," from "Ode XIII," in *Vers Lyriques* (1549).]

brevity) are partly right and partly wrong. The latter are right if they treat the majority as the supreme judge only *over time*; the former are right if the latter want the majority to be the judge not only over time but also *in every given and current historical moment.*

I will explain.

All that exists and is a work of man—from material objects to ideas—is nothing but the more or less modified imitation or repetition of an idea already invented by a superior individuality. Just as all of the words in our vocabulary, which are today very common, were once neologisms, all that today is common was once unique and original. Originality—it was very wittily said—was nothing but the *première* of triviality. If this originality does not have the conditions of life in itself, imitators are missing and it dies in oblivion, like a booed comedy at its first show falls back into nothingness; on the contrary, if it has in itself a single germ of usefulness, a soul of truth, then the imitations will increase to infinity like the stagings of a vital drama.

The foundation of ideas we despise today as being too vulgar because they are regurgitated by everyone is, therefore, formed by the intuitions—once miraculous, today outdated—of the ancient philosophers, and the commonplaces of the most ordinary discourses began their career as brilliant sparks of originality. What was not worthy to live died, and what today forms the wisdom and conscience of the great mass of the public is the best that geniuses have invented throughout the centuries.

It is, therefore, right to say that *over time* the only judge of every idea is the majority. It alone, with its slow and late verdict, gives supreme sanction to what great men have created or found.

But if, from the point of view that I will call *dynamic*, it is necessary to recognize in the majority the right to judge, can we equally recognize this right from the *static* point of view? In other words, is the majority that is able to judge—and is actually the only judge of—an idea from 100 or 1,000 years ago also able to judge a contemporary thinker's idea? Were temporal distance to be suppressed, can we say that the other conditions remain equal in this collective phenomenon of thought?

Evidently, the response cannot but be negative. The same ones who bow to the majority's opinion on a current debate cannot disavow that this viewpoint is often, or at least sometimes, wrong, while everyone necessarily bows to the view of the majority—formed by slow evolution—on an idea that arose many centuries back. Numbers are, therefore, the supreme judge from the dynamic point of view; it is not the case from the static point of view. And to express myself with a sentence that is perhaps partially inexact, but in a relative sense carves out my thoughts, I will say that, if to judge an idea it is enough to *count* the votes of posterity, it is necessary to *weigh* those of our contemporaries.[117]

To maintain that *the many*, in a given historical moment, are always right, and *the fewer* are always wrong, is a politically undeniable fact (and fatally necessary), albeit not fair. Instead, minorities in the world as well as in parliaments have always been the glory of every country.

A priori, then, the majority's right, applied as it is to our political life, seems to clash with logic, because the opinion of the many is not always the best opinion. It clashes, in particular, when one considers that this right of the majority is exercised through parliaments, that is, the numerous assemblies of men, which—as we tried to demonstrate earlier—always reduce the intellectual value of the decision to be made, by the fatal law of collective psychology.

And not only does it necessarily reduce the value of the results, but these can depend on sudden and unexpected causes, disproportionate to the effect they produce. Any word, gesture, or act can suddenly change the tendencies of an assembly, as of a crowd. The instantaneous contagion of an emotion changes everyone's viewpoint in a moment, like a gust of wind that bends to one side all the tops of a cornfield. Therefore, in addition to the *lowering* of its intellectual value, an assembly can be subjected to an instantaneous intellectual backsliding: it can give results not only of *lesser* value than what each of its members would give, but also of a *totally different* value.

This happens in every assembly of men, and all the more reason in parliaments, which, because of the way that they are formed and make decisions, represent and reunite two phases of collective psychology that overlap or, to use a more chemically exact expression, combine.

Indeed, not only the votes of members of parliament but also their elections are attributable to the gamble of collective psychology.

What are the most important coefficients that contribute to the election of a member of parliament—omitting the buying of votes on which it is useless to insist because it is already showing its own damage? They are speeches and newspapers.

---

117 Champfort has said that *foreigners are the contemporary posterity*. This phrase, which contains a contradiction, is very profound and confirms what we have been saying, given that foreigners, precisely because they are removed from the collectivity of the nationals, can be more dispassionate, freer, and more correct in their judgments.

Now, these two means of persuasion or, better, suggestion of the public, are the strongest and at the same time the least secure, that is, those that can give the most unexpected and illogical outcome, precisely because they act (and above all the former) by taking advantage of the surprises of collective psychology.

Yet, to better clarify my concept, I must ask the reader to follow me through a brief detour on that easily observable but not so observed phenomenon, which is the physiology of success.

## *III*

In the intellectual domain, a renowned figure, depending on the type of art or science he is dedicated to, achieves notoriety and fame at different speed. Disregarding, once again, the publicity that can be purchased, we can say that suggestion over the masses, and therefore *success*, can be *slow* or *immediate*, and generally it is *slow* if suggestion is exerted in a *diffuse* way, that is, over one individual at a time, while it is *immediate* if it acts in an *intense* way, over a crowd of individuals.

A book, for example, is never judged like a dramatic play: the former is read by individual scholars who, in the solitary calm of their rooms, can spontaneously form a sincere opinion; the latter is felt by spectators gathered in one place who mutually and unconsciously suggestionize one another and all together form a monster with one thousand heads that seems to impose this terrible dilemma on the poor author: entertain me or I will devour you!

The conditions of judgment are evidently different. Which is the best?

Before responding, let's ask another question. Have you ever subjected to an analysis of psychological chemistry those uncontrollable bursts of enthusiasm in a theatre or auditorium that sometimes drown out the end of a dramatic scene or the final words of an eloquent speech under a hurricane of applause?

In that moment, the audience believes it is right and sincere, because it truly feels the emotion it manifests. But is it really just thanks to the drama or the orator if the spectators have attained such a degree of frantic approval, or is there not, instead, perhaps some other drug that contributed to making this inebriating wine of enthusiasm bubble?

No one ignores the psychological law of indisputable truth—that the intensity of an emotion grows in direct proportion to the number of people who feel it in the same place and at the same time. Alfred Espinas, in his splendid volume *Des Societés animales* [Animal Societies], gives mathematical proof for this phenomenon: "Let's suppose"—he writes—

> that the emotion felt by a given orator when he faces the public can be represented by the figure 10, and that, upon his first words, in his first flashes of eloquence, he communicates at least half to his listeners, who will be—let's say—300. Each of them will react with applauses or by doubling their attention and this will produce what in the reports is called a movement (*sensation*). But this movement will be felt by everyone at the same time, since the listener is no less preoccupied with the audience than with the orator, and his imagination is immediately struck by the spectacle of these 300 people all prey to an emotion. This spectacle cannot but produce a real emotion in him. Supposing that he only feels half of this emotion, the shock he suffers will no longer be represented by 5, but by half of 5 multiplied by 300, namely 750.

Now, if I am not deceived, these words suffice to demonstrate that all of the crowd's judgments are inevitably exaggerated, because the listener's single opinion is elevated to the *n*th power *by the sole fact* of the others' presence. In this case, the number is the first and most important coefficient of *success*, which is certainly not created by him, but is, however, developed by him in proportions that sometimes touch the peaks of the unlikely.

Not accidentally, Ludwig of Bavaria, who was crazy but also a great artist and above all a great artistic consciousness, wanted to attend the performances of Wagner's works, alone in his deserted theatre. He felt that only in that way, free from any suggestion, could he sincerely judge and enjoy the manifestations of genius.[118]

For a scientist or artist who addresses a *scattered* public rather than a *united* public, the effects and measure of success are substantially different.

Has it not happened many times to each of us to be moved after reading certain sublime pages? But that gush of admiration that rose from our hearts and, if we had been in a theatre or a crowded hall, would instantaneously have led to a delirium of applause by the sole virtue of

118 [King Ludwig II of Bavaria (1845–1886), also called the Swan King and the Fairy Tale King, is renowned for his many grandiose and eccentric architectural projects, such as the Neuschwanstein Castle, on which he lavished his revenues, and for his patronage of composer Richard Wagner.]

contagion, dried out in the solitude of our soul and within the walls of our study.

The author of a book does not see or know these isolated manifestations of enthusiasm; he does not know the scattered public that admires him and, if he does hear its single voices, he does not, however, hear its collective and grandiose voice. He can never be like an orator or the author of a drama or melodrama, the fire where all the impressions felt by a hundred listeners converge in a unique instant, multiplying by 100 its effective value, because of the presence of other listeners. And this is why he never enjoys the acute and supreme voluptuousness of seeing an entire public moved and delirious at his feet, as they see, instead, orators and dramatic artists who are often worth much less.

Hence it is one thing to act on a *united* public; it is another thing to act on a *diffuse* public. Which one—I repeat—is the best condition?

Subjectively, I would not know. The response depends on individual temperament. There is the person who prides himself on being overwhelmed by a crowd's ovations; then there is the person who is content with indirectly discovering a public's admiration for him by indirect means. Mascagni and Zola can be equally satisfied in their vanity or in their just pride. The former has witnessed that epileptic attack of enthusiasm that struck the Viennese at the representation of the *Rustic Chivalry* and *Friend Fritz*; the other learned from his editor Charpentier that *The Downfall* reached 150,000 sales in a few months. They are two plebiscites, with different manifestation and similar significance.

Objectively, there is no doubt that the judgment of a scattered public is the most certain and truthful. I have already demonstrated that the judgment of a crowd is always exaggerated because of the influence of numbers, which necessarily elevates the tuning fork of single individual opinions. I believe I can add that this judgment is also often wrong. Collective psychology is rarely guided by logic and reasonableness. Circumstances, fortuity, and the unconscious[119] determine in most

119 [The noun that Sighele uses in Italian is "l'incosciente" (*Contro il Parlamentarismo* in *La delinquenza settaria* 252), a term that, before Freud's "unconscious," had begun to emerge in Italian psychology and philosophy as a translation of the German "Unbewussten" especially after the publication of philosopher Eduard von Hartmann's 1869 seminal work *Philosophie des Unbewussten* [*Philosophy of the Unconscious*]. See, for instance, Adolfo Faggi, *La filosofia dell'incosciente: Metafisica e morale* (Firenze: Successori LeMonnier, 1890)].

cases its manifestations. A shout from a single person forces everyone else to shout. The contagion of applause or of disapproval is instantaneous, just like when a minimal flapping of wings produces an irresistible panic in a flock of birds. Therefore, the judgment that ensues and that we believe to be the sum of everyone's judgments is nothing but the viewpoint of one, which, because of the unknown phenomenon of suggestion, has suddenly become the random and instantaneous despot of an entire crowd.

The judgment of a *scattered* public—which pertains to books—does not present these dangers. Of course, even for the book, a collective verdict gradually forms because all the *diffuse* readers exchange their impressions, and their single viewpoints merge like single notes rising to one chord. But this is a unison that arises more gradually, bringing together more pondered, and hence less easily modifiable opinions, rather than being caused by a sudden burst of unconscious collective psychology.

Analogous to the effect that a speech produces in front of hundreds of gathered individuals is the effect of an idea or a person praised in a daily political newspaper.

For collective psychology, one can say that a newspaper, in these cases, is equal to a speech. Indeed, the *instantaneity* of an orator's impression on *assembled* people is substituted by a *very brief space of time* (the two or three hours by which *all* will have read a newspaper after its distribution), when the impression left by an article or piece of news spreads among the people *close by* and in communication, by necessity of life.

It is enough to have witnessed only once—in the capital or province, in a café or pharmacy—the arrival of an expected newspaper, to convince oneself of how big and immediate the effect of suggestion really is when a piece of interesting news is anticipated.

The content of an article passes from mouth to mouth with a promptness almost equal to the propagation of an emotion in a crowd; the comments—favourable or unfavourable—have the suggestive force of the applause or disapproval that welcomes a speech, and, consciously or unconsciously, everyone's thought is subject to a veritable constraint, like that of every single spectator in a theatre or assembly. In other words: the newspaper's effect is, like that of a speech, *exaggerated* and often *misleading*.

## *IV*

Now, after that digression, let us return to the point from which we departed.

I have said that the election of a member of parliament is attributable especially to the forces of suggestion coming from these two means: *oratory art* and *daily newspapers*. It is the result, in other words, of the two means that construct more easily and quickly that edifice called *success* (a not very solid edifice, certainly, if it is not deserved, but its solidity and duration are of little importance for the effects that prompt us to study it) and that mainly perturbs, by the law of collective psychology, the voter's independent and sincere determination.

What occurs then? It happens that the voter, who places his ballot in an urn and seems to perform a free and self-contained action, is nothing but a victim under suggestion of some hypnotic force that today can be a speech and tomorrow a newspaper.

If he were influenced by an idea or by a person with a certain value, suggestion would then be socially useful! But even without being sceptical we can affirm that such cases are rare.

In our happy country of rhetoric, many are those who know how to stitch together an effective speech, and the mass is ignorant enough to admire those who declaim great phrases, even if they do not know how to make any flash of thought shine.

Oratory art, which is among the noblest and most difficult of arts, often comes down to the triviality of a simple artifice employed to attract uncultivated and naive listeners. "A flood of words above a desert of ideas"—this terrible but true phrase can in many cases define the speeches of candidates and those of their great constituents. The suggestive power of these second- or third-order speeches is demonstrated by the huge number of lawyers who flock to Montecitorio.[120]

As for the daily press—who does not know the value of the praises it bestows? These praises are either paid for (with money or favours), or obtained through the friendship of some newspaper editor, or are written by the ones being praised. The good, provincial public believes in the sincerity of the publicity, and it does not suspect the meanness and humiliation the candidate had to endure in order to put a laudative adjective next to his name. And down there in the tiny village, when one reads a newspaper, the magnifying effect is inevitable.

This is how, unfortunately, members of parliament are produced and given the illusion of being great men thanks to the thousands of votes obtained in such ways (and I do not talk about criminal means).

120 [The Montecitorio Palace in Rome is the seat of the Italian Chamber of Deputies.]

And when, in a moment of sincerity and discouragement, one examines the parliament's physiology, and sees that it is mostly composed of unknown or insignificant personalities, one claims, almost with petty satisfaction: the fault lies with the country; it was interrogated and responded with this choice.

The fault lies with the country, we are in agreement, but it responds in this way, that is, poorly because it is interrogated and obliged to respond with the deceitful means of collective psychology. If one could interrogate each individual in isolation, the result would be—I believe—different, just as the absurd verdicts of a jury would be less frequent if each of those twelve worthy men could give his vote without being subjected to the mutual suggestion of his colleagues, of the accuser, the defender, and the public.

The trouble is that this remedy is impracticable, or at least I do not see a way of implementing it.

Once parliament is formed, it functions, still and always, according to collective psychology. And the intellectual level of whoever composes it, which is already low, goes even further down because of the law that we enunciated before. The offices, councils, and committees—small parliaments within the larger one—multiply the probability for mediocre results and painful surprises. Political reason often allows the smuggling of many inconsistencies and injustices to pass under its banner. Articles of law are suppressed or modified without thinking that they function in relation to other ones that should, in their turn, be suppressed or modified; sometimes an *entire* project is approved only because *one part* is optimal and must be approved. And in solemn moments, the appeal to the great names and great ideals of patriotism is never missing, so that, by co-opting feelings, it can be possible to storm an approval that rationality would probably refuse to grant.

It follows that parliament can in many cases be compared to an inverted filter: instead of improving, bills worsen as they traverse all those phases to which they are subjected.

Let's look at an example. The text of a law is being discussed. It will certainly not be a masterpiece, and, in this respect, one can deplore that the projects are not assigned to a specialist.[121] But in any case, the text has been redacted by competent people and presents a certain cohesion.

---

121 In Austria, to cite a relatively recent case, the drafting of the project for a Code of Criminal Procedure was assigned to an illustrious legislator, and the result was excellent precisely because it came from a *single* and strong mind.

Well, immediately a shower of amendments pours over that hapless project. Perhaps some are inspired by a sincere desire to improve the law; and most, to be sure, are dictated by ulterior political motives and insidiously take this law as a pretext to set a trap into which the ministry will fall. The seduction of a felicitous phrase, the pressure of some newspaper, the momentary need to not displease one's opponents, thousands of reasons unrelated to the real topic of discussion may ensure the endorsement of a first amendment. Then, the day after, for different but still unrelated reasons, they will welcome a second amendment, often in contradiction with the first one, which is then voted on by members of parliament who were absent the day before, hence not informed about the discussion. And so on, until the moment when the law will be nothing but a confused conglomeration of heterogeneous articles, a monster that will scare the Chamber and will ultimately be sent back into nothingness.

We should add that collective psychology—in this respect similar to feminine psychology—is made of contradictions and cruelty, and passes, or, better, jumps, so fast from one given feeling to its opposite. And just as an actor or an orator who mispronounces a word can compromise the outcome of a comedy or speech by provoking cruel laughter even in the most serious of moments, so a representative or minister can see their most loyal and affectionate friends change into enemies because of an infelicitous phrase.

In short, the Chamber is psychologically a female and often a hysterical one.

To prove the truth of this humiliating definition, it should be enough to observe the difference that exists between the members of parliament when they are in the Chamber and in the corridors. The extraordinary mobility of their psychology has no other comparison than in hysterical temperaments. The men that you saw a minute before threatening one another with voices and gestures, challenging one another with their eyes, now you see approach one another with smiles and friendly handshakes. If a minister passes by, those who earlier covered him with offences now welcome him cheerfully, congratulate him on his brilliant reply, and perhaps (and here is the poison) they find a way to beg him for a favour.

Relationships, and even words and rulings, have changed. Speeches that were applauded, the proposition that was supported by one's own vote, become the object of bitter criticism. One of them speaks ironically about the doctrine he defended, and resentfully about the people he has defended. Another expresses himself with great moderation about the men and ideas he had violently attacked. The hackneyed phrases that were proclaimed in the Chamber as axioms now are ridiculed. Whoever screamed that salvation was in freedom, now implores a man, namely a dictator, to save the situation. Truth on this side of the door, error beyond it. On the one hand a stage, on the other the reality of things.[122]

Paul Bourget, I think, says that life is "a volume by Labiche interleaved with some Shakespeare."[123]

Parliamentary life can, a fortiori, be described in this way. A farce in the corridor, a tragedy in the Chamber.

## *V*

If these are the probable intellectual results of a parliament, what will the moral results be? Will the assembly of many also weaken the energy of character as it reduces the force of the brain?

Unfortunately, today it is no longer possible to discuss whether parliament as a whole responds to the highest ends of morality: very painful recent events exclude doubt on this subject.

The discussion is, therefore, possible only by looking at the causes of this immorality.

The first and most evident cause can be found in the way many members of parliament are elected. Thrown to the seat of representatives of a nation with the support of Tom or Dick—rather than for their own merits recognized by the population—they necessarily drag with them the chain of forced gratitude, which translates into favours that are biased and unjust. For the member of parliament it is an obligation to reciprocate the proofs of devotion that he received; for the voter, it is a right to receive this reciprocation. The legislative mandate is thus denaturalized from the bottom and paves the ground for new and greater immoralities.

These—given such a predisposition—do not wait long to appear.

---

122 On this topic, see the article "Explorations parlementaires," by E. Melchior de Vogüé in *Revue des deux Mondes* (1 Sept. 1894). In this article, Vogüé, repeating a concept he expressed elsewhere, which I mentioned earlier, writes: "I decline to plead against evidence, against the unanimity of judgments. To the witnesses of our sessions, we offer nothing but the choice between two diagnoses: sheer madness and general paralysis."

123 ["La vie ressemble à un volume de Labiche interfolié avec du Shakespeare." See Paul Bourget, *Physiologie de l'amour moderne*, in *Oeuvres complètes de Paul Bourget*, vol. II (Paris: Plon, 1901), 342.]

It is already known that company of whatever kind increases the small or great tendency to evil, which incubates latently in every one of us, like fire under the ashes.

Look at the children: when they find themselves together, it is then that they become naughtier and crueller. A rather bold joke, a petty theft, the climbing of a low wall, which no one would dare carry out or even think about when alone, are devised and accomplished when children are in a group. We adults, too, must recognize that if there is a circumstance when we can infringe the laws of delicacy or compassion, it is, indeed, when we are more than one, because then the courage to do evil comes out in us and we judge lightly the improper action that we would have not been able to carry out alone. Who does not have, in his youth, some episode that confirms the exactness of what we are saying? What gentleman does not remember having committed along with his companions—and solely because he was with them—some mischief that verges on being an immoral action, if not a crime?[124]

The reason for these facts—which are so common that they do not need evidence—is, above all, arithmetic. As the average of some numbers cannot evidently be equal to the highest among them, so a human aggregate cannot reflect in its manifestations the highest faculties possessed only by some of its members: it will only reflect the moral faculties shared by all of them. Giuseppe Sergi would say, with one of his beautiful and biologically exact similes, that the ultimate and best stratifications of character—those that civilization and education have managed to form in some privileged individual—are eclipsed by the average stratifications that are the patrimony of everyone, and, in the total sum the average ones prevail while the others disappear.

What we observed earlier from the *intellectual* point of view, indeed, occurs from the *moral* point of view. Company weakens both talent and moral sentiments. This is due also to another reason.

In an aggregate of men, it is enough to have an evildoer for turning disciples into imitators. Men, Bagehot says, are guided by models, not by reasoning. And he says it well, but forgot to add that they are guided, above all, by evil models. It is the rotten pear that corrupts the healthy ones: the contrary to this has never been witnessed. The microbe of evil has a power of expansion infinitely greater than that of the microbe of good, provided that the latter exists—because, while unfortunately we

124 See the *Confessions of Saint Augustine.*

know that many diseases are contagious, it is not equally proven that health is, too.

It is much easier to fall sick by suggestion, rather than to heal. It is, therefore, much easier to be socially corrupted than to reinforce one's own character—all the more so because moral corruption greatly attracts interest. A minimal rip to conscience can signify an immense economic advantage—and, in the bourgeois epoch we are living through, money shines too brightly not to hypnotize even those who believe they are, and who are to a certain extent, honest men. The environment surrounds them like a coil, and it is truly a boa constrictor that gradually suffocates their delicacy, honour, and even remorse.

Who can analyse the ways in which this degeneration happens? First, the life of the member of parliament—I mean the hours spent in the corridors of the Chamber—is certainly not made to fortify character. Amid these speeches, which pretend to formulate political ideas but are often nothing but gossip, will melts into words. By constantly approaching opponents, the better-tempered convictions smooth out and mollify themselves. Sarcasm from the most astute colleagues at first humiliates the naive and honest politicians; the spontaneous rebellion that the latter modestly start is met with scepticism, teasing, and indifference; confronted with that adverse plebiscite, their rigid honesty starts to vacillate, and they wonder: what if the others were right? Once doubt insinuates in their minds, the victory of immorality is secure, since, in the face of honour, to doubt means to be defeated. A favour first, a very small injustice later: the breach is open. And as they proceed on this course,—which is so steep that, once they set foot on it, they are sure to plummet to the bottom—conscience tries to justify its transformation with the most Jesuitical and useless of consolations: *everyone is doing it! My responsibility, if it does exist, is infinitesimal.* And in such a way, in the fact of being many, they find the illusion of an excuse, the last damage beyond the cause of corruption.

The very few who are spared this leprosy—the refractory ones—cannot diminish the epidemic. They rarely denounce it, because the good individual is compassionate and—I regret to say—also pusillanimous in certain cases. His cowardice derives from the virtue of being merciful. Judging the others like himself, he imagines and represents to himself the pain and humiliation of the evildoer who is put to shame—and he does not dare throw an accusation in his face.

To be a hero on the battlefield, one must be a bit cruel; likewise, to be courageous and frank in the political world, one must be deprived of a certain delicacy of sentiment. And only a high, imperative duty can win over this discretion and turn a colleague into an accuser.

The consequence is that the good ones, with their negative behaviour, facilitate the suspicious endeavours of the evildoers and of all those weaklings—those shrub men, as Balzac would say[125]—who bend where the wind blows and where the strong want.

An unacknowledged, latent association—unconscious too, we might say—gradually takes shape, extending its invisible network over public life as a whole. It is a power that nobody dares mention, but that is known. It is a force one does not see but feels. It resembles groundwater, which is not suspected from the earth's surface but which makes possible the vegetation that grows on the soil.

And that vegetation is favouritism, immorality, crime.

The public knows that, to obtain something, it is enough to address a member of parliament—even against justice, it does not matter. And the member of parliament asks, begs, imposes, and obtains. He obtains from the government by pledging his vote (even though he is then ready to betray as soon as he perceives he had put a wager on the loser); he obtains from the banks, selling the smoke of his influence; he obtains from bureaucracy, making the gold of his little medal shine, as well as his little deserved honourable title. In ministries, there are volumes containing recommendations by members of parliament and no one wonders why. And the government, which knows and tolerates all these things because it is advantageous, does not fear certain opponents in the Chamber, because they are too tied to it by unmentionable connections to have the audacity to tell the entire and complete truth. Under the strongest invectives from opponents—just to show off, to deceive the naive—there are agreement and the conspiracy of silence. They cannot reveal all the crimes of their opponents because they themselves would be swept away by ruin, as accomplices.

This is the real modern political criminality, made of subterfuges and hypocrisies—the sectarian criminality of those few who reach the peak—and it makes a worthy comparison to the sectarian criminality of the lowest social classes.

The latter—the franker—adopt violence, and their means of fighting are called murder and dynamite; the former—more Jesuitically civil—adopt shrewdness, and their means of fighting are called misappropriation, perjury, fraud.

---

125 [See *The Criminal Crowd* 70 and *In Art and in Science* 394 for source and additional recurrences of this image.]

Immorality of person, immorality of party, immorality of government—all of these are necessary and fatal consequences of a system that seems to have been created for the purpose of making men worse rather than better.

The member of parliament, before becoming such, stigmatized the behaviour and conduct of those who were members of parliament at the time, just like the ministers, before being such, that is, from the opposition's benches, screamed against the government. Not yet taken into the gears of the fatal wheel, they had the illusion of being able to resist. They did not know that politics is a slow depravation from which very few know how to escape. And even the best, when they came from far away provinces with high ideals and promising dreams, did not suspect that the light that attracted them would burn their honesty.

## *VI*

The indictment is over and the modest prosecutor who pronounced it should now, instead of requesting a punishment, indicate the remedies to the evil he complained about.

Truly, this evil has such profound causes and is so rooted in human nature that it seems difficult to eliminate. It could be compared to death, the inevitable phenomenon of which one always wants to attenuate the severity, but which one cannot abolish.

Who would dare fight the majority's supreme right and, consequently, the power of parliaments?

And what remedy is possible for the fact that every assembly, every group of men is morally and intellectually inferior to the elements that comprise it, if social life is nothing but the result or the complex of all these infinite groups that bustle in it, and that are called classes, churches, associations, or parties?

The remedy is evidently not there, and the acknowledgment of this painful truth is, perhaps, the most pessimistic hypothesis that has ever been formulated. To unite—in the human world—means to get worse; what is more distressing?

Gabriel Tarde—when I expressed such an idea for the first time[126]—with his logical acumen, which is not the least of his talents, drew a rather bold deduction. "I wish to point out, without insisting,"—he writes—

126 See my volume *La folla delinquente*, 2nd ed. (Turin: Bocca, 1895).

> the unexpected scope of this idea if we extend it beyond humankind. Everyone knows that organisms were rightly considered societies of cells,and cells societies of molecules. Now, we suppose that our principle applies to these biological or chemical societies. In other words, we suppose that also in these the aggregate is not superior to its elements, that it is, rather, inferior or at most equal. We then see the entire universe appear in a new light, and it is to the perfecting of the microscope, not of the telescope, that we will have to demand the revelation of the world's most admirable marvels. Perhaps, indeed, it was in virtue of a pure unjustified prejudice that the *I* of the *atom* had always been thought of as simpler, more miserable, and lower than the animal or human *I*. Perhaps, fundamentally hidden in living beings, in their elementary intimacy, much more intelligence and art lives and invisibly spreads than on the surface.[127]

But let's stop on the slope of this paradoxical conjecture. The unlikelihood of our theory, when it is brought to its extremes, takes nothing away from its truth when it is applied to the cases like the ones examined so far. That an assembly of men is, in its collective results, worse than the average of its individual components is a statement of which we are proud to have provided evidence, and we are content with it.[128]

As for the majority's right, although omitting to note that it explicates itself by means of the parliaments, that is, of collective psychology, it was also theoretically and practically opposed.

Indeed, the majority's right is precisely the first fundamental reason for our current political baseness.

The "government of mediocrity," [John] Stuart Mill writes, cannot but be a "mediocre government. No government by a democracy or a numerous aristocracy, either in its political acts or in the opinions, qualities, and tone of mind which it fosters, ever did or could rise above mediocrity, except in so far as the sovereign Many have let themselves be guided (which in their best times they always have done) by the counsels and influence of a more highly gifted and instructed One or Few."[129]

---

127 G. Tarde, *Les crimes des foules* (Lyon: Storek, 1892).

128 On this argument, which I only hint at here, see my polemic with Gabriel Tarde, Enrico Ferri, and Silvio Venturi in *Critica Sociale*, nos. 21, 22, and 23 (1894). There my thought is explained better and more clearly than I can do here.

129 [John Stuart Mill, *On Liberty* (Boston: Ticknor and Fields, 1863), 128.]

Thus, [John] Stuart Mill absolutely condemns a government of many, with the possibility of only one exception: when the sovereign population allows itself to be guided by a genius.

But, in such a case, rather than an exception, is it not perhaps the confirmation of the established rule?

We know, too, that political assemblies can often rise to sublime heights of thought or feeling, when the captivating words of a Mirabeau or the grandiose idea of a Camillo Cavour inflames them. But what do these facts prove in favour of the majority's right?

They prove nothing, because in such cases it is not the voice of the majority that imposes itself, but the despotism of only one, a despotism that thrives on unconscious suggestion rather than on material force, as in the past.

Every time an assembly proclaimed a truth or conquered a right, in short, every time it was not *mediocre* in its manifestations, it had to follow a man who charmed and intellectually possessed it, like the hypnotized does with his hypnotist. You can say—in such cases—that the result is attributable to the assembly or to its majority. This is an illusion. *Only one* desires that result, and *by suggestive force* he imposed that result on those surrounding him.[130]

Social life—and, therefore, also political life—is founded on the phenomenon of suggestion. Happy are the epochs and people that possess a genius who polarizes all the desires, aspirations, and feelings, and blindly drags the crowd behind him!

---

130 To avoid misunderstandings, and to prevent people from thinking that I give too much importance to the *individual* and too little to the *collectivity*, or rather to the *environment*, I underline that I am speaking from a *current* and *static*, rather than *dynamic*, point of view. *Dynamically* it is true that geniuses are a necessary product of the environment from which they arise, wonderful parts of the collectivity, unconscious views from a given historical moment—I have elsewhere acknowledged it too many times for having to repeat it here. But *statically* it is also true that geniuses are, more than actors, authors of the human drama, or as Sainte-Beuve calls them, kings that create their population. To those who deny this influence of the *great man* on the masses, remember Bagehot's words: "There is an odd idea that those who take what is called a 'scientific view' of history need rate lightly the influence of individual character. It would be as reasonable to say that those who take a scientific view of nature need think little of the influence of the sun." *Physics and Politics* 96.

But these are rare cases in the life of nations, and when the genius is not there, when this fire, which attracts all individual energies, is lacking, we truly have a reign of mediocrity, because the force of suggestion—instead of individualizing itself—diffuses and disperses itself, producing the thousand surprises of collective psychology.

It is in these cases—which are the most common and normal—that the painful effects we noted in parliament occur, and it is for these cases that a decrease in the number of parliament members could constitute, if not a true remedy, at least a mitigation of evil.

If, for example, the representatives of a nation were reduced to 100, it is certain that the average of these 100 would be intellectually and morally superior to the average of the 500 current members of parliament. Why? Because by limiting their number, the good ones would hardly be excluded, while, luckily, the bad ones easily would. When the spots are too many, the ballast almost inevitably creeps in. The member of parliament must be elected! And if nobody deserves the office, we must be content with the firstcomer. What happens with seats in parliament also occurs with chairs at universities. As long as there are too many, we will see too many professors who do not deserve their position. Once the chairs decrease, the best will come forward and occupy the positions. Hence the average of the teaching body will be better.

Furthermore, with fewer members of parliament we can avoid another inconvenience. Today it is enough that a person is renowned in any branch of science or art, and his province or city—which often boast of their fellow citizen, like mothers do when their son has been successful—believes it is obliged to throw him into the boiler of Montecitorio. He is a man of genius. And this is fine. But just because he writes beautiful lines or good books, will he also be an industrious and useful politician? Generally, quite the contrary happens. This is how a mediocre member of parliament is created, depriving art or science of an excellent artist or an illustrious scientist. This is unacceptable. Anybody can dedicate himself to politics if so desired, but voters should send to parliament the person who has demonstrated political abilities. We do not believe that ingenious people are enough to rule the population or to promulgate laws. A special kind of genius is necessary, as in all professions. Otherwise, we will see lawyers, ministers, or vice ministers in the navy or at the treasury, engineers at the Ministry of Justice, and gentlemen who cheerfully rave to the Ministry of Public Education.

With a limited number of posts, this *sorting* will be rarer and not so easy, and everybody will gain thanks to the law of work specification.

Let's add that it will finally be possible to pay a subsidy to members of parliament, requiring them to do nothing but be a member of parliament. The quality of representative of the people, which is now a *sinecure* only useful to obtain hat doffing and facilitations everywhere, will become an office demanding work. Responsibility divided among 100 instead of 500 will be much more strongly felt, and the elected will have to take care of important things and of truly general interests, letting every province look after its own interests autonomously and independently, allowing, above all, the fixers to work in Rome as the electors' clerks and correspondents, looking after their petty and personal needs.

Therefore, perhaps, there will be some improvement, and this by-now-old parliamentary organism, by simplifying itself, will be able to live yet for some time without infamy and perhaps even with praise. I believe that one can speak of it as one would about certain poisons, which either kill or reinforce, according to the applied doses.

Now the dose or, beyond metaphors, the extension and importance that parliamentarism has taken on is so great that it threatens to kill public life. Who knows whether a smaller dose can strengthen it, instead of killing it!

# 4 From *The Intelligence of the Crowd*

## Chapter 2: "Art and the Crowd"

*Art* and *crowd* are two nouns that to many of us must seem contradictory and not associable, because while the first represents the aristocracy of thought, the second means nothing but the vulgarity of numbers.

Can the crowd understand and judge art? Is its judgment one of those verdicts with no appeal, *pro veritate habentur* [sic]?[1] Or vice versa, as many assert, is the art that the crowd likes not art at all or, at most, nothing but an inferior form of art?

This is the rather old problem that some recent studies have made trendy once again; an interesting and important problem, not only for the solutions it could have but, moreover, and above all, for the psychological analyses that are necessary to resolve it. It is collective psychology, this immense, profound and mysterious sea that must be probed in order to discover not the intimate and ultimate reason, which is elusive, but at least some causes of its ebb and flow, of its calm and of its sudden tempests.

### *I*

Some smile at the moralizing role that Guyau[2] first and Tolstoy later attributed to art, and they do not admit it could aim at the progressive

1 ["Res iudicata pro veritate habetur," meaning that "a thing adjudged is held as truth."]

improvement of humanity, following from time to time the reforms that sprout up in the social environment. They deny that there is conservative and revolutionary art, realist and republican art, militaristic and anti-war art, because true art—they say—looks at all of these and many other small phenomena of the contemporary soul from above, and oftentimes treats them with disdain.

It could be. I do not claim the right to define *true* art, and I humbly confess to ignore whoever has the monopoly on this definition. But I feel that art, like a mirror, reflects the religious, political, and scientific currents that traverse the human psyche, and therefore affirm—with the due modesty of a layman—that art follows, in this sense, the thoughts and feelings diffused in the collective soul and, I would say, it almost feeds off of them. Art represents among human phenomena what the *mimosa pudica*[3] represents among vegetal organisms. With its extraordinary gift of perception that no one else has and that seems to be foreknowledge, it averts all that happens around it, or it reacts to the phenomena of the external world and absorbs them, but always with limpid, synthetic evidence.

This is proven by the problem I put forth as the objective of this study, which today returns to occupy the human spirit. This search for relationship between art and the crowd, this question as to whether the former can be judged by the latter, is nothing but the artistic form of the great disagreement between individualism and socialism that troubles contemporary consciousness. In this disdainful pride of the creative artist who denies the crowd the right to consecrate him to fame or oblivion, we see the return of the eternal duel between the individual and society; we feel the great doubt ferment out of whose mists the new century arises, that is, whether progress is the exclusive merit of some brilliant individuals who dragged the crowds behind them like sheep

2 [Jean-Marie Guyau (1854–1888), a French philosopher, sociologist, and poet, was inspired by Epicureanism, stoicism, and utilitarianism. His most famous work, *Esquisse d'une morale sans obligation ni sanction* [*Outline of a Morality without Obligation or Sanction*] (1885) influenced Nietzsche.]

3 [The term that Sighele adopts in the original Italian text is "sensitiva," that is, the common name of *mimosa pudica*, which highlights even more this plant's sensitiveness: when touched or shaken, indeed, its leaves fold inward.]

behind a shepherd, or, rather, the wonderful unconscious work of all, a kind of immense pyramid to which every man who ever lived contributed his stone.

Therefore, in the field of art, as in politics, we face two opposing and irreducible parties: one exalts the crowd, the other despises it; one deems it worthy to be the judge of any individual work and, therefore, also to govern, the other denies it any intellectual ability, and would thus want to treat it not as a judge and a despot, but as a handmaid and a slave, dominated always and in everything by one or by very few.

In politics, the party that despises the crowd is by now restrained to rather narrow confines; its superb and selfish thesis is by now difficult to support in its rigid pureness, because it clashes against a state of affairs that one cannot change: the right to vote. It is, moreover, necessary to add that politics, being the social phenomenon in which sincerity and frankness are scarcer, does not permit the clear and fair division of parties that exists elsewhere, and it rather manifests itself with uncertain gradations, not with resolutely pronounced colours. Indeed, in politics it is rare to find a staunch individualist, namely, a despot; likewise, it is rare to find a staunch socialist, namely, a man who denies any and all influence or right to the isolated individual. Both are intimately tormented by a contradiction that, although not confessed, can be easily laid bare: the individualist will find that adhesion and success in the public, which he scorns with words; the socialist will fight for that egotistical drive to overtake the others and to accumulate for himself, which he theoretically condemns.

In art, the party that despises the crowd is bigger. Without lingering on the extreme and pathological phalanx of the supporters of the superman theory, those who refuse the multitude's right to judge any artistic manifestation are undeniably many, and they grant it, at most, to a clique of experts who go by the name of critics. Also, in this case, the contradictory phenomenon occurs whereby those aristocrats of thought are ultimately not too displeased if the crowd fills them with praise and applause, although, however, basking in the popular aura that caresses them, they do not cease to scorn it, and when that aura is against them rather than in favour, they are not dismayed, but rather they smile with their incontestable superiority. This supreme contempt of the artist-individual towards the idiot crowd is one of the most common phenomena—from the ancient Greek orator who, when the crowd applauded him, interrupted himself, ironically asking: "*they applaud me? Have I thus said nonsense?*" to the Italianness of Arrigo Boito's modern genius[4] who, during the memorable night of the first showing of *Mephistopheles*, impassive in his conductor's seat, responded to the public's whistles, saying with a smile to his neighbours: "*what honour they give me!*"

Yet, is it always a logical and just phenomenon? Here is, finally and truly, the problem.

## *II*

Some have stated, and it is by now repeated daily by everyone, that the crowd is morally and intellectually inferior to the individual. The author of this book collaborated, or, better, was the first to highlight this truth, and had the pleasure to see his ideas reproduced many times. These reproductions, however, whether unconsciously because of near-sightedness or consciously because of partisanship, forgot that if I formulated a law, I also ascertained the not-rare exceptions.

Moral exceptions, above all.

The crowd is, without doubt, a terrain in which the microbe of evil develops rather easily, and in which vice versa the microbe of good almost always dies, not finding favourable living conditions. You are always fearful of a crowd, you rarely hope. Unfortunately, everyone feels and knows from experience that the example of an evildoer or a madman can drag the crowd to crime; far fewer believe, and it happens rarely, that the voice of a pacifist can induce the crowd to calm. In history, the work of a crowd was more a work of hatred and destruction than of creation or love, because the crowd, an unconscious and impulsive organism, acts inevitably more with the instincts of the savage and brute than with those of a civilized man.

But, one cannot deny that sometimes the multitude attains high psychological levels that the isolated man would not know how to reach, or manifests a generosity so sublime that no individual could explain it.

> When the greatest of orators manages to convince the Athenians that the man who had provoked irreparable disasters, persuading them to arm themselves against Philip of Macedon, deserved not punishment but a laurel

4 [Arrigo Boito (1842–1918) was an Italian librettist, composer, journalist, and novelist. He is still renowned for his libretti of Giuseppe Verdi's operas, and for his own opera *Mefistofele*. Together with his brother Camillo, he also contributed to the literary movement of Scapigliatura.]

> crown; when he glorified himself for having saved the honour of his country at Marathon, and persuaded the shopkeepers and artisans that their honour had to be dearer to them than life, that day offered the most beautiful triumph the human word had ever gained, and the Athenian people proved that a multitude is not always mediocre and that great inspirations sometimes can find the road to penetrate its soul. Every citizen perhaps, in isolation, would have resisted the eloquence of Demosthenes, but he was speaking to a crowd and the crowd gave up.[5]

Likewise, on the celebrated night of 4 August, the assembly of France, by throwing away its hereditary rights, gave proof of a collective altruism, unequalled in the history of individual altruism.[6]

Analogously, the inebriated crowd of Parisians at the epoch of the Revolution had flashes of sentimental sweetness in the middle of the obscure storm of its beastly ferocity. When Sombreuil,[7] condemned to death, appeared among the lines of bayonets, and his daughter clung to his neck begging the executioners to spare him or to kill her with him, a yell of grace arose among the multitude. And they agreed to spare his life on the horrible condition that she would immerse her lips in a cup full of aristocratic blood. The daughter took the cup with her steady hand and emptied it, with a toast to her father. Her supreme gesture worked a miracle. There are surprises of nature even in crime; there are unforeseeable revolutions in the abyss of the human heart. Those monsters, still tainted with blood, brought Sombreuil and his daughter in

---

5 V. Cherbuliez, "La théorie d'un positiviste italien sur la foule criminelle," in *Revue des deux Mondes* (15 Dec. 1892).

6 [On the night of 4 August 1789, during the period of the French Revolution, the newly formed National Assembly issued the Declaration of the Rights of Man and proposed reforms to abolish class privileges. The aristocracy and clergy abandoned their feudal rights, among them exemption from taxation.]

7 [Charles François de Virot, marquis de Sombreuil (1723–1794), lieutenant general, was sentenced to death by the Parisian revolutionary tribunal during the Revolution. His daughter Marie Maurille, comtesse de Villelume was immortalized as the "heroine of the glass of blood," a legend according to which, when her father was arrested for his anti-revolutionary activity during the 1792 September massacres, she begged for mercy interposing herself between the crowd and her father, and shouting that in order to get to him they would have to kill her first. Sombreuil's life—the legend continues—would be spared only if she agreed to drink the blood of beheaded aristocrats. In fact, Sombreuil ultimately died on the scaffold, on 17 June 1794.]

triumph all the way to their building and swore to defend them against any enemy.[8]

Therefore—to pass from the true and lived tragedies to false and represented ones—one cannot deny that in the most misunderstood societies, in the masses comprised of the worst elements, there is a collective sentiment of honesty and justice that beats out the most perverse individual instinct. I recall the indignation that pervaded an audience of convicts, whom the director of the penitentiary had allowed to attend a play, when the traitor Golo made two murderers kill the pious and virtuous Genevieve of Brabant along with her baby.

Hence, there is no doubt that, although having to affirm, in general, that the crowd is morally worse than the individual, it is also necessary to recognize how, sometimes, the crowd surpasses the individual in the manifestation of the highest faculties of the human soul. The crowd, like woman, has an *extreme* psychology, capable only of excesses, admirable at times for self-abnegation, often fearfully ferocious, never or almost never mediocre and balanced in its sentiments.

Now: can we say that the crowd has— even intellectually—this extreme and contradictory character? Can we say that its intelligence, like its psychology, reaches high peaks or profound abysses unknown to the isolated individual?

Here the problem becomes more complex and difficult.

At first it seems that the law I formulated, according to which a collectivity's intellectual product is always inferior to what any of the individuals within the collectivity would have delivered, does not contemplate exceptions. Twelve sensible men gathered together to form a jury often formulate verdicts devoid of common sense. Ten or twenty artists or scientists gathered together to form a commission often make decisions that are contrary to the most elementary principles of science and art. Hundreds of geniuses gathered together to form a parliament collectively behave in a way that often feeds disdain or derision rather than respect. Company, in conclusion, weakens—in regards to the overall result—both the force of brilliance and that of good and pitiful sentiments. Yet, there is an aggravating factor, detrimental to the intellectual product: while company generally lowers the moral level of individuals, sometimes, as we have seen, it can exceptionally raise it, but it can *never* raise the intellectual level. Actually, collectivity can sometimes be ingenious from the point of

8 Lamartine, *Histoire des Girondins*, vol. III, book XXV, 254.

view of emotions; it can never be such from the point of view of thought. Indeed, there are collective heroisms but no collective masterpieces. The crowd can attain supreme manifestations of virtue, but it cannot reach supreme manifestations of creative intelligence. In no political, scientific, or literary history do we find the example of a crowd that had a brilliant idea—by itself, in a given moment, and without external suggestion. Who could cite a council of war that conceived a battle plan comparable to Napoleon's? Who could cite a council of ministers that issued one of those political reforms that was the epoch's glory and made the names of Machiavelli, Richelieu, or Bismarck famous? Who could cite a congress of scientists in which one of those world-changing discoveries happened and rendered a Laplace or Galileo immortal?[9]

Here is why the enemies of the crowd can base their disdain towards the multitude on undeniable scientific reasons. The multitude is generally not only composed of ignorant and incompetent people, but even when it is formed by learned and competent individuals, its intellectual product merely represents the numeric product of mediocrity. The sacred fire of the genius's thought has never come out of the collective soul: it is the exclusive gift of the individual brain.

## *III*

At this point, however, an observation of great importance must be expressed, which most have neglected. Everything we have said about the crowd refers only to its mode of thinking and acting considered from the *static* point of view. When we note that assembled men are always of intellectually lesser value than the isolated man, we actually mean to apply this principle uniquely to those collectivities that form, more or less, suddenly and sporadically at a given moment, which are, indeed: *multitudes in the square, theatre audiences, juries, commissions, parliaments*, etc. We certainly do not intend—and it would be absurd—to apply this same principle to a crowd considered from the dynamic point of view, meaning to all human society in its historical development.

Therefore, it is necessary to establish very clearly this distinction that, having been misinterpreted by most, caused many misunderstandings: the psychology of the crowd is one thing when the crowd acts almost by improvisation at a given and brief moment, and another when the crowd acts slowly over the course of centuries. In the first case, its manifestations

9 See G. Tarde, *Essais et mélanges sociologiques.*

are always inferior to those of the individual, while in the second case, not only are they not always inferior, but sometimes they are superior.

If, indeed, no collective masterpieces exist that blossomed almost miraculously, all of a sudden, from an assembly of men, wondrous works exist, gradually created by the crowd with the help of time, to which one would search in vain to impose the seal of a unique genius. Canvases, statues, poems, some scientific discoveries, can and must individualize themselves through a name: Raphael or Van Dyck, Dante or Shakespeare, Phidias or Michelangelo, Kepler or Newton. Yet, certain complex creations, unquestionably of immense importance—like language and writing, for example—cannot have had a single author. They are the result of the work of millions of men, and no one could have accomplished them alone because they surpass the genius and life of any individual. They are a collective work, fluctuating and elusive like the water of a river, eternal and formed by an infinite number of small unknown streams, which nevertheless, all together produce a colossal effect. It is the crowd that was able to elevate the first imitative forms of the human voice all the way up to our extraordinary richness of expression. It is the crowd that, without the smile of glory that is granted only to individual genius, was able to extract from the small vocabulary of primitive languages that monument that is the latest dictionary by Flügel containing 94,000 words.[10] It is the crowd that, in passing from pictographic writing to phonetic and alphabetic writing, enabled us to sculpt and paint our emotions and thought with the subtlest gradations, and to transmit them to posterity with an accuracy that beats photography.[11]

And what to say about the legends, about the heroic cycles that every population possesses when it makes its first appearance on the stage of history? The Homeric poems of Greece, the rhapsodic creations of every country are nothing but slow intellectual formations created or transmitted by the crowd.

But this is not enough. The intelligence of the crowd, latent and dispersed in an infinity of individuals, also has other manifestations. Collectivity often precedes, I daresay, announces—the individual's precise and determined discovery in a vague and undetermined way.

---

10 [Johann Gottfried Flügel (1788–1855) was a German lexicographer widely renowned for his two-volume German-English dictionary *Vollständige Englisch-Deutsche und Deutsch-Englische Wörterbuch* (Leipzig, 1830).]

11 See on this topic the excellent studies by Pasquale Rossi: *Psicologia collettiva* and *L'animo della folla.*

What are proverbs, if not the unconsciously accumulated and synthetically expressed experiences of the crowd? What are the all-too-common, brilliant foresights of the population, albeit mostly neglected? When a genius discovers a new scientific theory, one can say that the crowd had already glimpsed and anticipated it. Before graphology and graphologists, writing was called *character*, almost as if to signify the relationship with the moral faculties of the person. Before Lister,[12] in the mountains of Calabria, wounds were healed with the turpentine gushing from the bark of pines. Before Lombroso stated his theory on the symbiosis of crimes, a *fabliau* had the intuition, telling the story of an astrologer who, having read in the stars that a child would become a murderer, advised the father that this child should become a surgeon, in order to gratify his cruelty instinct in a useful manner both for him and others.[13]

According to this point of view, the genius is thus the detector of truths that are dormant in everyone's consciousness. It is he who finds the formula and provides the demonstration of what the collective soul only drafted or sensed it in its obscure and anonymous work. He is the great reflector where thousands and thousands of rays converge, and from which the light spreads with a hundredfold intensity.

Great men—Bourdeau[14] says—do nothing but accomplish a social function; they are active, but it is the crowd that leads them; and in the mysterious destiny that elevates them to glory and makes them fall back down into nothingness, one must see only the convergence of the people's wills and aspirations. Political, artistic, and scientific men believe they lead a people and impose their own tastes and ideas on them; in fact, they do nothing but follow the impulse that comes to them from the people.

And one must not only recognize that every collectivity creates its own genius, just as every sentiment creates its expression and every confused, diffused idea is summarized in a symbol. It is, moreover, necessary to recognize that the collectivity corrects, develops, and elevates the individual genius's conquests of thought and sentiment.

The genius is the present, namely, the son of the past, of the obscure and collective work of all mankind; yet, like the present, he is not only the son of the past, but also the father of the future. Therefore, like all

12 [Baron Joseph Lister (1827–1912) was a British physician who introduced pioneering sterilizing procedures that inaugurated antiseptic surgery.]

13 See Rossi, already cited.

14 [Jean Bourdeau (1848–1928) was a French writer, translator, and supporter of socialist theories.]

fathers, he must submit to the inevitable law of evolution according to which his ideas and conquests will be judged and modified by the crowd of his descendants.

It seems to me that, from these simple observations, a conclusion clearly emerges that is neither uncertain nor contradictory as the premises might lead one to believe: the crowd that is inferior to the individual in the *static* moment, when he expresses his ideas or puts the energy of his will into action, is, on the other hand, useful and necessary to the individual not only in the past, to shape him, but also in the future, to correct and improve his ideas and actions. I would gladly say—and pardon me for the comparison—that, in history, collectivity has the same function as the seed in vegetable life: it produces wonderful fruits, the geniuses; when these fruits embalm the atmosphere, you must recognize that they are equal to nothing, neither in taste, nor in smell or beauty. The seed is, in this minute, undeniably inferior to its product; but in the cycle of life you must recognize that these fruits are far inferior to the seed because they would not exist without it, and because if the soil did not fecundate their inherent germs, their magnificence would be useless, just as the work of a genius would be useless if the crowd did not fecundate his thoughts.

## *IV*

I think also that such a conclusion begins to throw light on the problem of the relationships between art and the crowd, and, above all, helps overcome the disagreement between these two terms, which today seem irreconcilable opposites. This disagreement is not so much a contrast between the artist and the public, a duel between *the one* and *the many*, as it may appear: it is, essentially, only a question of time. The artist, indeed, can rebel against the judgment of the contemporary crowd, but not against the judgment of posterity. He can despise the multitude in which he lives, but not the multitude that will come after him. In the world, there are not and cannot be criteria for judging any intellectual manifestation other than the endorsement of the many: undoubtedly, a slow and remote endorsement, rather than immediate, but which reflects, nonetheless, a collective judgment, a crowd's judgment. No man could expect to be a genius if his successors do not recognize him as such, because his pride would be futile and laughable if future generations covered his name in silence and oblivion. In the field of science and art, the despotic system does not have the same force as it once had in politics; one cannot actually create principles in spite of and against the majority's will. Science and art function according to plebiscitary systems that are all the more secure and conscientious because they are promulgated by future generations, hence, they exclude any suspicion of corruption and suggestion.

And if, as I think, this is a truth of axiomatic evidence, I confess that it always seemed to me not only unjust, but strange that the artist, for the sole fact that the crowd does not know at first glance how to interpret and understand him, launches against it the anathemas dictated by his pride.

Yes, we recognize it. The public very often does not understand the work of art it is called upon to judge. It booed Rossini at the premiere of the *Barber of Seville*, and booed Wagner at almost all the manifestations of his extraordinary musical genius. The public silently ignored or ferociously fought other works of painting, sculpture, or literature that later became gems of eternal splendour in art. Even considering all of that and omitting that sometimes, next to the crowd's absurd verdicts, there are logical and just verdicts, I only want to ask the superb artists: why do you only flare up at the crowd's slowness in comprehending you, while this slowness of the collective soul towards the intuitions of individual genius is an inevitable and also beneficial necessity, not only regarding art, but also for all intellectual manifestations?

Even in science, politics, and whatever realm of human activity, it has never happened—or rather rarely, for one of those exceptions that confirm the rule—that the public, the crowd, all of a sudden embrace without hesitation a new idea announced by some seer or a new discovery by some individual genius. Napoleon smiled when he was presented with and informed about the model of a steamship. Thiers affirmed in a full French parliament that steam power and railways were a utopia, and that the world would never have another means of transportation other than the horse-drawn carriage. Aristotle did not accept that men are born equal, and believed that there would always be a division between slaves and freemen. And yet, no one—I believe and hope—will want to qualify Napoleon, Thiers, and Aristotle as mediocre. Thus, why do artists—painters, sculptors, or writers—claim the right to insult whoever does not immediately admire their works, and do not rave the first moment they see, read, or hear them? Why—at the risk of being accused of ignorance—upon hearing Wagner, should the crowd have that promptness of intuition that Napoleon and Thiers did not have in the case of Watt's discovery?

The truth is that any idea, before being victorious, must go through a period of conflict and adversity. All those who have fought in politics in order to achieve an ideal know this; all those who fought in science for the conquest of another part of the unknowable, which is still infinite, know this. And yet, in the period of conflict, neither the apostles and martyrs nor the scientists dared to draw reasons, from the opposition in their surrounding environment, to disdainfully insult the crowd that could not understand them immediately. Indeed, being more modest, because stronger and worthier, than certain superb, modern artists, they understood that in the crowd the effect of an idea or an image cannot always be obtained immediately—like the spark that ignites from sudden friction—but must propagate gradually, just as, when throwing a stone into water, always bigger ripples slowly reach the shore. They understood that hereditary habits and misoneism—more than ignorance or a narrow brain—prevent the public from making the best out of the novelty that is announced, and that perturbs it with an undefined sense of surprise and fear. And, patiently, they expected from time that applause and allegiance that their contemporaries denied them, without stigmatizing as incompetent and idiotic—as now seems customary—those who did not understand them.

Let's repeat it once again: from the crowd, one cannot expect a great promptness of intuition before a work of art, and one must insult it for this. Even the isolated man does not possess this promptness of intuition before works of art, or other intellectual manifestations, or other problems. Not all the poets are extemporaneous, not all men of genius are improvisational orators, but this is not a good reason to disdain whoever lacks this faculty. Rather, perhaps the true poet and the true scientist—who will remain in history for their eternal works—are those who lack these striking and suggestive talents. The crowd in its immense, collective soul is like one of these individuals whose genius does not know how to manifest itself instantaneously, and that, caught off guard, makes a worse impression than he would have deserved, but, with more time and reflection, can deliver a masterpiece.

Therefore, instead of the antithesis that a large part of superior individuals feel between themselves and the crowd, instead of the disdain they pour on it, as though it were nothing but the *corpus vile* on whom geniuses can perform their experiments, like doctors in hospitals, I would like a sentiment of love and solidarity to develop between artists and the crowd. This sentiment would produce a fruitful modesty, rather than the bad plant of a sterile pride, teaching us that, just as thought is nothing but the mysterious work of thousands of brain cells that would accomplish nothing in isolation, so the brilliant artist and his work are the individual and symbolic result of the collective work of millions of men, each of whom, if isolated, could not think, act, or live. Solidarity would dispel the black cloud of contemporary pessimism—which prompts certain supermen to condemn the crowd as a huddle of brutes, unworthy even to receive the gift of a work of art—and would, instead, develop the limpid and steady light of healthy optimism, in the name of which one would feel the fraternal duty to work for the intellectual elevation and the moral redemption of the crowd. Ah! I do not know how there can still be such sceptics and pessimists who maintain that life is not worth living, since the man of genius is not understood and the honest man is overpowered by the clever one. But this is a myopic and utilitarian calculation! And whoever makes it cannot be but a perverse and sick man. There are many miseries, many pains, much ignorance, and one does not feel that it would be worthwhile living only for the divine poetry of alleviating one of those miseries or one of those pains, of fighting only one of these manifestations of ignorance? And must it be art or the artists who give this sad example of pride and egoism, scorning the crowd and backing away from it as from a mephitic environment?

No. A much better example must come and will come from the serene field of art—I am sure. The artists, these millionaires of brilliance, must not imitate certain millionaires of money who hold onto their wealth and despise whoever does not possess equal amounts. They must recognize, above all, that their richness, their genius, is like gold for the capitalist, the fruit of the unconscious and hereditary work of thousands and thousands of men, and not their personal and exclusive merit. Furthermore, they must feel that their duty is to throw this richness into the crucible of the collective soul in order to make it fecund, as the duty of the rich is to put their gold back into circulation in order to increase the prosperity of a country. What does it matter if, at first, they are not understood, as the rich man who dispenses his money at first collects not gratitude, but ingratitude?

Gratitude, which is rare in the individual, is always certain, albeit rather slow, in the crowd, and it has a name to which even the most rigid aristocrat, the most logical individualist, and the most superb artist must bow, because it is called *Glory*.

## Chapter 4: "Public Opinion"

What is public opinion? In naming it, all have the illusion of knowing what it is; yet, no one would—and perhaps could—know exactly how to define it.

It is in the world what God is in the sky: an invisible judge, impersonal and feared; like religion, it is an arcane power in whose name the most sublime heroisms and the most abject iniquities were performed; like the law, it is wrongly or rightly invoked and interpreted in every moment of life; like strength, it is sometimes a supporter of what is right, more often of what is wrong; ultimately, like a flag, it is ready to turn in whatever direction the wind blows. And if one were to hazard a definition of it, one should apply the ironic quote that Pauline de Grandpré applied to the woman: "*We can say all we want about her, we will always find a reason.*"[15]

Perhaps, it is because of its undefinable character that public opinion has been poorly studied so far. Socially, it is an elusive phenomenon, I would almost say—if the word did not make you laugh—that it is psychologically an eel, because when you believe you have caught it, it slips away in all directions.

What are the causes that produce it? What are the laws that govern it? And above all, who and how many compose it?

We will try to respond to these questions.

## *I*

Ruggero Bonghi,[16] in a memorable speech held at the Chamber in 1873, attempted to put some initial order to this study by writing: "One should not believe or pretend to believe that every manifestation of the soul truly expresses a public opinion. In order for public opinion to have authority, it must be true, certain, and have its foundation *in the most general consensus of the educated minds of a country.*"

Golden words, but useless words.

Is it always possible—in practice—to distinguish Bonghi's definition of true public opinion from what is lacking in the characters he believes are necessary to form it? Who and where is this supreme judge who will rule, from time to time, that a given current of the public spirit deserves or does not deserve the name of public opinion? With what arithmetic means can one assuredly affirm that the majority thinks in a given way,

15 [In French in Sighele's text, from Pauline de Grandpré's *La Prison de Saint-Lazare depuis vingt ans* (1889). See Sighele's *The New Woman,* 265n1 in this volume.]

16 [Ruggero Bonghi (1826–1895) was an Italian writer and politician. Appointed Minister of Education in 1873, he tried to suppress the privileges within the academic system.]

and with what sociological criteria can one definitely distinguish the educated minds of a country from the uneducated ones?

And even granted that, as an unlikely hypothesis, this very difficult operation of psychological mathematics were possible, what would the outcome be in practice?

It is well known in many cases that the prevalent public opinion is not founded *on the most general consensus of the educated minds of a country*; but would this perhaps be enough to disregard that opinion?

Individuals or collectivities, subjects or rulers, all are oftentimes at the mercy of so-called public opinion, whatever it is and in whatever way it is formed. It is naive to try to ascertain whether it truly represents the majority of educated people. One fears it or follows it, even having the certainty that it does not possess the characters that Ruggero Bonghi wanted it to have; and governments have to be concerned with it, no matter whether it comes from the ignorance of thousands of peasants or from the intelligence of some superior personalities.

Let us take two relatively recent examples to better explain our thought.

After the disaster at Adwa, a public opinion emerged in Italy about the new direction that our foreign policy with Africa should take, and, with the support of the same radicals and socialists, it contributed to the Marquess of Rudinì's[17] appointment as prime minister. Was this a true public opinion? We do not dare to say; but we note the fact that it completely changed two years later, so much so that Rudinì's ministry had to resign.

Now, even if the public opinion of 1896 or 1898 were false—and one of the two must be for sure—one thing is beyond doubt: in both cases, politics surrendered to public opinion, without too much quibbling over whether it was or was not constituted by the majority of educated minds. It was public opinion, and it was enough to guarantee obedience, as to a despot.

---

17 [The battle of Adwa (1 March 1896) was the decisive event in the first Italo-Ethiopian war. The Ethiopian Empire defeated the Kingdom of Italy, and General Oreste Baratieri, who led the Italian troops was judged unfit for his role. At the disastrous news of Italy's debacle, violent demonstrations broke out in many cities, leading to the resignation of Prime Minister Crispi. His successor, Antonio di Rudinì, initiated peace treaties with Ethiopia, with the aim of stopping Italy's colonial campaign in East Africa. Yet, precisely his anti-expansionist stance became the main reason why he was overturned two years later, in addition to the excessive military force used by his government against demonstrators in Milan during the May 1898 riots.]

The second example I want to give is even better fitting. It deals with the Dreyfus affair. What part—in this infamous and famous affair—did French public opinion play? At first, it was unanimous in denying a retrial, but almost unanimous, afterwards, in demanding it loudly. The earlier public opinion was wrong: it was neither true nor certain, as Bonghi wanted it. It was the pathological result of a suggestion imposed by the perfidy of some, and endured by the patriotic naivety of almost everyone: and yet, would it have been possible not to take that opinion into account? You saw it: in a memorable session—on 7 July 1898—all of the French Chamber bowed like sheep to that public opinion, decreeing that Cavaignac's speech be displayed in all the communes of the Republic.[18] And Ruggero Bonghi should have admitted that the Chamber of Deputies represented the educated minds of a country, and therefore that one of its plebiscites is conscious and sensible. I modestly judge the parliaments in a different way, but this is not the place to explain why, and the reason is not actually important for my current thesis.

The consequence I wanted to reach, and it seems I did, is this:

1) Public opinion imposes itself even when it is not formed by the more general consensus of the educated minds of a country;
2) Even the thought of educated men can be the offspring of a sudden, erroneous, or rectifiable impression (as in the case of the French Chamber), and therefore it is not enough to recognize the authority of public opinion to demonstrate that it is founded on the majority of educated people. Like the ignorant, they too can be wrong.

In a brief but acute article, the lawyer G.A. Pugliese realized that Bonghi's definition of public opinion was not complete, and he proposed to add another parameter to Bonghi's, that public opinion relies on a constant mood. In this way—he thought—one would not mistake

18 [Alfred Dreyfus (1859–1935) was a French officer of Jewish origins who was charged with treason, imprisoned in the penal colony on Devil's Island, in French Guyana, and ultimately exonerated of all allegations against him. The episode represented one of the major political and legal scandals in late nineteenth-century Europe, in which public opinion and the press played a pivotal role. The French politician Jacques Marie Eugène Cavaignac (1853–1905), during his tenure as minister of war (1898), read a document to the Chamber that incriminated the Jewish captain Alfred Dreyfus. Even after the discovery that the document had been forged, he insisted on Dreyfus's guilt.]

the French public opinion, which denied Dreyfus's retrial, for true public opinion, since it was not constant. And he added: "It is said that in public works contracts the real test comes from time; well, it seems to me that even the baptism of true public opinion must come from time."

The simile is beautiful, but I am tempted to repeat in this regard: golden words, but useless words.

First of all, one could ask lawyer Pugliese: how much time is needed ... for the test? When will one be able to say that a given public opinion is true and certain? After ten years, twenty, thirty? Second—provided that one has this time frame which in my view is unrealistic—would that not be a purely platonic satisfaction? Supposing, for instance, that today a current of public spirit manifests itself, must we, and can we, neglect it and peacefully wait until a quarter of a century goes by? Third, is it not evident that such a public opinion would rather be something that strongly resembles tradition? What is tradition, indeed, if not a public opinion that is established and crystallized in the population?

Therefore—if I am not wrong—Bonghi's and Pugliese's proposed definitions are not complete, and if they were, they would not be practical.

In conclusion, the two cited authors limit themselves to affirming that true public opinion is that which wise people, time, and events have identified as correct. A definition, as you can see, that could carry Mr de La Palisse's[19] signature, but that, although truthful, has no consequence.

I believe that, in our current problem, one does not have to look a priori for definitions, which—as Lombroso wittily says—apart from geometrical ones, are all incorrect. Rather, one must try to study in what way public opinion is formed and by which strange and obscure psychological laws is it governed.

The definition is nothing but the synthesis of a phenomenon's description, and wanting to state the synthesis before doing the analysis is manifestly an error.

To distinguish true and certain public opinion from what is untrue and uncertain seems to me a rather difficult undertaking before we first establish what public opinion is. And to establish the meaning of public opinion, one must first of all know—or at least try to know—what the public is.

19 [That is, a comic truism or a tautology, as in the well-known misreading of Jacques de La Palisse's epitaph, which generated many popular satirical songs.]

Thus, loyal to the ideas of the positive method, we will first analyse the collective entity called the *public,* and we will attempt to isolate it from the other collective entities with which it is generally and easily confused. Second, we will study how the various opinions of the public are formed, whether gradually or all of a sudden, physiologically or pathologically. In the end, we will try to determine the parameters from which one can recognize whether a given opinion of the public is reliable, and whether it does or does not have to be respected and followed.

In our humble opinion, this is the only path to follow, not to entirely unveil (the affirmation would be superb), but at least to render less vague that mystery of collective psychology called *public opinion,* which in the modern world has such a great and dangerous influence.

## *II*

*Public* is a word that, like all those words that do not designate a materially defined object, has a very vague and elastic meaning. We generally know what it means, but we would feel very inadequate to specify it.

We say: the public of a theatre or an assembly;—in this case the word *public* has a determined value, restricted to those people who were in the theatre or who attended the assembly, and this is synonymous with *crowd.*

We say: the such and such book had such a great success among the public. In this case the word *public* has a less specific value; it no longer refers to a given number of assembled people, and it is, therefore, no longer synonymous with crowd, but comprises a portion of the population that is spread out rather than gathered, and that is versed and interested in art, literature, or science.

We also say: on a given political issue—let's say a war—the public has a given opinion; and in this case the word *public* has an even more general value. It does not refer only to a portion of the population, to that or this class or caste or school or party, but comprises the entire population, sometimes many peoples, sometimes all of the civilized world.

In which of these meanings is the word public to be understood?

To respond to such a question, one must retrace a bit the evolution across time of that complex and undetermined organism that today we call the public.

If we take a look at the lowest kingdoms of the animal world, we see that in them the dominating character is absolute individuality. "Beings of multiple species"—Espinas writes—, "in an amazing number live in the water, on land, and on other animals in a state of complete isolation. Many foraminifera, whose shells have formed continents, are physiologically isolated. Such beings are weak, not only because they are small, but also because they are alone."[20]

In these lowest stages of animal life, where there is no association, there evidently cannot be even the distant embryo of the public.

Nonetheless, association appears as soon as one ascends the tree of life only a little. At first, it is a simple material aggregate, purely physical. All association consists in an *action of presence*: if the individuals back away to the point of no longer being able to see one another, or if they remain distant from one another for a certain time, for this sole fact they cease to be associated. In a word, association is, in these cases, synonymous with *physical contact*.

As inferior forms ascend and become superior forms in the association among animals, we find that physical contact is no longer the necessary condition to constitute a society. Even though the single organisms are distant, the association subsists; the tie that holds them together is no longer only material, but it is also spiritual and becomes moral and intellectual. The animals placed more highly in the zoological ladder form these aggregates that could be called tribes or populations (the bees with their queen), and they have a division of labour, remote signals, and a voice that—if it is not the human word—is, however, a powerful means of communication.

In these societies, we can glimpse not only the embryo of the *crowd*—namely, individuals who are physically in contact—but also the embryo of the *public*—namely, individuals who are physically separated, yet, according to Tarde's astute expression, united by a moral cohesion.

The physio-psychological phenomenon of the *crowd* can be observed, for example, in a flock of birds, where the minimum disturbance of one bird's flapping of wings produces an irresistible panic in all of them, like a man's alarming cry in a street or a crowded square induces fear in all those who are near and makes them run away.

The phenomenon of collective psychology, which we call the *public*, can be observed—to use a more distant and less clear analogy—in the behaviour that some species of animals have towards one member of their group. Admired or hated, followed or avoided, even the animal experiences the social reflex—if I can say so—of its congenital talents or defects, and this reflex is nothing but the embryo of the public. The elephant, because of bad instincts, is always isolated and does not ever

20 A. Espinas, *Des Sociétés animales*, 2nd ed. (Paris: Germer, Baillière, 1888), 227 [in French in Sighele's text].

live in the company of others; this depends, in part, on its spontaneous desire and, in part, because the others want to leave it alone. And this is undeniably a judgment of the public.

If from animal associations we move to human associations, the evolution of the phenomenon we are analysing appears identical, albeit immensely magnified and complicated.

As in the lowest animal societies, where the social tie is constituted by simple physical contact, the *so-called public* is reduced to the *crowd* in the first human societies, since it is constituted only by individuals who are physically in contact. And as in more evolved animal societies, where the social tie is not only material but also moral and intellectual, the public is *a true public* rather than simply a crowd in the most modern human societies, since it is constituted by individuals who are not physically assembled, but, rather, who are distant from one another in space and, nonetheless, connected by an idea, a common sentiment, and an invisible, mental cohesion.

The following examples will clarify this thought better than my words could.

In Greek-Roman antiquity (to avoid researching more distant times or barbaric populations) can we say that a public existed?

*Crowds* existed, but *publics* did not. Everything that referred to politics was discussed in the forum, in assemblies, in *comitia*—namely, by the *crowd*. The rulers of states, the tribunes, the innovators had no means to circulate their thoughts and inoculate them in sparse and isolated individuals. They were forced to act on the assembled and present public, that is, on the *crowd*. Jesus Christ only had the word to disseminate his doctrine; from the first nucleus of people to whom he spoke the disciples arose, who in their turn spoke to other nuclei of people. The new word thus spread—from crowd to crowd—always enlarging the circle of those who were instinctually called on to hear it, just as a stone thrown into the water extends—wave after wave—the effect produced by its fall.

All that refers to art and science did not have, then, a *public* in the sense we understand it today: it simply had an *audience*, namely, a crowd. Were the poets not perhaps orators … in verse? Were their poems not perhaps *said* before multitudes larger or smaller, which would not know them unless going en masse to hear them? How did scientists spread their science, if not by revealing it out loud to some gathered disciples?

One will say—and it is true—that if this was the general rule, it had an exception, namely those single readers of hand-copied manuscripts in some dozens of exemplars containing poems of Virgil and Homer, or the histories of Tacitus and Caesar. But can we affirm (and this is Gabriel

Tarde's observation)[21] that these single readers had the consciousness to form a social aggregate, as do, these days, the readers of the same newspaper or even of the same trendy novel? Certainly not. They were the distant forerunners of the public, but they did not have the consciousness to be one, and they were too few. Because of number and unawareness, they, therefore, represented a negligible quantity.[22]

Did a public exist in the medieval era? Tarde denies it, maintaining that there were merely fairs, pilgrimages, and tumultuous multitudes, where—from time to time—religious or war frenzies, frightening rages, or vile fears unfolded. It is enough to consider the Crusades and the terrors that preceded the end of the first millennium, in order to understand that, in those times, any manifestation of a social movement was determined by the crowd and by its strange psychology.

It is certain that, at that epoch, the influence of the individual on the mass was exerted almost solely by the spoken word. The great agitators influenced bystanders, above all, and, on the other hand, men expressed their hate and collective loves always in the compact and brutal form of the crowd. Yet is also unquestionable that this distant forerunner of the public, which we have identified in the times of Greece and Rome, was gradually becoming more conscious and larger. The isolated readers of manuscripts increased; and under the intermittent and violent thought of the crowds, the continuous and peaceful thought of the public was taking shape—a less visible and more neglected thought, but not negligible, which, thanks to an imminent discovery, would soon become visible and very important.

This discovery was the press.

For the rise of the public, the invention of the press was what a political revolution is for the rise of a new social order, namely, the historical moment in which an organ becomes active and transforms its existence from potential to actual.

---

21 G. Tarde, "Le public et la foule," in *Revue de Paris* (15 July and 1 Aug. 1898), republished with other studies in the volume *L'opinion et la foule* (Paris: Alcan, 1901).

22 We must note, for historical accuracy, that in the Roman era there existed not only the exemplary handwritten copies of the works of poets and scientists but also newspapers. Journalism was born with the *Acta diurna*, which had a small number of readers, and thus a public. Cicero talks about a journalist, Chrestus, who enjoyed a great reputation. According to Tacitus, the newspapers were read avidly by the military. Suetonius does not mind drawing facts for his *History* from the annals of the Roman press. On this topic, see the articles published in *La Revue des revues*, 2nd semester (1897). —That does not, however, invalidate our argumentation.

This new organ was collective consciousness, which until then was forcedly constrained to close itself off in ignorance or silence and whose viable manifestation—both to learn the thought of whoever directed it and to approve or fight this thought—consisted of the meetings of parliaments, assemblies, fairs, or crowds.

The press brought the voice of even the distant meneurs to all civil men, and, simultaneously, offered a way to make the will or desires of the population heard by these *meneurs*, without the need for it to be assembled and present and shouting its threats under the windows of a royal palace, or committing excesses in a street or a square.

We, who were born when the press had already been a hereditary habit for some centuries, cannot, without effort, imagine the impact that its invention had in the world.

The books, published and disseminated for the first time in thousands of copies, gave to whoever read them the sensation of forming a new class of people—people who, although not knowing one another and being distant from one another, felt nonetheless tied by the invisible, intellectual thread that comes from reading an identical volume and the reflections which that reading awakened in them.

Until that moment, men, in order to feel their solidarity and to manifest it, had only one means: *to assemble in a crowd*. The press allowed their solidarity to be felt, and rendered its manifestation possible without the need for them to gather; it substituted *physical contact* with *moral contact*; it substituted the *crowd* with the *public*.

Unquestionably, the public at its birth was not such a complicated and powerful organism as it is today. As everything that lives, it traversed various phases before reaching the current phase.

If one can say that it dates back to the sixteenth century, after the great development of the press, one must then recognize that it had an extension and importance infinitely smaller than what it became thereafter. At first, it was an almost exclusively literary, scientific, or religious public; and, essentially, it was always formed by a minority of cultivated people. In the second half of the eighteenth century, the true political public arose, formed not by a minority of educated men, but by the great majority of the population, and it gradually absorbed all the other more or less special and restricted publics. The French Revolution gave this public a new extension, as it is, indeed, in that epoch that journalism took a leap, a big leap for that time.[23]

---

23 See Tarde on this topic, art. cit.

The press, however, despite having created the public almost as a substitute for the crowd, could not offer the public the advantage that the crowd enjoyed: timeliness. Let me explain. Those who read the newspapers knew about what happened in the world, but inevitably they knew it with a certain delay.

Among the many differences that exist between the crowd and the public, the major one was this: that the members of a crowd were all simultaneously struck by a piece of news, and they thus felt bound together—as well as by physical contact—by the thought that each of them had identical impressions in an identical instant. By contrast, the sparse individuals who composed the public were distant not only in space but also in time, as they learned the news not all at the same moment, but many hours, days, sometimes even many weeks later. Communication was not frequent or fast, and the distant provinces had to be content with finding out much later what had happened in the capital.

This lack of contemporaneity in learning the news rendered the public's influence weaker and less active. It deprived the public of the great prerogative and major secret of the crowd's dangerousness: its *unison.*

But what the invention of the press could not offer was provided by other discoveries, no less fraught with incalculable social consequences: the railroad and the telegraph, and, to be sure, the telephone and the wireless telegraph. With the first, distances shrank and newspapers could reach faraway places in a short timespan; with the other ones, distances were almost completely erased and a piece of news was able to travel hundreds and thousands of kilometres in a few minutes.

The railroad, the telegraph, and the telephone gave wings to the press, and gave the public that sense of participation in current events that it had never possessed before.

It has been said egregiously that the transport of force across space is nothing compared with the transport of thought.[24] Of course, the telegraph and telephone ensured that the reading public was, in terms of immediacy, almost equal to a crowd of listeners, as the time that the word of a man or the news of an event takes to reach the eyes of whoever reads a newspaper is—in its social relations—only a little longer than the time an orator's voice needs to reach the ears of whoever listens to him. Today, in the entire civilized world, one can know in a few hours what the President of the United States or the Czar said, or what happened in Paris or Buenos Aires. The public has actually conquered *that unity of*

24 G. Tarde, art. cit.

*time* that it has lacked so far, which made it, in a certain sense, socially inferior to the crowd.

Furthermore, the crowd was an aggregate that necessarily had limits: the number of people who composed it could not exceed a given figure. Let us take, as an example, the Coliseum, the largest amphitheatre of antiquity, which allegedly accommodated 100,000 people. Let us also take, as an example, the innumerable individuals that formed—outdoors—the audience of a Peter the Hermit. However generous our imagination can be, we can estimate, at the very most, two or three hundred thousand people.

The public instead—and I mean the modern public—does not know limits. A ruler or a genius, by means of the great discoveries—press, railways, telephone, and telegraph—today speaks simultaneously to millions of individuals, to the entire literate world.

## *III*

I hope that the little I have said so far will help raise some awareness about the evolution of the public and establish its differences from the crowd.

The public is nothing but a transformation of the crowd, slowly accomplished by civilization, which—as it progressed—always discovered better means to ideologically bind men together, without the need for physical proximity.

The crowd is a simple and sudden aggregate, hence, in a certain sense, an animal formation; the public is a more difficult and slower aggregate to form, thus a more human one.

The crowd is nothing but the assembly of psychic contacts, essentially produced by physical contact; the public does not need a close proximity of bodies to be an intricate complex of communications from soul to soul.

The crowd, in sum, is an eminently *barbaric* and *atavistic* collectivity; the public is an eminently *civil* and *modern* collectivity.

If the simile did not seem far-fetched, I would say that the difference between the crowd and the public is identical to the one that exists between the savage horde and present society. Progress, which was able to gradually transform the savage horde into the modern state, also managed to gradually transmute the crowd into the public. In both cases, it was a matter of substituting a shapeless human agglomeration that felt, thought, and acted impulsively and tumultuously, with another human agglomeration that feels, thinks, and acts with more reflection, under the restraint of certain laws.

The evidence of this difference between the crowd and the public is plentiful.

It is an axiom that the simpler an organism, the more susceptible it is to the forces of nature. The civil man protects himself from the elements better than the barbarian, and the periodic variation of the seasons has a smaller influence on his social life than on the barbarian. For the same reason, the barbarian knows and can offer greater resistance to the physical environment and greater defence than the superior animal, and the same applies to the latter, in its turn, with respect to the inferior animal.

Thus, crowds are simple and primitive organisms because their actions greatly depend on the state of the atmosphere and the seasons. A rainy day is enough to ward off the danger of a public gathering; and not accidentally, all the superintendents and prefects of police, following Bailly's example,[25] bless the bad weather that empties the squares and streets, rendering the gathering of crowds, and hence demonstrations or riots, very difficult, if not impossible.

The public—a more complicated and civil organism—is not at all affected by the instability of the atmosphere: no matter whether it pours or the sun shines, it remains identical in substance and efficacy.

Hence, heat or cold, summers or winters, so influential on crowds, do not affect the public. In this regard, we may refer to Fournial's observations[26] and, above all, to those of Lombroso and Laschi[27]: they say, with the precise and unassailable language of numbers, how crowds are more or less frequent and large according to the seasons and temperature.

By contrast, all of that is indifferent to the public: and the proof is, as Tarde observed, that the most acute crisis of an overexcited public, that of the Dreyfus affair, broke out and spread in the winter.

Another sociological axiom posits that the imprint of race is weakening more and more as organisms ascend the social ladder. And this axiom is so evident that it needs no explanation. The more social influences multiply and intersect, the more difficult it is to identify the hereditary

25 [Jean Sylvain Bailly (1736–1793), astronomer, mathematician, and politician during the Revolution, was also mayor of Paris from 1789 to 1791. In his *Mémoirs*, he writes that, since crowds are dangerous hiding places for criminals, rainy days were always cause for great joy, since they discouraged people from gathering. See *Mémoirs de Bailly* (Paris: Baudouin Frères, 1822), vol. II, 233.]

26 Fournial, *Les crimes des foules* (Lyon: Storek, 1891).

27 Lombroso and Laschi, *Il delitto politico.*

stigma of race—hidden, assuaged, or transformed by additional causes or contributing factors. We can act with a certain confidence on the vegetable kingdom and the animal kingdom (excluding man), relying only on the inevitable efficacy of race and heredity. Plant and animal breeders know it. With their grafts and hybridizations, they obtain—with almost mathematical accuracy—what they want: the qualities of the stamen and the pistil, of the father and the mother, combine and reproduce in their offspring with a wonderful precision. Can we act in an equal way on individuals? Certainly not. For them, if race and heredity matter a great deal, the environment in which they are born and live—in other words, social influence—matters even more. Supposing that, as an unlikely hypothesis, we could perfectly know the moral and physical features of parents and their ancestors, we could still not trace a priori the physical features of the child, and much less describe his moral and intellectual physiognomy.

Now, let us transfer this observation from the individual organism to the collective organism, and ask ourselves if it is not evident that race has a bigger influence on a crowd than on a public.

Who could not distinguish an Italian crowd from a German crowd? Who could confuse a "*meeting*" of Englishmen with a "*meeting*" of Neapolitans? Who does not know that a Venetian crowd would never attain the excesses of cruelty we find in crowds from Calabria or Palermo? Having once attended a show in a German theatre, and having compared the behaviour of its spectators with how Italian spectators ordinarily behave, is enough to understand how crowds are under the absolute empire of the race from which they come. They are calm or enthusiastic, cold or boiling, according to whether they are German or Latin.

The publics of various nationalities, of course, do not display such pronounced differences. And this is because—while in crowds the individuals smooth the edges of their single personalities so as to show only the outline of their nationality type—in publics there is no neutralization of the individual to the advantage of the racial character, precisely because in publics—more civil and modern aggregates—the social factor rather than the atavistic one predominates.

A third sociological axiom—also intuitively evident—posits that the superiority of an organism—be it individual or collective—is measured by the greater capacity for reflection underlying its manifestations. Individuals and peoples are more or less civilized, according to their ability to overcome—thanks to the power of inhibition that education and civilization developed in them—those atavistic and wild instincts that would lead them to act impulsively.

Now, who will want and be able to deny that *crowds* are much more impulsive and, therefore, more violent than the *public*? Let us compare, for example, female crowds to female publics. Psychologically, there is an abyss between the former and the latter. Female crowds are the quintessence of cruelty and barbarism: in their excesses, they by far exceed male crowds. Open a history book of any epoch, and you will read repugnant episodes about the unbelievable degree of bestiality that women can attain when they descend and assemble in the street. The French Revolution offers, in this regard, a great number of facts that inspire horror and terror; and also, without going back to distant times, whoever was present at the riots in Sicily in the winter of 1893–94 and the sad days in Milan in May 1898,[28] does not need to learn from others that women in a crowd are worse than savages, they are cannibals.

What is, rather, more civil, in the good and bad sense of this word, than female publics? The female readers of newspapers and fashionable novels, and those of newspapers and feminist magazines are indeed passionate and, at times, also somewhat fanatic; but their passion is wisely held in check by a non-negligible dose of cunningness, and their manifestations resemble much more the fox's behaviour than the tiger's. For this I said that female publics are civil even in the bad sense of the term: of civility they have not only the gentleness, but moreover—pardon me ladies—also the Jesuit duplicity.

And now that we have, or at least we believe we have, demonstrated the inferiority of the *crowd* with respect to the *public*, as the former represents a barbaric and atavistic aggregate and the latter a modern and civil aggregate, it is necessary to ask which role is played in the current social movement by these two diverse and indefinable organisms that synthesize the entire mysterious yet mighty collective psychology.

Years ago, Doctor Le Bon,[29] and I with him,[30] proclaimed that our epoch is "*the era of the crowds.*" Gabriel Tarde, instead, maintains that our epoch is "*the era of the publics.*"

---

28 [In connection with the riots of the Sicilian Fasci, which he had already mentioned in *The Criminal Crowd* and *Sectarian Criminality*, Sighele here alludes to the violent food riots in Milan (6–8 May 1898), and their repression. They started as a series of massive organized strikes against high food prices, but the crowd became violent. Di Rudinì's government declared a state of siege in Milan and Lombardy at large, and, under the command of General Fiorenzo Bava-Beccaris, troops restored order by killing numerous demonstrators and by sentencing many hundreds to prison.]

29 Le Bon, *Psychologie des foules* (Paris: Alcan, 1896).

30 Scipio Sighele, *Psychologie des sectes* (Paris: Giard et Brière, 1898).

All of us were partially wrong. Our epoch is at the same time the era of the publics and of the crowds.

Without a doubt, the public's rise and evolution diminished the frequency of crowds, but it has not suppressed them. It opened, so to speak, a new valve for the population's need to express their sentiments and thoughts, but it did not close the ancient valve. *Beyond* the crowds today there are the publics, but not *solely* the publics.

Progress modifies reality and, in so doing, improves it: but it does not totally erase its atavistic habits.

Carlyle says that civilization is nothing but bark within which the savage passion of man can burn alive, with its infernal fire.[31] And the truth of this affirmation is confirmed daily by facts: we see people—who behave in normal life according to the norms taught by civil life—burst all of a sudden into a cruel act that uncovers the human beast within them. This is the so-called crime of passion.[32] Confronting a provocation, the bark of civilization cracks to let out the sap of barbarism.

What occurs to individuals occurs to the collectivity as well.

Civilization morphed the crowd into the public, but the public, in turn, reverts to crowd, when the sentiment that dominates it is so strong that it can no longer be contained and needs its atavistic form in order to manifest itself.

Every day we see the phenomenon of a public producing a crowd.

When, for example, the idea that moves a party, that is, a political public, has reached a very high degree of expansion, almost by spontaneous generation, a crowd is born to that public, which makes demonstrations, riots, and revolutions.

When the religious sentiment pervading the public takes on its acute form, namely, superstition, religious crowds emerge from the public of devotees who make pilgrimages to a sanctuary, or are delirious in front of some Madonna or some miraculous saint.

Whenever love or esteem, or, vice versa, hate or disdain for a certain person trespass certain limits in the public, crowds materialize from this public, who scream with enthusiasm and admiration or execration and ferocity, around a ruler, a general, or an artist.

---

31 [See *The Criminal Crowd* 39n73.]

32 [See Lombroso's definition in *Criminal Man*: "the so-called crimes of passion which might be better labeled crimes of impulse, since all crimes flow from the violence of certain emotions." *Criminal Man*, translated by Mary Gibson and Nicole Hahn Rafter (Durham: Duke University Press, 2006), 105.]

The public, thus, in certain cases, reverts to a crowd, as the civil man, in certain cases, reverts to a barbarian. In this sense, we can, hence, say that the crowd today is nothing but an acute and pathological form of the public.

## *IV*

At this point, after having, in the briefest and clearest way possible for me, attempted to explain what the public is, isolating it from the other collective entities with which it could be confused, it is necessary and less difficult to return to the object of our study and to ask how public opinion is formed.

From all I have shown, it is evident that sometimes public opinion is not the opinion of the public in its most rigorous sense, but the opinion of the crowd.

If nowadays, as we have seen, the thought and sentiment of the collectivity normally express themselves by means of the newspaper and, therefore, reach out to sparse and distant individuals, they also express themselves abnormally by means of multitudes, which can say and impose in a statically violent way what the public thinks in a dynamically peaceful way. Speeches, meetings, electoral reunions, demonstrations in the square, are other forms of *crowds,* that even today have a great influence upon the formation of public opinion. Behind these crowds there is always—we are in agreement—a party, namely, a public, which is their cause and, so to speak, the cocoon from which they break out. But, unquestionably, it is the crowds that, all of a sudden, with the immediate and very strong suggestion that emanates from them, have the heart and brain of the individuals who otherwise would have taken more time to convert.

Thus, to respond to the question "How is a given public opinion determined?," it would be necessary to analyse not only the psycho-physiology of the public, but also that of the crowd.

Nevertheless, we have studied the psycho-physiology of the crowd elsewhere,[33] and we do not like to repeat ourselves. We will hence try to examine that of the public.

A first division of the public takes form spontaneously when we consider, on the one hand, the diverse degree of culture, and, on the other hand, the diverse interests of men. *Birds of a feather stick together,* says a

33 See *I delitti della folla,* 4th ed. (Turin: Bocca, 1910).

proverb, and that is true not only for crowds, but also for the public. A similar education, an identical scope, bring the individuals together in an intellectual bundle, just as an identical feeling pushes all to agglomerate in a street or square.

We have, therefore, the *judiciary, industrial, agricultural, literary, scientific, religious,* and *political* publics, according to the individuals belonging to the magistracy, industry, agriculture, literature, science, religion, or politics. These publics do not differ from one another solely in the goal that each pursues, but also in their extent and technicality. The narrower the public is, the more technical it is; and the more powerful and, therefore, dangerous it is, the more general the interest it defends.

In the past, the diversity of culture and interests entailed divisions of another kind in society, called corporations, crafts, classes, or castes. They were more stable and better defined divisions, above all, because they were sometimes founded on heritage, and, second, because whoever was a member of one of them could not easily leave, and whoever was not a member could not easily penetrate one. In a sense, they were closed fields in which one could count the number of soldiers, and where emigration and immigration were almost impossible.

The current publics, which have substituted these divisions, are much less stable and defined; they are, if I can say so, fluctuating organisms, because one cannot ever specify either the quality or the number of individuals who comprise them. A public is today a kind of nebula where, if it is easy to distinguish its central nucleus, it is very difficult to determine the boundaries. Whoever wants to enter and exit can; and the hereditary and traditional reasons are almost or totally useless in trying to convince such and such person to be a part of a certain public. We can say that the public is—to social life—what a waterfall is to the view: it always makes the same impression although the drops that compose it constantly change. The drops of the public are the individuals.

Not only is there a continuous variation in the drops forming the cataract or—to abandon the metaphor—in the cells forming that collective organism called the public; this same organism increasingly loses the characteristics of stability and unbreakability it once possessed.

Compare—and not only in Italy—the political parties from half a century ago with the current ones. *Right* and *Left* were then two names which, in the Chamber and in the country, responded to two currents of ideas following independent paths. Any confusion between those two parties, and among the men who represented them, would have seemed impossible, or, if it had occurred, it would have been judged a cowardly act or a betrayal. The division was clear-cut and intangible. The drops, that is, the men, necessarily changed, but the cataract, namely, the idea, remained intact and immobile. Can we say the same of current parties? It is a pity not to respond to this question, because everyone, unfortunately, sees and knows how little cohesive force and how little impermeability (excuse my pun) political parties have these days. They are nothing but a label that man keeps stuck until it suits him, and throws it far away when it is better for him to let it be forgotten. Among the various parties today, there is permanently a phenomenon of osmosis and endosmosis; the ideas of one penetrate into those of the other and vice versa, and the men who supported them do not find it strange, but, rather, logical to become allies after fighting against each other.

However, this continual mobility of current parties or publics (which, according to Tarde, is one of their principal characteristics) should not be judged too severely, since its causes excuse it a great deal, if not even justify it.

In the first place, it is evident that men today cannot be tenaciously loyal to an idea as they were able to be, and were before. In the past, every man at birth already had not only a career planned for himself, hence his place in the world, but also the set of theories to which he had to be rigorously faithful. Only in the case of a very serious event, for example, would an aristocrat nourish different feelings from those of his caste (and, in any case, it was a very strange phenomenon). Today, instead, every man being born is to a great extent an unknown variable, because it is impossible to know with certainty the career he will choose or the ideas to which he will be devoted. Furthermore, while in the past, generally, people would get old and die with almost the same ideas as in their youth, today it is more than probable to change one's ideas or at least to modify them every few years. The increasing speed of progress renders changes in opinion almost forcibly necessary, and a philosopher rightly observed that he who never changes opinion must be one who does not want to or cannot learn anything.

Another cause of the public's mobility, which is connected to the previous one and is a different facet of it, consists in the fact that today anyone's opinion is put to test by the daily threats of the spread of different or even contrary ones. A man preserves his honesty all the more easily if the occasions that tempt him are fewer; a man adheres more easily to a given viewpoint, the fewer the opposing viewpoints around him. An adamantine character was certainly not necessary way back to retain loyalty to that patrimony of ideas in which one was born and grew up, since it was not frequent to have a new current of ideas clash with and disrupt traditional and hereditary trends. By contrast, today the change of opinion is not synonymous with fickleness, as our social life offers anyone infinite forms of suggestion, which drag people to think and feel in one way rather than another.

Among these forms of suggestion, the most important one, that which summarizes and concentrates all the others, is undoubtedly the press.

There is no profession, no party, no artistic, religious, or scientific school that does not want to have its own newspaper or magazine, just as how there is no regiment that does not have its flag. In the modern world, any newly born idea requires, above all, to establish itself through a newspaper, as it is with every interest that does not want to be suffocated by rival ones. Therefore, a statistics and a psychology of our social life could be made just by counting and examining the newspapers that are published. Feeling the imperious necessity to own a newspaper implicitly proves that every party knows and believes that it is the best way to form a loyal following. In other words, it knows and believes that men side with an idea, not so much for hereditary and traditional reasons as in the past, but for current reasons of immediate persuasion.

Nevertheless, at this point we have to tackle the following daunting question: is it the newspaper or the journalist that forms the public, or vice versa?

I say the question is daunting not so much because it truly is in my view, but also because writers generally consider it so. In sociology, we have many of these questions, which could all be reduced to one: namely, whether it is the environment that has a greater influence on the individual or the individual on the environment. Ultimately, these problems only serve to reveal the psychological acuteness of individual opponents who, in order to support their theses, flaunt beautiful arguments and comparisons, albeit exaggerated and paradoxical. Let us take, for example, the so-called *theory of the great man.* According to Spencer, who ridiculed it, it is an error to attribute a great social influence to the man of genius. He is but the necessary product of the environment in which he arose and, so to speak, a son of his time—a man who is not active but *representative,* as Emerson defined him: an actor, not an author of historical drama. According to others, instead—primarily Carlyle—everything we see that is good and beautiful in the world we owe to heroes, namely, to the *great men.* The soul of all history is but their own story: they are, to repeat the expression by [John] Stuart Mill: "the salt of the earth; without them, human life would become a stagnant pool."[34]

---

34 [John Stuart Mill, *On Liberty*, 124. See *The Criminal Couple* 78n8.]

Who is wrong or right?

Before responding, allow me to resort to a simile that, however banal, has the merit of being clear.

Every man is the product of his parents; without them he would not exist, and with different parents he would be different from what he is. On that matter, we undoubtedly are all in agreement. Therefore, we certainly concur that every genius is the product of his own epoch, and that different epochs produce different geniuses.

Now, even if we accept these premises, which seem axioms to me, would we deny that every son—as soon as he is a man—can exert a great influence on his parents? Or, for the simple fact that he is the physiological and psychological product of his father and mother, should we deny the possibility of this influence? We should not, right?

The same, if I am not wrong, should be said of the genius. Napoleon and Garibaldi, Dante and Shakespeare, arose at a certain time because inevitably they had to, and in this sense it is true that they are sons of their times, the unconscious glimpse in which humanity in a given epoch is, so to speak, symbolized. But who will want to contest that, although being necessary products of history, they themselves imparted a new direction to history, exerting a great material or moral empire in the world?

Let us descend from these heights where one speaks of geniuses and historical epochs, and, going back to our more modest argument, let us speak of journalists and publics.

The names will be different, but the reasoning will not change.

Without a doubt, every public produces journalists who have its instincts, its tendencies, its talents, and its flaws; they are, in a word, its creatures. Yet, once the public has, so to speak, given birth to its journalist, he, like the son towards his parents, will start to influence the public, to guide and modify its opinions.

In this case, one can say that the public's psychology resembles that of the crowd. What are the *meneurs* of the crowd, if not the unconscious and instantaneous products of the crowds themselves? In an assembled and throbbing multitude, you all of a sudden hear a voice or cry, behind which the entire crowd immediately runs with blind and uniform credulity in order to vent their feelings of hate or love. The agent responsible for that scream or cry is not the man who emitted them, but the mysterious soul of the crowd, which forced him to. The *meneur* is thus created by the collectivity. But as soon as he is created, he acquires such a despotic power over those who surround him that he can lead them wherever he wants, to excesses or crimes that the crowd would have never wanted or considered committing.

The journalist is nothing but a *meneur* of his public. Created by it, he can drag it beyond where he himself wanted to go.

## V

If logic thus serves something, I believe that it gives us the right to affirm that public opinion is, if not completely created, certainly moulded, modified, and led by journalists.

In what measure?

Here is the problem. A very difficult problem to solve, given that—although the phenomena of collective psychology resemble chemical phenomena a great deal, for their unexpected *precipitates*,—nevertheless, what is possible in chemistry is impossible in collective psychology, namely, to know the required dose of the various substances to obtain the new substance.

Leaving metaphors aside: how can one determine the role of the personal work of a certain journalist in creating a given public opinion, and the role played by the anonymous, collective, and instinctive work of the population?

For example,[35] subscription statistics are considered an excellent thermometer—often consulted—that warns the editors of a newspaper about the line of conduct to follow. In this case, it is the public that, with an economic sanction, imposes its viewpoint on the journalists, not the other way around. And there is, in this regard, the famous example of *Le Figaro*, which in 1897, after having published the first articles by Émile Zola in defence of Dreyfus and of his supporters, changed sides so as not to disgust its subscribers and readers.[36]

Without resorting, after all, to such a notorious fact, which at least occurred with a forthrightness that could mitigate its gravity, each of us—however little expertise we have of the journalistic world—is aware of analogous episodes. That is, we know of newspapers and, even worse, of journalists who have changed or modified their opinions because the public's mood, hence the amount of the proceeds, humbly advised to modify them.

Despite these facts, I am, however, inclined to believe the journalist's influence on the public to be more frequent and intense than the

35 G. Tarde, art. cit.

36 *Le Figaro* then changed sides once again and became the main authority on the need to revisit the Dreyfus trial.

public's on the journalist. And not only is that influence, in my view, more intense, but it can also be more morally damaging. And here is the reason. The public may change the orientation of a newspaper. We recognize that this is an ugly thing for a newspaper's character and independence, given that it is, after all, a form of corruption. But it is a corruption that affects only one type of victim: the simple consciences of the converted. Therefore, it deals simply with a question of individual morality. If, to stick to the cited example, the readers of *Le Figaro* wanted their newspaper to defend the French Staff and upheld its sentence of imprisonment to Devil's Island, and if the administrative board of the big Parisian newspaper decided to please them, too bad for those readers and too bad, I repeat, for the consciences of the journalists and for the independence of the newspaper that abided by that change. There is nothing to deplore.

By contrast, the influence of the journalist on the public can be morally and materially much more damaging, since the journalist can lie, and make the public believe untrue things, hence leading its judgment astray. He can, in short, commit crimes against the public, taking advantage of its credulity and loyalty. Is there perhaps the need to show examples in order to prove how many shady businesses—financial and political—were passed off as good by the wise art of journalists? The French and Italian *Panamas* demonstrate it. With money, very much money, one can create any public opinion.

Let us then not speak of the electoral periods during which, beyond money, thousands of not-entirely noble and pure passions are at stake. There are candidates or their electors who lie to the *crowd* that listens to their speeches, promise things that they know they cannot maintain, and defame their adversaries. Likewise, there are journalists, on both sides, who lie to their *public* in order to convince it to vote for Tom rather than Dick. Having to acknowledge these painful facts leaves us with only one consolation: newspapers, like orators, use one another as antidotes and neutralize one another. But it is no less true that the *public* is, in very many cases, like the soft clay in which the journalist's hand imprints itself.

Gabriel Tarde with his habitual precision says that—almost as a psychological counterbalance to these crimes committed *against* the public—there are also the crimes committed *by the public.* And it is true.

Yes, that phenomenon of collective moral worsening that I acknowledged in the crowd also inevitably occurs in the public, which is nothing but a diffused crowd.

The individuals that comprise a crowd or a public—taken one by one—are generally good and nice people. When they gather together, one could say that their best qualities cancel each other out and hide, exposing the worst qualities and letting them have the upper hand. In collectivities, be they static like a crowd or dynamic like a public, the lowest instincts reawaken, and out of the stratifications of character, the earliest, most animalistic and savage ones rise to the surface. The crowds are more ferocious and brutal in the manifestation of these instincts precisely because they are atavistic organisms; publics are less brutal and ferocious because they are modern and civil organisms. The former, in their paroxysm of hate, resort to murder; the latter limit themselves to insult and defamation. The former kill materially, the latter limit themselves to killing morally.

Must we say—for this—that the crowds as much as the publics are incapable of noble, generous, and heroic impulses? Not at all. But these impulses are rare, and the rule is that, in collectivities, the good instincts remain asleep.

Take, as an example, the most restricted and common forms of the public: salons, clubs, etc. In a conversation try to say something good about a person: someone will echo it, the others, if they do not contradict, will remain silent, and the dialogue will die very soon.

Try instead to say something bad: it will be a chorus. Everyone will have their small pebble to add to the avalanche of gossip, and you can be sure that the conversation will not dwindle as quickly.

We must confess it: the biblical legend is psychologically very true; the fruits of the tree of evil are much more flavourful than those of the tree of life.

Let us shift from restricted to vast publics, from the salon to journalism.

In the press, if one truly wants to awaken the interest and curiosity of the public, it is necessary to create for it not an object of love, but an object of hate. Actually, the public likes idols, too, and it burns incense to them with great prodigality, but it gets tired of them. Yet, it is not always too malicious to suppose that the public creates idols just for the pleasure of destroying them.

An observation that I did not hear anybody make at the time and that yet seems very simple to me is that the Dreyfus affair gathered new momentum and intrigued the public of the two worlds much more when the brother of the wretched captain accused Esterhazy of being the author of the *bordereau.*[37] He found *the object of hate* to offer to the public as

37 [Ferdinand Walsin Esterhazy (1847–1923) is the French officer who betrayed Dreyfus by forging a letter (the famous *bordereau*) containing information about an alleged case of espionage in favour of Germany, which was ascribed to Dreyfus.]

nourishment. Until then, the battle was for the innocence of a man, but the name of the real culprit was unknown; it was a *negative* campaign, the nobility of which could not be felt by everyone, but only by those who were ideally passionate about truth and justice. The majority of the public, like the crowds in a theatre, wants the dramas to finish not only with the triumph of the innocent, but also with the condemnation of the culprit. And, in order to grow, the sympathy for Dreyfus had to ignite the fire of hate against Esterhazy.

Tarde says it very well: "To discover or to invent a new and great object of hate for public consumption is yet one of the surest means to become one of the kings of journalism. In no country, in no epoch, has apologetics had as much success as defamation."

And it is this consideration, and no other, that can explain the enormous success of the defamatory press, of the Drumonts, of the Rocheforts,[38] and of all the other literary tigers of France and elsewhere.

The public, then, is in itself somewhat criminal, because it has low and impure instincts and passions.

In the historical periods during which progress accelerates and takes on acute revolutionary forms, the public can really become criminal. Then it may easily shift from verbal to material ferocity and attempt to strike, not only with words, its *objects of hate.* Then it may easily applaud whoever proposes, and pushes to propose banishment laws, convictions, massacres, and persecutions of any kind. Without the existence and provocations of a certain public, the horrors of the French Revolution, as of all revolutions, would not have been possible.

In the normal historical periods, the criminal character of certain publics is different, less noticeable, but not necessarily less effective. In those cases, the public, more than an author, is an accomplice to crimes; it does not commit them, but tolerates leaders committing them, and it attempts to hide or attenuate them according to a special morality that is nothing other than a party interest. From that we get the conspiracies of silence on the not-so-beautiful actions of certain political figures; and we get also the rescue attempts when all their sins find them out and the

---

38 [Édouard Adolphe Drumont (1844–1917) was a French writer and journalist. He founded the newspaper *La Libre Parole* and the Antisemitic League of France in 1889.

Victor Henri de Rochefort-Luçay (1831–1913) was a French journalist and politician, notorious for his radical, extremist views (anticlericalism, nationalism, and hostility to Dreyfus), which he disseminated through journals like *La Lanterne*, *La Marseillaise*, and *L'Intransigeant.* He was repeatedly tried for defamation and condemned to prison, but managed to escape in 1874.]

fearful hour of the investigation strikes. But the theme is embarrassing, and insisting on it is neither easy nor perhaps beautiful.

If there are criminal publics, there are also insane publics or, at least, unconscious ones. The public is sometimes suddenly seized by a fit of madness, without reasons to explain it: this phenomenon finds no other comparison than in those gusts of wind that all of a sudden disturb the quiet atmosphere. The Greek public, which some years ago imposed on its government the war with Turkey, was in the throes of one of these fits; and after the disaster at Adwa, perhaps even the Italian people experienced a phase of recklessness when judging the responsibility of the war and when deciding the conduct that its ministers had to hold.

Less severe and less socially important, yet psychologically similar, these *engoûments* [*infatuations*] are also the characteristic of the publics, not so much the political as the artistic and literary ones. At times, a moment comes when a literary figure suddenly becomes *fashionable*, and for some time people only speak and write about him: he is the king of the day. Maybe he has not produced anything new, or his most recent book is inferior to his previous ones; and yet, only then does the public seem to recognize his celebrity.

In all these cases, the psychology of the *publics* resembles, once again, the psychology of *crowds*, where nobody knows how or why certain impulses are born and certain violent, criminal, or crazy actions break out, which no human force can moderate.

And precisely in these cases the question returns more imperious: behind every public are there not perhaps always publicists who incite them, just as behind every crowd there is always a sect that is practically its yeast?

Whatever response one wants to give to this question—and a clear, categorical response would be impossible in my opinion—it would have relative importance for the scope of our study. It is enough for us to have noted that sometimes—I would say many times—it is the journalist who forms public opinion. Only in these cases can one attempt to propose some suggestions that render the influence of the newspaper more honest and useful, hence making public opinion more conscious and true.

For the other cases, when it is not the newspaper that exerts its power of suggestion on the public, but, rather the latter on the former, I do not see the possibility of remedies or advice, perhaps apart from a vast and long process of popular education and instruction that would transcend the limits of our work.

If, indeed, you believe that any opinion manifests itself in the public without the influence of some publicist's voice, for an incomprehensible phenomenon of spontaneous generation, you can at most study the way and the forms in which this opinion manifested itself, but you cannot propose any means for modifying that opinion. It would be a fatality against which it is vain to fight.

But, I repeat, while the degree of influence of the press can be discussed, the actual reality of this influence cannot. Therefore, we will look for a way to discipline it, so that it can fulfil its very difficult task of creating public opinion with greater morality and more conscience.

## *VI*

It is apparently a somewhat strange phenomenon that, while the state requires intellectual and moral guarantees to authorize the doctor, the lawyer, the engineer, or the clerk to practise their professions, it requires none for the journalist.

One would say—and forgive me for the paradox—that the state leaves the highest and most difficult functions at the mercy of incompetent people. It leaves, indeed, to the jurors (who have no obligation to be jurists or psychologists) the task to judge the life and the honour of individual citizens. It leaves to members of parliaments (who are not expected to have studied sociology) to judge the nation's collective interests; finally, it leaves to the journalists (who do not have to take any exam or present a clean criminal record) the terrible power to form public opinion.

With that—and I wish to declare it right away—I do not intend at all to invoke laws that restrict the right to become a juror, a member of parliament or a journalist. I do not believe—or at least barely at all—in the official evaluation of aptitudes. I believe instead that—above all in the intellectual field—the law of selection and of the survival of the fittest dominates. The state can distribute diplomas and honours: whoever is not worthy of them, despite having obtained them, dies nonetheless of hunger or drags along in an obscure and exhausting existence. Anything with a government stamp—a degree, an exam, a competition—is ultimately nothing but a means for the diffusion of that crisis of mediocrity that is now affecting the notables of the bourgeoisie.

It seems to me, however, that while it would be useless—as well as ridiculous—to require a degree to become a journalist, it would not at all be useless to require a guarantee of a journalist's morality and intelligence. The diploma is an indirect responsibility that the state takes and that does not exist in practice; the obligation to sign articles would be—if I do not deceive myself—a personal and direct responsibility, which would have in practice a great and beneficial effect.

We all know the fetishism that people have for all that is printed. Most of those who read a newspaper believe what they read with blind faith; they deem it possible and probable; they repeat it, they talk about it, they amplify it, they twist it. One could say about every printed piece of news what one says about slander: even though there is nothing truthful, something will always remain.

Now, it seems to me that the public's unconscious credulity should not be exploited too much, and that the most elementary feeling of loyalty should advise to place a name—that is, a person responsible for it—at the bottom of every article. In this way, the reader would have a guarantee in that name, or at least an index suggesting a greater or lesser degree of trust in what one reads.

When in newspapers I see certain violent attacks against a person, a society, an institution, and I do not find a name at the end of the article, I am inclined to think—by association of ideas—of an anonymous letter.

I know: it could be objected that *the newspaper organism* is responsible for what is printed in its columns. But to what is this responsibility reduced? In most cases, nobody wants or can prosecute anyone because the extremes of the crime are missing in the article. Yet is it right, then, to lavish praises or discredits without disclosing who is hiding behind them?

Where a trial does take place, we have the small consolation and the very useless sanction represented by the condemnation of the newspaper manager, who is never guilty, or of the editor, who might not be, or—a very rare hypothesis—of the author of the anonymous article, if he feels the need to disclose his identity at the last moment, while, out of loyalty, he should have gone public.

Yet, anyway—it is said—the financial responsibility of the newspaper's administration would remain. Apart from discussing how real this responsibility is, I ask: is it just and civil to reduce to collective, anonymous, and only financial responsibility, the crimes that can be committed by means of the press? Would this not amount to reviving the Lombard period when even murder sentences were served by paying money, or, even worse, the barbaric era, when responsibility for a crime was not limited to the criminal who had committed it, but encompassed his entire family, his *clan*?

Let us be clear: I believe the newspaper's administration has to respond before the civil law of all that its newspaper publishes. But I do not believe this responsibility is sufficient, nor do I believe it is fair that the pitiful veil of an anonymous collectivity can cover the unpleasant conduct of the man who wrote things worthy of conviction or even only of blame.

The pillory is, among the ancient punishments, the one that, once civilly transformed, still seems to me the most fair. Let the name be publicly known of he who, out of vengeance, envy, or other base motives, discredited a person or deceived his readers and led them astray.

This, according to my conscience, seems the criterion with which we should understand responsibility..

Nevertheless, the supporters of the anonymous article have other arguments in favour of their thesis. The anonymous article, they say, is more effective on the public, since it reflects not the single opinion of one writer, but that of a party, and it allows the newspaper to maintain a consistent editorial line.

Is it more effective on the public? Perhaps. But what type of effectiveness?

I think that a signed article is comparable to the voice of an orator, and the anonymous article to one of those unknown cries that often emanates from a crowd.

I do not deny that this outburst can suggestionize the multitude more than the orator's word can persuade its audience. But which is the more conscious and more honest suggestion?

After all, one can affirm that the anonymous article reflects not the opinion of a person, but, rather, that of an entire party. In fact, the article is always written by one person or at least along the lines of ideas suggested by one single person, and hence the desire to present it as a collective work … like the poems of Homer, is a fiction.

No one, more than I, recognizes, and I have already said it, that the true journalist is, like the true artist in another field, a man who understands, synthesizes in himself, and expresses needs, desires, and thoughts that lie confused and diffused in the collective psyche. But if he has this felicitous gift to interpret the feelings of many, why hide his name? First of all, he could be wrong, and in such a case it is good to know that the opinion or stated judgment originate only from one and not from many individuals. Second, if he truly says what many think, where is the danger that his signature would create? Newspapers have a big role, but so do books in the formation and transformation of ideas and feeling. And books, especially the books that *have remade the people*, are not anonymous.

As for the consistency of the newspaper's editorial line, I recognize that the system of writing without signing is … the ideal system.

Since no one knows who writes, no one can reproach Tom or Dick for writing today in a newspaper the opposite of what he wrote yesterday in another. On the contrary, I wish that articles were signed precisely to prevent journalists who work anonymously from *conforming to a newspaper's editorial line*, which they opposed shortly before in another newspaper, without falling into disrepute. On the other hand, although recognizing that one can honestly change one's own opinions, I wish that these natural modifications of political thought in individual journalists were acknowledged openly and with the frank loyalty of whoever is not ashamed to have altered opinions.

The anonymous article is a specialty of the daily political newspaper; scientific or literary magazines contain only signed articles, except in very rare cases.

And yet, or indeed, the public opinion formed by magazines on whatever technical, scientific, or literary issue is always fairer, more measured, and more conscious than the political public opinion formed by daily newspapers.

Why?

The reasons are evident. First of all, because the writers of magazines are considered more honest than the anonymous writers of newspapers, in the sense that it is believed and known that they always express their own sincere opinion, not the one that, at a given moment, could please the public, and much less that which could be imposed on them, or perhaps paid by whoever might have an interest in its triumph. Second, because the writers of magazines are intellectually better, that is, more competent in the subject they deal with, and they *do not write an article* (unlike journalists) on whatever topic they might have ignored an hour earlier.

Now, this moral and intellectual superiority that the magazines incontestably have over the daily newspapers is, ultimately, attributable to the fact that, in magazines, articles are signed.

If you also require the signature for daily newspaper articles, then the articles will be better, morally and intellectually.

## *VII*

Having reached the end of my essay, I myself foresee two objections.

First, it might be argued that, if the press has so much importance in the formation of public opinion, it is not, however, the only cause. Second, even supposing that the mere requirement that articles be signed can be a remedy, it is a petty remedy in the face of journalism's potential evil.

I partly accept the first objection, but I respond with the following words by Max Nordau:

> The statesman who, approximately sixty years ago, said that "the press is the fourth power" believed to have stated a paradox: unconsciously he pronounced a prophecy. The press without wanting it, almost without knowing it, enters into vital competition with constituted powers. It tends to seize the crimes of the government, parliament, and the academy. Naturally, these bodies defend themselves. They hate the press because they feel it is somewhat like their impatient heir. But their hate will be impotent. The press will be the strongest because it is the daughter of these new conditions of civil life, while the other powers were created by a civilization that did not yet know railroads, telegraphs, telephones, or obligatory and universal instruction. The sociological basis of all the institutions of a democracy is public opinion, namely, the emotion and will of the majority of the public. All the mechanisms of parliamentarism: electoral agitations, elections, the Chamber, regulations of the sessions, debates, votes, are nothing but putting public opinion into effect. But how heavy and unfashionable is this machine! And how elegant, mobile, efficacious, to the contrary, is that of the press! As an incarnation of universal suffrage, it is infinitely more adapted to modern inventions than is parliamentarism![39]

We can, thereby, be forgiven if, in this first draft on a study of public opinion, we have stopped to consider the influence of the press, which is at the same time the most profound and true cause and expression of public opinion.

To the second objection I reply that, even if undoubtedly there will be many more radical reforms to correct the flaws and hence the influence of the periodical press, these reforms would target the laws that govern the press, not the people who embody and represent it. But I modestly think that today it is, above all, necessary to change the people rather than the laws.

Even optimal laws are useless, if not harmful, when the people who apply them are mediocre or evil. And even if one could devise an optimal law on the press without damaging the principles of freedom, this would

39 [Here Sighele is, in fact, vaguely referring to scattered ideas in, but not directly quoting from, Max Nordau's *Conventional Lies*, in particular the last chapter, "Miscellaneous Lies," where Nordau discusses the influence of the press, its repercussion on public opinion, and the "despotic power of the journalist." See Max Nordau, *The Conventional Lies of Our Civilization* (Chicago: L. Schick, 1884), 324–40.]

remain ineffective if the publicists did not have a greater conscience, and did not feel greater responsibility for their mission.

Now, in order to develop this conscience and to make this responsibility felt, I do not know a greater incentive than the one that would come from requiring the publicist to always put his name next to his words.

By eliminating the unworthy and mediocre, the moral and intellectual level of the periodical press would gradually rise, and the well-deserved influence on the public would be granted to that intellectual elite still representing the only form of aristocracy that can have rights over the people. Indeed, if it is true that in order to judge the value of an idea it suffices to count the votes of future generations, it is equally true that it is necessary to weigh the contemporary ones.

And no matter how much one wants to and must lower and diminish the efficacy of single individuals on the surrounding environment and to attribute all the honour of human progress to collectivities, it must be recognized that a man still has the power of personal suggestion, and it would be harmful to deprive him of it by requiring that he always hide behind anonymity.

To understand what the name of he who supports and divulges an idea can do—more than the idea itself—it is enough to think about the famous "J'accuse!" by Émile Zola.[40]

The extraordinary force of suggestion of that superbly beautiful act was not so much in the feeling and thought as in the man who expressed them. And the immense good that letter did to the cause of justice and humanity by overturning an unfair public opinion depended not on the content of the letter, but on the signature.

---

40 [On 13 January 1898, Émile Zola published an open letter with the title "J'accuse!" [I accuse!] in the newspaper *L'Aurore*, in which he denounced the French government's antisemitism as the main cause of Dreyfus's wrongful condemnation, and laid bare the many inconsistencies and judicial errors in the trial.]

# 5 From *The New Woman*

## "Excellent or Awful?"

### *I*

These days I have been reading a very interesting volume by Pauline de Grandpré, a good and cultivated woman, entitled *La Prison Saint-Lazare depuis vingt ans*, and I found in it this perhaps banal, but largely true phrase: "*Nothing in the world has been more praised or blamed than woman. I maintain that we can say all we want about her: we will always find a reason.*"[1]

This is perhaps a banal phrase, as I said, and above all a very convenient one, because it justifies the opinion of both pessimists and optimists, and it turns the *eternal feminine* into a kind of psychological Proteus, who today shows one face, tomorrow another, and authorizes the strangest and most disparate judgments.

I do not believe, however, that we can resign ourselves to this very undetermined and hence very superficial diagnosis. And it seems impossible to me that amid the surprises and great diversities that the study of

1 [In French in Sighele's text. Pauline Éléonore Michel a.k.a. Pauline Chevalier de Grandpré (1828–1908) was a French writer and philanthropist. In addition to authoring several literary works, such as *Le Marquis de Valbert* (1863) and *Le Jeune apôtre de l'Océanie* (1868), she devoted her life to the rehabilitation of former female prisoners through "L'œuvre des Libérées de Saint-Lazare," an organization that she founded in 1870. Saint Lazare was the only prison for women in Paris.]

the female soul undoubtedly offers, it is still so difficult to capture some common notes able to set the tone, so to speak, of woman's way of thinking and acting, and to give a glimpse of some aspects of her character.

A philosopher once said that crimes are like the shadow of society, and that, although it may seem reckless to judge a body from its shadow, its profile never fails to offer some useful lesson.

I, too, believe that an analysis of female criminality can illuminate the psychology of she who—at least for us men—is the more beautiful half of the human race.

Just as the temperament of a population reveals itself—better than in monotonous everyday life—in the pathological moments of great social commotions, such as riots or revolutions—so the intimate nature of a class of individuals or of a sex—more than in simple everyday facts—becomes apparent in the abnormal phenomena of existence, in insanity, in suicide, and in crime.

Now, the indisputable fact that blatantly emerges and catches the attention of whoever takes even a cursory glance at criminal court statistics is this: woman commits crimes infinitely less frequently than man (in France out of 100 accused, 14 were women, in Italy 9), but when she does commit a crime, she is more cynical, more cruel, more brutal, and more depraved than man.

Combine this fact with another one—that woman rises higher than us in moral greatness, because there is no virtue, devotion, or heroism where she does not surpass us—and you will draw this consequence: that female psychology knows heights of peaks and depths of abysses that man neither could nor would ever reach.

If hence an overall judgment on woman were allowed, it could be said that hers is almost always *the psychology of extremes.* The middle path is unknown to her, in good as well as in evil. The pale and dull figures, a bit good and a bit bad, that never have either the energy for a generous act, nor the audacity for crime, belong above all to the male sex. Woman, instead, is awful or excellent, and even when she does not seem to be either one, and apparently falls into that grey zone wherein the majority lies, it is enough that an occasion awakens her from her apparent torpor, to make her immediately unveil her character, which has neither uncertain nor confused hues, and to make her appear as an angel or a demon, terrible in her perfidy or sublime in her sacrifice according to circumstances.

To what can we attribute this strange characteristic of female psychology?

In my view to the restricted sphere in which the activity of woman takes place, to the morally and intellectually small environment in which she lives.

While man has a very vast field on which to bestow his feelings and thoughts, woman, in our current society, only has the very limited field of the family. A man lives, fights, fears, hopes for *ideas* and for *things*, in addition to people; by contrast, woman generally does not live or fight but for *people*. He *spreads* his affectivity on very many individuals; she *concentrates* it on very few: the husband (or lover), the children. Hence it is natural and, I would say, necessary that her affectivity is indeed *more intense*, for better or worse, because it is *less diffused*, and that her heart has flashes of ardour and the obscurities of a cavern, sublime impulses of tenderness and brutal bursts of refined cruelty.

You see, in the intellectual field a phenomenon occurs that is analogous to what was observed in the moral field.

Woman's intelligence overall is very inferior to man's, but the former surpasses the latter, and is truly acute and subtle, in the analysis of certain delicate feelings and generally in the psychological intuition of moods. A woman of mediocre talent sometimes reads the human heart better and more deeply than a brilliant man. Schopenhauer magnificently said that "she is afflicted by a myopic intelligence that allows her to see the things near to her with great penetration; but her horizon is limited; what is distant escapes her."

Well, what is the reason for this myopia? Evidently, the cause cannot be but one: given the restricted circle in which she lives, her intelligence, so weak in judging the things that do not concern her, those vast fields where she never pushes her gaze, refines and specializes in the observation of nearby things, and her cerebral activity becomes more intense where it can apply itself, precisely because it is not so diffused.

Is it bad or good that civilization and evolution have formed the female brain and heart so differently from ours, fossilizing woman in a circle of thoughts and feelings beyond which she arguably does not live, but within which she lives more intensely than us?

I do not know. Of course, from the point of view of male egoism, I would reply that it is a good thing. In the difference of her nature, in the hopes and dangers that her unpredictable and inconstant manifestations of hate and love raise, is enclosed the secret of her charm, the reason why we love her.

Emancipate her (actually it would take a long time to destroy the result of centuries), allow her to live our life and spread her intelligence and affection over all the petty and great things that interest us, and you will render her morally equal to man. Between the two sexes only the physiological difference will remain, and, in this way, the highest and most human of her charms will be removed from love. "We dislike the woman who resembles us"—Renan said; "what we seek in the other sex is the opposite of ourselves."[2]

## *II*

So far I have tried to grasp the fundamental note of feminine psychology, and I think I have found it in exaggeration. Woman, I said—and the facts prove it—always exaggerates in good and in evil, in hate and in love, in pity and in cruelty. This is, of course, a dangerous but, after all, agreeable feature. Extreme temperaments give great pains but also great joys, and they appeal, indeed, because there is something energetic and absolute in them. They are like certain profiles with sharp and marked lines, whose beauty may be debatable, but which are attractive because they reveal a thought and a character.

Now, in order not to complete but to make this study less imperfect, I wish to highlight other sides of female nature.

It will be—as it is usually said—the downside, because the psychological notes we shall discuss will cast some shadow on this rapidly sketched portrait.

It is a common observation that woman fights in life with more ferocious and less fair weapons than man. She prefers guile, deceit, and hidden paths to frankness and to clear and open ways.

The reason for this phenomenon is totally physiological. The weak being, and such is woman, must help herself out of necessity with means able to paralyze the faculties of he who is strong. She must be a fox to win, and sometimes a lion.

This is why female psychology is largely made of cleverness, betrayal, and intrigue. Woman knows better than a spider (ladies please forgive me for the vulgar comparison) how to weave an invisible web wherein man gets caught more easily than a fly. The vendettas she prepares are almost never carried out fairly, but they are planned in the semi-obscurity of the elegant sitting rooms. She simulates and feigns not only when she plots small and mysterious conspiracies, but also when, as she directly confronts her enemy, she seems to be acting and speaking sincerely. In this latter case, she had studied … *la scène à faire* [the scene that needs to be staged]. And the habit of not telling the truth has penetrated so deep into her nature that frankness always disarms her—as Bourget wittily observes—since this is the thing that she least expects!

2 [In French in Sighele's text.]

Precisely for this reason, foreign and internal *politics* have been much and egregiously served by the subtle womanly arts. The history of many governments says this, and even today, I believe that many wasps buzz around the police and the diplomatic chanceries.

There is yet another fact that explains the reason why woman acts almost always in the shadow. Since, out of despotism or of necessity, the *foreground* (I adopt the painter's jargon) on the canvas of social life is occupied by man, only the background remains for her to occupy, which is less visible and has but minor importance. Yet precisely as in paintings it serves much more often to shed light, life, and movement on the figures that are at the forefront.

In criminality, for example, the woman always has secondary, or better, background roles. The man, stronger and more naive, acts; the woman, weaker and cleverer, limits herself to helping, instigating, suggesting. She knows that traces of moral complicity almost never remain, and she rarely experiences a scruple or remorse for abandoning in the hands of justice whomever she pushed to crime.

There have been—it is true—two women in New Caledonia who were condemned to forced labour for life (although they deserved a minimum sentence) for following their lovers, the murderers Vrignault and Chevalier,[3] but the case is rare. Generally the woman abandons her accomplice, when she does not accuse him first.

The woman informant is, in fact, a frequent phenomenon in criminal psychology (a phenomenon that, in any case, also occurs in normal psychology), when she does not like her lover anymore or she has lost esteem for him because he was caught.

The most vulgar form of this betrayal is the anonymous letter, the consolation of all betrayed or jealous women. The anonymous letters sent to the prefecture of the Paris police have been mainly identified as female handwriting; and I believe that one would obtain the same result when examining the letters received by private citizens.

One could perhaps attribute this form of denunciation to the great facility with which women always reveal the things that they should not reveal. "*There's nothing like a secret weighs;*"—La Fontaine said—"*Too heavy 'tis*

3 [Two women, Piat and Conturier, although innocent, allegedly asked the Parisian police to be arrested so as to be transported to New Caledonia together with Vrignault and Chevalier. See Arthur Griffiths, ed., *The History and Romance of Crime from the Earliest Time to the Present Day* (London: Grolier Society, 1900), 209.]

*for women tender.*"[4]—The secret of a crime must then be more unbearable than anything else, and it is, therefore, natural that women are unable to keep it. The clever delinquents know that one should trust female secrecy very little, and not accidentally the famous Abadie,[5] among the sixty articles of his gang's rules, inserted one that said: "only the leaders have the right to keep a woman with themselves; the other associates can only have lovers for a day."

However, this too well known and too much noticed defect still does not explain the reason for certain abandonments and certain sudden revelations.

When Émile Zola was interviewed by Edmond Le Roy on the reason that pushes women to denounce their lovers and accomplices to a crime, he replied: "It is not remorse that pushes the female accomplice to denounce the culprit, her lover. It is—on the one hand—the need to be talked about, to occupy the public's attention ..."[6] and so far Zola is fully right.

Gabrielle Bompard's remark to the investigating judge, Dopffer, became famous: "It seems that the press is nice to me!" "Here is the desire of female vanity!" Zola continued: "... Then, it is profound indifference that [women] reserve to those who have ceased to please them."[7]

And here I no longer agree with Zola. It is not indifference, it is hate. Whoever is indifferent does not care about others. Is Gabrielle Bompard, who came from America to denounce Michel Eyraud, perhaps indifferent? Is Eugénie Forestier, who enjoyed revealing Prado's infamies one by one, perhaps indifferent, or Antoinette Sabatier and Jeanne Blin, who, at their hearing, both repeatedly ordered to Pranzini and Prado: "But confess, then, confess!" and were delighted to see them defeated and annihilated under the weight of their revelations?[8]

---

4 [In French in Sighele's text. Jean de la Fontaine, in "The Women and the Secret," in *The Fables of La Fontaine*, trans. by Elizur Wright, Book VIII, Fable VI (Adelaide: University of Adelaid Library, 2014)]

5 [See *The Criminal Couple* 82n17.]

6 [In French in Sighele's text.]

7 [In French in Sighele's text. For Bompard, see also *The Criminal Couple* 109n80.]

8 [Eugénie Forestier lived with Luis Prado, a Spanish criminal who moved to Paris after squandering his wife's wealth. When he was arrested for theft in 1887, Eugénie, resentful for being abandoned, declared that he was also the murderer of Camille- Marie Aguétant, a prostitute who was killed earlier that year. In 1888, Prado was condemned to death. See also *Criminal Couple* 105n70 in this volume. Likewise, Henri Pranzini (1857–1887), guilty of slaying three women – the notorious 1887 murder of rue Montaigne in Paris – was made to confess by the sentimental and dramatic rhetoric of his lover Antoinette Sabatier. See Albert Bataille, *Causes criminelles et mondaines de 1888* (Paris: E. Dentu Editeur, 1889), 302; Albert Borovitz, *Blood and Ink: An International Guide to Fact-based Crime Literature* (Kent and London; Kent State UP, 2000), 89.]

No—I repeat it—it is hate: it is a transformation of ancient love, which only the female soul can give, so sudden in its contrasts, so terrible in its revenge.

Even when honest women (and I say honest from the point of view of criminality), for whatever reason, get rid of their lover or are set free by him, they do not forget him, they never become indifferent towards him: they follow him with their thoughts and, if the occasion presents itself, they know how to make him understand that they are still alive.

If you break your relationship with a gentleman, you are sure that this gentleman, once the dispute is over, will never try to hurt you. If, instead, you break a relationship with a woman, you do not have the certainty that she will leave you in peace; you rather feel that she will hurt you if she can. Women have everlasting hatred if they have brief love. You will have made a ferocious enemy out of a previous friend, for the same reason that an accomplice to a crime may become an informant at any moment.

It is still and always the psychology of extremes that reveals itself in the female soul.

A dangerous psychology, which, nonetheless, instead of turning people away, attracts. Why?

Risk is the attraction of every undertaking: what is certain and sure cannot provide real emotions. The same happens in love: man finds in woman—in this capricious and treacherous being from whom he must expect the greatest and most painful surprises—that sensation of danger that today, unfortunately, is so rare and that constitutes a great charm for whoever feels life poetically.

## "The Woman Question"

By now the woman question is no longer the sentimental resource of some journalist in search of a theme for his daily article. It is no longer the occasion for some witty or poisonous *boutade* by idle writers in the summer calm. It represents a real need in our restless life, and, after setting fire to the four corners of England, it threatens to burn France and thus to spread the heat of its flame even among us.

In the battle that has begun, after the light cavalry of journalists and readers, even the heavy cavalry of scientists takes the field, the weapons of the spirit become blunt against the armours of scientific ideas, and the fire of jokes goes out under the hailstorm of machine guns heavy with thought.

Science is a rude lady who ignores the Jesuitries of etiquette and the conventional lies arraigned by Max Nordau.[9]

If you ask her what she thinks of woman, she replies that woman is of lesser *anthropological* value than man.

And since *some truths are better left unsaid,*[10] women hate science, that irreconcilable enemy of religion, and, echoing Brunetière, consider it responsible for the present corruption and the low level to which morality has sunk at the end of this century.

Nonetheless, one must also grant the right to speak to this rude lady, who does not argue unless on the basis of facts and figures, and who perhaps resembles the surgeon who heals by hurting.

An influential interpreter of science is Professor Moritz Benedikt[11] from the University of Vienna, a friend and admirer of Italy, of which he speaks the language well and knows the intellectual movement perhaps much better than most Italians.

In one of his articles, where he summarizes the ideas that he would develop in a voluminous work entitled *Psychology as Experimental Science,* he establishes a comparison between the two sexes—a comparison largely advantageous to man, the reason why women will say … that comparisons are always hateful.

For Benedikt, the decisive points that determine the psychological difference between the two sexes are the following:

1 In man the impression of observation and perception is preponderant, in woman the impression of the sentiment is;
2 In man the transformation of the will into movement occurs more easily than in woman;
3 Finally, woman is incompletely organized for the highest investigations of thought.

---

9 [Sighele is here alluding to Nordau's provocative book *The Conventional Lies of Our Civilization,* which presents the existing social, religious, political, and economic institutions in Europe and America as deeply deceptive. See also *The Intelligence of the Crowd* 263n41.]

10 [In French in Sighele's text.]

11 [See *The Criminal Crowd* 69–70n137. The Italian title that Sighele gives of Benedikt's book is *La psicologia come scienza sperimentale* [Psychology as Experimental Science]. We have provided the English equivalent even though none of Benedikt's books seems to exist in English with that title.]

If some facts may contradict the truth of these principles, it is necessary to remember that exceptions serve only to confirm the rule, and it must be taken into account that no man descends solely from a man, and no woman solely from a woman, hence the parents' qualities are transmitted to the children in varied, countless combinations. A woman can essentially have male characteristics, as a man can psychologically and intellectually be a female. The natural dispositions in such cases are inverted, and these *incartardes* [deviations] against nature are, indeed, called *perversions.*

Taking as a term of comparison a normal man and a normal woman, we must recognize that the former has a creative intelligence, the latter at most an assimilating intelligence.

The intellectual patrimony that society hands down across centuries, which increases proportionally and at great speeds, is due to men. In the construction of this glorious edifice, woman has had but a minimum part, and can be considered a negligible quantity. Let us look at an example. For centuries, we have taught women music. Therefore, they cannot say in this regard that it is a lack of instruction that leaves them inferior to man. And yet, their musical compositions are very rare and all very mediocre. Where do you find a woman who is equal to, I do not say a Wagner or a Verdi, but a Mascagni or a Leoncavallo?

The counter-evidence that the intellectual difference between males and females is to be attributed uniquely to the sex lies in the fact that as a child, when the sex still *does not speak,* the female is more intelligent than the male. Indeed, you can find that intuition and perception are much more developed in an eight- or ten-year-old girl than in a boy of the same age.

Female development halts with growth, while male development continues for life.

In man, other character qualities add up to intellectual inferiority, which are a powerful help for the intellect: I mean, objectivity and impartiality.

Given, as a hypothesis, a man and a woman of equal intelligence, the first will always represent a *social force* superior to the second, since, being less irritable and less impressionable, he will not be carried away by momentary passions; he will strip himself of his *I* in order to judge things and men; he will be, in a word, more impartial and more objective.

It would be vain to expect these qualities in a lady. Woman ignores what is *theoretical* discussion, in the absolute sense of the word. A subjective individuality par excellence, she embellishes her ideas in line with her feelings; she brings to opinions the current and often mutable state of her soul; she cannot judge a fact by detaching it from the person who accomplished it; and she always assumes in other people's words those personal references that are never lacking in her own.

If we move from the intellectual to the moral sphere, the conditions change and the comparison works to woman's advantage.

Professor Benedikt says that woman tolerates pain with greater resignation than man. I will not dare to contradict him, but I wish to remind him of what Professors Giuseppe Sergi and Paolo Mantegazza asserted: that woman actually feels less than man. The resistance to pain would hence be reduced in her to a minor sensibility.[12]

It is very probable that ladies will rebel against this crude scientific truth, because it will seem to them that their weeping and nervous crises are proofs of a delicacy of feeling that man does not know. But they forget that they are a weak organism, and that weak organisms have much livelier exterior manifestations than strong ones. They forget that crying is a liberating outlet, while silent, tearless suffering represents a victory over oneself, which only the strong can attain and which increases pain.

One must not confuse feelings with what the French call *sensiblerie* [sentimentality].

In this, without a doubt, women have no rivals.

"But, are you not perhaps too severe?" This question that even men could ask me has an easy answer. I speak about the majority of women, not indistinctly of all women.

I attempt to grasp the general lines of female psychology as science traced them, but I do not claim that this portrait resembles all physiognomies. All the more so, because the moral physiognomy of woman is—like the physical one—of a strange variability, and in the woman of today, you could not always recognize the woman of yesterday.

---

12 See, e.g., Giuseppe Sergi, *Per l'educazione del carattere* [For the Education of Character], 2nd ed. (Milan: Dumolard, 1893), 233. [Mantegazza, in fact, often also maintains that women are more sensitive than men, yet at the same time, since his first book *Fisiologia del piacere* [Physiology of Pleasure], he also underlines that women are inferior to men in the enjoyment of the pleasures of taste and of sight, as well as of intellectual and sexual ones. In his *La donna delinquente, la prostituta e la donna normale* [*The Criminal Woman, the Prostitute, and the Normal Woman*], Lombroso endorses Sergi's and Mantegazza's views.]

Morally, woman has an unstable equilibrium that allows her to go through the entire range of human emotions in very little time, passing from the best to the worst with a self-confidence and a promptness that would surprise a man … little versed in psychology.

And this instability, this easiness in reaching *extremes*, typical of every woman is reflected collectively in the entire female sex, which, as a whole, can be considered—and always rightly so—either much better or much worse than the masculine sex.

You speak to me of heroism? For many cowardly men whom we saw in the French Revolution, history records only one example of female cowardice: du Barry.[13]

You speak to me of ferocity? No man has ever attained the lascivious and beastly cruelty of certain females during riots or street demonstrations.

You speak to me of love and affection? Few fathers love their sons with the devotion with which a mother loves them—but judicial records register just one cruel father out of 100 females who torture their children like hyenas.

An extreme temperament that surpasses man in goodness and perversity: this is, thus, woman, an extreme temperament created by her own weakness and inferiority, and an individual who, despite being man's consoling angel, needs nonetheless his guidance and support.

To end this wandering through female psychology with a practical and positive idea, if man had not instituted marriage, woman would certainly find herself alone and miserable in the last part of her life.

Age, disease, and maternity reduce in woman, much more than in man, the conditions of a happy existence. It would be unfortunate if marriage were not there to restrain masculine whims! Of course, laws (on divorce, for example) can render the ironclad ties of marriage more elastic, but any law on marriage, no matter how strict, is an immense advantage for woman. The woman who asks for free love is blind and an unconscious enemy of her own sex, because free love for her means a period of freedom followed by the certainty of abandonment and misery.

13 [Jeanne Bécu, comtesse du Barry (1743–1793) was the last mistress of King Louis XV of France. She is associated with cowardice because she did not face execution with the same calm and dignity displayed by other noblewomen, such as Marie Antoinette. Accounts of du Barry's final moments on the scaffold, indeed, describe her attempt to escape from the scaffold, her many pleas for life, and her shrieks.]

# 6 From *Modern Eve*

## "Woman and the Injustices of Legislation"

*We will speak against senseless laws until they are reformed and, meanwhile, we shall blindly submit to them.*

—Diderot[1]

For anyone who wants to objectively discuss this topic, which has stirred and still stirs raging polemics, there is first of all a simple but important observation to be made: "*women are the only people whom nowadays our laws exclude from certain capacities, for reasons of birth.*" Like the slaves in ancient times, like until very recently black people in America, women come into life with the indelible mark of a juridical inferiority.

I do not argue with it, for now. I limit my research to the causes of these legal provisions.

The main and most obvious cause consists in the widespread opinion that woman is inferior to man. I will not repeat what has been said with such boring insistence! From the Fathers of the Church to the most illustrious representative of modern positive science, from poets to physiologists, from socialist to conservative writers, it is a chorus that, to conclude with Leopardi, says that woman

1 [In French in Sighele's text.]

(...) naturally
is less than man in everything. For if her limbs
are softer and more tender, she's also given
a mind that's less capacious and less strong.[2]

What is strange is that woman's enemies are in agreement with her most valid defenders on the consequences of this claim. Indeed, the second reason why woman is always considered a perpetual minor consists in the opinion of those who consider her such a noble and pure creature that she needs to be held apart from the reality of life, so as to avoid being profaned.

The former said: woman is a morally evil and intellectually inferior being; she cannot be granted all the rights man has. The latter said: woman is an almost divine being, the flower of our existence, the light of our path, but precisely for this reason she must be protected as one protects a flower or a child. And the former out of disdain, the latter out of admiration, have resolved to keep her juridically subdued.

How has woman been able to carry her chains?

She has imitated the angels who, in Raphael's canvas, free Saint Peter;[3] she did not try to break the solid iron bars with her fragile, white hands; she simply lulled and hypnotized the watchmen ...[4]

Why should she care if she was excluded from the crafting of laws, if she directed those who crafted them?

Why should she care if she was considered less than man, if this proud and overbearing male who denied her certain rights, was, by contrast, in front of her, as humble as a servant and as obedient as an automaton?

They say it is a historical law that the conquered peoples take revenge against their conquerors by corrupting them. Woman historically took revenge on male oppression not only by corrupting man, but also by making him act according to her will and leaving him only the illusion of independence.

2 ["(...) dell'uomo al tutto / Da natura è minor. Che se più molli / E più tenui le membra, essa la mente / Men capace e men forte anco riceve." Giacomo Leopardi, "Aspasia," in *Cantos*, translated and annotated by Jonathan Galassi (New York: Farrar Straus Giroux, 2010), 240–41.]

3 [*The Liberation of Saint Peter*, painted in 1514 by Raphael Sanzio together with his assistant Giulio Romano.]

4 See E. Ollivier, *Le féminisme*.

If I were asked which force has contributed the most to the world's progress, after the swords of the great captains and the discoveries of geniuses, I would say that it was women's seduction and charm.

This is an obscure and latent force that did not have the clangour of fame like every beautiful or perfidious thing made by man, but a force that invaded and pervaded through the centuries all the meanders of social life, just as those subterranean waters that spread quietly throughout the fields are the hidden and perennial reason for the fertility of certain terrains.

I do not know whether all the works of man are owed to feminine inspiration. I know for sure that man alone, man without woman, is nothing but half of himself; to be complete he must have felt close to him the vibration of the heart of a mother, a sister, a lover, and of all those graces, all those affections, all those flowers of the soul fused together in a single perfume like vine clusters. He must have known how to create for himself a strong and good soul, the daring soul of the brave individual who tries any challenge for the love of a woman, the generous soul of the one who feels he owes the best of his being to her, to the woman who stays by his side and whom the law places so much beneath him![5]

But, unfortunately, only rarely are men aware of their relative value, and anyway this is not enough. Woman cannot be satisfied with this silent role as a hidden inspirer. It is undoubtedly a great moral satisfaction for her to be able to say, when seeing men bustle and rush on the stage of life: "it is I who behind the scenes direct their movements." Yet, beyond the satisfactions of self-respect, effective satisfactions are required, and woman wants to get out of the legal and political shadow under which she has been relegated thus far. She wants to conquer her place in the sun; she wants to act not only with the indirect weapon of her charm, but also by means of the rights the law must grant her.

And here—then—is feminism.

Feminism's point of departure is this: man and woman are equal in birth and in death; the physiological differences exist in their bodies, but they do not exist at all in their moral constitutions; the heart and brain do not have a sex. As a consequence, all must be equal between man and woman.

I venture to believe the premise of this theory to be scientifically wrong.

In the woman question, as in any other, the point of departure must not be equality, this political glory that is also the scientific error of our

5 C. Pelletan, *La femme.*

times. The law regulating the world is not equality, but inequality. This does not signify inferiority and oppression, but difference and hierarchy.

Woman is not equal to man, not according to the unwise prejudice of Canon law, which said "mulier non est facta ad imaginem Dei";[6] nor because of the most unwise reason adopted by Proudhon[7]—a socialist!—who affirmed there cannot be a closer association between man and woman than that which is possible between animals of different species. Rather, this is so because, as Spencer says, to suppose that the soul and intellect of man and of woman can be identical while the body displays many differences between the two, and while in life the paternal and the maternal functions are so diverse, amounts to supposing that special faculties should not correspond to special functions, which frankly, would be a unique example in nature.

Let's, therefore, leave to simplistic psychologists the dream of equivalences between the two sexes that daily observations easily disprove, and acknowledge that it is not necessary to start from such a wrong premise in order to reach the absolutely right consequence of the juridical equality between man and woman.

If woman is, indeed, different from man, she is not perforce inferior; she is different from him, but equivalent to him, and as necessary as he is. Hence she must not suffer any diminution of rights.

After all, the profound congenital diversity between the psychic gifts of the two sexes has been preserved and even magnified by the long centuries of barbarism and obscurantism, during which woman was considered little more than a slave, and was kept away not only from public life but also from every light of culture and intellectuality.

Who can say what woman would have become if Oriental systems of education had not atrophied so much of her energy? Who can say what sense of measure and relativity her mind, which is still today impulsive and absolute, would have acquired, if men had not stiffened her brain in blind obedience to the husband's despotism or embittered her heart in the solitude of convents? Who can say what dignity and what proud self-defence she would have learned from experience, if the codes of law had not considered her—as they still do—a minor or insane?

---

6 ["Woman is not made in God's image."]

7 [Pierre-Joseph Proudhon (1809–1865) was a French politician, author of the famous treatise *What Is Property?* and founder of mutualist philosophy, upholding a society where each individual can possess means of production.]

I do not believe there are biblical curses that forever condemn a race, and even less a sex, to inferiority. We, people of the white race, are now realizing what the yellow race can do and where it has managed to arrive in few years, although certain pseudo-scientists had already labelled it as refractory to any kind of progress! We will see—if we are able to educate woman and to allow her to freely open up in the sunshine of civilization—what the female sex is able to do and how far it can get!

Everything moves and evolves in the world, and there are no so-called inevitabilities—or at least there will no longer be, one day—that history did not refute.

Woman, who until now has remained stationary or progressed rather slowly, enters now a period of more rapid evolution, and—by improving herself—she conquers in few years what earlier she took centuries to conquer.

The philosophers of history affirm that woman's self-evolution and her ascent towards better legal conditions have always accompanied every population's progress, and is the infallible sign of the passage from barbarism to civilization. I believe that this general principle includes some exceptions, given that the barbaric laws punished, for instance, some crimes by women with more clemency, and vice versa they punished the offences committed by men on women with greater severity. In so doing, they demonstrated they were applying, perhaps with more justice and certainly with more courtesy, the difference of the sexes that the Roman laws, and in general the laws of civilized populations, applied—and still do—in a much different way!

But, without insisting on particulars and limiting myself to highlighting the main stages of the journey made by woman's legal condition in the world, I will say that if in Roman laws, as in all the laws of their time, woman at the beginning counted little or nothing because she could not dispose of herself or of her property, and was completely absorbed by paternal or marital authority, in Rome itself she gradually broke free from this absolute servitude. In Cicero's time, woman was a proprietress: at the end of the Empire, the customary right had overlapped with the laws, and woman, free from all tutelage, could buy, sell, and manage her property at will.

All the work of Roman jurists thus consisted in detaching Eve from Adam's rib, so as to give her an autonomous existence. Arguably, the idea of equal dignity for the two sexes is a Roman idea, later confirmed by Christianity. This, however, is a more theoretical than practical idea, since it was only partially applied, and, in order to translate effectively into reality, it had to let the dark epochs of the Middle Ages and feudalism pass, and wait until the rise of the French Revolution.

It was, indeed, the French Revolution that revolutionized also private law.

The new female private law, whose foundations were laid by the Legislative Assembly and whose entire system appeared in the Napoleonic Civil Code, was truly founded on the equality of the two sexes, much more so than in Roman law.

In homage to this principle, the laws sanctioned for the first time:

Equality between woman and man regarding the capacity to acquire and to possess;

The abolition of the Senatus Consultum Velleianum,[8] that is, of the prohibition for woman to stand surety for other persons;

Equal freedom to end and dissolve marriage;

The right to intestate succession for daughters, on equal terms with sons.

It was not everything, but it was a lot. It was not a true female conquest, either, since those reforms, although being favourable to women, had not been dictated by feminist theories. They were the logical and necessary consequence of the abolition of the rights of primogeniture and other privileges of feudal and aristocratic origins. If woman was favoured, it was a corollary, not the objective.

The French Revolution—and I mean both those who intellectually conceived it and those who carried it out—did not have time to care about woman and her rights. Rousseau, in the *Social Contract*, does not speak about them; Montesquieu, in *The Spirit of the Laws*, opposes them; Robespierre, this mystical and bloody tyrant, despised woman and he wanted the man to be a dictator within the family.

Therefore, if the French Code of Law sanctioned and brought to the world woman's legal equality along with the rights of man, it did not entirely extinguish that residue of masculine feudality, which the Code itself reveals by enslaving the wife to the husband's iron will.

According to the Code, indeed, if the woman is unmarried or if she becomes a widow after getting married, she is legally capable and free to own, to buy, to sell, to negotiate, to trade, but the wife, alas, is incapable to do so, in the sense that she can do nothing without her husband's authorization.

8 [A decree of the Roman Senate enacted in 46 AD, under the consulship of Velleius Tutor and Marcus Silanus, according to which married women were prohibited from making contracts.]

The male dominating spirit and the Jacobin spirit of the petty politician lie entirely in this difference between the woman with a husband and the woman without one. Indeed, when commenting, on the provisions of his Code, Napoleon said that "there is one thing is not French: a married woman's freedom to do what she likes."[9]

Well, we can paraphrase the emperor's brutal assertion and say that "there is one thing that is not logical and it is a woman legally capable on the eve of marriage who becomes incapable the morning after." On the contrary, her dignity as a spouse and her glory as a mother should increase her rights, not diminish them!

I know that if the spouse has been condemned to an incapacity that starts with marriage and finishes with it, this did not happen out of hatred for women or uniquely as a consequence of the feudal prejudice whereby the man is the absolute boss in his house. There was also a higher and undeniably respectable reason: to prevent domestic discipline from weakening, to hold the family's unity intact.

The jurists say and everyone's common sense repeats: a direction is needed; we cannot conceive a boat without a pilot, a state without a king, an army without a general, a society without a director, an assembly without a president, hence we cannot conceive a conjugal society without a leader.[10]

We are in agreement. But we cannot conceive, either, that today, when everyone's economic conditions, and especially woman's, have changed, woman has little or no authority over her own money, money she earns! We cannot conceive, either, that the legislator still wants to keep the wife's economic tutelage in the Code of Law today, when woman works not only within domestic walls, but also in factories, in workshops, and has acquired a commercial and industrial value that she did not have before. She is no longer the luxury object providing a few hours' pleasure, but, rather, the male's valid help in bearing the family's material and moral burdens. This tutelage is often the origin of marital discord, and sometimes even of the ruin of families.

This is not the time to further specify what I am saying, to cite articles of the Code and to comment on them, but I want to say, to our credit, that, with regard to the wife's economic conditions, the Italian Civil Code is better than the Napoleonic Code, against which a league of intellectuals is rising in France today. It is even better than other European civil codes, but not enough to satisfy the needs of the feminists, which I deem legitimate.

9 [In French in Sighele's text.]

10 See the already cited Ollivier.

Even in Italy, marriage is a deep sleep for woman, as far as property is concerned: a sleep from which she is often suddenly awoken by the sound of a disaster.

The husband, accustomed to not depending on anyone, rarely asks the wife's advice on business matters ... even when her own money is at stake. The wife, in part obliged by the law and even more conforming to customs, remains estranged from all that is not daily domestic business.

And this lethargy of female activity is not only an injustice, but also an error, because woman has more prudence than man, and, being more conservative by nature, she would never be in favour of that inconsiderate largesse that gradually corrodes patrimonies, nor of those risky speculations that suddenly swallow them.

Nevertheless, it is not only as a wife and proprietress that woman could complain about the Civil Code. It is, above all, as maiden and mother that she could protest against the injustices of legislation.

A strange and sad irony! The legislator, in order to justify the legal tutelage subjecting woman, resorted to her weakness and her need for protection. Yet he totally forgot this female weakness and this need for protection when woman had to be protected from masculine seductions ... In other words, the legislator took all the precautions to safeguard woman's economic patrimony, and made sure that not only she but also her husband would be responsible for it. Yet he did not bother at all to safeguard the maiden's moral patrimony, her honour, and he said to the man who compromised her, smiling: "Don't worry! You are not responsible! The search for paternity is prohibited!"

Is this logical? Is it right? Is it humane? I read in our Civil Code, article 1151: "any man's action that causes damage to others obliges he who is responsible for it to pay for the damage."[11]

This article protects our windows, our doors, our furniture, the gates of our gardens, the produce of our countryside, our dogs, and our horses ... but it does not protect woman!

Before the Code, woman is less than our animals![12]

And yet, does seducing woman not cause damage to her, does it not make her suffer, does it not destroy, perhaps forever, her beauty and

11 [Sighele is here referring to the Italian Civil Code of 1865.]

12 Rivet, *La recherche de la paternité.* [Gustave Rivet (1848–1936) was a French politician, playwright, and poet, who discussed the issue of the search for paternity in the bourgeois drama *Le Châtiment* (1879) and in his renowned essay mentioned by Sighele. In 1910 the French senate, under Rivet's influence, approved a law in favour of the identification of the father.]

health, leaving her with the double cross of dishonour and the material obligation to nourish and raise the child?

Oh, I hear the voices of prudent and serious men who have so much respect for the legal family, and thus little for illegal families that love creates and condemns to unhappiness. I hear the harsh and cold voices saying: "the woman was weak, she should have reflected before surrendering, what fault has the man if she could not resist him?" And I even hear the malignant voices whispering: "it is naive to believe that it is always man who seduces! In most cases, it is woman who seduces!"

And so? And even if that were true? In what treatise of logic or morality can we find the principle that only one of the two accomplices to an action must pay the penalty and bear the consequences? And allow me to claim, at least, that if man is not the primary author of evil, he is undeniably the necessary accomplice. And why can this necessary accomplice, after doing what he meant to and sucking the flower's honey, leave undisturbed, free like the wandering bee, with one fewer thought and one more triumph, leaving in neglect, in pain, in shame, she who gave him the best of herself?

But those severe and prudent voices still repeat: "the Code cannot worry about all these infinite small dramas of love in which man accomplishes his male experience by assaying female virtue; these cases do not depend but on conscience!"

Well, I indeed believed that the law had to be the conscience of those who did not have one![13] I believed that the law had to re-establish the equilibrium between man's responsibility, which is now null, and woman's responsibility, which is now too much, not only to obey a criterion of justice and to diminish that tribute of souls and female bodies that humanity pays to the Minotaur of masculine egoism, but also for reasons of social welfare.

Do you know what happens to all the abandoned maidens and illegitimate children?

What happens to all the betrayed maidens is easy to imagine. Apart from the few heroines who possess the wise sweetness of resignation, and who, with honest work, know how to rebuild a life for themselves, which man's deceit threatened to shatter forever, apart from the few energetic ones who, in the pain for their cowardly abandonment, find the criminal courage to retaliate against their lovers with a knife, a handgun, or vitriol, all the others more or less slowly descend the ladder of vice, poor candid leaves of magnolia that upon first contact turn yellow forever!

---

13 See Rivet, already cited.

And what happens to the children? To that army of illegitimate creatures that rise every year to threaten society, of which they expose the vices with their birth, and of which they represent vices and crimes with their lives?

A small number of illegitimate children immediately pays with their violent death for the guilt and shame of their birth.

Infanticide is the extreme aberration of the betrayed maiden, who could not kill herself or avenge herself on her lover, and who suppresses the innocent, the living and screaming proof of her dishonour. And jurors acquit the horrendous crime—33 acquittals for every 100 infanticides—not only because they feel that in this case the crime is not the consequence of evil passion, but rather the bloody testimony of a legitimate revolt. Indeed, they acquit also because they have only the young single mother in front of them; they do not see the man, the necessary accomplice who is far away, and this injustice disarms them, rendering them indulgent …

Furthermore, when infanticide is not committed by the mother, the hostile society does its share by committing it on illegitimate children.

Coming into the world after months of anxiety and pain, deprived of every hygienic and moral care, they are sentenced to death; and, indeed, 11% die in the first month and 21% in the first year.

Then … then … the others who remain—without a name, without a position, incapable of pride—traverse life with a latent hate against the injustice they are victim of, and they populate our hospitals and our prisons!

Therefore, in the presence of these children who become social dead weights if they are not killed or do not die of starvation, in the presence of the many women who fall into disrepute if they do not end up in prison for avenging themselves on their lover, I would like to repeat the question that Senator Rivet asked the legislators of his country. I would like to ask the most serious politicians—who, in matters of commerce and customs, are so often angry protectionists—if they still find it useless to protect woman from male seduction, and if they are still in favour of the free exchange of abandonments and of infanticides, saying with blissful indifference: "*laissez faire, laissez passer!*"[14]

14 [Sighele's original Italian expression here—"lasciate fare, lasciate passare!"—polemically echoes that of the French physiocrats—*laissez faire, laissez passer!*—and, by extension, the motto of nineteenth-century European liberalism, with its emphasis on a passive state that, apart from protecting private property and administrating justice, does not intervene in the lives of its citizens.]

Perhaps—since male egoism is so great—we will not be able to ensure that men provide, at least economically, the first necessities for illegitimate children, until women will, like men, obtain the right to vote and thus the right to make laws.

This is also what Beaumarchais acknowledged, with the witty smile of a teasing philosopher, when in *The Marriage of Figaro*, alluding precisely to the way that the Code treats the woman who sinned in love, he wrote:

Of this absurd injustice
Shall we tell the cause?
The strongest have made the laws![15]

This question of the female vote, around which feminism's major effort revolves, seems to me among those political problems—and, alas, they are many—that frighten society more out of ignorance of their consequences than out of knowledge of their underlying causes.

We are often fearful of words; we sometimes have an instinctive aversion for certain reforms that we imagine full of who knows how many and which dangers. Even adult men, like children, have their *nightmares*. But when the sun appears, the ghosts disappear, and when certain problems are studied closely, under the quiet lamp of scientific observation, they make us realize that they were not as revolutionary as our timidity and misoneism feared.

The female vote! To be sincere, I begin by declaring that I do not believe our current laws recognize it. Those who believe so cannot but be a partisan who exchanges his desire for reality, or a lawyer who, as usual, maintains that the law sanctions his client's opinion!

No: our laws do not recognize woman's right to a political vote … but they could, they should recognize it.

I read many pages in favour and against the female vote, and, of course, even the speeches recently delivered at the Chamber of Deputies, where, miraculously the extreme right of Luigi Luzzatti agreed with the extreme left of the honourable Mirabelli,[16] in an act of courteous chivalry towards

15 ["*De cette absurde injustice / Faut-il dire le pourquoi? / Les plus forts ont fait la loi!*" These lines, from Act 5, scene ix of Beaumarchais's *Marriage of Figaro*, do not appear in the English edition of the play. We have provided our own translation.]

16 [Luigi Luzzatti (1841–1927) served as prime minister of Italy between 1910 and 1911. Ernesto Mirabelli (1850–1924) was a professional soldier and undersecretary of the Italian minister of war; he served as a deputy from 1911 to 1919.]

the ladies. But I confess I have not found anything better, in terms of neither logic nor clarity, than the arguments that Condorcet developed no less than 120 years ago in the *Journal de la société de 1789.*

For men, the right to vote and to be elected is based on their character as intelligent and free creatures.

Are women not also such creatures?

Men's only limits to that right are the condemnation to an afflictive penalty, defamation, and mental disability.

Well, did all women perhaps have to settle accounts with justice, or does article 240 of the Civil Code not state that every individual of either sex comes of age at 21?

Will anybody, perhaps, argue about woman's alleged mental inferiority? It is absurd, because—even if such inferiority existed—are less intelligent men deprived of the right to vote? The lowest employee at the lowest administrative ranks has the same political rights as Guglielmo Marconi!

Will anybody argue about woman's physical weakness? If this objection mattered, one would need to submit voters to a jury of doctors, and since the electoral medical examination has not been instituted yet, and neurasthenics, epileptics, and alcoholics can vote, it seems to me that—as far as health is concerned—also women could vote.

The main objection—everybody knows and feels it—consists in observing that by opening political life to women, they are distracted from the family.

But do manual and commercial professions not also distract them from the family, much more than the hypothetical participation in political life? Is it not our hasty and feverish life that throws maidens, wives, and mothers into workshops, warehouses, and administrative offices? Is it not the terrible spike of economic struggle, is it not the anxiety of earning, is it not the inevitability of the great industry that removes the female worker from her hearth, from her child, from her duties as mother and wife, to segregate her all day where the monster of civilization needs her work?

We may as well protest against this immense and harsh necessity, but we should not accuse the political vote of producing damage that capitalism, the machine, the creation of big factories, have already produced. The small white ballot is not what would remove woman from home and family. The big industry and the black workshop already did that.

In order to vote,—or to learn how she must vote with conscience and liberty—should perhaps a woman use those eight or ten hours of work per day, which today she subtracts from her family ... without the antifeminists' protest? Or is it, perhaps, that the antifeminists do not worry about the woman who must earn her living with her own work—which is the large majority—and they only have in mind the wealthy woman, practising a comfortable armchair sociology, just as Paul Bourget is the psychologist of millionaires, who only studies human souls with an annuity of at least 100,000 liras?

Therefore, I confess, I do not see a single argument that can, in theory, validly oppose women's right to vote.

As for practice, that is, its immediate realization—regardless of those who fear a reactionary revival from women's vote—it is women themselves who demonstrate they do not feel any imperious need. In Austria, women of high nobility have had, for more than thirty years, the right to vote, but they exercise it rarely. In France and in Belgium, more evolved countries than ours, this daring reform has yet to be attempted. In Italy, it would be enough to acknowledge the indifference with which most of the female public has followed the recent parliamentary debate—which actually was more a rhetorical exercise than the eloquent expression of a sincere sentiment—to be convinced that the enthusiasm of a few is not followed by everyone's full and warm consensus. It would be enough, above all, to take a look at the frightening statistics of illiterate women—50% of Italian wives cannot even sign their own name on the marriage certificate!!—in order to understand that too many other things among us are more urgent for the true emancipation of woman!

* * *

Therefore, the tactic of a fruitful feminism should be to proclaim all rights, to avoid submitting to the authority of any of them, albeit remote and noble, and to pursue more needed and useful conquests with tenacity. Woman may as well be expected to be equal to man, but she must be elevated through the education and instruction for which she has longed.

Indeed, more than the woman voter, more than the woman politician, it is urgent today to vindicate woman in the simplicity of her sacred function, namely, the loving woman.

I do not believe in spurious feminism, which wants to declare war on man under the guise of a battle of the sexes, it wants to masculinize woman, it wants to convince us that she can live without man. All this is against nature, against beauty, against love!

I believe in a feminism that exalts woman, that opens all paths to her in such a way that her mind can expand as far as where her eye has never arrived, while keeping all of her feminine attractions intact.

It is precisely when woman is really woman, and not a hybrid champion of the third sex, that she can create masterpieces. The women who wrote books that withstand the test of time are not the women who killed their sex in themselves in order to measure up better in the brutal competition with the male, but they are the women who loved. If there is feminine poetry that moves, it is that which expresses passion; if there is a woman's work of art that imposes itself, it is that which was inflamed by love. Guizot said that one day, while researching with Macaulay what was the female literary work closest to perfection, they agreed that it was Madame de Sévigné's letters, and both attributed the superiority of that masterpiece to the fact that it was the work of a mother.

Therefore not a feminism that extinguishes what is purest and most sacred in woman. Not a feminism that divides and hates, but a feminism that equalizes and strengthens the spiritual ties between man and woman.

Let us grant woman all the rights to which she is entitled—she will determine whether or not to exercise them. But, above all, let us grant her that free and bold education she lacks, which is necessary for her to understand that she must not be our competitor, but our ally, and that her improvement means doubling the intellectual forces of humankind, and hence the probability of a happy life.

As man and woman are physiologically necessary to create life, so the accordance between them—by now equal in culture, in dignity, in rights—is necessary to create progress.

This is the truth, and this, I believe, is even poetry!

One of the most illustrious Italian feminists, Anna Maria Mozzoni,[17] exclaims: "poor rebels we are, who love our enemies!" The best conclusion to our problem resides in these words, since, if it is true that a man is not moved to act other than by the desire to offer all that he conquers—fame, honours, wealth—to the woman he loves, even feminism cannot and must not be but the vindication of a woman's personality, so that she can most nobly offer it to he whom she has freely chosen.

---

17 [Anna Maria Mozzoni (1837–1920) is considered the initiator of the Italian woman's movement, and a leading advocate of universal suffrage in Italy. She translated John Stuart Mills's *The Subjection of Women* in 1879. See also the introduction to this volume, xxxviii.]

## "The Education of Woman"

We must bring up the girl with the constant thought that one day she will be the man's companion.

—Mme De Staël[18]

It is said that one day, when Legouvé[19] was asked at what stage in his children's lives he began their education, he answered: "*Before they were born.*"

Unfortunately, few fathers could respond with such philosophical depth and provident affection as Ernest Legouvé; and, of course, no government has ever wanted to push the education of its citizens so far back.

Governments, in general, do not think about education, but only about instruction, and not always successfully and completely about the latter, either.

If statistics was defined as a kind of scientific bromide, since with its cold shower of figures it calms the excited nerves of our curiosity, there is a statistics that should irritate our nerves rather than calm them, and make the flames of shame for our inferiority rise up to our face. I am referring to the statistics of illiteracy.

While in Germany there are only 2.45 illiterates out of 100, in England 3.45, and in France 3.50, we Italians break the sad record of savagery, even in comparison with Russia, since Russia has 36 illiterates out of 100, and we have 52.93.

Unfortunately, these overall statistics—if one wanted to distinguish by sex—would be much worse for woman than for man.

Indeed, taking demographic data of marriages before civil registrars as a term of comparison (if religious marriages were also consulted, it would be even worse!), we find that out of 100 bridegrooms, only 35.50 could not sign the nuptial agreement, while out of 100 brides, 47.95 could not.

---

18 [In French in Sighele's text.]

19 [Ernest Legouvé (1807–1903) was a French dramatist who supported the improvement of women's and children's education, and advocated for women's rights, topics on which he lectured extensively and published numerous volumes, such as *La Femme en France au XIXe siècle* (1864), *Messieurs les enfants* (1868), *Nos Filles et nos fils* (1877), and *Une Éducation de jeune fille* (1884).]

Therefore—and it is really painful to say so—*half of Italian wives and mothers cannot even write their own name*!

Let us imagine the culture of most of the other half! And, out of mercy for my homeland, I overlook the fact that in Germany, in France, and in England, wives who did not know how to sign the marriage act barely reach 2, 3, a maximum of 4 per cent.

In front of these realizations—which are shameful and socially dangerous, while apparently our politicians seem accustomed to considering them with Olympian indifference, like a necessary evil that a third of Italy inherited from the papacy— a naive person would be prompted to ask: "But is there or is there not a law for compulsory education in Italy?"

The law has existed for more than 30 years, because precisely from 1877 it has been a part of the collection of the Kingdom's innumerable laws and decrees, but ... who applies it?

This law of ours—which had the unique merit of preceding the analogous ones in France and England—made, among others, the very serious mistake of limiting compulsory education from six to nine years of age for financial reasons.

This period of three years was too short not only for the direct objective of education, but also for the indirect objective of social prevention at which the school should aim. All civilized countries had required a longer period, at least double: In France education is compulsory from 6 to 13 years; in Austria, in Hungary, in Germany, from 6 to 14 years; in England, from 5 to 14 years; in Switzerland, from 6 to 16 years. And a question arises spontaneously: what will happen to male and female Italian children, who at nine years old are no longer mandated to attend school? (I speak, of course, about children from the lowest social classes who, unable to afford the luxury of continuing education on their own, send their children to school—if they do!—only during the period fixed by law.) The street will evidently be schools for these children, since the father and the mother, peasant or labourer, are busy working in fields or workshops, and leave them to wander, glad to have one fewer thought or nuisance for some hours ...

Minister Orlando recognized our country's inferiority, which amounted to a social danger, hence, with the law of 8 July 1904, he extended compulsory education until the 12th year, and provided municipalities with the means to institute courses of secondary elementary education.

A very noble intention, but it remained simply ... an intention. One can say, indeed, without being excessively pessimistic, that the law of 1904 is not enforced in practice. This is because penalties for parents who break it are milder than elsewhere (a fine of 50 cents!),[20] and, furthermore, they are very rarely applied. Therefore, not only is the law on compulsory education not observed, but it is also completely useless, since in Italy school is attended only ... by those who go to school spontaneously.

In England and in the United States, thanks to a better educated population and to the inflexible Anglo-Saxon rigour with which the contraveners to the law are punished, there is no appreciable difference between the number of pupils who should attend school and the number of those who effectively attend it. By contrast, unfortunately for us, *one-third* of Italian pupils who should attend school abandon it.[21] Mind you, we are talking about a million, *a million* girls and boys who should attend school and do not. And our nature is so apathetic that no one demands an explanation for this neglect, which constitutes a crime. No one asks who is guilty if the law on compulsory education is not enforced. No one thinks that a million children in the street between the ages of six and twelve means a very serious, future social danger, it means illiteracy, with its fatal consequences: vagrancy and delinquency!

And while, inside and outside of parliament, it is easy to find those who fiercely protest against every irregularity and against every abuse—as long as they are, of course, committed by political opponents, because when they are committed by coreligionists, even crimes are excused,—it is very difficult to find people who feel the need and duty to rise from the stagnant swamp of political gossip and petty parliamentary scandals, to face the real problems affecting the life of the nation, and to demand that the function of schools—where the population's best energy and future health resides—be not abandoned to the ignorance of the majority and to the indolence of the government!

Pardon me if, to close this argument, I still insist on figures: they will be the last ones.

The number of pupils, for both sexes, reaches around 20 per cent of the total population in all civilized nations: it is 20.70 in Switzerland, 20.38 in the United States, 20.00 in Bavaria and Saxony. For us it is only 7.89 per cent. Advanced sociology is not necessary to recognize this axiomatic truth: that the maximum percentage of the number of pupils is

---

20 [Cent [centesimo] here refers to one-hundredth of a lira, the Italian currency from 1861 to 2002.]

21 In France, 4 out of 5 children attend compulsory school. And this is considered a poor result. What should we say?—See G.L. Duprat, *La Criminalité dans l'adolescence* (Paris: Alcan, 1909), 220.

the tangible index of the highest level of civilization, in other words, of the countries where material well-being is greater, industry is more widespread, and the number of crimes is lower.

There are many excuses or justifications that attempt to explain our inferiority. But, overlooking secondary ones, the principal causes of this painful phenomenon can be reduced to two, one being social and the other strictly economic.

The social and, in part, racial cause—which hopefully can weaken with time, while today it is still very strong especially in southern Italy—consists of the fact that Italian parents do not understand the usefulness of school for their children. They prefer to exploit them with work and mendicity even at an early age, or allow them to idle in the middle of the street ...

Vice is in the blood, and laws can do very little! In Belgium, for example, compulsory education does not exist; and yet, schools have high attendance there. Another race and, let's say it, another level of civilization!

Since, as I said, authorities in Italy do not bother to fine parents who do not send their children to school, this bad example spreads and the sore turns to gangrene.

Therefore, at the bottom, we find incredulity towards the advantages of education; at the top, indolence in repressing violations. These are the obstacles between which the problem of school is caught in our country.

But the main obstacle is economic, the financial difficulty. It is well known that, in many municipalities, schools are in such a deplorable state that it almost justifies those who do not attend them.

We are constantly being told that there is no money for the Minister of Public Education, whose budget is notoriously the Cinderella of Italian budgets.

I believe that, just as newspapers resort to the excuse of the tyranny of space in order to justify the non-publication of what they do not want to publish, so governments hide behind the excuse of financial tyranny in order to never spend money where they do not want to spend it.

We are still victims of the prejudice that for the greatness of our homeland it is necessary to create rifles and cannons rather than heads and men, and we forget that the victories of the German army are attributable to the culture of their soldiers. For this reason Germany, which knows how to prepare its victories from afar, does not skimp on money for public education; for this, the Kingdom of Prussia alone spends 356 million a year just on public education, and even the most conservative German press claims it is too little, while we are happy, instead, with a public education budget of around 100 million, of which the state pays less than half and the rest is paid for by municipalities!

I do not want—nor would I know how—to discuss whether today in Italy genuinely committed politicians could persuade the government to do more for public education than we currently do; but I know for sure that the great reform that the nation is waiting for is the increase in material resources for school.

This increase is all the more urgent insofar as—beyond and together with the males—a female army advances, which was once not only absolutely excluded from secondary schools and, heaven forbid!, from universities, but also excluded, if not in an absolute way, at least on the basis of custom and habit, from primary school.

In the past, no right to education was recognized for women. Women were not only juridically but also intellectually subjected, and men wanted to leave them in the most blissful ignorance.

"A woman always knows enough," Molière says,

> when the ability of her mind enables her
> to distinguish a doublet from a pair of breeches.[22]

In a letter to a friend, Goethe writes that the education of women has to limit itself to the most elementary notions, and advises to trust the care of the kitchen and of the garden to girls, and make those who preferred to sit do needlework.

Is the citation perhaps a bit too antiquated?

Elizabeth of Austria confesses to her loyal and maybe only friend Dr. Christomanos:[23] "The less women learn, the more worth they have, since they extract all their science from their *I*. The rest does nothing but denaturalize them: they unlearn a part of themselves and imperfectly appropriate a bit of grammar or of logic."

---

22 [In French in Sighele's text. From Molière's *Les Femmes savantes* [*The Learned Women*] II, vii, ll. 575–78.]

23 [Princess Elisabeth of Austria (1837–1898), also known as "Sissi," was the wife of Emperor Franz Joseph I. Uneasy in Habsburg court life, she developed a very close friendship with her much younger Greek tutor Konstantinos Christomanos (1867–1911). A scandal erupted when pages from Christomanos's diary were published in a newspaper, disclosing his attraction to her.]

This aversion to culture may be surprising in the mouth of a very cultivated empress, who perhaps uttered those words on a day of sadness or irony; but that was the mood until about thirty years ago. Until that epoch, indeed, only a small minority of girls attended primary schools. And, after all, does each of us not have painful documents of what female education was during the previous generation? Do we not find today a great majority of illiterates in the elderly women of inferior classes, and do we not find also in the women of wealthy classes, especially of certain provinces, a culture so low as to allow every sort of superstition to germinate?

The concept of educating woman—not for simple embellishment as in certain convents and certain boarding schools about which we will speak very shortly—in order to improve her intellectually and morally, is hence relatively new. Likewise, it is a recent fact that woman dares to leave the family in order to receive an education, and mingles with boys in public schools.

Only a few years ago, the number of male pupils in primary schools was much greater than for girls; now they tend to be equal, and in some states, for example, in France and in Bavaria, females outnumber males.

In our country—and the phenomenon is reassuring—the number of girls who attend elementary schools is gradually and regularly growing, and since the latest statistics from a couple of years ago showed a minimal difference between the two sexes, it is probable that now the army of little female pupils has numerically matched the male army.[24]

There is another observation to make (after having highlighted the bad, it is also beneficial for us Italians to call attention to the good of our country), and it is that Italy can be considered the most progressive of Latin countries regarding the co-educational system of pupils of the two sexes, the so-called *scuola mista* [mixed school], which is universally adopted in the United States but still partially or totally rejected in the European countries. I believe in the intellectual and moral efficacy of the mixed school, since it promotes more liveliness and colour, and greater inspiration to work; and, as an expert educator has said, "[I]t eliminates hysteria and restores the ozone of natural life to an atmosphere that was rendered deleterious by ancient monastic customs."

24 [Here Sighele adds a table with numbers of male and female children enrolled in elementary schools for the year 1901–02, distinguishing between day and evening schools, public and private, weekend and autumn schools. See *Eva moderna* (Milan: Treves, 1910), 172.]

A sad habit has lasted until now—and strangely still prevails in the very daring France—namely, the desire to keep girls and boys distinct and well separated in the first years of life, when the sex does not yet speak, and then to allow them together in social life, precisely when the dominating sentiment in both is love! If they are accustomed to interact with one another since childhood, males and females acquire that frank, free, and fraternal *camaraderie* without ulterior motives, which, if it may frighten timorous souls, is certainly more loyal and healthier than those wise, Jesuit reluctances that sometimes condense all the modesty of certain girls.

The co-educational school in Italy was not an act of will: it was the public's unconscious victory over the government. It arose almost by surprise, inadvertently. It began, in some cities where female institutes did not exist, when some father was granted the favour of his daughter's admission to a *ginnasio*[25] or a vocational school; and the bold initiative, initially criticized and opposed like all initiatives, was gradually imitated. Men are rebels on principle, but then, and fortunately in this case, they revert to sheep.

Today, according to the most recent statistics, beyond the 20,000 female pupils of teacher's training schools, we have more than 9,000 girls in technical schools and more than 500 in technical institutes, more than 2,000 in *ginnasi* and more than 400 in *licei*. And every year we see a constant increase.[26]

Progress was slower in universities. No woman graduated in Italy before 1877. In that year, and in the following three, there was one female graduate per year. The number remained very low until 1893 when there were 15, and then it went up to 52 in 1900.[27]

---

25 [According to the so-called Legge Casati, which in 1859 modified the Italian secondary school, two tracks were available at the end of primary school: either the *ginnasio* (five-year preparatory course of study leading to three years of *liceo*) or the *scuola tecnica* (a three-year vocational school leading to three years of *istituto tecnico*).]

26 [Here Sighele provides a table with the number of girls enrolled in normal, secondary, classical, and technical schools, both public and officially recognized schools. And he adds the following comment:] I owe these data to Commendatore De Negri, general director of statistics, who wanted to compile them for me on the official bulletins of the Ministry of Public Education. [See *Eva moderna*, 174.]

27 It was impossible for me to track down the exact number of female graduates after 1900. The figures of female students in 1905–06 were as follows: [table with number of female students enrolled in the universities, single university courses, and other higher education institutions for that academic year. Not reproduced in this volume.].

Given this momentum, it is easy to foresee that the increase will continue in always greater proportions. We will not catch up with, or even get close to the United States, where the number of female pupils attending secondary courses (or rather, our *ginnasi* and *licei*) is greater than that of male pupils, where in 1900, in addition to 130,000 boys who said they studied Latin, there were 190,000 girls who studied it, and where, beyond co-educational universities, there are 13 university colleges intended solely for women, counting 5,100 students. Yet, undoubtedly, we will also follow the great main road that allows woman to obtain the strong educational background that can render her not only equal to man but, what matters most, independent from him.

Tocqueville, writing when the conditions of American women had not yet attained the present level, was already struck by the progress of the feminist movement in America, and avowed: "If you ask me to what I attribute the singular prosperity and the evermore growing force of the American population, I will reply that the cause is the intellectual superiority of its women."

Will we also deserve, in a more or less distant time, a similar praise by another great historian of the future?

Before responding to this question, one must posit another. We must ask ourselves: why do these female students study? Why do these intellectual sisters come with us to fight that great battle of science against the unknown, or of art for beauty? Why do we find them in our steps, as kind and feared competitors who give us the smile of their company, but who often steal from us the palm of triumph?

They may come among us because the love of learning pushes them, perhaps without economic needs.

Today, woman, too, like man, feels the desire for her own individual expression. She feels the need to affirm herself by herself, with her own work, with her own brain, to become independent. I would say that she craves a *human* life in the widest Latin sense of the word, and she does not want to remain enclosed any longer in the simple *sexual* life, where history has confined her until now. She wants the world for herself, and not solely the family.

Is it good? Is it bad? It does not matter. It is inevitable!

Woman had always lived in a kind of economic parasitism. Her only hope and her only career was marriage. The maiden's psychological state was waiting; and this condition of having to wait for a husband was nothing but a form of mute mendicity for her. Therefore, if she did not get married, and the cloister did not host her deluded virginal hopes, she would remain in the social environment like a dry branch amid the glory of the green blooming forest, like an organ that failed in its function, like a useless burden on her own family.

And already many years back, Holtzendorff[28] had sensed the social seriousness of this unjust condition, and, with the cold calm of a German jurist, he brutally posited the problem in the following terms: either polygamy, or offer women excluded from marriage other means of honest and lucrative placement.

When Holtzendorff was writing, there were more than two million unmarried women over the age of 25 in Germany,—"*a living indictment*"—he says—"*of the carefree egoism of men.*"

How many will there be today, and not only in Germany, of those honest girls who, not wanting and not being able to get married, have nonetheless the right to an existence different than the demeaning, useless, and parasitic life of the old maid?

There must certainly be more, since in our epoch, when all is reduced to the common denominator of money, and the needs of every class have grown out of proportion, man cannot get married as easily as before. There is a crisis of marriage—smaller among us than elsewhere, but not negligible—caused by the fact that to maintain a family today is an economic problem that not everyone can solve.

She who drives male activity is still and always, as was and will be in eternity, woman, and Rudyard Kipling can sing: "as long as our women must walk in streets all well-dressed, and money is needed to buy their jewelry, the whalers will run year after year across the seas, trusting to luck"—but it is the lover of a month or an hour who induces her man to these sacrifices and heroisms; generally, he does not have either these thoughts or these energies for his wife!

And since the maiden feels this psychological truth, since she is aware that the hard, economic necessity renders marriages less frequent, since in the dignified rebirth of her personality she disdains to wait like a slave for man to throw her his handkerchief, almost as if he were a sultan, she has wanted, and in part has been able, to become independent. She said: "I will study, I will work, I will be sufficient unto myself, like a man."

A new type of woman has arisen, who perhaps has not found her precise expression yet, but she undoubtedly transcends the three big

28 [Joachim Wilhelm Franz Philipp von Holtzendorff (1829–1889) was a German jurist who distinguished himself in the domains of criminal and international law.]

categories within which Alexandre Dumas has the illusion of confining all kinds of women.

Dumas says that women are *vestals*, *matrons*, or *courtesans*, that is, women of the temple, of the hearth, or of the street.[29] Well: for those who would be ashamed to be courtesans, for those who do not want to be vestals, for those who cannot become matrons, another category must also exist: the severe and arrogant category of the woman who does not exploit her sex and charms in order to please, but rather resorts to her brain and work in order to lead a respected and independent life in the world.

Nevertheless—although the phenomenon I have spoken about is serious and interesting, and represents one of the most acute cases of our social malaise—it must be recognized that it is, in a sense, an exceptional phenomenon within the greater problem of the education of women. After having observed, with Anatole France's witty words, that "science can well have, like religion, its virgins and deaconesses,"[30] after having recognized that it is right for the maiden to find her conditions of existence outside marriage, we must also say that, if it is a duty of society to facilitate them for her in every way, it is otherwise right and, I would say, society's even greater duty to commit to shaping the maiden into a wife and a future mother.

Does the education we impart today to the girls in our schools perform this high task? Is the state aware of this great duty?

Unfortunately, we must confess that, beyond the scanty compulsory schooling, female education in our country, as well as in other civilized nations, becomes a privilege that, because of its cost and of innumerable other hurdles, very few are able to enjoy. Indeed, secondary school in Italy is attended only by 1/10 of the total number of girls.

And there is another more painful aspect. The state—I still believe because of its terrible financial tyranny—was unable to gain the trust of families, a vast majority of whom abandons public schools and institutes to send their daughters to private institutions.

In 1898, the number of girls in Italy who attended the state schools was 21,335, and the girls who completed their education in monasteries numbered, instead, 95,404!!! In other words, more than three-quarters of Italian girls are educated by nuns!

29 [Sighele is here referring to Alexandre Dumas (Fils), whose classification of women appears in his *L'Homme-femme* (1872). See *Man-Woman: Or, The Temple, the Hearth, the Street*, translated by George Vandenhoff (Philadelphia, 1873), 20.]

30 [In French in Sighele's text.]

Far be it from me the idea of engaging in a discussion of principles regarding these figures. I respect all faiths and opinions and, precisely because I unswervingly but serenely support my own, I do not react to others' opinions with those verbal furies or those Jacobin despotisms that are mistaken for manifestations of energy, but that, in fact, are sometimes only convulsions of uncertain souls hoping to drown their tormenting doubts in violence.

But allow me to deplore that the state leaves the education of woman, with such indifference, to those who, even without irremediably spoiling her ideas, certainly cannot instil in her that sentiment of Italianness and of modernity that we also want to teach to the males in public schools.

Perhaps this is wherein lies the germ of that dissonance of convictions and tendencies between the two sexes that prevents them from having common and concordant ideas. And perhaps the more useful educational work would, indeed, consist in eliminating this dissonance, in re-establishing the unison between man and woman, who now, unfortunately, feel, think, and thus act in a contradictory way!

If, however, I leave aside this difficult problem, and I limit myself to speaking about female education as it is now, I believe we can raise two opposite objections that, according to the circumstances, will be recognized as real.

In female institutes, pupils are made to study either too much or too little. We find either an excess of serious study that kills happiness and health, or certain frivolous studies mainly for embellishment and for ... attracting a husband, a frivolity that corrupts a girl's character and diminishes her sense of dignity. Some institutes teach, above all, what is needed to make an impression, to allure, to conquer. They offer, I daresay, a sprinkling of superficial culture, so that the ephemeral fragrance of this culture can deceive whoever approaches it. They do not teach anything of what truly nurtures the brain, of what strengthens conscience, of what prepares for life. These institutions produce those dolls that sing and play music, who coquet and flirt in three or four languages, and whom society welcomes with a smile as the models of a perfect education, without ever wondering if these constructions could not be more accurate or at least more solid!

These dolls traverse life doing more bad than good, often being very harmful with the calmest irresponsibility, because they only love themselves and they believe that the world was created solely so they can have fun ... "Delightful and terrible little beings"—so De Ryons defines them in *L'Ami des femmes* [The Friend of Women]—for whom we ruin ourselves, we dishonour ourselves and we kill ourselves, and whose only preoccupation—in the middle of this universal carnage—is to dress sometimes like umbrellas and sometimes like bells!" [31]

What a contrast between the ambiguous figure of these perfidiously light women, and the profile of the serious girl who devotes all her youthful, sincere enthusiasm to studies, and who wants to draw from them not a battery of seduction techniques to hook into a husband, but an intellectual patrimony only useful to her!

And yet, just as there is exaggeration in evil, there is also exaggeration in good!

Not many girls, but also devoted fathers, and even mothers, today, are increasingly influenced by the belief that the more one studies, hunched over school benches with their noses in books and dictionaries, the better it is.

The abuses and excesses of the school—it is not I who says it, but Senator Angelo Mosso[32]—are like fatal ivy that now clings even to the organism of woman, and saddens her existence by drying up the springs of its life. We make girls learn how to extract cube roots, and we deny them a courtyard where they can run and get some fresh air, stretch their legs, and longer feel their schoolmates' elbows in their side! It is the prejudice of pedantic and anti-hygienic intellectualism that violates the laws of health! It is rebellion against ignorance that, although originally absolutely right, reaches up to exaggerated and illogical consequences!

We must re-establish equilibrium between the development of the brain and that of other human faculties. For moral education, we must adopt the harmonic concept that the Greeks had for physical beauty. Unlike ours, ancient art did not worry only about the breadth of the pensive forehead, the ironic fold of the lip, the contraction of the irritated eyebrow. In their time, the expression of beauty would emanate from all the limbs, not only from the head, unlike today, and the entire

31 [De Ryons is the protagonist in the Alexandre Dumas comedy, *L'Ami des femmes* (Paris: Cadot, 1864): "... ces charmants et terribles petits êtres pour lesquels on se ruine, on se déshonore et on se tue, et dont l'unique préoccupation, au milieu de ce carnage universel, est de s'habiller tantôt comme des parapluies, tantôt comme des sonnettes" (19).]

32 [Angelo Mosso (1846–1910) was an Italian physiologist famous for his studies on pulse variations and blood circulation in different emotional and mental states. He is credited with the first conceptualization of neuroimaging techniques. He became president of the Italian Gymnastics Society in Turin, the oldest in the nation, and, as a senator, he committed to the improvement of physical education facilities in Italian schools.]

human person would speak to the imagination of the artist and of the population.

Well: we must apply this artistic criterion also to social life. We must develop all the limbs and faculties of the individual, not only the brain, because progress is not the unique and monstrous fruit of that rare plant of intelligence, but, rather, the beneficial harvest that mankind reaps when physical and moral health join intellectual health.

This thought, this preoccupation for physical health should be dominant in the question of women's education, above all because physical hygiene is also moral hygiene. Wherever, as in England, in the great parks adjacent to schools, girls alternate their hours of study with hours of play, they feel this pure air that envelopes their body even hovers around their soul, and, as their organism becomes stronger, so their discourses become purer and healthier. Silly gossip does not take root, nor do indecent allusions, which instead, blossom like moss in the humid shade of schools where girls sit still for long hours.

This is the reason why, especially abroad, a movement is gaining ground that would want to move schools and institutes of education outside of the smoky and loud cities, to the green and calm environment of the countryside. Likewise, beyond teacher's training schools, *ginnasi*, and all-female high schools, we should also develop those *female agricultural schools* that the most ingenious Italian poetess advocated about three years ago.

Seeing that despite the overcrowded teacher's training schools,—where the number of graduating teachers will soon be greater than that of the pupils to be taught—the problem of female unemployment remains unsolved, Ada Negri[33] asks: "Why not attempt also in Italy to open a path to healthier and more serene activity in the open air for women, among the pure and simple things of the earth, supporting their natural instinct and physiological development? Why not steer towards agricultural schools all those modern, anemic girls who now impoverish their blood on the benches of urban schools?"

And the poetess was right not only because today, for woman as for man, a technical and practical education is more valuable than those learned, purely embellishing futilities that one teaches in certain schools;

33 [Ada Negri (1870–1945) was an Italian poet and writer who started her career as a schoolteacher and became the first woman admitted to the Reale Accademia d'Italia, the elitist cultural organization created by the Kingdom of Italy during the Fascist regime to celebrate the highest achieving Italian scholars, scientists, and artists. Negri's poetry emphasizes emotions and the maternal instinct.]

she was right, above all, because, to whoever sees it from afar, the problem of woman's education, coincides today with the problem of race.

If we want future generations to be physically healthier, hence morally more balanced than our generation—in which nerves are the terrible despots of our organism, and neurasthenia is, more than a morbid exception, the sad general rule—it is necessary for us to educate woman in such a way that she can transmit to her children a blood purified by the oxygen of free air and the fresh, healthy smell of the land.

Unfortunately, while our Latin initiative is fertile in works of charity, it is almost sterile in works of prevention.

We have tears and money for all the diseases and human faults. Old, sick, crazy, blind, deaf and dumb, feeble-minded, rachitic, scrofulous, tuberculous, criminal, every physical and moral sore is classified and healed in this immense hospital that is the world. Our posthumous pity is almost as great as our misery!

Yet, only quite rarely do we have the money and thoughts to prevent all those ills and pains! We do not reflect on the fact that, if we knew how to educate, many of these miseries would disappear and all of them would diminish.

They would diminish, above all, if beyond a religious education, a worldly education, and a scientific education, woman could receive a social education.

We must open her brain to the major problems that agitate man's mind in such a way that she can be not only his understanding companion, but his guiding conscience. We must also expand her sensitivity, so that she can learn—during the age when it is easy to learn good and generous things –that her destiny and her mission are not enclosed in the mediocrity of selfish well-being, but must stretch farther and higher.

Undoubtedly, woman's first need is to create happiness around herself, in her family: to create it with honesty, to maintain it with sweetness. But this duty is not enough: woman must go beyond it. She must integrate the purest ideals of socialism with facts, with her example; she must provide—not under the impulse of unconscious pity as in the past, not as a fashion or a sport like today, but as a conscious duty, almost like a specific task of femininity—that support, that material and moral comfort which, beyond the familiar horizon, acts upon the pains and injustices that do not affect us closely.

Beside a man who fights, she must be the fairy who attenuates and alleviates the inevitable consequences of struggle: she must help souls socialize in order to bring people together,—a much worthier work than socializing property in order to suppress classes.

## "For Our Children"

We wonder where the tedious classical studies that we impose on the young bourgeoisie lead: they lead to the café.

—Maurice Barrès, *Les Déracinés*[34]

There are two great categories of duties towards childhood. The first pertains to all those provisions of charity, of assistance, of prevention that we strive to multiply to the advantage of the children of *others*, of unhappy children, be they victims of crimes or the delinquents themselves, be they miserable people or vagabonds, sick or degenerate. The other category pertains to all we can and must do *for our own children*, for happy children, for those, that is, who, after being born, do not lack any of the conditions necessary for life, and who ask from us only wisdom and a patient education to face the world with health, confidence, and combativeness.

Now, of these two opposite sides, which together represent the serious problem of childhood, it seems to me that today the former is more studied than the latter, and that our greatest and best energies are consecrated to it. Arguably, we listened to the laments coming from the street, rather than to the small voices from our house; with a magnificent impetus of altruism, we felt our duties towards society, beyond and perhaps more than those towards the family.

It was right, furthermore, and it was inevitable that this would happen.

Too long was the period of contemptuous disregard towards the wretched little ones, who suffered in silence or unconsciously set forth on the sad path of degeneration. Too timid and empirical were previous charity attempts, almost all directed to hospitals and hospices, to the old and sick. Therefore, our epoch feels the need to remedy the past by devoting its fecund care above all to underprivileged childhood. Finally, too sad and serious were the statistical revelations, hence inevitably—out of pity and, perhaps, also fear—we did not try to oppose stronger dams than those already built against abandonment, vagrancy, and juvenile delinquency, which are dramatically increasing.

The statistics say that the number of abandoned children in Italy surpasses 30,000 per year, and that every year 70,000 minors go to prison,

34 [In French in Sighele's text.]

one-tenth of whom are younger than 14! And every day the news reports which crimes are committed not by but against childhood, what tortures are suffered by their souls and bodies not only in slums, but also where no one would have dared imagine, in those convents and religious shelters in which some degenerate exploits the mystical cloak of faith to cover his obscene vices against nature.

It was thus natural that societies and institutes would proliferate everywhere to remedy these evils and prevent these infamies. The urge to study, above all, what is dangerous and faulty in the problem of childhood was legitimate for writers. The desire of the wealthiest and most cultivated classes to exert their pity by alleviating pains, curing miseries, protecting and educating the children of the poor was spontaneous and beautiful.

It is a very noble example of due solidarity, which is not diminished by the ironic scepticism with which some judge it. A foreign female writer dared to say that our philanthropy, which was never, before now, so extended and intrusive, is incense burned at the mouth of a sewer: the perfume attenuates the miasma momentarily, but cannot destroy it. This is an unjust judgment of a just work, because even if it were true that all this philanthropy does not provide practical results—while, in fact, it does, abundantly and daily!—, it would be enough, to its credit and as proof of its utility, to spread that sense of human brotherhood that makes us feel connected to one another, and guilty of not having done our duty if we only think of ourselves rather than devote some of our time and money to whoever is unhappier than us!

However—allow me to be sincere—we should not forget that, beside this great and widespread social activity, there is also a family activity, more modest and intimate, that demands our attention. We must remember that the merit of being part of charity committees for either category of disadvantaged children does not exonerate us from the obligation to take care of own children. In short, we must recognize that the exercise of philanthropy is not and must not be a kind of *excuse card* with which one buys the right to neglect other duties, as some unfortunately believe.

There are rich people who every year give a sum in alms, and, with this act of administrative generosity, they believe they have appeased their consciences. Likewise, there are people who fervently do charitable work all year round, and with that they believe they have exhausted all obligation, and have almost acquired the right to not worry about surrounds them more closely, above all their children, who feel the nostalgia for these too busy and distant parents. Let us distrust these illogical forms of altruism that are too dispersed and not concentrated enough, and let's claim loudly and strongly that only when we have worthily taken care of our children, can we consider ourselves worthy of praise by also taking care of the children of others.

It is a mistake to separate these two duties, almost removing humanity from the family, because only those who know how to love the few a great deal truly know how to love the very many a little.

This is the reason why I prefer to narrow down my topic to modest boundaries, and to limit my research to our obligations towards the childhood that grows out of us and with us. Therefore, leaving the main road of social duties, by now too beaten, I will try to explore the lesser known paths of our simplest family duties towards children.

It has been a rather long time since Herbert Spencer, in his book on education, described with the somewhat heavy but profound humour of his race, the country gentlemen and provincial officers, all busy after lunch discussing the breeding of chickens, the art of fattening and strengthening an ox, the transformation of a horse into a good trotter, and added: "none of them thought or spoke about the art of helping a child attain the maximum of his vigor and moral energy."[35]

Thenceforth, much has been thought and said about this art of *human breeding*. Actually, mankind seems to have not only listened to Spencer's reproach, but also appropriated, at least in words, Emerson's rather crude and vulgar claim that the first condition of man's success in the world is to be a good animal. The old sentimental and poetic prejudice that used to make us scorn health and instilled in girls the desire to be pale, "like a beautiful autumn evening," is by now far and forgotten amid the fogs of romanticism. Today we are convinced—perhaps because we see increasingly weaker and more nervous generations rise around us—that physical health is the basis for every education. We are so convinced of this that the doctor has become in our families and societies what the priest was in the families and societies of earlier times: a kind of spiritual director who, if he does not judge our thoughts and actions, does set, however, the timetable of our life and dictates its hygienic norms.

Now, I do not know whether there is perhaps a bit of exaggeration in this dictatorship of doctors, and we are not all somewhat victims of the professional mania that wants to substitute, as Bourget wittily says, "*the*

35 [Sighele is alluding to Herbert Spencer's 1860 volume *Education: Intellectual, Moral and Physical*, which supports self-development and the creative aspect of instruction.]

*box of pills for the page of the Gospel.*"[36] I do not know, either, whether the Anglo-American passion for every form of gymnastics and sport (which has invaded us, as well) acquires the pathological tint of fashion, and whether or not Nansen[37] was right in his criticism as he observes that "while the aim of a simple and healthy life is to make us live in nature, the aim of sport is, very selfishly, only to make us reach the goal a few seconds before our competitors." I know that all this deference to medicine should be put into practice not only and not simply for all that pertains to the aesthetic side, the physical development of children, but also and, above all, for the psychological side, their moral development.

One of our most serious flaws in education is to never remember that a child's temperament depends on his health and that most of the times a bad child is synonymous with an unhealthy child.

We know all that, in theory, because this is certainly not a new thing, and we have read it endless times. But … we almost always forget it in practice, and while we rush to call the doctor for our child's tiniest throat ache, we never or almost never call him to ask advice on the cure—which is much more important!—to correct our children's tantrums, insubordination, and obstinacy.

And yet, one should insist ad nauseam upon this great truth: the child's morale, like the man's, is so strictly tied to its organs' conditions, that only by taking care of or modifying them, a way can be found to render children better and men wiser.

Perhaps to recognize this close and inevitable link between the organism and the manifestations of the soul may appear repugnant to some, especially to mothers, because it tastes too much of materialism. They may think that, by recognizing it, one diminishes and desecrates the concept of the good and of goodness they would want to hold high. But these mothers ignore that the conquests of physiology are by now universally recognized, even by spiritualists, and that—if science has demonstrated that our thoughts and feelings, in a word, our soul, manifests itself in and, so to speak, is embodied by the materiality of our nervous system—science, nonetheless, allows everyone to let their immortal

36 [In French in Sighele's text.]

37 [Fridtjof Nansen (1861–1930) was a Norwegian scientist, explorer, diplomat, and Nobel Peace Prize winner in 1922 for his aid to displaced victims of the First World War. He led the first expedition across the Greenland cap in 1888, and reached a remarkable northern latitude in his subsequent North Pole expedition from 1893 to 1896.]

Psyche soar above the human apparatus that serves as mediator to the exterior world.[38]

Once we win this prejudice that makes us ascribe the children's flaws and bad tendencies to a specific perversity uniquely attributable to free will, that is, once we recognize that they are morally what their physical organism allows them to be, the problem of education would appear simpler, and we would become not only more skilled educators, but above all, more dispassionate and fairer judges. In other words, we would humbly welcome that great lesson of modesty that comes to us from the law of heredity.

For example, I have heard many times—and every reader can verify the truth of what I am about to say—some parents get surprised and angry at the undisciplined, disobedient, irritable character of their child, as if they were not responsible for all this small soul and body thinks and does.

Do they not perhaps know that everything the child is, he owes to his parents and ancestors? Do they not know that our sons are what we are? And do they not understand that against bad temperament, against the tendency to either betrayal or violence, anger or lies, the child cannot fight with anything other than those instructive suggestions that we ourselves will exert on him, and hence—also for this reason –we are the ones truly liable for his actions?

And yet, such reasoning of intuitive logic and elementary justice is very often forgotten. In acknowledging our children's flaws, we never think that they are mostly due to us. In correcting them, we often let ourselves be overcome by a severity and an unconscious irritation that resemble the stupid wrath with which a floriculturist might want to beat his plants and flowers because they grow poorly!

If only this severity were at least the consequence desired by a system, our brain's calm response to what seems worthy of punishment, or the fulfilment of what we believe to be a duty! But most of the time, unfortunately, it is not like this. One must have the frankness to avow that often our acts of severity towards our children are anything but calm or wise, intentional or conscious. They are—simply—the reflex of our state of transient nervousness.

Perhaps it is one of those days in which, for barometric causes or personal reasons of bad mood (and our life offers us many!), there is

38 See Maurice de Fleury, *Le Corps et l'âme de l'enfant* (Paris: Armand Colin, 1907). I am referring once and for all to this volume, and to that of Dr Toulouse, *Comment former un esprit* (Paris: Hachette, 1908), from both of which I have drawn throughout this chapter. [For Toulouse see 313n13, this chapter.]

an electric tension in the air and nervous tension in our temperaments; and then it happens that the sound of the child's games, the uproar they make, their innocent mischief—which at other times were for us reasons for pleasure and cheerfulness—annoy and tire us. We raise our irritated voice reproachfully; the children disobey; we insist, but they rebel, and this rebellion triggers our fury. Since words are not enough, more persuasive arguments are necessary; and very soon it is no longer an educator who punishes with the sole objective of correcting the child, but it is an excited nervous system that vents as it can, blindly, with yells and beatings.

Later, we realize the humiliating spectacle we have shown our children, and we feel remorse and shame. Then we try to remedy with exaggerated affection, we try to compensate the momentary lightning and thunderbolts of our fury with a shower of caresses and kisses. But the remedy is useless, because the child understands and judges us with a lucid, precocious intuition, and feels this tacit confession of our wrongdoing. The remedy is not only useless but also wrong, and has deleterious consequences, because it is precisely our oscillations of energy that disorient the children, render their desire incoherent, and does not allow them to understand when we are really right. Hence they suppose that each of our rebukes, even the most just, is nothing but the effect of our bad mood and nerves.

Therefore it happens that severity, which aspires to be the best means to hold our authority up, is often a means to deprive ourselves of authority …

Many parents are aware of this negative result, and to remedy it, or perhaps simply and selfishly to get rid of a responsibility that weighs on them and would take too much time from their days … full of many other things, they decide to lock up the child in a boarding school whenever his education presents some difficulty.

I will not be so unjust and absolute as to formulate a single judgment on all boarding schools! Some, today, are as valuable as the best of families—but unfortunately, most of them are not in Italy!—and create healthy and strong men, modernly prepared for life and its struggles, and not typically filled only with culture … But disregarding its intellectual and didactic merits, the boarding school as it once was everywhere and now generally still is in Italy, that is, the college enclosed in the city, a sort of barrack and convent—elicits moral sadness. The child, suddenly plunged into that unknown crowd, is pervaded by a sensation of cold and thinks about his mother.

Have you read *Sous le fardeau,* by Rosny[39]? Have you meditated on the eloquent pages that describe how much a delicate infantile soul can suffer in a boarding school? And do you remember Sully Prudhomme's verses that contain such a sad and just rebuke:

We see in the gloomy schools
Little children always in tears.
*Oh mothers! Absent culprits!*[40]

Mothers had better—much better –not be the *absent culprits,* if they truly want to deserve the sweet name their child calls them! Better for him and for them if they do try to personally fulfil their duty as educators! To leave their own children's first education to strangers—except in undeniably necessary cases—is family cowardice. One must overcome the obstacles if there are any, support the inevitable burdens of education, modify one's own temperament, arm oneself with that *maternal serenity* that Sofia Bisi Albini[41] so effectively describes, and understand that what we owe to our children are not harshness and punishments, above all, not the dangerous alternation between reprimands and kisses, but, rather, *calm* and *firmness,* so that they can find respite and support in us, and can harbour that respect towards us which is a *loving fear.*

Generally, instead, what education lacks is, indeed, the union and, I would say, the fusion between these two qualities: we are unable to be at the same time *calm and serene* towards children, and we only know the two opposing and exaggerated systems of too much severity or too much indulgence.

The first system, that of rough discipline, creates little, always trembling beings, and mechanically shapes them in compliance with passive obedience. It is, undoubtedly, very convenient for us, but not equally useful for the children, since it extinguishes or atrophies their sense of

---

39 [Joseph Henry Rosny is a pen name for the Belgian brothers Joseph and Séraphin Box, who wrote numerous novels focusing on sociological problems, among them *Sous le fardeau* [Under the Burden] (1902).]

40 [Sully (René François Armand) Proudhomme (1839–1907), French essayist and poet, was the first writer who received the Nobel Prize in Literature, in 1901.]

41 [Sofia Bisi Albini (1856–1919) was an Italian writer and journalist devoted to the problems of education, with particular attention to women. She was the founder and director of the journal *Rivista per le signorine,* and authored numerous children's stories. See also xliin24 in the introduction to this volume].

initiative, the consciousness of their own personality, that healthy individualism without which they will do nothing worthy in the world. And many times, at the outset of life, it also produces a dangerous reaction, because in the impetus of liberation from an excessively strict discipline, the young child shifts impulsively to a life of disorder.

The second system, that of a too lenient education, all condescension and weakness, which leads the child to believe he is the family's small despot, has in itself its own evident self-condemnation. By making the child too happy by never denying him anything, it inevitably makes him an unhappy man, who will not be able to bear contradictions and overcome the obstacles that life prepares for him, for which no one in his family prepared him.

The greatest trouble for both these systems is that they do not always draw their justification—as it could appear– from the concept the parents formed about the way they educate their children, but rather from their unconscious egoism. In other words, it is not a meditated intellectual judgment that leads us to follow either the system of severity or that of indulgence, but simply our personal advantage. If we keep our children under a rigid discipline, it is mainly because we would be bothered by always having them in our rooms, where we want to be free and independent at all times. If, on the contrary, we blend them into our lives, keeping them too often with us and among us, and satisfying them in every way, it is because most of the time our affection degenerates into morbid sentimentality and cannot achieve what duty would dictate.

In a word, what we do for our children has the appearance, nay I would say, the etiquette of being done for their well-being. In fact, however, it is often done for our own convenience, to automatically follow the not-always-reasonable impulses that our instinct suggests.

And even when we truly, profoundly, love our children, we love them—without realizing it—more for ourselves than for them. Indeed, our way of understanding their happiness is so inevitably selfish that we do not accept to see them happy without us.

In our affection towards them, we sometimes know how to touch the highest summits of altruism, but normally we are incapable of making those daily sacrifices—more humble and, therefore, more difficult—that, while contributing to the child's happiness, would detach him from us. The same mother, who is sublimely devoted to her sick child and, at his bed, does not calculate her labours and forgets herself, happily and unconsciously risking her life for him, will be unable to forget herself or risk the ephemeral pain of distance by later allowing this child to find a way in life and to construct his happiness away from her. While heroic in exceptional cases, she will not have even the tiniest courage to forget herself in normal cases.

Desmolins[42] said very well that one of the greatest obstacles to education reforms in Latin countries is the mother's too-exclusive tenderness. And, I dare add, too illogical as well.

Some mothers, who sometimes allow their very young children to enter a boarding school without much pain—as long as it is nearby!—then refuse to let them leave when they grow up, precisely when they would need truly to shake off the sentimental power of their house and learn, by travelling, how to form their character and gain a position.

We have inverted—if I can say so, and with the due exceptions—the law of nature that wants the child near the parents in his first years, and free afterwards. And while, in certain cases, the idea of abandoning our child's first education to others, to strangers, does not repulse us too much, once this child becomes a youth and an adult, we want him to spend his life always next to us.

This inversion is due to our egoism, to our Latin sentimentality, which is quite far from understanding and even partially adopting the broad vision of English education, where children, at a certain age, leave the family nest, almost like birds apparently ungrateful for forgetting it, only to return to it later, proud of a worthily lived youth, pleased to have given to the country, in distant countries, that treasure of energy that makes it great in the world.

Now, it would be evidently absurd to claim that the Latin family is, like the Anglo-Saxon family, ready to truncate its very sensible nerves, and only cares that their own children find wealth far from their own home. Our race, our social and economic constitution would oppose it. I, too, recognize that in our way of conceiving life there is a perfume of poetry and gentleness that compensates, perhaps in part, for the material advantages of English insensitivity.

42 [Edmond Desmolins (1852–1907) was a French pedagogue and director of the journal *La Science sociale*. After travelling to England to visit non-conventional schools, he published *À quoi tient la supériorité des Anglo-Saxons?* [What Accounts for the Superiority of the Anglo-Saxons?] (1897) and founded the École des Roches (1899), a boarding school located in Normandy that, drawing inspiration from British models, adopted the innovative method of active pedagogy, replacing regular courses with scientific and artistic activities from which students could draw the notions and principles needed for their education.]

Yet, if not everything, we could learn at least something from foreigners—this above all: to let our children's tendencies to manifest themselves; to let their initiatives take place; to let their originality expand. We should learn to direct their nature, rather than, as we all too often do, struggle to correct and stifle it in order to follow the aprioristic concept that we have made of their career and future.

Unfortunately, this is not so.

If we look at our systems of education and instruction, we realize that their characteristic is desolate uniformity. One would say that all the boys are thrown into the same mould that produces a single type of intellectual: the office worker, the professor, the professional, stuffed with a more or less digested culture.

Years ago, a great reactionary gust came from France against this system of education, but it barely made some leaves rustle in our quiet, immobile, intellectual landscape. It did not shake the sturdy trunks or disturb the firm ancient roots. Very few felt how much sincerity there was in this gust of rebellion; believing it was attempting to attack the untouchable right that the study of Latin or Greek has in our culture, most people branded the desire to give a more practical and socially more useful education to our children as the opinion of barbarians or the vulgar preoccupation of shopkeepers.

I am sorry to say that these people did not understand anything or pretended to understand nothing. They ignored, above all, that the chief of that cursed crusade was not a barbarian or a shopkeeper spirit, but one of the most illustrious academics of France, one of the most didactically and politically orthodox writers, Jules Lemaître. Furthermore, they forgot that the crusade did not fight Latin and Greek, but only the way these languages … and many other things! are taught.

Let us put a hand on our heart and confess that we know very little Latin and almost no Greek, after studying it for five or eight years! Dr Toulouse[43] has said, and I can repeat his words verbatim: "I am 40 years old and for 30 years I have worn myself on books and on the observation of facts; but I could not, at the moment, find in any of the disciplines that I studied those responses that we require from students, and which I myself have provided to my epoch several times."

43 [Edouard Toulouse (1865–1947), French journalist and psychiatrist, was editor of the journal *Demain*, creator of the *Comité d'hygiène mentale* [Committee for Mental Hygiene], and an innovator in the domain of experimental psychology.]

Here is an observation on which those who prepare school programs, draw up exams, and believe in their efficacy should meditate.

Current instruction consists in transmitting cognitions, while its scope should be to form spirit and character. In school today, one learns everything except thinking and acting; today one forgets that the effort of every kind of education must consist not in imposing culture, but in forming attitudes. True superiority in every environment is to create, not to know; and in this respect, the tradesman who manages to give life to a company that is better adapted to the customers' needs accomplishes a creative work equal to, and perhaps more useful than that of a writer's beautiful book.

It is on these premises that we protest against the uniformity of an education that gives the illusion and not the reality of culture, that creates more fools than individuals capable of transforming the classic food that nourished them into juice and blood.

And yet, parents—and here I mean the parents of higher classes—out of vanity, habit, or indolence continue to send their children to those classical schools that are famous for automatically forming the so-called cultivated youth, as if, for the satisfaction of creating some scholar, one had the right to throw a crowd of mediocre, useless people into the world, or as if we were expected to be merely an immense people of philosophers, novelists, writers, a people of pure spirits, who lived … on literature, and for whom all other human activities and energies almost did not matter at all.[44]

How many are those who worry about developing and determining the child's natural tastes at the right time … if by chance he is not inclined to the study of Latin and Greek? How many are those who have the instinct and tact to understand his inclinations? The idea that there is in the child's soul, as there is in his face, something that distinguishes him from the others, and that would, therefore, demand a special study on our part does not even flash into most people's heads.

Actually, I correct myself. We sometimes perceive some of the so-called natural dispositions of our children. We perceive them in order to bask in our instinctive paternal or maternal pride or to vainly show them off to acquaintances and friends. But we do not go deeper into the analysis of these faculties that break the equilibrium of the infantile psyche; we

44 "Human societies no longer live on art and literature as in the past; nowadays, they live above all on science and industry"—M. Berthelot, *Science et morale*, 124. [In French in Sighele's text.]

do not wonder whether it would not, perhaps, be our duty to give them all our care, changing, if I can say so, the educational orientation of the child. We do not calculate the damage in abandoning at its source, along the thousand rivulets of distraction, a vein that could become fecund, and without remorse, without a doubt, we insist on the old, usual system: that is, we send the child to the school that seems to us the most useful for him, where, being required to study subject matters that he does not love, he will often achieve mediocre or very poor results.

Perhaps it is here that we need to look for the reason why certain schools give results of which we cannot boast too much. And when Alexandre Dumas—making, indeed, a cutting remark against the school system—wonders "*why are there many intelligent children and many idiotic adults?*" he has intuited that this curious and painful transformation occurs because the school, instead of developing the child's individual qualities, atrophies them, hence, instead of forming the man, it deforms him.

This is the great pedagogical crime of our days, a crime that not only teachers in school, but also parents in the family commit daily, and it extends not only towards young children, but also towards youth.

When the time comes to choose a profession and a career—which should be the most important moment in a youth's life because his happiness depends on it—how many fathers care about giving free rein to their children's innate inclinations, of which they were proud in the past? How many are those who realize that, in life, he who does what nature intended at creation tolerates every labour and difficulty more easily, while he who is forced into a profession that his nature refuses will eternally harbour an intimate sadness and rebellion that will embitter his work and make it very difficult for him to reach a high goal?

The majority of parents have no qualms about oppressing their own child's nature to replace it with a different one. They want to produce a lawyer or an engineer, a professor, a magistrate or a clerk, according to family tradition, the supposed economic advantage, the opportunity of the moment, without worrying at all that, in so doing, they are suffocating a brain and violating a soul. And if you dare to alert them to this error, they arm themselves with seemingly victorious arguments, and they tell you it is useless to worry about the youth's individual inclinations, because true vocations make their way *all the same*, through all obstacles, and they quote Voltaire, who was a clerk in an attorney's study, and Musset, who was a bank clerk ... which, undeniably did not hinder their careers.

But these too logical fathers forget that the laws and methods of education are not for the exceptional individuals, who always find a way to stand out; rather, they are for the infinite number of average and normal individuals who do not have the strength to remove the leaden cloak that oppresses them, and of which they remain lifelong victims.

Here is the greatest misunderstanding that dominates the great problem of our duties towards youth.

We are all persuaded that our first duty is to give happiness to our children or, since happiness is unattainable, to direct them at least towards the path leading to it. But, generally, people believe that happiness lies in the placid security of a job, and do not understand, instead, that it is a prize that one conquers little by little with the free development of one's own energies.

We want to turn the young into precociously old and calculating people, who content themselves with a small, secure, nearby job, rather than take risks, which are the poetry of life. As a sort of reverse suggestion,[45] we inoculate in them the germs of a utilitarian pessimism, which numbs consciousness and ardour, and renders them timid in front of every obstacle, only concerned about gaining a mediocre position that can guarantee a peaceful future.

Thus we do not feel how much more beautiful and useful, more dignified and proud it would be, instead, to instil the sense of free initiative in them, and to fecundate the first and best gift of youth, which is enthusiasm; to let them free to follow their natural inclinations and to interpret the inner voice that *dictates to us*: "let us stimulate their enthusiasm, that is, the love for whatever idea they support, with a brain that calculates but with a heart that does not calculate at all, like a soldier who counts his enemies but then forgets the number while thinking of the beauty of his flag ..."

Such I think should be the ideal of education, and it is, perhaps, recognized as such by everyone in the intimacy of the soul. But far fewer dare to apply it. Why?

Because one of the strangest and most contradictory phenomena of our psychology is that, while we are modernly audacious in thought, and we endorse the boldest ideas raised by books and recent studies, we are still fearful in action. While our brain lucidly sees the new path we must take, our will cannot be independent enough to suddenly abandon the

45 [Here Sighele is applying his theory of suggestion in a context where the effects are opposite to the exaltation produced by the crowd. The consequence of collective influence, in this case, is the torpor of conscience, hence a weakening of reactions, rather than their exponential increase.]

old path, to which we are tied by a thick network of traditions and prejudices. In this way, that omnipresent eternal disagreement between theory and practice, which is a consequence of the fact that man acts as he feels and not as he thinks, has repercussions even on the problem of education.

One day I was attending a conference on the *New Education* by one of our illustrious female writers. There were great crowds of ladies in the room and huge applauses. While exiting, I overheard this dialogue between two mothers: "Those things are so true"—said the one—"but how can one put them into practice?" "Right"—replied the other—"I certainly would not want to be the first!"

So it is. We have a sacred horror of isolated actions, and not one of us wants to be the first to apply certain principles, to experiment with certain methods and ideas on our own children. In the case of any act of our life, we never ask whether it is good to accomplish it: we always only ask whether it is generally permitted to do so. And for fear of being the first, for the terror of taking an initiative that could be criticized, we continue with the old *routine.*

We need to destroy this antithesis between theory and practice; one would need to have the courage to make this effort to be able to reconnect ideas with facts and to render our actions logically worthy of our thoughts.

Lemaître says: "It is enough that the privileged classes begin, the others will inevitably follow."

I believe it, too, and therefore I wanted to repeat here what too many others, and much better than I, have said.

## "The Soul of the Child"

When we pronounce the noun *childhood,* it wakens in our memory a stack of recollections that have the charm of a novel.

It is our youth that is revived, as in a dream; it is our experience that sees and recounts it, mixing the poetry of reality with the attraction of distance, deforming episodes that time magnifies in our consciousness, as space enlarges in our eyes—through the branches of the trees—the profile of the stars that rise ...

This alteration of the truth is so spontaneous, so unconscious, that not only do we believe in all that our fantasy recalls, which sometimes tinges the first period of life with too much pink and sometimes with too much black, but we also dare to explain and judge all the complicated mechanism of our own small, childhood soul with our superb adult psychology.

Perhaps the least true pages in certain writers' autobiographies are those that recall their childhood—pages that effuse a comfort or a regret, the far away echo of innocent joys or incomprehensible pains, but in which, while the description of an epoch or a milieu is often admirable, the moral figure of the protagonist is almost never exact, precise, or sincere.

Even if it were, we would have the psychology of *a* child, thus not the psychology of *the* child.

To attempt this, one must hence keep away from the superior and exceptional beings who often also want to present their childhood on the stage of glory;[46] one must not place too much importance on one's own memories, which are overly subjective, and one must, instead, multiply the serene and dispassionate observations around us, among the families surrounding us, as well as among the anonymous crowds of the street and the school ... Only in this manner—with a minute and diffuse analysis—was it possible for modern science to extract at least some secrets from that eternal sphinx that is the soul of the child.

Rereading—as I had and wanted to do—a good portion of what has been written about childhood, I am convinced that, until some years ago, child psychology could be summarized by two diametrically opposed and equally absolute opinions.

On the one hand, there were the detractors for their own sake, who defined children as all selfish, rebels, liars, and cruel; on the other hand, there were the eulogists who, nonetheless, defined them as symbols of perfection, angels of goodness and innocence.

Among the first ones who said the worst things about childhood, La Bruyère, a celibate, and Dupanloup,[47] a bishop, stand out. And it can be easily explained—I say it without malice—that a theologian, who had every interest in upholding the doctrine of congenital depravation, and an old bachelor to whom the children of others must have seemed like little demons, boring and tormenting, labelled them so severely.

---

46 George Sand (*Histoire de ma vie,* vols. 1, 3) confesses: "When we talk about ourselves, we end up bragging, and this happens very unintentionally."—Analogously, Renan (*Souvenirs d'enfance et de jeunesse,* Preface) writes: "What we say about ourselves is always poetry."—Rousseau even claims to have invented events: "I was already old when I wrote my *Confessions.* I would write them by heart: my memory would often fail, and I would fill the lacunae with details that I imagined." [All quotes in French in Sighele's text.]

47 [Félix Antoine Philibert Dupanloup (1802–1878) was the bishop of Orléans and a religious educator, author of works such as *L'Énfant* (1869) and *De l'Éducation* (1872).]

Among the ones, those whom I would call the courtiers of childhood, Rousseau excels, with his claim that the child is perfect out of the Creator's hands, and that only our false education deforms and ruins him. And his optimism is as explainable as the pessimism of the others. The philosopher-poet, seduced by infantile grace, and more so perhaps by his antisocial bias, has idealized an age that all poets before and after him had wrapped in the azure charm of legend.

Without discussing for now how exaggerated both these opinions are, it is first necessary to acknowledge that they start from a false point of view.

They claim to give a *moral* judgment on the child's psychological activity, which is an equivocation and an illusion. They should not ascribe to the child specific motives which he does not have. They cannot interpret his feelings, impulses, and tendencies, as we interpret ours. What is meaningful to us has no meaning for him. His conscience ignores all that constitutes the hinges of our own. He begins life without understanding it, like a plant that sprouts from the soil; and in the morning twilight of his existence, he instinctively affirms his natural energies, ignoring that later these must be judged and directed by a moral light, just as every grass and every tree rises and freely unfolds its stem and trunk at dawn, ignoring that soon the sun's rays will strike and transform them.

Let us thus leave to theologians, philosophers, and poets the platonic satisfaction of judging the soul of the child like that of an adult, and instead of embellishing childhood with illogical praises or covering it with an even more illogical contempt, let us modestly and simply try to explain the *reason* for its strange and contradictory psychology.

One of the least discussed physiological laws by now, and thus worthy to be held almost as an axiom, is that *ontogeny* reproduces *phylogeny*. These somewhat obscure words, translated into an impoverished language, mean that the individual, from the act of conception to that of birth, reproduces the phases through which the species has evolved.

Before attaining that state of relative civilization, of which the most remote history preserves details for us, men lived for thousands and thousands of years in conditions and under forms that we attempt to evoke today, reconstructing the least fantastically possible—thanks to the flashes of light that come to us from science—the long Via Crucis through which our ancestors gradually stripped off their animality in order to acquire human features and consciousness.

Well: every individual fetal development retraces in a few months this road that was laboriously travelled by the species over centuries, and the life of the embryo can be considered the summary, *at great speed* (allow me this expression), of the journey made by the world species.

From this physiological law, which Haeckel[48] splendidly illustrates, it seems to me that, by analogy, and as an almost spontaneous corollary, another law of psychological order can ensue. Just as in fetal development we reproduce our ancestors' physiology in skeletal forms and anomalies, in the first years of life we reproduce their psychology in the attitudes of our mind and will. The child, in other words, feels and acts like a primitive and a savage, and all of his incoherent, impulsive psychology that surprises and disturbs us is nothing but the resurrection, fortunately transitory, of the ancient psyche, as though to remind us—thereby humiliating us—whence we came.

If it is thus true, as is commonly affirmed, that in the child there is, potentially, a glimpse of the future man, it is equally true that there is, in fact, a glimpse of the primitive man, the summary of an entire atavistic psychology that we have by now surpassed.

This scientific observation is not only the platform on which all studies related to childhood must be based, but it is also, in a certain sense, the implicit explanation of every form of child activity. Indeed, by examining the child's feelings, thoughts, and actions, in all of them we find the echo, the memory and, I would almost say, the photograph of a distant and vanished moral world.

The most typical characteristic of the infantile soul is without a doubt the potency of its imagination. Childhood is the age of the dream, during which this world we still ignore is dressed in the most brilliant colours. It is the age when the greatest enjoyment consists in listening to fables and extraordinary tales.

Therefore, is it not perhaps during *the world's childhood* that myths and legends were formed, these histories of an infant mankind, destined to cover under a lush fantasy the paucity of human knowledge?

Imagination—in the child as in the savage—is so great that it transforms objects into conscious and sensitive beings; it infuses the breath of life into inanimate and inert things. A four-year-old child attributed a kind of soul to stones and pitied them because they had to remain always immobile in the same place. Likewise, the savage believes that the

48 [Ernst Haeckel (1834–1919) was a German biologist, naturalist, and philosopher who formulated the so-called biogenetic "law of recapitulation," according to which "ontogeny," that is, the biological development of an individual, condenses "phylogeny," that is, the evolutionary development of its species.]

rustling tree encloses a spirit, and attributes not only a body, but also a soul to the wind that screams in the night.

Who does not observe every day the adorable manifestations of sympathy that a girl lavishes on her doll, as if it were alive? She speaks to it, kisses it, dresses and undresses it, and at night she wants it next to her in bed to avoid leaving her alone and frightened in the dark!

Who does not know that children, in their games, sharpen this power of their imagination, not only lending a personality to things that do not have one, but even to the point of changing their own personality, the total illusion of metamorphosis? A five-year-old boy, who loved so much to play coalman, lived his fictitious character with such complete illusion that he demanded to be called coalman rather than his real name, and at night, in his innocent prayer, he would say to God: "*O Lord, help me to be a good coalman tomorrow!*"

I know and I foresee this: we should wonder to what extent this illusion is complete. Is the child truly a victim of his own imagination? Is he not perhaps sometimes a precocious artist who plays a role and wants to make fun of us?

The response is difficult and, as we may easily understand, an answer can only be given case by case. There are imperceptible *nuances* in these illusions, which go from the blindest of faiths to the first glimmer of incredulity springing out with a smile. There are grades, psychological nuances, according to the age and to the more or less intelligent or obtuse temperament of the child. But one thing is beyond doubt: in many children the illusion is sincere and absolute, because the imagination exerts such a despotic influence on their psyche that it is truly, as Pascal said, "the sovereign creator of errors and falsehoods."

It is in this power of child imagination that we must search for the origin of one of the most serious and dangerous characteristics of the child: lying.

It is claimed that children are born liars, and this is right, but the mechanism of their lies is not always interpreted well.

Ellen Key,[49] the author of one of the most suggestive and profound books about childhood, wittily distinguishes children's lies into *cold lies*, namely, conscious and therefore guilty ones, and *hot lies*, the expression of a momentary excitation and an ardent fantasy. Without knowing it, she popularized in this way an element of experimental psychology that Sully and Ribot had highlighted, that is, between imagination and

49 [See xlvii in the introduction to this volume.]

hallucination there is only a difference of degree, and they often touch and coincide.

Certain *hot lies*—to adhere to Ellen Key's vocabulary—in children are nothing but transitory hallucinations, totally unrelated to bad faith. When you hear a playing child declare that he is a coachman or a soldier, you can be sure that, in that very moment, he is convinced he is such, and does not lie. When a girl is suddenly asked: "who gave you such a thing?" and she replies confusedly: "my doll," quite probably she is not guilty of a true lie, but, rather, is the victim of an illusion.

Undoubtedly, from these small lies told as jokes, the child advances to *cold lies*, to lies meditated with that great cunning and subtle perfidiousness that are sometimes enclosed in his small soul. But do we not, perhaps by example, teach him to persevere and perfect his lies? We are greatly scandalized by the child's lies, but are we—his alleged models and teachers—sincere in our life and, above all, in front of him? What should he learn from us, if our speeches are always ambiguous, if our social life is a thread of clever lies, and if our most frequent and relished occupation is slander about everyone, especially our friends? An act of contrition would be more appropriate, in this respect, than an indictment!

And after all, even in those conscious lies that hurt us and surprise us the most in the child, what is the role of perversity and what that of suggestion and hallucination?

There is an entire literature—volumes and volumes by physicians and psychiatrists—on the lies and false testimonies of children; and all the authors indistinctly conclude that they are the consequence of autosuggestions.[50]

In certain cases the power of autosuggestion is such that the child begins to believe that the events he dreamed of are real, to confuse his memories, to mix reality with his fictions. And when he recounts a fact, he transfigures it: he creates a legend and believes it. The judicial annals are full of terrible errors with which the false testimonies of children have prolonged or diverted trials. It is enough for a child to be the spectator to a crime, and his imagination immediately embellishes reality with the spontaneous generation of a thousand new details. It is enough for someone to simply recount a fact before him, and the child fancies he has witnessed it, being ready to declare it and swear it.

50 [The term "autosuggestion" begins to spread after French psychologist and apothecary Émile Coué (1857–1926) developed a psychological technique relying on the influence of one's imaginative power over one's own physical and mental conditions.]

It is the strange, mysterious, and dreadful prestige of the imagination that alters the child's psyche and leads him, unbeknownst, to the frontiers of crime!

Unfortunately, however, the child approaches crime also through other means, and one can say that his psychology is often that of the criminal.

Indeed, childhood is not only organically a liar, but also organically cruel. *This age is merciless,*[51] La Fontaine writes, and perhaps few men have attained the absurd and useless cruelties of children, apparently for the mere pleasure of seeing others suffering. When a poor bird, cat, or insect unfortunately falls into their terrible little hands, children inflict the most atrocious and prolonged torments on them with an unconscious joy that really deserves the name of moral insanity. There is like a fury of destruction in them, which does not think about or calculate the sufferings it inflicts. It is like the impulsive outburst of an instinct for domination, the voluptuousness to entirely possess—at whatever price—the victim who awakened their desire. It is the atavistic return to the psychology of the savage who knows no restraint to his appetites. It is also the individual glimpse of that cruel and egotistical collective psychology of certain civilized populations that do not respect the rights of the weak, and that want to subjugate and oppress them at all costs. It is, in other words, a small imperialism.

It is the imperialism of an unconscious despot, or, better, the caricature of imperialism, that lashes out not only on people and animals, but—out of revenge—also on inanimate objects. How many times do we see a child beat the seat or the table he banged into, which injured him? This brings to mind the ridiculous vendetta of Xerxes who, irritated because a storm had prevented his army from crossing the sea, ordered his soldiers to beat the Hellespont with sticks, in retaliation.

Sometimes cruelty against things—which manifests as purposeless destruction—is determined in the child by a curiosity that becomes a kind of iconoclastic mania. It is out of curiosity that many children break their toys, like Goethe, who confessed to having thrown, as a child, all the china of the house from the window, just to see how it broke on the sidewalk, or like Ruskin, who narrates that in his childhood he would rip and snip the flowers, in absolute amazement.

But what most offends and surprises our soul in the study of the child's soul, is, on many, too many occasions, his profound insensitivity to

51 [In French in Sighele's text.]

moral pains. The child is indifferent and impassive in the face of misfortunes, of others' diseases, even of death. He is often the symbol of the most absolute egoism. He only thinks of himself and his games. In this regard, I remember a peculiar anecdote. One summer day two boys were swimming in the sea. The mother was observing them from the beach; her youngest, a six-year-old girl, was next to her. Suddenly, the boys, who had gone out too far, were no longer visible. The waves swept them away. One can imagine the mother's anxiety when she sent boats to save them. The small girl, calm and smiling, seeing that the brothers did not reappear, said: "*Don't think about them any longer, mamma! By now it's certain they have drowned: it's noon, let's go eat!*"—

I have cited this anecdote to prove the moral analgesia of children, because this comes from my personal experience, but I could tell many analogous ones!

Nevertheless, the observation I quickly made at the beginning returns here very pertinently: having verified this absence of pity, this cynical predominance of egoism in the child, can we judge him as we would judge a man? Can we apply our morals to children?

Evidently, there is a great difference between being impassive in the face of misfortune, knowing what it is and representing all the consequences to ourselves, and being indifferent because we do not understand the value of it and do not foresee the results. We project our psyches onto the infantile psyche, and we imagine that children must be instinctually aware of our pains, or that, at least, they can understand when we express them openly. Now, that is illusory, that is nothing but mental colour blindness. Our anxieties and preoccupations leave children indifferent in most cases for the simple and single reason that they go beyond children's capacity for sympathy.

For example, do we know what idea children have of death? Do they understand its meaning and terrible consequences? Do they have that sensation of irreparability that is the saddest and most distressing for us? I do not think so. In this regard an English lady, Mrs. Burnett,[52] offers us an eloquent document. She recounts her impressions of the two times death visited her house while she was a child. The first time she only had one desire: to touch the body, to know what the phrase she had heard meant: *as cold as death.* The second time, in front of the body of a

52 [Sighele does not offer any additional clue about the identity of this lady, but she might be Frances Hodgson Burnett (1849–1924), author of *The Secret Garden.*]

three-year-old girl, blonde and beautiful, she merely had a pleasurable impression offered by the poetic spectacle of the white bed all covered in flowers! And Mrs. Burnett adds: "I was not moved, I was not able to shed a tear, although earlier I imagined I would cry a lot!"

It is thus absurd, I repeat, to expect that, confronted with pain or misfortune, the child expresses emotions he does not feel because his brain does not understand them yet.

And it is absurd, for the same reason, to judge other sides of infantile psychology with our own criteria, with our severity that presupposes a consciousness.

Theft, for example, is frequent in children. Every time they can steal a sweet without being seen, they do so. But do they perhaps—in the very first years—know what *mine* and *yours* mean? Anything the child sees or touches, he cries impulsively that it is his, as the savage impulsively takes what happens to be within his reach; and to appropriate what surrounds him, what excites his desire at a given moment, is a natural tendency for the child; it is, if I may say so, *an extension of his personality*. Later, without a doubt, he comes out of this unconsciousness and learns that there are limits to his own desires and to the rights of others, which must be respected, and at that point, but only then, if he steals, can we say that he is truly a thief.

Thus, when we claim that most children are disobedient and rebellious, we affirm the truth, but we do not always interpret correctly the reason for their disobedience and rebellion. For the child, the principle of authority and its consequence, which is punishment, are things that should not exist. He does not understand love other than the way we understand it ... when we are in love, that is, under the form of caresses and kisses, of the immediate, humble, and voluntary satisfaction of each of our desires ... He does not understand that the love of those around him can be expressed, for his own good, as scolding and refusals. And the mother or father who denies him something, in his fantasy turns into cruel beings who torment him and make him unhappy. This antagonism of the infantile soul against every rule and against every authority is so strong and violent that the desire of children to grow is dictated, after all, precisely by the hope of escaping this law, this control. To become an adult, for the child, means above all, to be dispensed from the obligation to obey, to be free to do what he wants. In the meantime, before he can be free, he lets out his instinct of insubordination with those revolts that we call *capricci* [tantrums], a word with which I intend to define an impulsive act without reason, as free and unexplainable as the wind that blows.

And yet—like the wind that blows—even tantrums have their causes and conditions. And it would be good, from time to time, to study them. It would be good especially to remember that the soul of the child is not logical, reflective, conscious like ours; rather, it is a small, anarchic soul, and the child is an unconscious disciple of Rousseau, who only sees in our educational attempts an annoying and useless intervention upon the child's natural development.

But at this point, I feel a question arise in you. You might tell me: whether or not the child is conscious of what he feels and does, no matter whether the explanations and justifications offered so far are true or false, the picture you have traced of infantile psychology is very sad and obscure: and is it also accurate? Is it, indeed, true that only egotistical, deceitful, rebellious, and cruel instincts palpitate in the child?

I respond that in life, and above all in psychology, nothing is absolute because nothing is simple. The human organism is a complicated, delicate, mysterious machine. No men exist who are either totally perverse or totally excellent in their deeds because nature penetrates the most abject souls with flashes of light and darkens the best souls with patches of shade. Likewise, no children exist in whom the poison of atavistic impulses always circulates, and the candid flower of sweetness and serenity never blossoms. Each of us preserves in memory—if we are not fortunate enough to have the living proof nearby—the recollection of gentle, very sensitive children, who enclose in their delicate organism the most exquisite manifestations of the heart, moral clairvoyants, if I can say so, that respond with affectionate quivers if we only touch them. Even beyond these sentimental exceptions, it is certain that every child knows altruism and sympathy, if only because he imitates what he sees, and cries if he sees someone cry. Every child has leaps of tenderness towards the dog and the cat that are his companions in play, and that perhaps in another moment he can martyrize. Every child has treasures of affection and the charm of caresses for the people surrounding him, and he knows how to be forgiven for the delightfully disheartening insensitivity of his temperament and the flashes of his ferocious egoism.

But this normal psychology that brings him closer to us, gradually develops in him with age, as the psyche of the future man emerges and develops from his atavistic psyche, like a butterfly from a cocoon. It is—if I can say so—a slow work of embroidery on which education gradually refines and transforms the too coarse fabric of his original nature.

The basis of his soul remains as I have tried to describe it. Of course, I do not assume to have been either complete or precise, but I hope I have approached the truth.

What happens in painting happens in psychology. When making a portrait, we must limit our scope and focus in order to capture the subject's inner and most vigorous and dominant expression. That is, one must strike what is characteristic in a person's physical and moral physiognomy, inevitably neglecting many particulars on which, instead, the gaze of pedantic and myopic viewers focuses.

Now, the portrait of childhood can be depicted only with the colours that the positive and scientific research offers us, without resorting to the ideal nuances of poetry and its exaggerated rhetorical tints.

But what is comforting is that this portrait is transient: it is one of those portraits that no longer resemble their subjects, over time.

All that psychology recalling the primordial phases of mankind in the child slowly fades with the years, and vanishes during puberty. In life, apart from exceptional cases of congenital criminality, it is a mere physiological parenthesis, the salute, the memory, the admonition of distant miseries from which we ascended to civilization, a kind of disease—as there are many!—that we must suffer and overcome as children, and out of which we emerge healthier, stronger, and morally better. Indeed, it is not rare that those who were the most violent, capricious, wicked children later become the wisest and most remarkably good men, and the most honest and austere women.

However, in order to obtain this result, we must know how to understand the child, and, in order to understand him, we must love him.

We must love him not with an exaggerated sentimentality, perhaps made more of words than substance, which is fashionable today. We must love him not with our ridiculous and nervous anxiety that trembles for every sip of unboiled water and for every biscuit in excess. We must love him but not spoil him or even impose the yoke of a schedule on his studies and entertainment, which goes against his nature. We must love him in order to merge with his soul, to live his life of impulses and contradictions, to explain the lack of unity and consistency in his psychology, to understand, ultimately, that he is like a field with ancient roots of poisonous plants that need to be suppressed, and new germs of fertile plants that need help to evolve without being suffocated by the harmful ones.

Above all, we must be serene and generous towards him; we must forget that he is insensitive to our pains because he does not understand them, and try, instead, to understand his own.

Our major fault towards the child is the fact that we often repay him with the same mental indifference he shows towards us.

We smile at his pains because they seem negligible to us, and we do not realize that the terms of comparison are wrong. What seems futile to us is serious for the child, just as what is important to us is not even comprehensible to him.

In those small souls there are great and fearful tragedies, which we define as tantrums. There are, in a nutshell, all the passions that tear apart the human heart, and that we naively believe we are able to appease with a scolding or a punishment, while in fact, we only exacerbate them. There are strange, precocious intuitions that allow the child to see, to feel, to judge all the injustices we commit against him, deluding ourselves into thinking that he does not understand them. For example, pride and jealousy, these very precocious human passions, perhaps make children suffer more than adults, and they create the frequent type of child enclosed in his silent sadness and stubbornness, who bears the pain of his wounded pride with misunderstood dignity. Stupidly and perversely we throw our severity at him, claiming to correct a defect in him while ignoring the causes.

Finally, beyond these considerations, there is a higher and broader one that today should modify not only the judgments about the soul of the child, but especially the parenting methods.

I have traced some lines of childhood psychology, analysing childhood in itself from a scientific point of view, almost isolating it from time and environment. The analysis, I confess, is not complete. I forgot that in the study of any organism one cannot disregard the environment from which it arose, and that—be it a work or a man, an individual, or a collectivity—all of them, like plants, feel the influence of the terrain that produced them.

Today, also childhood feels the influence of the epoch in which it lives beyond hereditary and congenital causes; it is subject to the moral temperature of its surroundings, and it is illuminated by the reflection of that great world stirring around it. And its soul unconsciously throbs with the heartbeat of our own soul.

Modern children are different from the children of fifty years ago, because they cannot avoid and ignore the fever that dominates our hasty civilization. Today they enter life too early; too soon do they strain their brains with studies; too soon do they waste their adorable, infantile simplicity, partaking in society of the complicated, irritated, busy existence of adults. Today what they hear in the family, the great deal they read, the overload of vileness they see in the streets, the same distressing preoccupation of the parents that reverberates in them and agitates them, the consciousness of becoming the most important person in the house,—this inebriating mixture of pride and vanity deludes them into being someone while they are still nothing, and already pushes them to stand out in a world that still ignores them. All of this makes them accelerate and skip the physiologically normal periods of their development, rendering them precocious and nervous.

All distances are shorter today, in the physical world as well as in the moral world. Our sovereign law is haste. To abolish those ancient obstacles called time and space, as long and as much as possible, is the goal towards which we frantically run.

And we are abolishing or shortening childhood.

Just as we become old prematurely, so the child becomes a man prematurely. Under the violent pressure of emotions and sensations above his age, he becomes a man through desires, ambitions, and passions, not through force and consciousness.

And it is from this imbalance between wanting and being able, from this antinomy between the law of nature and the needs of civilization, that the most dreadful and painful drama sometimes erupts from the infantile soul: suicide!

We believed that the refusal of life was only possible in whoever knew life; we believed that this moment of courage, which perhaps conceals a dormant cowardice, was a consequence of the pains and preoccupations of maturity. In fact, however, the suicide epidemic also spreads among children, and statistics record its regular increase every year. We see and read that not only fifteen- or sixteen-year-old youth commit suicide, but also ten-, eight-, even six-year-old children![53]

Alas, who will ever be able to imagine the storm of all-too-grand ideas in those all-too-small brains? Who can ever retell the torment of those souls before they commit the fatal act?

The atavistic theory cannot help explain this mystery! Neither heredity nor nature is guilty! The fault is ours because our too intense, feverish, and cerebral civilization tarnishes and poisons even the child's innocence, and excites all of his nervous system to a pathological level.[54]

---

53 The cases of suicide among children or adolescents are especially frequent among secondary school students. Maurice Barrès in the preface to his book *Un homme libre*, dedicated "to *some schoolboys of Paris and of the province*," writes: "Schoolboys are almost the only human beings with whom we can commiserate ... At school, they are subject to a discipline they have not chosen: this is abominable. In the last six or seven years, I have recorded with pity the names of children who committed suicide. It is a long list that I do not dare publish" [in French in Sighele's text].

54 [After having highlighted the main and most problematic effects of modern existence —the acceleration of time and experiences, the shortening of distances, the inadequacy of the individual vis-à-vis the pressures of civilization, the increase in nervous

We should feel this remorse, and be conscious of this responsibility. We should finally understand that the first duty of education is to create a morally healthy and beautiful environment around the child, where the echo of all the anxieties that torment us does not penetrate, and where the soul of the child can freely develop according to the laws of nature, without being too quickly suffocated or martyrized by the thoughts and sensations of our soul.

And only then—once we give back to childhood its serenity and peacefulness, and we see it bloom around us as a symbol of hope—, only then will we be able to understand and deserve the phrase by Amiel[55] that the little bit of paradise we find on earth we owe to the presence of a child!

illnesses and ultimately in suicide cases—, Sighele hence maintains that such a degree of complexity and the ensuing behavioural anomalies cannot be mastered by the principle of atavism underlying the Lombrosian criminal theory.]

55 [Henri Frédéric Amiel (1821–1881) was a Swiss moral philosopher, essayist, and poet, best known for his *Journal intime*, a journal that he kept for over four decades, in which he exposed his quest for values against the scepticism of his time.]

# 7 From *Tragic Literature*

## Chapter 1: "The Work of Gabriele D'Annunzio before Psychiatry"

### *I The Rights of Criticism*

I do not know if the title of this chapter will generate some curiosity. I know for sure that very many will say: "here is another outsider to art who has the audacity to speak about an artistic work!" Eveyone's thought will swiftly go to Cesare Lombroso and to Max Nordau—the terrible dissectors of the brain and the psyche of geniuses—, and one will believe that I want to proudly imitate the research methods of those two scientists who were undeservedly named by artists *the enemies of art.*

None of that.

The disciple is too aware of his nullity to attempt what is legitimate solely for the masters. He does not dare judge, from a psychiatric point of view, the overall work—and a fortiori the personality—of a living artist whom his very detractors must recognize as the comforting proof that Italy still produces priests of ancient beauty. The disciple simply wants to limit himself to studying whether or not the types of degenerates that D'Annunzio shows us in his dramas and novels correspond to scientific truth.

Such is my very modest task. But if I narrow it to these short confines, I do not deny the right of others to range over vaster fields. I do not associate myself with those—and there are many of them—who, confronted with the patient study of a scientist who examines the hereditary predispositions or diseases of an artist to find the origin of his genius, cry profanation, almost as if the genius were the only human phenomenon that the scalpel of science cannot touch, and almost as if knowing the causes of a work of art meant to belittle it.

The sun is always the sun, even if astronomers describe its spots, and its light does not decrease, even if they reveal to us the quality of its material component. The pearl is always admired as the most elegant of jewels, even if the naturalist tells us that it is nothing but a disease of the oyster shell. And geniuses will always be the torches that illuminate the path of progress, even if doctors discover some sign of insanity or degeneration in their organism.

Were there perhaps scientists who, in their diagnoses, trespassed the proper limits by assigning the label of insane or degenerate too profusely? Perhaps. No one is infallible in the world, and much less does science claim to be, as it denies the dogma of infallibility to everyone—hence also to itself. But the errors or exaggerations of the few do not undermine the valid arguments of the many, and even less the principle that the artist can and must be an object of scientific analysis.

If some scholars and artists rebel against this principle, and they do not want science to discuss them, it is because they are somewhat afraid of science, just as those who fake illnesses fear the doctor. They are afraid that science might tell them—and reveal to the public—this important truth: that in art there are false artists as there are false political delinquents in criminality. There are mediocre brains who delude themselves into imitating Wagner or Ibsen, Zola or Verlaine, as there are common criminals who act as political martyrs, copying—according to the epochs and their intellectual capacity—a Mazzini or Pietro Micca, a Lassalle or Bakunin; and they exploit their degeneration or their abnormality as a symptom that allows them to resemble great men, yearning to be their worthy disciples, while they are nothing but caricatures.

Science clips the wings of pride off those mediocre ones, since it demonstrates that there are two kinds of degeneration or abnormality: the first is typical of men of genius or of the apostles who glimpse a new truth or who sacrifice themselves for an ideal; the second is that of the half-crazy[1] who exaggerate truth through the oddest distortions or disfigure

1 [Sighele's original term—"mattoidi"—corresponds to one of Lombroso's variations to the category of the insane criminal. Literally, "half-crazy," the mattoid is a person with eccentric behaviour—unstable, but heroic—and mental characteristics bordering on psychosis.]

an ideal in its most odious applications. Certain symbolists, certain decadents, certain satanists are as intellectually far from the models they claim to copy, as the crime of a Ravachol is morally and politically far from the crime of a Charlotte Corday.[2] Undoubtedly they are all degenerates, but some of them are on this side, and others on the other side of the subtle line that separates the sublime from the ridiculous, and heroism from infamy.

Just as some deny scientists the right to study artists individually, there are people who would want to deny them the right to analyse works of art sociologically. However, this is wrong because art is a social function, hence if artists are competent to judge the beauty of an artwork, philosophers are competent to judge its utility. This is wrong as well because art and science are two grandiose rivers, which, despite having different courses, come from an identical source and flow towards a single—invisible and perhaps unattainable—estuary.

This common origin of art and science manifests itself as soon as one decides to take a look at modern literature.

What surprises us in it?

We are surprised by the fact that every novel and drama is a study of vices rather than of virtues, an analysis of abnormal rather than normal sentiments, in short, a work that, instead of singing a simple hymn to what is good and beautiful, describes what is ugly, morbid, or evil.

Take the naturalist novel by Zola or the psychological one by Bourget, take Nordic symbolism or the psychiatric reports that comprise Dostoevsky's volumes, or, lastly, take all the works by our D'Annunzio and tell me if these literary forms–with different means and goals—do not reflect all the pathology, rather than the physiology, of the social body.

Why? Certainly not out of a spontaneous whim of their authors' monstrous brains—as Pierre Loti naively claims—but, rather, because the movement of modern thought necessarily had to produce this consequence in the field of art.

Not in vain has experimental science opposed the belief in free will, which so far has too comfortably appeased the research into the causes of human phenomena. Crime, prostitution, vagrancy, alcoholism, every form of misery and degeneration, until not many years ago, were

---

2 [For Ravachol, see *Sectarian Criminality*, this volume, 150n4. Charlotte Corday (Marie-Anne Charlotte de Corday d'Armont) (1768–1793) was executed by guillotine for having murdered Jean-Paul Marat, the Jacobin leader during the French Revolution.]

considered the effects of man's free will. Today, science affirms that they are nothing but the inevitable result of anthropological and environmental conditions, painful symptoms of moral diseases attributable to the individual as physical diseases, although unfortunately, they are more difficult to cure than the latter.

It was, therefore, natural that the fear and hate of evil–vile sentiments that our century, like the previous ones, had known–would be replaced by a sentiment that is, undoubtedly, less dangerous and more noble: compassion for evil.

Rather than merely punish vice and crime with a useless posthumous revengeful hatred, it was crucial to eliminate the germs before they blossomed in the mud like poisonous flowers; and in this saintly work of prevention and cleansing, only the artist could validly help the scientist.

Sores do not heal if they are not uncovered; and, in order to reveal to the world of honest and happy people that other unknown world of criminals and wretches who represent society's dead weights, we needed not the arid and scarcely read book of the scientist, but, rather, the passionate book of the artist, which, by seducing through form, could produce a shudder of pity in the souls of its many readers.

The naturalist novel is—as in another field the socialist novel—an ally of modern science. The moral and economic crisis we are traversing could not help resonating in literature. A warm whiff of altruism permeates the contemporary conscience; what today interests and occupies everyone's mind is—on the one hand—that army of wretches who have so far suffered in silence and whose silence we have rewarded with carefree nonchalance or disdain, and—on the other hand—that army of criminals whom we despise without studying them and believing instead that their illusory punishment in prison could be a sufficient remedy. Today we feel—perhaps prompted by fear—that it is time to abandon that nonchalance and disdain; hence we try to contain increasing poverty and criminality with dams that are stronger than ever.

Could art have remained unaffected by this general preoccupation? Should it have held its eyes fixed on the ideal, while sad reality asked its help? Was it fair to insist on describing the beautiful and good, while unhappiness and guilt let out their loud cry of pain?

And yet, could even those literary schools that do not have humanitarian worries or intentions, and rather disdain them by proclaiming the privileges of the superman, describe types of honest individuals or extol virtues, while in this frightening outset of the century we are all—or believe so—more or less neurotic or deranged or sick?

Certain writers were defined—and not wrongly—as "the Mithridates of art, who get used to nourishing themselves with morbid thoughts"[3]; and they inevitably adjust to it, given that the poison does not exist in them alone, but has spread throughout the entire environment in which they live.

Here, then, is why artists are mostly reduced to playing the role of clinicians who study and analyse pathological cases, and why, in our days, literature has become a type of psychopathology.

Yet, I foresee this facile criticism: "everything you have said"—one might object—"is true, but is not new to our epoch." Art has always been psychological, hence also psychopathological. Next to the classical types of beauty and virtue, which painting, sculpture, and poetry bequeathed to us, we have the classic types of deformities and of physical and moral monstrosities. To remain within the literary field, and to cite only one example, did the genius of Shakespeare not give us perhaps in Othello, Macbeth, and Hamlet the three insuperable types of the criminal by passion, the born criminal, and the insane criminal?[4] Nothing new, then, under the sun, critics say; and they are partially right. Nothing is new under the sun, we agree, but in substance, not in form or, better, in method. And method is everything, in art as in science.

Thanks to a fortunate gift of nature, the artists of the past could intuit the manifestations of that unknown disease of the spirit they wanted to represent. The artists today do not need to intuit: they know. Shakespeare wrote before the birth of psychiatry and criminal anthropology. Zola has acknowledged he read the works of Lombroso, and none of the truly great novelists of our day can ignore the achievements of psychiatry and experimental psychology in the last fifty years.

All that was once done unconsciously through divination today is done —or at least can be done—consciously through the culture acquired from books.

Here is the *novelty* that it would be vain to deny in art, and this is why even the most obscure scholar can have the luxury to examine whether the ideal types of criminals or degenerates coming from an artist's fantasy are scientifically true.

---

3 [Mithridates, King of Pontus and Armenia Minor, was one of the worst enemies of the Romans. He is remembered for his immunity to poison, which he obtained through regular ingestion of small doses of lethal substances.]

4 [Sighele is here classifying Shakespeare's characters according to the main categories in Lombroso's *Criminal Man*, just as he later refers to the Lombrosian occasional criminal to define Tolstoy's Nikita (*Tragic Literature* 340, in this volume)].

## *II The Prose Works*

### 1 "The Character Types Giovanni Episcopo, Tullio Hermil, and Isabella"

Rereading, as I had and wanted to do, all of Gabriele D'Annunzio's prose works in chronological order, I experienced a crowd of strange and diverse emotions that I would like to summarize as follows. Artistically, it seemed as though I had left one of those classical music concerts, of which the layman always understands and admires the grandiosity of the style and the difficulties its form overcame, but cannot always grasp its intimate, mysterious beauty. Intellectually, I thought I had finished reading some obscure pages of Nietzsche or some lucid pages of a Greek philosopher, as the flavour of ancient wisdom mixed with the sometimes brilliant but more often crazy ideas of a modern, infamous philosopher. Morally, I wondered if all the progress of civilization was truly useless and if, after having defeated so many tyrannies, we still had to subjugate ourselves to the quite new and immoral one of the superman.[5]

Just as my impressions of D'Annunzio's overall work were diverse and contradictory, so were—among them—the main principal character types, which in his work stood out like figures in the background of a painting: some evidently drawn from the daily reality of life, others conceived by an imagination that became unlikely and unnatural in its desire for originality.

Among the first ones, I do not hesitate to place Giovanni Episcopo, Tullio Hermil, and Isabella, the insane character in *The Dream of a Spring Morning.*

Regarding *Giovanni Episcopo* and *The Intruder*, literary criticism accused D'Annunzio, if not of plagiarism, at least of an exaggerated Russophilia; and there is no doubt that in those two stories, that is, in those two criminals' confessions, one feels and often finds the words of the spirits of Dostoevsky and Tolstoy hovering over. But that is not important to us. If it is imitation, the imitation is well done, because—just as the characters of Nikita in *The Power of Darkness* and Raskolnikoff in *Crime and Punishment* are alive and real—so are their intellectual brothers, Giovanni Episcopo and Tullio Hermil.

---

5 [While Sighele now sounds hostile to the idea of the superman, he will later write an essay on Nietzsche (published posthumously in *Letteratura e sociologia*) that explains the superior individual as a result of a Darwinian evolutionary process, hence finding connections with his own positivistic approach.]

In Giovanni Episcopo, we have the type—I dare say scientifically perfect—of the moral neurasthenic,[6] whose addiction to drinking makes his already weak volitional faculty even more obtuse, and who, all of a sudden, becomes a murderer as a consequence of one of those psychological hurricanes that, just as they can shake the firmest conscience, also turn the rabbit into a lion.

And, for his cowardice, Giovanni Episcopo truly is a rabbit. He not only endures, without even a trace of rebellion, the wound that Giulio Wanzer inflicts on him by hurling a glass against his forehead, but, from that day on, he also becomes the slave, *the object*, of his despotic friend. "The only attitude I could have toward him"—Episcopo avows—

> was that of a frightened dog. (…)—He robbed me of all sense of human dignity, just like that, suddenly, with the same facility with which he would have tweaked out a hair.
>
> And I wasn't in a daze. I was aware of everything I did, I was conscious of everything: of my weakness, my abjection and, especially, *of the absolute impossibility* of escaping from that man's power.
>
> (…) Confronted by my executioner, I *no longer had any will* (…) O sir, who will be able to unravel this mystery for me before I die? So there are indeed men on earth who, when they meet other men, can do what they wish with them, can make them their slaves? So the will can be taken away from a man, just as one takes a blade of straw from between a man's fingers? Can one do this, sir?[7]

Science responds to the anxious question of the neurasthenic, and does so in the affirmative. Yes, there are imperious and evil characters on earth that know how to impose themselves on a weakling and to make him do what they want. There are *degenerate couples*, with a strong individual (the *incubus*) who suggestionizes a weak one (the *succubus*), annihilates his will and drags him to vice, to crime, to every abjection, like an automaton.[8]

---

6 [Neurasthenia is a category that Moritz Benedikt introduced to explain criminal behaviour. Unlike the atavistic hypothesis that Lombroso couples with epilepsy, Benedikt's theory presupposes a native psychic weakness that entails moral debility.]

7 [Gabriele D'Annunzio, *Giovanni Episcopo*, in *Nocturne and Five Tales of Love and Death*, translated by Raymond Rosenthal (Marlboro, VT: Marlboro Press, 1988), 95–97. Hereafter cited parenthetically in the text as *Episcopo*.]

8 [Here Sighele is analysing literary characters according to the psychological categories that he coined in *The Criminal Couple*.]

Gabriele D'Annunzio has admirably reproduced in art one of these *degenerate couples*, of which scientific literature offers many examples, and, even in the catastrophe of his narratives, he intuited the tragic ending that often in life breaks this strange bond of domination and servility.

It sometimes happens that the weak person—when the measure of his patience is full and the strong person demands a new act of renunciation or cowardice from him, beyond every human possibility—rebels and retaliates against his master with a single act of energy that is all the more ferocious the longer his passive resignation lasted. This individual phenomenon is parallel to the collective phenomenon of certain populations, which, after bending their necks in silence for years and centuries under a despot's yoke, finally one day find in themselves the strength and audacity to make a bloody revolution.

Hence Giovanni Episcopo, after tolerating Giulio Wanzer's theft of his wife—an extreme proof of supremacy like that of the feudal lord over his subjects—after accepting the role of the two lovers' compliant servant, and allowing Wanzer not only to rob him of his wife, but also to beat her in his own home—suddenly, like an angry rabbit, finds a moment of ferocity. One day, he hears the sharp cry of his son, the poor, small Ciro, from the nearby bedroom, and he imagines that cry was caused by Wanzer's blow. Pushed by a prodigious force, he runs towards the two, and, upon seeing Wanzer's big hands on his son, he grabs a knife, and "Two, three, four times [he] drove the knife into his back, right up to the handle" (*Episcopo* 151).

The victim retaliated against his executioner, and the vendetta was psychologically very natural, just as, in the entire story, the analysis of that neurasthenic's life was of sculptural evidence and rare scientific precision.

Very different from Giovanni Episcopo—and yet equally real—is the figure of Tullio Hermil in *The Intruder*. He does not commit infanticide in an impetus of passion, but, rather, out of cold calculation. He is a born criminal, not brutal and atavistic, that is, not one of those who have the courage of their own crimes and accomplish them with naive and dangerous means like poison or the knife. Rather, he is refined and civil, one who Jesuitically leaves to the cold, nocturnal air the task of killing his wife's baby, and not his own. All of his faculties are always alive and very acute. He lacks only one, the result of congenital atrophy: moral sense.

He is an egoist in the most absolute and repugnant sense of the word; he proclaims that the dream of all intellectual men is to "be constantly unfaithful to a constantly faithful woman."[9] He enjoys torturing the soul of his wife Giuliana with the frequency and the insulting fanfare of his betrayals. And he borders on the absurd as he maintains that he was right to make his wife suffer so much, since she could thus become heroic in her own resignation. In conclusion, he is one of those elegantly dressed scoundrels who frequent high-society salons, and who veil their perfidy behind gentlemanly impeccable manners and behind the charm of an uncommon, pleasant ingenuity.

These types—which are not as rare in reality as we might think—apparently remain honest before the penal code, until their egoism encounters an obstacle. At that point, they get rid of it with a crime.

For Tullio Hermil, the obstacle is discovering that Giuliana, the *turris eburnea*,[10] has also surrendered to guilty love, and has become pregnant. This revelation disturbs not so much his husbandly affection, as his manly egoism. He, therefore, does not harbour rancour towards the adulteress, but, rather, towards the innocent baby, whose birth will hinder the renewed happiness he now feels he could enjoy with Giuliana. Indeed, for the sake of a mere sensual reward, after many infidelities, he still loves his docile wife, for whom he has had a "sisterly" affection for years; and his erotomania—so frequent in degenerates like him—renders him indulgent, out of egoism, towards Giuliana, who is by now necessary to his pleasure, and, vice versa, renders him implacable, again out of egoism, towards the intruder who would be an obstacle to that enjoyment.

One day, he hears the newborn cough, and that cough reveals to him the way he will kill the baby. He will make him die of pneumonia, exposing him from the window to the cold north wind.

And it should be remarked that the idea of crime, like a sinister lightning, sometimes traverses even the clear sky of an honest conscience. Perhaps many husbands, in the case of Tullio Hermil, would have directed a cruel prayer to God that that cough might lead the baby to the grave. But on the pure crystal of an honest character, the criminal idea slides away without leaving a trace, while it undermines and corrodes the impure soul of a degenerate.

From that day, indeed, Tullio Hermil's premeditation of infanticide begins: "The fixed idea"—he narrates—"possessed me absolutely with

9 [Gabriele D'Annunzio, *The Intruder*, translated by Arthur Hornblow (Boston: Page, 1897), 47. Hereafter cited parenthetically in the text as *Intruder*.]

10 [The ivory tower.]

inconceivable power. (…) My perspicacity seemed to be trebled. (…) There was not a single moment of relaxation in my circumspection. I said nothing, I did nothing that could awaken suspicion or cause surprise. I dissimulated, ceaselessly (…)" (*Intruder* 280).

Here in these words is proof of congenital delinquency: there is no passion, excitement, or a burst of remorse, but, rather, an intellectual lucidity, a horrifying moral indifference. And more serene and calmer he turns out to be in the act of committing the crime: —"… I returned to the door, I opened it, assured myself that the corridor was deserted. I ran to the window (…) A blast of icy air came in (…) I drew back, approached the cradle; (…) I took the infant up very gently; I bore him to the window; I exposed him to the air that was to make him perish. *I did not for a moment lose my presence of mind; not one of my senses was dulled*" (*Intruder* 301 [Sighele's emphasis]).

Who, if not a born criminal, would thus not lose themselves and not feel their senses obscured in that instant?

Tullio Hermil—it is true—acts less basely when, in front of the parents witnessing the newborn's sudden agony, he screams, like Tolstoy's Nikita, in the last scene of *The Power of Darkness*:—"Do you know who killed this innocent?" But, while Nikita does confess his crime because he is an occasional criminal, Tullio Hermil's cry, where one would expect a confession, dies on his lips and in his conscience. He keeps quiet, he lets his brother carry him away, and after a few hours, he gets comfortable with what he did, he attends the funeral two days later, and then he delights in talking about it in its tiniest details with the moral analgesia of a Lacenaire, who described his most atrocious crimes and his victims' throes while laughing.[11]

I do not know if a Tullio Hermil has ever existed in real life; but I do know that he has all the psychological characteristics of a real criminal.

Third, and lastly—as I said—among the types of degenerates successfully intuited by Gabriele D'Annunzio is Isabella, the madwoman of *The Dream of a Spring Morning*.

This tragic poem seems more like a *dream*, that is, implausible for the public who hears it recited and for many of those who read it. And it is undoubtedly implausible for its scenic representation, just as certain episodes are unrealistic, and the secondary characters are counterfeit,

11 For a discussion on Tullio Hermil, see *I delinquenti nell'arte*, by Enrico Ferri. [For Lacenaire, see *The Criminal Couple* 82n17.]

especially that doctor who is not a doctor but a mystic, not a modern alienist but a medieval doctor, who, instead of curing the demented female, thinks she is an enlightened mind, according to ancient prejudice. But the fundamental features of Isabella—or, better, of her insanity—are designed with a rigorous, psychiatric accuracy.

First of all—and here I expose the viewpoint of one of the most distinguished Italian alienists—D'Annunzio is scientifically correct in making the protagonist's mental disease depend on the atrocious and very sad cause that had thrown her soul from the apogee of happiness into the abyss of sorrow and terror. Her lover was killed in her arms, and she stayed for a long time in bed with that corpse and that blood.

Her brain—struck by an affective stimulus of such extraordinary intensity—had fallen into a state of astonishment. And as the astonishment necessarily allowed the brain's nervous elements to rest, it later allowed them to resume their functions. Isabella, indeed, gradually wakes up and communicates with the external world; but all that struck her in the supreme moment is erased in her consciousness. Nothing remains in her but a few superficial constraints connected with the past, for instance, the perception of red, namely, the colour of blood, which is always accompanied by a distressing emotion. And D'Annunzio was brilliant in imagining the sedative effect that the vision of green has on the demented, precisely because green is complementary to red. Likewise, the vague delirium in the insane person's usual discourses is represented through the frequent and insistent reappearing of a few ideas, and always those that are reawakened by fortuitous associations. The doctor, for example, says: "*I am old.*"[12] Isabella then looks at his hair, which is white, thinks by contrast of hers, which is red, and says that she would have liked it to be white, "like the bundles of flax on the threshing-floor" (*Spring* 19).

But the most beautiful, artistic effect—because more scientifically plausible—that the author obtains in his poem is when the demented woman recognizes her lover's brother in Virginius, and this recognition is like the miraculous key that suddenly opens the casket of her memories, which madness had closed.

All the particulars of the tragedy, unfolding with such rapidity, remained barely impressed in her violently shaken soul, and the subsequent period of astonishment had apparently erased them. But they lay in the

12 [G. D'Annunzio, *The Dream of a Spring Morning*, in *Poet-Lore: A Quarterly Magazine of Letters* XIV, 1 (Oct. 1902), edited by Charlotte Porter and Helen A. Clarke (Boston: Poet-Lore), 19. Hereafter cited parenthetically in the text as *Spring*.]

unconscious, and seeing Virginius was enough to clearly awake the image of her lover, which, in its turn, released a long trail of mnemonic images chained together. Isabella was hence prompted to narrate the entire drama, conjuring up the lover's mother and fearing her curse, which made her scream out all of her pain, all of her horror, all of her passion, with true sincerity.[13]

This dramatic scene makes up for the many improbabilities and many absurdities of the other scenes, and it is a wondrous artistic resurrection—I daresay, almost a photograph—of what sometimes occurs in asylums.

## 2 "Giorgo Aurispa, Claudio Cantelmo, *The Dead City*"

Unfortunately, after the figure of Isabella, one would vainly search in Gabriele D'Annunzio's work for other character types equal—in scientific verisimilitude—to those already described. One would say that the author—too confident in himself and too disdainful of his reality—wanted to give free rein to his fantasy, which, without the restraint and control of experimental observation, went on to create not true men, but characters who are the exaggeration or the caricature of reality.

In this regard, I recall a very beautiful comparison by Achille Loria:[14] "the imagination of a scientist or artist"—he says—"can sometimes rise up from the ground of reality, as a mettlesome horse that takes a leap; yet, like the horse, it must touch the ground again afterwards." It is, in other words, legitimate—and, rather, it is a proof of ingenuity—to depart from what is certain and tangible in order to launch ourselves towards a philosophical synthesis or an artistic creation, but we must then return to the world of real phenomena; that synthesis or that creation must find further confirmation in facts.

Now, Gabriele D'Annunzio deserved this simile for his creations of Giovanni Episcopo, Tullio Hermil, and Isabella, since, while these characters came out of his imagination, they were then recognized by science

---

13 For an analysis of the character of Isabella, I adopted the sharp observations by the late Professor Ezio Sciamanna [(1850–1903), who was professor of neurology at the University of Rome and director of a psychiatric clinic separate from the asylum. He was a disciple of Jean-Martin Charcot and of Moritz Benedikt].

14 [Achille Loria (1857–1943) was an Italian professor of political economy and senator, who interpreted social history and economic development in deterministic terms.]

as true, and if with his flight the artist had shortly soared in the aerial field of imagination, he soon also came back down to the terrain of positive truth. But he seems no longer worthy of that simile for the creation of the other characters in his dramas and novels. His imagination can no longer be compared to a horse taking a leap, then returning to the ground from which it departed, but, rather to a non-existent hippogryph, which, after taking flight, goes nobody knows where, and loses itself in the distant clouds.

For example, Giorgio Aurispa, the hero of *The Triumph of Death*, does not fit a precise, anthropological classification among the types of true degenerates, if not perhaps—like Enrico Ferri said—that of abortive madness.

He is a "superior degenerate," one of those intelligent but unfortunate men—rather, unfortunate perhaps because they are too intelligent—who employ their brain to torture their soul, with a psychological self-analysis that has all the cruelty of an anatomical knife, since it mercilessly scrutinizes and searches the most intimate fibres of one's organism. He can never be content with life, and his pathological heredity sharpens his pessimism. He has taken excessive and vulgar sensuality from his father, a refined, exquisite sensibility from his mother, the suicidal mania from his uncle, and, by grafting these three tendencies onto the trunk of his strong intellectual capacity, he manages to compose a life of love and torment for himself, not ever managing to enjoy the fleeting hour and the people passing by, and always torturing himself in search of an absolute happiness, which of course, he cannot find and knows he will never find. Therefore, when—upon finishing the novel's final page—you think about that man who has had neither the generosity to kill only himself, or the criminal courage to kill his lover, but wanted to commit a double suicide and die with her, falling into a ravine while clutching each other, you hence admire the ingenuity of the author who knows how to make you interested in a similar drama, but you do not hear within yourselves that voice—that is the intimate seal of great artistic creations—telling you: "yes, this type is true and human; if I have not met him, I could meet him."

Still less real—better, outside of every reasonable verisimilitude—is Claudio Cantelmo, the protagonist of *The Virgins of the Rocks*, a man possessed by the ambitious dream of being destined to perpetuate his aristocratic race by giving life to a perfect son, and who, in fact, does not know how, does not want to, or cannot choose among the three virgins the one who will realize his dream through their union. He should be a "superior degenerate" like Giorgo Aurispa, but his profile is surely not drawn in the same way. In the book, his figure does not stand out; his character is as nebulous as his ideas, and the nightmare of a hereditary and collective madness hangs over the entire story. In fact, all eight characters of this novel—which is the most musical, but also the most incomprehensible and emptiest of Gabriele D'Annunzio's novels—turn out to be insane, or people on the verge of insanity; and the strange thing is that even those who in the author's conception should be mentally sane, speak and act like madmen. I do not know what D'Annunzio's objective was in writing this book, but if I am allowed to judge the work based on what shows through it, I affirm that it attains the opposite of its intended goal, because instead of proving the vitality of an aristocratic race, more or less legitimist or Bourbon, and the superiority of its representative, it proves its sterility and its moral and intellectual impotence.

And what to say about *The Dead City*? In this tragedy—which, as always, I admire and do not discuss for its form—we find the idea that traversed D'Annunzio's previous works, now finally expressed in all its criminal audacity, namely, the idea of guilty love between brother and sister. We have seen in *The Intruder*, then in *The Triumph of Death*, and then in *The Virgins of the Rocks* that the author delighted in giving an acrid, almost incestuous taste to his characters' loves, calling the lover *sister*; it was the pathological leitmotif of his erotic symphony. In *The Dead City*, this becomes the motif of the entire drama and leads a disgraced brother to crime, the murder of his sister in order to keep her pure. But the figure of the murderer and his victim seem to us outside the psychological realm, just as the buried Mycenae where the tragedy unfolds is far from and outside our modern life.

## 3 "The Theory of the Superman"

*The Dead City* is Gabriele D'Annunzio's final work of prose in which these types of criminals or madmen can be found. In *The Dream of an Autumn Sunset* there is nothing but the description of an exceedingly furious jealousy; and that tragic poem is notable solely for the visual impression of the colour red, which the final battle and the final fire leave in the reader. This is an artistic and well-imagined contrast to the impression of the colour green, which is left, instead, by *The Dream of a Spring Morning*, since it is right to have red as the dominating tonality of sunset and autumn, just as green for morning and spring.

In *Gioconda*, it is almost impossible to recognize the D'Annunzio of his other works, since the character types are so relatively normal and the plot of the tragedy so logically human. He reveals himself only in his form—always harmoniously the same—and in that *concordance* that concludes the volume symbolizing its meaning, and, above all, in the theory of the superman, resumed and incidentally affirmed by Gioconda Dianti.

And it is by speaking very briefly about this theory that I believe I can summarize this first critical look at the Dannunzian oeuvre.

After examining some of its types in light of psychiatry and criminal anthropology, it seems, indeed, logical to examine the concept that shapes all the artist's prose under the light of morals. It will be another profanation, another act of pride that a humble philistine will dare to perform in the temple of art.

That theory—which fortunately is not Italian, but has been imported among us with the ease with which we copy the few bad things from abroad together with the many good ones—makes its first appearance in *Pleasure* by Gabriele D'Annunzio, where it is nothing but an egotistical, vulgar consequence of an Epicurean philosophy. It returns in *The Intruder*, expressed in a more intellectual manner and attributed to the protagonist, yet without the author's explicit approval. It reappears in *The Virgins of the Rocks*, where it is diminished and warped, because, while until then the superman believed he owed his preeminence only to his intellectual aristocracy, in this novel he is also and above all the expression of the aristocracy of blood, the most unjust of all. The theory of the superman is ultimately revisited in *Gioconda*, where it is proclaimed in the sacred name of art. And after such insistence, it is no longer possible to suppose—even for other literary and political manifestations by D'Annunzio—that this theory is not his moral and intellectual *belief*.

Perhaps—and here I express my doubt more than my firm thought—the artist let himself be gradually suggestionized by the abnormal idea he was studying. Initially, he must have only wanted to analyse the certainly not common yet true phenomenon of the superman; subsequently, the disease he was observing must have been transmitted to him by contagion, and he must have been the victim of that psychological poison that—in the fever of research—he had subjected to examination.

And what he experienced from the artistic point of view must also have happened from the moral point of view. More than the idea, he adored so much the form it acquired that, like an ingenuous believer prostrated before the image of the Madonna, he ended up having faith not so much in divinity as in its material symbol. In this regard, he resembled the unhappy anarchist Taillade [*sic*],[15] who did not see the substance in a murder, namely, the horror of the savage action, but only the form or the artistic expression of the *nice gesture.* Therefore, he has fallen so much in love with the thesis of the superman that, instead of limiting himself to studying it as a pathological case, he has made it his own and believes in it.

He believes in it and ostentatiously shows that he does. He is sincere and courageous in this, like certain past artists of ours who still surprise us, one does not know whether more for the marvels they created or for the crimes they committed. He is a Benvenuto Cellini of the word, whose scalpel has no rivals and does not know difficulty, and who, just as Cellini confessed his crimes in his autobiography with the most cynical indifference, proclaims his immoral theory in his novels with the proudest audacity. He wants freedom, privilege, and omnipotence for the supermen, who do not have to submit to the yoke of common laws made only for the humble and mediocre crowd.

Now, we rebel against this superb and aristocratic theory, since we think that, if superiority of ingenuity gives greater rights in a sense, it also gives morally greater duties. And without resorting to science—which teaches that the function of modern society is to provide well-being to the greatest possible number of individuals, rather than keeping it all for the monstrous exceptions of some superior brain—in front of that contempt we affirm with our heart and mind our love for the crowd of the humble.

We do not bow to the incontestable, intellectual superiority of a Gabriele D'Annunzio, but if he finds poetry in the extolment of the rare and luminous virtues of the strong, we find it in the extolment of the obscure virtues of the weak and in the support of their still unrecognized rights. His is, without a doubt, a more intellectual and aristocratic poetry, but ours—I feel—is more human and true.

---

15 [Laurent Tailhade (1854–1919) was a French anarchist, satirical poet, and provocative essayist, who, in 1893, endorsed a terrorist attack on the Chamber of Deputies by the anarchist Vaillant. Focusing on the aesthetic aspect of the violent act, Tailhade declared that the victim has no importance if the gesture is beautiful.]

## *III The Works of Poetry*

### 1 *"Francesca da Rimini"*

In the note that Gabriele D'Annunzio adds at the end of the magnificent edition of his *Francesca*, he warns us that "the work of the painter, the sculptor, the engraver, the goldsmith, the gunsmith, the draper, accomplished with sagacious discipline and love, all contributed to the apparatus of the tragedy in an extraordinary way." And he continues: "Equal care was given to the printing of this volume, so that it can remain a document of the sincere and courageous effort that two concordant wills accomplished in their homeland in order to attest at least their aspiration towards those multiple ideal forms which once made of Italian life the ornament of the world."

It is certain that, just as the collaboration of minor artists with the author contributed a great deal to the success of the tragedy on stage by highlighting the poet's ideal and individual work with their patient material and collective work, so the quality of the edition greatly contributes to the more measured and reasoned admiration that invades the soul of whoever reads the book.

Printed on a different paper with the usual modern typographic characters, without embellishments, *Francesca da Rimini* would have appeared to the reader as a literary and moral anachronism. This edition instead prepares our soul to find in the volume a feeling and language that by now have been dead for centuries, and, with a visual suggestion that goes from the eye to the brain, leads us unconsciously back, if not to the times in which the tragedy took place (when the printing press did not exist), at least to times that were also psychologically closer to that turbid epoch than to ours.

This work of editorial suggestion[16] was all the more necessary to transport us to an environment that our modern souls repel and from which they feel detached. The tragedy's greatest worth consists, indeed, in the perfect reconstruction of such an environment. We must be able to understand this wondrous, dramatic reconstruction, where the poet violently enclosed a decade of the dense history of Romagna, or else we must give up admiring anything in the tragedy.

16 [Sighele here applies the key concept of his collective psychology—suggestion—to explain the influence that not only the content of the work, but even its paratext can have upon readers.]

Indeed, the types of the protagonists, which the public imagined to be the most incisive, did not stand out as clearly as other ones, and the guilty, bloody passion of Paolo and Francesca, which had to be the central nucleus according to general expectations, almost the lively flame from which the work of art received all its warmth and splendour, turns out to be a colourless episode, a simple note of poetry and love in the clamorous concert of a combative and ferocious medieval life.

One of our greatest critics noted that the figure of Francesca is evanescent. It is lost in the dream; she is intangible and elusive, and traverses the drama, of which she is the origin, like a symbol of gentleness and feminine weakness. Nothing in her reveals strength and will; she is an instrument, not a cause, and even her love—despite being the world's most celebrated love!—seems to be the consequence of a set of small circumstances rather than the spontaneous and irresistible impulse of one whole soul towards another.

Paolo (who has praised the figure of Paolo in this tragedy?) is a man whom Francesca likes for his beauty, and whom the public dislikes for his effeminacy. He is so palely designed, in comparison to his brothers' strong prominence, that he inspires neither sympathy nor compassion.

And all the scenes that unfold between the two lovers—where there are also lines of exquisite harmony—do not seem able to elicit (as happens in theatre, too) that intense commotion that a great artist's description of a great love normally evokes.

Dante, and the legend that thrived after him, had idealized Paolo and Francesca's adultery so much that no one thought about the two cousins' guilt; their passion went beyond the obstacle of the moral law that should condemn them, and they appeared as perfect and admirable types in whom the purest and strongest love was engraved.

Not having attained Alighieri's poetic height, Gabriele D'Annunzio has inevitably brought back to the more modest proportions of reality the legend that had excessively ennobled and sublimated adultery. In his work, Paolo appears simply as the type of lover that has always existed and will always do, and Francesca is nothing but a weak and gentle girl imbued with dreams and poetry, who, forcibly given in marriage with deceit to an ugly man, fatally falls into the arms of a beautiful man, whom she thought was the husband designated for her.

However, there must exist a reason why Gabriele D'Annunzio—whose bow always knows how to hit exactly where it aims—did not succeed, as he did with other characters in creating the types of the "two cousins." The reason—advanced with great modesty by a very modest psychologist—

seems to be that Gabriele D'Annunzio's artistic temperament is such that it attains the highest summits of art when he wants to represent exceptional individuals or pathological souls, but remains inferior to itself when he designs morally sane individuals and normal souls.

Retrieve all of his literary production, and you must confess that the types that have remained in your memory and deserve your admiration are, indeed, those in which D'Annunzio symbolized a crime, a disease, or a form of degeneration. Giovanni Episcopo, the neurasthenic murderer, Tullio Hermil, the Jesuitically modern parricide, Isabella, the madwoman of *The Dream of a Spring Morning*, Leonardo, the incestuous brother of *The Dead City*; here are the Dannunzian figures that have a life of their own and will defy time. Even in his other works—from *Pleasure* to *The Triumph of Death*, from the *The Virgins of the Rocks* to *The Flame*—the best pages are those that describe something repugnant or perfidious, and the characters D'Annunzio creates and delineates more confidently and vigorously—be they called Andrea Sperelli or Claudio Cantelmo, Giorgio Aurispa, or Stelio Effrena—are nothing but "superior degenerates," in whom he delights to represent or to pathologically exaggerate a facet of his own soul.

Love, furthermore, is always portrayed morbidly or tragically by D'Annunzio. He never sings or describes the pureness of an idyll or the sanctity of a fecund union. He is the wondrous artificer who paints the slow rising or the impetuous irruption of an immoral and abnormal passion with all the colours of a very rich palette; he enjoys muddying the limpid source of the sexual instinct with the blood of a crime or suicide, or with the poison of an impure thought. Indeed, in his novels—as I have already remarked—love almost always has an acrid taste of incest, because the man calls his lover *sister*, and this pathological refrain becomes the dominating motif in *The Dead City*, where it could be argued that the nebulously incestuous sentiment, which slithered throughout his previous works, bursts out with open sincerity, subsides, and extinguishes itself in fratricide.

Now, it is easy to understand how such an artistic temperament cannot feel, and therefore, cannot reproduce a normal passion like that of Paolo or Francesca, in a way worthy of its fame. And I claim this passion is normal, although it is adultery, because it is not vice but fatality that made it arise, and because adultery is too light and common a crime to be considered the index of degeneration in whoever commits it. It is the *political crime* of the family, as Raffaele Garofalo wittily wrote, a crime that the law punishes as a platonic homage to an ideal principle, but that custom strikes with contempt, and even encourages with envy.

Men of perverse or ferocious instinct, passions that degenerate into crime or madness, epochs of iron and blood—here is what Gabriele D'Annunzio's genius is best suited for, here is the material with which this Benvenuto Cellini of the word magnificently works.

Some smiled at the excessive care the poet placed in the "staging" of his tragedy, the extraordinary exactness of the reproduction of every weapon, every dress, every object. They smiled, above all, at his preoccupation that in the second act—where, from the Malatesta tower, fire is set to the houses of Rimini—the mangonel work with a perfect illusion of reality, and the spectators have the frightening sensation of finding themselves before an actual battle.

Of course, there was something more in Gabriele D'Annunzio than just every author's reasonable desire to have his work appear in a worthy and appropriate environment. There was a kind of obsession in him that, beyond his characters' words and actions, the sensation of *the historical moment* could reign supreme over the public. He himself told me that a young friend of his worked and studied for a month with the objective of finding the fires and fumes chemically most appropriate for the stage representation of light and heat, of the fog and confusion of a true battle. If these studies did not theatrically create a felicitous effect in the second act, we must, however, recognize that the reproduction of the medieval milieu in the tragedy, of that life centred only on ideas of conquest and feelings of cruelty, is admirably perfect, both in the poet's words and in every act or design of his collaborators.

Seeing the play or reading it, we feel dragged by a mysterious force—which is the sovereign prestige of art—towards that century that was so morally obscure and so bright with the extraordinary actions of male will and of conscious ferocity. We lose or forget our psychology as modern men, and ancient man is gradually revived in us so that we not only are in a state of admiration, but we feel overtaken by those emotions that the poet managed to stir in front of us. Isidoro del Lungo[17] says in this regard, in an insuperable way: "… to the strained ear an echo of voices from six hundred distant years returns, and the illusion of images and sounds connects with the scenic illusion. The impression is that art this time has grasped its eternal object: the true."

---

17 [Isidoro Del Lungo (1841–1927) was an Italian historian, literary critic, and senator. He was the first president of the Accademia della Crusca and also president of the Società dantesca italiana.]

Art grasped the truth because Gabriele D'Annunzio's soul was in unison with the soul of the epoch he evoked—to such a degree that the poet gave his best in designing the types that best summarize and symbolize that epoch (Ostasio, Gianciotto, and Malatestino), and he was inferior to himself in creating the two types (Paolo and Francesca) who are removed from and transcend that epoch, being not medieval, but simply and eternally human.

The public's judgment was unanimous in admiring—perhaps above all the others—the scenes of the first act when the figure of Ostasio appears, and those of the fourth act, when the figures of Gianciotto and Malatestino delineate and illuminate themselves through the psychological lightnings of a verbal duel.

The former of these three men is the son of Guido Minore da Polenta, the others are the sons of Malatesta da Verucchio, and all truly and worthily represent the families from which they descend, the environment in which they live, and their epoch's dynamic morality. They are three violent men whose ideal is to extend their dominion, their right on the tip of their sword, and all of their psychology in arrogance. They are three types of men who today we qualify as criminals, and who were then nothing but the symbol of the squires and warlords that infested Italy.

The scene between Ostasio and Bannino is brief, but it is so dense with psychology that nothing else, I believe, equals it in the tragedy. The legitimate son of Guido vents his contempt and hatred against the bastard with a biting irony: and his words stab like daggers.

Ostasio says to Bannino, returning unscathed from a bout with the Forlivians:

"(...) You
Have not a scratch upon your white face,
O mighty man of valour in your words!"[18]

And since Bannino wants to defend himself from a cowardly accusation, Ostasio addresses him indignantly: "(...) Speak then, if you know how to wound a man" (*Francesca* 42). When Bannino threatens to reveal Ostasio's attempted poisoning of his father, these lines follow:

18 [Gabriele D'Annunzio, *Francesca da Rimini*, translated by Arthus Symons (New York: Frederick A. Stokes, 1902), 41. Hereafter cited parenthetically in the text as *Francesca*.]

"No, pour out
Your gall, that is now painted on your face,
Or I will wring you up as if I wrung
A wet rag out." (*Francesca* 42)

And finally, after Bannino utters the accusation, Ostasio wounds him on the cheek, but only superficially (a final irony imposed with the sword after the irony imposed with the word), and says to Ser Toldo:

"I have only pricked the skin;
Not in a bad place, no: and not in anger,
I pricked him just a little
That he might learn not to fear naked steel,
(...)
He is from another nest, and he was hatched
Not by the eagle, no, but by a jay." (*Francesca* 44–45)

The contrast between the two brothers is rendered with unsurpassed art, and the criminally courageous type, Ostasio, the legitimate son of his father and of his time, acquires greater vividness of colour from the livid cowardice of the bastard.

But the figure of Ostasio is remarkable for another reason. Through him, D'Annunzio also wanted to insinuate in this tragedy, albeit covertly and incidentally, the suspect of a love that is more than fraternal between brother and sister. The lines where Ostasio describes Francesca are of such passionate poetry that it surpasses the affection and admiration every brother owes to a sister—even if very beautiful. And in the entire tragedy, no one, not even Paolo, knows how to speak of Francesca as Ostasio speaks of her. For example:

Ostasio (absorbed)
"Ah! Is she
Not worth a kingdom? How beautiful she is!
There never was a sword that went so straight
As her eyes go, if they but look at you.
Yesterday she was saying: 'Who is it
You give me to?' When she walks, and her hair
Falls all about her to her waist, and down
To her strong knees (she is strong, though very pale)
And her head sways a little, she gives forth joy

Like flags that wave in the wind
When one sets forth against a mighty city
In polished armour. Then
She seems as if she held
The eagle of Polenta
Fast in her fist, like a trained hawk, to fling him
Forth to the pray. Yesterday she was saying:
'Who is it you give me to?'
Why should I see her die?" (*Francesca* 37)

In the third act, Francesca interrupts the slave who had uttered the name *sister*, saying:

"O, that name
Is like a poison here." (*Francesca* 128)

She alludes to Paolo and Malatestino, but also Ostasio—if she had known—perhaps would not have been unworthy of the allusion.

Malatestino is the tragedy's most vigorously drawn figure and the most original, not only because he is Gabriele D'Annunzio's direct creation who did not have—as for Paolo and Francesca—the terrible Dantesque comparison, but also because in Malatestino the type of the fourteen-century man of war is more exaggerated than merely symbolized. This exaggeration is perhaps not artistically damaging, since, just as the orator needs to strain his voice to make himself heard, so the artist needs to accentuate the traits of a character in order to make everyone understand it and to keep it in everyone's memory.

If his brother Gianciotto is a violent man, Malatestino is a true criminal, whom today we would call a born criminal. And D'Annunzio depicts him in this way, without undermining his criminal character not even for a minute.

In the second act, when he is wounded in the eye and appears for the first time on stage, carried in the arms of armed men, Malatestino has neither a complaint nor a cry of pain. His first words, which he utters like one who suddenly wakes up, do not tell his suffering, but only his regret for not being able to kill the prisoner he had taken. And the ferocity and analgesia of the true criminal are sculpted in this episode. He has lost his eye and the sore is horrendous. His parents would like to heal it, but he screams with the insensitivity of great criminals, which resembles heroism:

"No time to weave new linen with old thread.
Put on a bandage, quick,
Give me to drink, and then
To the horse, to the horse!" (*Francesca* 112)

In the fourth act, Francesca, who, upon contact with him, like a sensitive plant[19] withdraws into herself out of repugnance, defines him in sculptural terms:

"Your cradle, of a surety, was hewn out
From some old tree-trunk by a savage axe
That had cut many heads off before them." (*Francesca* 164–65)
(...)
"You are athirst for blood
Always, always at watch,
The enemy of all things." (*Francesca* 164–65)

And the story of the falcon's killing by Malatestino is successfully imagined, as he reveals, with the eloquence of a confrontation, the absolute lack of moral sense inherent in this perverse boy. Her cousin decapitating a falcon seems like a great cruelty to the sweet Francesca, and she scolds him for it. What will she think knowing that Malatestino would cut off the prisoner's head with the same supreme indifference with which he cut the falcon's head off? For Malatestino, there is no difference between the two victims. They are both his own things. He can kill them, and he does kill them. Humanity does not speak in him.

Even love is cruel in Malatestino. Jealous of Paolo, he is ferocious not only against him, but also against Francesca. He is terrible in his irony towards his sister-in-law when, as she pushes him away, she shouts:

"You do not touch me madman, or I call
Your brother!" (*Francesca* 167)

He replies with an insulting question: "*Which one?*"

19 [See *The Intelligence of the Crowd* 222 and 222n3, and, infra, 365.]

He is outrageously deceitful when, as she withdraws in the window recess so as not to hear the prisoner's screams, he says to her, almost intending to render her a service:

"Well, I will go. I will see that you shall have
A quiet night and an untroubled sleep" (*Francesca* 169)

and he goes towards the tower holding the axe and the torch.

Finally, he is a master of guile in his conversation with Gianciotto. This principal scene of the fourth act has the only flaw of too closely resembling a scene between Iago and Othello. But how much more superbly full of pride is Malatestino than Iago! The former is a vulgar traitor and a mediocre soul even in evil; the latter has the very strong temper of a criminal who commits evil not out of fear, but out of will. Iago trembles before Othello. When Gianciotto, who is by now suspicious, orders him "*Speak!*" Malatestino responds haughtily and with that scorching irony that is the verbal outlet of his ferocity:

"Not for threats. You frighten me, I say.
Because I wore no visor, I was made
Blind of one eye; but you must wear indoors
Visor and headpiece, chin-piece, eye-piece, all
Of tempered steel, without a flaw in it!
You will see nothing, nothing can come through
The iron-barred approaches to your brain." (*Francesca* 183–84)

And what precautions he can imagine and recommend to his brother so that the ambush can succeed! Malatestino considers gagging the slave, and to prevent Gianciotto from being heard by Paolo or Francesca when he returns at night, he gives him this acute advice:

"Saddle your swiftest horse, and take with you
A little linen
To bind about his hoofs, in case of need,
Because at night the stones
Upon the noisy way
May well be traitors, brother." (*Francesca* 187–88)

And he instructs him on how to contain himself with his wife and Paolo, in order to not raise suspicion:

"But can you find out the way
to cheat, to smile? Ah, no, you cannot smile." (*Francesca* 186)

To which Gianciotto responds beautifully:

"Let my revenge teach me the way to smile,
If my delight could never." (*Francesca* 186)

And the vendetta, indeed, teaches everything—not only the smile—to this man, to this type of blind husband, unconscious of his ugliness, unconcerned with his wife's aversion towards him, certain of her honesty, he who would go far away, as *podestà* of Pesaro, for a long time without regret, without desire, without jealous fear, preoccupied solely with waging war and with acquiring power and glory for his house.

The archer in the second act defines him rather well:

"The Lamester is well made
To ride astride upon the Omodeo,
To batter strongholds, and to ford the streams,
And to force palisades,
To plunder and to pillage all the earth,
But not to labour in the lovely vineyard
That God has given him." (*Francesca* 70)

Now, however, that he feels and suspects that another is working in the lovely vineyard, he returns psychologically a husband, and he will give death to the woman to whom he had never given a flower.

These three character types—the brother, the brother-in-law, and Francesca's husband—comprise the entire medieval environment. They express the thoughts and feelings of that obscure epoch. When they appear, there is a roar of weapons and a silence of hearts; they are the voice and symbol of strength and violence, without ever any light of a noble impulse or a high ideal.

Paolo and Francesca speak and act in the tragedy, but with a life of their own, almost detached from the environment. They are, if I can say so, a sentimental current that traverses the drama without mixing with the life of the other characters, just as certain underwater currents traverse the ocean without ever sharing with it either their colour or their heat.

Ostasio, Gianciotto, and Malatestino are, instead, lively figures that you cannot detach from the background of the picture from which they stand out. And it is they who, together with the minor figures, create what is truly beautiful and perfectly successful in the tragedy: the exact reproduction of a historical period.

This is a historical period that Gabriele D'Annunzio likes, since in the valedictory tercets appended to the tragedy's text he declares he wants to draw the voice of Sigismondo Malatesta from the marble of Leon Battista Alberti:

> ... the long-haired Sigismondo
> The stormy imperial soul
> Who had a few castles but not the world.[20]

And there is no doubt that he will give us a new poem of tears and blood, recalling the figure of this fifteenth-century warlord.

We deplore how an artist like Gabriele D'Annunzio lets himself be entirely possessed by the suggestion of the past, without feeling how much poetic flame exists also in our epoch, and gives his time and genius to the reproduction in masterpieces of what was, rather than describe what is and to foresee what will be. Nevertheless, we realize, once again, that if he turns to the past, and can revive it with the prestige of art, this is because his soul feels the passions of the past better than those of the present. The individualist arrogance from medieval times responds more to his temperament than the fraternal and socialist spirit of our times.

D'Annunzio is intellectually one of the greatest modern men, but morally he is a man from the sixteenth century.

## 2 "*The Daughter of Jorio*"

As happens to those who are guided more by inspiration than by a conscious will, Gabriele D'Annunzio has not yet kept his promise to draw the voice of Sigismondo Malatesta from the marble of Leon Battista Alberti, and he has appeased the public's anticipation and desire with two tragedies: *The Daughter of Jorio* and *The Torch under the Bushel.*

In both, the past relives—, an imprecise past in the *The Daughter of Jorio,* where he expresses the date in this way: *in the land of Abruzzi, many years ago*; a less imprecise past in *The Torch under the Bushel,* described

20 [Our translation. These lines, from D'Annunzio's final "Commiato," are not included in the English translation of *Francesca da Rimini.*]

in this phrase: *in the Paelignan land, within the territory of Anversa, next to the gorges of the Sagittario, the eve of Pentecost, at the time of the Bourbon King Ferdinand I.*[21]

And this distance in time, customs, and language must be taken into account when reading the two tragedies, in order to understand—I would almost say to forgive—the oddities of the form, which are sometimes obscure, sometimes infantile, and always shrouded in a fog of *implausibility*.

There are crimes—and many—in these tragedies, but there are no true criminals. Blood drips, but the people who hold the homicidal weapon do not have the psychological prominence that should make them throb like living people.

*The Daughter of Jorio* appears as the laborious story of a horrible dream; in it we find that imprecision, that confusion, that tumult of ideas characterizing nocturnal nightmares.

*The Torch under the Bushel* seems a vulgar news report clad in poetry and ennobled by the aristocratically difficult names of the characters and the pompous descriptions of an old palace in ruin.

In *Francesca*, Gabriele D'Annunzio gave us a historically accurate environment and some truly human character types; their profiles were well engraved, just as the places and times were well determined. In *The Daughter of Jorio* and *The Torch under the Bushel*, fantasy took history's place. Not only location and time, but also the souls and thoughts of the protagonists are vague, nebulous, and uncertain.

Who is the shepherd Aligi? He is a mystic, lost in his visions and religious hallucinations; he commits parricide in order to save the woman he spiritually loves from her father's dirty appetites.

Parricide, which is—theoretically—the most horrible of crimes, does not induce great horror in this case. It is the fatal consequence of an outburst of jealousy; it is an act Aligi performs not only out of jealousy, but as the immediate, legitimate defence of a person he loves intensely. Lazaro di Rojo, the father, who follows Mila di Codra up the mountain and would like to take her with him against her will and against his son's

---

21 [The Paeligni were an ancient Italic population that lived in the central region of the peninsula—the current Abruzzi and Umbria regions—before being subdued by the Romans. D'Annunzio is hence using archaic overtones to describe the geographical setting of his drama, which, in fact, takes place at a much later age, namely, between 1759 and 1825, the period of Ferdinand of Bourbon's reign over various areas of southern Italy. Anversa is a town in Abruzzi, close to the calcareous gorges of the river Sagittario.]

prayers, suddenly reveals a sensual fury at the end of the second act, of which the previous scenes gave too feeble notice. He is a repugnant and insignificant old man who deserves the fatal strike of the axe with which his son knocks him down, dead.

Aligi killed in a passionate impetus that blurred his reason, and *he could not* reflect on his action. This dreamlike creature woke up from his psychological lethargy to brandish a weapon. His humanity, his verisimilitude lie entirely and uniquely in that instant of ferocity and blood. Until that moment, he sleeps the isolating sleep of the mystic. He claims this himself when he appears for the first time in the scene, and finds his house celebrating the nuptials that his mother Candia della Leonessa arranged with Vienda, his silent fiancée:

> "Mother, mother, I have slept years seven hundred,
> Years seven hundred! I come from afar off.
> I remember no longer the days of my cradle."[22]

And he always talks "in a dazement" (9) (like Candia tells him), or rather with a weak mind and wild eyes. When Mila di Codra, Jorio's daughter, the lost female, enters Lazaro's house gasping out of exhaustion and fear, having escaped the crowd of harvesters who would like to take and torment her, Aligi keeps silent for a long time listening to what she says in terror, what the harvesters yell in their fervour, what the scared women scream, because they fear that the sad female, the daughter of a magician, might have desecrated their hearth. And he gives a sign of life, he gets up and speaks "with a mixture of dementia and dismay,"[23] only when his mother repeatedly orders him to open the door and throw Jorio's daughter outside. But since she walked away from him in fear, cursing and crying, he suddenly gets down on his knees with open arms and exclaims:

---

22 [Gabriele D'Annunzio, *The Daughter of Jorio*, translated by Charlotte Porter, Pietro Isola, and Alice Henry, in *Poet Lore: A Quarterly Magazine of Letters* XVIII (Spring 1907) (Boston: Poet Lore), 9. Hereafter cited parenthetically in the text as *Jorio*.]

23 [We are providing our own translation of this phrase, to reflect more faithfully D'Annunzio's original terms—"*Un misto di demenza e di sgomento*," which will make Aligi speak "come chi delira" [like someone who is delirious]. The deranged mental and emotional state that D'Annunzio describes is much closer to Sighele's area of investigation than the attitude emerging from the English version—"perplexity and sorrow" (27)—with which Aligi "speaks as one in a dream" (27).]

"Mercy of God! Oh give me forgiveness!
I saw the angel, silent, weeping;
He is weeping with you, O my sisters!
At at me he is gazing and weeping.
Even thus shall I see him forever,
Till the hour for my passing, yea! past it." (*Jorio* 29)
(...)
"And I saw the silent angel
Stand behind her. With his eyes I saw him,
These mortal eyes that shall not witness
On this day the star of vesper.
I saw him gazing at me, weeping." (*Jorio* 83)
(...)
"Harm you not who has harmed you never!
Nor let the false enemy beguile you
Any longer with his potions." (*Jorio* 31)
(...)
"I wished not to harm her.
Spurred on I was by these voices;
And those who to this wrong have brought me
Shall suffer for many days greatly.
Mila di Codra! sister in Jesus,
o give me peace for my offences." (*Jorio* 29)

In these verses we have the description of the hallucination, which gives new direction to Aligi's thought, polarizes him, so to speak, towards pity, while earlier, under his parents' suggestion, he was polarized towards contempt and condemnation of the intrusive female.

The young mystic (of that vague mysticism that has its natural roots in peasant ignorance, where religion is formalism and superstition, and that is pathologically reinforced and sublimated in the shepherd's solitary life) thought he was acting well and serving God by throwing out of the house the woman who had "bewitched" it with her presence and whose name was men's laughing stock. But as soon as he raised his hand against her, the "silent angel" appeared to him, that is, he had a vision that diverted him from his cruel act, and suddenly, by instantaneous psychological revolution, restored the sentiments of pity and forgiveness that are, or should be, the foundation of the Christian religion.

The vision has therefore converted the hallucinating man. He was, until then

(...) like a man on the other
Bank of a river, seeing all things as yonder
Afar, past the water flowing between,
The water that flows everlastingly. (*Jorio* 39)

From that moment, in the nebula of his dreams, a central nucleus stands out more and more clearly: the thought of Mila. He escapes from the house, leaves his mother, leaves his sister, leaves his spouse still intact, and goes far away to the mountain. To find Jorio's daughter? Perhaps this is his objective, but he does not say it. And, indeed, he finds her, one day, as he himself recounts:

"On the morning of San Teobaldo.
On the rock out there was sitting this woman
And she did not arise, for she could not,
So sore were her feet and bleeding.
  Said she: 'Aligi,
Do you know me?'
  I answered: 'Thou art Mila.'
And no more word we spoke, for no more were we
'Twain. Nor on that day were contaminated
Nor after, never." (*Jorio* 42)

For many mystics, the final transformation of their mysticism is love. This happened to Aligi. His love is pure and very chaste, and has something religious in itself. The veneration that inspires the loved one restrains the impetus of the senses. The superstitious core of his soul makes him almost believe that the woman he knew by miraculous apparition is divine, hence intangible. It was the *silent angel* that revealed who Mila di Codra was to him, Mila against whom everyone inveighed; and he loves her more with the fearing adoration of the believer than with the passion of the man. Therefore, he respects her and does not touch her during the long days in which he is alone with her on the mountain. Therefore, when his father Lazaro di Rojo means to rape her, it seems a sacrilege to him:

"The Saviour will judge me, father:
But this woman I shall not abandon,
Nor unto your wrath shall I leave her,
While living. The Saviour will judge me." (*Jorio* 61)

And when the furious Lazaro di Rojo has two herdsmen tie him up and lead him away, out of the cavern, so that he can be alone with Mila, he struggles with himself and prays to God (the struggle of the mystic is prayer) that his hand will not strike his father:

"Christ my Saviour, help Thou me!
That I may not uplift my hand against him
That I may not do this to my father!" (*Jorio* 62)

He feels the obscure, terrible thought of parricide in his brain; he feels it would be wrong to attack his father, but he also feels that what his father has done to him is awful, and what he has done against Mila is horrendous. After Ornella loosens the rope with which the herdsmen had tied him, Aligi returns to the cavern where Lazaro and Mila are. He hears Lazaro offer money to the woman and sees him jump on her to take her; hence he brandishes a weapon, "blind with fury and horror" (*Jorio* 65), yelling to his father: "Let her go! For your life!" (*Jorio* 65) and strikes him dead.

From the psychiatric point of view, Aligi's parricide could thus be defined as *the crime of a mystic*. This is demonstrated not only by the precedents, but also by the consequences of the crime. Aligi's clinical type never contradicts itself. What he was before the parricide, he is also afterwards. His repentance is imbued with religiosity and superstition. Femo di Nerfa describes his behaviour before the Judge:[24]

"He fell on his knees and remained so
And upon his own hand stayed gazing,
And at times he would say 'Mea culpa';
And would kiss the earth before him." (*Jorio* 70)

Remarkable in the line "upon his own hand stayed gazing" is the symbolism (that already recurs in other scenes of the tragedy) depicting how the culprit believes that the cause of the crime is not in himself, but more precisely in the limb that acted and struck the blow.

24 [Sighele's original term here is "Giudice del Maleficio," that is, a judge who, in the 1300s, was in charge of criminal cases, appointed by the *podestà*, that is, the local administrator and magistrate in Italian medieval cities. See 363.]

All of Aligi's words when, "robed in gray, the head covered by a black veil, both hands manacled in heavy, wooden fetters" (*Jorio* 75), he goes to his mother to drink the cup of consolation before the execution, are impregnated with mysticism. And, in the final scene, his congenital, mystic inebriation gradually merges with the inebriation produced by the wine mixture.[25] Therefore, when Jorio's daughter suddenly appears and accuses herself in his place, and the community believes her and throws her into the fire, freeing Aligi, now presumed to be innocent, Aligi by now out of his mind and dizzy, curses Mila, and falls in his mother's arms.

He had appeared in the drama almost like a sleepwalker who spoke and acted feeling estranged and far from the environment where he lived. He vanishes from the drama like a drunkard, after having just one glimmer of humanity by making the axe glisten on his father's head. He is a type that does not contradict any scientific possibility (perhaps it would not be difficult to find one who resembles him in the history of asylums), but he is an implausible type because of the way D'Annunzio presents him to us. In the land of Abruzzi, nobody knows which, and in an undefined time, this young shepherd does not have a solid enough ground under his feet; nor does he have a sufficiently delineated family around him to render him a living figure. Beyond and more than his soul and his word, turbid are those men and things that surround him; and everything in the drama stirs and palpitates with the exaggeration and confusion typical of dreams, not of reality.

Jorio's daughter Mila is more believable, because she is more human. The uncertainty of the settings and dates does not harm her, since she is the eternal type of woman who—after having sinned a great deal with the senses—rehabilitates and renews herself in the flame of a great love. In the land of Abruzzi or elsewhere, in one century or another, the exceptional psychology of these sinners, who convert and redeem themselves by attaining the heights of heroic sacrifice, is fundamentally identical. Balzac wrote that "the humanity of a courtesan in love begets such magnificence as might put even the angels to shame,"[26] and all those artists and scientists who studied the soul of those women discredited by

25 [An alcoholic beverage offered to criminals to numb them before being executed.]

26 [In French in Sighele's text. English translation in Émile Faguet, *Balzac* (Boston: Houghton Mifflin, 1914), 203.]

misfortune recognized that Balzac's claim contains a great truth. It is love or maternity—these two poles of female life—that saves prostitutes. In the case of Mila, it was love.

Before meeting Aligi, what was Jorio's daughter?

A harvester tells Candia, when Mila seeks refuge in her house:

"O Candia della Leonessa,
Know you whom in your home there you harbour,
In your home there with your new-found daughter?
The Daughter of Jorio, the daughter
of the Sorcerer of Codra!
She-dog roamer o'er mountains and valleys,
A haunter of stables and straw-stacks,
Mila the shameless? Mila di Codra.
The woman of stables and straw-heaps,
Very well known to all companies." (*Jorio* 20–21)

Love allows this shameless woman's rebirth—a psychologically and sexually different love than what she had known too well until then. Mila, like Aligi, does not want to surrender to her senses. But while Aligi's abstinence is—as we have said—due to mysticism, Mila's abstinence depends on another cause. There arises in her, with noble passion, the nobility and purity of thought; there arises modesty, the sentiment of dignity, the desire to be *different*, namely, pure in front of this lover, different from what she was in front of others. In her, it is the soul, not the body, that offers itself. She says to Aligi:

"Like a sacred lamp before your faith burning,
With immaculate love before you shining." (*Jorio* 36)

And the third scene of the second act—the most beautiful in the tragedy—describes with suave delicacy this restraint, which the two lovers have, in surrendering to the fever of the senses.

Mila speaks to Aligi:

"Give me that hand of yours, so I may kiss it.
'Tis the drop that I yield to my thirst." (*Jorio* 45)

And later on:

"(...) give leave this one night
more

That I leave with you, here, where you are here,
breathing
That I hear you asleep and be with you,
And over you keep, like your dogs faithful vigil!"
(...)
"Ah! We tremble, we tremble. You are frigid,
Aligi. You are blanching ... O whither
Is flowing the blood your face loses?" (*Jorio* 46)

Since Aligi extends his hand towards her, and the two lovers kiss, overcome by passion, they fall together to their knees and ask forgiveness from heaven for their sin. And Mila prays:

"O Holy Virgin! Grant me this mercy:
That I may stay here with my face to earth bowed,
Cold here, that I may be found dead here,
That I may be removed hence for burial.
No trespass there was in thy eyesight.
No trespass there was. For Thou unto us wert
indulgent.
The lips did no trespass. (To bear witness
There wert Thou!) The lips did no trespass." (*Jorio* 47)
(...)
"Mother clement! I was never sinful
But a well-spring tramped on and trodden.
Shamed have I been in the eyes of Heaven,
But who took away from my memory
This shame of mine if not Thou, Mary?
Born anew then was I when love was born in me.
Thou it was willed it, O faithful Virgin!
All the veins of this new blood spring from afar,
Spring from far off, from the far far away,
From the depths of the earth where she rests,
She who nourished me once in days long ago, long ago.
Let it also be she who bears now for me witness
Of this my innocency! O Madonna, Thou also
bore witness!" (*Jorio* 47–48)

This rebirth, the result of love, transforms Mila from a female dedicated to pleasure into a sensitive plant, as she feels that one kiss is to have sinned a great deal, and into a heroic woman who sacrifices first her happiness, and then her life, for the man she loves.

She sacrifices her happiness by advising Aligi to return to his house next to his abandoned spouse, and forcing herself to depart, to escape without leaving any trace. For this, she can say to Ornella (Aligi's sister):

"(…) I am sinless before your brother,
Before the pallet of your brother clean am I!
(…) But this is the loving Mila.
This is but my love, Ornella.
(…) All paths know the daughter of Jorio;
Already her soul ere your coming
Had started,—ere now, O Innocent one!" (*Jorio* 54)

She sacrifices her life—she confesses to being the perpetrator of the crime Aligi committed. And since people at first hesitate to believe her, in a magnificent impetus, Mila makes her false and holy confession:

"Oh now must you heed me, God's people!
(…) It was close upon night in that ill-fated
Lodging. Lust-crazed then his father
Had seized me to drag toward the entrance,
When Aligi threw himself on us,
In order to save and defend me.
I brandished the axe then with swiftness.
In the darkness I struck him.
I struck him again. Yea, to death I felled him!
With the same stroke I cried: 'You have killed him.'
To the son I cried out: 'You have killed him.
Killed him!' And great in me was my power.
A parricide with my cry I made him—
In his own soul enslaved unto my soul.
'I have killed him!' He answered, and swooning,
He fell in the bloodshed, nought otherwise knowing." (*Jorio* 84–85)

Beyond her sculptural beauty, Mila's ability is admirable in this story. In order to gain credibility, she takes advantage of her fame as "the sorcerer's daughter" (*Jorio* 81): "there is no sorcery that [she does] not know well" (*Jorio* 81). In her sacrificial voluptuousness, she finds invention is more believable to the people's superstitious fantasy. She—namely, the sorceress—pretends she has diabolically suggestionized Aligi, convincing him he was the author of what she had done by herself.

This is perhaps the point when Gabriele D'Annunzio's tragic intuition is most powerful and brilliant. This is when the chaste love of a female sinner is sublimated up to the peaks of martyrdom; this is when we feel the protagonist's soul in unison with that of "The land of Abruzzi (...). Many years ago" (*Jorio* 2). And this is also when the spectator's or the reader's soul is more enthralled by the charm of the drama, because if Jorio's daughter was really not the one who killed Lazaro, it is also true that Aligi killed him for her. Mila di Codra atones at the stake for a crime that is not hers; but something great and obscure, God or fate, seems to punish her because, through the infamy of her past and the love that redeemed her, she turned the mystic Aligi into a parricide.

## 3 "*The Torch under the Bushel*"

One of the greatest qualities of *The Daughter of Jorio* is the adaptation of form to its subject: mystical, sad, tragic is its dominating thought, and such are also, according to the circumstances, the lines that express it. The poet never forgets the psychological nobility and delicacy of the protagonists' types, and all the drama is suffused with sweet melancholy.

If the conception of *The Torch under the Bushel* is vulgar, its expression is even more so. There are phrases and blatant similes that were already rightly berated by Francesco Pastonchi.[27] But all the vulgarity is summarized, sharpened, and symbolized in Angizia's type, the servant who:

> (...) was sweeping between two doors, with naked
> Arms and her skirt raised at the hips,
> And the airstream
> Was lifting the garbage around her,
> Throwing it back against her face.[28]

This female figure, who certainly cannot claim any originality or refinement, could at least have become grandiose and terrible in her perfidy. All human iniquities concentrate in her: as the master's lover, she kills his wife in order to marry him, and, now married to Teobaldo [*sic*]

27 [Francesco Pastonchi (1877–1953) was an Italian literary critic and poet heavily influenced by D'Annunzio's decadent style, and founder of the periodicals *Il Piemonte* and *Il Campo*.]

28 [All translations from *The Torch under the Bushel* are our own. The play has never been translated into English.]

di Sangro, attempts to poison his son Simonetto, while becoming the lover of his half-brother Bertrando.

Gabriele D'Annunzio perhaps wanted to make this woman a tragic creation: the evil genius of the family. He only succeeded in making of her a creature good for the prison and for the street, like those one finds in the news section and at theatre shows of the lowest order.

From the day when Angizia, Luca's girl, dominated the senses of her master, the timid and cowardly descendent of a strong and courageous race, there is only misfortune in the ancient house of Sangro. The walls crumble and people fall sick. It seems that fate wanted the ruin of things and of men, and the extinction of the name. This material and moral debacle is, however, more *described* than *felt*; for sure, she who causes it does not have that aesthetic superiority, that dramatic importance she should have over the other characters. She is always and solely a servant—not enough to accomplish or have others accomplish what has occurred in the play. Her lips only know insolence against everyone: against her husband, her accomplice whom she despises; against Gigliola, her judge whom she fears; against Serparo, her father of whom she is ashamed. Her soul only emerges out of an impudent cynicism and clever calculation: she calmly confesses her crime to Gigliola (her stepdaughter), because by accusing herself together with Tibaldo, she knows—or is deluded into thinking—that his daughter will not dare avenge her own mother by retaliating against her father.

When, on the anniversary of the homicide (Act I, scene vi), Gigliola stubbornly stares at her face, here is how Angizia confesses the truth:

"Do you believe I ignore
What your eyes always say
When you stare at me? They say:
'It is you, you, you!' Indeed, yes,
it is true ...
... it is true. It is
me. I shout this to you and I do not lower my eyes.
Here I am. I have answered you
Without trembling. It is I who did it. One year today."

And since Gigliola exclaims:

"My mother, my mother, holy soul
(...) Support me. I promised:
I will keep my word. I will be strong."

Angizia interrupts her:

"And what will you do?
What can you do to me?
I am protected by your father. There are,
there were two of us.
...
Hear me: two of us. I am telling you
So that you understand
That before touching me you must
Go through your father."

Tibaldo, who is present at the scene, attempts to contradict Angizia by screaming that she is a "mad beast, a rabid bitch," who has the dizziness of hate and does not know what she says, but his knees tremble and bend before his daughter.

This Tibaldo di Sangro recalls other Dannunzian types, in a worse version, though, just as all copies recall the original for the worse. He is the type—by now common in life and thus not rare in literature, either—of the weakling, of the neurasthenic, of the sick person who, from his physiological misery, is gradually and inevitably drawn to moral misery. He is a cowardly character, the soul of a slave onto whom the surrounding strong evildoers exert their sovereign power. He is, in short, a failed and implausible *Giovanni Episcopo*. Giovanni Episcopo had only one master, Wanzer, and got rid of him through crime. Tibaldo also gets rid of Angizia, the sad woman who dominates him; but he has other masters beyond Angizia, other people to whom he surrenders, whose charm wins him over, whose feet he allows on his neck.

For example, when he appears for the first time in the tragedy, we see him argue with his half-brother Bertrando Acclozamòra about some topic of interest. The scene, which becomes violent not only with words but also with events, is a reproduction of the scene between Ostasio and Bannino in *Francesca*. Ostasio, Guido da Polenta's legitimate son, insults Bannino the bastard, who remains humble and resigned in front of him. In *The Torch under the Bushel*, Bertrando Acclozamòra, the oldest brother, insults Tibaldo, the son by a second marriage, in the following terms:

"Flabbiness without
A skeleton, born of an old man's seed

whose heartache renders him even more cowardly than the fear for his crimes does."

The two scenes resemble one another for the quality of the protagonists and for the fraternal hate that emerges. It is the ancient theme of envy and rancor between those who have a common but not identical origin. They share blood from one parent, but not of both. And as Ostasio dominates Bannino with his contempt, so Bertrando is Tibaldo's despot. They are two couples of equal characters, revealing the eternal psychology of the *incubus* and *succubus.*

But Tibaldo does not solely bow his forehead and soul before Angizia and Bertrando. He is one of those weaklings who bow before the least important person who speaks to them, when this person knows how to talk with the harsh pride of the strong addressing the coward. Therefore, after the scene with Acclozamòra, he beseeches Gigliola, ashamed before his daughter, in whom he reads the suspect of uxoricide; he defends himself from her horrendous doubt with infelicitous protests; and condescends to her desire to banish Angizia, the female who killed his wife and who now betrays him in his house, with his half-brother …

This rapid turn of the father towards his daughter, whom he had ignored until then, may seem like remorse, but it is also cowardice. Tibaldo understands, through a thousand signs, that *his* crime was discovered. Gigliola, this young feeble girl, who seems to carry around in the crumbling house not only the sore of her sorrow, but also the flame of her revenge, dared to interrogate him—and in what way!—about *his* participation in the murder. The other ones, his mother Donna Aldegrina, his son Simonetto, the wet nurses Benedetta and Annabella, do not speak to him, but there is more than doubt in their silence: there is certainty, condemnation. When he enters a room where the others are, they leave, they escape from him, they are afraid to talk to him.

Tibaldo understands all of this: he feels that the hour of truth, perhaps also the hour of expiation, is near, and he needs to know, to truly know, what those who watch him with diffidence and disgust think of him. He needs to overcome this state of anxiety, which is his martyrdom. And one day, the same day when Angizia accused him of being an accomplice to Gigliola, he interrogates his mother.

Donna Aldegrina was with Simonetto and the wet nurses in the vast hall of the palace. When Tibaldo appears, the wet nurses and Simonetto leave; the mother remains alone with him, and he says to her:

"Are you not leaving,
Mother? Do you not flee the leper, like the others?
Do you not plug your mouth
To avoid drinking
The infected air?"

And Donna Aldegrina:

"Son,
Do not repine. You have trodden on
The hearts that loved you."

Thus even the mother doubts him. He asks her:

"I am the murderer?
Do you believe so? Gigliola told you?
Is she accusing me before you?"

And she responds:

"... You are frightened by yourself
And are shouting irreparable words."

The scene is strangely implausible. Yes, its first improbability consists in its relative length. A son who is about to make a terrible confession to his mother does not waste time in telling her:

"I looked at my face in the mirror
And I did not recognize myself. Hence
I hit it and broke it. My soul
Went to one thousand pieces,
scattered on the floor;
and I see one thousand of my selves,
which I do not recognize ...
... and you who have given me this poor
Soul, you are helping me pick it up,
and patch it."

Second, his excessive humility is strange and illogical in one who also wants to support his innocence. Likewise, it is strange and illogical that he does not proclaim his presumed innocence loudly and strongly, but instead begs for it like a concession from the maternal lip.

The mother keeps silent, despite the reiterated pleas of her son, who implores her to tell him whether she believes he is a murderer. But the silence, which would be a sufficient response for anyone, is not enough for Tibaldo, who (and here is another great improbability) insists and wants Donna Aldegrina to hear from Angizia herself:

"What silent hand
Did suddenly push
The peaceful one?"

Angizia then enters the hall; she is furious with Serparo (her father, whom she did not want to recognize, because she is ashamed of him) and incites Tibaldo to throw him out.

Tibaldo responds to her:

"With a stick
Like a dirty beast
I will chase you away,"

since, under the suggestion of his mother and daughter,[29] he has rediscovered some strength in himself to finally react against the Marsican female. But Angizia, who knows him, is not afraid of his threats:

"You earlier
Wore the mask of the strong
Man before your daughter; and now
You wear it before your mother.
But you cannot deceive me. Behind it,
I behold your bloodless visage."

She calls him a liar and reveals all the pettiness of his soul:

"You implored me,
Crying, contorting on the ground,

29 [Sighele wrote "sister" ["sorella"] but, as we can see in the subsequent excerpt from the play, it should be "daughter" ["figlia"], as he is referring to Gigliola. We have hence corrected it accordingly.]

when I wanted to leave; you grabbed
my knees, you lay
your face in the dust, so that
I could press my heel on your nape."

Tibaldo does not deny his earlier cowardice, but he affirms that now "he has raised his head," and challenges his wife to give proof in front of his mother that she participated in the crime. To which Angizia responds:

"What evidence was there
Against me when your daughter
Was earlier repeating: 'I am looking at you'?
And the old woman is looking at you.
And you have no more colour
Of life, nor a drop
Of blood that is not frozen in your
Heart; and you make a desperate effort
So that your teeth do not chatter
—yet, your jaw is betraying you—
Like this night is the year, when
You secretly came barefoot
Into my dark room and, staggering,
looked for me, and came
To lie next to me, because
You could not be alone;
and I knew I had your tacit
consent and you knew that my hand
was ready to act.
And we clung to each other; and became
Two, for widowhood and for marriage.
Do you not remember? Are you convinced? Enough,
now. This had to be said
as a pledge for silence."

Donna Aldegrina neither moves nor speaks, and Tibaldo screams at her:

"I am your
Mad, and vile and lost son. And she mingles
Her sin with my madness, so that

I will never again be able to separate my soul
From it, nor save myself before you ...
... she
Is the nameless, destructive
savage beast,
that we must shatter ..."

And he rushes towards Angizia to strangle her. But Donna Aldegrina screams, and he:

"no, no, mother.
I let go. I let her go. Not in front of you."

His intent to kill her is deferred, not abandoned. He does not yet confess, but recognizes that everything accuses him. His guilt—even though it is not the direct guilt demanded by judges—is a moral guilt, enough for men to condemn him. It is the guilt of the weak, of the coward, of the *succubus,* who knew, who intuited what Angizia would do and allowed her to do it. And now, all the horror of his behaviour is clearly visible and the reaction of his weakness is—as always in the weak—ferocity. Like Giovanni Episcopo against Wanzer, Tibaldo will avenge himself on Angizia, who has demeaned and discredited him. He will kill her, hoping that a single act of criminal energy will redeem his long-lasting cowardice.

Even Gigliola—the least unlikely figure in the tragedy, as Serparo is the most beautiful—contemplates Angizia's death. She believes in her obligation to carry it out. She vowed she would; she wants to avenge her mother and save her family by liberating it forever from the one who brought shame and misfortune to them. In a very effective scene, she accepts a hairpin from Serparo that will help her to kill, and she will secretly take from Serparo the sack of snakes into which she will immerse her hand so as to be poisoned by the reptiles' bite, with the certainty of not failing, of not trembling in the supreme moment:

"I put death
At my heels,
As I seek my vengeance:
May I not come back
Nor turn around
Nor hesitate."

And she will tell her brother Simonetto—whom everyone ignored because he was far from the house when their mother was killed—the horrendous truth that she had kept locked in her heart for a year:

"It happened in Alcesti's room. The woman
Was there, looking for clothes
in the chest; and she seemed to find none. Then
She appeared on the threshold, in ambush; and called.
The chest was open;
the cover was lifted,
the trap was set,
the device was ready
for the deadly move.
She called to the door: our mother came,
entered unsuspectingly; she bent over
to look for things. The executioner
caught her off guard: she lowered
the cover on her neck:
she pressed down, and suffocated
the last cry ..."

Leaving Simonetto, to whom the sudden and horrendous revelation renewed the pangs of his illness, Gigliola goes—pale and confident—to her revenge. But in her stepmother's room she finds Angizia already dead and exits screaming, aghast:

"Where is
My father? Who killed her? Who killed her?"

Tibaldo had killed her—and Gigliola will die by poison, without being able to accomplish the vow that only her pure hands should have executed.

Gigliola's character unconsciously personifies the tragedy. The daughter fails at her vow, as the tragedy fails in its scope. The drama that would like to be grandiose is only terribly heavy. The crimes are too many and the criminals are not human enough, and not even specific to the environment in which the author makes them move and speak. Their lips insult too often, there is too much artifice in expression, and there are too few personal and local features that we could recognize as coming from one particular region or epoch. Even the environment is badly depicted, with exaggerated horror and melodramatic mystery. In addition to Tibaldo's first murdered wife (a crime that occurs before the tragedy and dominates it), to Angizia's homicide (a crime that closes the tragedy and completes it), to Simonetto's poisoning attempts, to Angizia's patricidal actions against Serparo, to Gigliola's suicide, there is Angizia's adultery with Bertrando, there is a locked-up madwoman whose scream they hear (just as in *Francesca* they heard the prisoner's screams), there is the crumbling palace, the family in poverty, and there is even … a hidden treasure!

It is not only the Sangro household, it is the reader and the spectator who feel oppressed under the implausible heap of so many infamies and oddities. The truth is lost among these horrors. The Tibaldo type, which basically could have been a felicitous creation, comes out as a second, worse edition of Giovanni Episcopo. And the Gigliola type, initially the simplest and most original, in psychologically terms, also deforms itself and loses her naturalness to put itself in unison with the coarse exaggeration surrounding her.

In short, in *The Torch under the Bushel* we do not feel the lion's claw to the same level as in *The Daughter of Jorio.* The artist is minor, or at least different from what has appeared so far. He is also different in his thought and in the objective he intends to convey and follow.

No intellectual light radiates from *The Torch under the Bushel.* In Gabriele D'Annunzio's prose works, we found the reflection of Nietzsche's theory; in *Francesca,* we recognized an adorer of the past, of the epochs of violence and will; in *The Daughter of Jorio,* in the absence of a new and strong thought, we could recognize a setting that was, according to Amiel's definition,[30] a state of mind. But in *The Torch under the Bushel,* who can find the core of an idea under the lucid surface of its poetic garment, or at least the exact reproduction of an environment? There is perhaps still, here and there, the cold perfection of technique, but the drama is intellectually meagre.

And from an artist like Gabriele D'Annunzio we expect works that not only make us admire the artificer's lines, but also discuss the poet's ideas.

---

30 [For Amiel see *Modern Eve* 330n55.]

# 8 From *In Art and in Science*

## Chapter 2: "Reading Balzac"

Some years ago, in an article in *Nuova Antologia*[1] Vincenzo Morello observed that, despite his efforts to summon the attention of the Italian positivists on Balzac's work, they had not yet devoted their studies to that multitude of psychological intuitions and anthropological divinations which is the *Human Comedy*: not Lombroso who, in his many citations of scholars, always forgot Balzac; not Ferri who, in his *I delinquenti nell'arte* [Criminals in Art] (where, nonetheless, he analysed volumes of many novelists and poets), only dedicated a line to Balzac; not Sighele who, in his *Criminal Couple*, did not cite the figures of Vautrin and Lucien de Rubempré as the most perfect psychological exemplars of the *crime à deux.*

Vincenzo Morello was right in his reproach. But if I did not listen to him before, it is because it was very difficult to find the necessary time to attentively reread, annotate, and comment on the fifty-five volumes that, in the edition published for the centenary of Balzac's birth, contain all the superb literary fecundity of a man who was rightly named as *professor of social sciences*, and who could without exaggeration boast of *having carried an entire society in his brain.*

1 Issue of 1 March 1901. [Vincenzo Morello (1860–1933) was an Italian journalist and senator. He worked for several daily newspapers—among them *La Tribuna*—and later was the editor of *La Tribuna illustrata*, *L'ora*, and *Il secolo*.]

Now that in a period of rural quiet I have had the comfort to dive once again into the *Human Comedy* and to relive the multiple and intense lives of his two thousand characters, I can reply to Morello's invitation with a scholar's serene conscience, and present my modest contribution to the analysis of what is perhaps the largest and most complete representation of life that ever came from a genius of the last century.

Balzac has been studied too much—from Lamartine's book up to the *essays* of Brunetière and of Bourget—for me to be able and willing to attempt a work of criticism on his life and oeuvre.

The man who fought and suffered during almost all of his existence, who wasted most of his wondrous energies running after the phantoms of projects and industrial enterprises he never achieved, ultimately died in the luxury and splendours of that wealth that he craved so much and that he had attained only a short time before. His life could resemble one of those cloudy, stormy days that end, almost miraculously, in the rosy light of a sudden, magnificent sunset.

In his youth he had written to his sister: "I have two single and immense desires: *to be famous and to be loved*."[2] This was for him (and for whom would it not be?) the perfect combination of happiness. God, in whom he believed, granted it to him. A foreign millionaire, a Polish woman who admired his genius, fell in love with him, married him, and gave him love and wealth. His dream to be loved was brief because death broke it; but his fame stretched and continued into the future, growing every day. Today he is recognized as a precursor and a master; today everyone turns to him when, annoyed by the mediocre works of their minuscule contemporaries, they want to see a giant again, and delight in the contemplation of a colossal work.

I will not write, I repeat, a work of criticism, but simply a work of exhumation. I will try to recall—out of the thousands of pages in which they are confused and hidden—those ideas with which Balzac summarized and synthesized not only the spirit and morality of his era, but also the

2 [Sighele is part of a long line of Balzac critics who, to a greater or lesser degree, have romanticized the French author's personality on the basis of some of his statements. Balzac's biographer Graham Robb underlines that, in fact, Balzac's tone is often more scathing and cynical. In particular, precisely this alleged pronouncement, taken from one of Balzac's letters, is an apocryphal alteration of the following (unpunctuated) statement: "I only have two passions love and glory and nothing has been satisfied yet and never will be." See Graham Robb, *Balzac: A Biography* (New York: Norton, 1994), 78.]

psychological, fundamental truths of our civilization. I will not, in short, perform other than the task of the miner, who brings the precious metal to light and life from the profound obscurity of a mine. I will be content to collect in only one necklace, with a goldsmith's patience, the pearls that Balzac's genius scattered in his works.

I believe that this is the best way—since it is the surest and sincerest—to honour and interpret a man. In front of the vast and multiform production of great writers who lavished the sparks of their genius with the prodigality of millionaires, the most useful and fertile comment is, indeed, the one that limits itself to gathering and organizing the ideas thrown here and there haphazardly and unconsciously. In other words, it should give a systematic unity and, I would almost say, a philosophical dignity to fragments that, taken individually, would only have a relative and partial value and significance.

## *I Woman and Love*

Lamartine wrote that there are two dominating qualities in Balzac's brilliance: truth and morality. I would like to add that his morality was not premeditated, tedious, and pedantic. Rather, it is a necessary consequence of the sincere picture he wanted to make of life, and it was always flavoured with humour or hidden under a pungent irony. Balzac is never a preacher because, unlike other authors, he almost never speaks in the first person. His moral is expressed by events more often than in words. And when you linger pensively over a profound observation, it is a woman's spirit or a journalist's scepticism or a criminal's cynicism that pronounced it. Balzac does not exist in his books: it is his characters that exist. He transfused himself into them by one of those miracles of autosuggestion he so magnificently describes in the first pages of *Facino Cane.* And in his work you do not find the author, you find *the entire society* that he had in his brain and to which he gave voice, action, and feeling, with an unattainable and never-attained naturalness.

Because these characters are many and varied, because they belong to all social classes, because they live in Paris and in the provinces, because they are of diverse races, and the crossbreeding of heredity and the environment's suggestions merge and spread in them, there is an entire world that stirs around you, that throbs, loves, suffers, cries, commits crimes, and dances a joyous or fearful jumble around your imagination, giving you the calm delight of a dream or the feverish anxiety of a nightmare ...

Bourget says, I believe, that life is "a volume by Labiche interleaved with some Shakespeare."[3] Even Balzac's work, which is a photograph of life, deserves this definition. A subtle vein of humour and spirit pervades and fecundates it, although it is interrupted here and there by the impetuous torrent of drama and tragedy.

Bixiou, Blondet, de Marsay, Rastignac—these *viveurs* to whom Balzac trusts the task of elegantly reciting the rosary of his philosophy as a man of the world—or the women, like the Princess of Cadignan, the Duchess of Maufrigneuse, or Mademoiselle de Touche—to whom he leaves the witty prerogative of criticizing the weaknesses of their sex—are characters full of spirit who decorate their pleasurable existence with a conversation studded with epigrams and *bons mots* that often enclose a profound morality. In France everything is done while laughing, Balzac says; and his characters laugh even when doing philosophy.

You want to know what these *viveurs* think of love? "Love is a religion, and his cult must in the nature of things be more costly than those of all other deities; Love the Spoiler stays for a moment, and then passes on; like the urchin of the streets, his course may be traced by the ravages that he has made."[4]

Eugène de Rastignac, who, in order to succeed in the art of seduction, wants to renew his modest, provincial wardrobe as soon as he arrives in Paris, consoles and justifies himself with this definition: "Love and the Church alike demand a fair altar-cloth" (*Goriot* 166).

The Baroness Nucingen, who supports Eugène de Rastignac, tries to win over the final scruples of her lover, who was still disgusted to accept money from a woman, with this curious reasoning: "Did not a lady in olden times arm her knight with sword and helmet and coat of mail, and find him a charger, so that he might fight for her in the tournament? Well, then, Eugène, these things that I offer you are the weapons of this age; everyone who means to be something must have such tools as these" (*Goriot* 229–30).

More serious than Delphine de Nucingen is the Princess of Cadignan, who does not give advice to her lovers, but pronounces judgments: "Some women"—she said—"put their lover before their children, just as most women are mothers rather than wives. The two instincts of wifely

3 [See Sighele, *Against Parliamentarism* 212n123.]

4 [Honoré de Balzac, *Old Goriot*, translated by Ellen Marriage (London: J.M. Dent and Sons; New York: Macmillan, 1913), 238. Hereafter cited parenthetically in the text as *Goriot*.]

love and motherhood, developed as they are by social conditions, often come into conflict in a woman's heart."[5] The princess was no longer very young when she expressed this truth: she was at the sunset of her mundane career, but she did not yet renounce testing the power of her charm over men. "I know something about these setting suns"—a journalist said—"They last for ten minutes on the horizon, and for ten years in a woman's heart."[6]

It is precisely the Princess of Cadignan who, in her pride as a great lady, finds this just definition: "it was the glory of civilisation that it had created Woman, when Nature stopped short at the female" (*Princess* 19). Palférine, the prince of *bohème*, establishes in a nutshell the comparison between the woman and the child that psychology would then develop and demonstrate scientifically: "Woman, in my opinion, is the most logical of created beings, the child alone excepted. In both we behold a sublime phenomenon, the unvarying triumph of one dominant, all-excluding thought."[7] This observation is completed by and integrated with this other one: "The characteristics of a true affection are frequently like those of childhood,—absence of reflection, imprudence, heedless improvidence, laughter, and tears."[8]

What is more changeable than woman and child? And yet, woman is more constant in love than man. And, among women, the most loyal are those who should be less so. The fallen females, the lovers of criminals, show devotion towards them that perhaps few honest women would know how to attain:

> It is female devotion, crouching faithfully at the doors of prisons, perpetually employed in thwarting the wiles of the police or, the examining judges, the incorruptible guardian of the blackest secrets,—which makes so many criminal cases obscure and, in fact, impenetrable. (...) In the language of

5 [Honoré de Balzac, *A Princess's Secrets*, translated by Ellen Marriage (London: Dent; New York: Macmillan, 1908), 50. Hereafter cited parenthetically in the text as *Princess*.]

6 [Honoré de Balzac, *Splendors and Miseries of Courtesans*, in *The Novels of Honoré de Balzac*, vol. 1, translated by Ellery Sedgwick (Philadelphia: George Barrie & Son, 1895), 409. Hereafter cited parenthetically in the text as *Splendors*.]

7 [Honoré de Balzac, *A Prince of Bohemia and Other Stories*, translated by John Rudd and Ellen Marriage (Philadelphia: Gebbie Publishing, 1899), 50. Hereafter cited parenthetically in the text as *Bohemia*.]

8 [Honoré de Balzac, *A Great Man of the Provinces in Paris*, in *La Comédie Humaine of Honoré de Balzac*, vol. 17, translated by Katharine Prescott Wormeley (Boston: Hardy, Pratt, 1904), 332. Hereafter cited parenthetically in the text as *Provinces*.]

> these women, *avoir de la probité* (to be honest) means not to fail in any duty to that attachment; to give all their money to the men *enflacqué* (imprisoned); to watch over their safety and comfort; to keep every species of faith with them; and to undertake for them all possible things. (...) No passion of a virtuous woman, not even that which a religious nature feels for a confessor, can surpass the attachment of the mistress who shares the peril of these great criminals.[9]

And in reality, few honest men have been loved almost as much as all great criminals. "[T]hat love which does not consist of an indissoluble friendship," Bixiou says, "seems to me a momentary libertinism."[10] But how many, among lovers, are the cases of this indissoluble friendship? Perhaps it is more easily found at the prison gate than in the salons.

If honest women, according to Balzac, love less intensely than others, then superior men are less able and less fortunate lovers than mediocre men and imbeciles. "A man may be great, and yet be a villain, and a fool may rise to sublime heights of love" (*Princess* 18), says the Princess of Cadignan, who perhaps needed to justify some of her particular adventures. And the Baroness Nucingen underlines her friend's thought by affirming: "[L]ove offers fools their only chance of growing" (*Nucingen* 58). It seems that the fools very often have this occasion to *aggrandize themselves.* Perhaps this is because they have more time than others. "There is no absolute virtue, but there are circumstances" (*Nucingen* 17), and the unoccupied imbecile has more time to ... exploit the circumstances, and to warm up by the flame of his passion the apparent coldness of those aristocratic dames who, as de Marsay says, are stoves "with a marble casing."[11]

And because anecdotes are the passports to every morality, and the anti-narcotic of all books, allow me to recall the dialogue between two women, one of whom had all the spirit that the other's husband lacked.

9 [Honoré de Balzac, *The Last Incarnation of Vautrin*, in *La Comédie Humaine of Honoré de Balzac*, vol. 19, translated by Katharine Prescott Wormeley (Boston: Hardy, Pratt, 1904), 56–57. Hereafter cited parenthetically in the text as *Incarnation.*]

10 [Honoré de Balzac, *The House of Nucingen*, in *The Novels of Honoré de Balzac*, translated by William Walton (Philadelphia: George Barrie's Sons, 1896), 15. Hereafter cited parenthetically in the text as *Nucingen.*]

11 [Honoré de Balzac, *Another Study of Woman*, in *César Birotteau, Nucingen and Co., Another Study of Woman*, translated by Katharine Prescott Wormeley (Boston: Little, Brown, 1899), 524. Hereafter cited parenthetically in the text as *Woman.*]

"Have you ever observed, my dear, that women in general do not love but the fools?"

"What are you saying, duchess! And how could you agree with this observation, with the aversion you have for your husband?"

The truth is, as Balzac says perhaps with some exaggeration, that women "would sooner hear say 'that is a very handsome man' than see [their] lover elected to the Institute."[12]

This is the philosophy—or the experience—of the rich, cultured, and carefree classes. It is not very profound because it only touches a part of human psychology, the psychology of the great world. But it is quite exact within its limits. We find more breadth and universality in these sentences: "The virtue of women is perhaps a question of temperament" (*Physiology* 46); "A virtuous woman has in her heart one fiber less or one fiber more than other women: she is either stupid or sublime" (*Physiology* 46). We find more morality and optimism in this simile: "it is as absurd to deny that it is possible for a man always to love the same woman, as it would be to affirm that some famous musician needed several violins in order to execute a piece of music or compose a charming melody" (*Physiology* 61). We will find more acute psychology in Blondet's claim: "Passion which does not believe itself eternal is hideous" (*Nucingen* 15–16) and in the painful, but truthful affirmation: "All passions are essentially Jesuitical."[13] We will find more wit in this affirmation: "It is easier to be a lover than a husband, for the same reason that it is more difficult to be witty every day, than to say bright things from time to time" (*Physiology* 65), and in the observation of Madame Rabourdin (the heroine of the story *The Government Clerks*): "in all countries society, before making up its mind about a man, listens for what his wife thinks of him."[14] There is more crude sincerity in de Marsay's irreverent aphorism: "There is always the soul of a monkey in the sweetest and most angelic of women!"

12 [Honoré de Balzac, *Physiology of Marriage: Petty Troubles of Married Life*, edited with introduction by J. Walker McSpadden (Boston: Dana Estes, 1901), 8. Hereafter cited parenthetically in the text as *Physiology*.]

13 [Honoré de Balzac, *Lost Illusions*, in *La Comédie Humaine of Honoré de Balzac*, vol. 16, translated by Katharine Prescott Wormeley (Boston: Hardy, Pratt, 1904), 19. Hereafter cited parenthetically in the text as *Illusions*.]

14 [Honoré de Balzac, *Bureaucracy*, in *La Comédie Humaine of Honoré de Balzac*, vol. 22, translated by Katharine Prescott Wormeley (Boston: Hardy, Pratt, 1904), 12. Hereafter cited parenthetically in the text as *Bureaucracy*.]

(*Woman* 531), and in the judgment of a novelist: "If there is any thing more ungrateful than a king, it is a nation; but (...) woman is more ungrateful than either of them" (*Physiology* 164).

Above all, we will find a more brilliant intuition of woman's ability to guess a hidden thought from a facial expression in the phrase that explains why Esther could penetrate her lover's secrets with a look: "The knowledge of a man's face is, for the woman who loves him, what the wide sea is for a mariner" (*Splendors* 359). Poor Esther! She was one of those women who "make up by an insensate luxury for the childish days when they lived on raw apples" (*Bohemia* 28), but she loved her Lucien like no other woman has ever loved her lover. The letter she writes to Lucien de Rubempré before poisoning herself and dying for him (after selling herself, for him, to Nucingen for the price of 750,000 francs) is perhaps one of the pages in which Balzac's art is most complete, since it unites the shiver of commotion with the elegance of humour. It is a letter that makes one cry, smile, think. All the cords of the human lyre are touched with a measure, with a delicacy that only genius and love possess. It is a woman's heart that reveals itself, mixing the cheerfulness of youth with the tears of a moribund person, as a flower softens the vivacity of its colours with drops of dew. Esther, in order to render her death less sad for her friend, comments in the Parisian way: "I said to you: 'Better die at thirty'; well, that day you found me thoughtful, and caressed me to distract my mind; and between two kisses I spoke to you again, and said, 'Every day pretty women go out from the play before the curtain falls!';—I have not wished to see the last act, that is all" (*Splendors* 108).

## *II Politics and Parliament*

I wanted to show, with some citations about a theme that lends itself to the simplest and most common of psychologies, what was the way and, I would say, the method that Balzac used to embroider his sometimes witty and sometimes profound observations on the canvas of his stories.

But my task is more specifically dedicated to researching Balzac's ideas of criminals and, in general, of all those problems of morality and sociology that the positivist Italian school years ago retrieved from spiritualist oversimplifications—like the very naive explanation in terms of free will.

If I wanted to continue in the entertaining, and perhaps useful, but unorganized work of citing the various definitions Balzac disseminated in his volumes about the most diverse arguments, many pages would not be sufficient. He talked about anything and made pronouncement on almost everything: on art, to him nothing but concentrated nature; on conscience, to him a stick everyone uses to beat their neighbour, but never uses on oneself; on instincts, nothing but "living facts, of which the cause lies in necessity that has been undergone" (*Splendors* 58); on jealousy, nothing but fear in love; on punishment, which the Catholic Church enshrines with the sacrament of confession, and which is just "a hypocrisy, an award given to immoral or guilty actions"; on resignation, "a daily suicide"; on misfortune, a sidewalk for the genius, a treasure for the able man, an abyss for the weak man; on the lottery, the "opium to poverty"[15]; on journalism, which he detests because it "is hell,—a pit of iniquity, falsehood, treachery, which no one can cross and no one can leave with a pure soul,—unless it be Dante under protection of Virgin's laurel" (*Provinces* 104); on bureaucracy, a "ponderous curtain hung between the service to be done and the man who orders it" (*Bureaucracy* 16); on diplomacy, "the science of those who have no other, and whose depth seems the greater because they are empty" (*Illusions* 48); on the big bank and its great bankers, who are conquerors sacrificing "great masses to reach some results" (*Incarnation* 244) and whose soldiers "thus sacrificed are the interests of individuals" (*Incarnation* 244), since, according to Blondet, "the money of fools is, by right divine, the patrimony of clever men" (*Nucingen* 78).[16]

Let us leave these *boutades*, and move closer to Balzac's thought on more important and vital problems.

What does he think—or what do his characters think—about parliament and politics?

As almost all the superior men who do not plead in the public's favour and who are, therefore, sincere in their brutal pride, Balzac is sceptical of parliament, not because he does not recognize its rights in theory,[17] and not because he does not appreciate the advantages that come from

15 [Honoré de Balzac, *A Bachelor's Establishment*, translated by by Clara Bell (London: J.M. Dent, 1898), 67.]

16 [Émile Blondet, a character that appears in several volumes of Balzac's *Human Comedy*, is an ambitious and unscrupulous journalist.]

17 In his introduction to *At the Sign of the Cat and Racket*, where he explains the origin, the plan, and the purpose of the *Human Comedy*, and where he openly exposes his conservative and in some cases reactionary ideas, Balzac says, "Without being an enemy to election, which is an excellent principle as a basis for legislation, I reject election regarded as *the only social instrument*." [Honoré de Balzac, "Introduction," *Honoré de Balzac in Twenty-Five Volumes*, vol. 1 (New York: Peter Fenelon Collier & Son, 1900), 17; original emphasis. Hereafter cited parenthetically in the text as *Cat*.]

exercising liberty, but because—as a profound connoisseur of collective psychology—he knows that, in practice, the crowd's sovereignty is often an equivocation or a danger: "To meet with a great prince is certainly a rare chance (...), but to trust to a whole assembly, even though it be composed of honest men only, is folly."[18] This sentence is nothing but the unconscious translation of an ancient adage: *Senatores boni viri, senatus autem mala bestia.*[19] And it is explained and justified by these other claims, where I think I see the embryo of that psycho-physiological theory of panic, which Espinas illustrated half a century later: "Most men are startled and reassured by nothing just as animals are" (*Splendors* 162).[20] And again: "Such persons are excited by vociferation, as vulgar palates are by strong drinks" (*Illusions* 102). Is there not in these words the *reason* for many rallies? Is there not the germ for that psychology of the crowd, which only in these recent times has been scientifically studied? But Balzac goes further, and glimpses not only the obscure mechanism that makes the assemblies and crowds speak and deliberate, but also the mechanism that makes them act and—unfortunately very often—commit excesses and crimes. "Parties *en masse* commit infamous actions which would cover a single man with shame and opprobrium" (*Rector* 91). Why do they commit them? And in committing them, why do they generate praise and admiration, rather than condemnation and contempt? For the simple reason that between private morality and political morality there exists an abyss that the journalist Blondet explains very clearly:

> There are certain arbitrary acts which are criminal between individuals, but which amount to nothing when they are expanded through any multitude whatever, like a drop of Prussic acid which becomes harmless in a tub of water. You kill a man and you are guillotined. But, with any governmental conviction whatever, you kill five hundred men, the political crime is respected. You take five thousand francs from my writing-desk, you go to the galleys.

---

18 [Honoré de Balzac, *The Village Rector*, in *La Comédie Humaine of Honoré de Balzac*, vol. 14, translated by Katharine Prescott Wormeley (Boston: Hardy, Pratt, 1900), 277. Hereafter cited parenthetically in the text as *Rector*].

19 [See *The Criminal Crowd* 8n14 and *Sectarian Criminality* 201.]

20 [In *Des Sociétés animales* (1877), Alfred Espinas, the French physiologist and sociologist to whom Sighele frequently refers in *The Criminal Crowd*, compares the crowd's sudden emotional explosion even before knowing the reason for the occurrence of something to the reactions of a flock of birds, for which the slightest beating of wings or any other imperceptible movement degenerates into veritable collective panic. Alfred Espinas, *Des Sociétés animales*, 2nd ed. (Paris: Germer Baillère, 1878), 187.]

> But with the pimento of a profit to make, skilfully put in the mouths of a thousand purse-holders, you force them to take the stocks of I-know-not-what republic or monarchy in default, (...)—no one can complain. These are the true principles of the age of gold in which we live! (*Nucingen* 72)

These principles are recognized as true even today, not only because Napoleon's conviction that "collective crimes involve no one" (*Provinces* 213) is true even now and will be in eternity, but, above all, because even today, despite the verbal protests of the naive and the Jesuits, we are all forced to recognize that the law regulating individual morality is not the same as that which regulates political morality. This is a painful affirmation, to be sure, but we cannot deny it if we do not want to repeat the silly psychology of the ostrich, which thinks it can avoid a danger by placing its head in the ground.

For multitudes, as for individuals, politics has a rather different code from that which guides private morality. It is nonsense to want to transport to parliaments or governments the rigid principles that govern us in our quiet familiar life. What would an ambassador do, on remembering that a gentleman should never lie? What would a great captain do, if he followed the Christian and Tolstoyan precept: *do not kill*? What would a Minister of the Interior do, if, during an election period, he allowed the will of the country to pass without any act of corruption or suggestion? All of those would be honest, but incapable. They would not be politicians.

When, years ago, I dared to affirm this truth—painful but, I repeat, undeniable—there was a chorus of disapproval, almost as if the culprit were the one who revealed a fact, rather than the one who accomplished it. Unfortunately, if many were shocked in words, fewer were shocked in reality, and the political life of our constituencies continued, and will continue to resemble that of Besançon (see the story entitled *Albert Savarus*), where having to choose between a modest member of parliament but a gentleman, and a member of great brilliance but without scruples, of course the second was chosen. "Was it not better"—says a voter—"that the town should be represented by a man evidently destined to govern, rather than by a mere voting mechanism? A statesman was an actual power; a commonplace deputy, however incorruptible, was only a conscience."[21]

---

21 [Honoré de Balzac, *Albert Savarus*, translated by Katharine Prescott Wormeley (Boston: Roberts Brothers, 1892), 143. Hereafter cited parenthetically in the text as *Savarus*.]

Already Montesquieu had claimed that *small morality*, meaning private, kills *great morality*, meaning political, because it produces honest but incapable men of government. Balzac repeats the concept, and perhaps, in repeating it, he exaggerates it.[22] He does so when, at the end of a banquet, among the fumes of the champagne, he makes Blondet spout the definition of the true politician: "A great politician"—says Blondet—"should be a blackguard in the abstract; without which societies are badly conducted. A politician who is an honest man is a steam-engine which has feelings, or a pilot who makes love while at the helm,—the vessel founders. A prime minister who takes a hundred millions and who renders France great and happy, is he not to be preferred to a minister who has to be buried at the expense of the state, but who had ruined his country?" (*Nucingen* 85–86).

Something rebels in us when reading these very sceptical and cynical words, and we wish they were not true. We wish we could cry that there have been brilliant politicians who never failed to abide by the laws of private morality. But would our rebellion be authentic? And, by the way, would the cases—more unique than rare—that we would be able to cite, not be exceptions that confirm the disheartening reality of the norm?

Balzac intuited the inverse relationship that exists between genius and morality, between brain and conscience. He intuited the obscure ongoing duel in the mystery of organisms, which can perhaps be explained as a law of distribution of human forces. "If it be equally distributed, intellect produces fools or mediocrity everywhere; if it be divided unequally it engenders those differences to which we give the name of *genius*, and which, if they could take visible shape, would appear as deformities. The same law rules the body: perfect beauty is almost invariably accompanied by want of animation, or stupidity" (*Splendors* 294).

This law of inequality, which above all becomes evident in politics, where geniuses—from Caesar to Napoleon, from Richelieu to Bismarck—certainly did not have the moral equilibrium of gentlemen, manifests itself even outside of politics, in the fields of science, letters, and art. In a physiological sense, it is true that "[a]ll great men are monsters" (*Illusions* 365), that is, exceptional products of the human species. And even in the psychological sense, the genius is often *a monster*, since next to his intellectual greatness he shows a great moral deficiency. Claude

22 In the "Introduction" to *At the Sign of the Cat and Racket*, Balzac writes: "[A]s Napoleon said, for kings and statesmen there are the lesser and the higher morality" [(*Cat* 19–20)]. Napoleon repeated the phrase to Montesquieu.

Vignon says to Lucien de Rubempré: "Genius is a horrible disease; every writer bears in his heart a monster, like a tapeworm in the stomach, devouring the feelings as soon as they unfold. Which will conquer,—the disease or the man? Surely the man must be great indeed to keep his balance between his genius and his nature. Talent grows, the heart withers. Short of being a colossus, or of having the shoulders of a Hercules, he must end without a heart or without a brain" (*Provinces* 409–10).

Magnificent phrases that almost herald, in poetic form, the Lombrosian theory on the relation between genius and madness.[23] *Genius is a disease*; this is the truth Balzac affirms without uncertainties or circumlocutions. This physiological approach to the intellectual or sentimental qualities of the man is not an isolated case in his work. Elsewhere he returns to this argument,[24] and in *The Rise and Fall of César Birotteau*, he writes: "Is it not carrying flattery of society somewhat too far to paint individuals always in false colours, to conceal in certain cases the real causes of their vicissitudes, so often brought about by disease? Physical ills, in their moral aspects and the influences that they bring to bear on the mechanism of life, have perhaps been too much neglected hitherto (...)."[25]

Here the scientific theory that morality is strictly tied to the body is thus stated even more clearly and limpidly; here a fiery strike is launched against the spiritualistic theory of free will. All of society is no longer depicted with romantic colours, but studied in its causes and conditions based on race and heredity. Man, his vices, his passions, his crimes, are explained not through rhetoric, but through physiology and anthropology.

---

23 [In his controversial 1864 study *Genio e follia* [Genius and Folly], and in his subsequent volume *L'uomo di genio in rapporto alla psichiatria* (1888) [*The Man of Genius*, 1891], Cesare Lombroso connects extreme intelligence and creative activity to insanity, treating them as instances of morbidity, often inherited, manifesting itself through epilepsy and further substantiated by shared physical peculiarities. For his part, Balzac does not consider mental derangement a necessary promoter of creativity, but, rather, one of the characteristics of genius.]

24 For example, in *Albert Savarus*, where he writes: "Physiologists and profound observers of human nature will tell you, to your great amazement, perhaps, that temperaments, characters, mind and genius reappear in families at long intervals, precisely like what are called hereditary diseases. Thus talent, like gout, often skips two generations. We have proof of this phenomenon in the illustrious instance of George Sand, in whom are revived the vigor, power, and congenital qualities of Maréchal Saxe, her grandfather" [(*Savarus* 19–20)].

25 [Honoré de Balzac, *The Rise and Fall of César Birotteau*, in *La Comédie Humaine*, edited by George Saintsbury, translated by Ellen Marriage (London: J.M. Dent; New York: Macmillan, 1896), 62.]

If genius is a disease, what will suicide be? “Suicide results from a sentiment which we will call, if you please, *the esteem of self*, in order that we will not confound it with the word *honor*. The day when a man despises himself, when he sees himself despised by others, when the reality of life is at variance with his hopes, he kills himself, and does homage in this way to society, in presence of which he will not remain when stripped of his virtues or of his splendor” (*Illusions* 354–55). It is worth noting that Balzac’s very fine psychological analysis would lead one to define suicide, in line with reality, *an act of posthumous self-respect*. “No matter what may be said, among atheists (for exception must be made of the Christian suicide) none but cowards will accept a dishonored life. Suicide is of three kinds: first, the suicide which is only the climax of a long illness and belongs, therefore, to pathology; next, the suicide of despair; lastly, the suicide of reason (...); often the three causes are combined, as in the case of Jean-Jacques Rousseau” (*Illusions* 355).[26] Therefore, according to Balzac, suicide, like genius, has pathological causes. They are not whims of nature or arbitrary acts of human will: they are physiological inevitabilities.

Given these premises, it will be easy to imagine what Balzac thinks of crime and criminals.

### *III Crime and Criminals*

I already observed our author’s scepticism, diffidence, and absolutism regarding politics and parliament. We find the same attitude towards justice.

First of all, he asserts this painful truth: “there is nothing less known than which everybody ought to know, namely, The Law” (*Illusions* 222). It would seem that the only remedy to this evil is education. But if Balzac deplores ignorance, not only of the law, but of every other useful thing to know, he is not otherwise in favour of the spreading of education. A strange contradiction from a man within whom the logic of ingenuity was still fighting against conservative prejudices! “Education, equally distributed through the masses, brings the son of a porter into a government office to decide the fate of some man of merit or some landed proprietor whose door-bell his father may have answered. The last comer is therefore on equal terms with the oldest veteran in the service” (*Bureaucracy* 21). That seems like a scandal and an injustice to Balzac, in

26 Here the facts contradict Balzac, because many believers do commit suicide.

whose veins flows the blood of a reactionary, and in whose words there is often a disdain towards the crowd and a devoted admiration for superior personalities. He who condemned "that spirit of social insubordination which underlies the word *equality*" (*Illusions* 306) conceived justice as the mission a privileged caste had to exert without the intrusion of popular will. Therefore, he considered the institution of juries an absurdity. This small parliament, transported from politics into the field of justice, seemed to him a mistake and a danger: "The jury—that institution which revolutionary legislators have thought so strong—is an element of social ruin, for it fails in its mission; it does not sufficiently protect society" (*Incarnation* 149). And it fails in its mission, according to Balzac, because it is incoherent and indulgent. "The jurors divide themselves into two camps, once of which is against the death penalty; from this results the total overthrow of equality before the law. A certain horrible crime (parricide) obtains in one department a verdict of *non-culpabilité,* while in another some far less heinous crime is punished by death" (*Incarnation* 149). And he adds with wonder and sorrow: "there are at the galleys twenty-three parricides to whom have been granted the benefits of 'extenuating circumstances'" (*Incarnation* 149). If Balzac were to live again today, he would console himself in seeing France invaded by a lust of severity that wants not only a more active guillotine, but also the introduction of floggings in prisons, a partial resurrection of torture! And, above all, he would console himself by realizing that, in France, the jury he accused of indulgence does not spare death sentences. It is the President of the Republic who has the weakness to *pardon* all too often!

Yet, it would be unjust not to take into account the causes that explain, if not justify, Balzac's severity and, I daresay, ferocity. He lived and wrote in an epoch in which France, and especially the city of Paris, saw the crime rate increase dramatically, and were spectators of the most horrendous misdeeds.

When the tide of crime rises, most people do not believe that there is any other dam than the severity of punishments. And Balzac contributed to the majority's opinion. For this same sentiment of necessary severity that was widespread in the air, for this need to defend oneself against the criminals who abounded and struck terror, Balzac is sceptical about judiciary errors. For him, not only is a condemned person always rightly condemned, but also every suspect, every accused person is a priori guilty: "... it seems to us well nigh impossible for an innocent man ever to sit upon the benches of the Court of Assize" (*Splendors* 10). And elsewhere: "The general rule; all criminals talk of mistakes! Go to the prisons. Question the prisoners; they are almost all victims of some judicial error. Thus this mere word raises an imperceptible smile to the faces of those who come into contact with *prévenus, accusés,* or *condamnés*" (*Splendors* 32).

This *general rule* is undeniably very true when we replace the absolutism of Balzac's pronouncement with the possibility of some exception. I remember that many years ago when I visited with Enrico Ferri the penal colony of Civitavecchia for the first time,[27] I was struck by the uniformity of responses by the many convicts we interrogated: "*I am innocent.*" Very rarely did they confess.

Yet, by contrast, they change behaviour among themselves. Rather than affirming their innocence, they boast of their crimes, they exaggerate them, they invent others. Just as when dealing with strangers they proudly claim to be victims of an error, so among their fellow inmates they make it a point of honour to appear as the most perfidious and skilful in the criminal career.

This diversity of behaviour is determined by a single reason: their interest. Towards gentlemen, they must hide themselves under the mask of innocence in an attempt to save themselves. Towards colleagues, they must beautify their atrocious endeavours to instil respect and terror.

Today, after the development of studies in criminal psychology, we are familiar with these two opposite sides; today, everyone knows that in prisons the most dangerous bandits want to exert, and they do exert, their suggestion and charm on the others, precisely by flaunting the infamy of their actions. Even crime has its aristocracy, which is followed, with envy, by the multitude of the mediocre. But it is remarkable that Balzac had exactly intuited, at that time, this characteristic of the criminal psyche. In *The Village Rector,* he made the murderer Farrabesque say: "Before I got there, as I was saying, two of my comrades told of me as a man able to do great things. At the galleys, madame, nothing is so valuable as that reputation, not even money. In that republic of miscry murder is a passport to tranquillity" (*Rector* 225). And in *The Last Incarnation of Vautrin,* after describing the influence that the murderer La Pouraille exerted on his fellow prisoners, he writes: "There, as everywhere that men congregate, there, as in schools and colleges, reigns physical force, and mental and moral force. There, too, as at the galleys, criminality forms the aristocracy. He whose head is in danger takes precedence of all the rest. The

27 [Enrico Ferri describes his visits to numerous Italian and foreign penitentiaries—among them Civitavecchia, and Tivoli—in the company of Sighele when Ferri was still a student of his—in *Sociologia criminale* (Turin: Bocca, 1900; 1st ed., 1881), 100.]

*préau*, as we can readily believe, is the criminal's law school; it is even a court where cases are tried" (*Incarnation* 45).

Like Eugène Sue—who in his *Mysteries of Paris* revealed a profound knowledge of the criminal soul[28]—Honoré de Balzac seems to have studied those same criminals and criminal environments in real life. In his descriptions, there is the accent of truth; in his observations, there is the spark of those theories that, over time, would gain the approval of the scientific world. When he talks about the murderer Tascheron, he makes an open allusion to criminal anthropology: "One feature of his physiognomy"—he says—"confirmed an assertion of Lavater as to persons who are destined to commit murder: his front teeth lapped each other" (*Rector* 142). When he presents Farrabesque to us (an affiliate to the gang of the *chauffeurs*, condemned to ten years of forced labour), he expresses himself in these terms: "Madame Graslin (...) looked at the man and noticed in his face (...) the signs of underlying ferocity; irregular teeth gave to the mouth, the lips blood-red, an ironical expression full of evil audacity; the dark and prominent cheek-bones had something animal about them. The man was of middle height, with strong shoulders, a thick-set neck, and the large hairy hands of violent men capable of using their strength in a brutal manner" (*Rector* 190). And he confirms and validates these allusions and partial observations with an explicit act of faith in anthropological fatality. Vautrin says to Esther: "My daughter, I have tried to give you to Heaven; but the church always finds a repentant woman a fiction and if there were one she would turn courtesan again in Paradise. (...) You are a courtesan, you will live a courtesan, and will die a courtesan. *In spite of all the attractive theories of trainers, here on earth, an animal remains what it is.* The phrenologist is right, you have the bump of love" (*Splendors* 90–91).

This allusion to Gall ("homme aux bosses"),[29] this fatalism that Balzac applies to fallen women (and which would be more justly applied only to a part of them), enlightens, by extension, his conception of crime and,

28 See in *Letteratura tragica* [*Tragic Literature*] the chapter "Eugenio Sue e la psicologia criminale" [Eugène Sue and Criminal Psychology]. This chapter is not included here in our volume.]

29 [Balzac's original phrase "homme aux bosses" (literally, the man of the bumps) is a reference to German anatomist and physiologist Franz Joseph Gall (1758–1828), who developed the method of cranioscopy (i.e., phrenology) in order to identify an individual's mental and moral faculties on the basis of the external shape of the skull. He assumed that the bumps of the skull resulted from the pressure of the brain, and he divided the brain into different sections, each associated with particular physical and behavioural features.]

in general, of every form of human activity. *Down here, one can only become what one is.* That is, there are irreducible individuals, on whom the influence of education and of the environment acts like the passage of the sea wave on the beach sand. That is: just as Balzac assumes the existence of the man who is honest by nature—the oak man[30] whom no wind can divert from the right path—, so there exists the born criminal, the man of evil instincts, whom no power will be able to modify and turn to goodness.

An unconscious precursor to what would become the cornerstone of the Italian positivist school—namely, the existence of the born criminal—, Balzac also managed to trace the first lines of the psychology of the great criminals, summarizing it into two vices: cowardice and sensuality. "Putting certain very rare exceptions aside, they are all cowards" (*Incarnation* 78). Despine, Lombroso, Ferri, Corre, after many observations, came to an identical conclusion. But why are great criminals all cowards? Balzac limpidly reveals the reason to us with an analysis that scientific experience has confirmed:

> Their faculties are continually strained to the uttermost by the excitement of robbery, and the execution of crime demands the employment of all their vital power, alertness of mind equal to the readiness of body, and an intensity that weakens the intellect. When the violent exercise of their will is past they become stupid, for the same reason that a prima donna or a dancer falls exhausted after a fatiguing step, or after one of these formidable duets, which modern composers inflict upon the public ear (...) After the success of *a job*, they fall into such a state of prostration that, yielding to the peremptory need of debauchery, they make themselves drunk on wine and liquor, and rush passionately to the embraces of their women, seeking in vain for calm amid the wreck of their strength and for forgetfulness of crime in the forgetfulness of reason. (...) When a crime has been committed, their difficulties begin, for they are as stupefied before the necessity of concealing their new wealth as they had been formerly prostrated by poverty. More than this, they are weak as the woman who has just risen from child-bed. Alarmingly energetic in their conceptions, when success comes, they behave like children. In a word their nature, like some savage beasts, is an easy prey when it has gorged its fill. (*Incarnation* 246–47, 248)

It would be long and useless to cite the pages of anthropologists, doctors, criminologists, who demonstrated the truth of Balzac's analysis with

30 [See *The Criminal Crowd* 70n139 and *Against Parliamentarism* 215.]

facts. Cowardice and sensuality are the two poles of the psychology of great criminals, and one is explained through the other. They are cowardly precisely because they are sensual, and they are sensual because the animality of their instincts—*le naturel des bêtes sauvages*—wants them that way. Ultimately, Balzac himself declares, "The excessive love which drags them, *constitutionally*, as doctors say, towards women, consumes all the moral and physical strength of these giants of energy" (*Incarnation* 224).

It seems to me more useful and important to observe that Balzac, after having intuited the born criminal, intuited another category, the habitual or professional criminal.[31] The born criminal is fortunately the exception in the world of criminality, while the professional criminal is the rule. The former represents aristocracy, the latter the plebs of criminality—"the *haute pègre* (...) is the faubourg Saint Germain, the aristocracy of this world" (*Incarnation* 53) for these people. If the attention of laymen is, above all, attracted by the deeds of the great murderers, the so-called human beasts, those who deal with criminality focus instead on the immense and ever increasing number of common criminals, who are like an army of microbes infecting and corrupting the social organism. This army is composed of thieves and prostitutes, the two instinctive, antisocial forms with which the male and the female can make a living. To steal and to sell oneself, here is what any man and any woman can do, when they do not have the means of subsistence and when a rock-solid honesty does not support and defend them against the thousand suggestions of the external environment. "Prostitution and thievery"—Balzac says—"are the two living protests, male and female, of the *natural state* against the law of society" (*Incarnation* 219). Unfortunately, these two protests are so common that those who lead them have formed a caste, a separate class that, by law of heredity in families and out of habit in individuals, possesses its special characteristics. Gabriel Tarde, when studying precisely this *professional criminality*, remarked how every profession leaves, in whoever practices it, an indelible character in the body and in the morale. Balzac preceded it with this observation:

> Thievery and the trade of the harlot are like the stage, the police, the priesthood, and the system of gendarmerie. Under these six conditions the individual assumes an indelible character.[32] He no longer has the power to

31 [As in the case of the born criminal, here Sighele is applying a Lombrosian category to Balzac's fictional world.]

> become other than he is. The stigmata of holy priesthood are quite as ineradicable as those of the soldier. The same truth holds good of other careers which are natural enemies, contraries in civilization. These violent diagnostics, strange, peculiar and sui generis as they are, render the harlot and the thief, the murderer and the discharged convict, as easy for their enemies, the detective and the gendarme, to recognize, as game is for the hunter: they have their own inalienable mien, bearing, complexion, look, color, odor, in short, their own unmistakable peculiarities. (Incarnation 220–21)

From here comes that science of disguise, which is so profound in criminals; from here also comes the jargon, this psychological means of defence that Balzac has broadly studied, the first among novelists, and later to be followed by Sue.

Thus, before any other writer, he intuited the relationship between madness and crime. "Crime bears some resemblance to madness"—he writes—"The prisoners in the yard of the Conciergerie are but a repetition of the madmen in the garden of an asylum. Both these classes of men walk up and down avoiding their comrades and casting from side to side strange or angry looks, according to the feelings of the moment. They are never happy, never quite serious; for they either know or fear one another" (*Incarnation* 211–12).

Therefore, in Balzac's work, we find in a nutshell many of the ideas that the Italian positivists would later develop. There is the profile of the born criminal and of the habitual criminal; there is a hint at the

32 I wish to quote another page in support of the naturalistic method with which Balzac approached society: "(...) society resembled nature. For does not society modify Man, according to the conditions in which he lives and acts, into men as manifold as the species in Zoology? The differences between a soldier, an artisan, a man of business, a lawyer, an idler, a student, a statesman, a merchant, a sailor, a poet, a beggar, a priest, are as great, though not so easy to define, as those between the wolf, the lion, the ass, the crow, the shark, the seal, the sheep, etc. Those social species have always existed, and will always exist, just as there are zoological species. If Buffon could produce a magnificent work by attempting to represent in a book the whole realm of zoology, was there not room for a work of the same kind on society? But the limits set by nature to the variations of animals have no existence in society. When Buffon describes the lion, he dismisses the lioness with a few phrases: but in society a wife is not always the female of the male. There may be two perfectly dissimilar beings in one household. The wife of a shopkeeper is sometimes worthy of a prince, and the wife of a prince is often worthless compared with the wife of an artisan. The social state has freaks which Nature does not allow herself; it is nature *plus* society" [(*Cat* 12–13)].

resemblance between crime and madness; there is the psychological study of criminal environments; in short, there is a conception of crime different from that which dominated at the time; there is the foresight of the artist who, by pointing at the path that science will later follow, more slowly but more organically, unconsciously enunciates those paradoxes that are nothing but the truth of tomorrow.

And—even more remarkable—Balzac's work contains even a judgment on the penitentiary systems which seems to have been written nowadays. The jail system, which was considered the best because it was socially the most secure if not always the most humane, today represents a costly cruelty that does not help the culprit improve, but, rather, leads him to the edge of madness. Well, Balzac has a magnificent page on the psychological value of isolation, which I wish to reproduce in its entirety:

> The tender philanthropy of modern times believes that the atrocious punishment of isolation is her invention; she is deceived. When torture was abolished in the very natural desire to reassure the over-delicate conscience of juries, the officers of prosecution conceived the terrible weapon that solitude gives to justice against remorse. Solitude is vacuum, and moral nature hates it quite as much as physical nature. Solitude can be dwelt in only by the man of genius, who fills it with his ideas, children of the spiritual world, or by some contemplator of divine works who sees it illuminated by the light of heaven and animated by the voice of God. With the exception of these two types, both on the threshold of Paradise, solitude bears the same relation to torture that moral does to physical nature. Between solitude and torture there is all the difference which separates nervous disease from the disease which can be cured by surgery. It is suffering multiplied by the infinite. The body touches the infinite through the nervous system as the spirit penetrates thither by the thought. (*Incarnation* 251–52)

Reading this page, our legislators and scholars of penitentiary studies can find an explanation of the causes of the degradation that people sentenced to life in prison reach after many years of that kind of solitude, "which is a moral torture."[33]

33 [Although this is not a direct quotation from Balzac, it synthesizes and rephrases the gist of the previous passage from *The Last Incarnation of Vautrin*.]

## *IV The Philosophy of "Vautrin"*

Until now, I have considered the *Human Comedy* uniquely from the sociological point of view. I extracted some ideas or some fragments of ideas but I did not consider it from an aesthetic point of view. I did not show which truly human types stand out, which lively and eternal figures Balzac, this great sculptor, successfully moulded.

Such a work of psychological analysis—as I said at the beginning of this study—was outside my task, not only because others had already attempted it, but also and above all because I would not dare, from my layman's view of art, to judge Balzac's work in artistic terms. In his work I am looking for thoughts, not for aesthetic emotions. I want to examine which scientific truths Balzac had already intuited; I do not want to linger on the admirable masterpieces he created.

Others have already said what these masterpieces are: *Eugénie Grandet*, the tragedy of the slow and silent cruelties of avarice; *César Birotteau*, the epic-comic poem of ambition; *Old Goriot*, the Shakespearean picture of a father's guilty weakness and of the unlikely ingratitude of his two daughters; *The Lily of the Valley*, the hymn to pure love, to platonic love, that is deformed into a kind of moral hermaphroditism.

But there is a masterpiece about which I believe I am able to say something. There is a figure that rises above the others with the lines of a Michelangelesque statue, and which I also wish to admire and to describe. This masterpiece, this Michelangelesque statue, is the character of Vautrin.

Vautrin is one of the names under which the convict Jacques Collin hides. Having been condemned many times, and having escaped many times from the penal colony, he had to perform his major crimes disguised as a Spanish abbot, the Abbot Carlos Herrera, and, thanks to the cowardice of men and to the brilliance of his perfidy, he ended up not under the guillotine but as head of the Paris police.

More than a man, he is a symbol, as are all the great artistic creations. "This man was the incarnation of the life, the strength, the cunning and the passions of the galley; he was its very worst expression" (*Incarnation* 190). He is not a *criminal*: he is the monstrous personification of *crime*; he is, if I can say so, the quintessence of all the most perverse and satanic instincts that have ever slithered at the bottom of the human soul.

In order for Vautrin to worthily play this role, Balzac describes him physically as a born criminal. And his degenerative characteristics were so pronounced that, despite his extraordinary metamorphic ability, while the investigating judge Camusot was watching him—dressed like an abbot and all unctuously busy reading his breviary—, he was forced to exclaim: "That certainly *is* the physiognomy of a convict!"[34]

Furthermore, it is not in the physical portrait of his characters that the art of a novelist best manifests itself: it is in their moral portrait. Vautrin, whose face was "the poet of an inferno, wherein all thoughts and passions that move human nature (save repentance) find a place" (*Goriot* 217), revealed himself with acts and words better than with physiognomy. He says to Eugène de Rastignac: "I am a great poet; I do not write my poems, I feel them, and act them" (*Goriot* 119). Indeed, he was the poet of evil. He was an artist who meditated, composed, and carried out his crimes with the same sincere passion and creative fever that agitates the brain and heart of whoever hopes to produce a work of art. More than a poet, he was a genius of evil. "Genius is, everywhere, Intuition. Below this phenomenon all other remarkable things are done by talent. In this consists the difference which separates persons of the first order from persons of the second order. Crime has its men of genius" (*Rubempré* 282).

Vautrin was this man of genius, because he had the *gift of intuition.* Intuition helped him not only to concoct crimes that to others would have appeared as the most improbable and most difficult, but also, and above all, to know people, to make them unconsciously serve his objectives, to adopt them as instruments and stools in order to make a fortune. A Napoleon of criminality—this is what Vautrin was.[35]

The first condition to make one's way in the world is not to worry if others are to be crushed while we rise. Vautrin possessed this supreme contempt of every scruple, an insensibility that is characteristic of the born criminal. "'[A]nd you may just as well know at once that I think no more of killing a man than of that,' and he spat before him as he spoke" (*Goriot* 111). (This phrase and this act remind me of the words of a famous French murderer:—*couper la caboche à un homme, qu'est-ce que c'est?*

34 [Honoré de Balzac, *Lucien de Rubempré*, in *The Works of Honoré de Balzac*, vol. 18, translated by Katharine Prescott Wormeley (Boston: Roberts Brothers, 1896), 321. Hereafter cited parenthetically in the text as *Rubempré.*]

35 [Sighele here fully grasps not only Balzac's own fascination with the idea of superiority and with its embodiment in charismatic, mysterious, powerful individuals, but also the French author's masterful depiction of the criminal's psychology, and its ability to captivate readers instead of repulsing them. This is an aspect that, by contrast, Lombroso does not take into consideration whenever he refers to Balzac (as, for instance, in *The Man of Genius*) and to literary depictions of criminals in general].

*c'est du chocolat, c'est du velours!*[36]) "Only when it is absolutely necessary to do so"—Vautrin continued—"I do my best to kill him properly. I am what you call an artist. I have read Benvenuto Cellini's *Memoirs*, such as you see me (...) From him I learned to follow the example set us by Providence, who strikes us down at random, and to admire the beautiful whenever and wherever it is found. And, setting other questions aside, is it not a glorious part to play, when you pit yourself against mankind, and the luck is on your side?" (*Goriot* 111). And here, in these final words, is an artistic vision of crime, the ambitious pride of the egoarch in feeling alone against everyone else, an exception of audacity among a herd of weaklings, a superman against the crowd. Vautrin conceives the world as certain degenerate artists do: he considers it the shapeless dough of which a few brilliant individuals constitute the yeast; he believes it is the arena in which some exceptional personalities can accomplish their deeds with impunity. Listen to this profession of faith: "Mankind is not perfect, but one age is more or less hypocritical than another, and then simpletons say that its morality is high or low. I do not think that the rich are any worse than the poor; man is much the same, high or low, or wherever he is. In a million of this human cattle there may be half a score of bold spirits who rise above the rest, above the laws; I am one of them" (*Goriot* 118).

Since he is one of those very few who place themselves above everything, even laws, Vautrin looks at life and at the world as the field for his conquests; and, from the top of his cynical and proud superiority, he renews the psychology of the medieval squire, who, from his eagle's nest on a mountaintop, dominated and extorted the rabble of his vassals.

What is Paris for him, this ocean of which one can never know the depth, not even by throwing a probe in? Paris is for Vautrin "a slough (...). And an uncommonly queer slough, too (...). The mud splashes you as you drive through it in your carriage—you are a respectable person; you go afoot and you are splashed—you are a scoundrel" (*Goriot* 51). And he adds: "Paris, you see, is like a forest of the New World, where you have to deal with a score of varieties of savages (...) who live on the

36 ["To cut off a man's head, what is it? It's chocolate, it's velvet!" This statement, quoted very frequently in late nineteenth-century criminal chronicles (Lombroso's among them) is by Victor-Joseph Prévost, the notoriously cold-blooded assassin who, in 1879, killed and cut up at least two people, scattering their remains throughout the neighbourhood. See also *The Criminal Couple* 141. French anthropologist Paul Broca sectioned and studied Prévost's brain, looking for morphological anomalies able to justify his criminal behaviour, and wrote the report "Le cerveau de l'assassin Prévost" [The Brain of Prévost the Assassin], *Bulletin de la Société d'anthropologie de Paris* 3, 1 (1880): 233–44.]

proceeds of their social hunting (...); there are many ways of hunting. Some hunt heiresses, others a legacy; some fish for souls, yet others sell their clients, bound hand and foot. Every one who comes back from the chase with his game-bag well filled meets with a warm welcome in good society" (*Goriot* 121).

Perhaps these words that sculpt the Parisian environment could also apply to other environments, because, unfortunately, in Vautrin's cynicism there is a truthful soul that transcends particular observation to attain the significance and the value of a general consideration. Vautrin is a philosopher, a turbid and bitter philosopher who has the effrontery to say out loud that which some individuals think and do without daring to boast. "Do you know"—Vautrin asks Rastignac—"how a man makes his way here? By brilliant genius or by skilful corruption. You must either cut your way through these masses of men like a cannon ball, or steal among them like a plague. Honesty is nothing to the purpose. (...) Corruption is a great power in the world, and talent is scarce. So corruption is the weapon of superfluous mediocrity" (*Goriot* 116–17).

Let us look around and confess that at a distance of almost eighty years (*Old Goriot*, from which I drew these words, dates back to 1834), Vautrin's philosophy is still alive and true—and not only in Paris. He is a convict who speaks, and his phrases enclose all the rancour and venom of a rebel against the society that condemned and defamed him. But how much truth is there beneath his exaggerations, how much wisdom is there beneath the poison of his invectives! Like Iago, he recites a *belief* in which all human egoism and pessimism scream, but cannot ignore some sparks of psychological geniality in the great obscurity of moral principles. "There are no such things as principles; there are only events, and there are no laws but those of expediency: a man of talent accepts events and the circumstances in which he finds himself, and turns everything to his own ends" (*Goriot* 122).

Once the moral law, the categorical imperative of conscience, is abolished—which in Vautrin does not exist—life for him is nothing but a race to fortune, to wealth, to pleasure, a path free from psychological obstacles called scruples, and where any other material obstacle must be eliminated. The world is a track where the unique scope is to gain a good first place; and on this track "honesty serves nothing"; what is useful are corruption and ingenious audacity. "Men and women for you"—Vautrin says to Rastignac—"must be nothing more than post-horses; take a fresh relay, and leave the last to drop by the roadside; in this way you will reach the goal of your ambition" (*Goriot* 85). And speaking to Lucien de Rubempré, he insists on this idea and develops it: "Regard men, above all regard women, as instruments only; but never let them see that you do so. Adore as a god the man who, being higher in station than yourself, may be useful to you; and do not leave him till he has paid a full price for your servility. In your dealings with the world be as grasping as a Jew, and as base; do for power that which the Jew does for pelf. Pay no more heed to a fallen man than if he did not exist" (*Illusions* 366).

This school of ferocious egoism is necessary, according to Vautrin, if one wants to succeed. To dominate the world, one must first obey and study it. Vautrin, ironically, contemplates the scientists and moralists who study books, and, through their imagination, form laws and duties and abstract principles to which only a few submit in practice. He admires the great politicians, to whom he feels like a brother, who leave books to the libraries and theories to the solitary and naive brains, and they study man as he is, his interests, the causes underlying his actions. And from this study he draws the arid and pessimistic conclusion, unfortunately sometimes true, that the world, society, men, all taken together, are fatalists because they do not consider their intentions, but they only adore the result. From whatever path you have attained wealth and power, you will be feared and envied. Success is the law of the world. "Success is virtue!" (*Goriot* 88).

If we wanted to judge history, above all political history, taking these criteria into account, we should recognize that Vautrin is right in many cases. The artistic beauty of this character and his profound morality consist precisely in the fact that Balzac entrusts a convict, a criminal guilty of the most serious crimes, with the task of demonstrating how unjust and immoral is the society in which we live. Vautrin is the unconscious ironist who, in unveiling his soul and thoughts, makes us reflect on how turbid our own soul is, and on the egotistical and evil intentions that pave our own civilization, of which we are so proud. Hearing him speak, hearing him justify the perfidy of his actions with philosophical aphorisms, we are forced to wonder: is the cynicism he flaunts and exaggerates not perhaps hidden, in minor proportions, in each of our thoughts? Are we truly, totally different from him, or, rather, is he not the monstrous symbol of that fever of money and power that overwhelms certain social classes, and that was—across time—the origin of every political greatness and also perhaps of many private riches?

I do not remember who pronounced the phrase that must sound bad to the ears of the fortunate businessmen: "every fortune, rapidly built, is the effect of a chance discovery, or the result of a legal theft" (*Splendors* 271). In more absolute terms, Balzac makes Vautrin say: "The secret of a great success for which you are at a loss to account is a crime that has never been found out, because it was properly executed" (*Goriot* 124). It is certain that when one makes a fortune politically or privately, when power or millions or billions are conquered, not too many look back to the ladder that helped them get to the winner's circle. There are two moralities: a severe one, for whoever commits evil but does not succeed; another one, quite indulgent, for those who achieve success despite committing evil. "To not succeed"—Balzac says egregiously—"is a crime of social lèse-majesté" (*Illusions* 66).

Therefore, there are two justices: a severe one, for the poor or the mediocre, who do not know how to give their crime the appearance that elevates it to a financial affair or a political action; the other one, very mild, for the clever ones, who know that the law, like society, does not punish *the substance* of a criminal act, but only the *form.*

Vautrin, also in this regard, is the lucid interpreter of such a painful truth: "All depends on form. Understand what I mean by form"—he says to Lucien—

> There are uneducated persons who, being pressed by want, take something by violence which belongs to another. These are called criminals, and they are forced to reckon with the law. But a poor man of genius discovers a secret, the application of which is equivalent to enormous wealth; he owes you three thousand francs (...); you torment that poor man with the law until you make him give you the whole or part of his secret; there is nothing to hinder you but your conscience, and your conscience doesn't accuse you of anything. The enemies of social order make use of such inconsistencies to yelp at justice and rail in the name of the People because the law sends the man who steals chickens at night to the galleys, while other men who ruin families escape (if punished at all) with a few weeks in prison. But these hypocrites know very well that in condemning the thief the judges maintained the barrier between the poor and the rich, the overturning of which would put an end to social order; whereas the bankrupt, the adroit purloiner of inheritances, the banker who trottles another man's enterprise to his own profit, are only making money change hands. (*Illusions* 371–72)

Who counts the years whence these words were said? They have not lost any of their relevance. Who considers that they come from a murderer's mouth? They could have been pronounced by the severe conscience of a moralist. Who remembers that they belong to the book of a conservative and reactionary author who did not hide his sympathy for the Bourbons? They have a flavour of liberalism and socialism, as if they came from the eloquence of a member of parliament from the far left.

Vautrin, in his cynical sincerity, is the interpreter of a sentiment that surpasses time, environments, and customs: he is the defiant asserter of truth, which the Jesuitic interest of the many does not want to confess.

He further provokes with his criticism of society and laws, and ironically asks:

> How is it that a dandy, who in a night has robbed a boy of half his fortune, gets only a couple of months in prison; while a poor devil who steals a banknote for a thousand francs, with aggravating circumstances, is condemned to penal servitude? Those are your laws. Not a single provision but lands you in some absurdity. That man with yellow gloves and a golden tongue commits many a murder; he sheds no blood, but he drains his victim's veins as surely; a desperado forces open a door with a crowbar, dark deeds both of them! (*Goriot* 124)

I believe that Balzac never sculpted with more conciseness, spirit, and delicate refinement of form, the immoral antithesis of our laws that severely punish the thief or the common homicide and, by contrast, are so indulgent towards the thieves of honour, towards those who perturb the interests of families and kill their peace.

## V *The Criminal Couple*

The type of Vautrin would not have been a complete creation if Balzac had not made the light of a human sentiment shine in the soul of this philosopher of evil.

Every pure and virgin conscience has its stains of shadow; likewise, every perfidious soul has its sparks of affection and kindness. The most ferocious of criminals, the most stubborn of rebels cannot always and solely hate; they must also live. And Vautrin, although he had the instincts of the beast and the savage in his character, felt that, like the beast and the savage, even man cannot totally isolate himself from his peers, aloof and hostile to everybody, but he needs someone on whom he can directly exert his influence; he needs *another one* to associate to his destiny; he needs to set his hopes, his pride, his future on another human creature. And since Vautrin, beyond being a criminal of genius, is a very profound analyst, he himself explains the *reason* for this necessity, to which he is subject, like everyone else. And he explains it in a page that could serve as the preface to a treatise on the psychology of association:

man has a horror of solitude. And of all solitudes, moral solitude is that which terrifies him most. The first hermits lived with God; they inhabited the most populous of worlds, —the spiritual world. Misers inhabit a world of fancy and possession; a miser has all, even his sex, in his brain. The first desire of man, be he a leper or a galley-slave, infamous or diseased, is *to have a sharer in his fate.* To satisfy that desire, which is existence itself to him, he employs his whole strength, his every faculty, the very sap of his life. Without that sovereign need would Satan have found companions? (*Illusions* 381)

This is the page that Morello reproached me for not having cited in my book *The Criminal Couple.* Indeed, it contains in a nutshell all the reasons that determine the formation of that psychological bond between two individuals, which is the first link of the broader human associations.

Vautrin hence wants *an accomplice in his destiny,* he wants to find a creature to love, "to fashion him, mould him to my needs, in short to love him as a father loves his child" (*Illusions* 382), and he affirms: "I have a mania, too, for devoting myself to some one else" (*Goriot* 176).

Chance makes him meet Lucien de Rubempré. This poet, as beautiful as a girl and as weak as a reed, will be his *succubus,* his victim, his instrument, and his love.

In order to establish one of those psychological rapports between two persons that form, according to the trite but true phrase, two bodies in one soul—as I demonstrated elsewhere—, one must exert a certain dominance over the other. It is necessary for one to be the head, and for the other to be the arm; one the master, the other the slave. To Vautrin's imperious will, Lucien de Rubempré represented precisely this type of almost feminine delicacy, easy and ready for all suggestions. His friend D'Arthez describes him in this way:

Lucien is a poetical being, but not a poet; he dreams, and does not think; he is emotional, not creative. In short, (...) he is effeminate, he likes to pose—the vice of Frenchmen. (...) *He would willingly sign a compact with the devil if it would give him a few years of a brilliant and luxurious existence.* (...) He will despise himself, he will repent, but whenever the occasion returns he will do the same thing over again, —for *will* is lacking to him; he is without strength against the allurements of pleasure, or against the satisfaction of his minor ambitions. *Lucien is a harp, the strings of which tighten or stretch according to the variations of his atmosphere.* (...) Anything and everything may be expected of Lucien. (*Illusions* 205–206 [Sighele's emphasis])

In these words, we find the psychology of all *succubi*: of those natures composed of diverse metals, like bronze, which can veer indifferently towards vice or virtue, *tabulae rasae* on whom destiny writes what it wants, types that Ball defined as *effacés* and that Ribot more energetically called the *idiots of the will*.[37]

Balzac writes: "… there are, no less, natures so robustly protetected, that this sort of projectile falls flat and harmless on skulls of triple brass, as cannon-shot against solid masonry; then there are flaccid and spongy-fibered natures into which ideas from without sink like spent bullets into the earthworks of a redoubt. Rastignac's head was something of the powder-magazine order; the least shock sufficed to bring about an explosion" (*Goriot* 107).

Lucien was one of these natures, which become shadows of the energetic natures that know how to dominate them, the automatic executors of each of their commands. He meets Vautrin disguised as the Abbot Carlos Herrera, the extraordinary delegate of H.M. the King of Spain to the Court of France, and he meets him in the saddest and most terrible moment of his life. Everything is collapsing around him: he has lost his position, the esteem of his friends, the affection of his family; he is in poverty and dishonoured and about to kill himself. Vautrin brings him back to life; he instils in him the passion for life. With an authoritarian move, he satanically seizes this soul which by now hopes for nothing except death. Vautrin performs a miracle of resurrection; but the man whom he saves from death will be his own work in the world, his unconscious accomplice. "If you will be a soldier"—he says to Lucien—"I will be your captain. Obey me as a wife obeys her husband, as a child obeys its mother, and I will guarantee you that in less then three years you shall be Marquis de Rubempré, and the husband of one of the proudest daughters of Saint-Germain, and you shall sit at some future day on the bench of Peers" (*Illusions* 375).

---

37 [Benjamin Ball (1833–1893) was an English-born, naturalized-French psychiatrist, the first holder of the Chair of Mental and Cerebral Diseases in Paris in 1877. His entry "Démence" in the *Dictionnaire encyclopédique des sciences médicales* (1882) is considered the source of the current concept of dementia. Théodule-Armand Ribot (1839–1916) was a French psychologist noted for his experimental approach to mental life, privileging physical over spiritual elements. He is remembered for his studies on the diseases of personality and of the will, the psychology of emotions, and creative imagination.]

The dream is beautiful. Lucien listens. Vautrin pressures him and insists: "you belong to me as a creature does to the Creator, as the Afrite to the genii, as the page to the sultan, the body to the soul" (*Illusions* 375).

And Lucien, gradually conquered by the mirage of a happy, rich, and glorious future, is about "to sign a compact with the devil" (*Illusions* 205) according to D'Arthez's prediction.

Vautrin becomes even more suggestive, and continues in his work as a seducer: "Child, (...) have you ever meditated over Otway's *Venice Preserved*? Do you understand the profound friendship of a man to a man, which binds Pierre to Jaffier, makes woman of no account, and changes all social terms?" (*Illusions* 380–81).[38] And he "fixed on Lucien one of those steady, piercing looks by which the will of a strong man is injected, so to speak, into a weak one. This fascinating glare (...) relaxed all Lucien's fibres of resistance" (*Splendors* 94).

With his magnetism, the terrible convict would win over many other resistances beyond Lucien's. Against him, the victory was simple and ready. The poet allowed himself to be conquered, or, better yet, he sold his dignity and soul, perhaps because—as his sister Eve sadly said—"I do believe there is, in a poet, a pretty woman of the worst kind" (*Illusions* 305). For the vain satisfaction of coming back rich to that Parisian world from which he had to escape as a beggar and full of debts, Lucien agrees to be supported by the Abbot Carlos Herrera, to live with him, and, with his money, to try his luck in that aristocratic world where he wanted to enter and settle by way of a great marriage.

Did Lucien perhaps have, every now and then, some bursts of rebellion? Did the *succubus* perhaps attempt to free himself from the suggestion of the *incubus*? These were flashes in the pan, flares of ephemeral energy. Vautrin, endowed with the genius of corruption, gradually destroyed the last residues of Lucien's honesty. He threw him into crude inevitable defeats (such as losses at gambling) and saved him from them by making him tacitly consent to dubious or infamous actions that, however, kept him apparently pure and loyal in the eyes of the world, since he

38 Otway's novel, which analyses the phenomenon of the *suggestion à deux* perhaps in even more detail than Goethe's *Elective Affinities*, must have deeply impressed Balzac. [Sighele here wrongly defines *Venice Preserved* as a novel, while in fact, it is a play—the most important tragedy of the English Restoration period.] Although in his one hundred novels and short stories he never repeats himself, he remembers *Venice Preserved* in three of his books: *Lost Illusions* [*Illusions perdues*, vol. II, 315], *Old Goriot* [*Père Goriot*, 178], and *The Two Brothers* [*Un ménage de garçon*, 174].

accomplished them in the shadows. "I am the author"—he said to him—"You shall be the play. If you fail it is I who shall be hissed" (*Splendors* 121).

But Lucien represented something more than the drama in Vautrin's fantasy: beyond and more than the work of the brain of his despot and of his author, he was the work of his sentiment.

Vautrin was forced to live far from the world where by now the law forbade him to return, weakened by vices and exhausted by all the terrible vicissitudes of his life. Yet, nonetheless, he was endowed with a wonderful resilience, and, although old, was still devoured by the fever of life. Vautrin, this ignoble and great character, obscure and famous, "lived once more in the graceful person of Lucien, whose soul he had made his own. He was represented in society by this poet to whom he gave his character and his iron will. To him Lucien was more than a son, more than a beloved wife, more than a family, more than life itself; he was his revenge. Thus as strong minds cling more closely to an idea than to reality, he was bound to him by indissoluble ties" (*Splendors* 117). What were these bonds?

While at first he allowed Lucien to believe that he was the Abbot Carlos Herrera, the ambassador to the King of Spain, he later confessed his true name and crimes to Lucien, and revealed to him that the money he gave him and that he was spending was nothing but the spoils of all the crimes committed by convicts for whom he was the treasurer. "With all his strength he was so feeble against the whims of his creature that he had eventfully entrusted with all his secrets. Perhaps this complicity, entirely moral though it was, made one more bond between them" (*Splendors* 117–18).

This was the indissoluble bond with which the convict had forever tied the poet to his wagon. This was the supreme proof of Vautrin's love for Lucien. Confiding in him, he was running the risk of losing himself. "[I]t is so fine to commit one's self! That's a pleasure of the soul" (*Incarnation* 132). He wanted to indulge in this new voluptuousness of the soul, forgetting for the sake of his friend, his son, his intellectual disciple, that prudence which had made his fortune in life. And he was becoming monstrously beautiful for that devotion "worthy of the canine race" to Lucien, for this abandonment of all egoism in his confidence in Lucien. "The ignoble convict, incarnating the cherished ideal of so many poets, Moore, Lord Byron (...) —a demon ruling over an angel, enticed into hell to refresh himself upon dew stolen from paradise—Jacques Collin (...) had for seven years renounced himself. His powerful faculties, absorbed in Lucien, were brought into being for Lucien's sake;

his delight was in Lucien's progress, in his love, in his ambition. For him Lucien was his visible soul" (*Splendors* 191–92).

Where can one find a more perfect analysis of *the criminal couple*? Who has ever known how to describe the phenomenon of *suggestion à deux* with a more profound truth? I, who dedicated an entire volume to this phenomenon, and collected and studied hundreds of true facts,[39] declare that Balzac was a precursor even in this domain, and that his genius has guessed what science later had to demonstrate.

And he also intuited how in life this impure and pathological bond of domination and servility can dissolve. He intuited that sometimes the slave, the victim, has an ultimate moment of rebellion against his despot, the stronger and more intense, the longer the period of subjugation and degradation. One could say that the daily renunciations accumulate at the bottom of the *succubus*'s soul, only to burst with more violence all of a sudden.

When Vautrin and Lucien are arrested for Esther's suicide, and Lucien confesses to the judge who the Abbot Carlos Herrera is and how his priest's robes hide the mark of the convict; when the dubious endeavours surface against the Baron Nucingen, to whom Vautrin and Lucien had sold Esther for 750,000 francs with the purpose of collecting the necessary sum for Lucien's marriage to the young Duchess of Grandlieu; in short, when the web of infamy on which the two accomplices lived is discovered, the poet cannot withstand the collapse of all his hopes, and finally glimpses the abyss into which Vautrin threw him. After deciding to kill himself, before executing his plan, he writes this letter to his corruptor, which is the swan's song of his conscience, the extreme protest of the victim who finally comes to know his executioner. Let us read this letter; it is a document of truth; it is the moral of the grim story, the moral that, as always, comes too late:

> There is the posterity of Cain as well as that of Abel. In the great drama of humanity, Cain is the enemy. (...) Among the demons of this race, there appear from time to time terrible beings whose vast organizations contain the sum of all the powers of man, and who are like those restless beasts of the desert that need the immense solitudes they inhabit. Creatures like these are as dangerous to society as lions turned loose in the heart of Normandy. They need a pasturage, they devour common men and browse upon the

39 *La coppia criminale* [*The Criminal Couple*], 3rd ed. (Turin: Bocca, 1908).

> money of fools. Their very games are so perilous that at length they kill the meek dog which they have chosen for a companion, for an idol. When God so wills it, these mysterious beings are Moses, Attila, Charlemagne, Mohammed, or Napoléon; but when he lets these gigantic instruments rust at the bottom of the ocean of a generation, they are but Pugatcheff, Fouché, Louvel, or the Abbé Carlos Herrera. Endued with boundless influence over sensitive souls, they attract them and grind them to powder. It is great, in its way it is beautiful. It is the venomous plant of gorgeous colors which fascinates children in the woods. It is the poetry of evil. Men such as you should dwell in caverns and never come forth. You have made me live this giant life and I have finished my full measure of existence. Thus I may draw my neck from the gordian knots of your projects to slip it into the running noose of my cravat. (...) My contempt for you was as great as my admiration." (*Splendors* 153–55)

Lucien hung himself, and Vautrin, who showed he had a heart only for him, cried tears of blood for him. "Ah! a devoted nurse never loved her only son so tenderly as I loved that angel" (*Splendors* 332)—he said to the general prosecutor.

But Vautrin's love for Lucien does not go so far as the sacrifice of life, unlike Esther's. Once the terrible moment has passed, the Abbot Carlos Herrera reverts to the criminal he is. With the death of his idol, his egoism rises again, fully and entirely, and he only thinks about himself. How to save himself? How to get out of prison? He possesses the compromising letters that many aristocratic women wrote to Lucien, this *enfant gâté* of the great world. And these documents will allow him to get out of a very dangerous situation. It is once again his victim who, from the tomb, offers him the way to fight and win his extreme battle. Vautrin threatens a scandal if they put him on trial. The most beautiful names of Paris, the most illustrious families of France, will be dragged into the mud of the Criminal Court. The investigating judge is afraid; the general prosecutor and the Minister of Justice retreat in the face of this danger. What to do? The investigation will close quickly with the decision not to prosecute him, and to buy Vautrin's silence they will appoint him as chief of police.

The critics said: that is improbable. These critics were ignorant, because they did not know that Vidocq, the famous *Chief of the Security Police*, was a common criminal in his youth, who was condemned many times. Balzac was, as always, true, and not implausible.

But these critics ignored the history of the judiciary police, which includes many cases similar to Vidocq's—wanting to form the police force with gentlemen officers rather than with criminals is like doing "the cooking in white gloves" (*Splendors* 173), the agent Peyrade said—, but they also proved they could not understand all the philosophy embodied in *Vautrin's final incarnation.*

This philosophy is an ironic insult to justice, revealing its cowardice and impotence. In the world there are neither laws nor magistrates: there are the weak who surrender to the strongest. Vautrin is the strongest, hence the executioner of a society that did not know how to punish him.

This is Balzac's morality. A sad morality that leaves an obscure sense of discouragement in the soul. But in contemplating and judging the world, can one perhaps be true without being sad?

# Index

## THE LORENZO DA PONTE ITALIAN LIBRARY

General Editors: Luigi Ballerini and Massimo Ciavolella

Pellegrino Artusi, *Science in the Kitchen and the Art of Eating Well* (2003). Edited and translated by Luigi Ballerini and Murtha Baca.

Lauro Martines, *An Italian Renaissance Sextet: Six Tales in Historical Context* (2004). Translated by Murtha Baca.

*Aretino's Dialogues* (2005). Translated by Margaret Rosenthal and Raymond Rosenthal

Aldo Palazzeschi, *A Tournament of Misfits: Tall Tales and Short* (2005). Translated by Nicolas J. Perella.

Carlo Cattaneo, *Civilization and Democracy: The Salvemini Anthology of Cattaneo's Writings* (2006). Edited and introduced by Carlo G. Lacaita and Filippo Sabetti. Translated by David Gibbons.

Benedetto Croce, *Breviary of Aesthetics: Four Lectures* (2007). Translated by Hiroko Fudemoto, Introduction by Remo Bodei.

Antonio Pigafetta, *First Voyage around the World (1519–1522): An Account of Magellan's Expedition* (2007). Edited and translated by Theodore J. Cachey Jr.

Raffaello Borghini, *Il Riposo* (2008). Translated by Lloyd H. Ellis Jr.

Paolo Mantegazza, *Physiology of Love and Other Writings* (2008). Edited and translated by Nicoletta Pireddu.

*Renaissance Comedy: The Italian Masters* (2008). Edited and translated by Donald Beecher

Cesare Beccaria, *On Crimes and Punishments and Other Writings* (2008). Edited by Aaron Thomas; Translated by Aaron Thomas and Jeremy Parzen; Foreword by Bryan Stevenson; Introduction by Alberto Burgio.

Leone Ebreo, *Dialogues of Love* (2009). Edited and translated by Cosmos Damian Bacich and Rossella Pescatori.

*Boccaccio's Expositions on Dante's Comedy* (2009). Translated by Michael Papio.

*My Muse Will Have a Story to Paint: Selected Prose of Ludovico Ariosto* (2010). Translated with an Introduction by Dennis Looney.

*The Opera of Bartolomeo Scappi (1570): L'arte et prudenza d'un maestro Cuoco (The Art and Craft of a Master Cook)* (2011). Translated with commentary by Terence Scully.

*Pirandello's Theatre of Living Masks: New Translations of Six Major Plays* (2011). Translated by Umberto Mariani and Alice Gladstone Mariani.

*From Kant to Croce: Modern Philosophy in Italy, 1800–1950* (2012). Edited and translated with an introduction by Brian P. Copenhaver and Rebecca Copenhaver.

Giovan Francesco Straparola, *The Pleasant Nights*, Volume 2 (2012). Edited with an Introduction by Donald Beecher.

Giovan Francesco Straparola, *The Pleasant Nights*, Volume 1 (2012). Edited with an Introduction by Donald Beecher.

Giovanni Botero, *On the Causes of the Greatness and Magnificence of Cities* (2012). Translated and with an introduction by Geoffrey W. Symcox.

John Florio, *A Worlde of Wordes* (2013). A Critical Edition with an Introduction by Hermann W. Haller.

Giordano Bruno, *On the Heroic Frenzies* (2013). A Translation of *De gli eroici furori* by Ingrid D. Rowland; Text edited by Eugenio Canone.

Alvise Cornaro, *Writings on the Sober Life: The Art and Grace of Living Long* (2014). Translated by Hiroko Fudemoto; Introduction by Marisa Milani; Foreword by Greg Critser.

Dante Aligheri, *Dante's Lyric Poetry: Poems of Youth and of the Vita Nuova* (1283–1292). (2014) Edited, with a general introduction and introductory essays by Teodolinda Barolini. With new verse translations by Richard Lansing. Commentary translated into English by Andrew Frisardi.

Vincenzo Cuoco, *Historical Essay on the Neapolitan Revolution of 1799* (2014). Edited and Introduced by Bruce Haddock and Filippo Sabetti. Translated by David Gibbons.

Vittore Branca, *Merchant Writers: Florentine Memoirs from the Middle Ages and Renaissance.* (2015) Translated by Murtha Baca.

Carlo Goldoni, *Five Comedies* (2016) Edited by Michael Hackett and Gianluca Rizzo. With an Introduction by Michael Hackett and an essay by Cesare De Michelis.

*Those Who from Afar Look like Flies: An Anthology of Italian Poetry from* Officina *to the Present* (2016). Edited by Luigi Ballerini and Beppe Cavatorta. With a Foreword by Marjorie Perloff.

Guittone d'Arezzo, *Selected Poems and Prose* (2017). Selected, translated, and with an introduction by Antonello Borra.

Giordano Bruno, *The Ash Wednesday Supper* (2018). A new translation of *La Cena de le Ceneri* with the Italian text annotated and introduced by Hilary Gatti.

Giacomo da Lentini, *The Complete Poetry* (2018). Translated and annotated by Richard Lansing. With an Introduction by Akash Kumar.

Remo Bodei, *Geometry of the Passions: Fear, Hope, Happiness: Philosophy and Political Use* (2018). Translated by Gianpiero W. Doebler.

Scipio Sighele, *The Criminal Crowd and Other Writings on Mass Society.* Edited, with an Introduction and Notes, by Nicoletta Pireddu. Translated by Nicoletta Pireddu and Andrew Robbins. With a Foreword by Tom Huhn.

www.ingramcontent.com/pod-product-compliance
Lightning Source LLC
LaVergne TN
LVHW090145080826
844660LV00013B/674/J

* 9 7 8 1 4 8 7 5 0 3 1 8 5 *